D1650246

BLACKWOOD

Praise for
Naming Monsters

'Very impressive... this is scary good.'   − Alison Bechdel

'A strange and haunting contemporary folk tale... It will stay with you,
incubus–like, long after you've finished it. Beware and enjoy.'
                                                             − Ian Rankin

'Striking visuals, hauntingly concise language, and incantatory pacing.
Cutting through the darkness and dysfunction are humor and hope...
an open heart anchors the work.'   − *Kirkus Reviews*

'A beautiful comic... the structure of the story is flawless and the
poignant combination of text and imagery is breath-taking in places,
capturing mundane moments that sit within the tensely wound space
of the narrative with a heartbreakingly honest depth.'   − *The Quietus*

'Beautifully drawn − a wonderful evocation of coming of age − unlike
anything I've seen.'   − Paul Gravett

'So inviting, so recognisable; peppered with sublimely rude humour,
intertwined with folklore and still able to spring powerful emotional
punches.'   − Hannah Berry, Comics Laureate

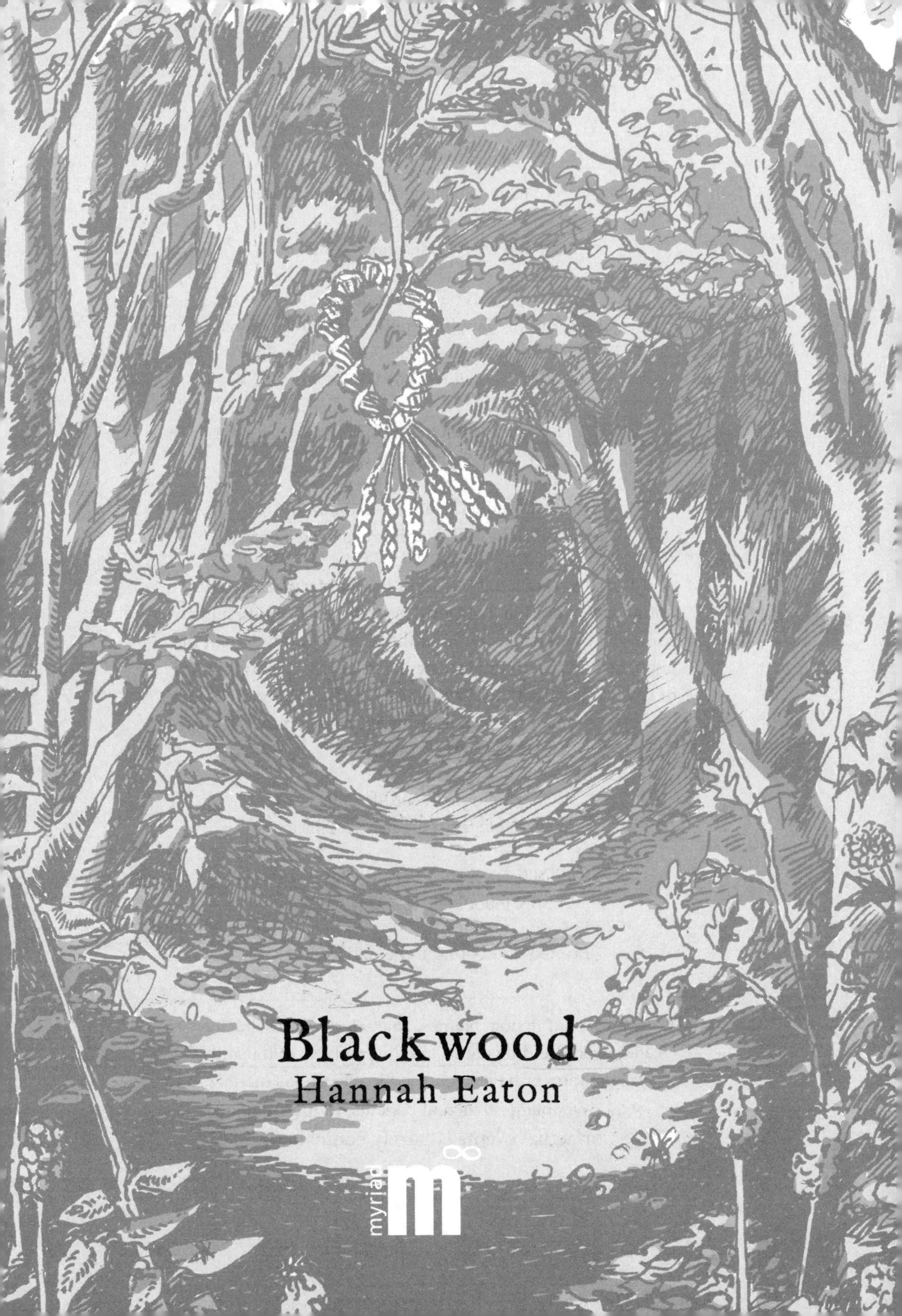
Blackwood
Hannah Eaton
myriad

First published in 2020 by
Myriad Editions
www.myriadeditions.com

Myriad Editions
An imprint of New Internationalist Publications
The Old Music Hall, 106–108 Cowley Rd,
Oxford OX4 1JE

First printing
1 3 5 7 9 10 8 6 4 2

A CIP catalogue record for this book
is available from the British Library

ISBN (paperback): 978-1-908434-71-5
ISBN (ebook): 978-1-908434-72-2

Printed and bound in Poland by Pozkal

This is a work of fiction. Names, characters, places, businesses, locales, events and incidents are the products of the author's imagination or have been used in a fictitious manner. Any resemblance to actual persons, living or dead, or actual events is purely coincidental.

In memory of my grandad,
Jack Walter Woodcraft,
1922-2016

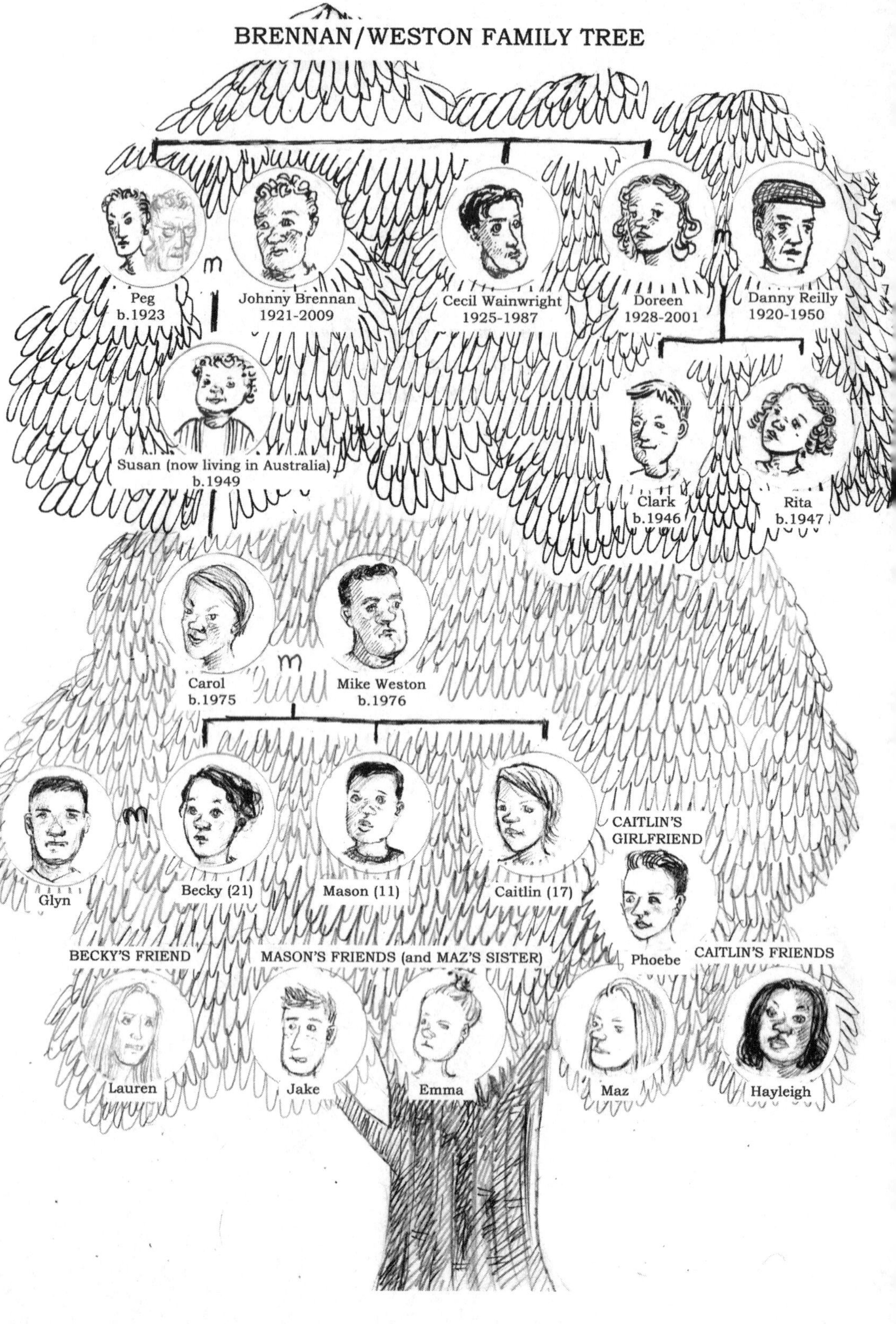
BRENNAN/WESTON FAMILY TREE
Peg
b.1923
m
Johnny Brennan
1921-2009
Cecil Wainwright
1925-1987
Doreen
1928-2001
m
Danny Reilly
1920-1950
Susan (now living in Australia)
b.1949
Clark
b.1946
Rita
b.1947
Carol
b.1975
m
Mike Weston
b.1976
Glyn
m
Becky (21)
Mason (11)
Caitlin (17)
CAITLIN'S GIRLFRIEND
Phoebe
BECKY'S FRIEND
Lauren
MASON'S FRIENDS (and MAZ'S SISTER)
Jake
Emma
CAITLIN'S FRIENDS
Maz
Hayleigh

TOWNSPEOPLE AND OTHERS 1950

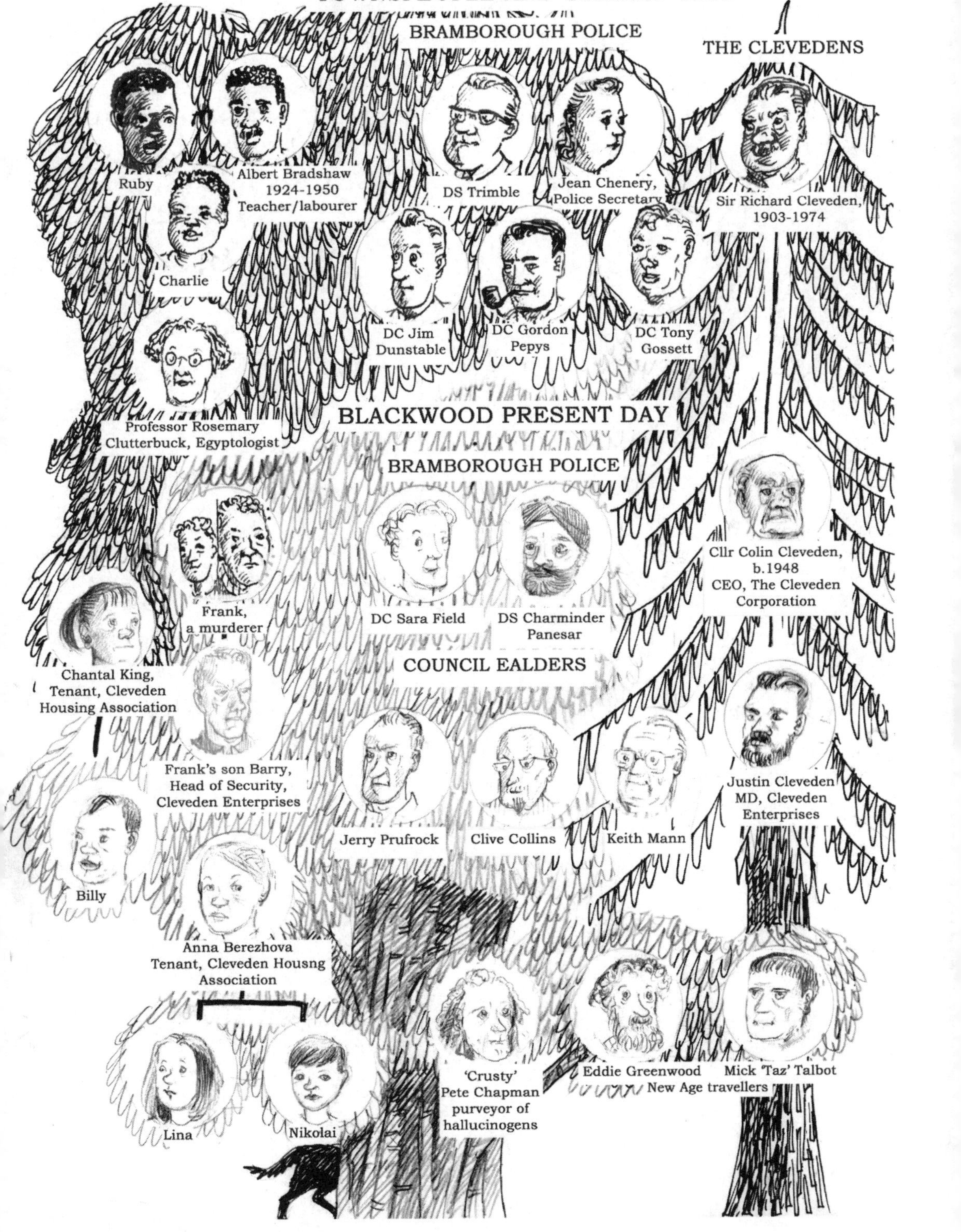
BRAMBOROUGH POLICE
THE CLEVEDENS
Ruby
Albert Bradshaw
1924-1950
Teacher/labourer
DS Trimble
Jean Chenery,
Police Secretary
Sir Richard Cleveden,
1903-1974
Charlie
DC Jim
Dunstable
DC Gordon
Pepys
DC Tony
Gossett
Professor Rosemary
Clutterbuck, Egyptologist
BLACKWOOD PRESENT DAY
BRAMBOROUGH POLICE
Cllr Colin Cleveden,
b.1948
CEO, The Cleveden
Corporation
Frank,
a murderer
DC Sara Field
DS Charminder
Panesar
Chantal King,
Tenant, Cleveden
Housing Association
COUNCIL EALDERS
Frank's son Barry,
Head of Security,
Cleveden Enterprises
Justin Cleveden
MD, Cleveden
Enterprises
Jerry Prufrock
Clive Collins
Keith Mann
Billy
Anna Berezhova
Tenant, Cleveden Housng
Association
'Crusty'
Pete Chapman
purveyor of
hallucinogens
Eddie Greenwood
Mick 'Taz' Talbot
New Age travellers
Lina
Nikolai

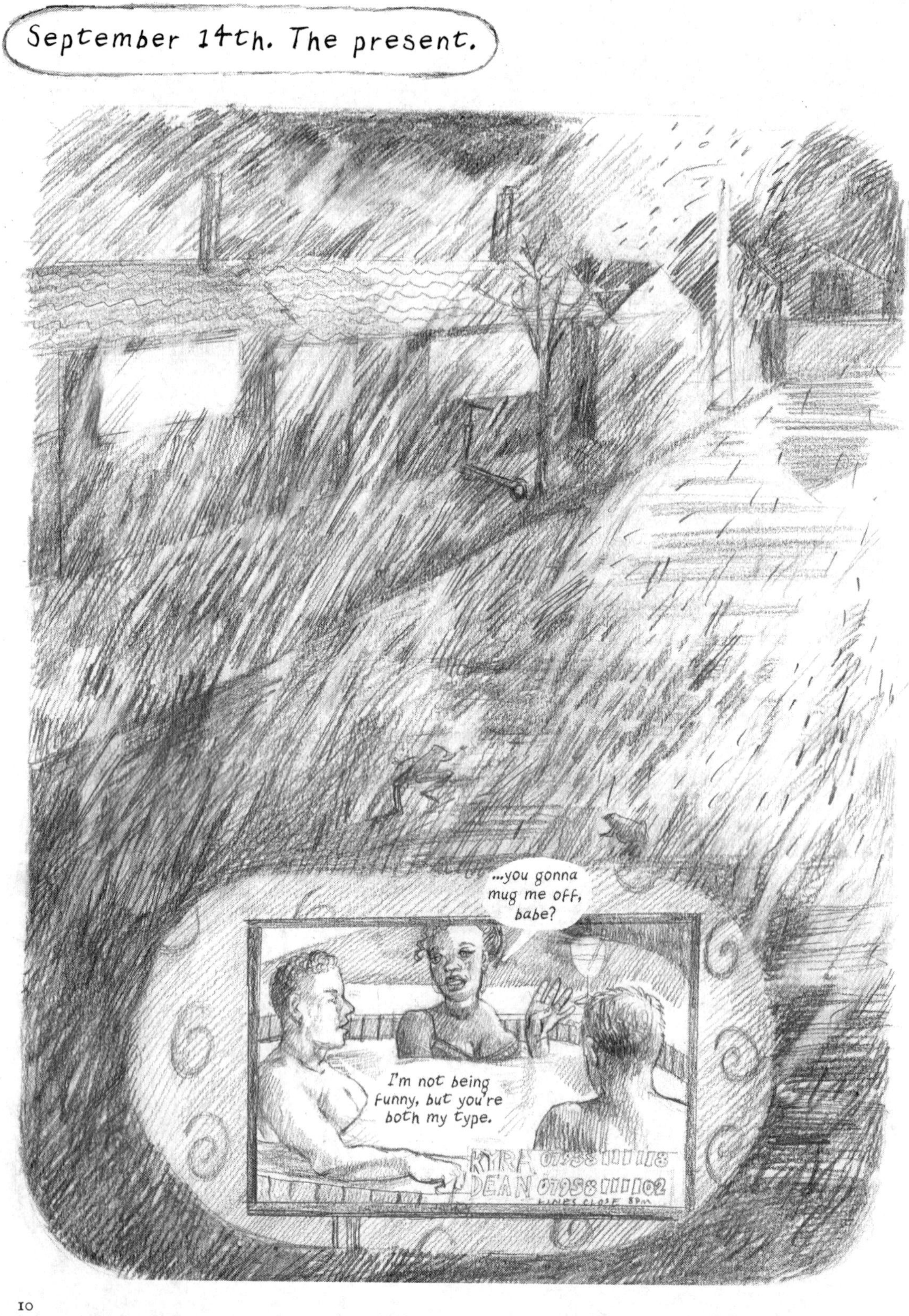
September 14th. The present.
...you gonna mug me off, babe?
I'm not being funny, but you're both my type.
KYRA 07958 111 118
DEAN 07958 111 102
LINES CLOSE 8PM

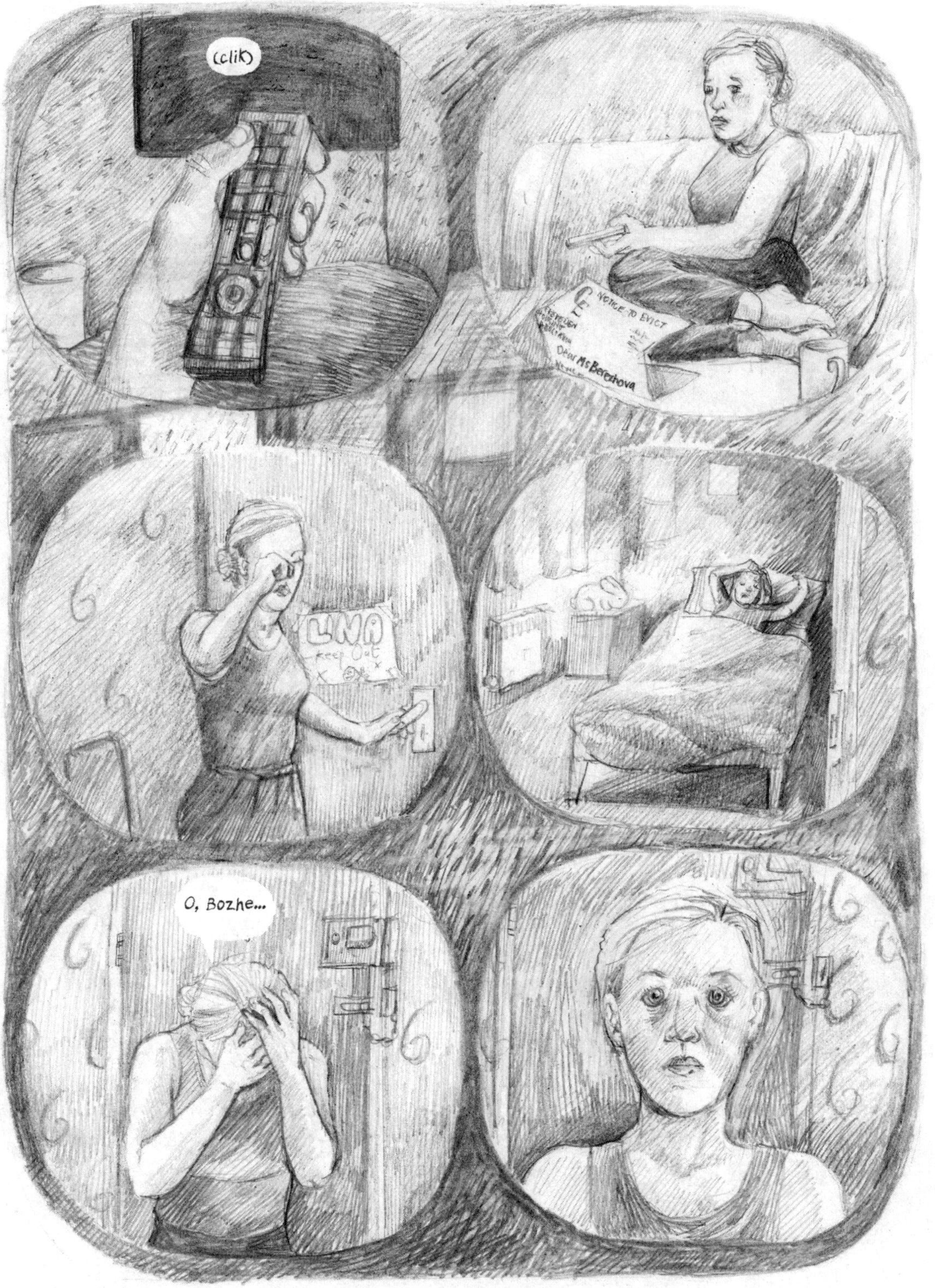
(clik)
NOTICE TO EVICT
Dear Ms Bereshova
LINA
Keep Out
O, Bozhe...

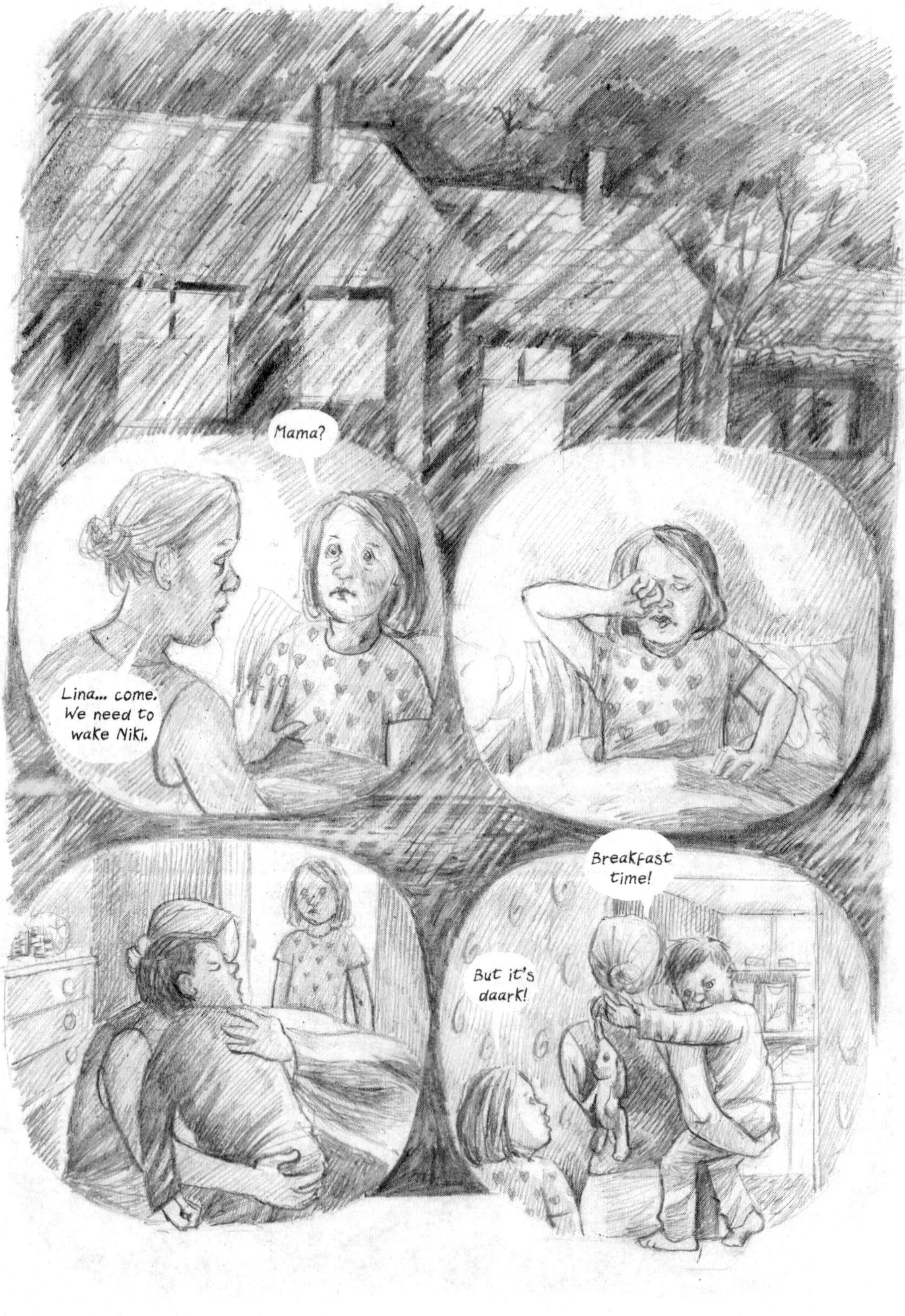
Mama?
Lina... come. We need to wake Niki.
Breakfast time!
But it's daark!

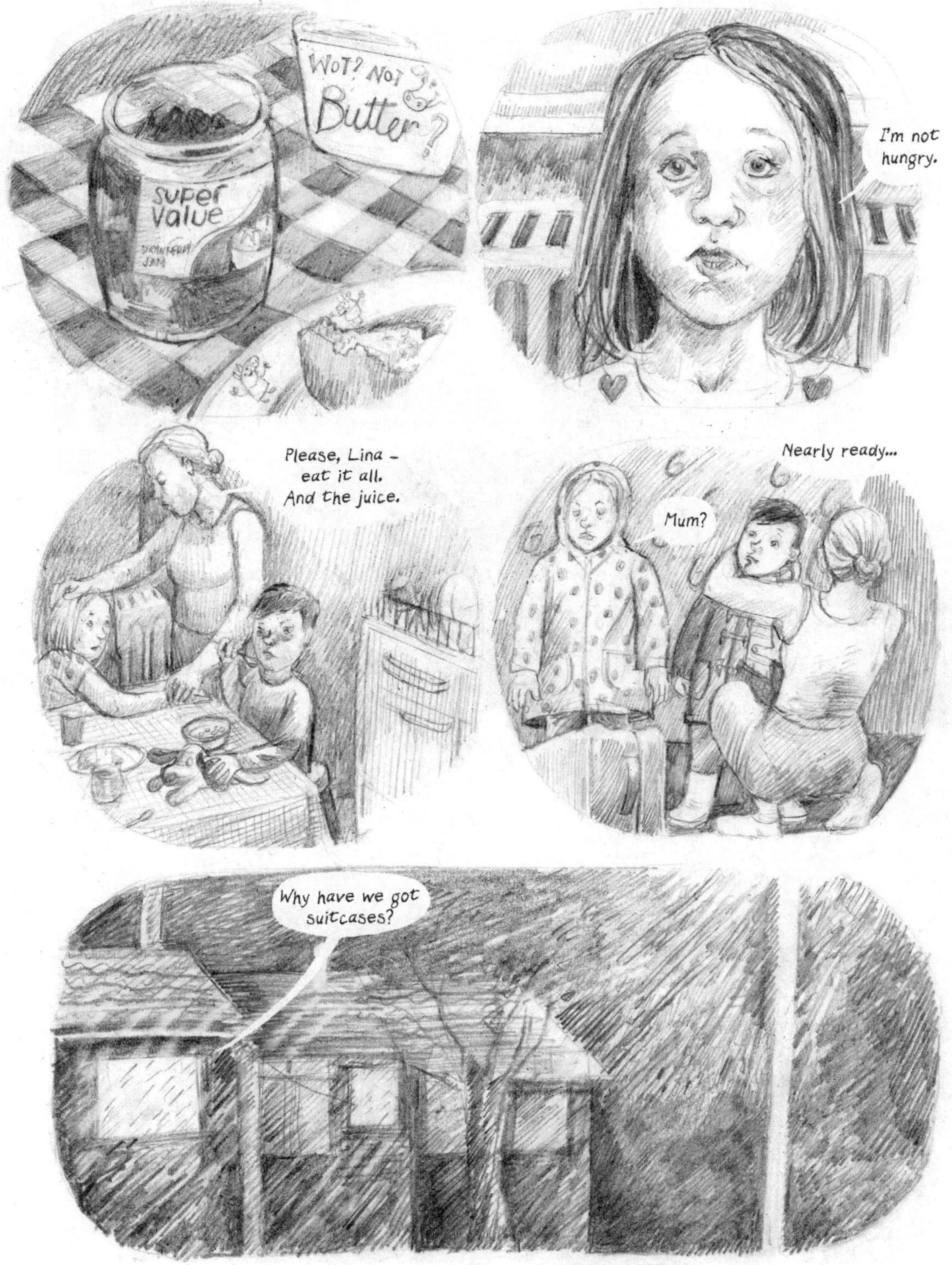
WOT? NOT
Butter?
super value
I'm not hungry.
Please, Lina - eat it all. And the juice.
Nearly ready...
Mum?
Why have we got suitcases?

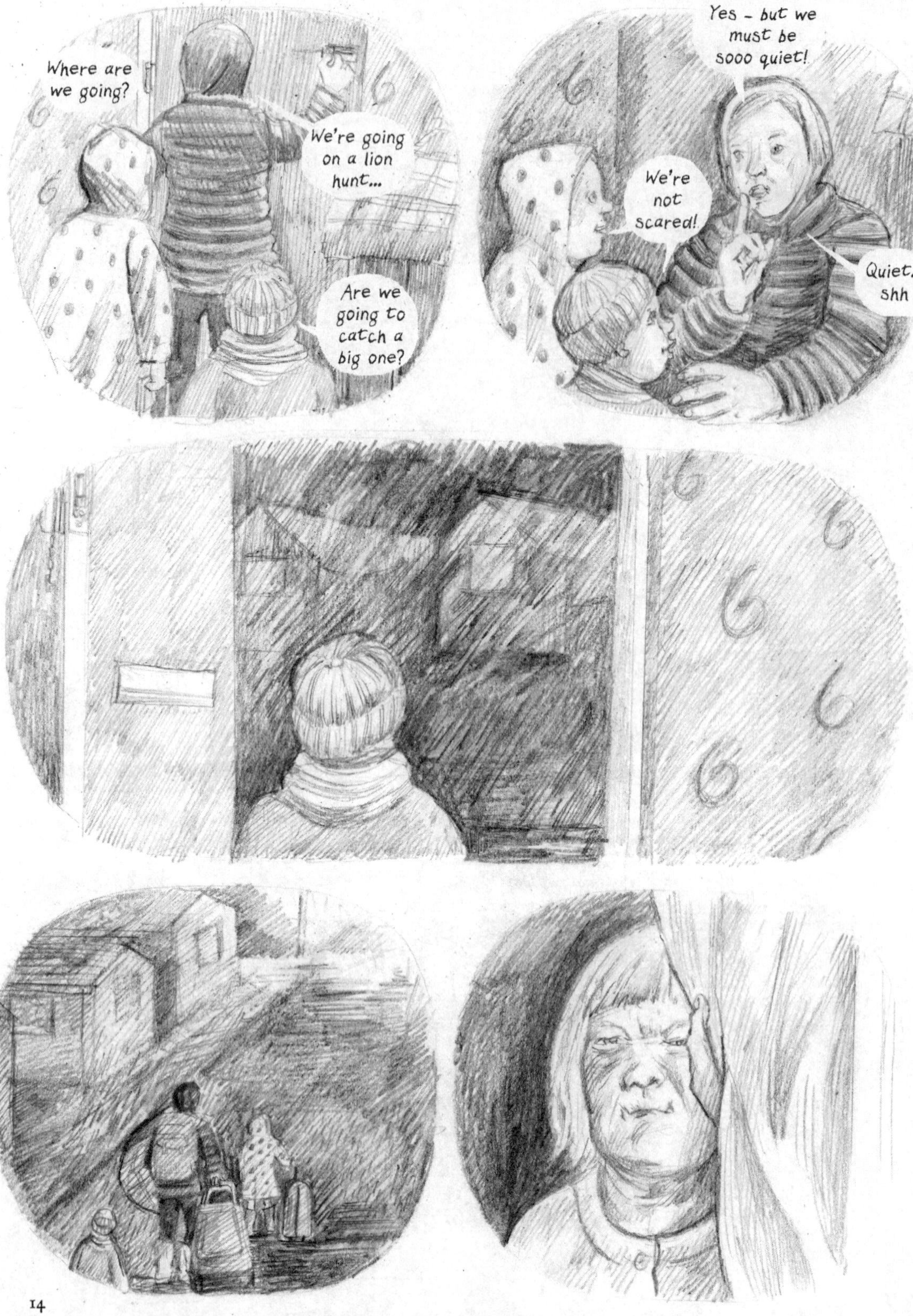

Where are we going?
We're going on a lion hunt...
Are we going to catch a big one?
Yes - but we must be sooo quiet!
We're not scared!
Quiet... shh

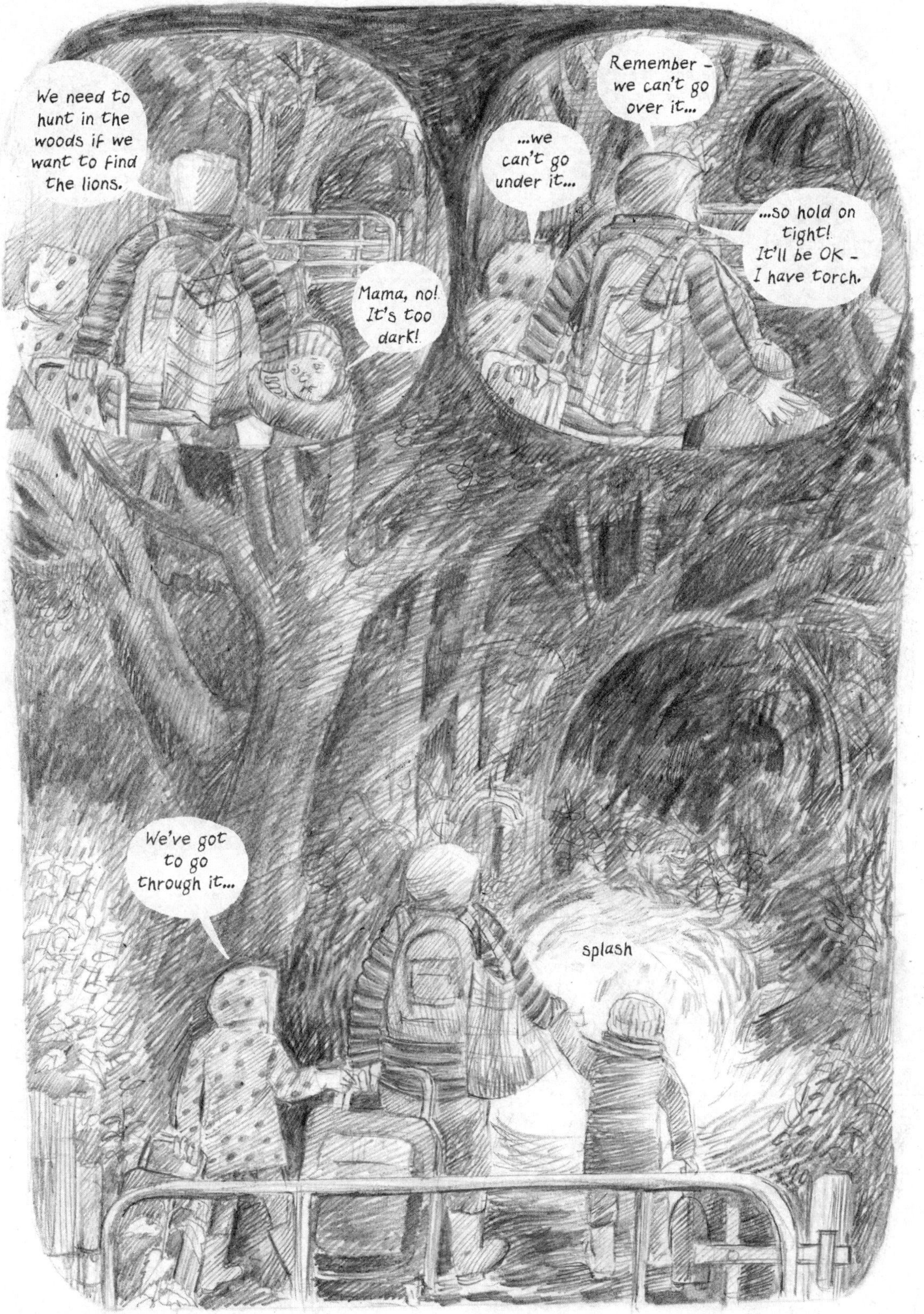
We need to hunt in the woods if we want to find the lions.
Mama, no! It's too dark!
Remember - we can't go over it...
...we can't go under it...
...so hold on tight! It'll be OK - I have torch.
We've got to go through it...
splash

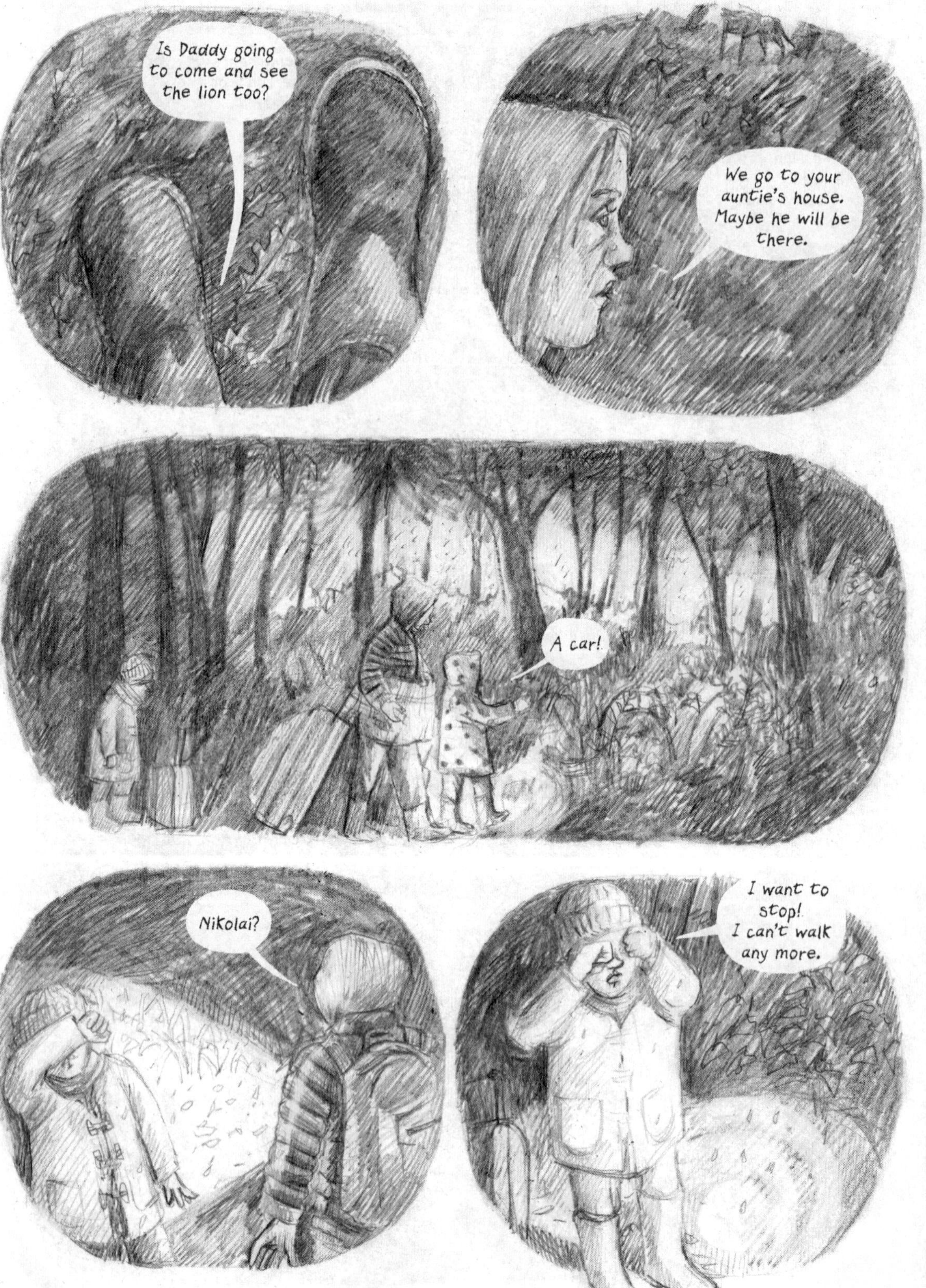
Is Daddy going to come and see the lion too?
We go to your auntie's house. Maybe he will be there.
A car!
Nikolai?
I want to stop! I can't walk any more.

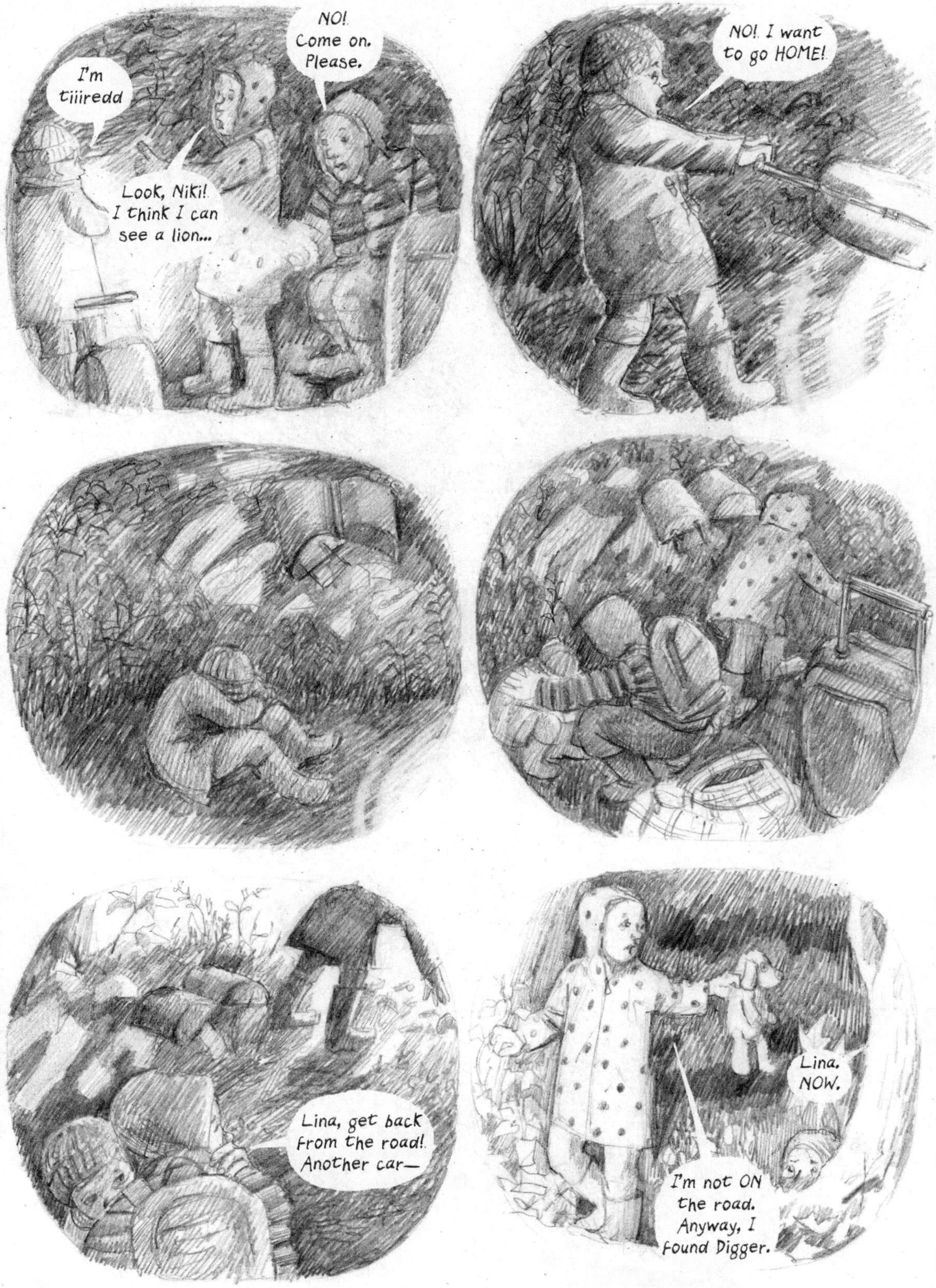
I'm tiiiredd
Look, Niki! I think I can see a lion...
NO! Come on. Please.
NO! I want to go HOME!
Lina, get back from the road! Another car—
Lina. NOW.
I'm not ON the road. Anyway, I found Digger.

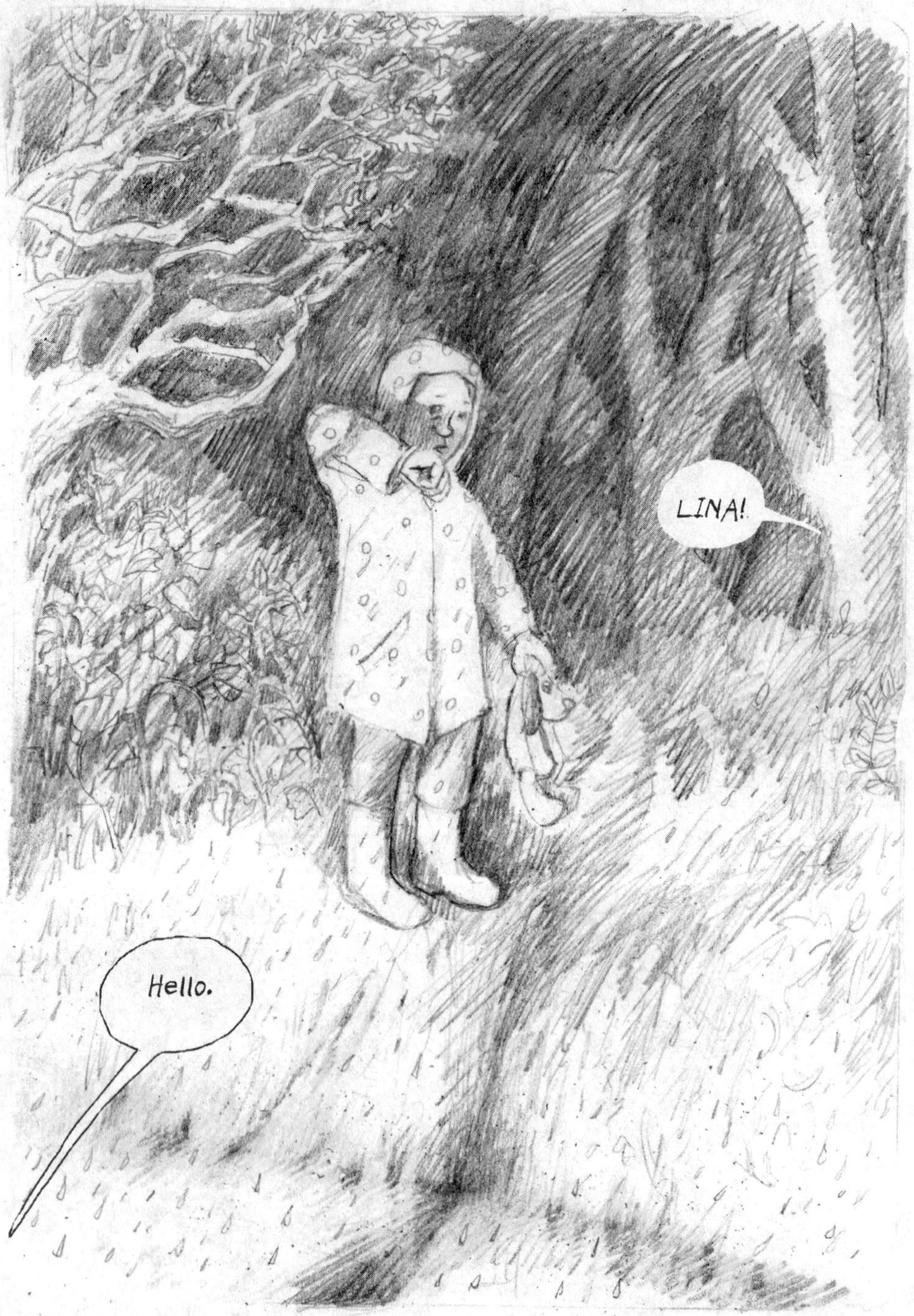
LINA!
Hello.

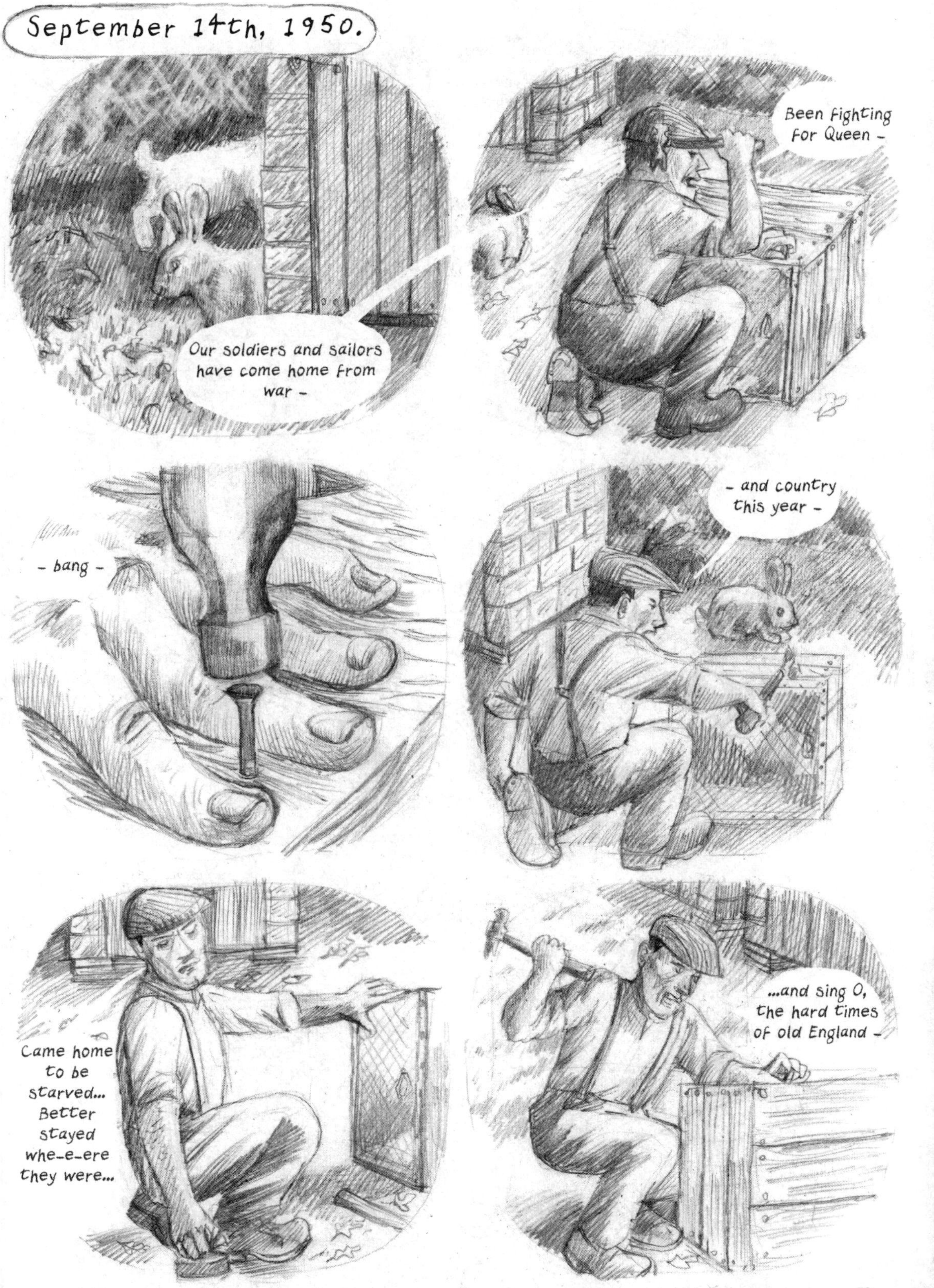
September 14th, 1950.
Our soldiers and sailors have come home from war -
Been fighting for Queen -
- bang -
- and country this year -
Came home to be starved... Better stayed whe-e-ere they were...
...and sing O, the hard times of old England -

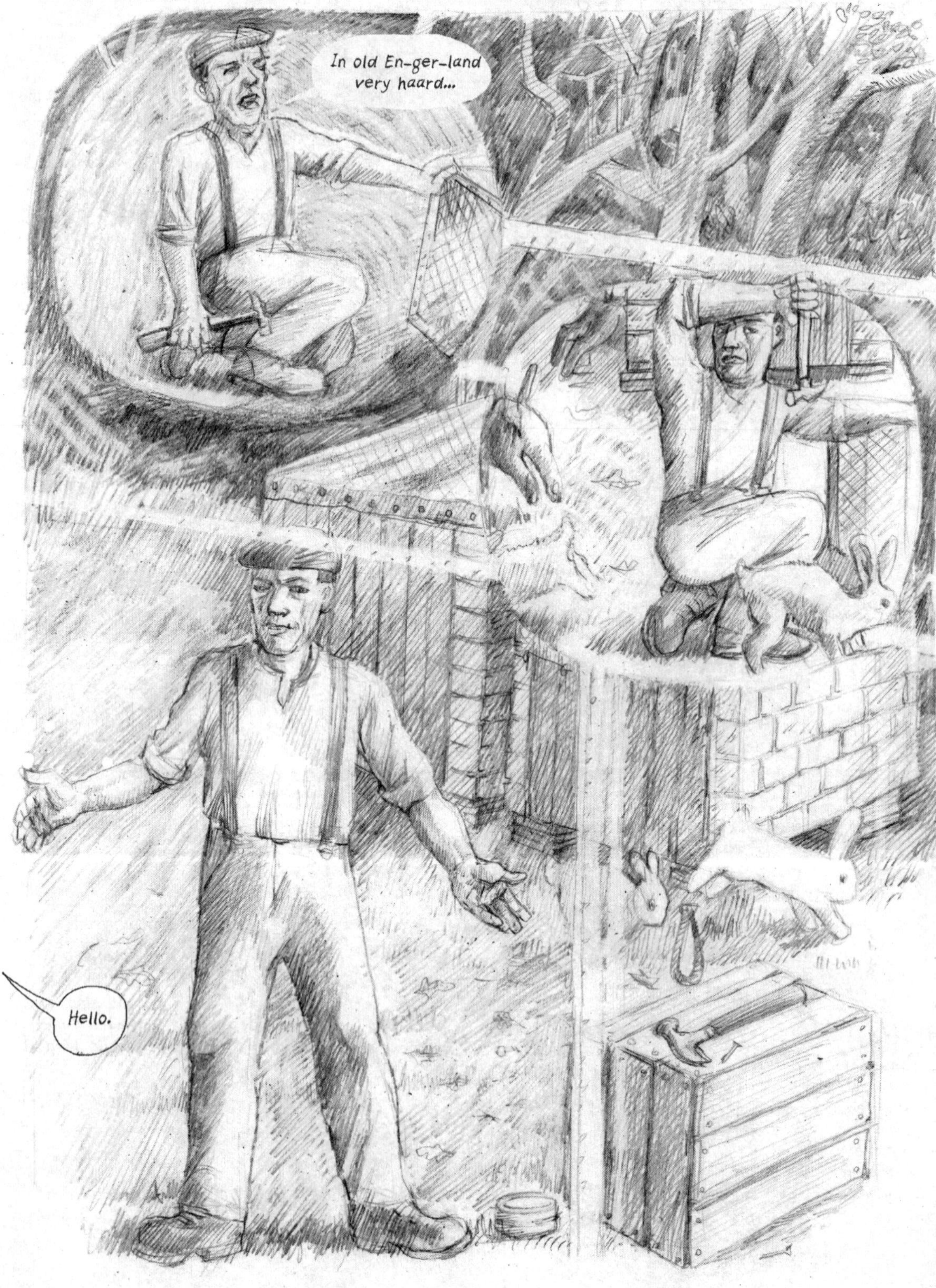
In old En-ger-land very haard...
Hello.

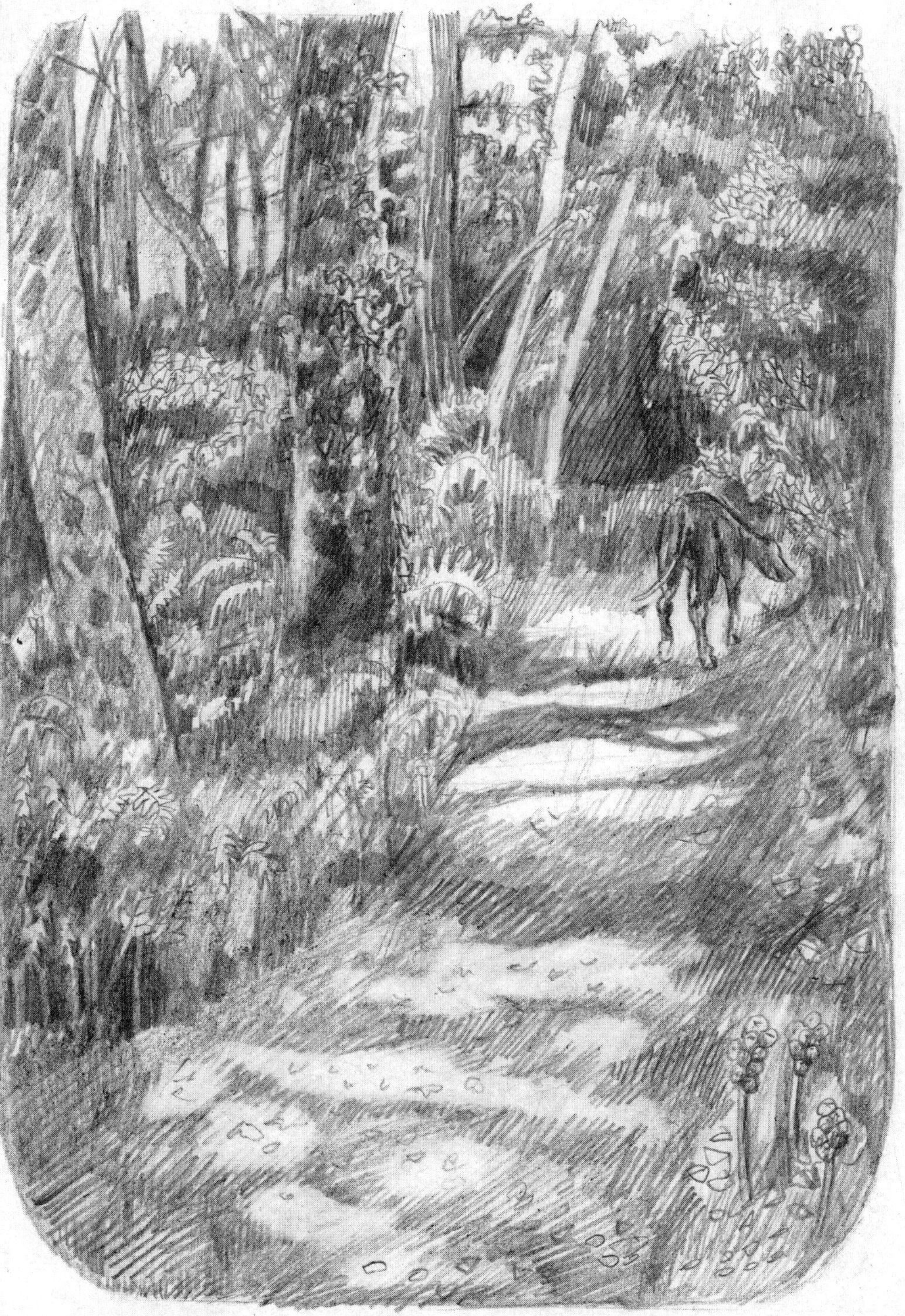

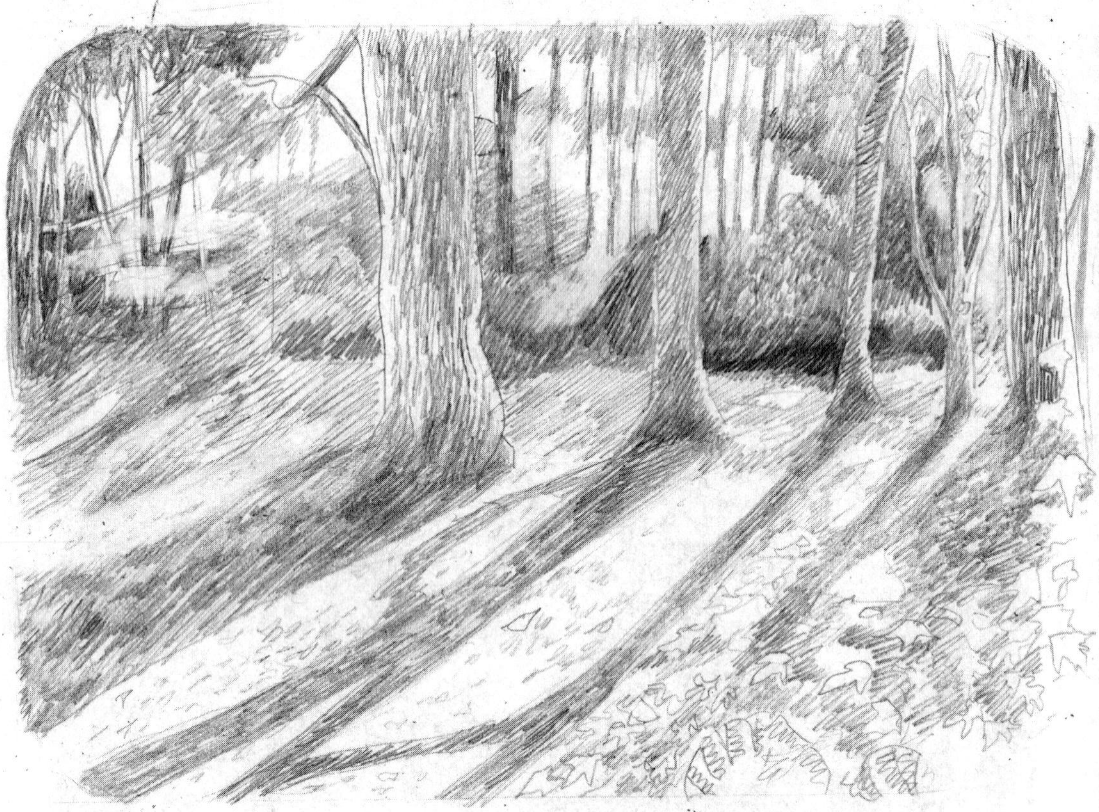

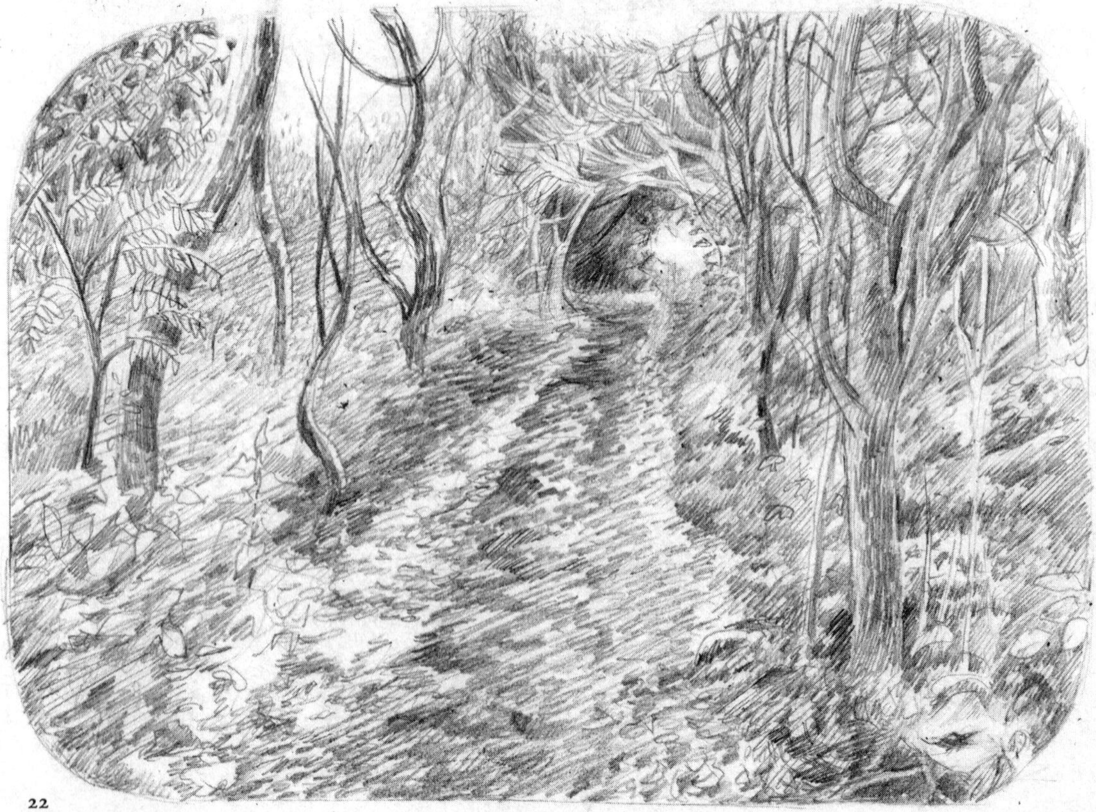

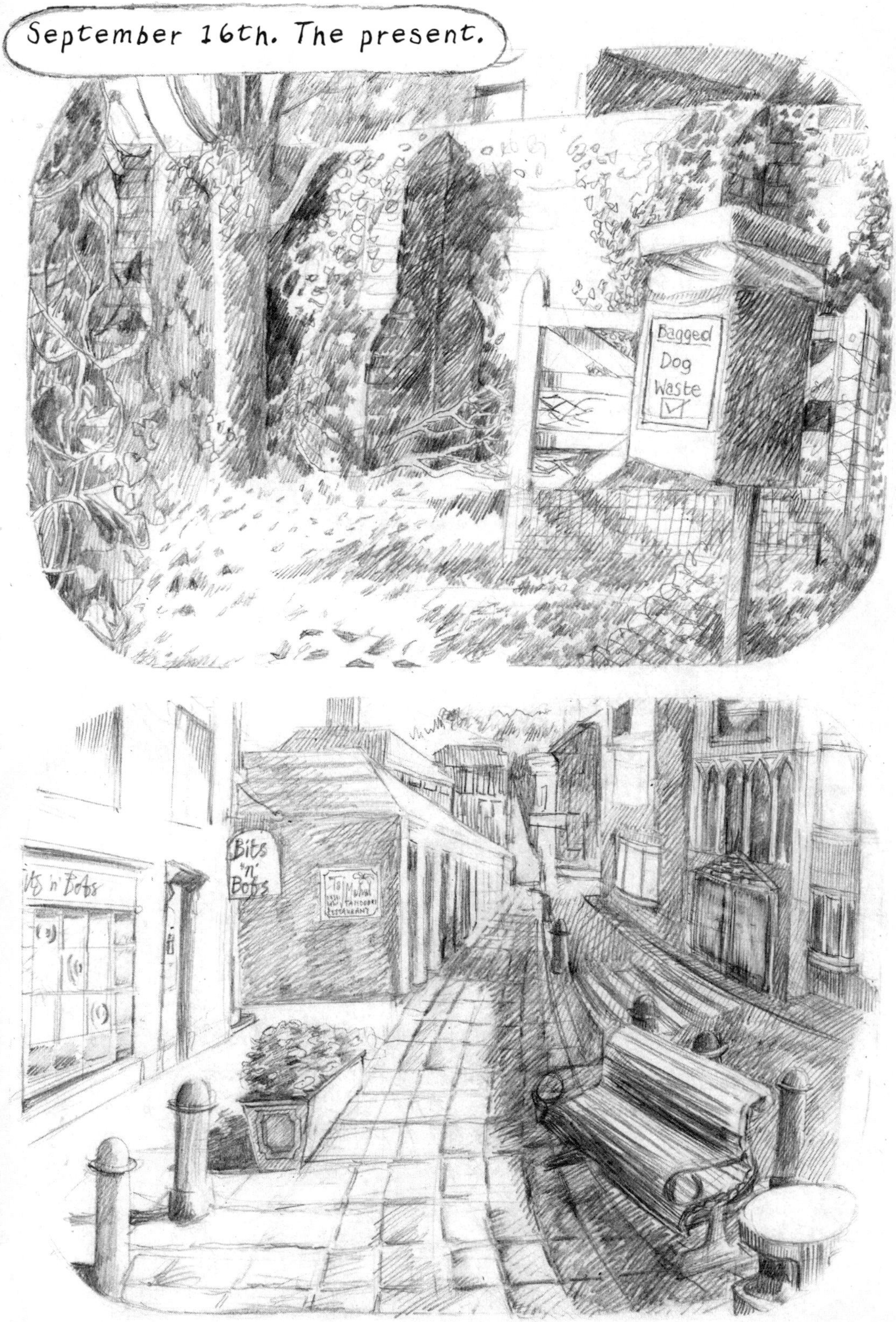
September 16th. The present.
Bagged Dog Waste
Bits 'n' Bobs

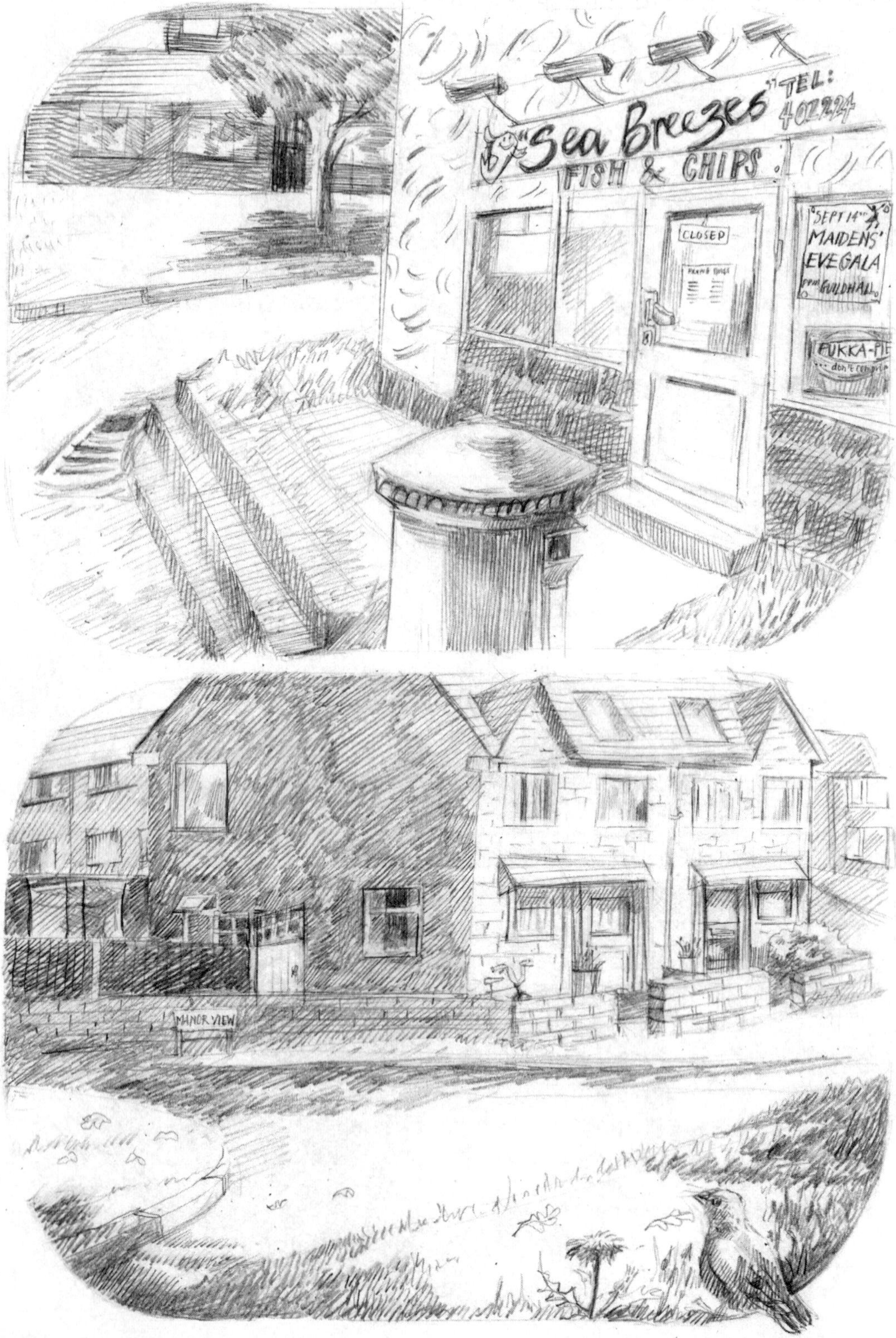
"Sea Breezes" TEL: 402224
FISH & CHIPS
CLOSED
"SEPT 14th" MAIDENS' EVE GALA GUILDHALL
FUKKA-PIE
MANOR VIEW

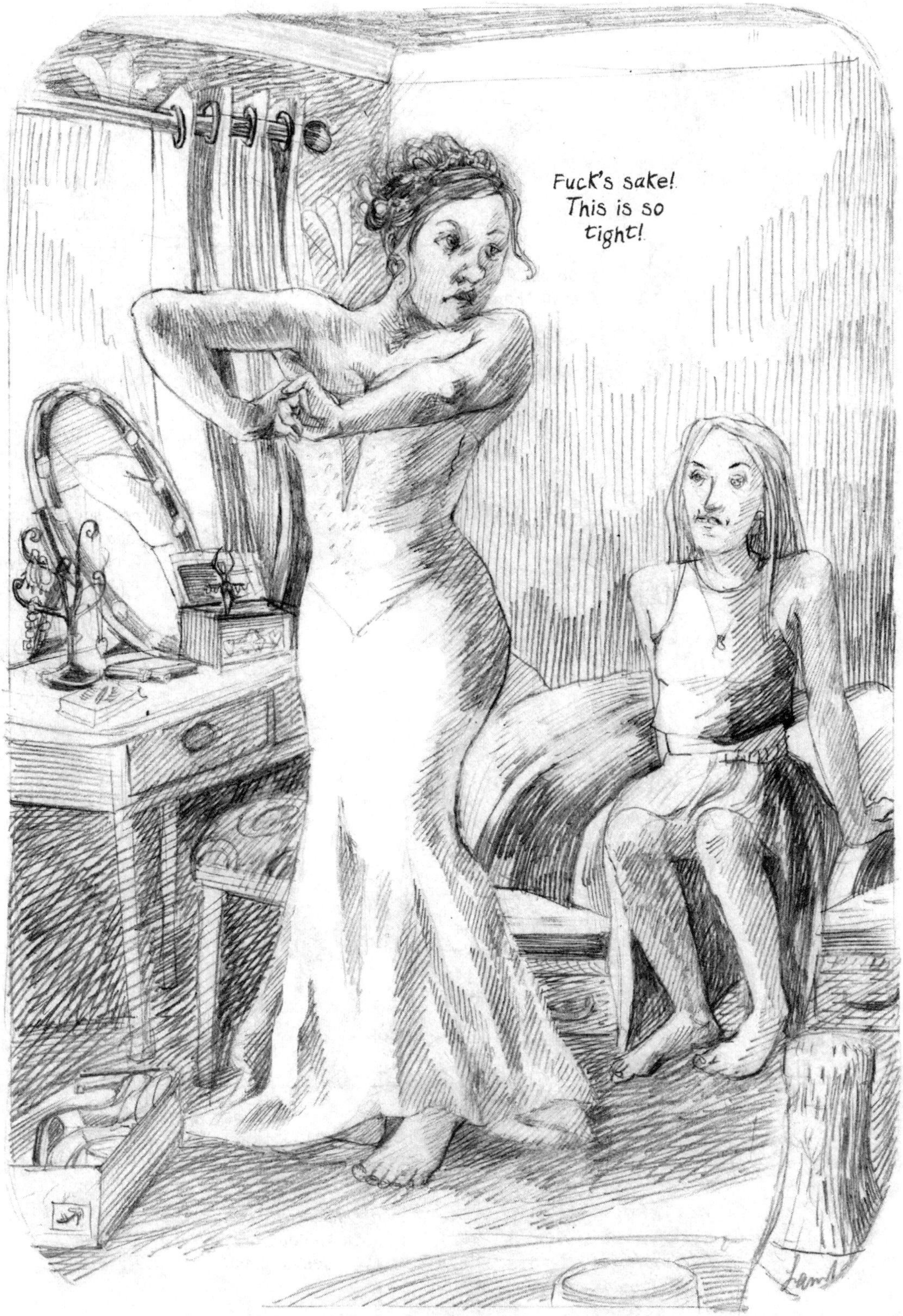
Fuck's sake! This is so tight!

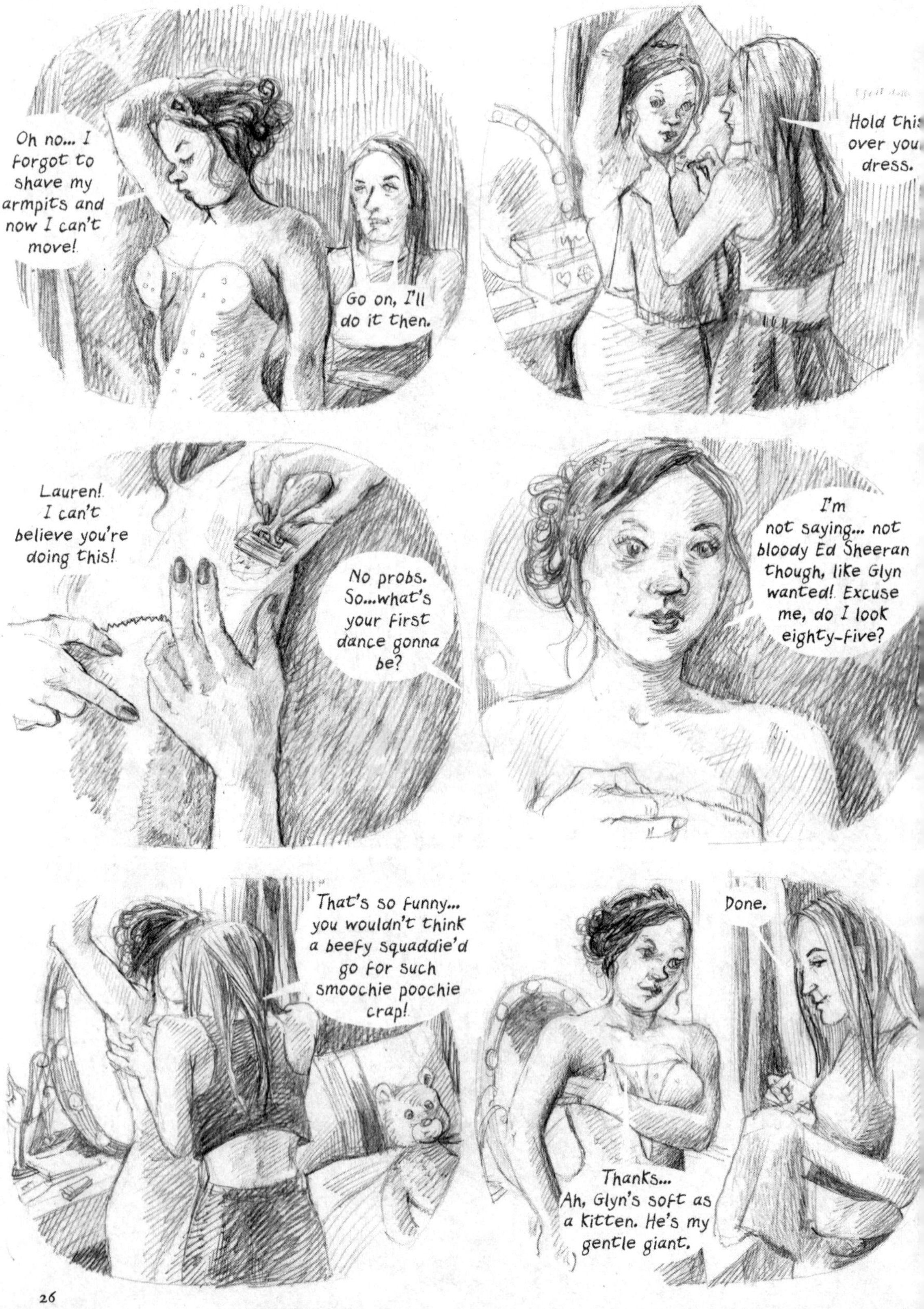
Oh no... I forgot to shave my armpits and now I can't move!
Go on, I'll do it then.
Hold this over your dress.
Lauren! I can't believe you're doing this!
No probs. So...what's your first dance gonna be?
I'm not saying... not bloody Ed Sheeran though, like Glyn wanted! Excuse me, do I look eighty-five?
That's so funny... you wouldn't think a beefy squaddie'd go for such smoochie poochie crap!
Done.
Thanks... Ah, Glyn's soft as a kitten. He's my gentle giant.

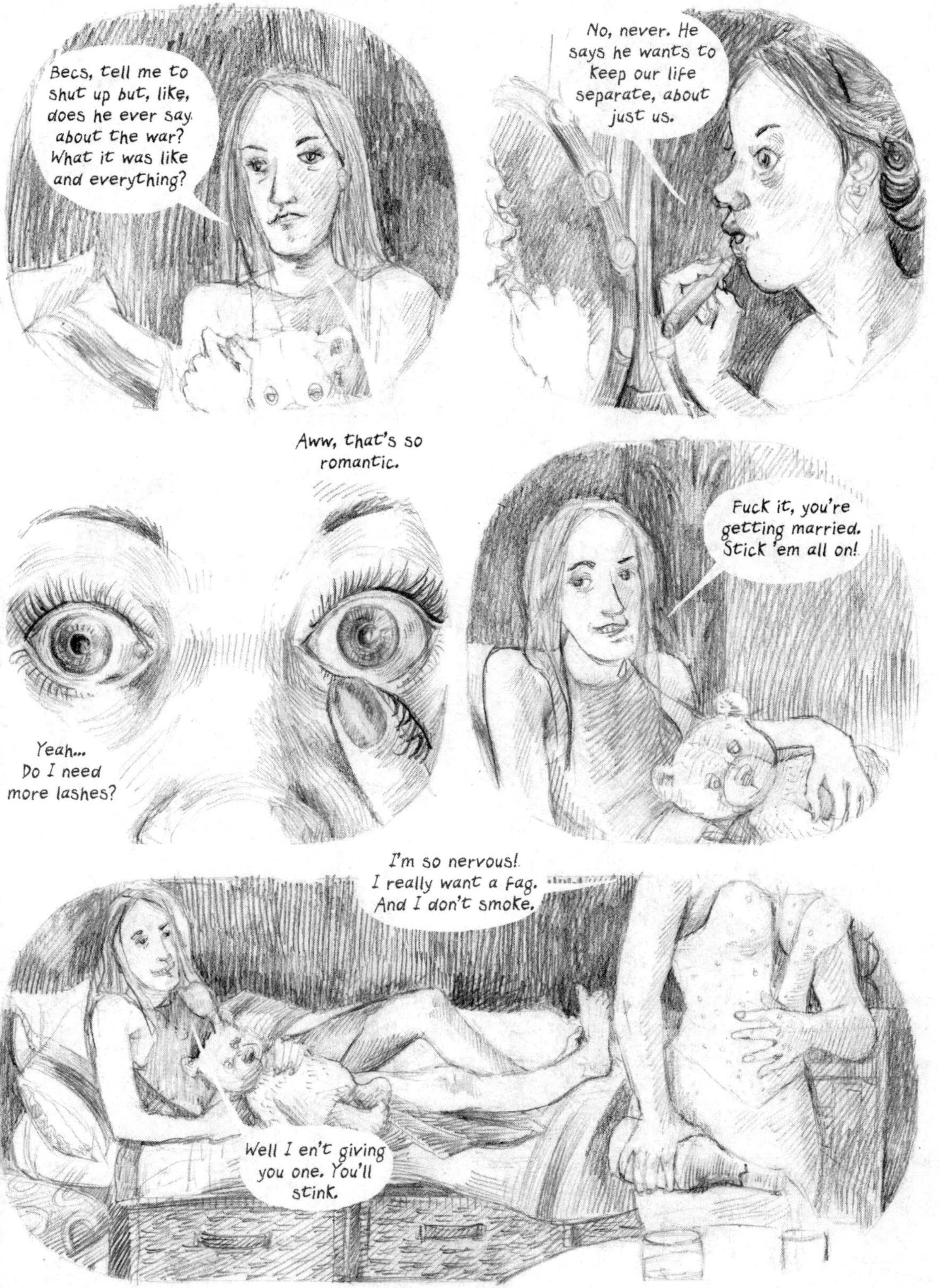
Becs, tell me to shut up but, like, does he ever say about the war? What it was like and everything?
No, never. He says he wants to keep our life separate, about just us.
Aww, that's so romantic.
Yeah... Do I need more lashes?
Fuck it, you're getting married. Stick 'em all on!
I'm so nervous! I really want a fag. And I don't smoke.
Well I en't giving you one. You'll stink.

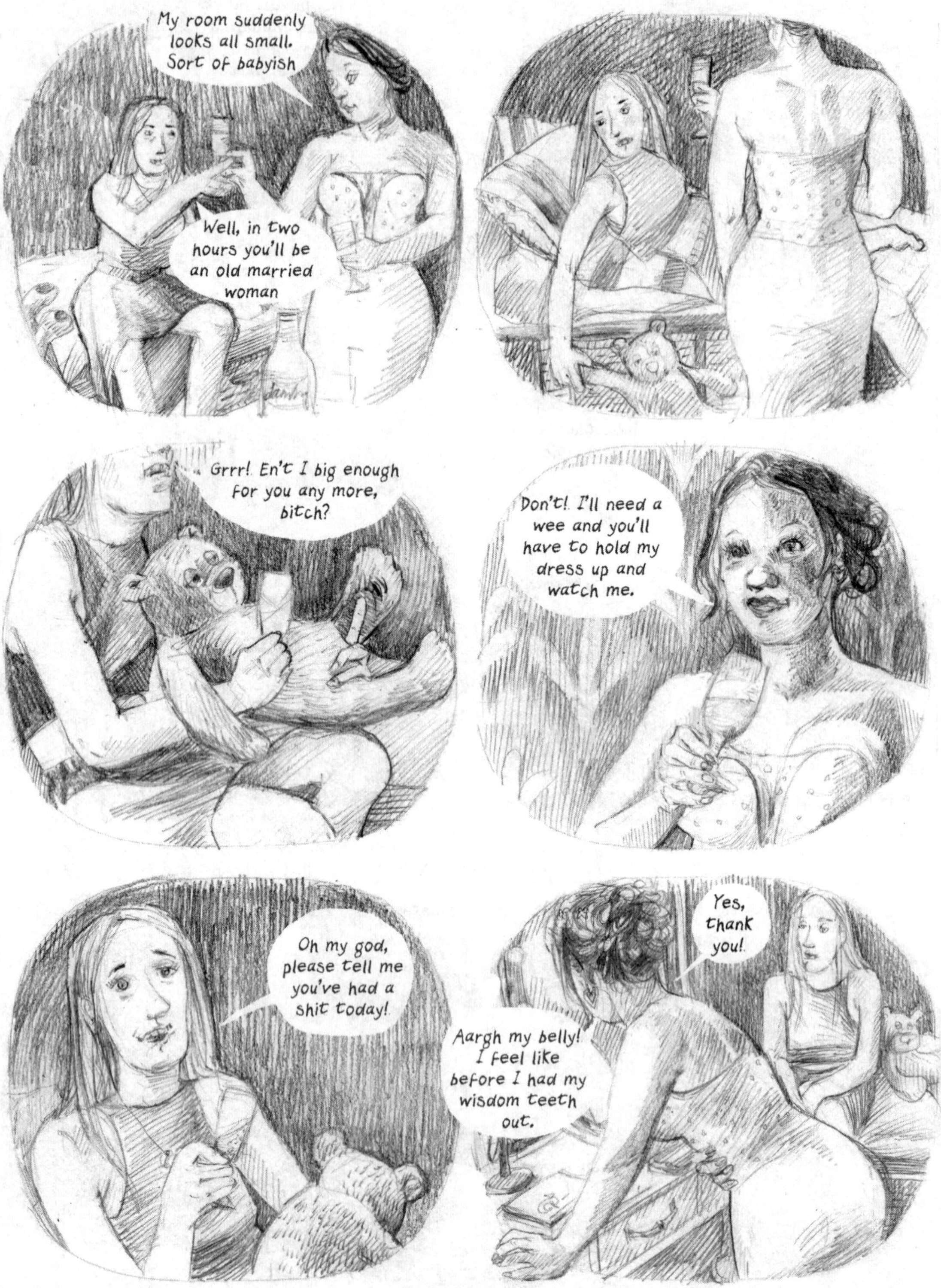
My room suddenly looks all small. Sort of babyish
Well, in two hours you'll be an old married woman
Grrr! En't I big enough for you any more, bitch?
Don't! I'll need a wee and you'll have to hold my dress up and watch me.
Oh my god, please tell me you've had a shit today!
Yes, thank you!
Aargh my belly! I feel like before I had my wisdom teeth out.

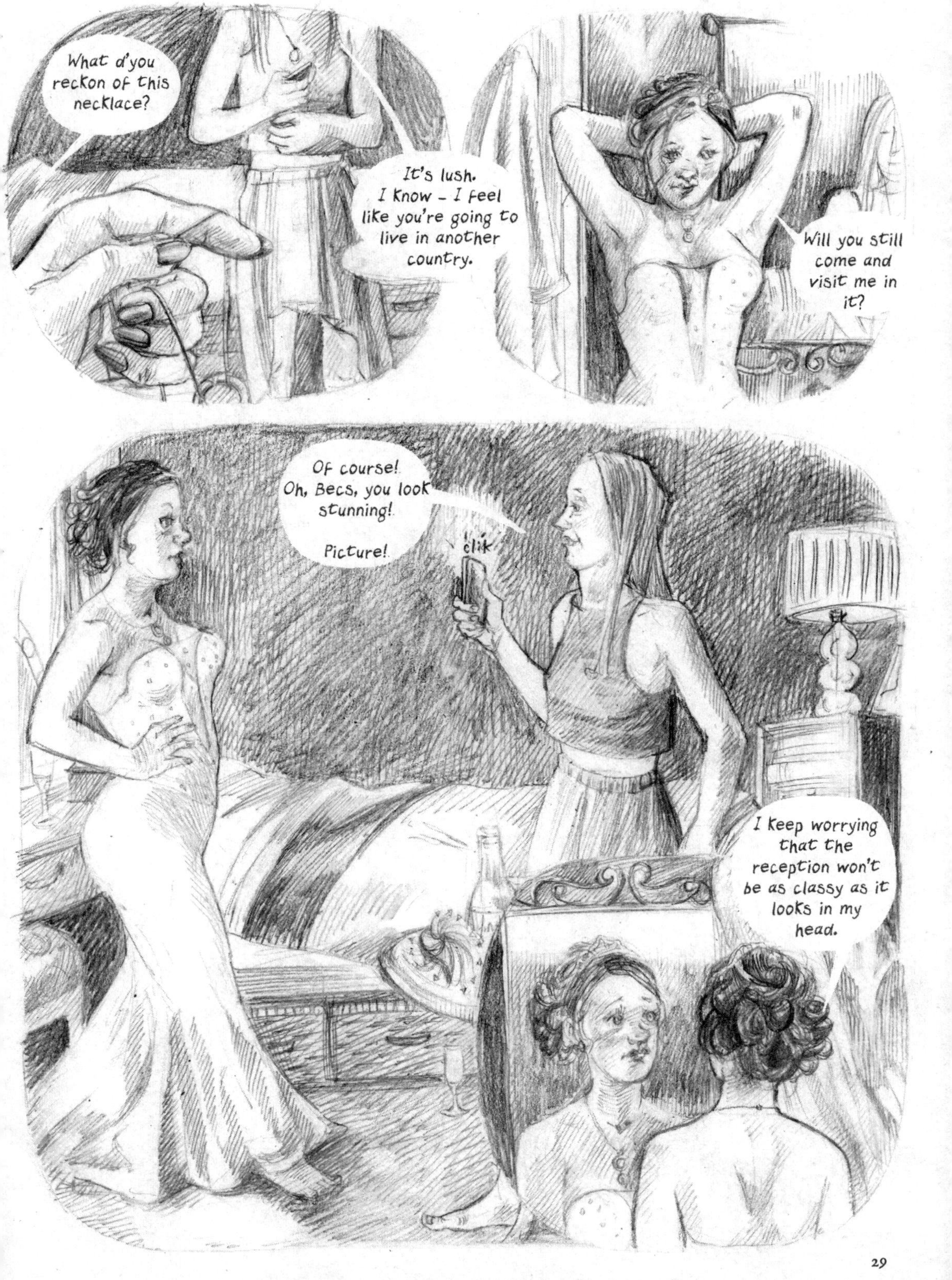
What d'you reckon of this necklace?
It's lush. I know – I feel like you're going to live in another country.
Will you still come and visit me in it?
Of course! Oh, Becs, you look stunning!
Picture!
clik
I keep worrying that the reception won't be as classy as it looks in my head.

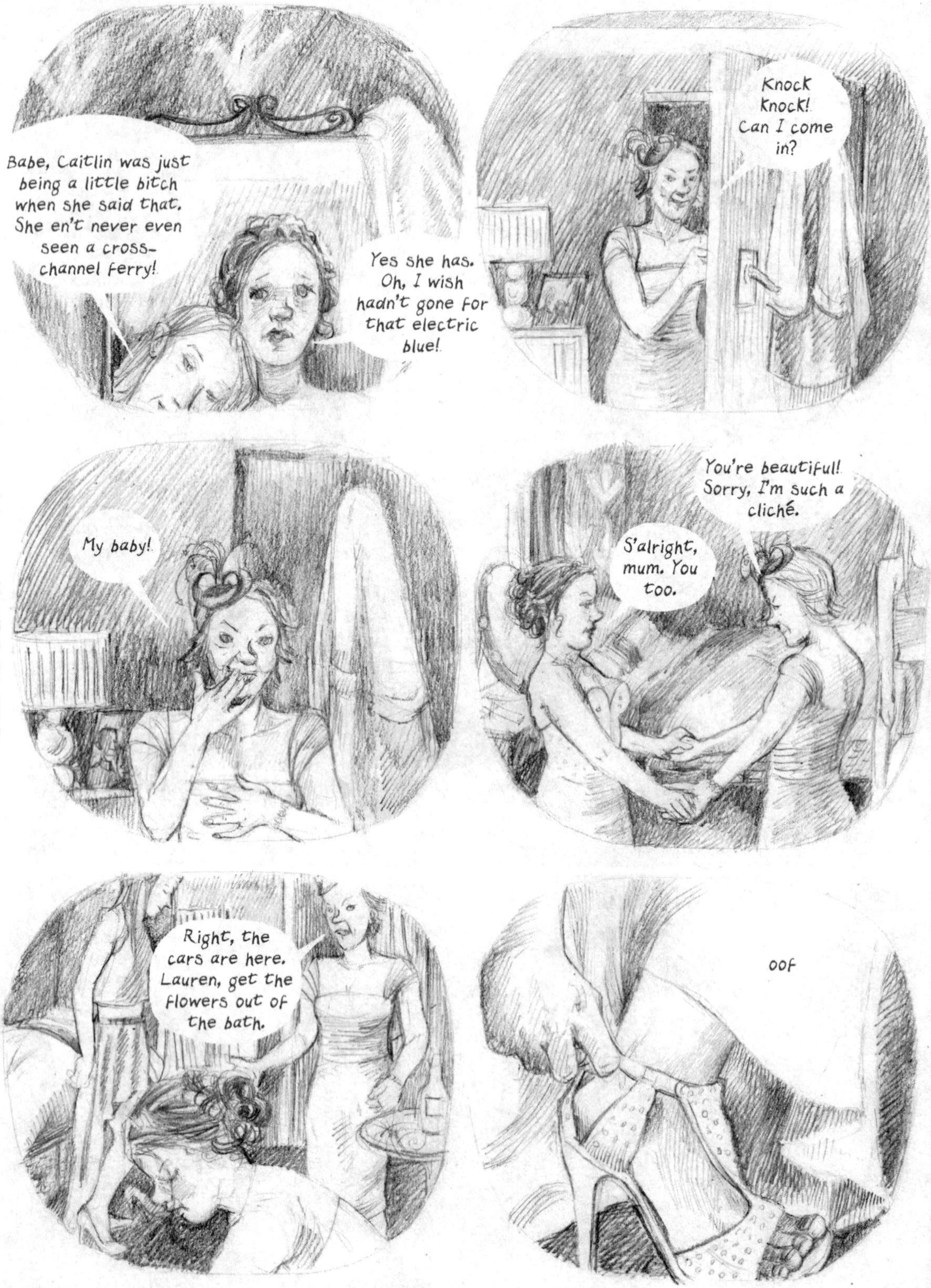

Babe, Caitlin was just being a little bitch when she said that. She en't never even seen a cross-channel ferry!
Yes she has. Oh, I wish hadn't gone for that electric blue!
Knock knock! Can I come in?
My baby!
You're beautiful! Sorry, I'm such a cliché.
S'alright, mum. You too.
Right, the cars are here. Lauren, get the flowers out of the bath.
oof

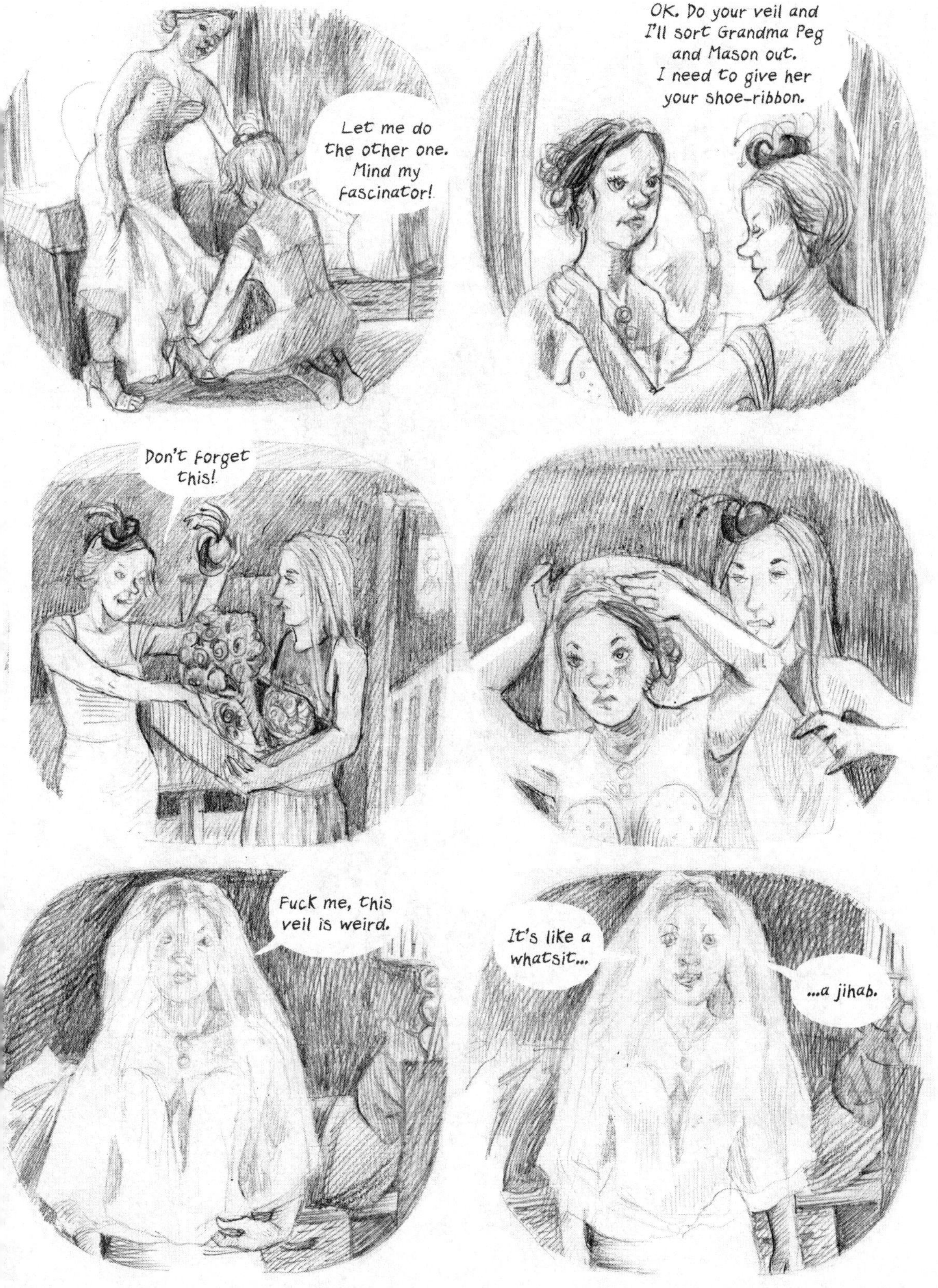
Let me do the other one. Mind my fascinator!
OK. Do your veil and I'll sort Grandma Peg and Mason out. I need to give her your shoe-ribbon.
Don't forget this!
Fuck me, this veil is weird.
It's like a whatsit...
...a jihab.

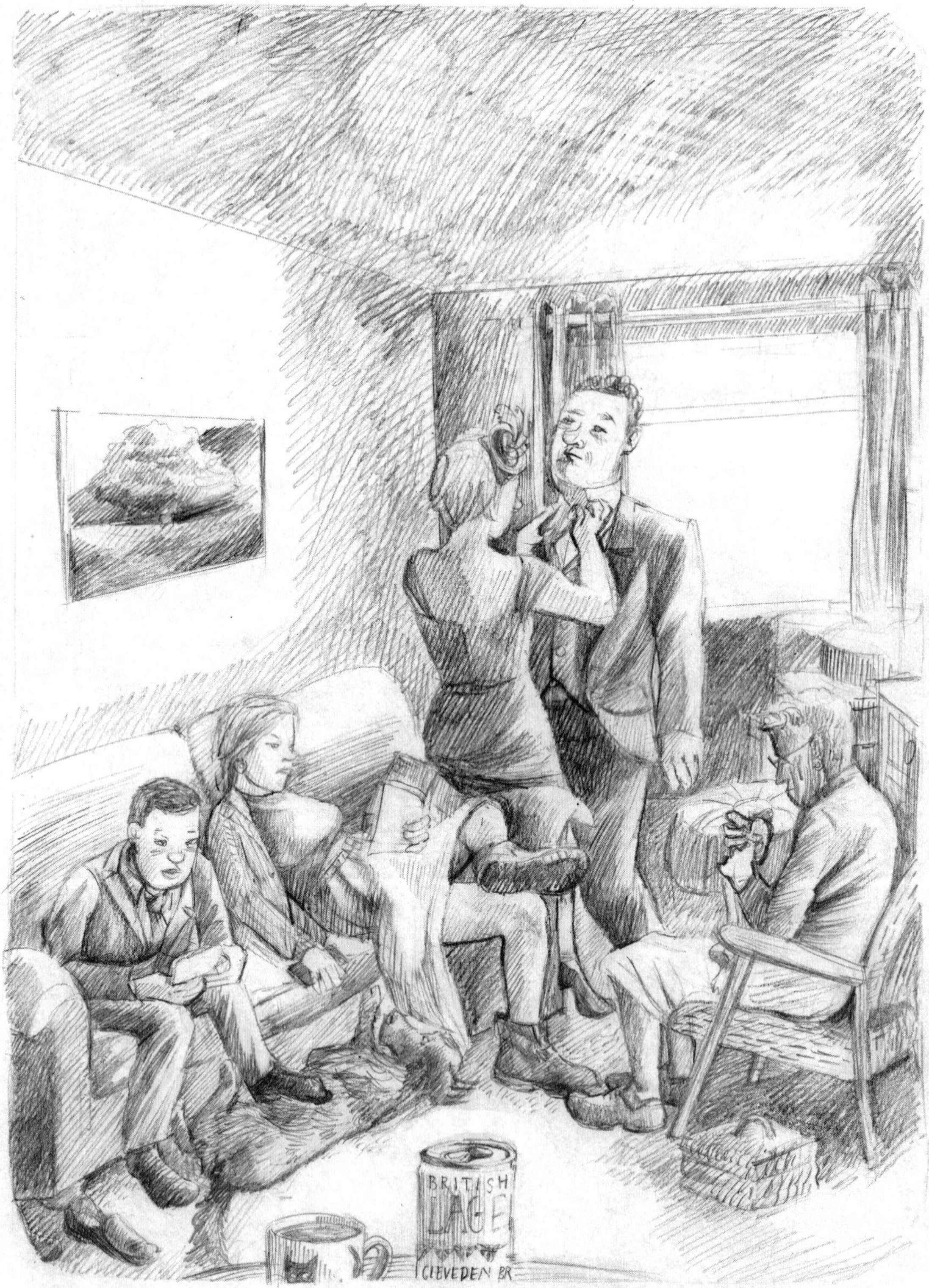
BRITISH
LAGE
CLEVEDEN BR

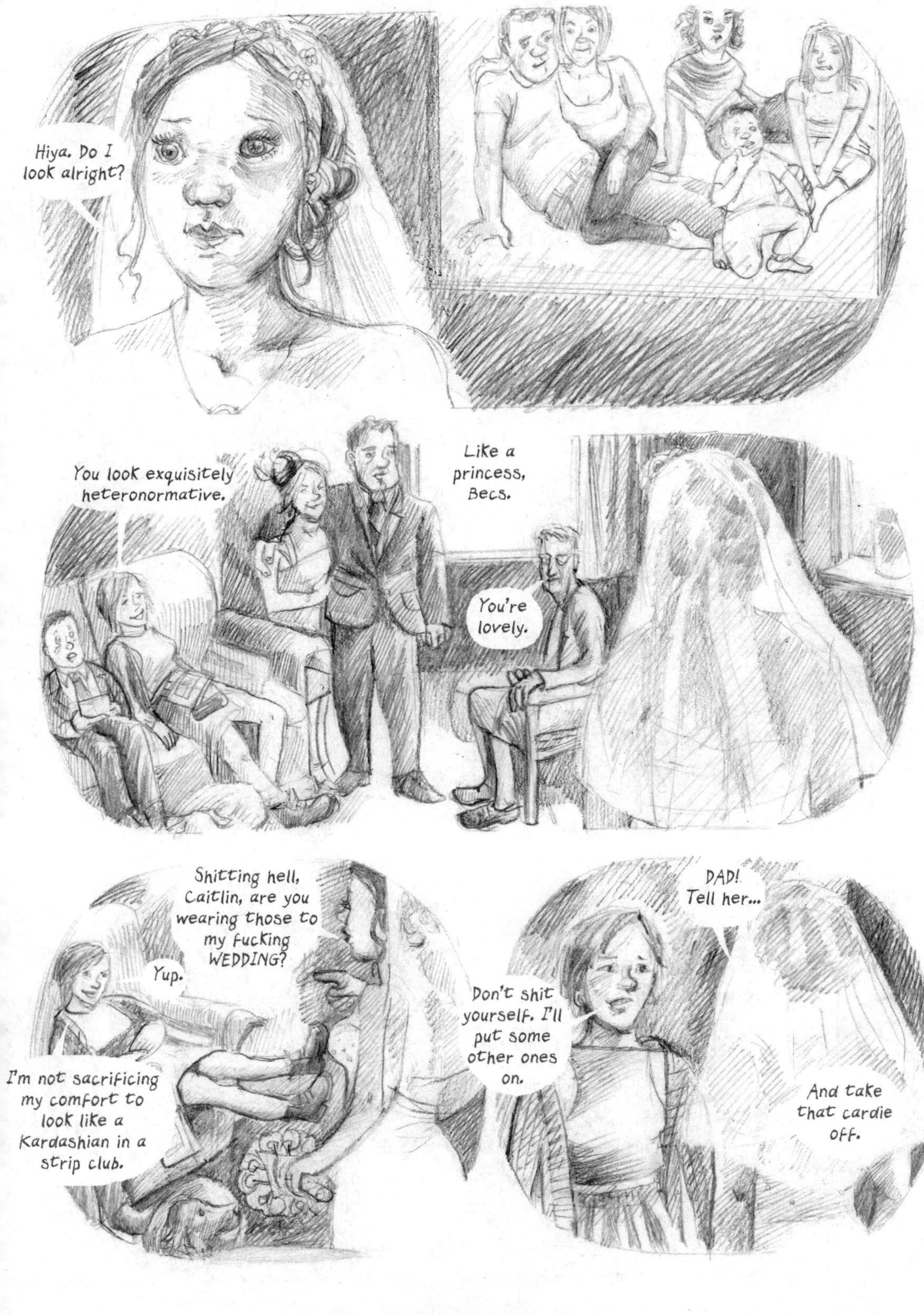
Hiya. Do I look alright?
You look exquisitely heteronormative.
Like a princess, Becs.
You're lovely.
Shitting hell, Caitlin, are you wearing those to my fucking WEDDING?
Yup.
I'm not sacrificing my comfort to look like a Kardashian in a strip club.
DAD! Tell her...
Don't shit yourself. I'll put some other ones on.
And take that cardie off.

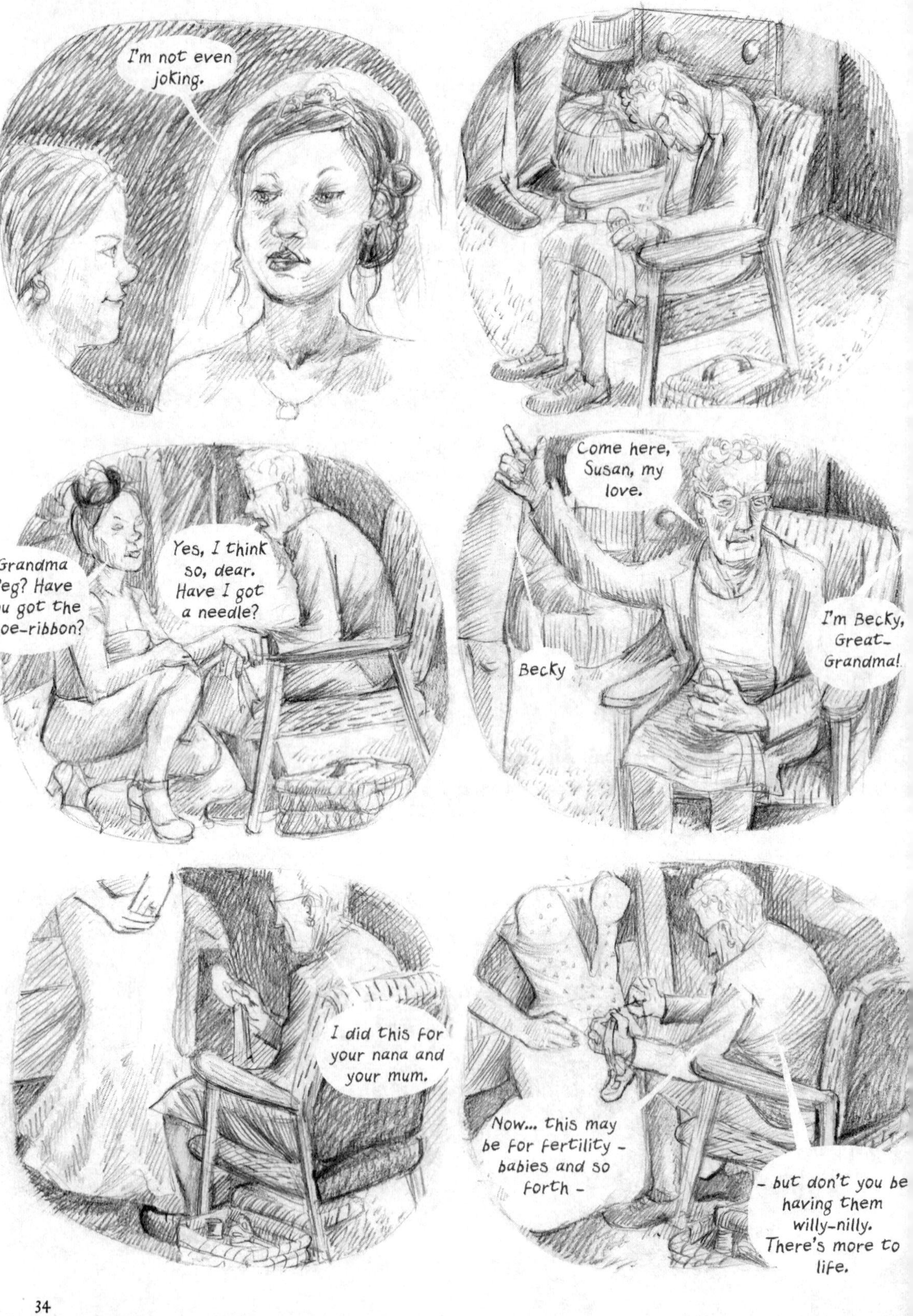

I'm not even joking.
Grandma Peg? Have you got the shoe-ribbon?
Yes, I think so, dear. Have I got a needle?
Come here, Susan, my love.
Becky
I'm Becky, Great-Grandma!
I did this for your nana and your mum.
Now... this may be for fertility - babies and so forth -
- but don't you be having them willy-nilly. There's more to life.

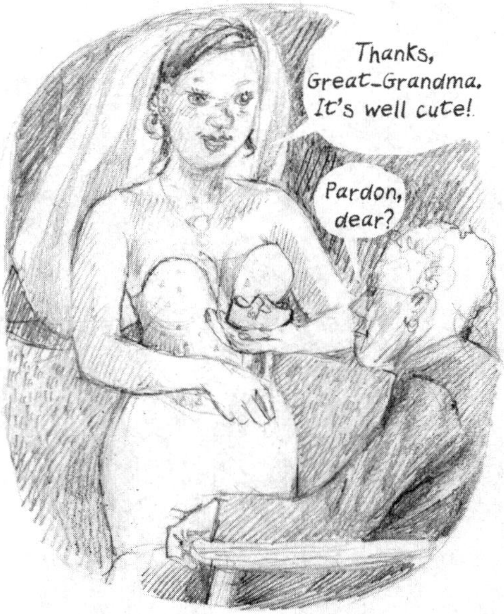
Thanks, Great-Grandma. It's well cute!
Pardon, dear?

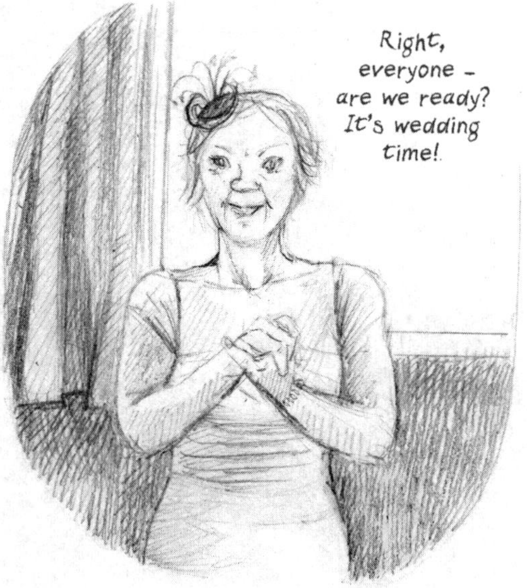
Right, everyone - are we ready? It's wedding time!

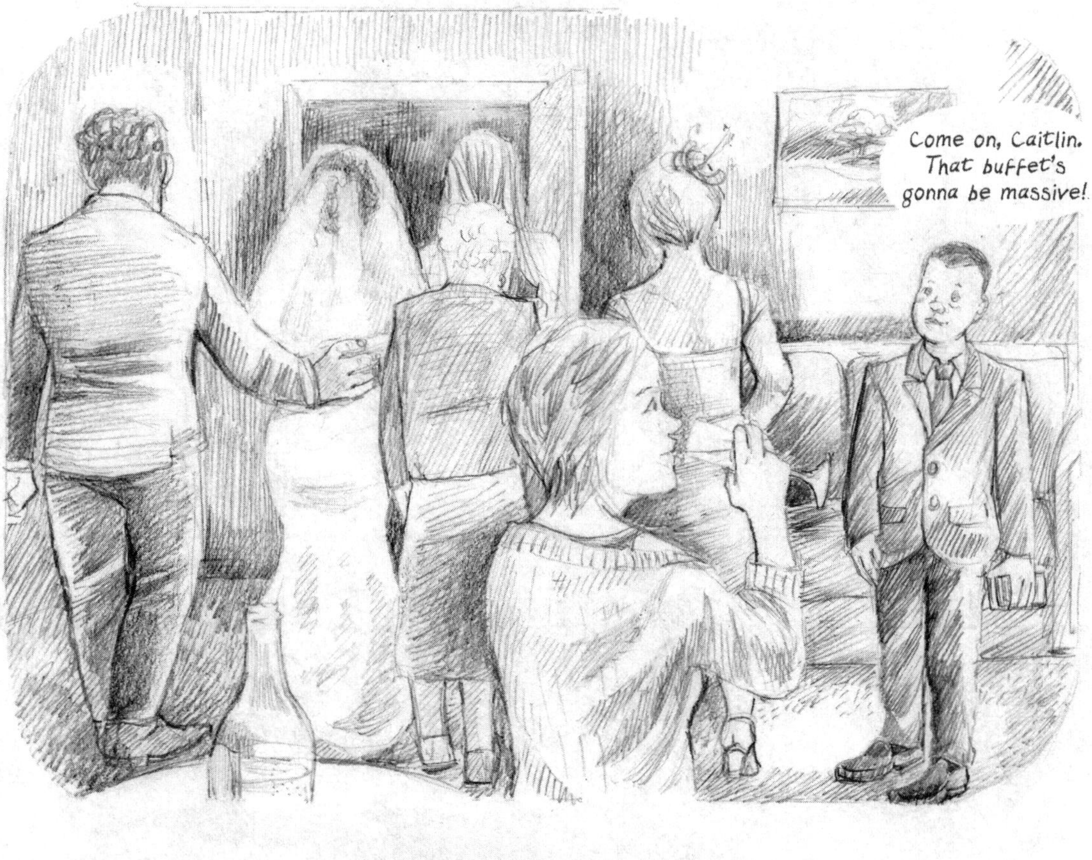
Come on, Caitlin. That buffet's gonna be massive!

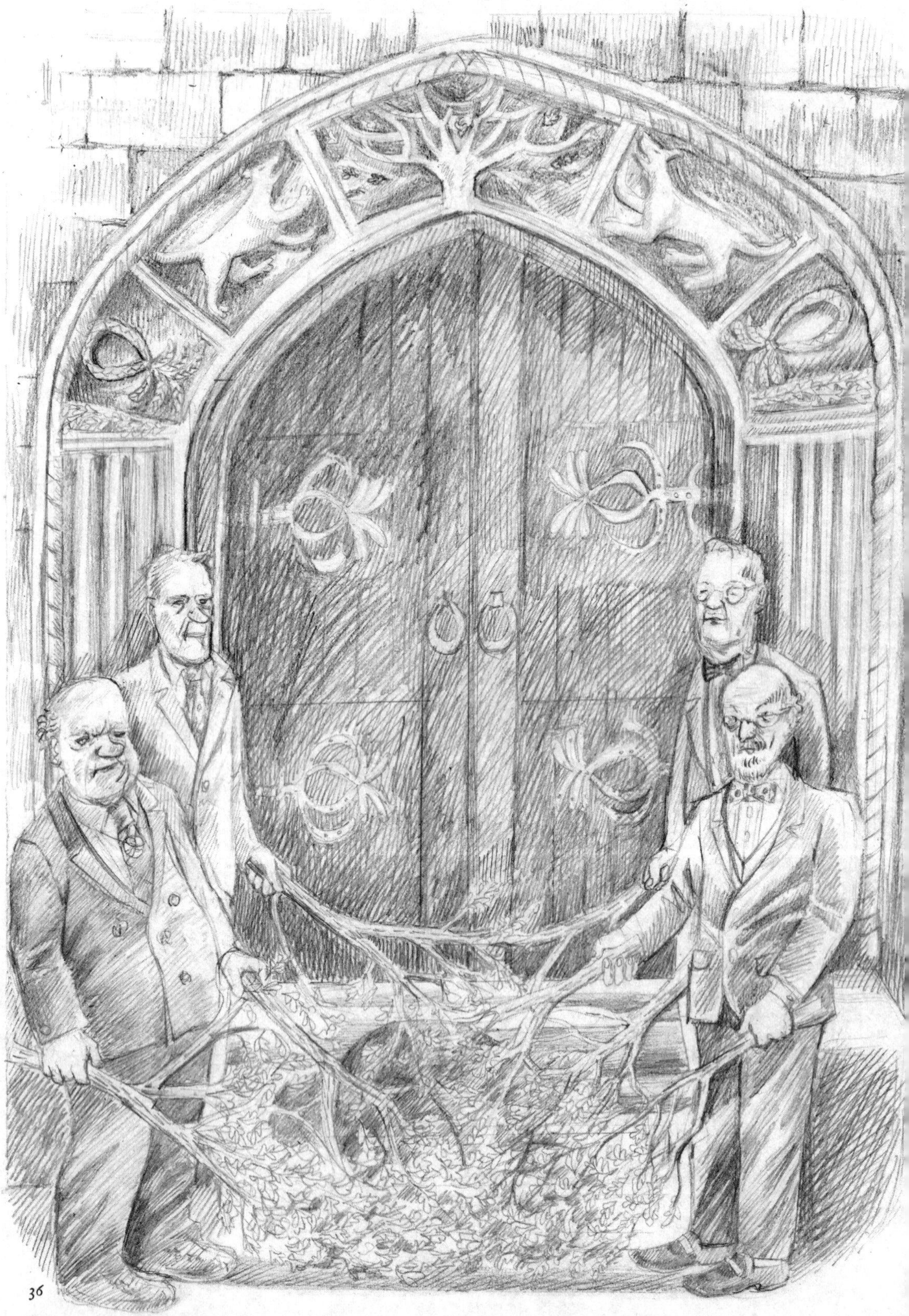

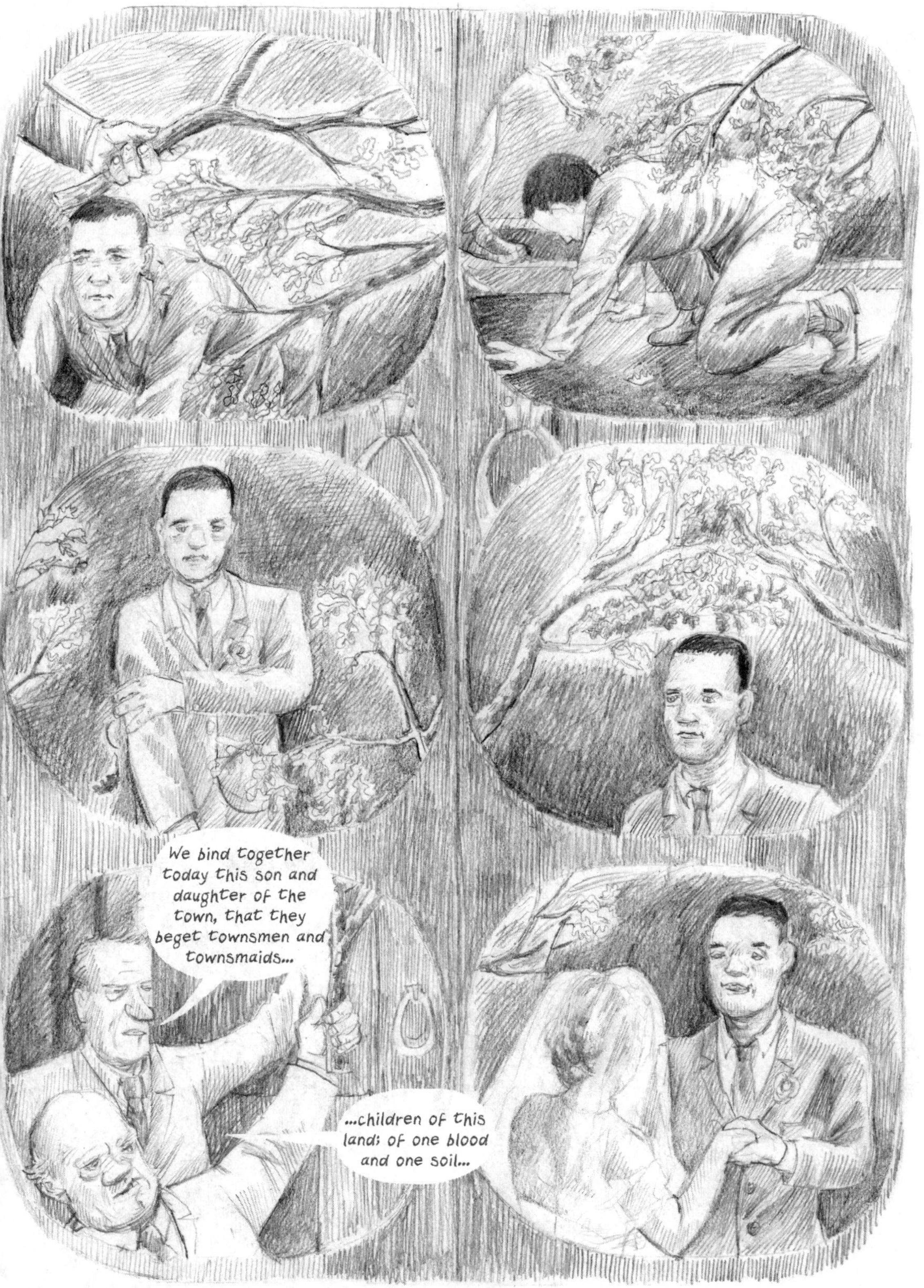
We bind together today this son and daughter of the town, that they beget townsmen and townsmaids...
...children of this land; of one blood and one soil...

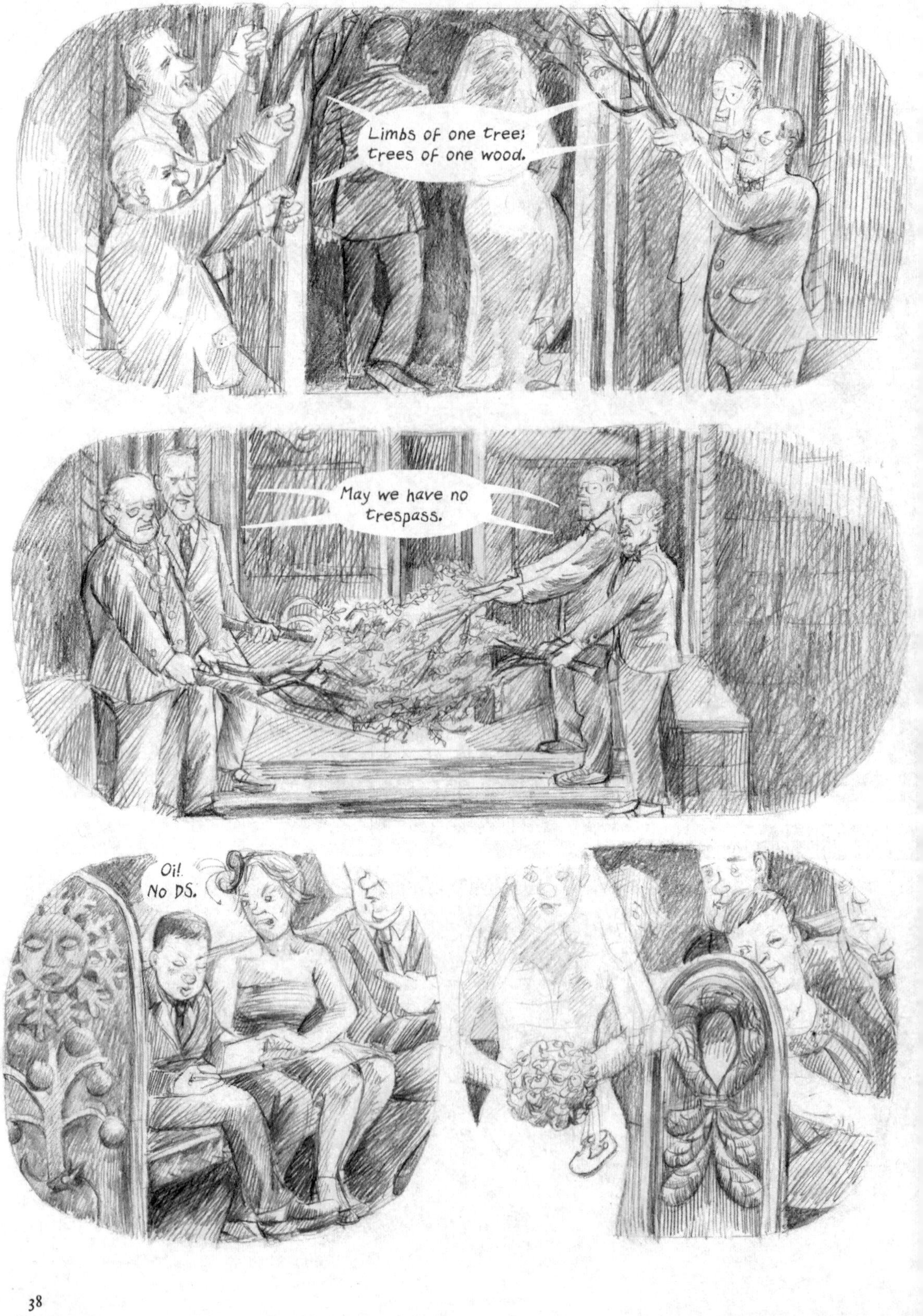
Limbs of one tree;
trees of one wood.
May we have no
trespass.
Oi!
No DS.

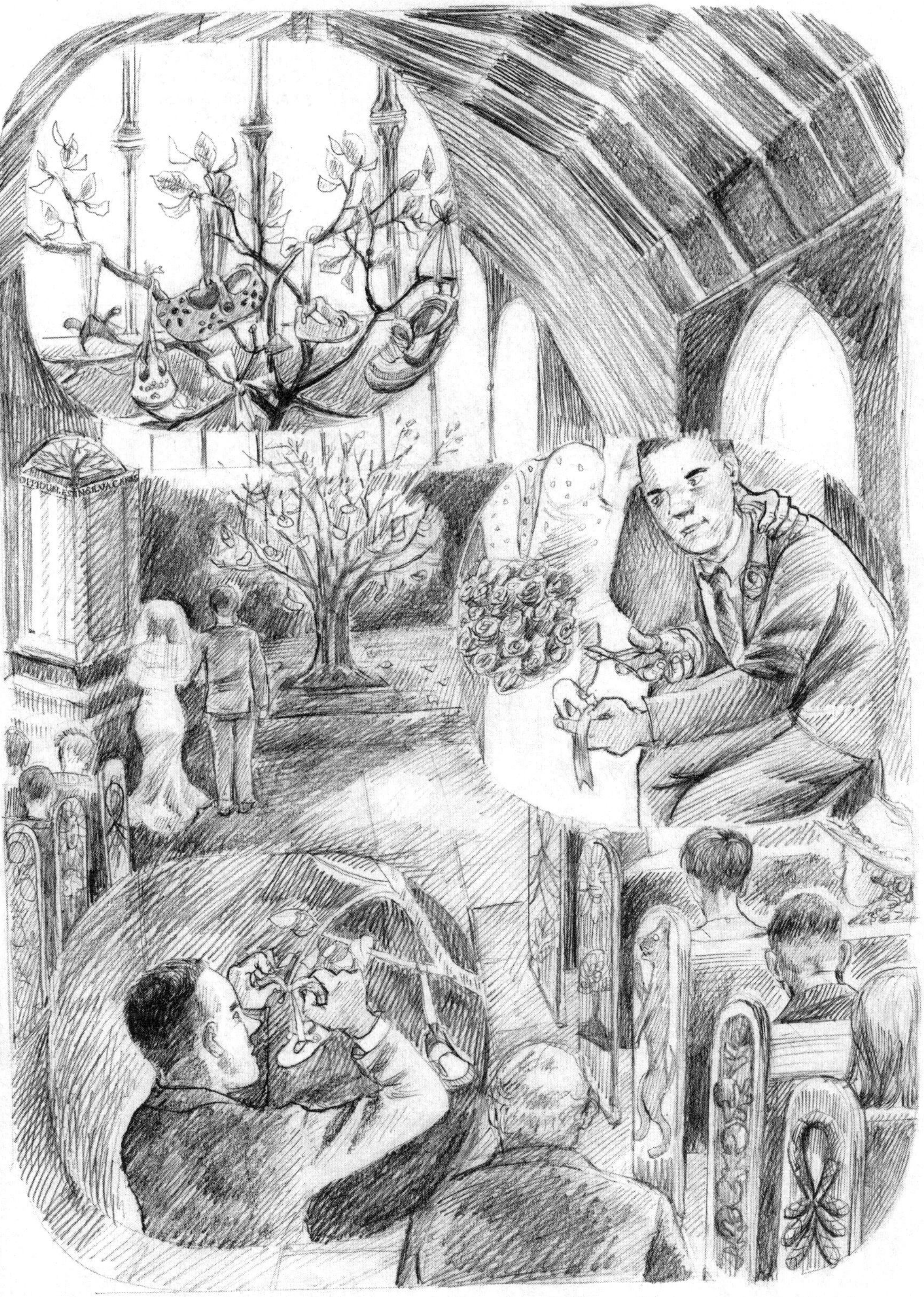
OPPIDUM EST IN SILVA

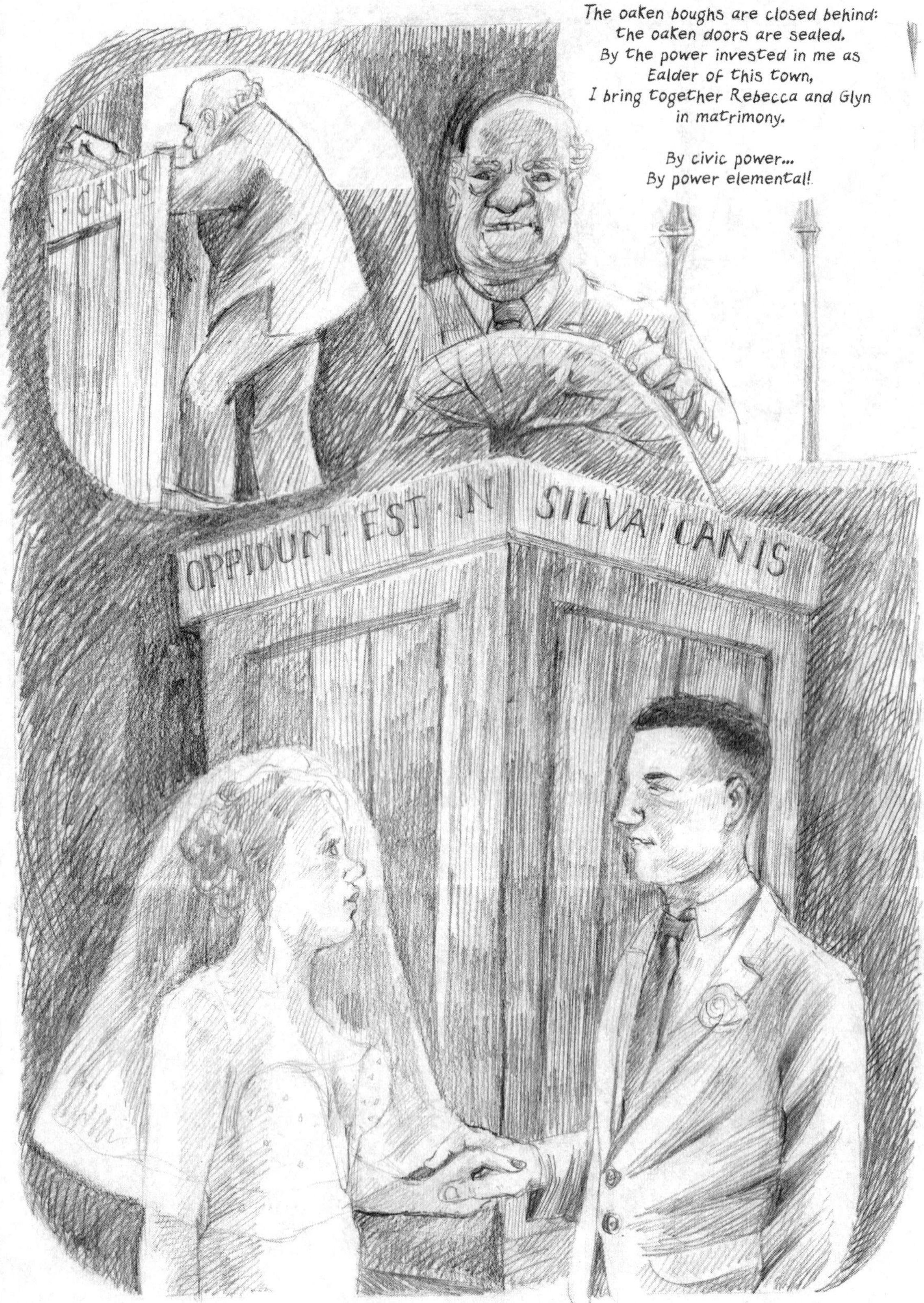
The oaken boughs are closed behind:
the oaken doors are sealed.
By the power invested in me as
Ealder of this town,
I bring together Rebecca and Glyn
in matrimony.
By civic power...
By power elemental!
OPPIDUM EST IN SILVA CANIS

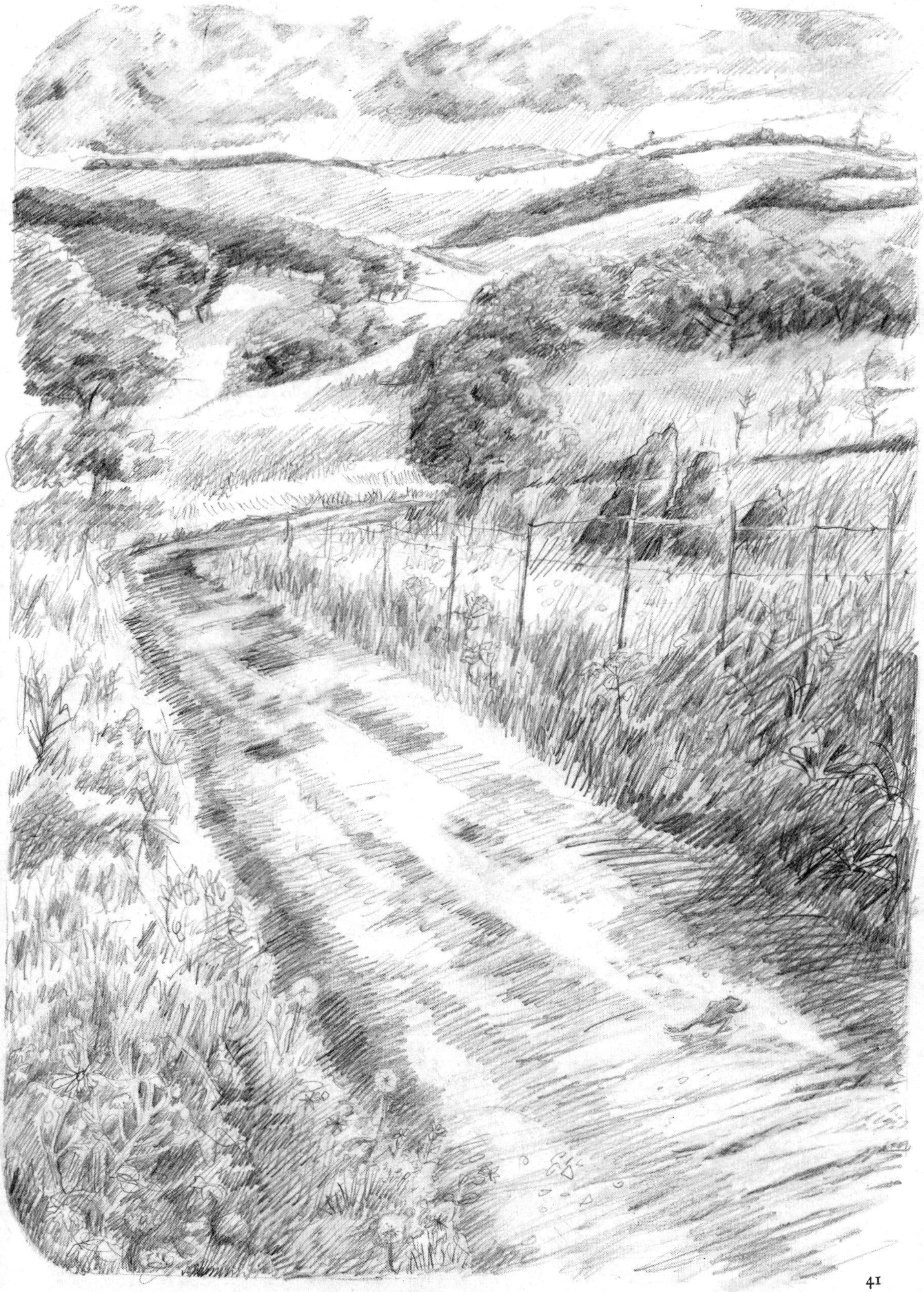

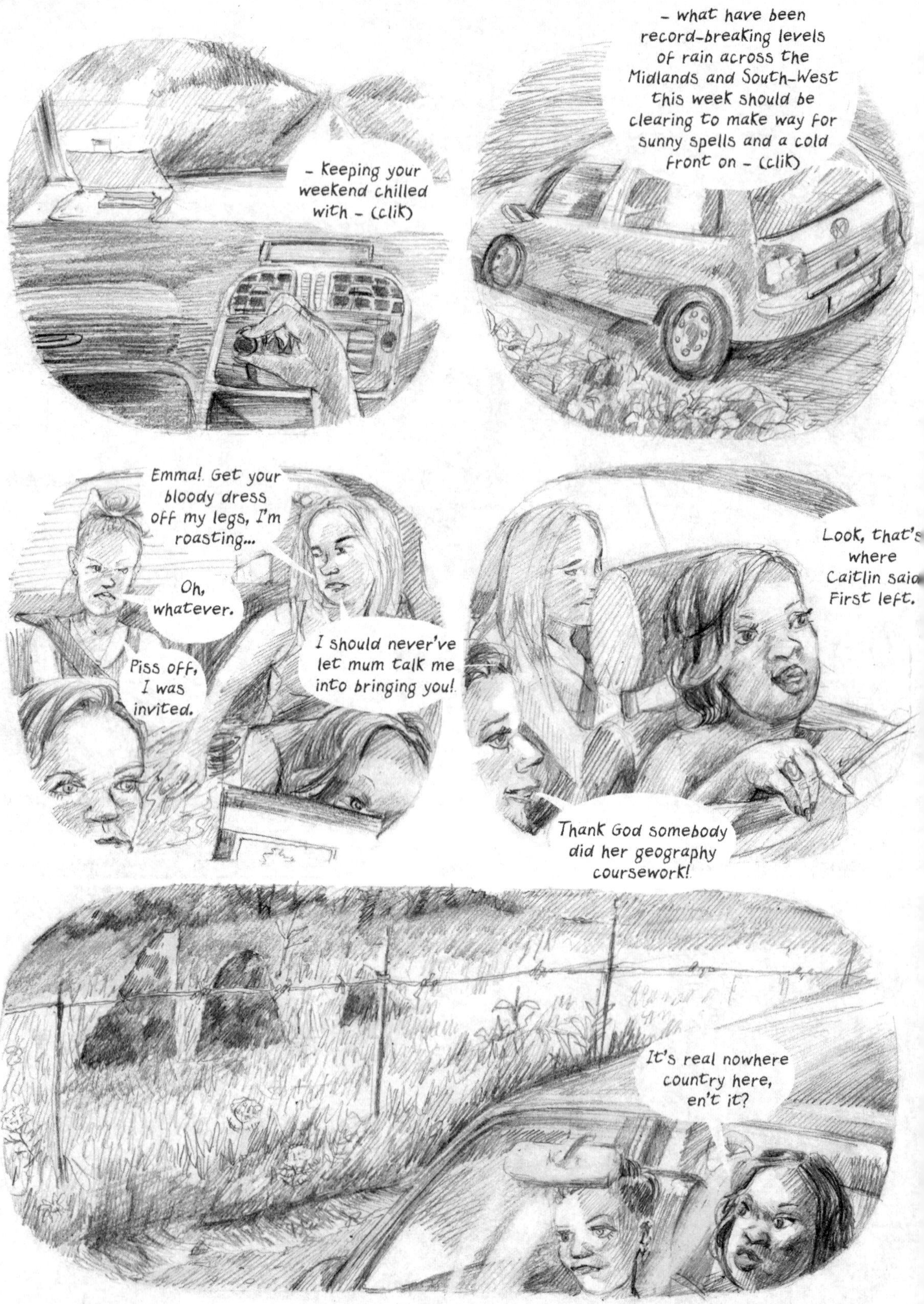

- keeping your weekend chilled with - (clik)
- what have been record-breaking levels of rain across the Midlands and South-West this week should be clearing to make way for sunny spells and a cold front on - (clik)
Emma! Get your bloody dress off my legs, I'm roasting...
Oh, whatever.
I should never've let mum talk me into bringing you!
Piss off, I was invited.
Look, that's where Caitlin sai First left.
Thank God somebody did her geography coursework!
It's real nowhere country here, en't it?

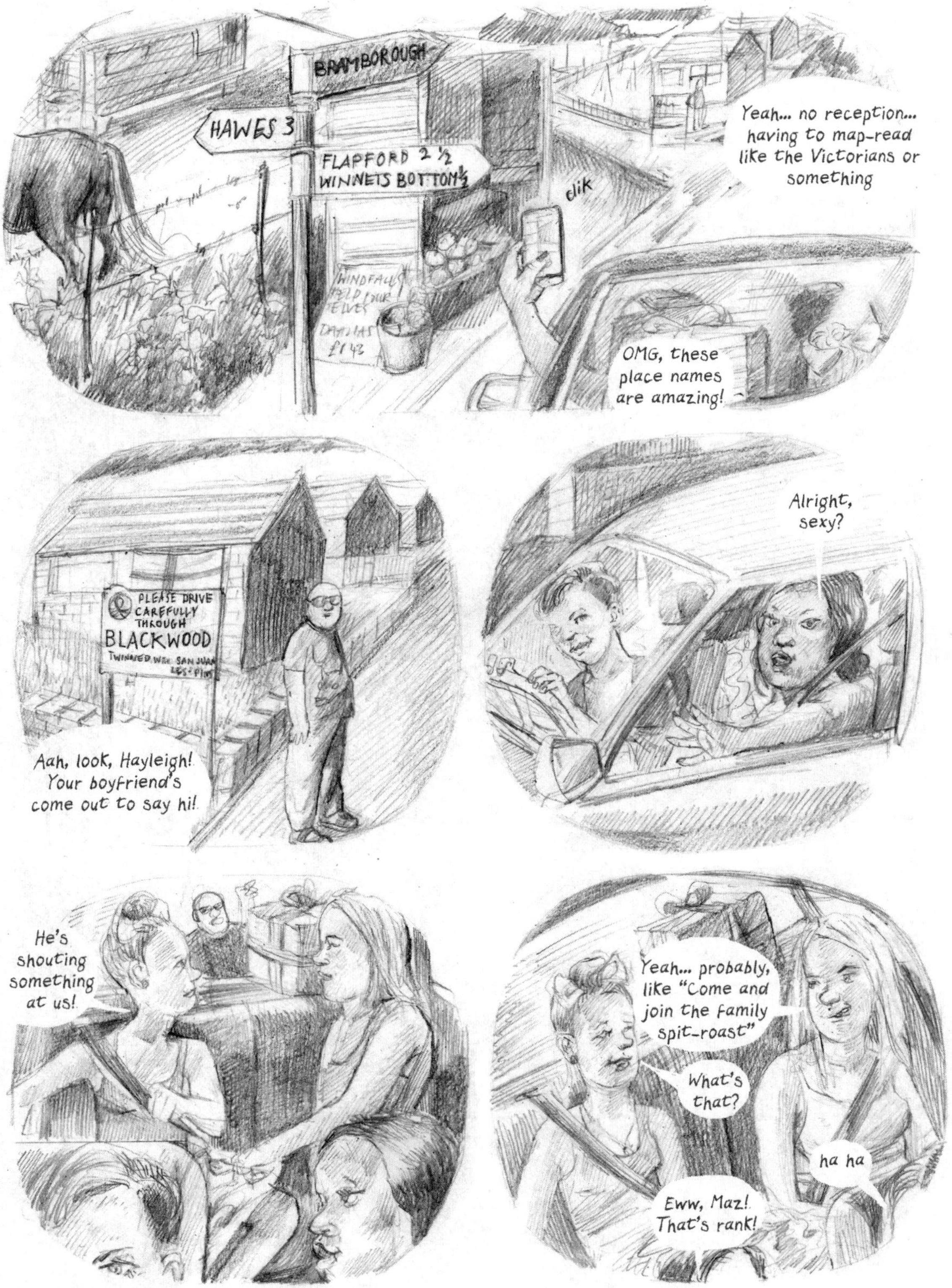
BRAMBOROUGH
HAWES 3
FLAPFORD 2 1/2
WINNETS BOTTOM 1/2
Yeah... no reception... having to map-read like the Victorians or something
clik
OMG, these place names are amazing!
PLEASE DRIVE CAREFULLY THROUGH
BLACKWOOD
Aah, look, Hayleigh! Your boyfriend's come out to say hi!
Alright, sexy?
He's shouting something at us!
Yeah... probably, like "Come and join the family spit-roast"
What's that?
ha ha
Eww, Maz! That's rank!

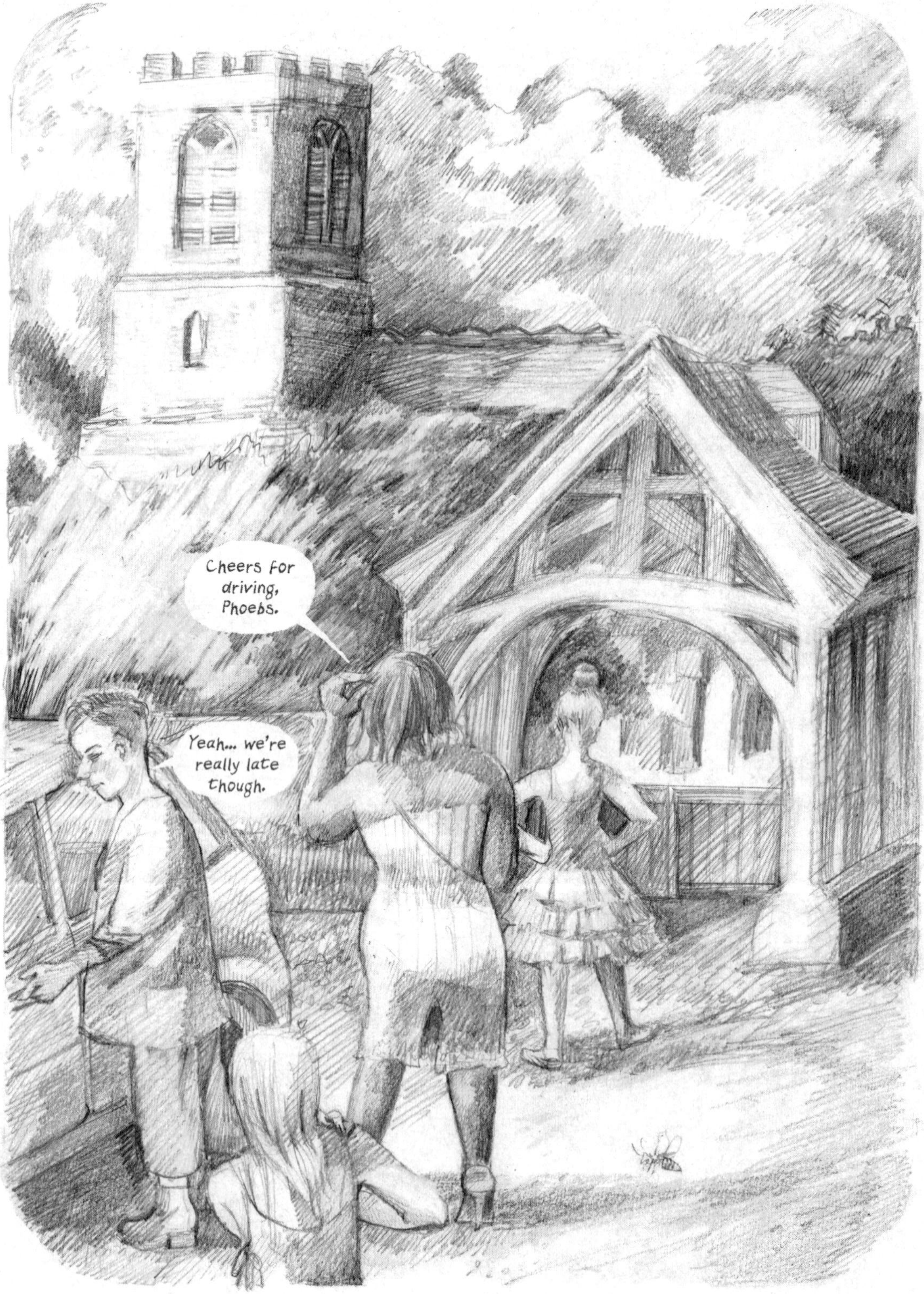
Cheers for driving, Phoebs.
Yeah... we're really late though.

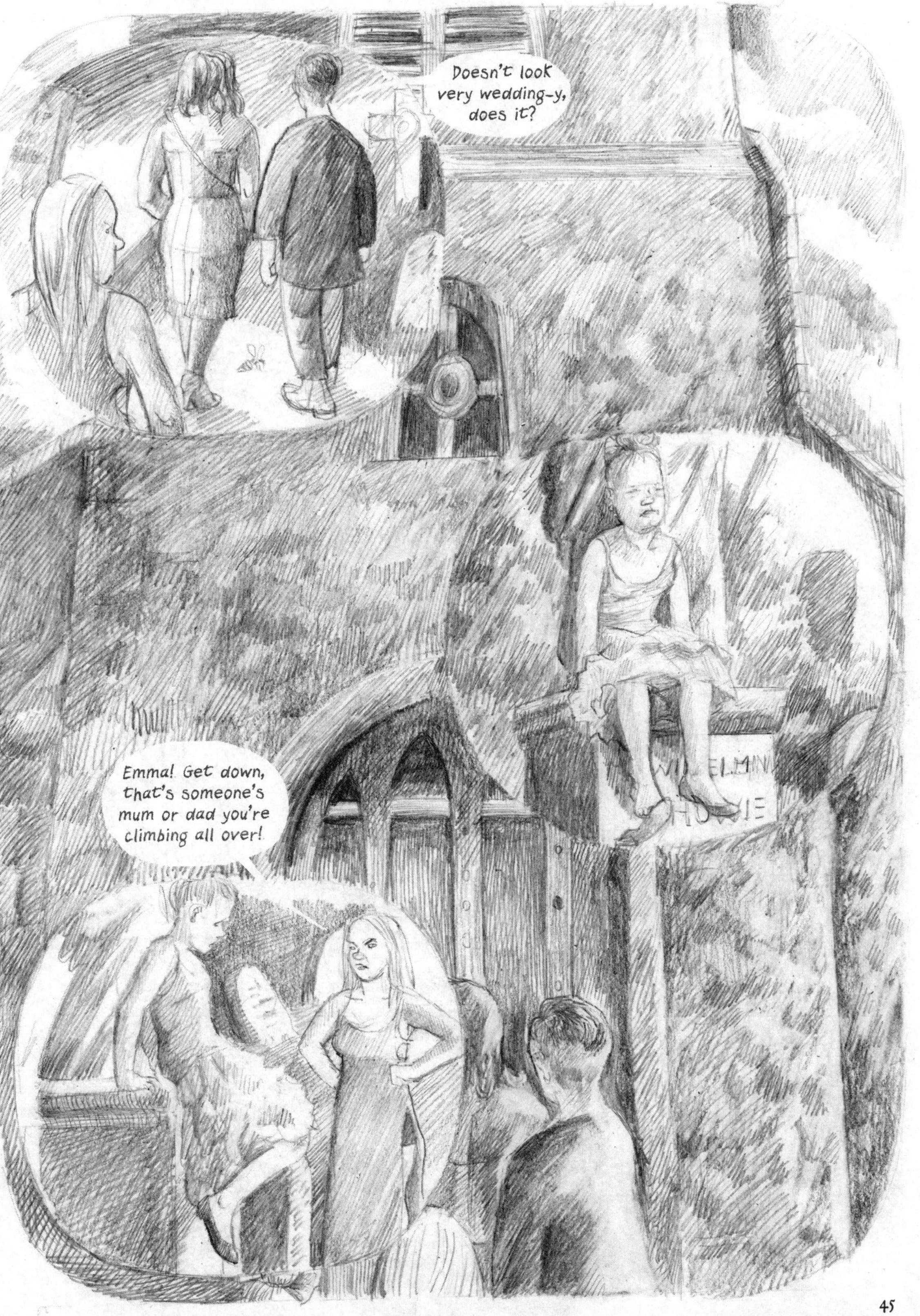
Doesn't look very wedding-y, does it?
Emma! Get down, that's someone's mum or dad you're climbing all over!

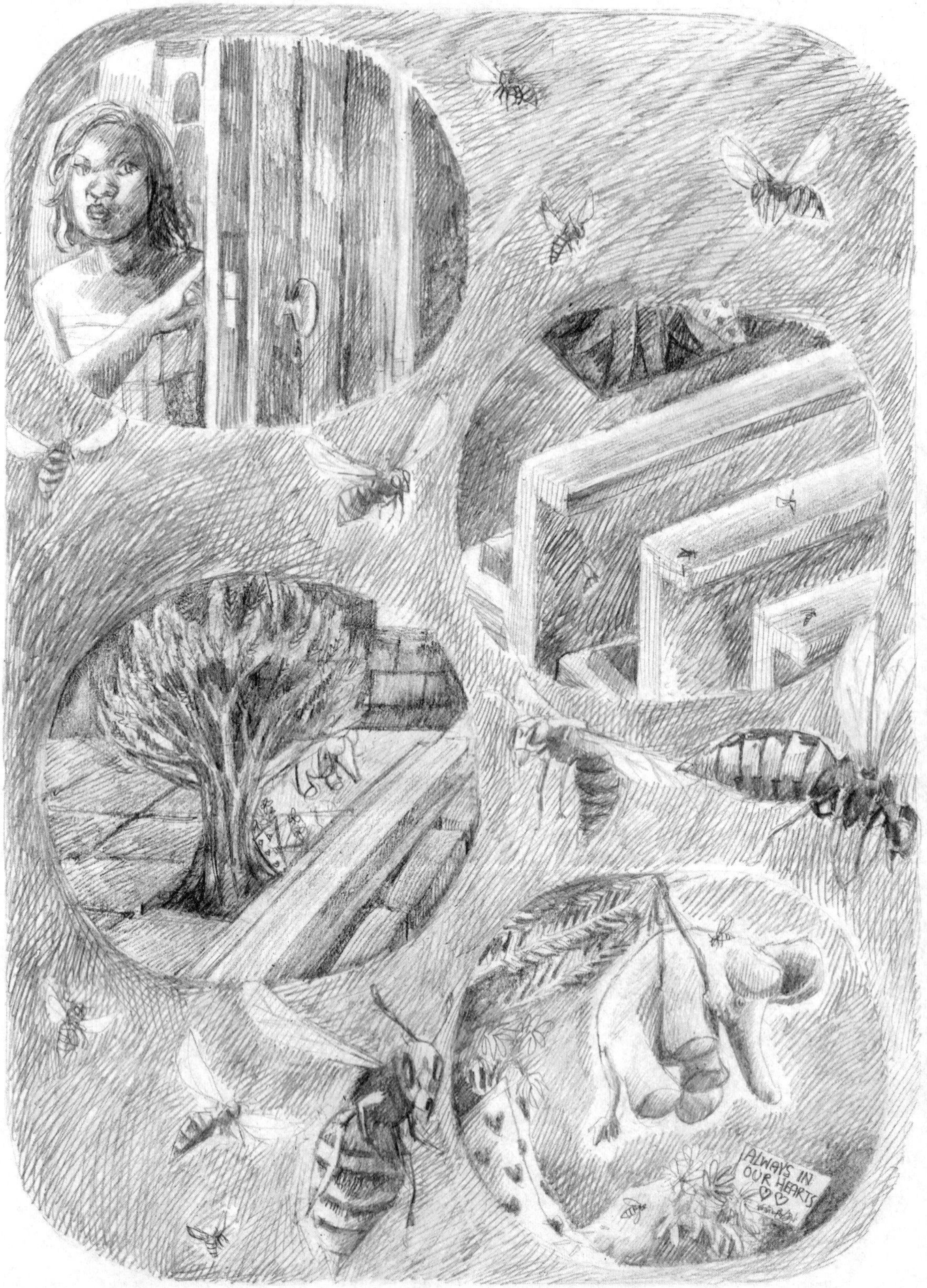
ALWAYS IN
OUR HEARTS

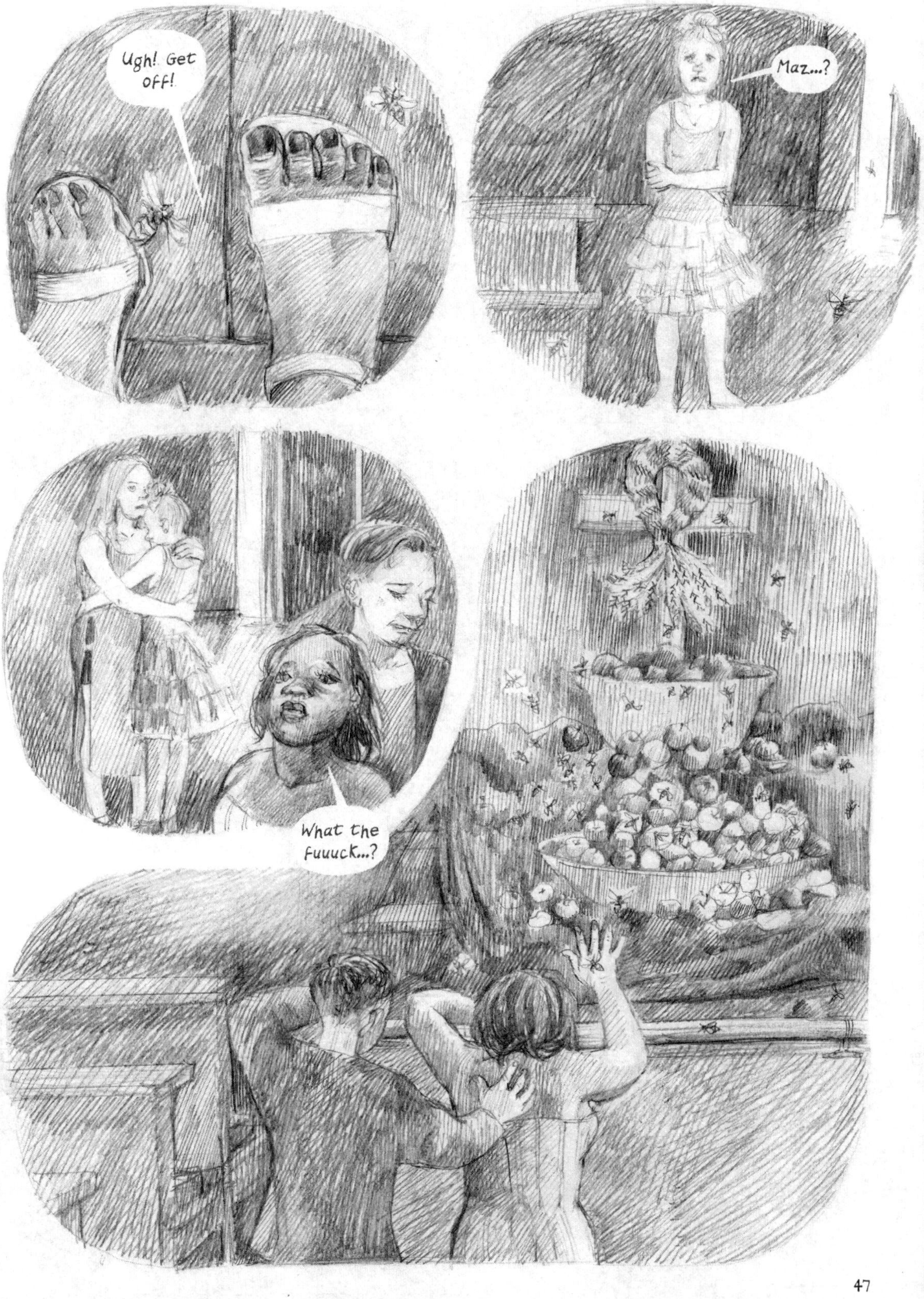
Ugh! Get off!
Maz...?
What the fuuuck...?

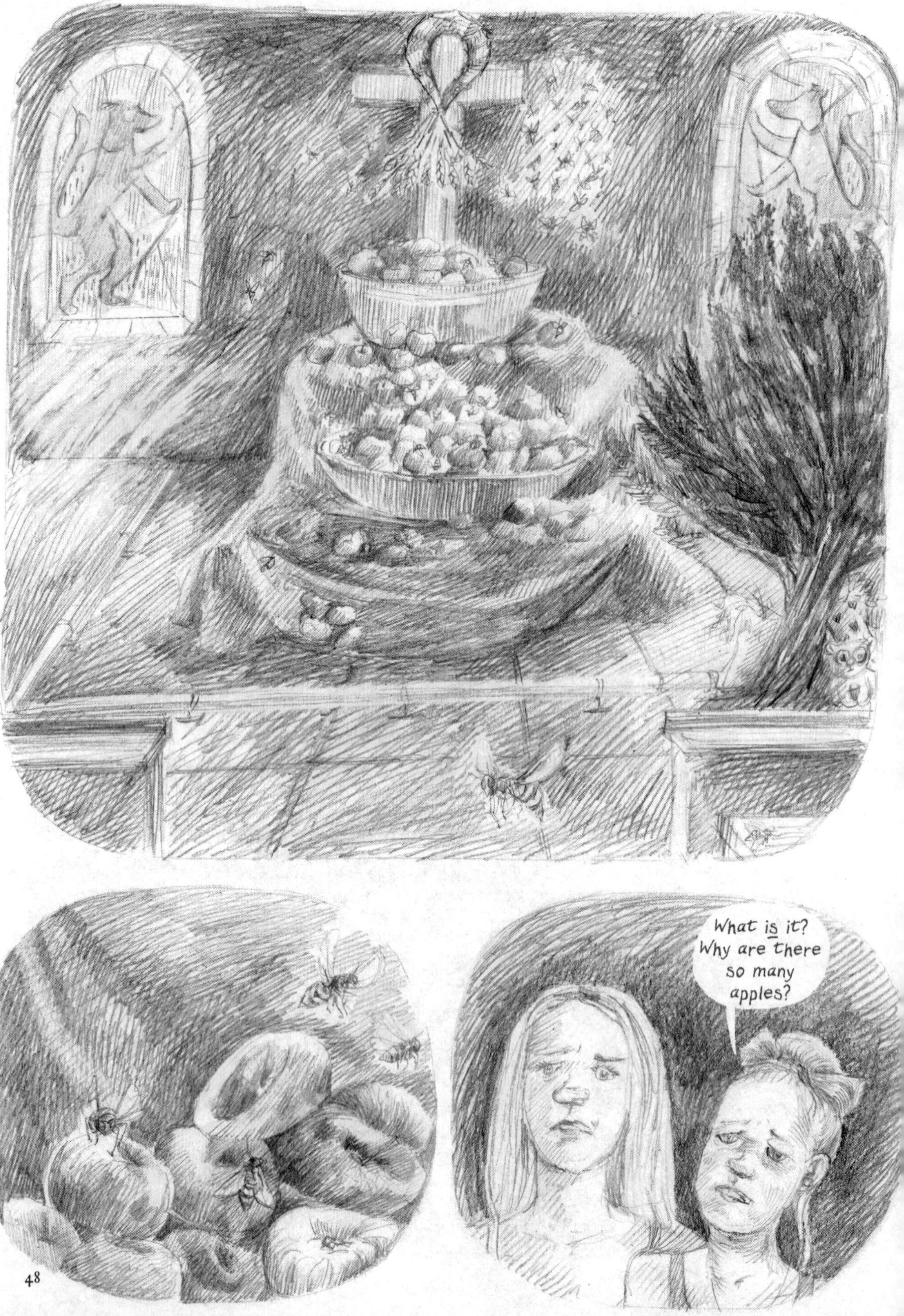
What is it? Why are there so many apples?

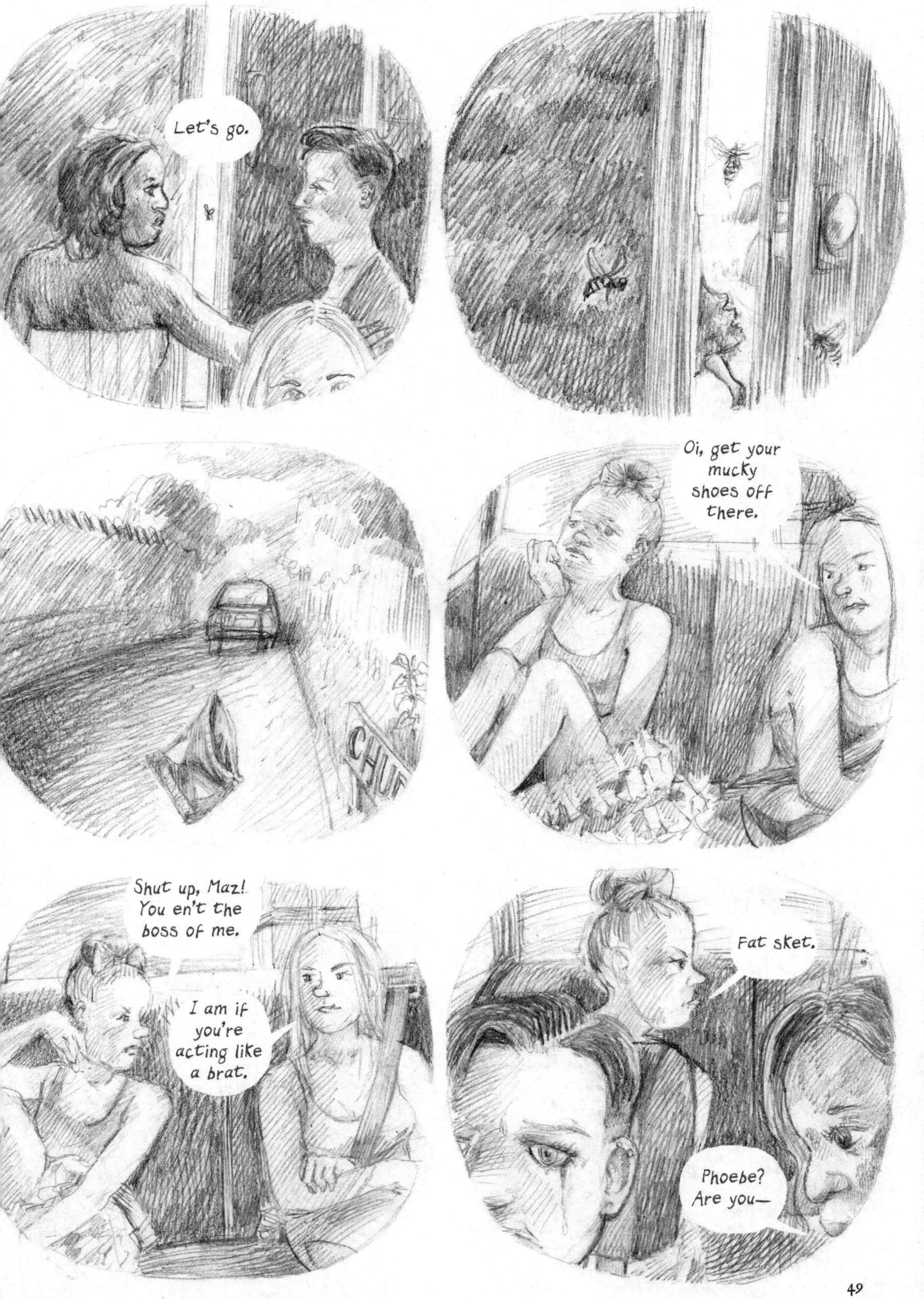

Let's go.
Oi, get your mucky shoes off there.
Shut up, Maz! You en't the boss of me.
I am if you're acting like a brat.
Fat sket.
Phoebe? Are you—

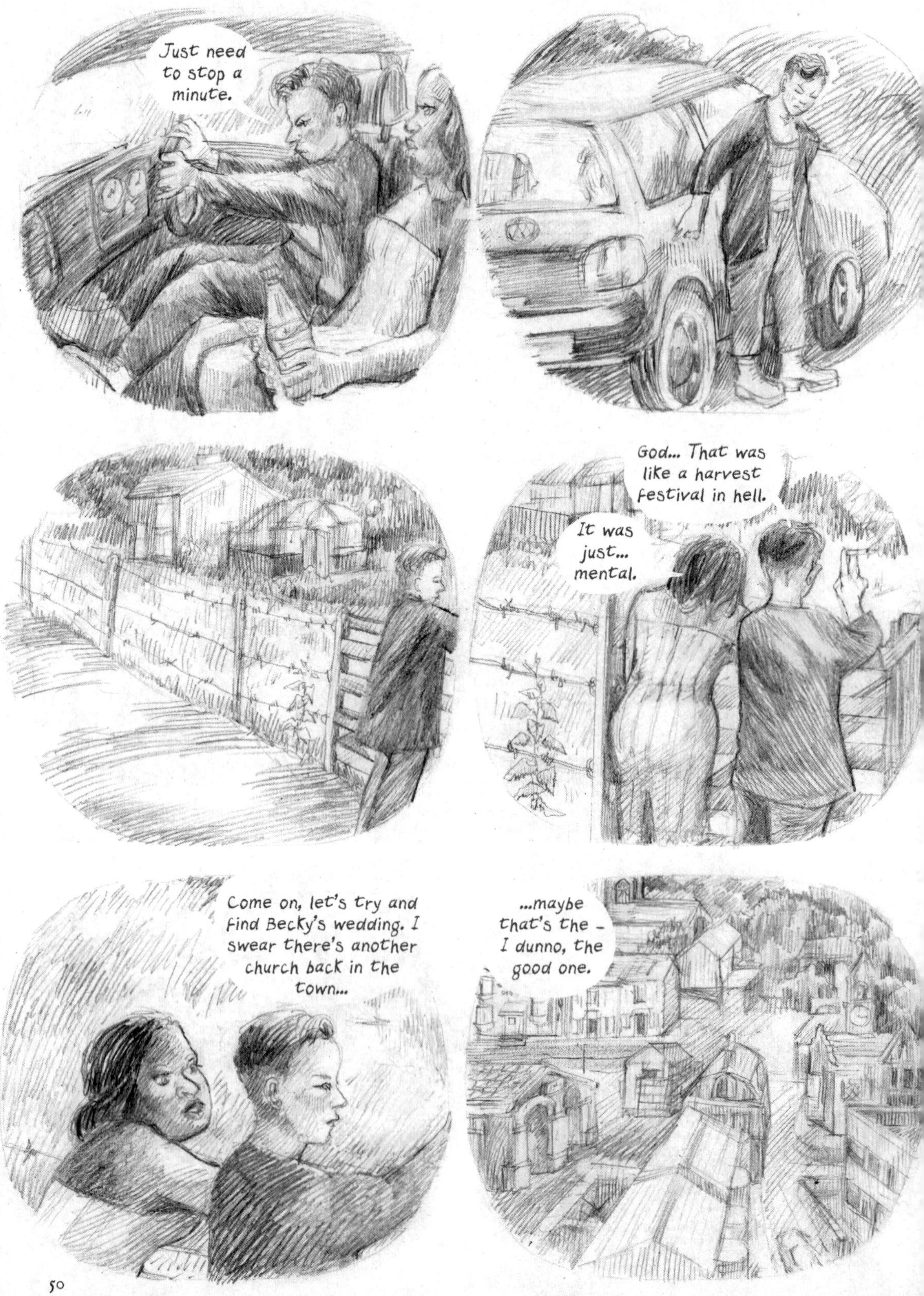
Just need to stop a minute.
God... That was like a harvest festival in hell.
It was just... mental.
Come on, let's try and find Becky's wedding. I swear there's another church back in the town...
...maybe that's the – I dunno, the good one.

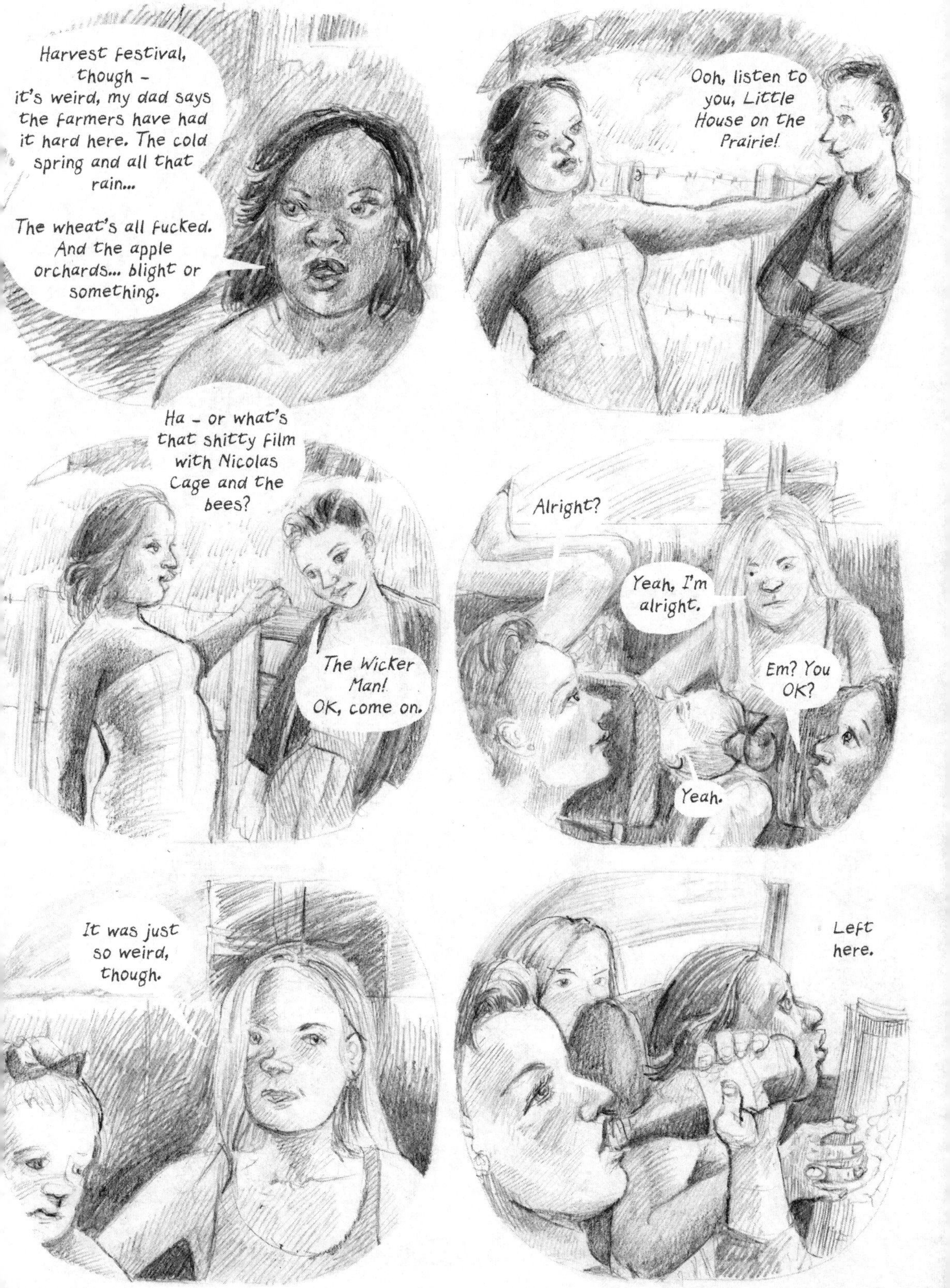
Harvest festival, though - it's weird, my dad says the farmers have had it hard here. The cold spring and all that rain...
The wheat's all fucked. And the apple orchards... blight or something.
Ooh, listen to you, Little House on the Prairie!
Ha - or what's that shitty film with Nicolas Cage and the bees?
The Wicker Man! OK, come on.
Alright?
Yeah, I'm alright.
Em? You OK?
Yeah.
It was just so weird, though.
Left here.

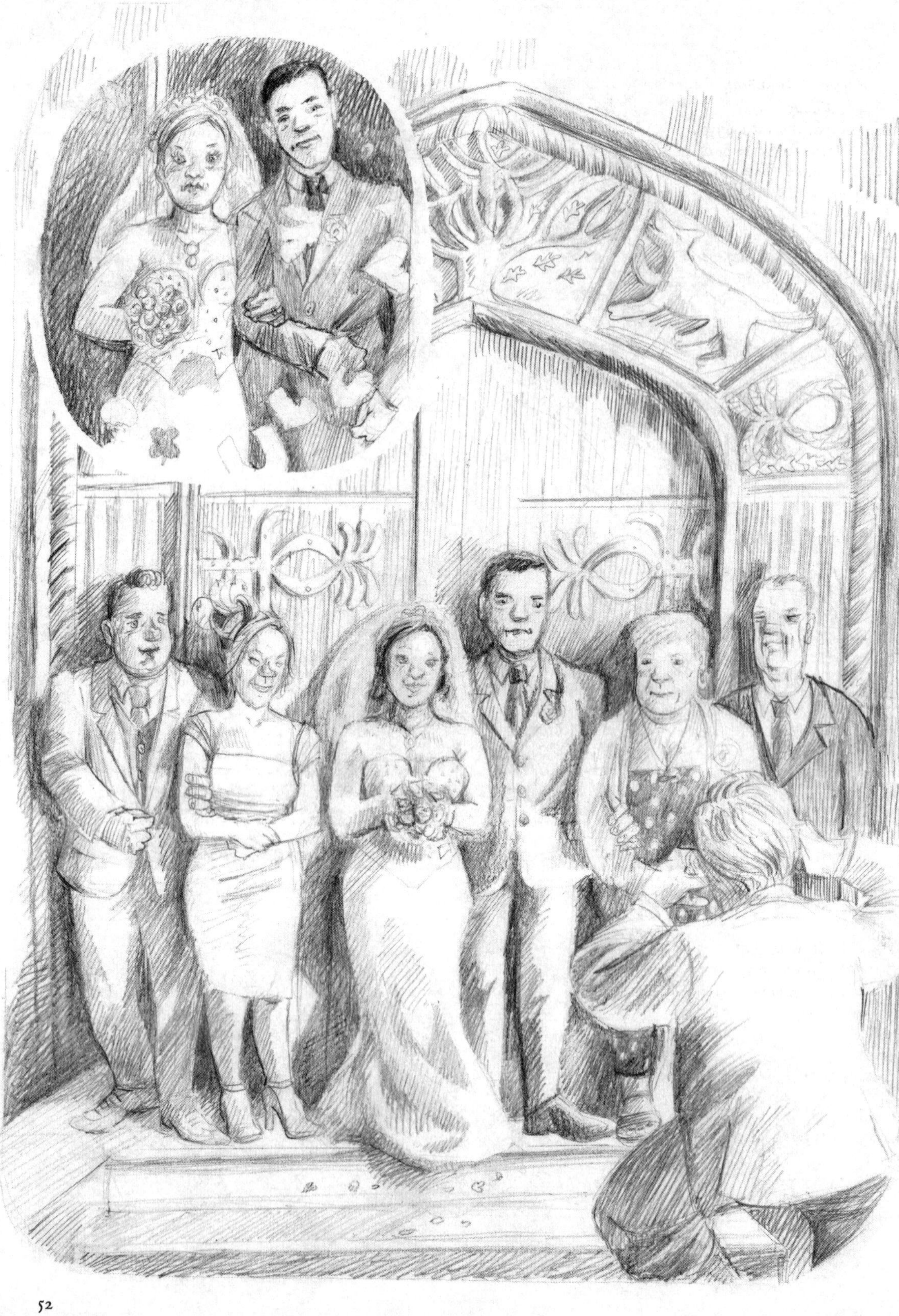

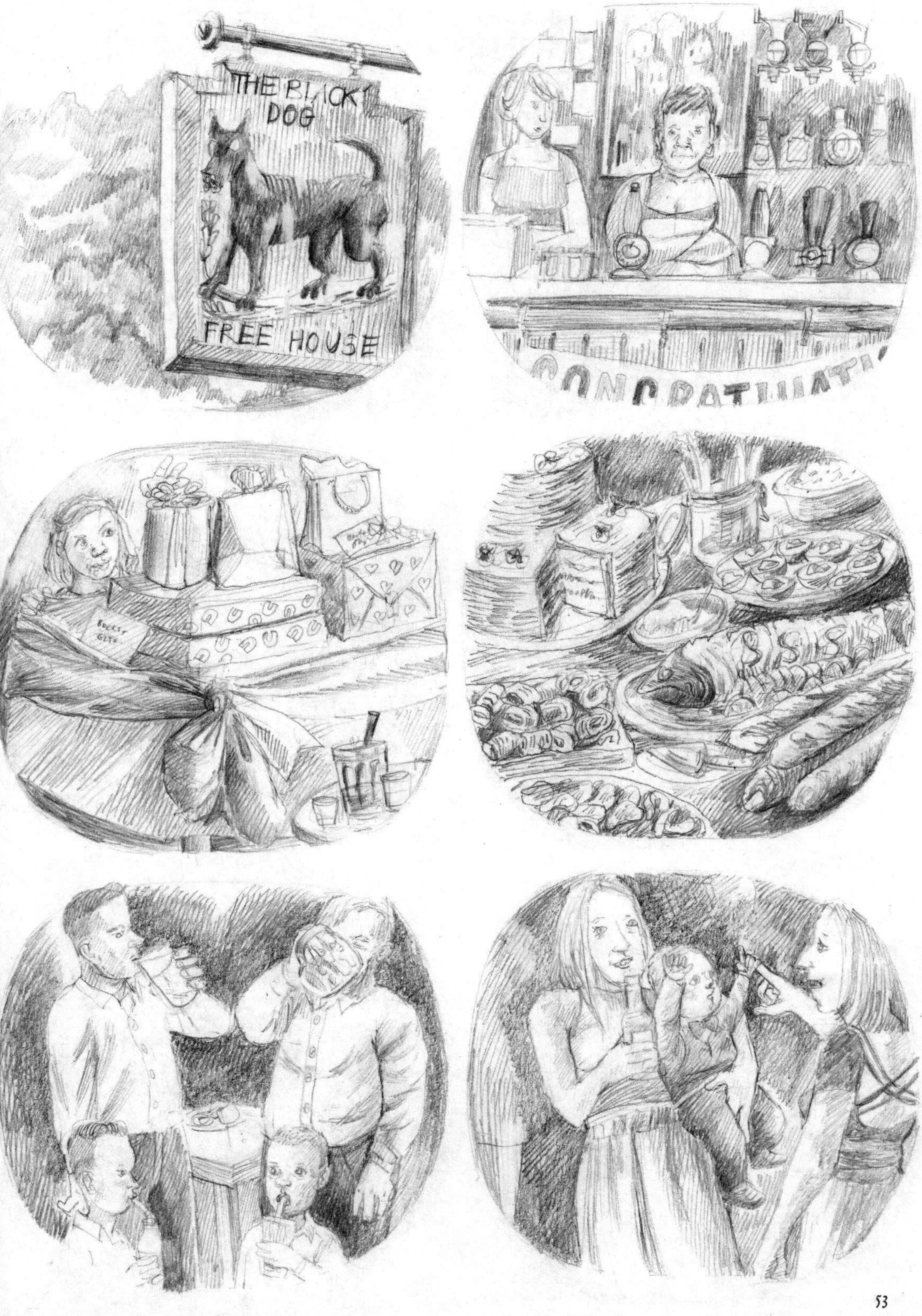
THE BLACK DOG
FREE HOUSE

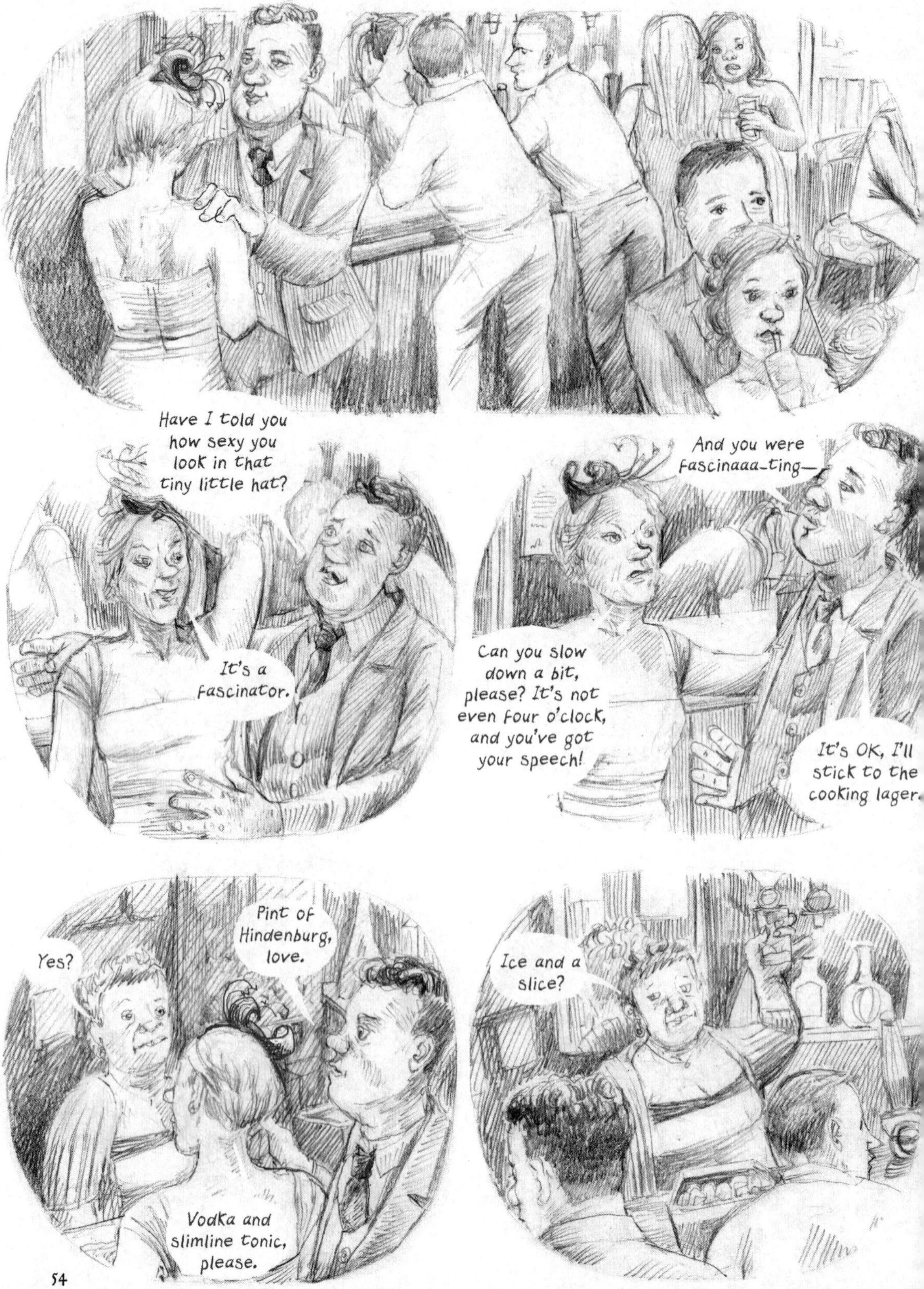
Have I told you how sexy you look in that tiny little hat?
It's a fascinator.
And you were fascinaaa_ting—
Can you slow down a bit, please? It's not even four o'clock, and you've got your speech!
It's OK, I'll stick to the cooking lager.
Yes?
Pint of Hindenburg, love.
Vodka and slimline tonic, please.
Ice and a slice?

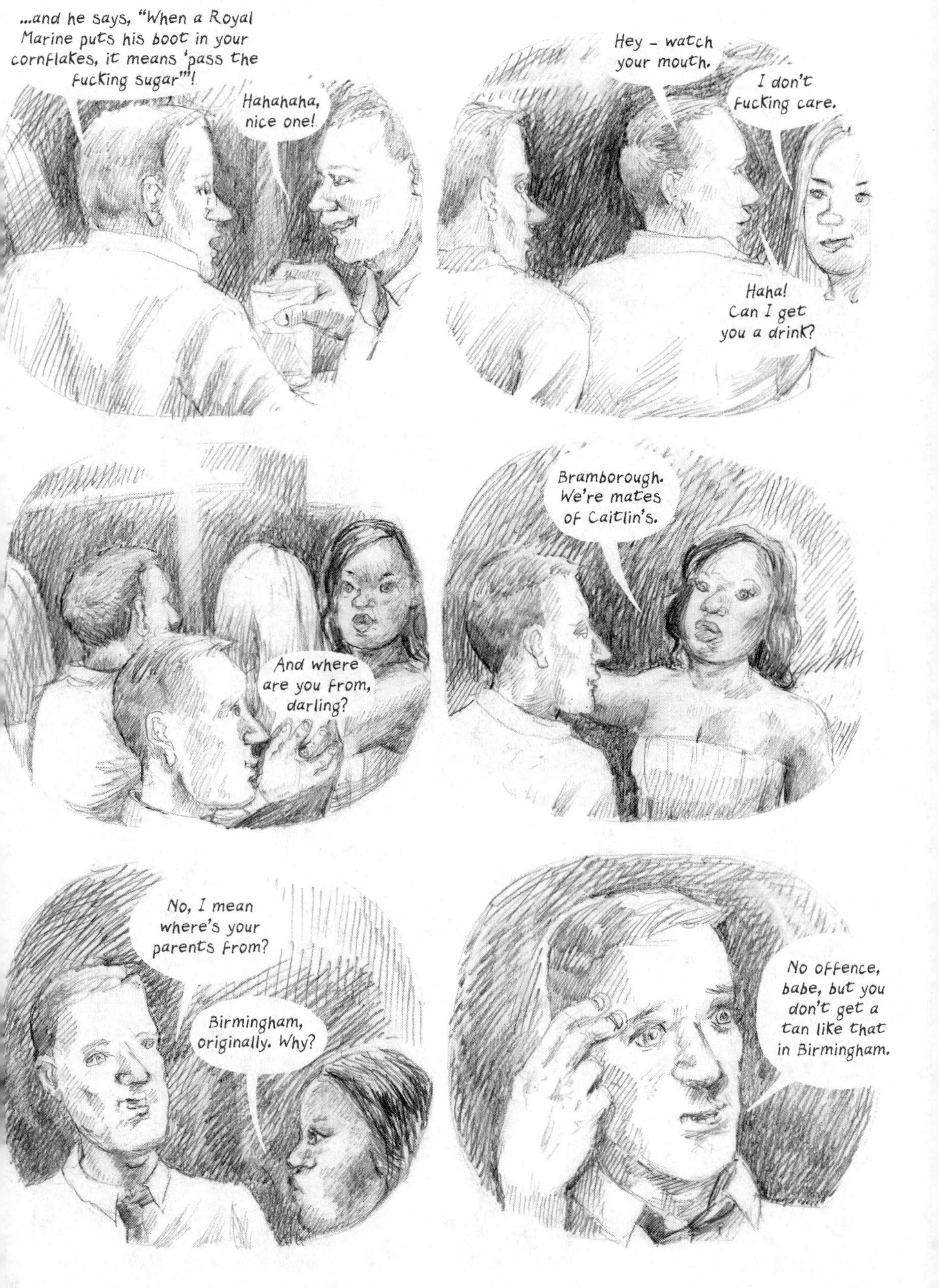
...and he says, "When a Royal Marine puts his boot in your cornflakes, it means 'pass the fucking sugar'"!
Hahahaha, nice one!
Hey - watch your mouth.
I don't fucking care.
Haha! Can I get you a drink?
And where are you from, darling?
Bramborough. We're mates of Caitlin's.
No, I mean where's your parents from?
Birmingham, originally. Why?
No offence, babe, but you don't get a tan like that in Birmingham.

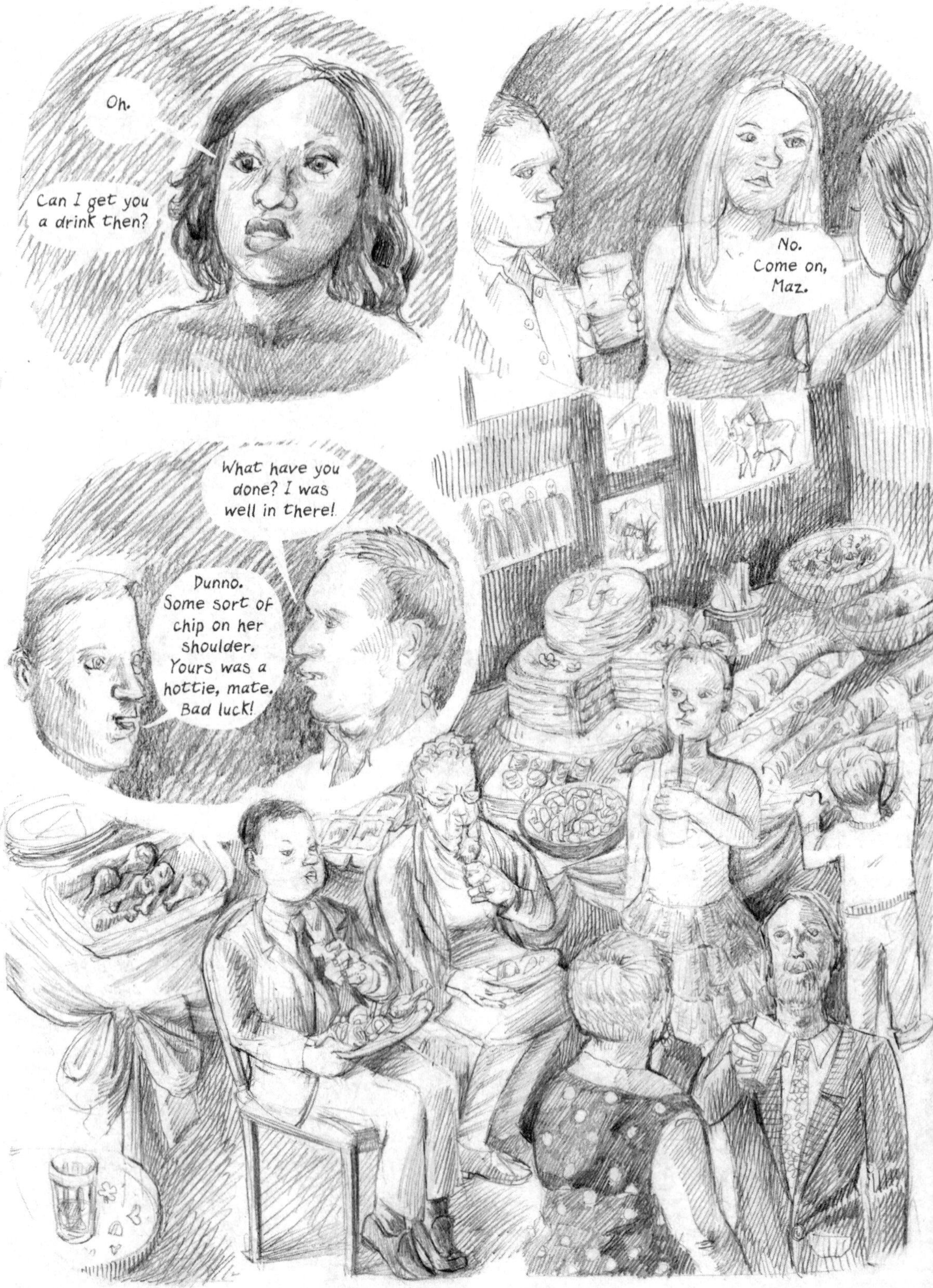

Oh.
Can I get you a drink then?
No. Come on, Maz.
What have you done? I was well in there!
Dunno. Some sort of chip on her shoulder. Yours was a hottie, mate. Bad luck!

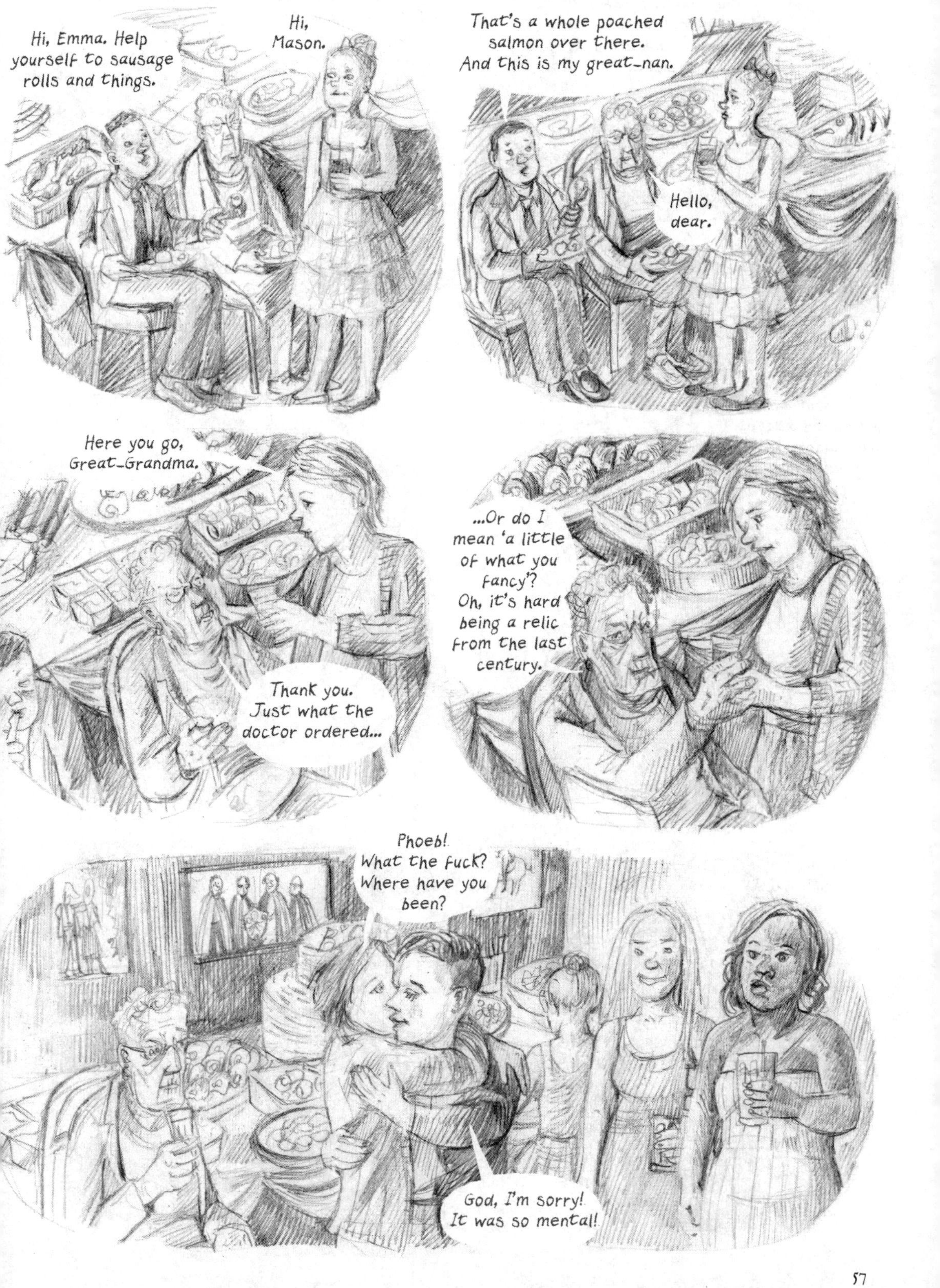
Hi, Emma. Help yourself to sausage rolls and things.
Hi, Mason.
That's a whole poached salmon over there. And this is my great-nan.
Hello, dear.
Here you go, Great-Grandma.
Thank you. Just what the doctor ordered...
...Or do I mean 'a little of what you fancy'? Oh, it's hard being a relic from the last century.
Phoeb! What the fuck? Where have you been?
God, I'm sorry! It was so mental!

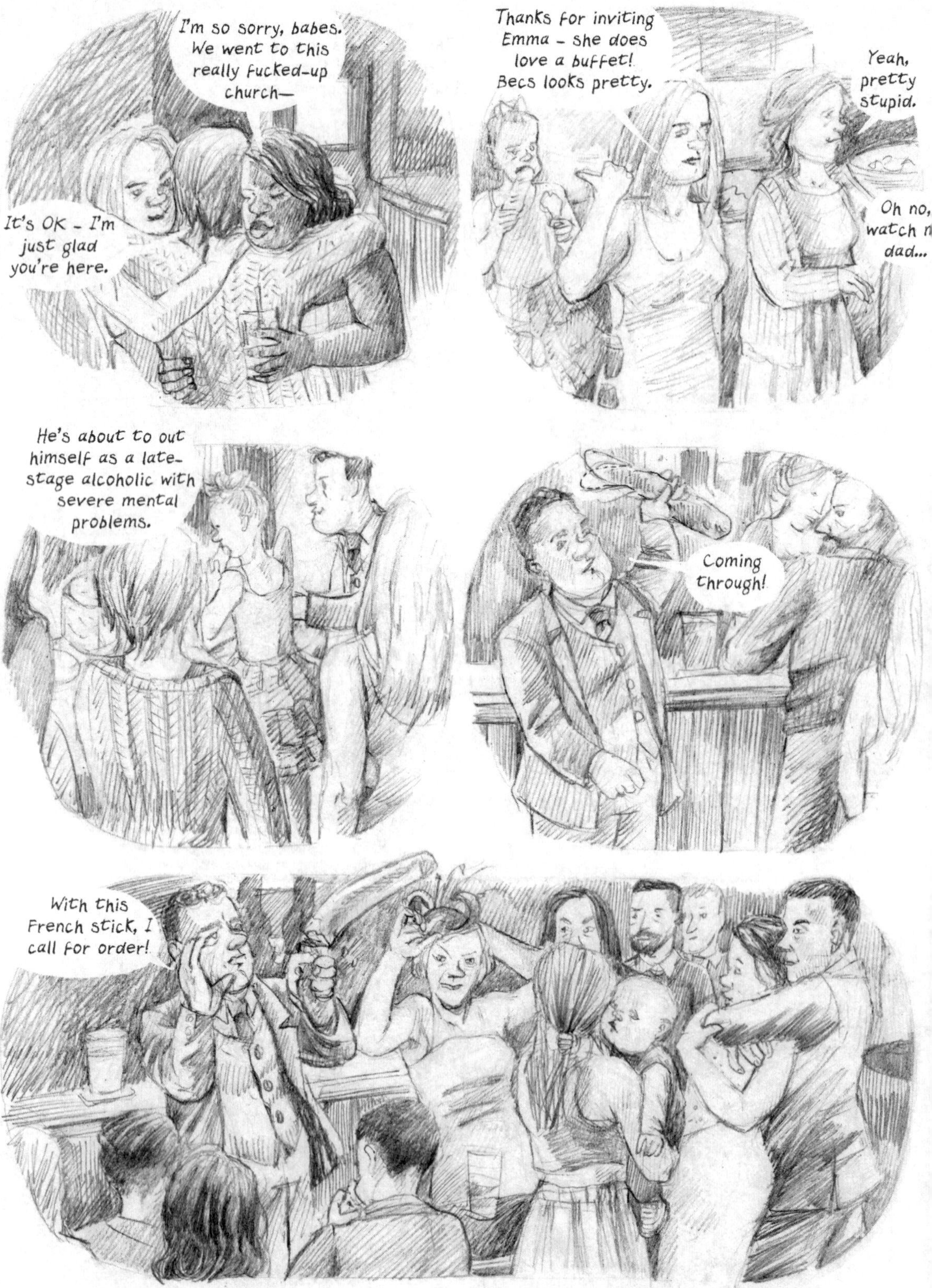
I'm so sorry, babes. We went to this really fucked-up church—
It's OK - I'm just glad you're here.
Thanks for inviting Emma - she does love a buffet! Becs looks pretty.
Yeah, pretty stupid.
Oh no, watch dad...
He's about to out himself as a late-stage alcoholic with severe mental problems.
Coming through!
With this French stick, I call for order!

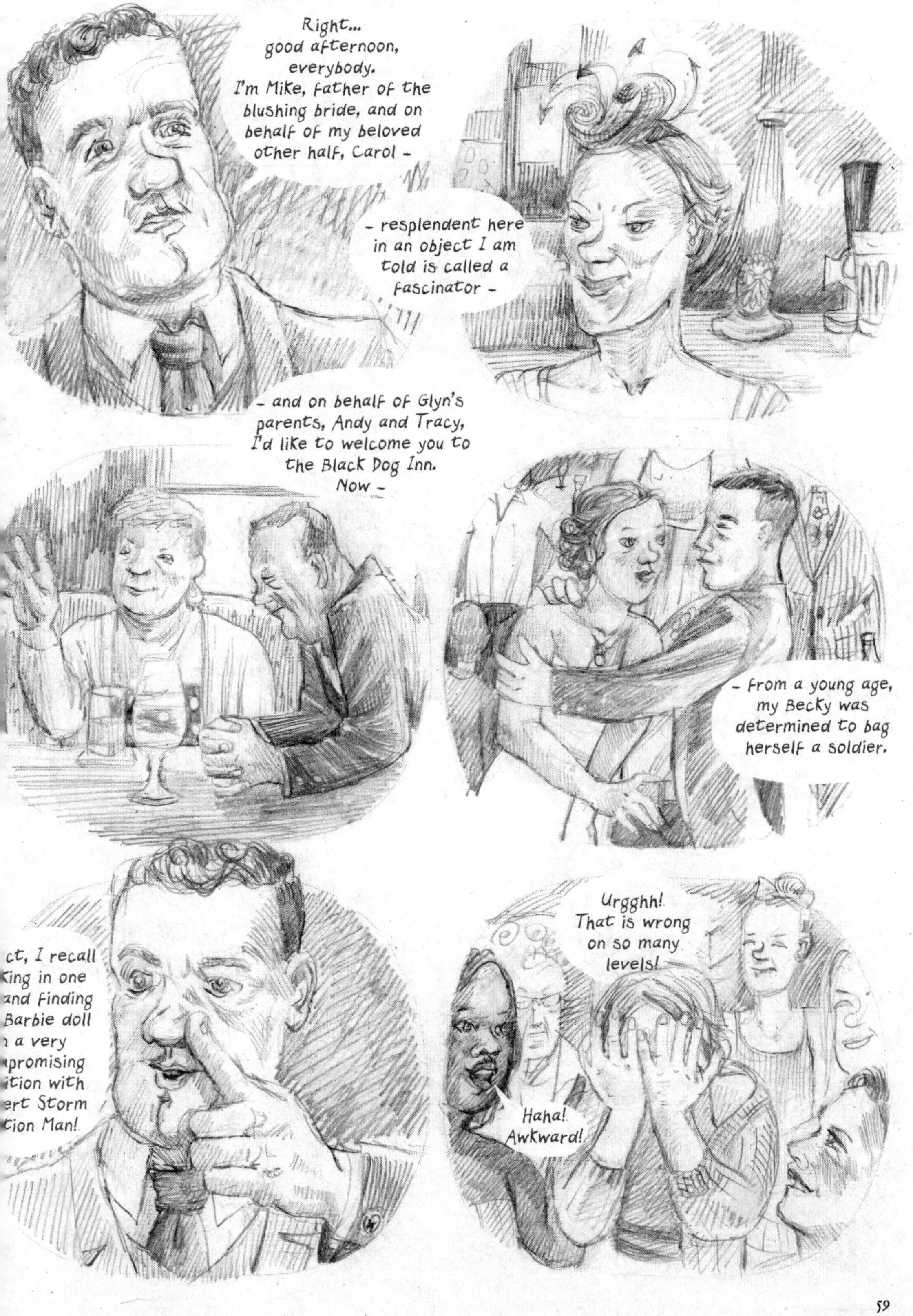
Right... good afternoon, everybody. I'm Mike, father of the blushing bride, and on behalf of my beloved other half, Carol -
- resplendent here in an object I am told is called a fascinator -
- and on behalf of Glyn's parents, Andy and Tracy, I'd like to welcome you to the Black Dog Inn. Now -
- from a young age, my Becky was determined to bag herself a soldier.
ct, I recall
king in one
and finding
Barbie doll
a very
promising
ition with
ert Storm
tion Man!
Urgghh! That is wrong on so many levels!
Haha! Awkward!

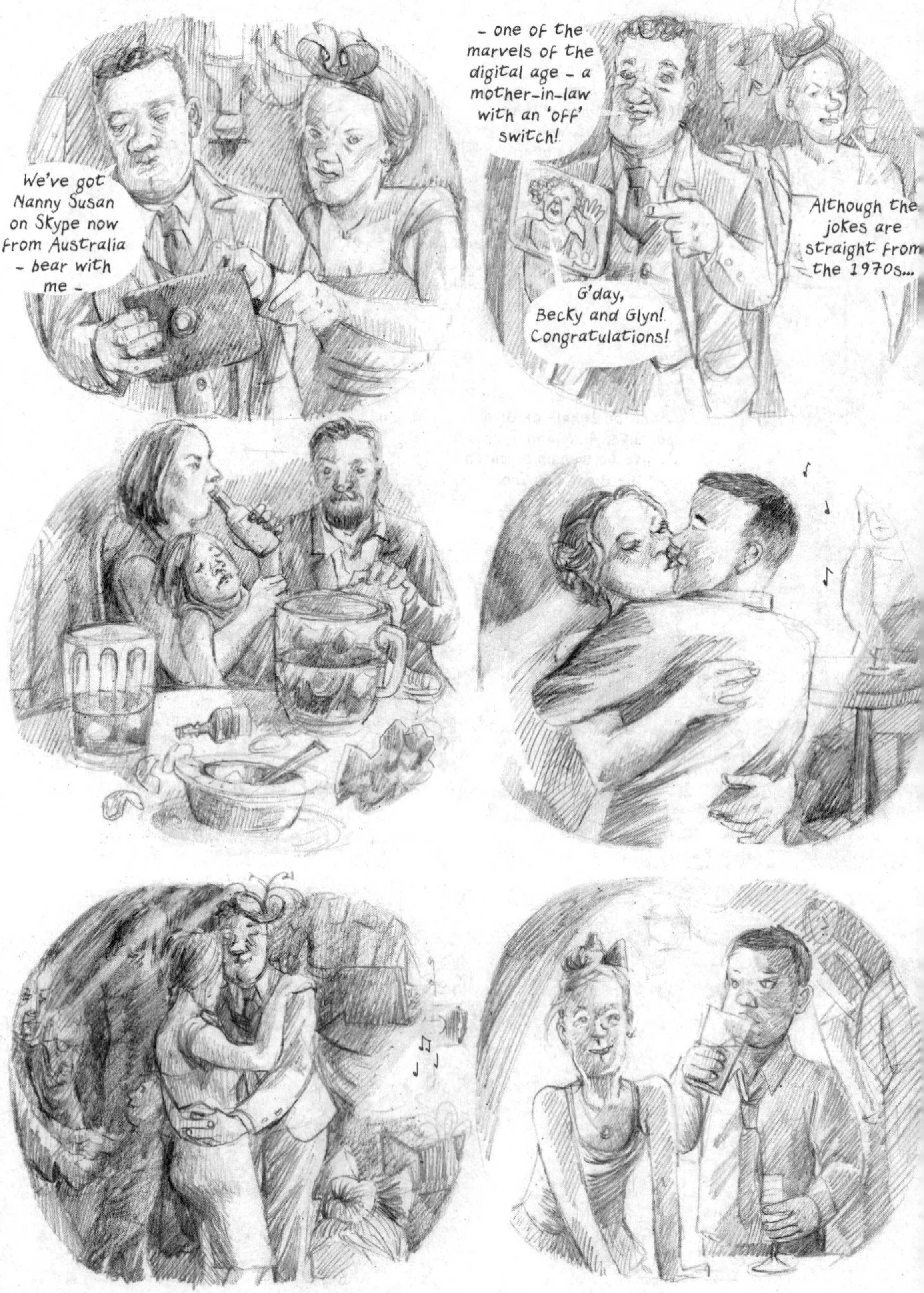
We've got Nanny Susan on Skype now from Australia - bear with me -
- one of the marvels of the digital age - a mother-in-law with an 'off' switch!
G'day, Becky and Glyn! Congratulations!
Although the jokes are straight from the 1970s...

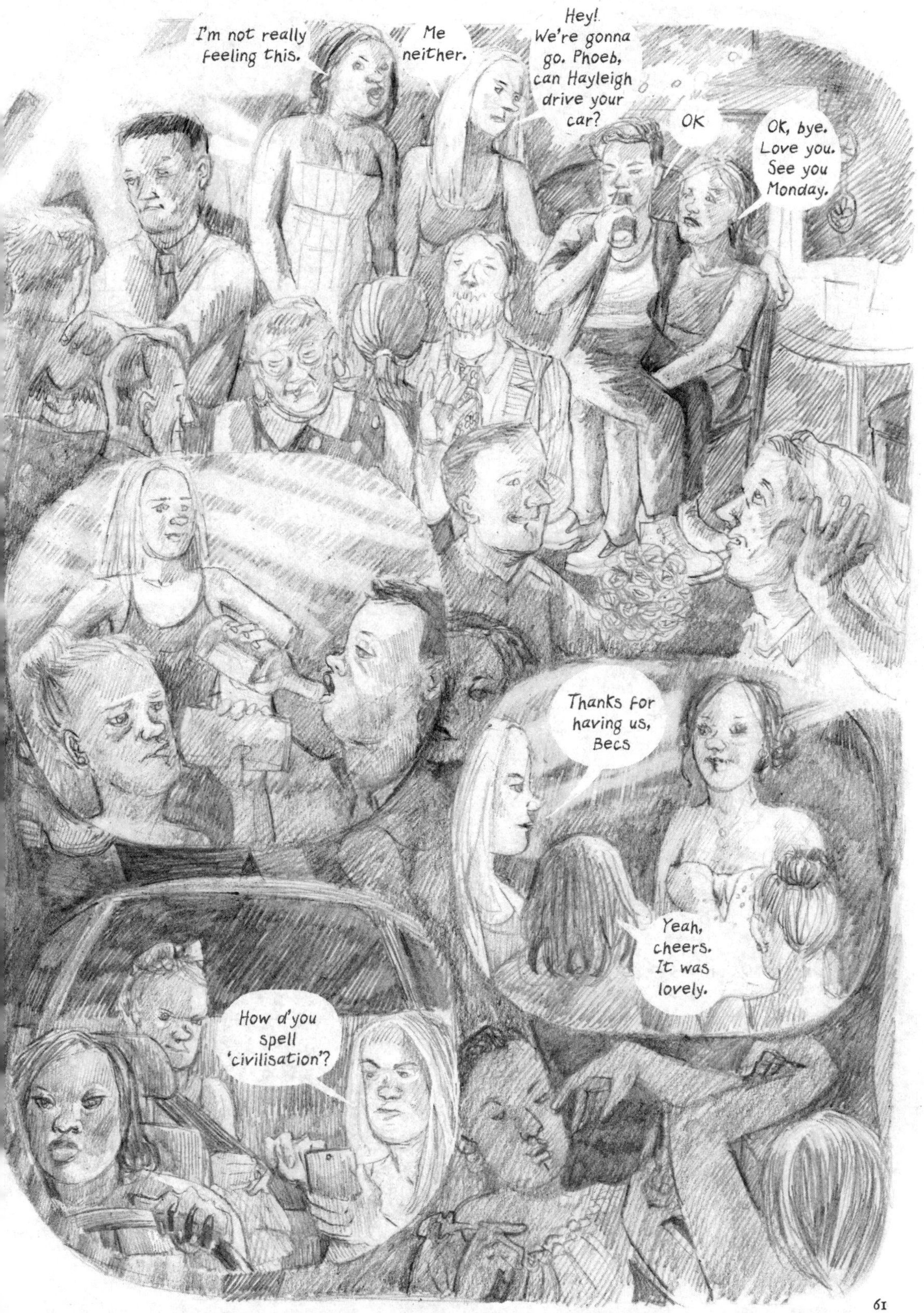
I'm not really feeling this.
Me neither.
Hey! We're gonna go. Phoeb, can Hayleigh drive your car?
OK
Ok, bye. Love you. See you Monday.
Thanks for having us, Becs
Yeah, cheers. It was lovely.
How d'you spell 'civilisation'?

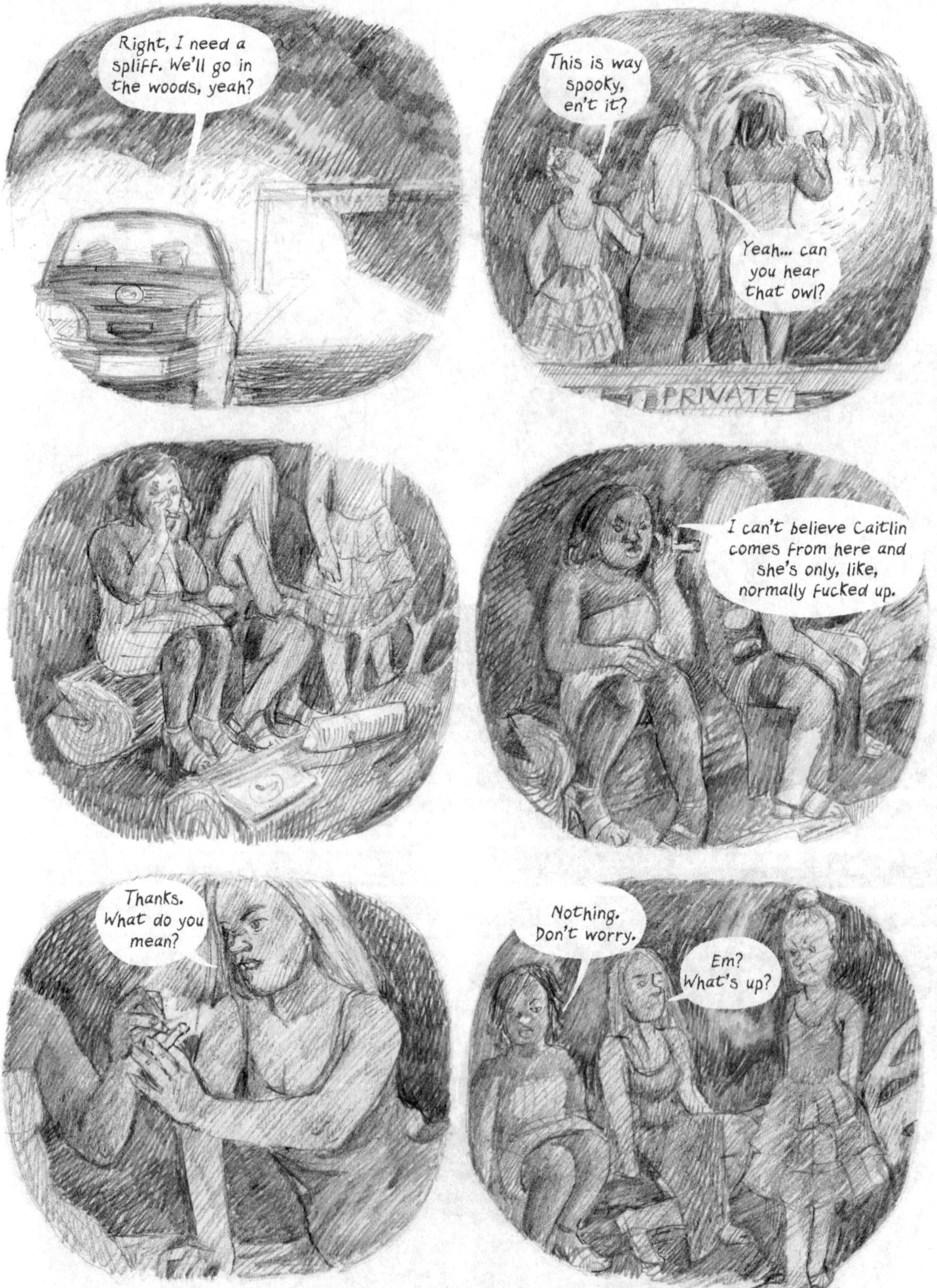
Right, I need a spliff. We'll go in the woods, yeah?
This is way spooky, en't it?
Yeah... can you hear that owl?
PRIVATE
I can't believe Caitlin comes from here and she's only, like, normally fucked up.
Thanks. What do you mean?
Nothing. Don't worry.
Em? What's up?

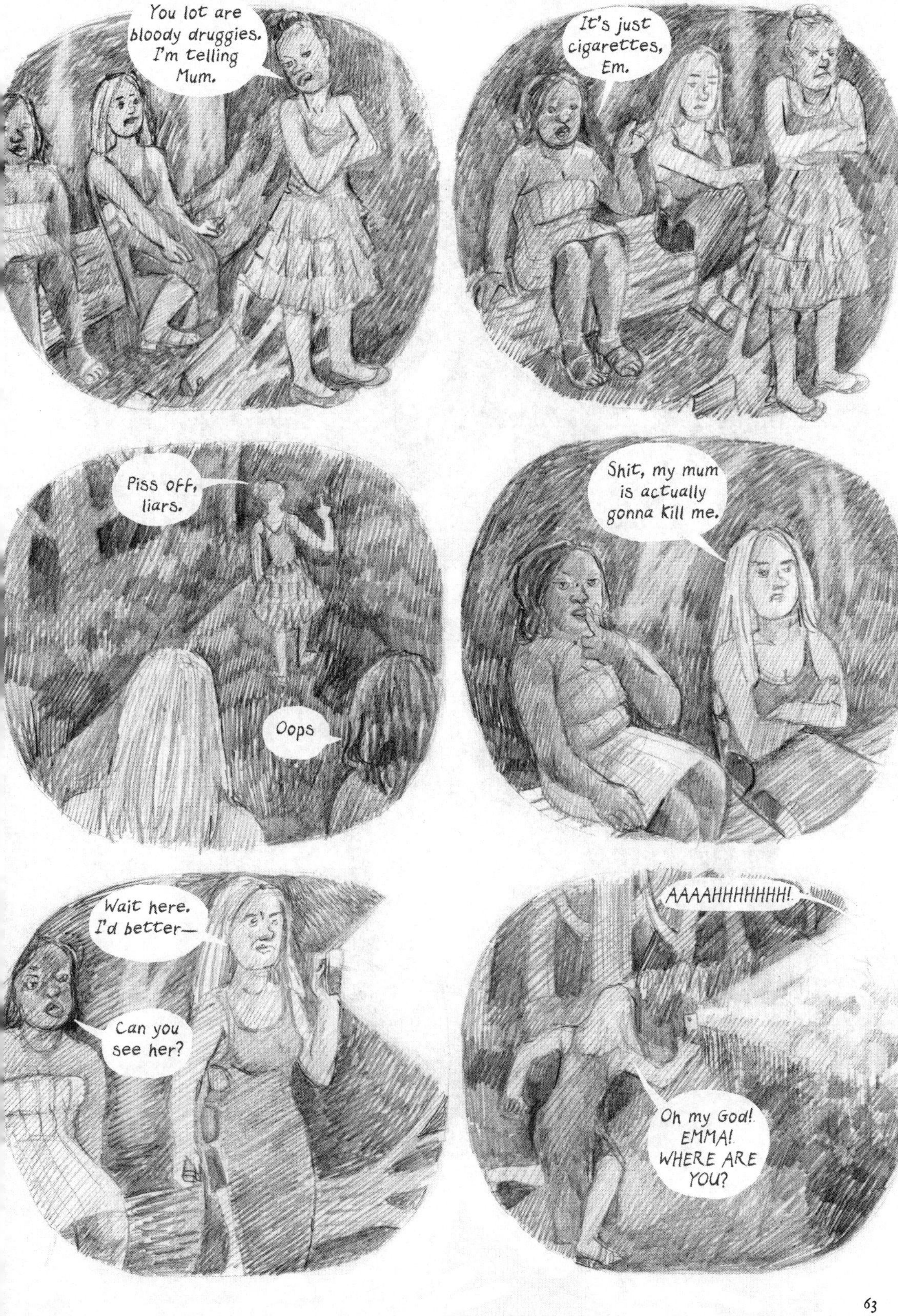
You lot are bloody druggies. I'm telling Mum.
It's just cigarettes, Em.
Piss off, liars.
Oops
Shit, my mum is actually gonna kill me.
Wait here. I'd better—
Can you see her?
AAAAHHHHHHH!
Oh my God! EMMA! WHERE ARE YOU?

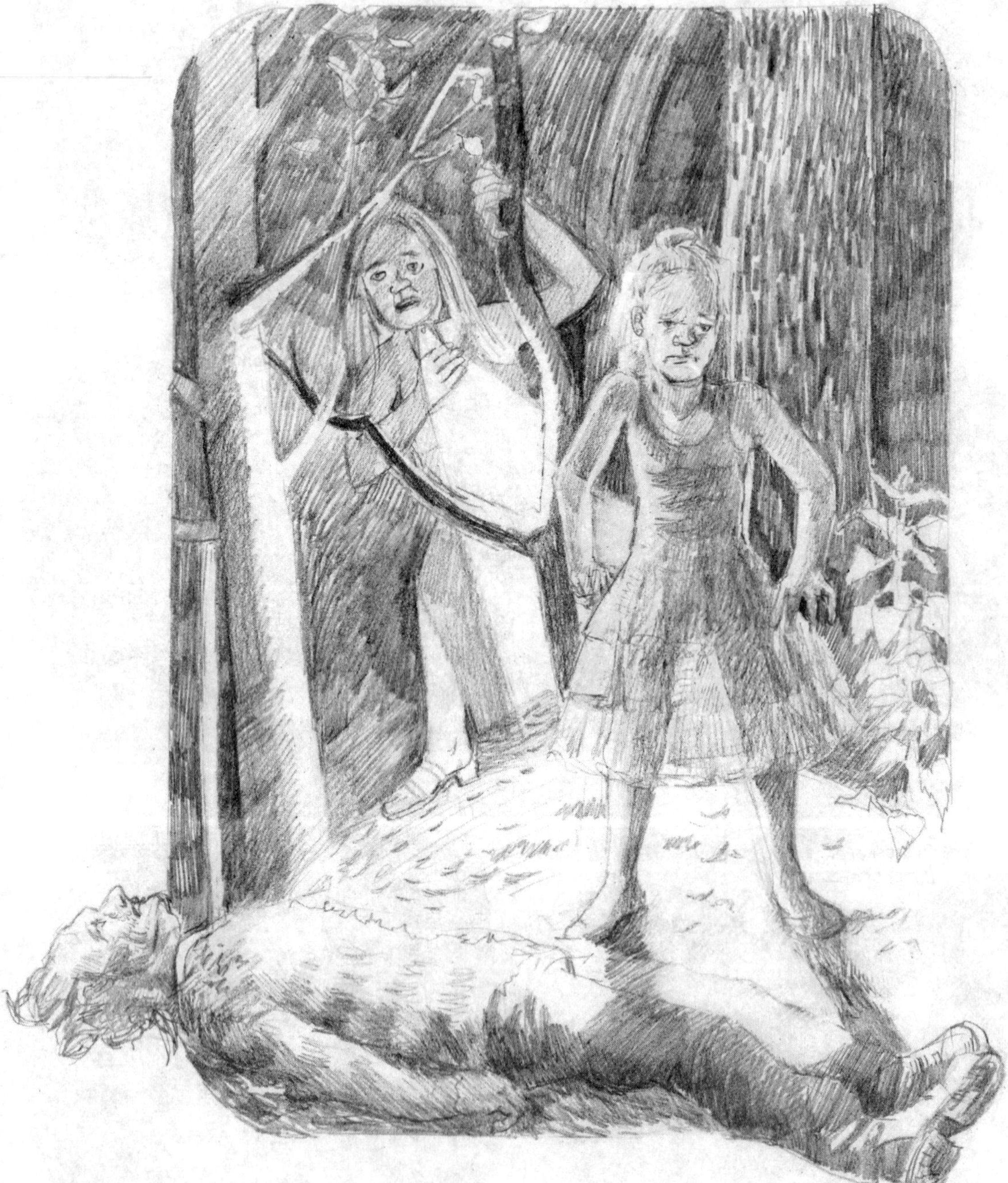

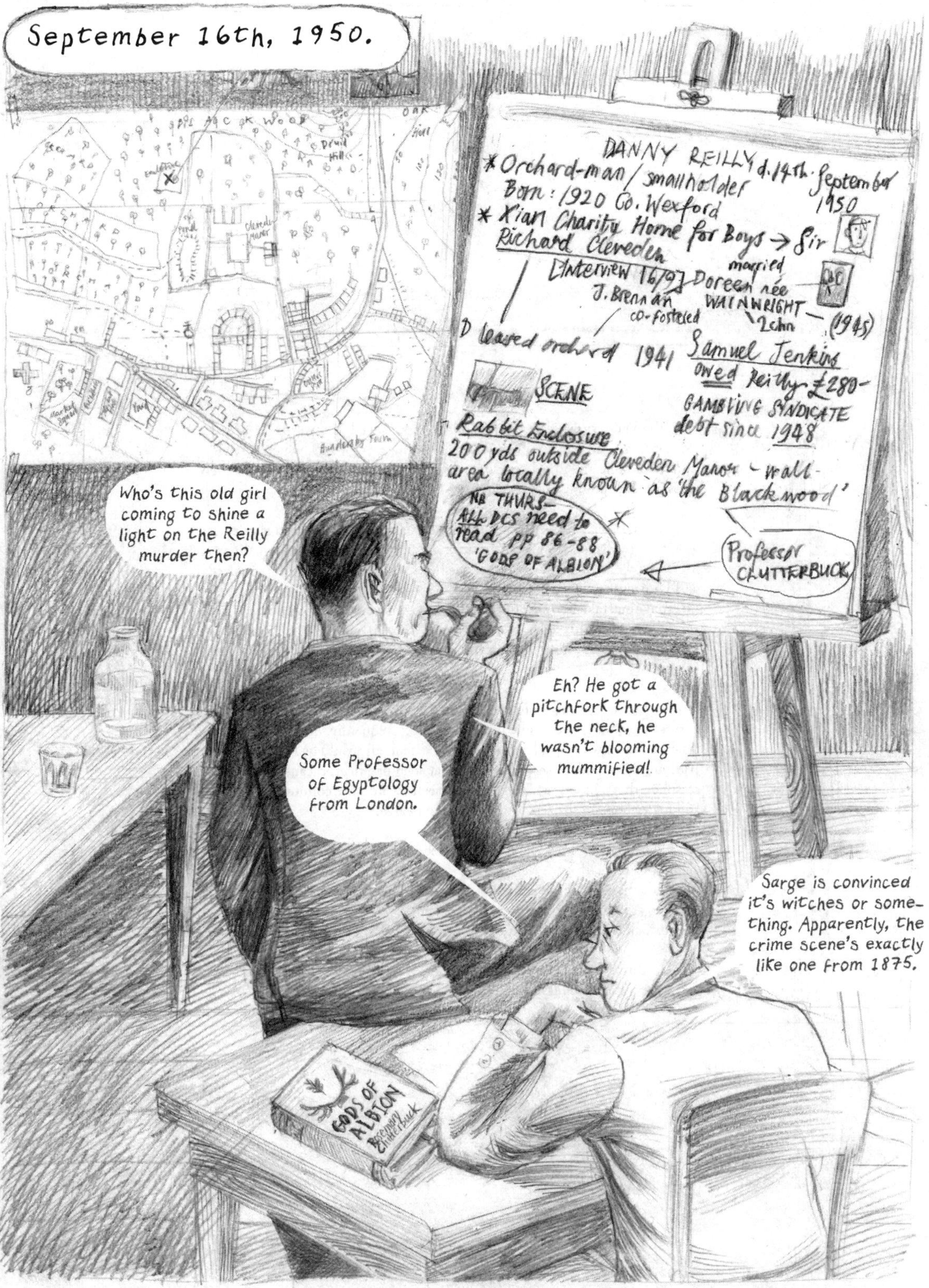
September 16th, 1950.
DANNY REILLY d. 14th September 1950
* Orchard-man / smallholder
Born: 1920 Co. Wexford
* Xian Charity Home for Boys → Sir Richard Cleveden
[Interview 16/9]
J. Brennan
co-fostered
married
Doreen née WAINWRIGHT
2chn
(1945)
leased orchard 1941
Samuel Jenkins
owed Reilly £280-
GAMBLING SYNDICATE
debt since 1948
SCENE
Rabbit Enclosure
200 yds outside Cleveden Manor - wall-
area locally known as 'the Blackwood'
NB THURS-
ALL DCS need to read pp 86-88 'GODS OF ALBION'
Professor CLUTTERBUCK
Who's this old girl coming to shine a light on the Reilly murder then?
Some Professor of Egyptology from London.
Eh? He got a pitchfork through the neck, he wasn't blooming mummified!
Sarge is convinced it's witches or something. Apparently, the crime scene's exactly like one from 1875.
GODS OF ALBION

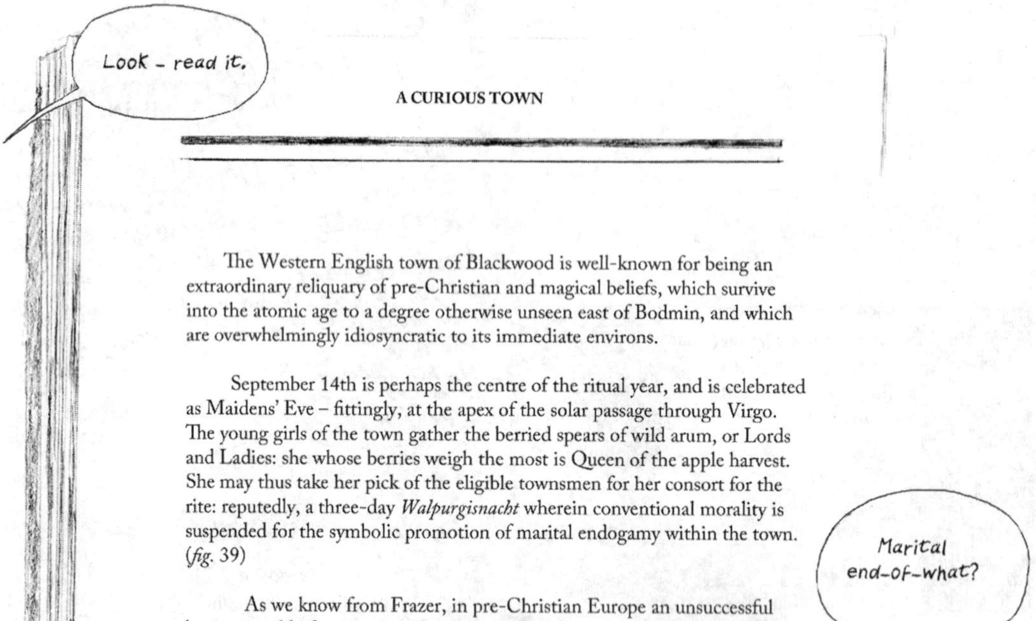
Look - read it.
Marital end-of-what?

A CURIOUS TOWN

The Western English town of Blackwood is well-known for being an extraordinary reliquary of pre-Christian and magical beliefs, which survive into the atomic age to a degree otherwise unseen east of Bodmin, and which are overwhelmingly idiosyncratic to its immediate environs.

September 14th is perhaps the centre of the ritual year, and is celebrated as Maidens' Eve – fittingly, at the apex of the solar passage through Virgo. The young girls of the town gather the berried spears of wild arum, or Lords and Ladies: she whose berries weigh the most is Queen of the apple harvest. She may thus take her pick of the eligible townsmen for her consort for the rite: reputedly, a three-day *Walpurgisnacht* wherein conventional morality is suspended for the symbolic promotion of marital endogamy within the town. (*fig.* 39)

As we know from Frazer, in pre-Christian Europe an unsuccessful harvest would often require a human sacrifice: frequently, during those wild times, a person who had been accused of witchcraft would be the scapegoat. Although our modern sensibilities balk at such practices, it can perhaps be reasoned that a blood sacrifice could be seen to promote community cohesion and foster hope in the fertility of the failing earth.

In 1875, Walter Burnside, a Blackwood farmer, bludgeoned his elderly neighbour to death and, *post mortem*, stuck a pitchfork through her neck. This hideous practice is known locally as 'staking': drawing the blood of a witch to stop her roaming after death and to reverse the damage done to crops or livestock by curses, or 'overlooking' in local parlance. (*fig.* 40)

Burnside claimed that the woman, Thomasina Wheelwright, had given his cattle the milk fever.

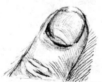

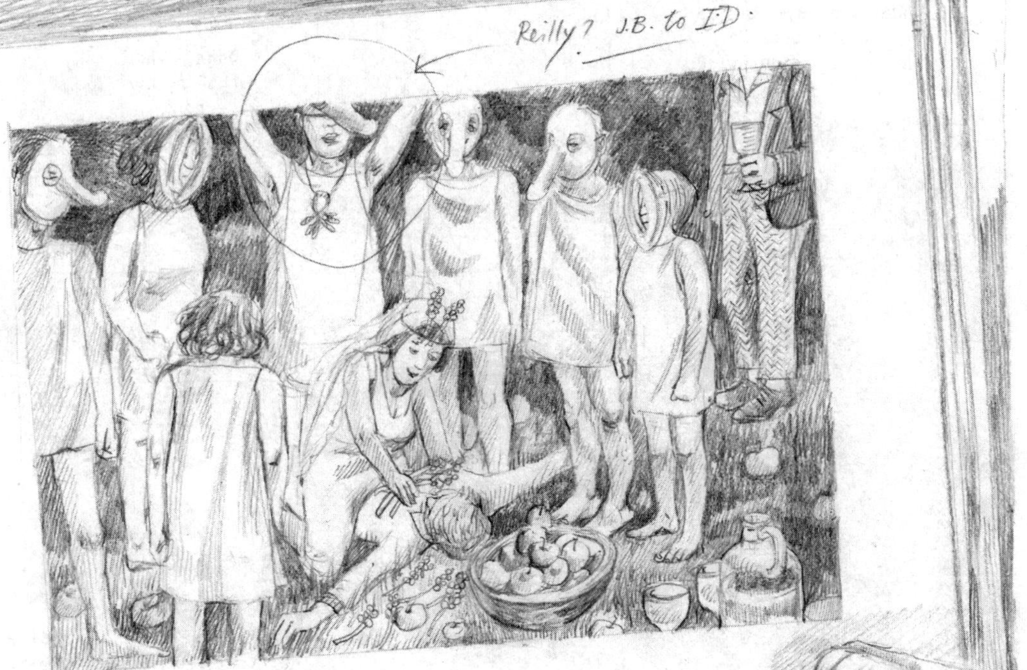
Reilly? J.B. to I.D.

fig. 39

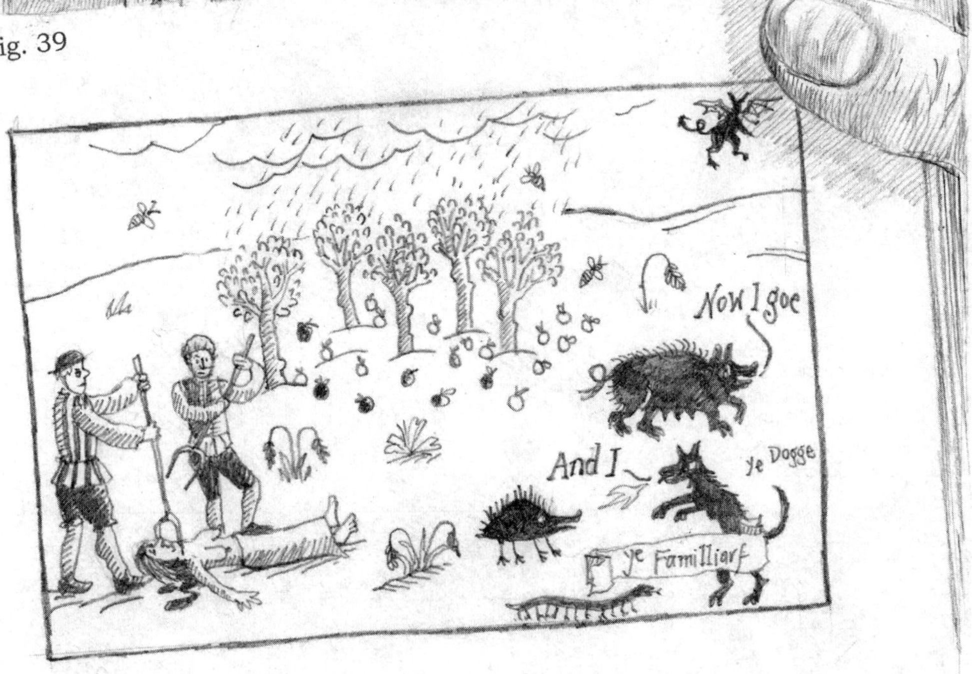
Now I goe
And I
ye Dogge
ye Familliars

fig. 40

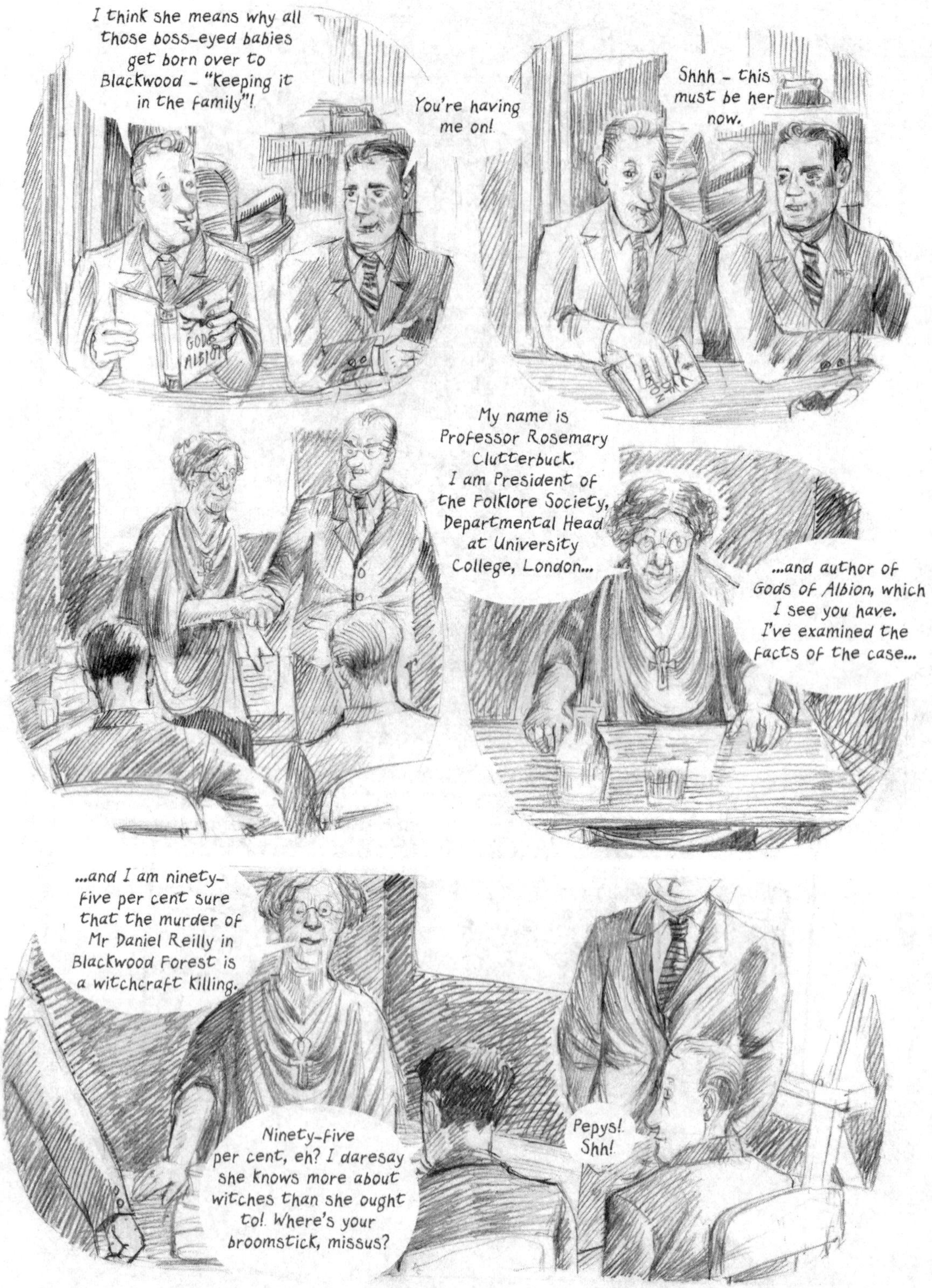
I think she means why all those boss-eyed babies get born over to Blackwood – "Keeping it in the family"!
You're having me on!
GODS ALBION
Shhh – this must be her now.
My name is Professor Rosemary Clutterbuck. I am President of the Folklore Society, Departmental Head at University College, London...
...and author of Gods of Albion, which I see you have. I've examined the facts of the case...
...and I am ninety-five per cent sure that the murder of Mr Daniel Reilly in Blackwood Forest is a witchcraft killing.
Ninety-five per cent, eh? I daresay she knows more about witches than she ought to! Where's your broomstick, missus?
Pepys! Shh!

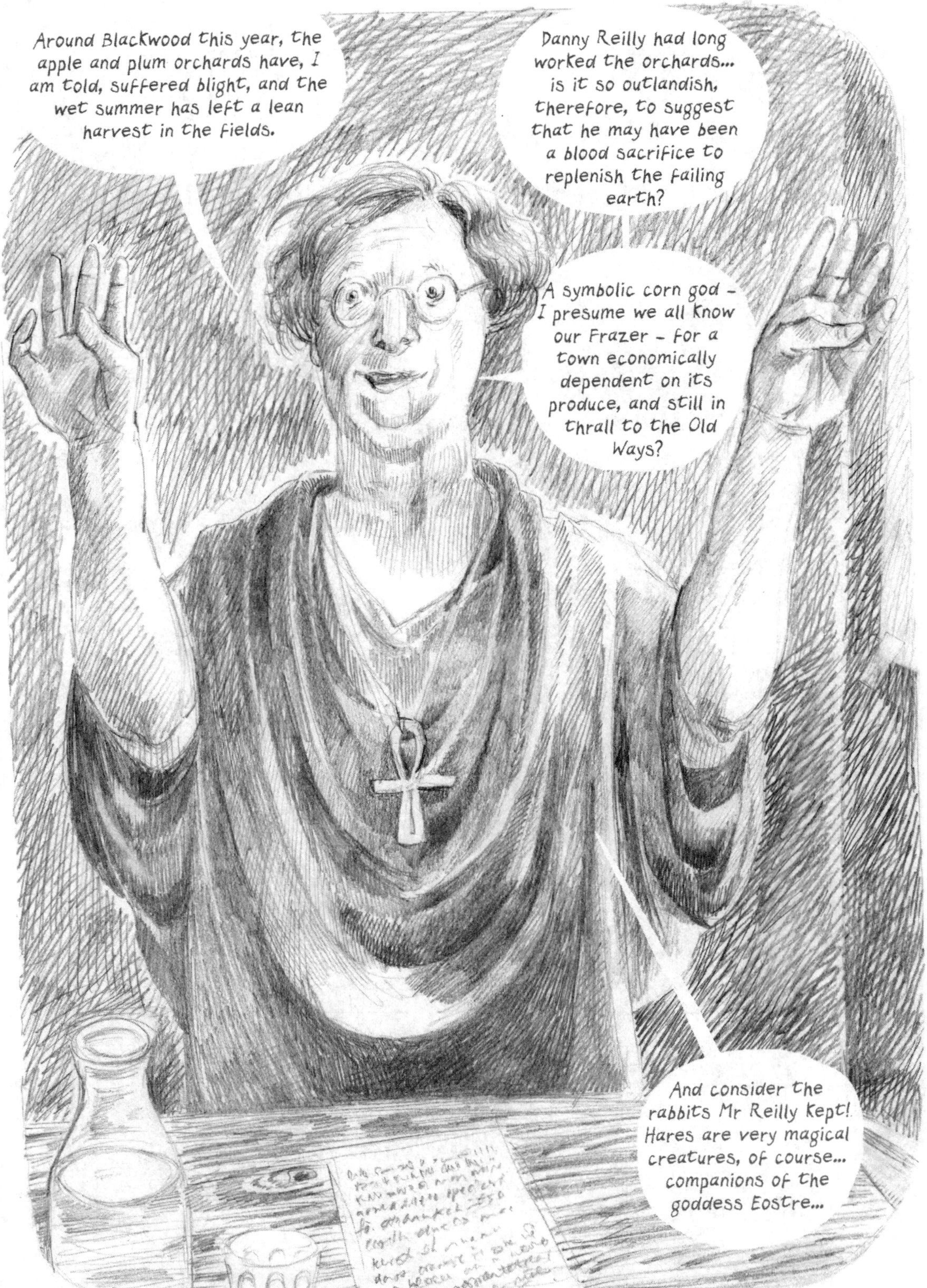
Around Blackwood this year, the apple and plum orchards have, I am told, suffered blight, and the wet summer has left a lean harvest in the fields.
Danny Reilly had long worked the orchards... is it so outlandish, therefore, to suggest that he may have been a blood sacrifice to replenish the failing earth?
A symbolic corn god - I presume we all know our Frazer - for a town economically dependent on its produce, and still in thrall to the Old Ways?
And consider the rabbits Mr Reilly kept! Hares are very magical creatures, of course... companions of the goddess Eostre...

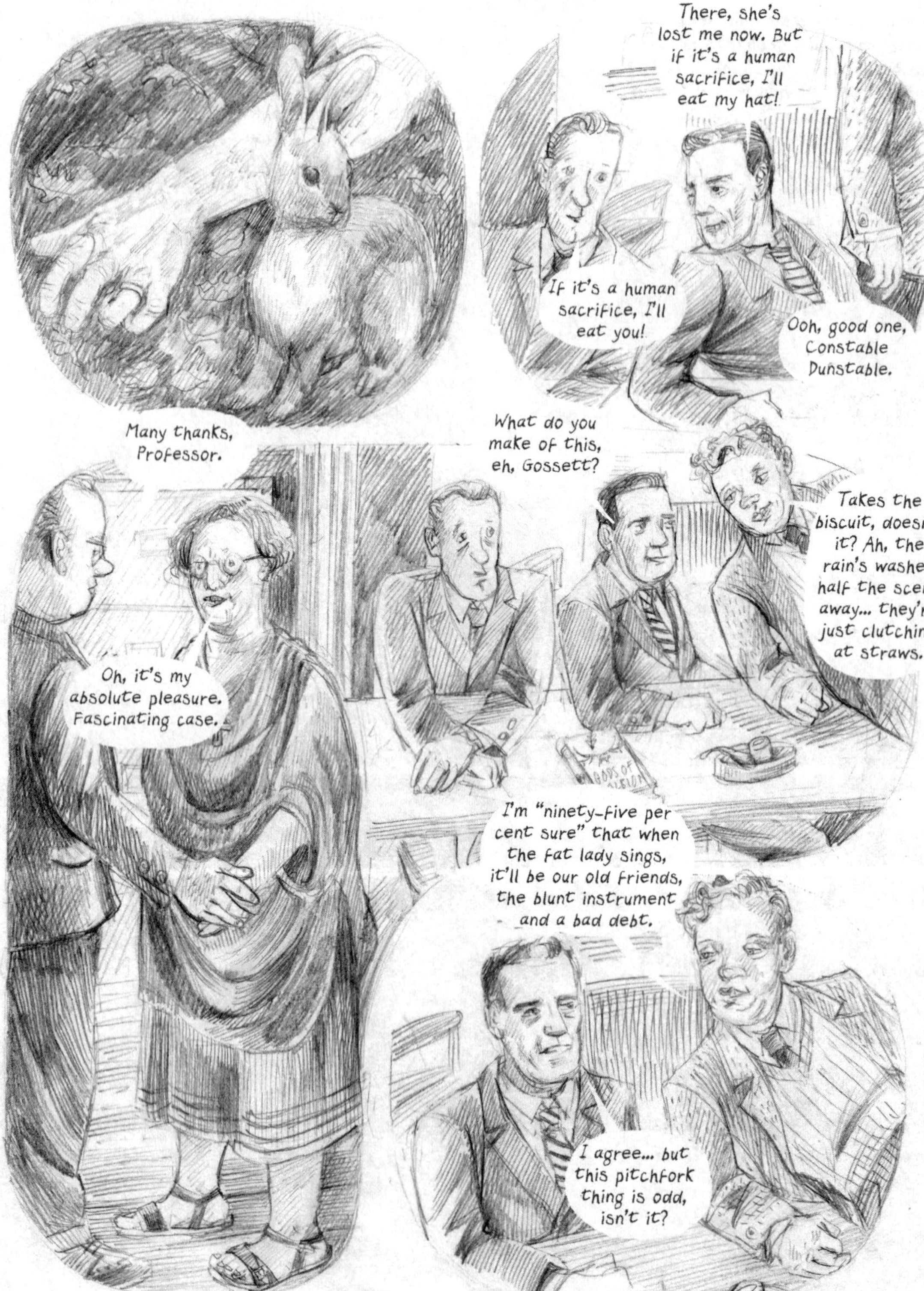
There, she's lost me now. But if it's a human sacrifice, I'll eat my hat!
If it's a human sacrifice, I'll eat you!
Ooh, good one, Constable Dunstable.
Many thanks, Professor.
Oh, it's my absolute pleasure. Fascinating case.
What do you make of this, eh, Gossett?
Takes the biscuit, doesn't it? Ah, the rain's washed half the scene away... they're just clutching at straws.
I'm "ninety-five per cent sure" that when the fat lady sings, it'll be our old friends, the blunt instrument and a bad debt.
I agree... but this pitchfork thing is odd, isn't it?

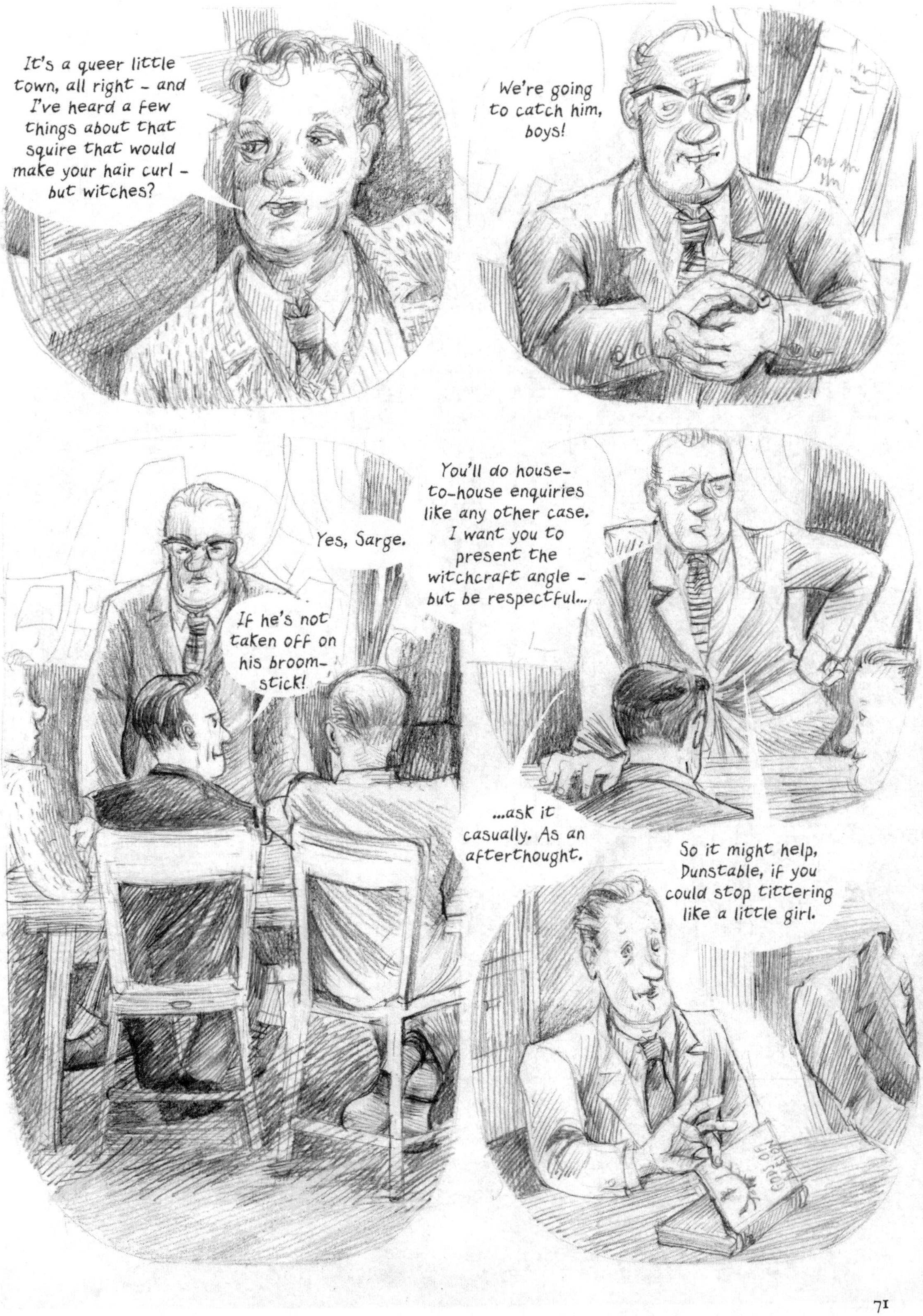
It's a queer little town, all right – and I've heard a few things about that squire that would make your hair curl – but witches?
We're going to catch him, boys!
Yes, Sarge.
If he's not taken off on his broom-stick!
You'll do house-to-house enquiries like any other case. I want you to present the witchcraft angle – but be respectful...
...ask it casually. As an afterthought.
So it might help, Dunstable, if you could stop tittering like a little girl.

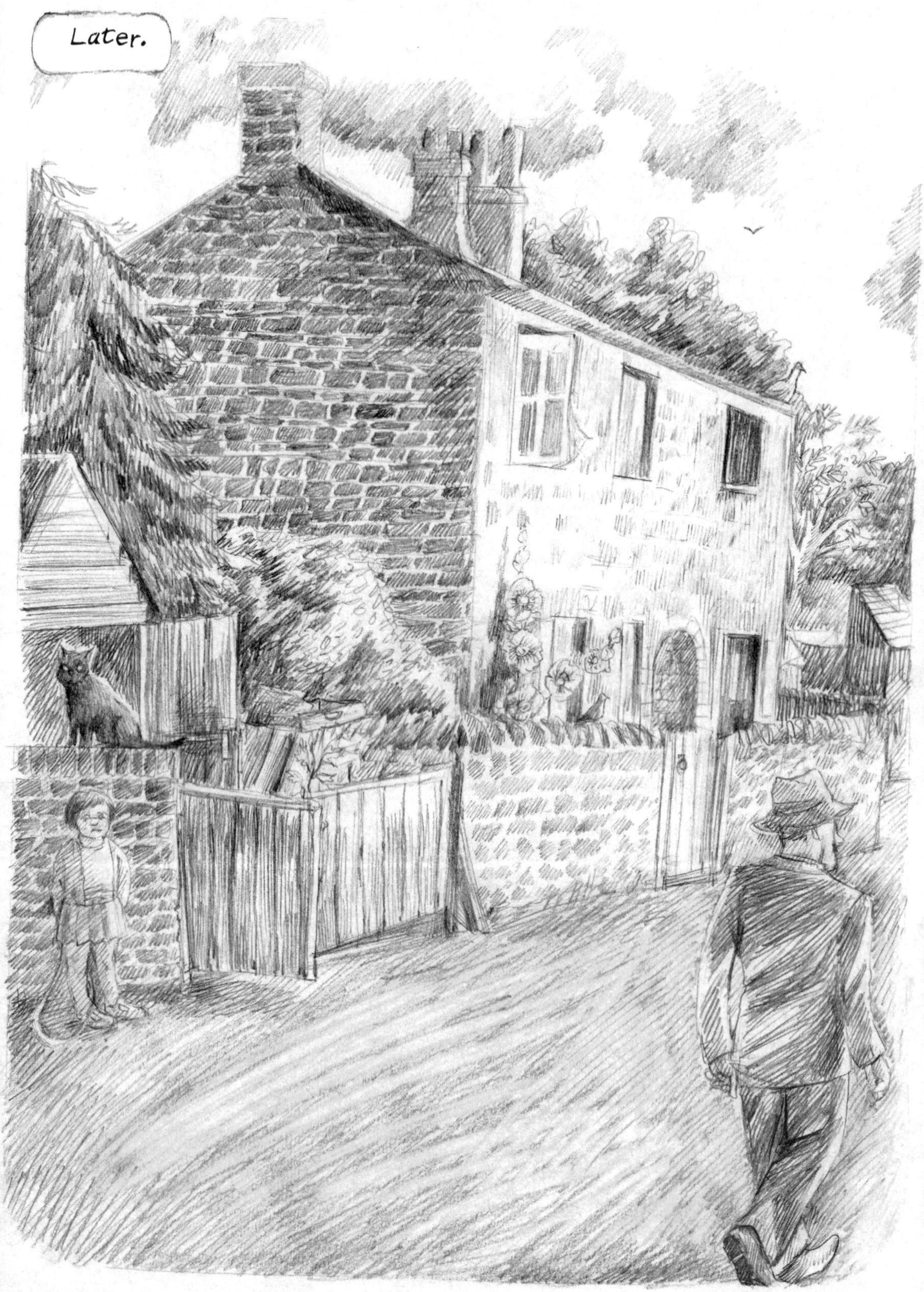
Later.

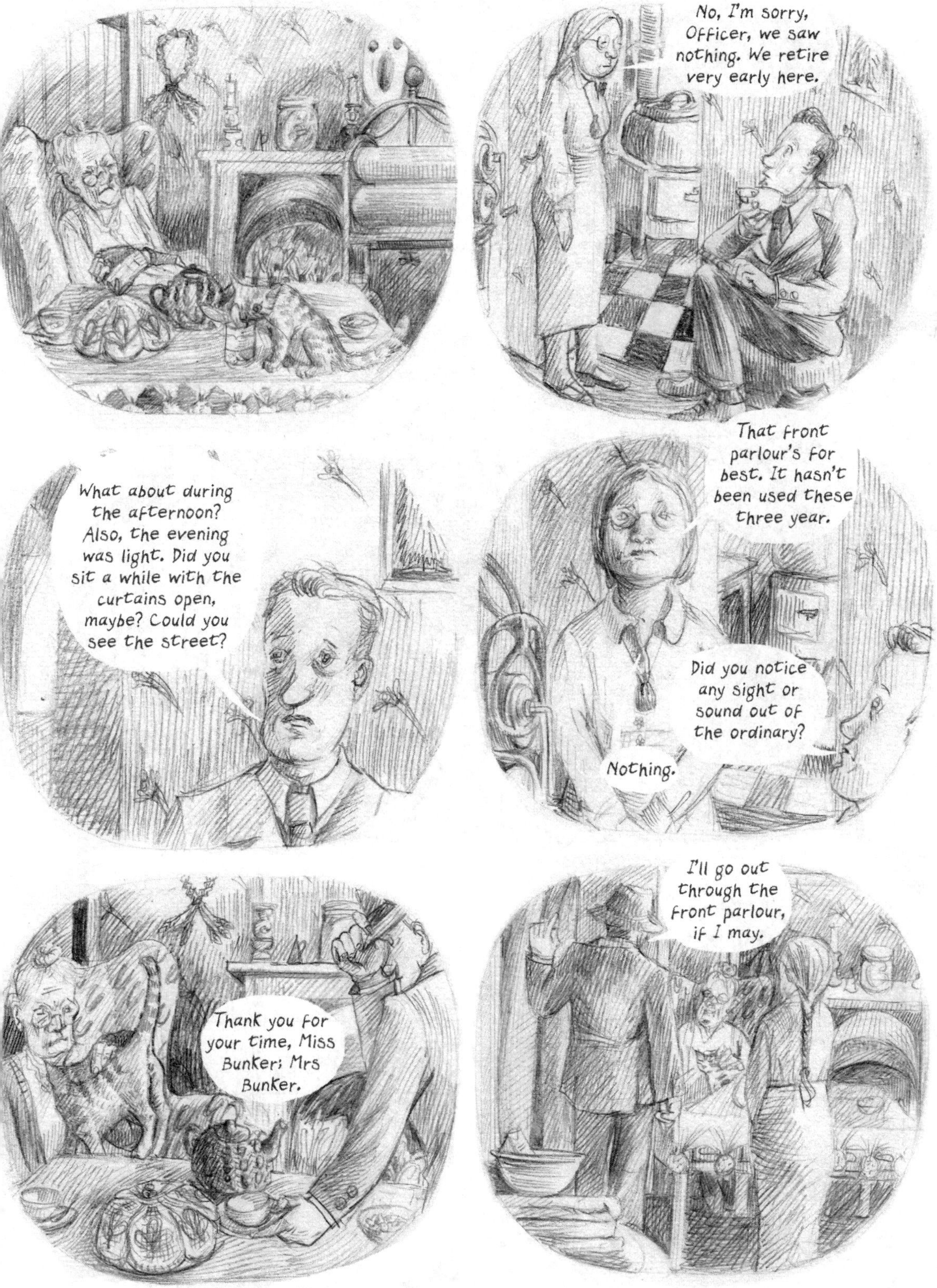
No, I'm sorry, Officer, we saw nothing. We retire very early here.
What about during the afternoon? Also, the evening was light. Did you sit a while with the curtains open, maybe? Could you see the street?
That front parlour's for best. It hasn't been used these three year.
Did you notice any sight or sound out of the ordinary?
Nothing.
Thank you for your time, Miss Bunker; Mrs Bunker.
I'll go out through the front parlour, if I may.

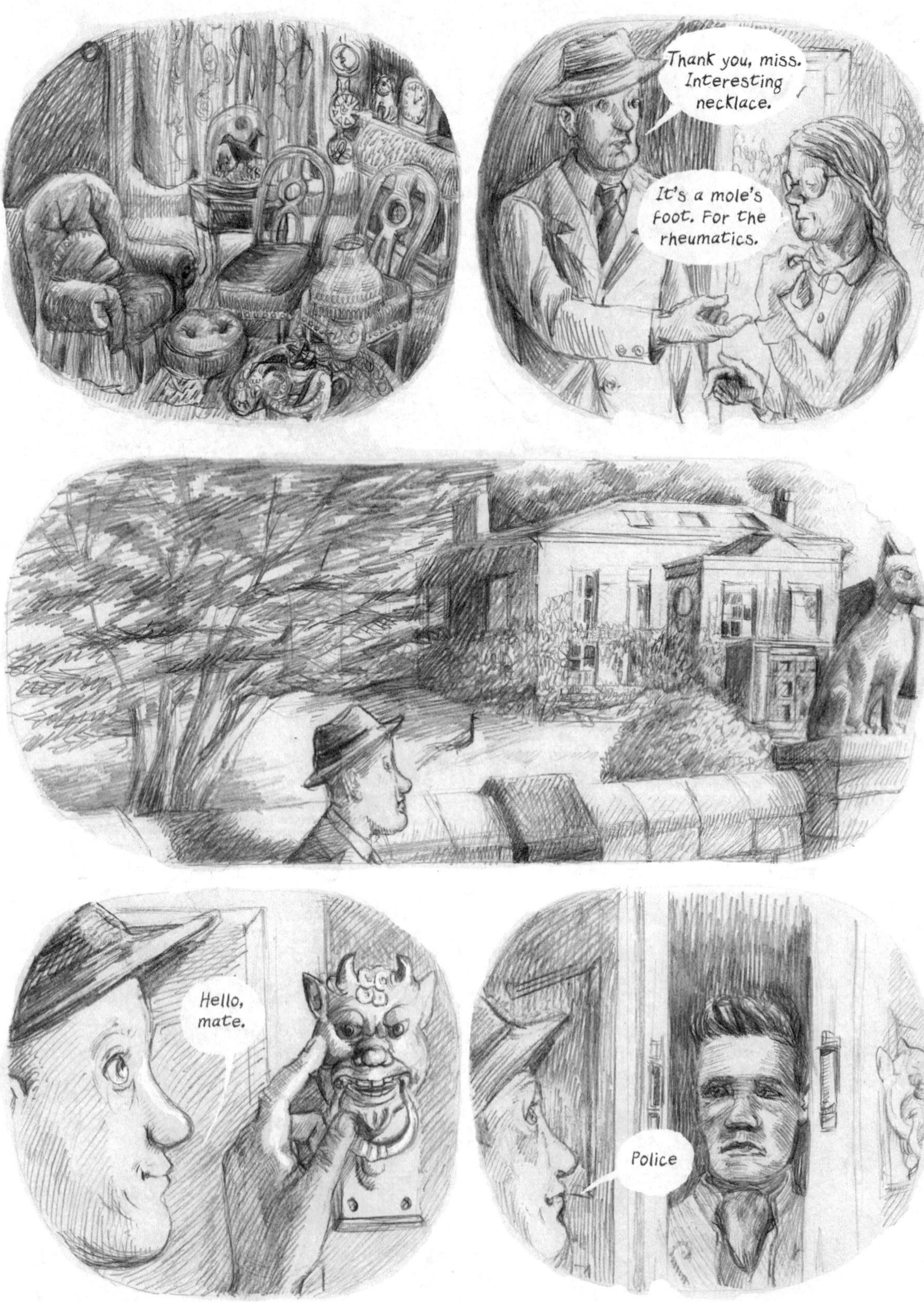
Thank you, miss. Interesting necklace.
It's a mole's foot. For the rheumatics.
Hello, mate.
Police

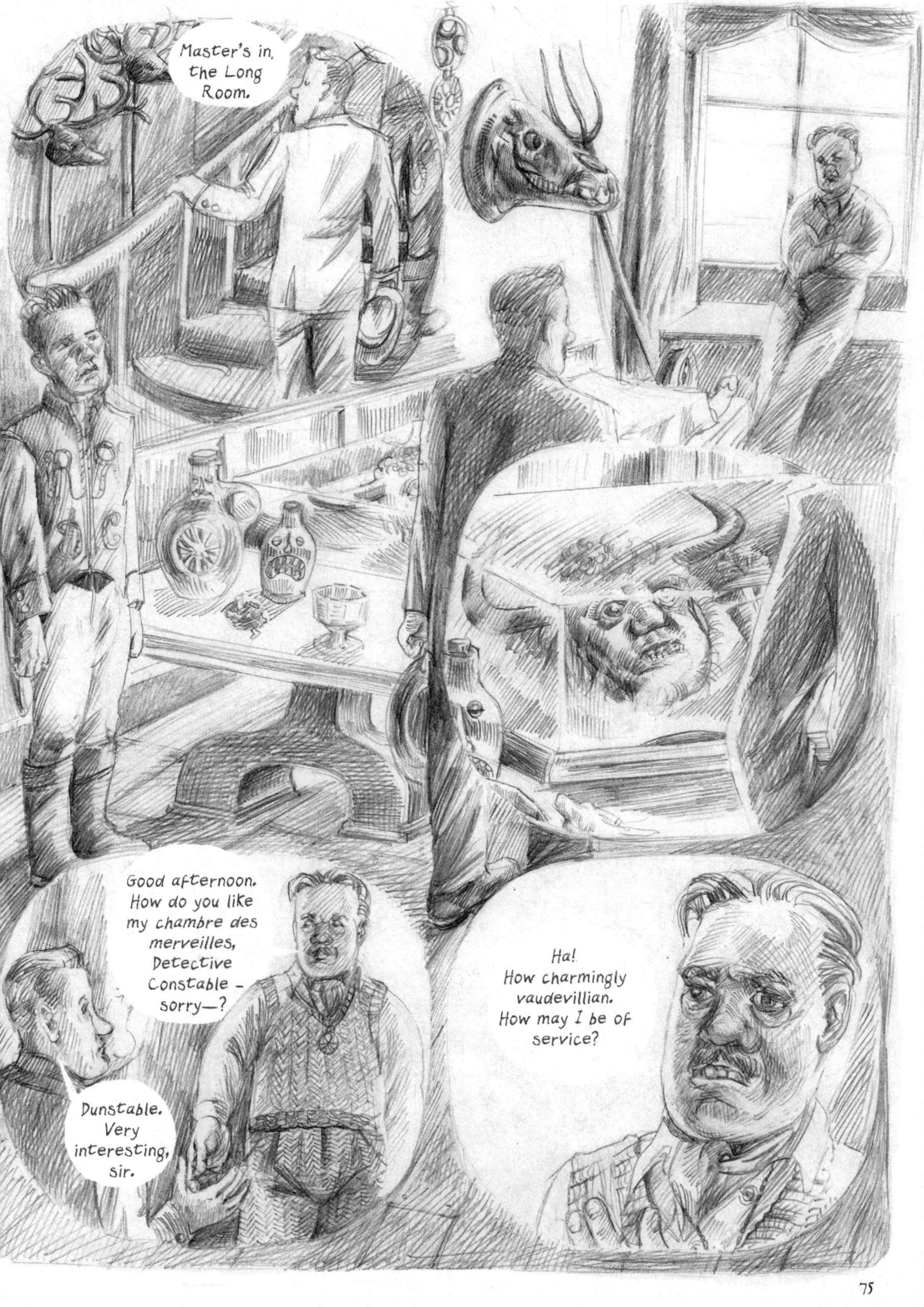
Master's in, the Long Room.
Good afternoon. How do you like my chambre des merveilles, Detective Constable - sorry—?
Dunstable. Very interesting, sir.
Ha! How charmingly vaudevillian. How may I be of service?

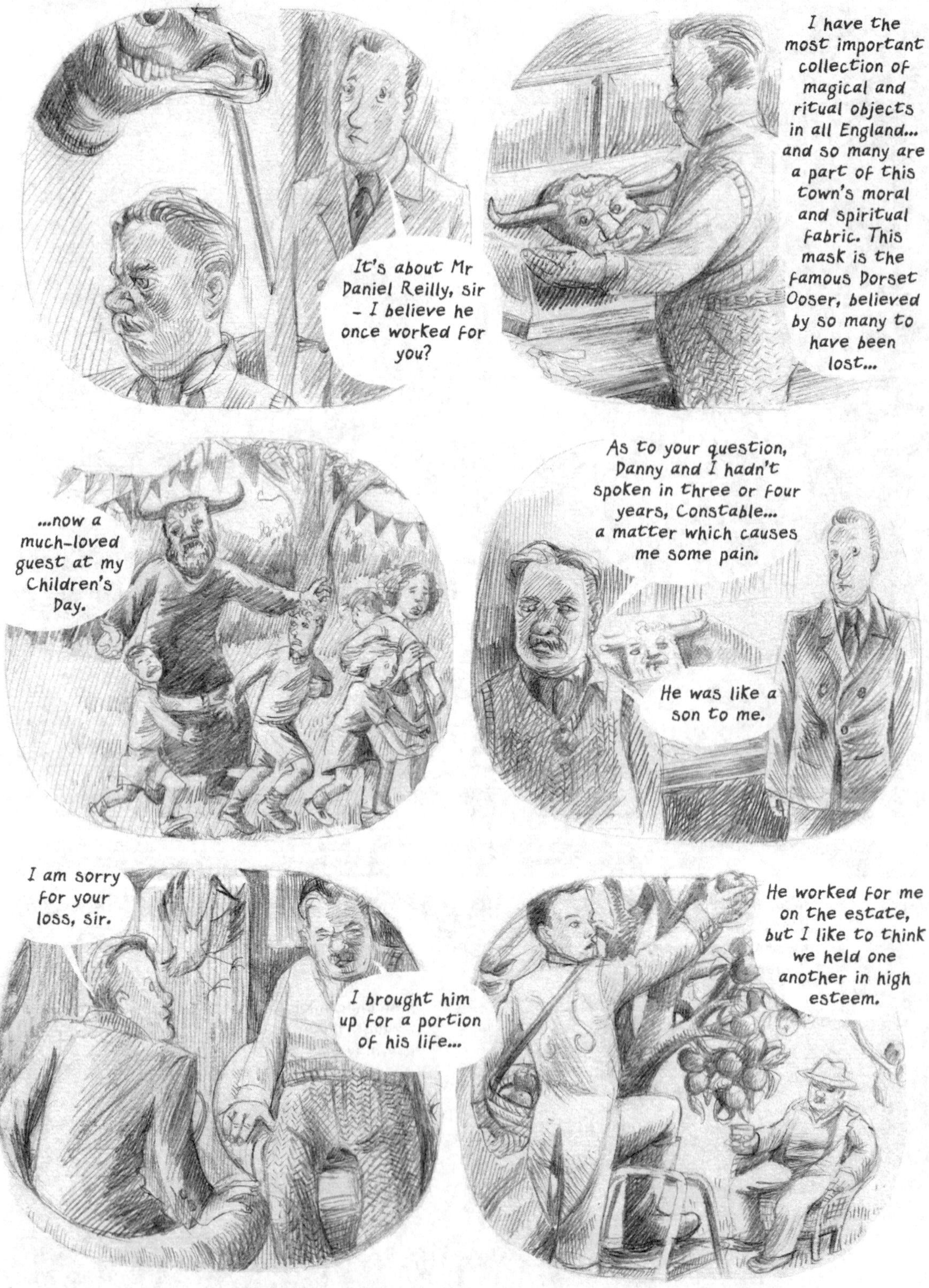
It's about Mr Daniel Reilly, sir – I believe he once worked for you?
I have the most important collection of magical and ritual objects in all England... and so many are a part of this town's moral and spiritual fabric. This mask is the famous Dorset Ooser, believed by so many to have been lost...
...now a much-loved guest at my Children's Day.
As to your question, Danny and I hadn't spoken in three or four years, Constable... a matter which causes me some pain.
He was like a son to me.
I am sorry for your loss, sir.
I brought him up for a portion of his life...
He worked for me on the estate, but I like to think we held one another in high esteem.

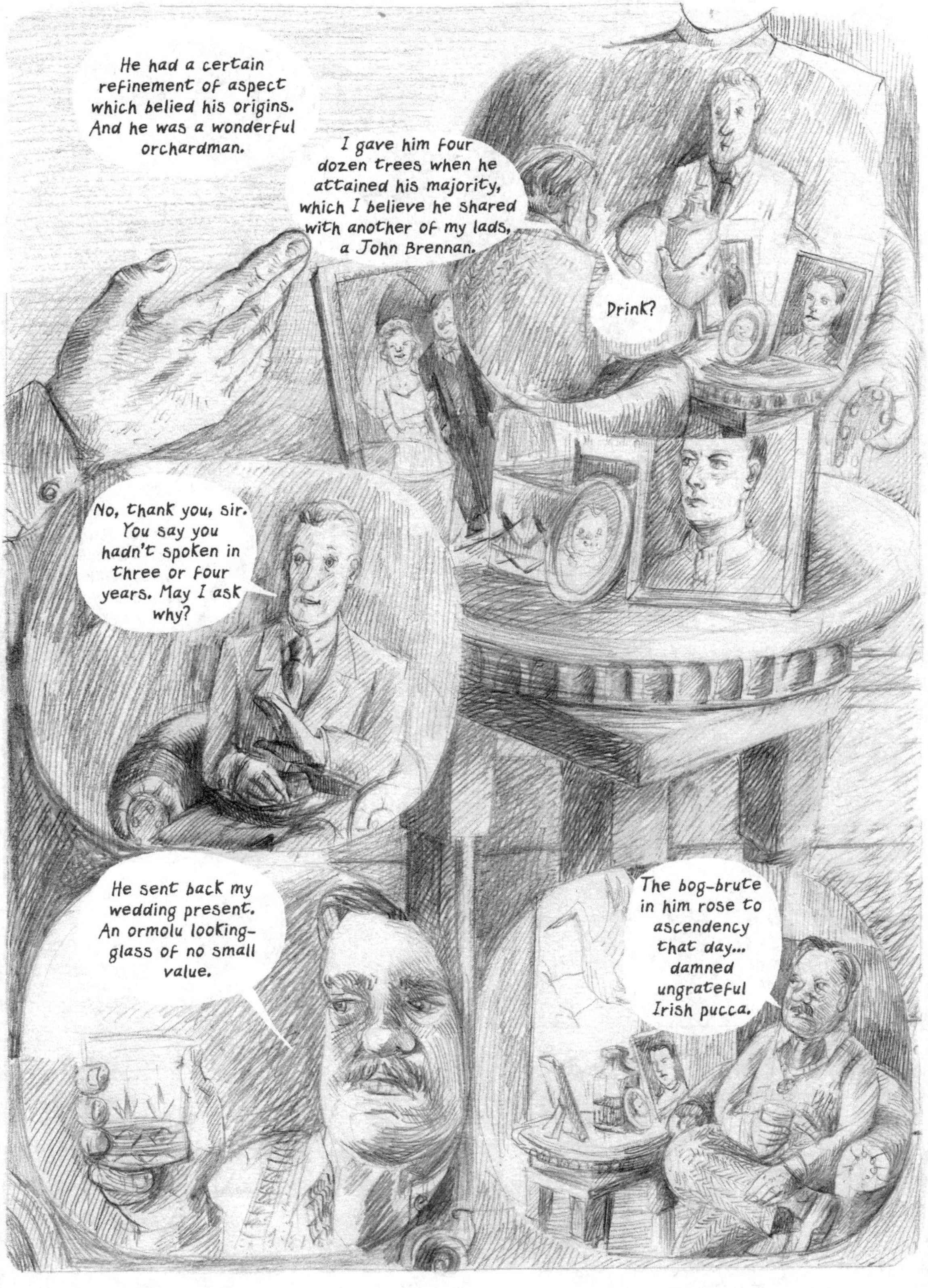
He had a certain refinement of aspect which belied his origins. And he was a wonderful orchardman.
I gave him four dozen trees when he attained his majority, which I believe he shared with another of my lads, a John Brennan.
Drink?
No, thank you, sir. You say you hadn't spoken in three or four years. May I ask why?
He sent back my wedding present. An ormolu looking-glass of no small value.
The bog-brute in him rose to ascendency that day... damned ungrateful Irish pucca.

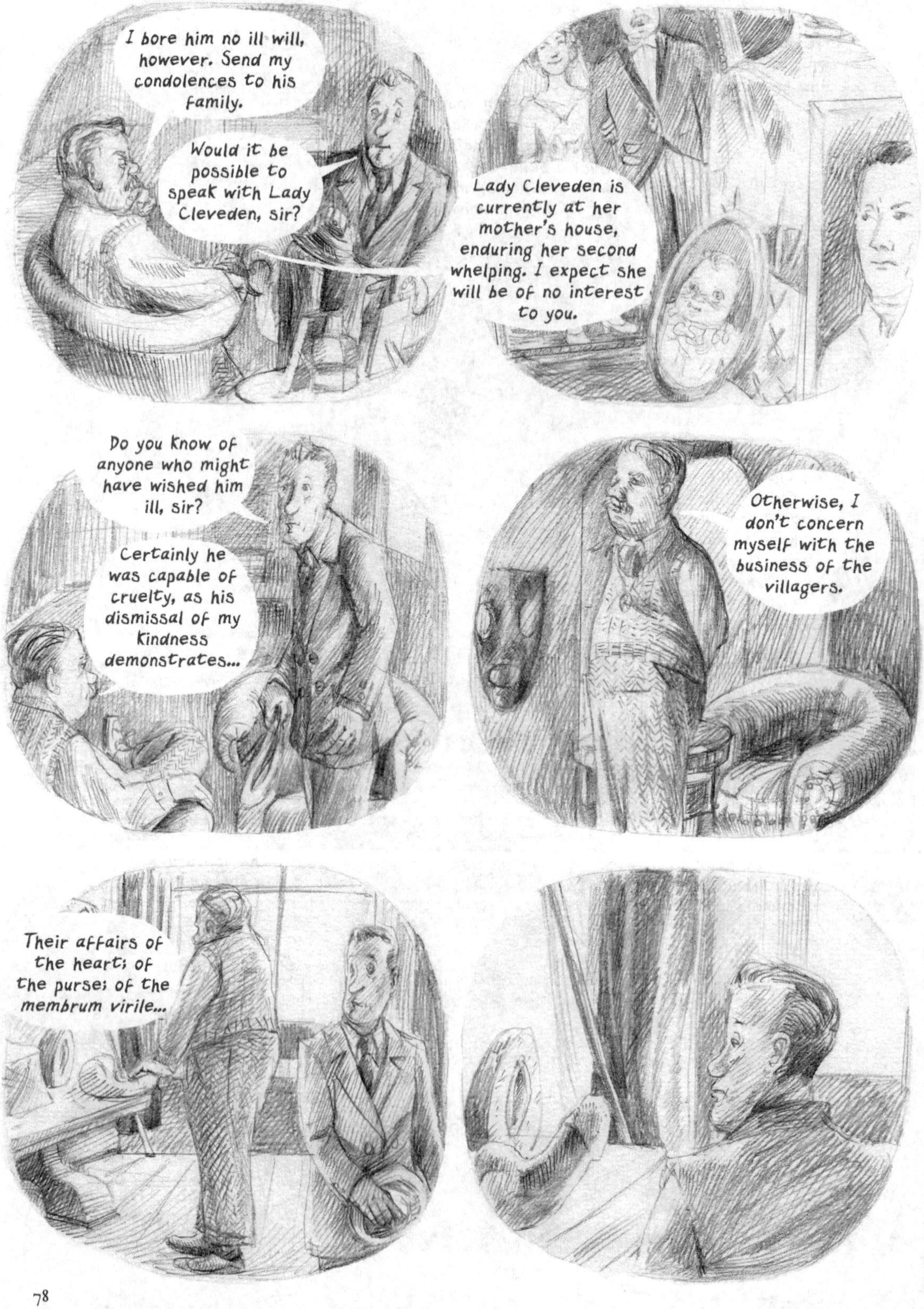
I bore him no ill will, however. Send my condolences to his family.
Would it be possible to speak with Lady Cleveden, sir?
Lady Cleveden is currently at her mother's house, enduring her second whelping. I expect she will be of no interest to you.
Do you know of anyone who might have wished him ill, sir?
Certainly he was capable of cruelty, as his dismissal of my kindness demonstrates...
Otherwise, I don't concern myself with the business of the villagers.
Their affairs of the heart; of the purse; of the membrum virile...

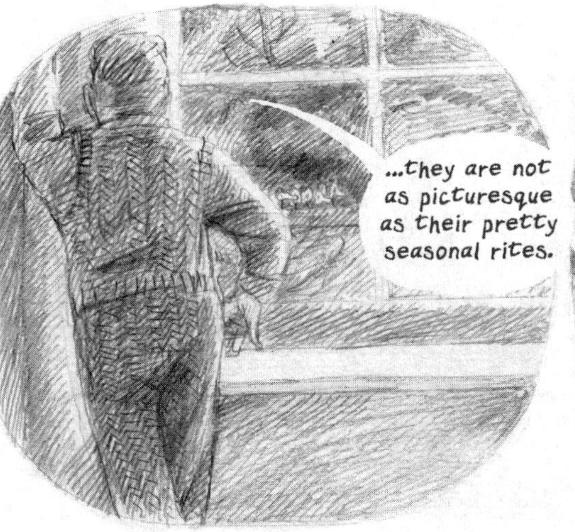
...they are not as picturesque as their pretty seasonal rites.

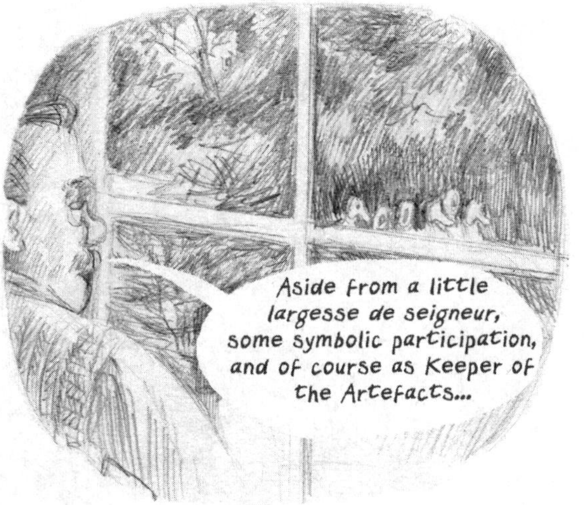
Aside from a little largesse de seigneur, some symbolic participation, and of course as Keeper of the Artefacts...

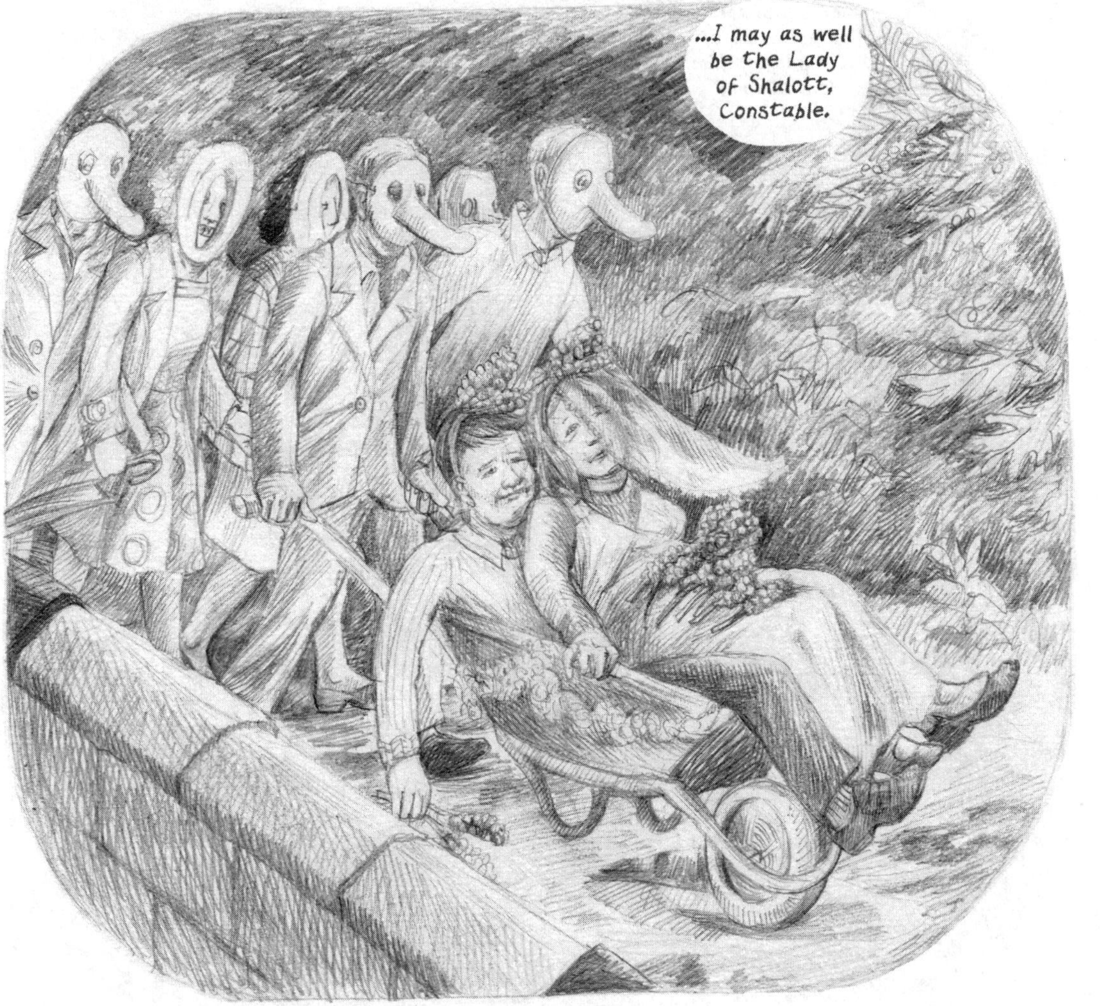
...I may as well be the Lady of Shalott, Constable.

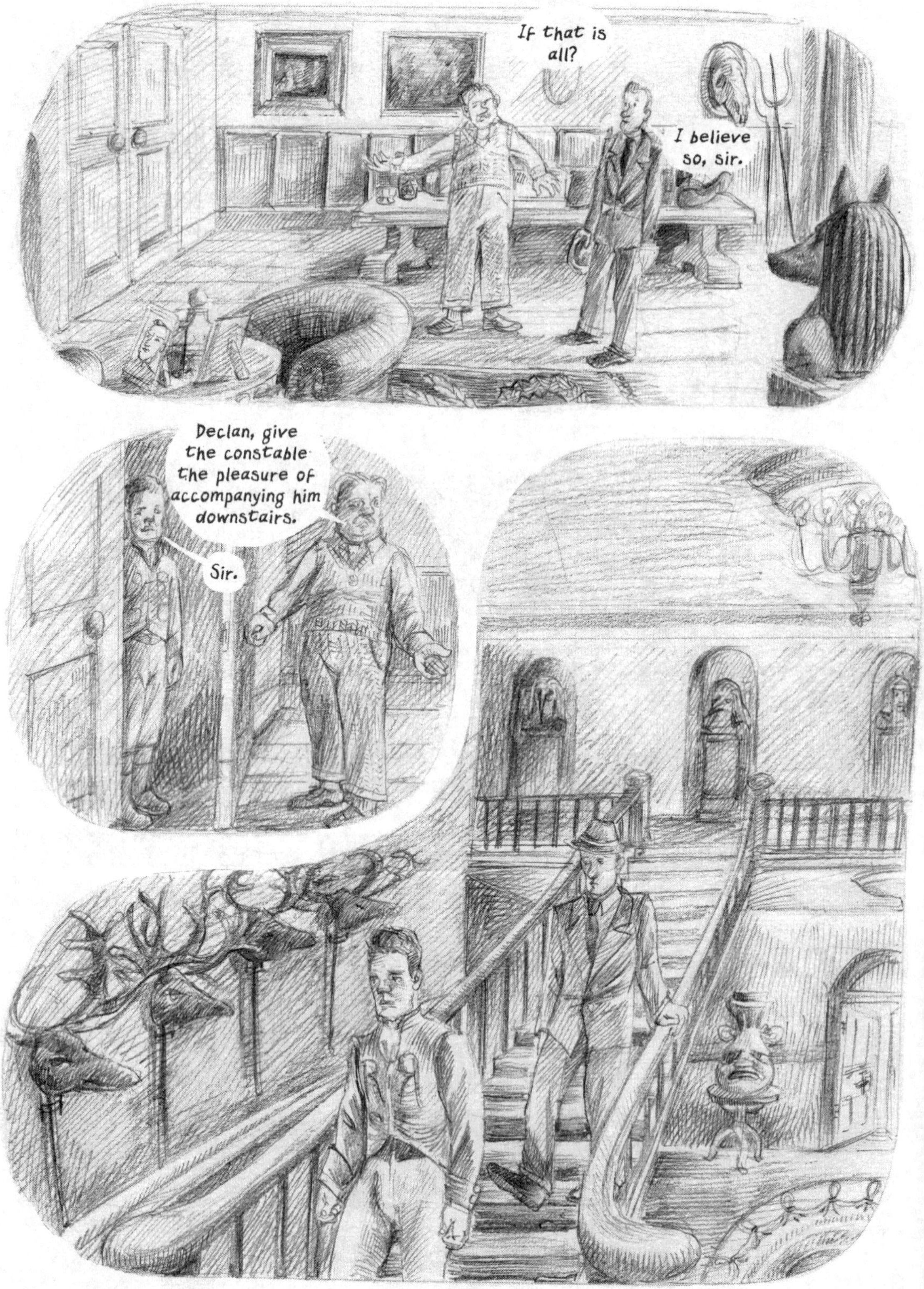
If that is all?
I believe so, sir.
Declan, give the constable the pleasure of accompanying him downstairs.
Sir.

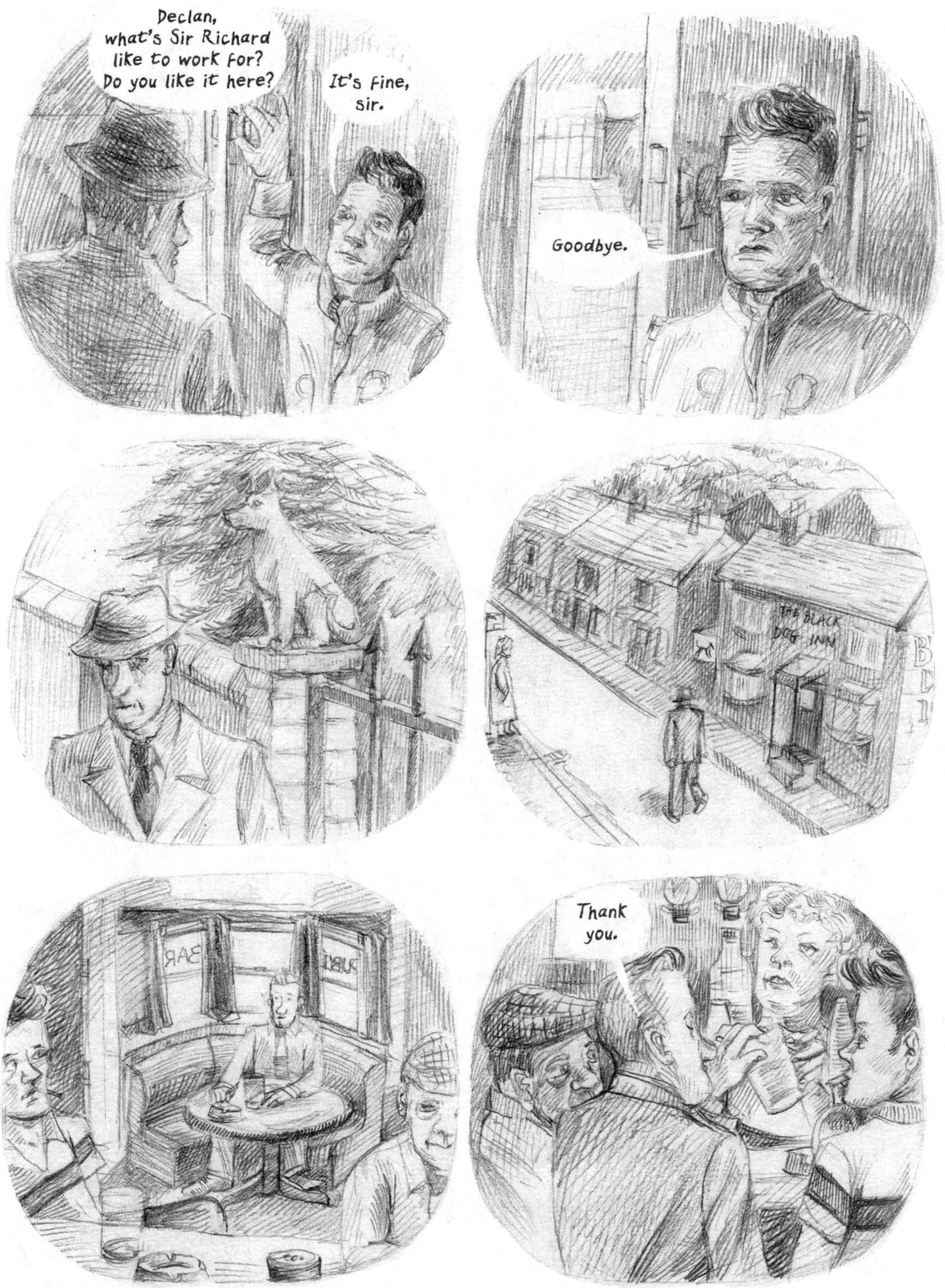
Declan, what's Sir Richard like to work for? Do you like it here?
It's fine, sir.
Goodbye.
THE BLACK DOG INN
Thank you.

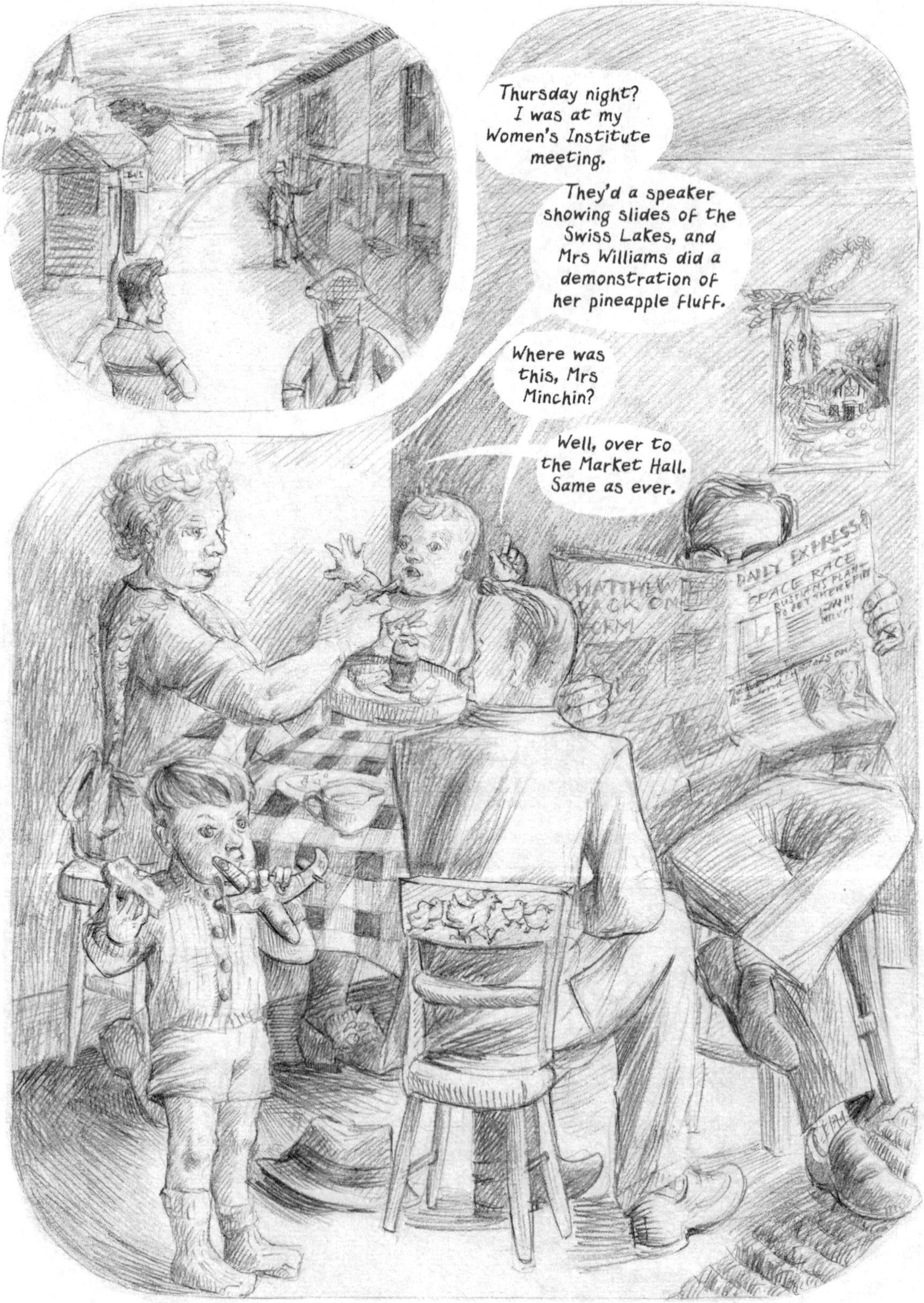
Thursday night? I was at my Women's Institute meeting.
They'd a speaker showing slides of the Swiss Lakes, and Mrs Williams did a demonstration of her pineapple fluff.
Where was this, Mrs Minchin?
Well, over to the Market Hall. Same as ever.
DAILY EXPRESS
SPACE RACE

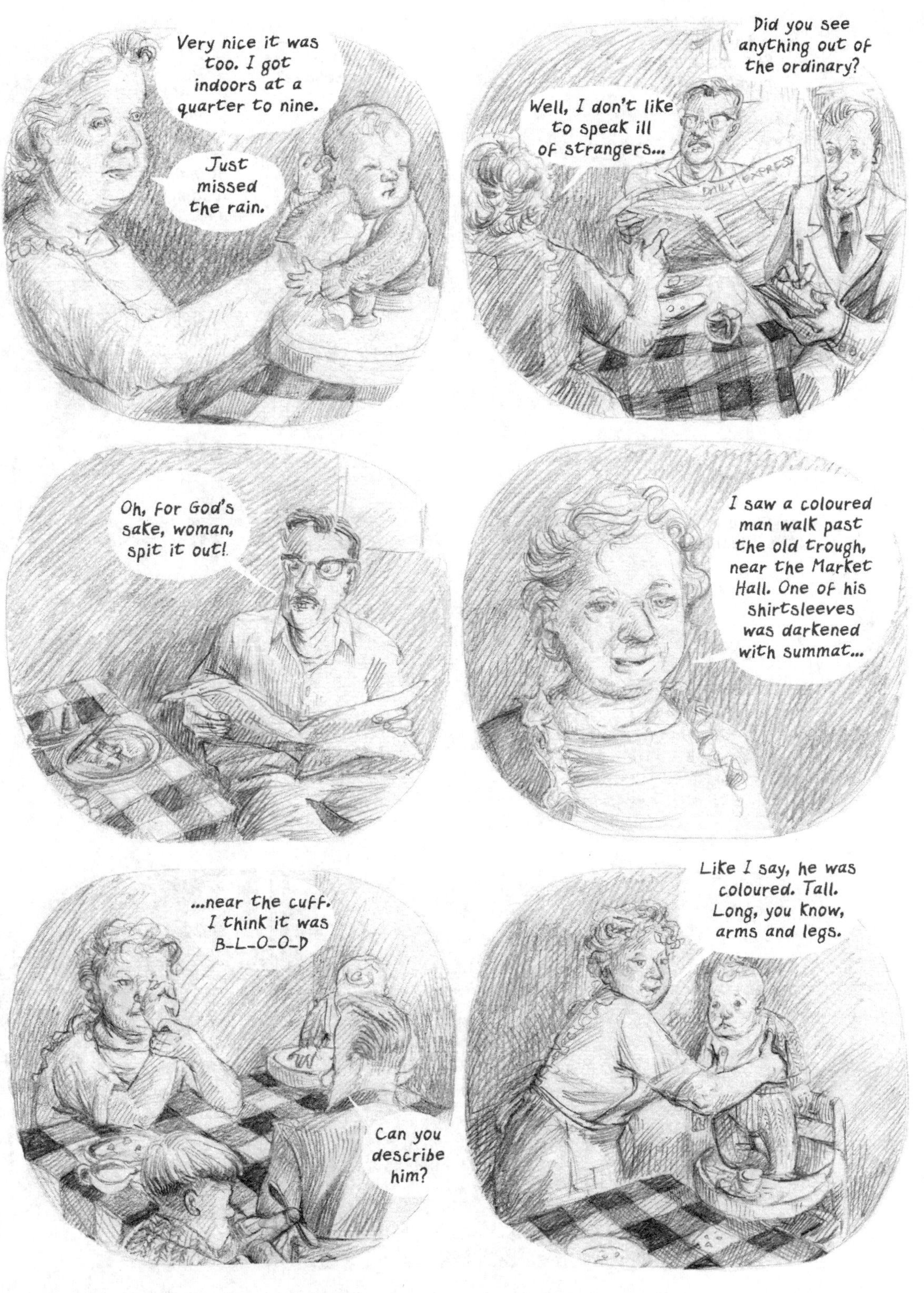
Very nice it was too. I got indoors at a quarter to nine.
Just missed the rain.
Did you see anything out of the ordinary?
Well, I don't like to speak ill of strangers...
DAILY EXPRESS
Oh, for God's sake, woman, spit it out!
I saw a coloured man walk past the old trough, near the Market Hall. One of his shirtsleeves was darkened with summat...
...near the cuff. I think it was B-L-O-O-D
Can you describe him?
Like I say, he was coloured. Tall. Long, you know, arms and legs.

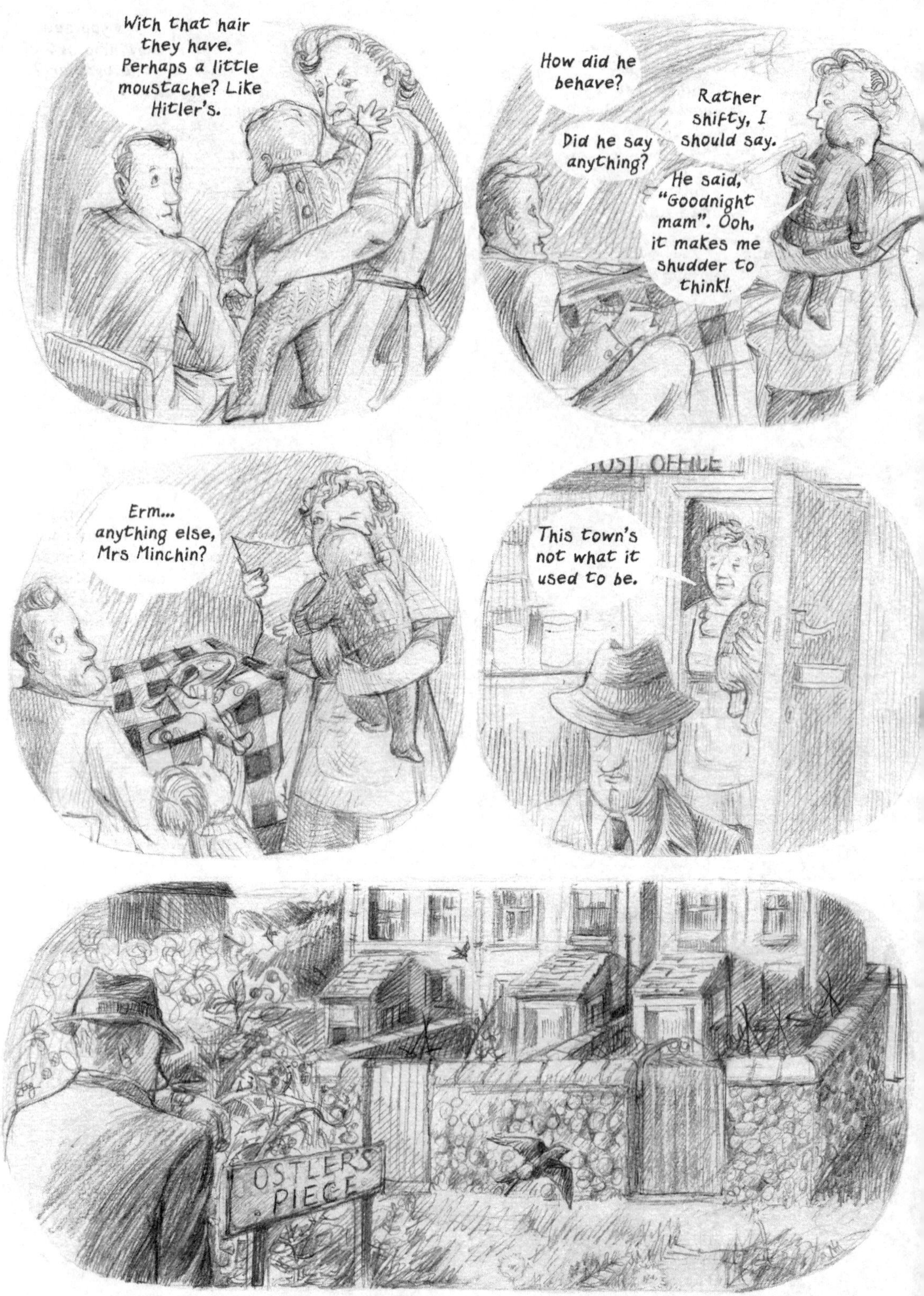
With that hair they have. Perhaps a little moustache? Like Hitler's.
How did he behave?
Did he say anything?
Rather shifty, I should say.
He said, "Goodnight mam". Ooh, it makes me shudder to think!
Erm... anything else, Mrs Minchin?
POST OFFICE
This town's not what it used to be.
OSTLER'S PIECE

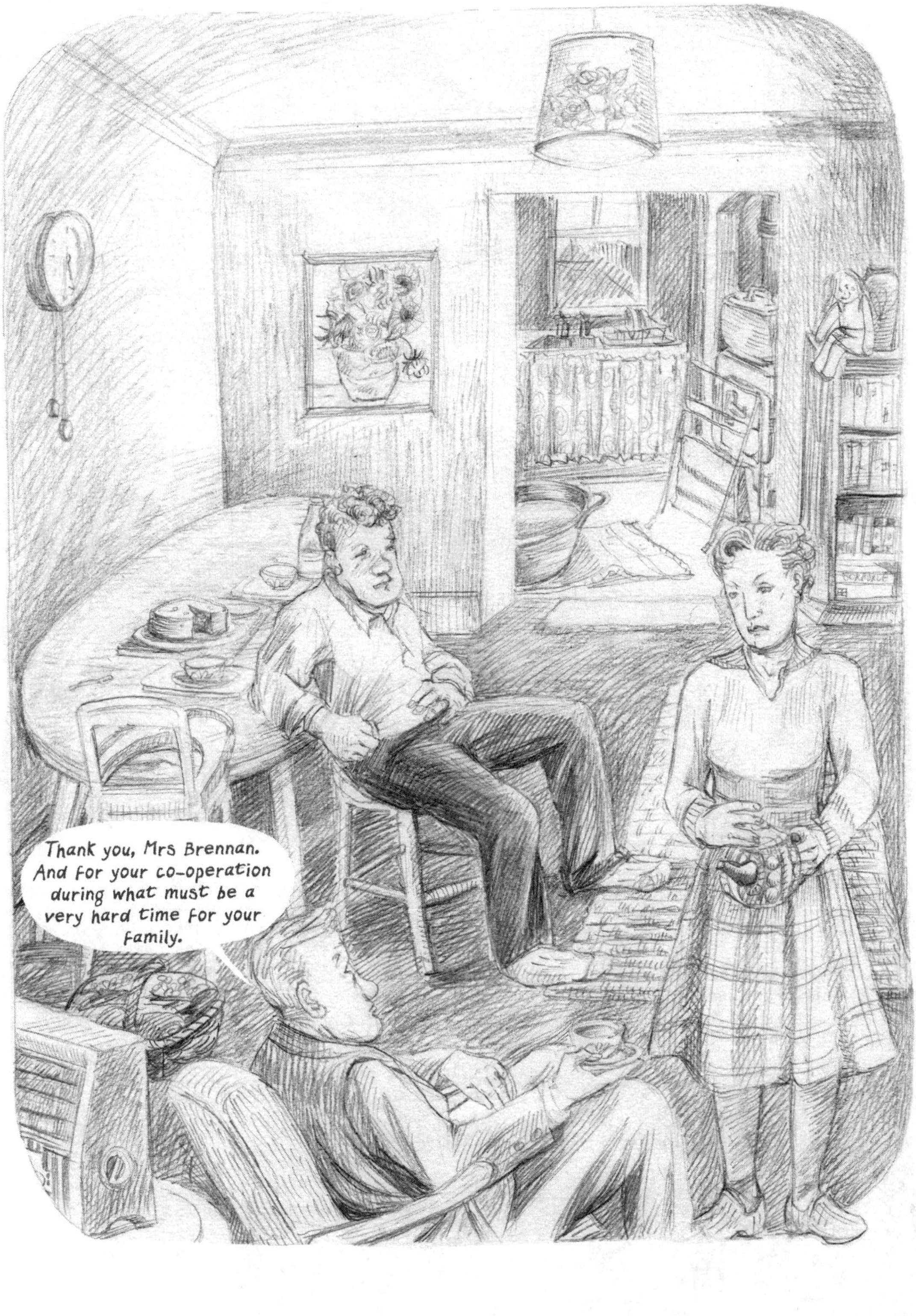
Thank you, Mrs Brennan. And for your co-operation during what must be a very hard time for your family.

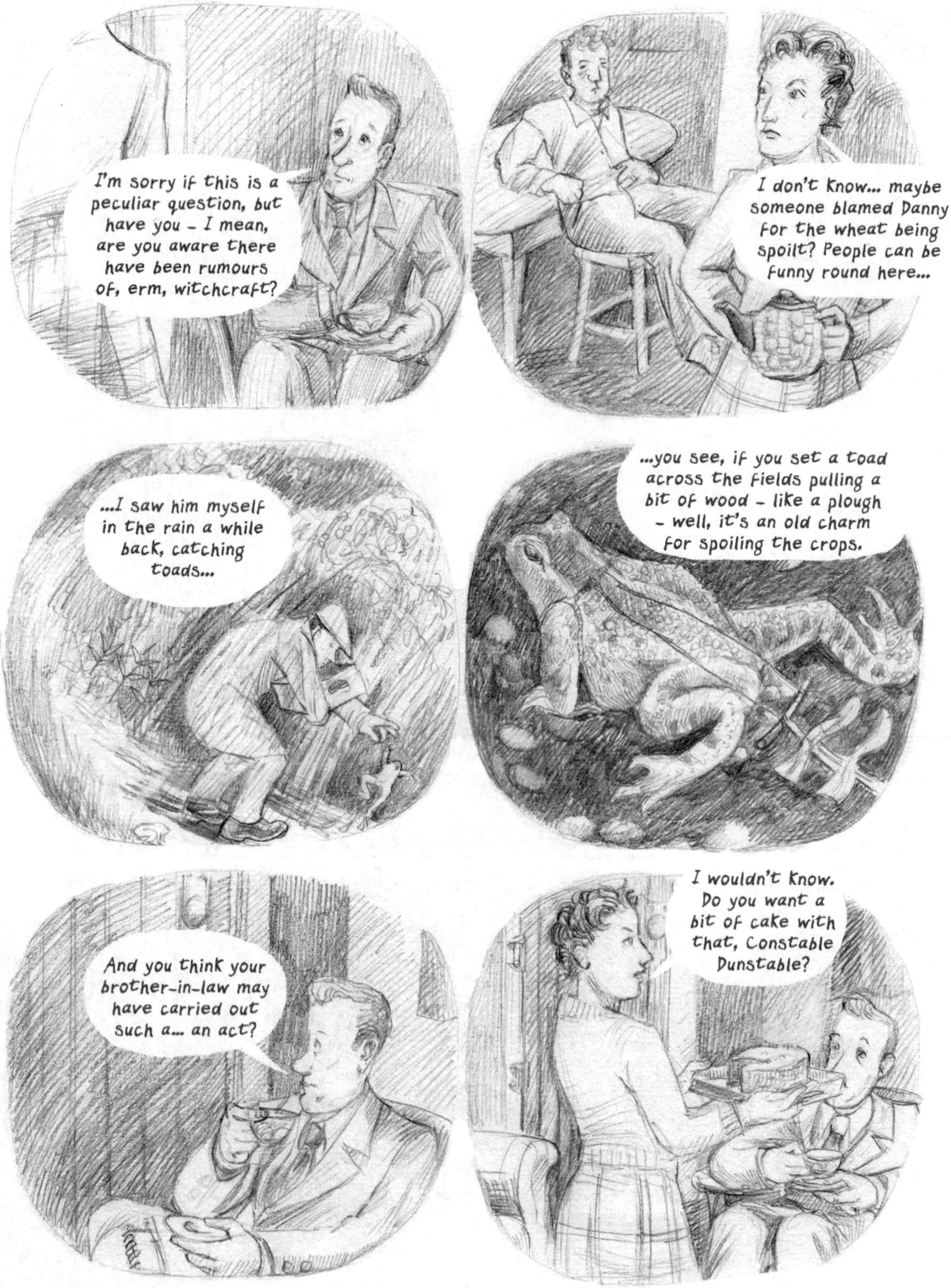
I'm sorry if this is a peculiar question, but have you - I mean, are you aware there have been rumours of, erm, witchcraft?
I don't know... maybe someone blamed Danny for the wheat being spoilt? People can be funny round here...
...I saw him myself in the rain a while back, catching toads...
...you see, if you set a toad across the fields pulling a bit of wood - like a plough - well, it's an old charm for spoiling the crops.
And you think your brother-in-law may have carried out such a... an act?
I wouldn't know. Do you want a bit of cake with that, Constable Dunstable?

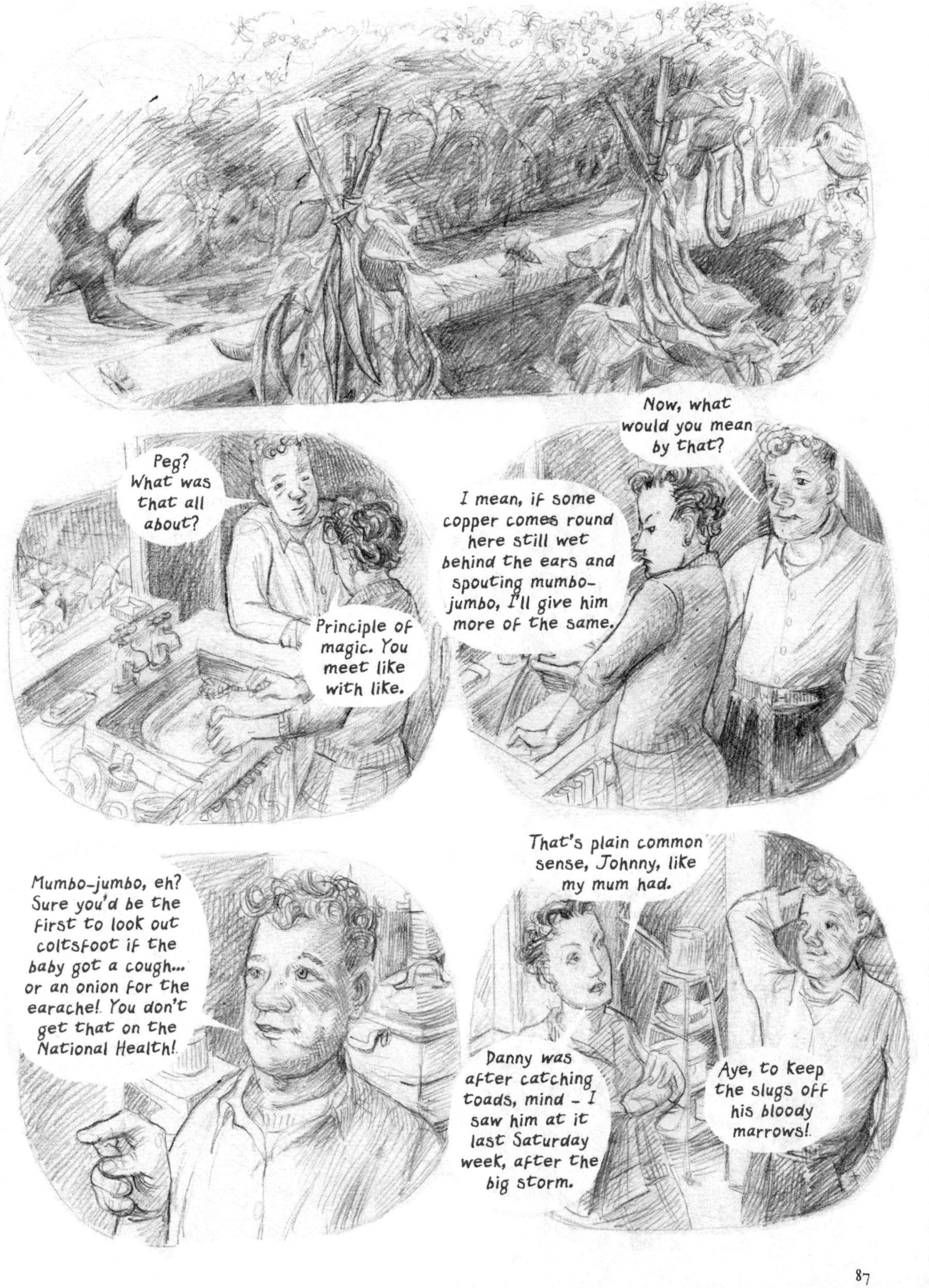
Peg? What was that all about?
Principle of magic. You meet like with like.
Now, what would you mean by that?
I mean, if some copper comes round here still wet behind the ears and spouting mumbo-jumbo, I'll give him more of the same.
Mumbo-jumbo, eh? Sure you'd be the first to look out coltsfoot if the baby got a cough... or an onion for the earache! You don't get that on the National Health!
That's plain common sense, Johnny, like my mum had.
Danny was after catching toads, mind – I saw him at it last Saturday week, after the big storm.
Aye, to keep the slugs off his bloody marrows!

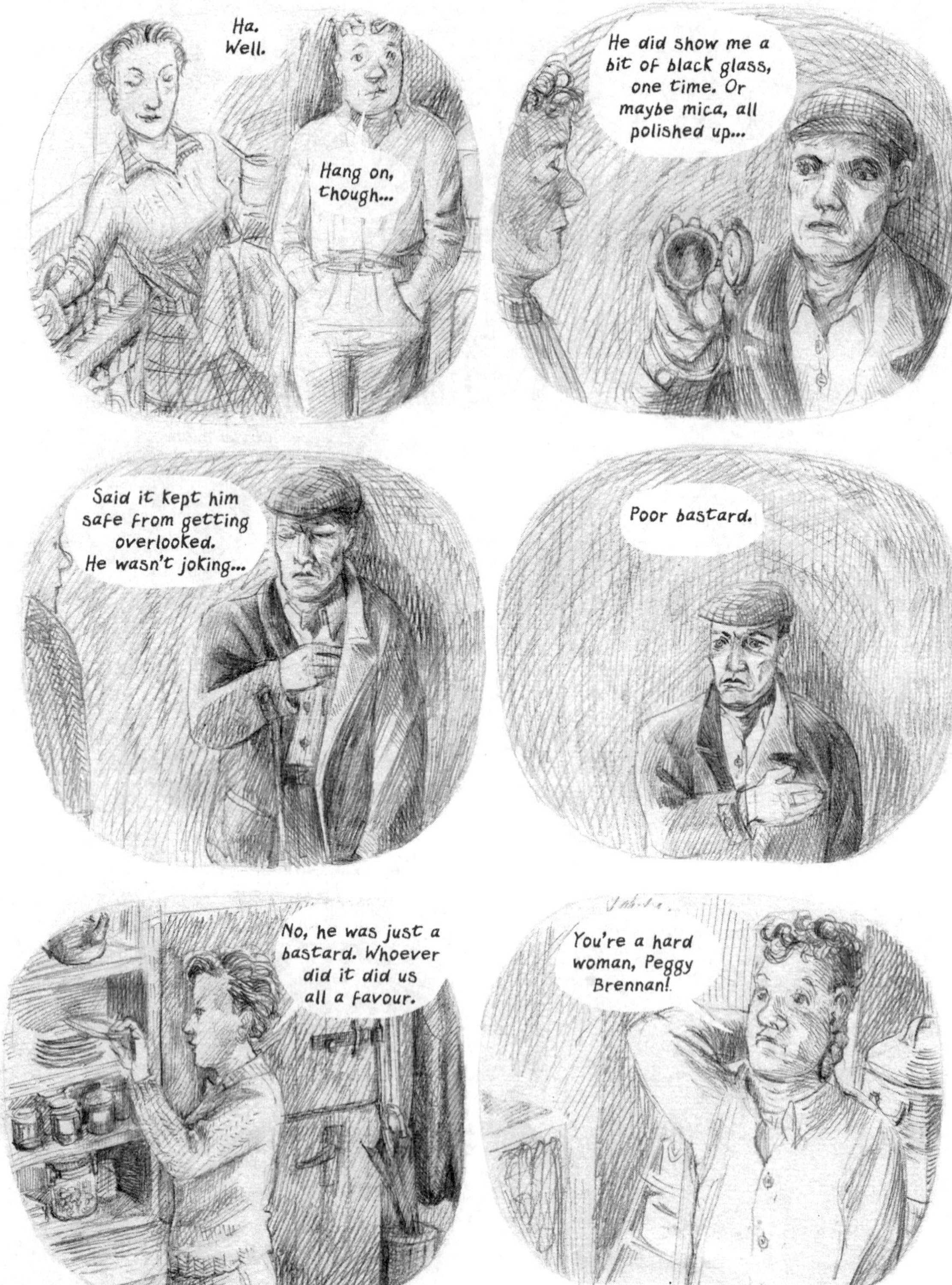
Ha.
Well.
Hang on, though...
He did show me a bit of black glass, one time. Or maybe mica, all polished up...
Said it kept him safe from getting overlooked. He wasn't joking...
Poor bastard.
No, he was just a bastard. Whoever did it did us all a favour.
You're a hard woman, Peggy Brennan!

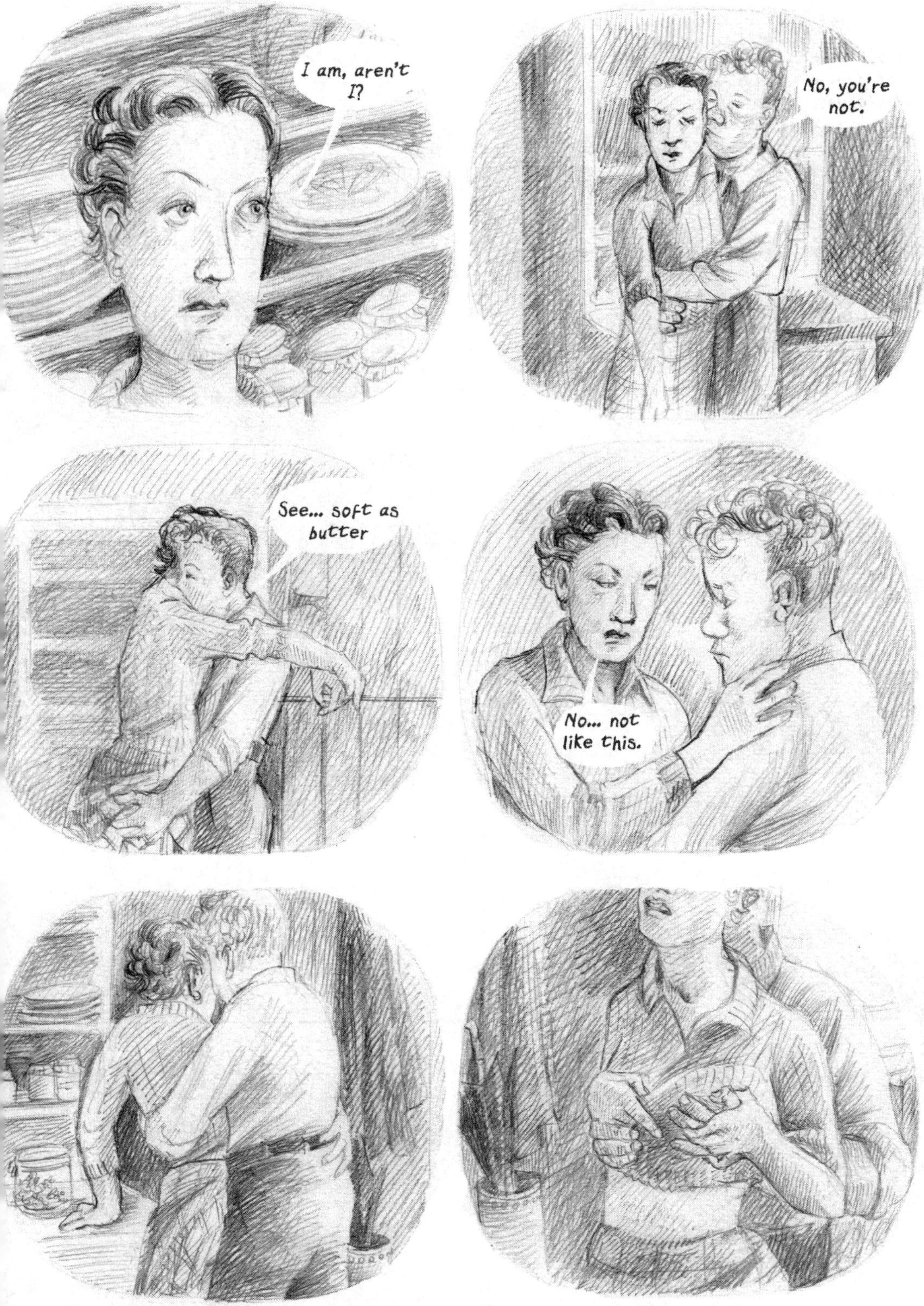
I am, aren't I?
No, you're not.
See... soft as butter
No... not like this.

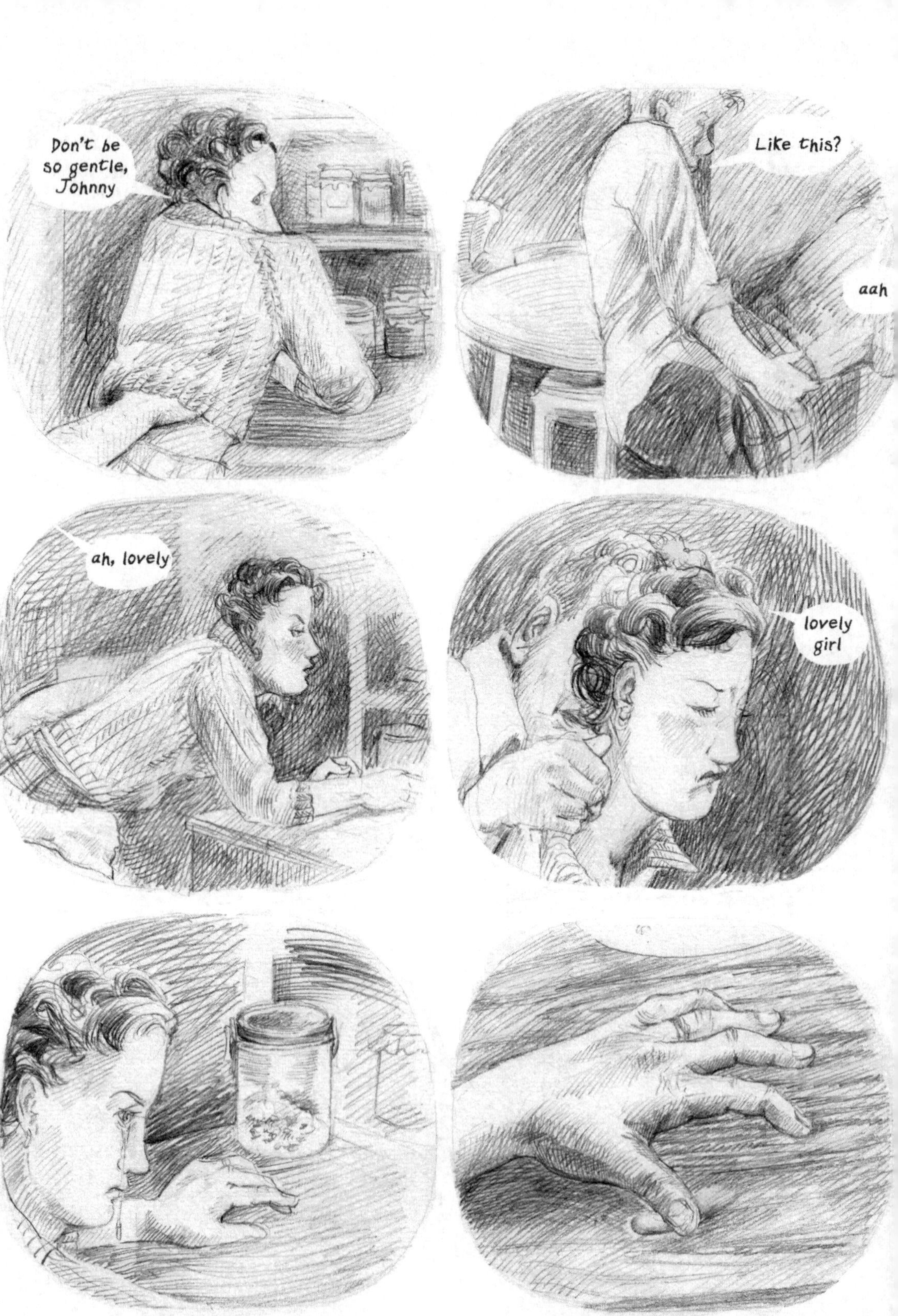
Don't be so gentle, Johnny
Like this?
aah
ah, lovely
lovely girl

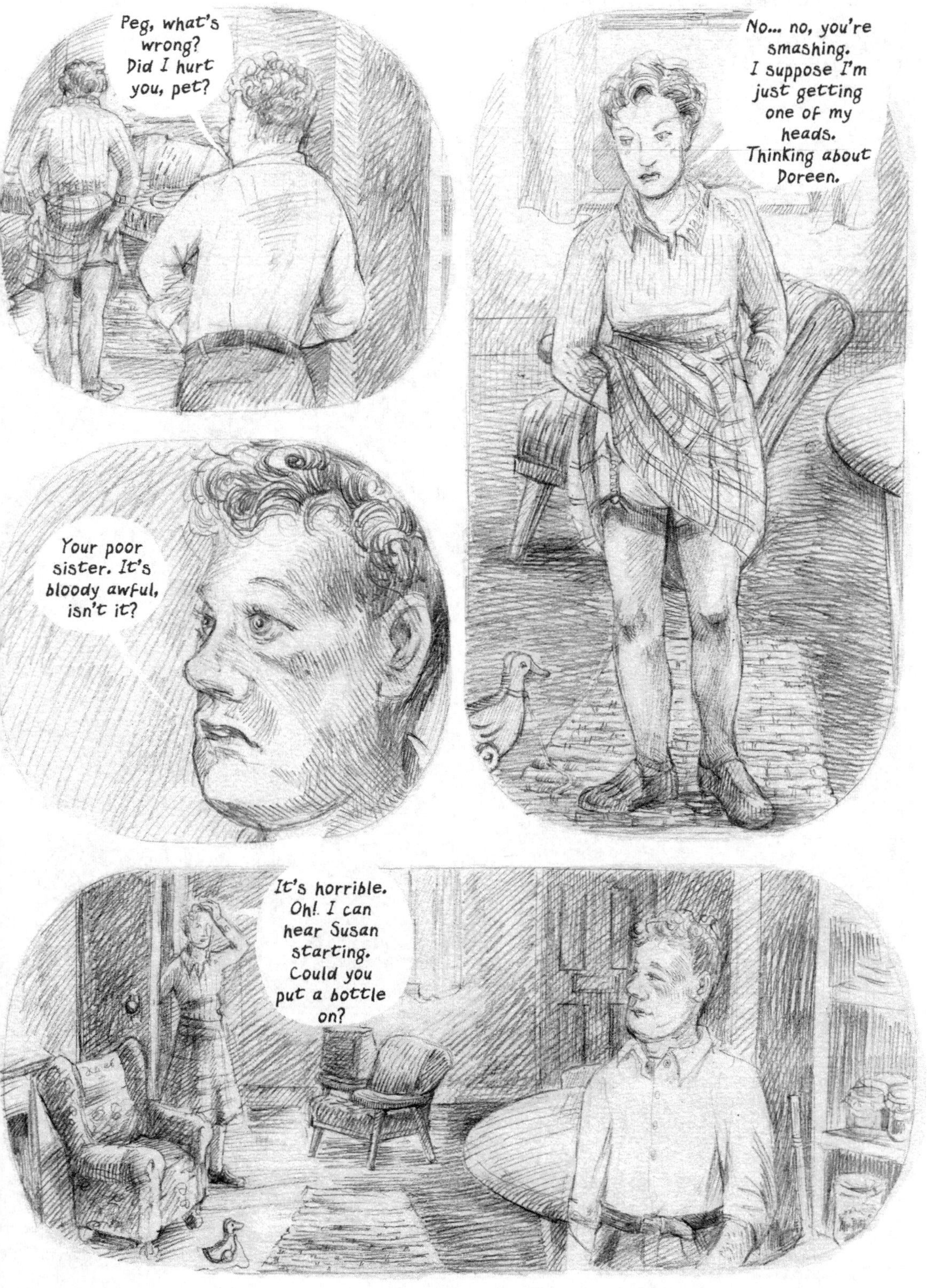

Peg, what's wrong? Did I hurt you, pet?
No... no, you're smashing. I suppose I'm just getting one of my heads. Thinking about Doreen.
Your poor sister. It's bloody awful, isn't it?
It's horrible. Oh!. I can hear Susan starting. Could you put a bottle on?

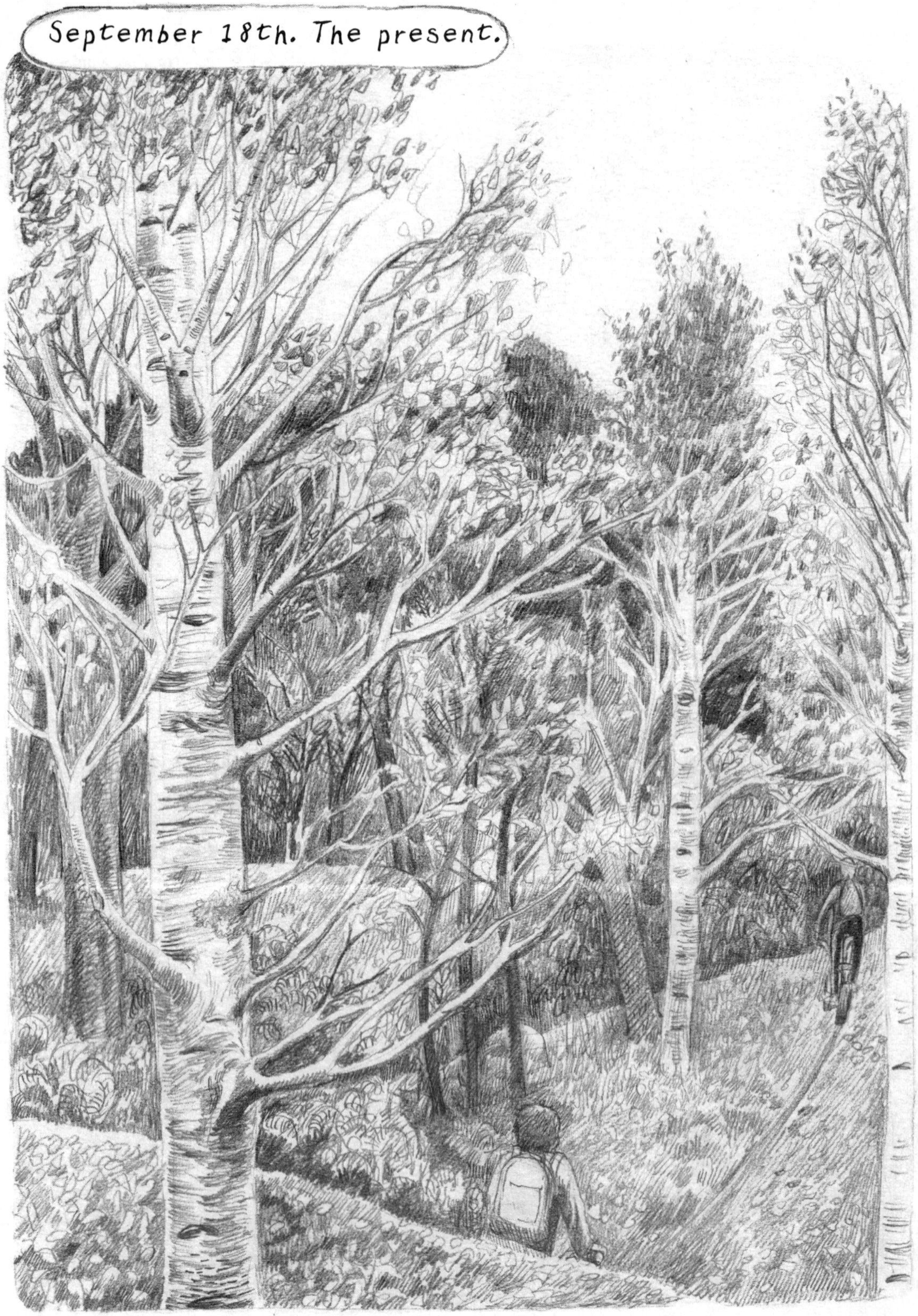
September 18th. The present.

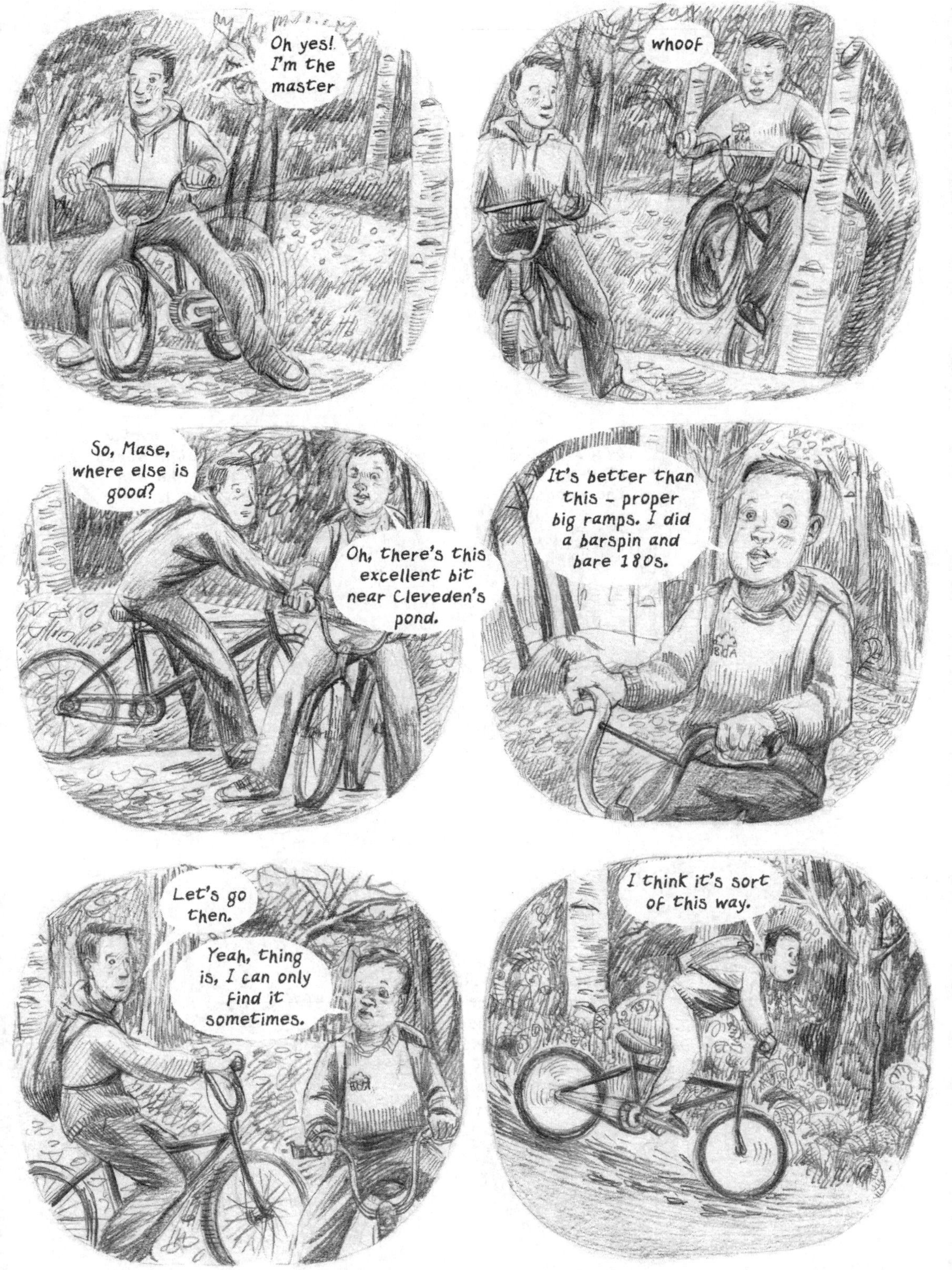
Oh yes! I'm the master
whoof
So, Mase, where else is good?
Oh, there's this excellent bit near Cleveden's pond.
It's better than this - proper big ramps. I did a barspin and bare 180s.
Let's go then.
Yeah, thing is, I can only find it sometimes.
I think it's sort of this way.

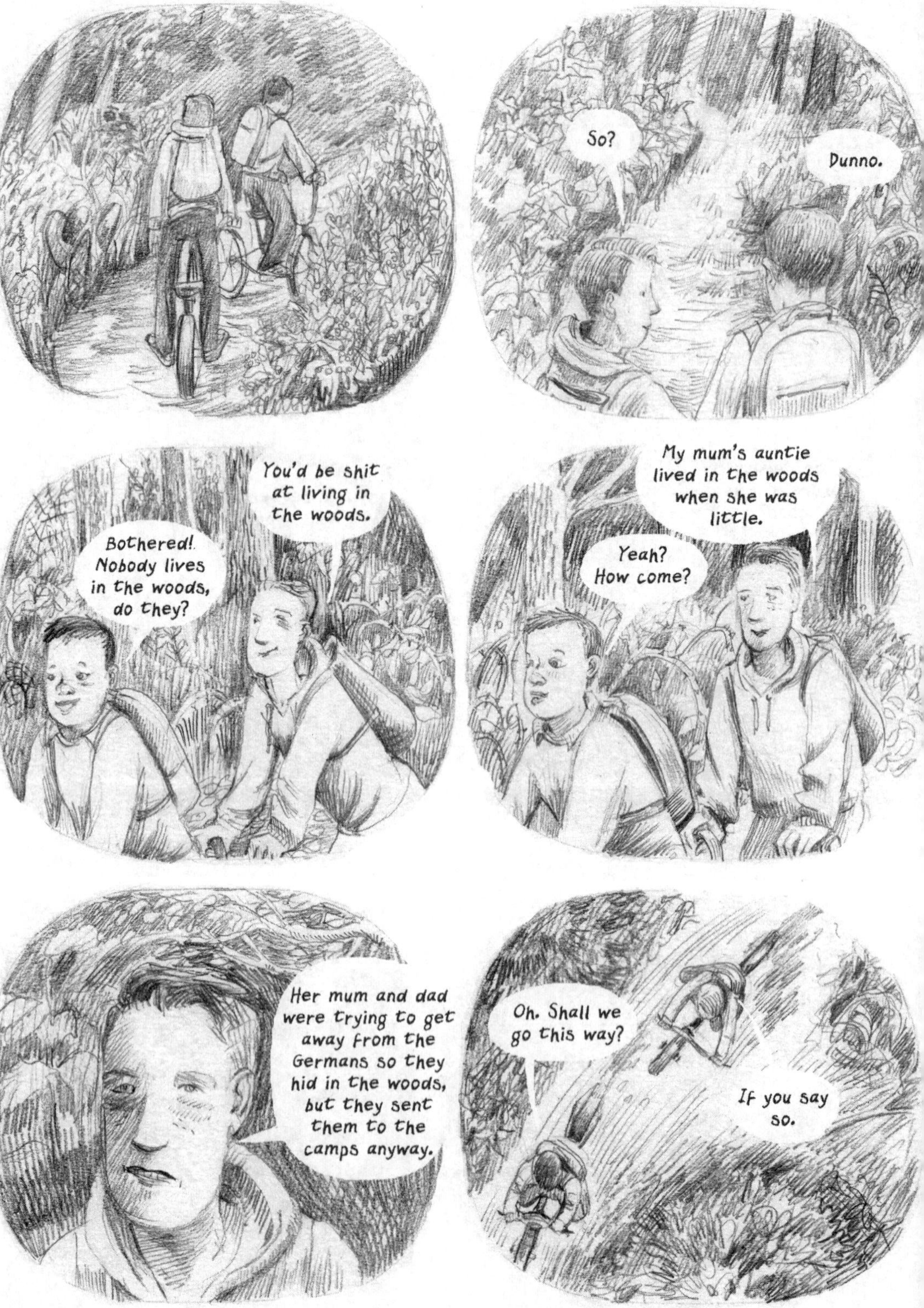
So?
Dunno.
You'd be shit at living in the woods.
Bothered!. Nobody lives in the woods, do they?
My mum's auntie lived in the woods when she was little.
Yeah? How come?
Her mum and dad were trying to get away from the Germans so they hid in the woods, but they sent them to the camps anyway.
Oh. Shall we go this way?
If you say so.

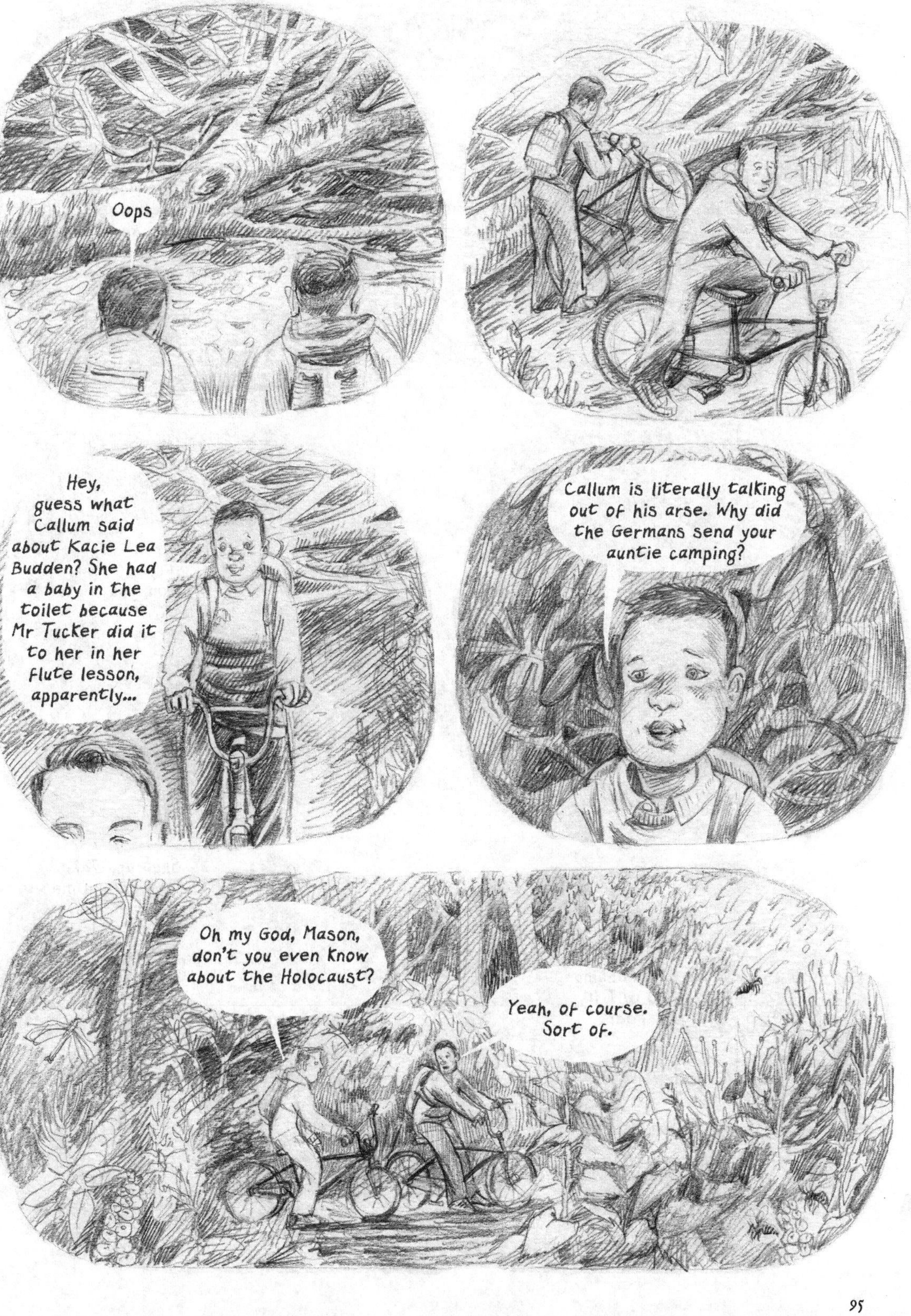
Oops
Hey, guess what Callum said about Kacie Lea Budden? She had a baby in the toilet because Mr Tucker did it to her in her flute lesson, apparently...
Callum is literally talking out of his arse. Why did the Germans send your auntie camping?
Oh my God, Mason, don't you even know about the Holocaust?
Yeah, of course. Sort of.

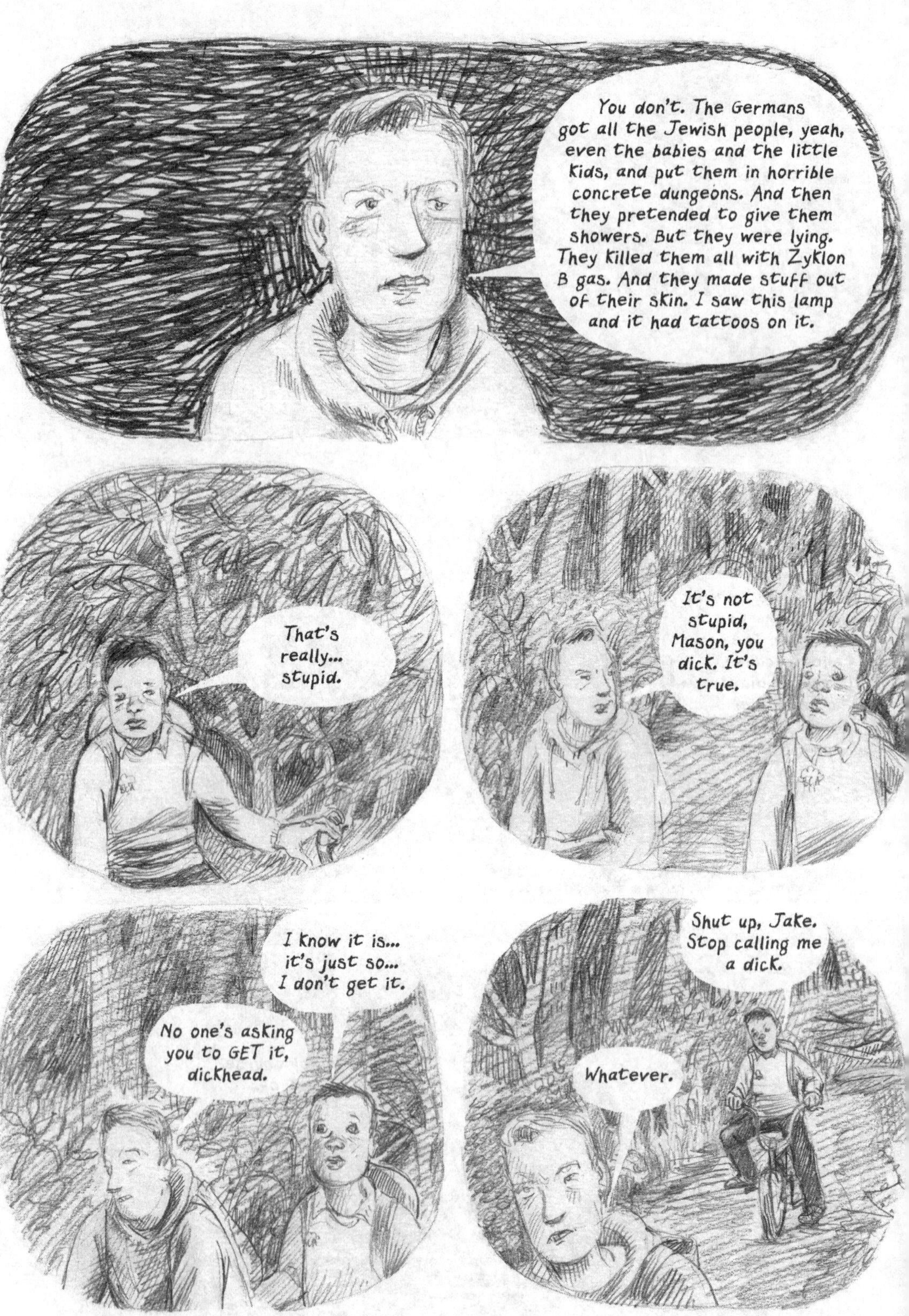
You don't. The Germans got all the Jewish people, yeah, even the babies and the little kids, and put them in horrible concrete dungeons. And then they pretended to give them showers. But they were lying. They killed them all with Zyklon B gas. And they made stuff out of their skin. I saw this lamp and it had tattoos on it.
That's really... stupid.
It's not stupid, Mason, you dick. It's true.
I know it is... it's just so... I don't get it.
No one's asking you to GET it, dickhead.
Shut up, Jake. Stop calling me a dick.
Whatever.

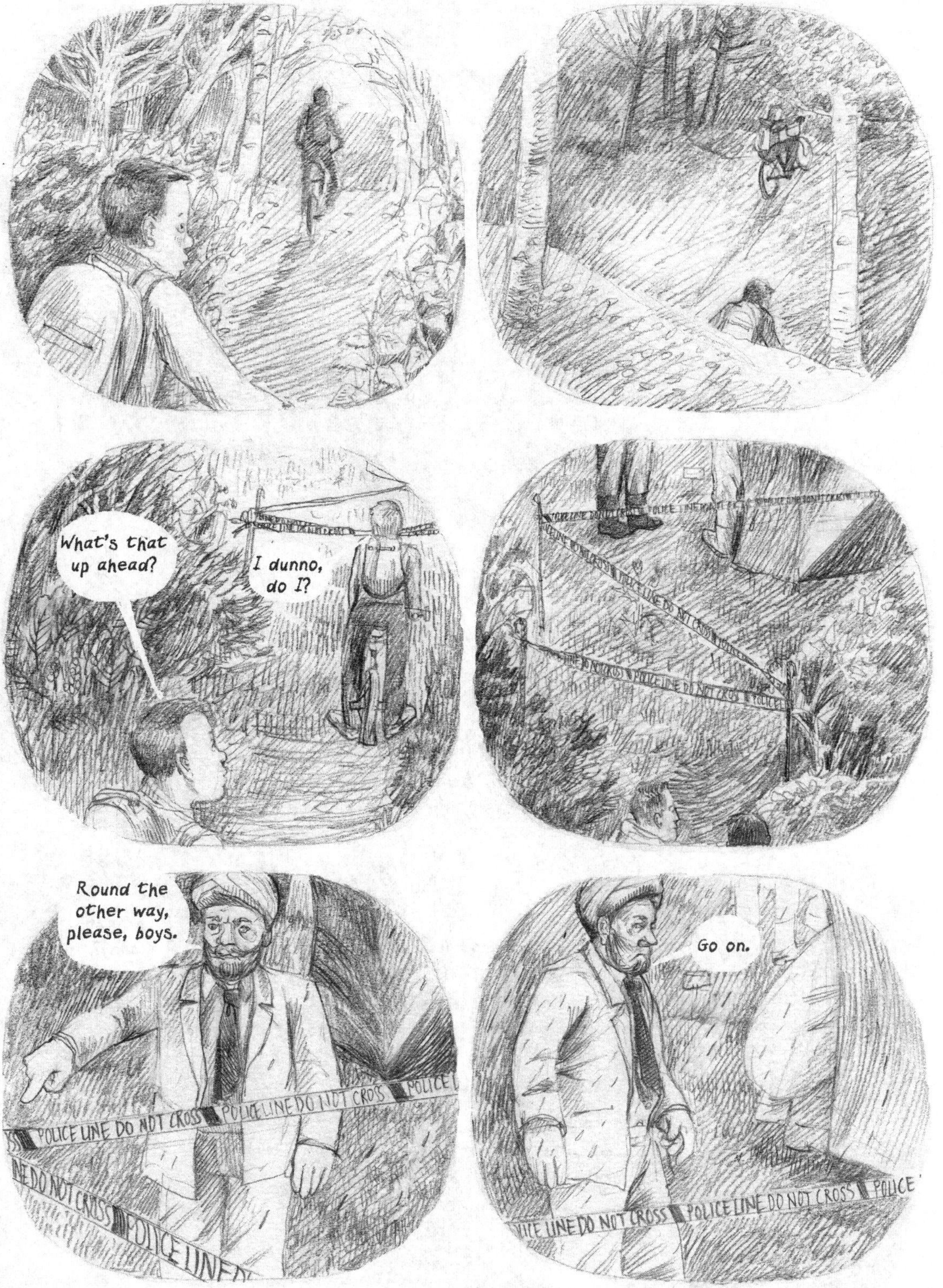
What's that up ahead?
I dunno, do I?
Round the other way, please, boys.
POLICE LINE DO NOT CROSS
Go on.
POLICE LINE DO NOT CROSS

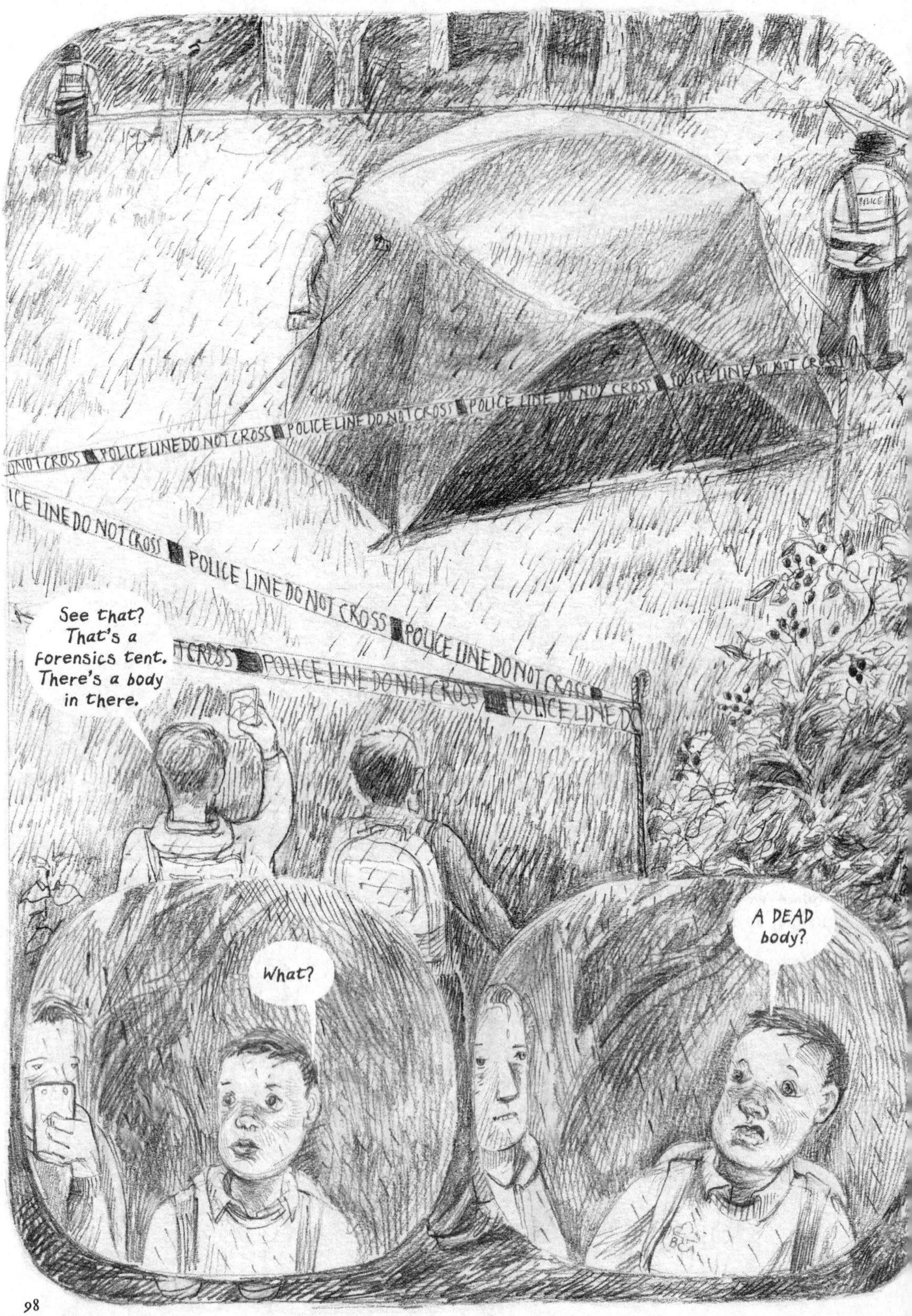
POLICE LINE DO NOT CROSS
See that? That's a forensics tent. There's a body in there.
What?
A DEAD body?

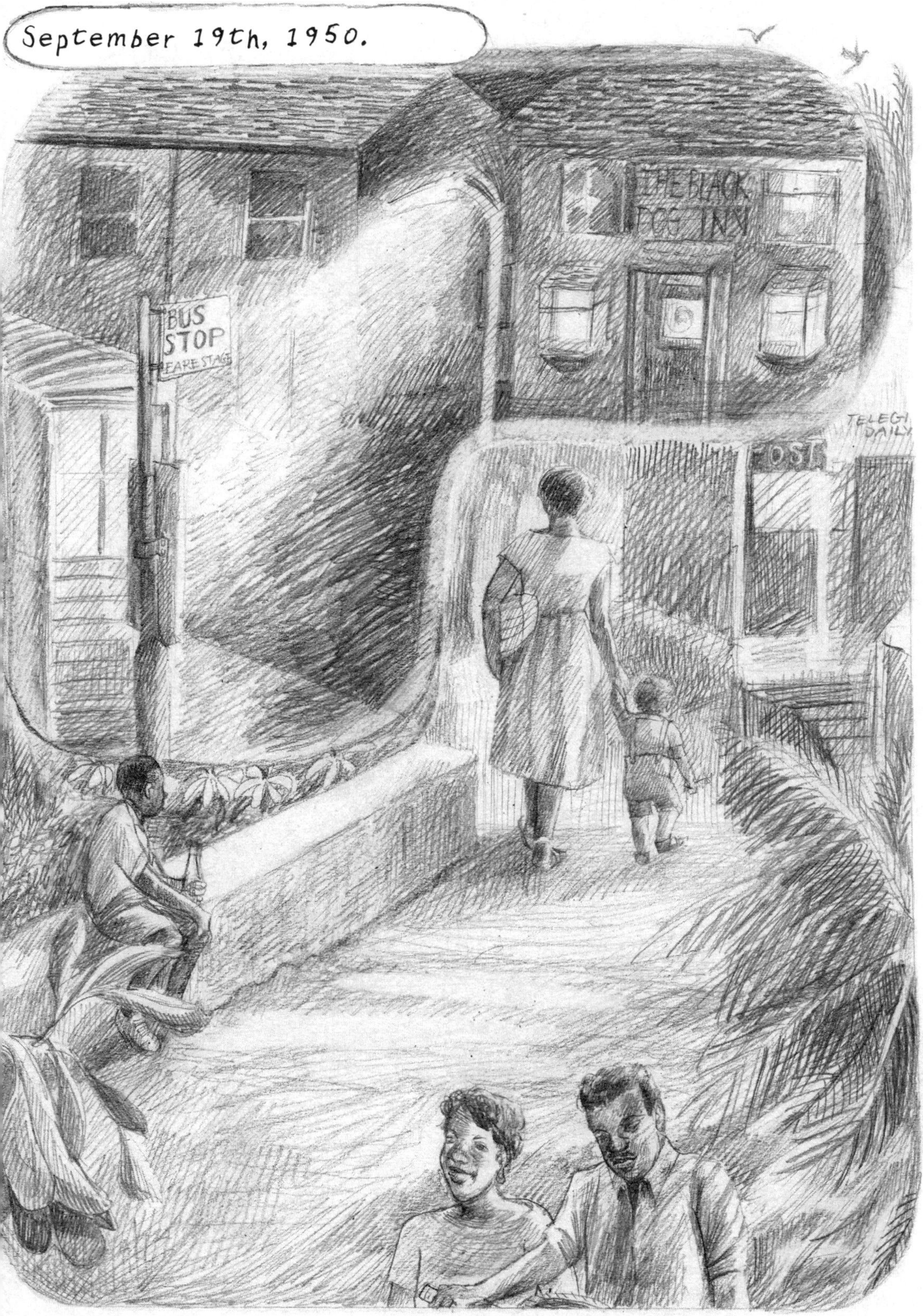
September 19th, 1950.
BUS STOP
FARE STAGE
THE BLACK DOG INN

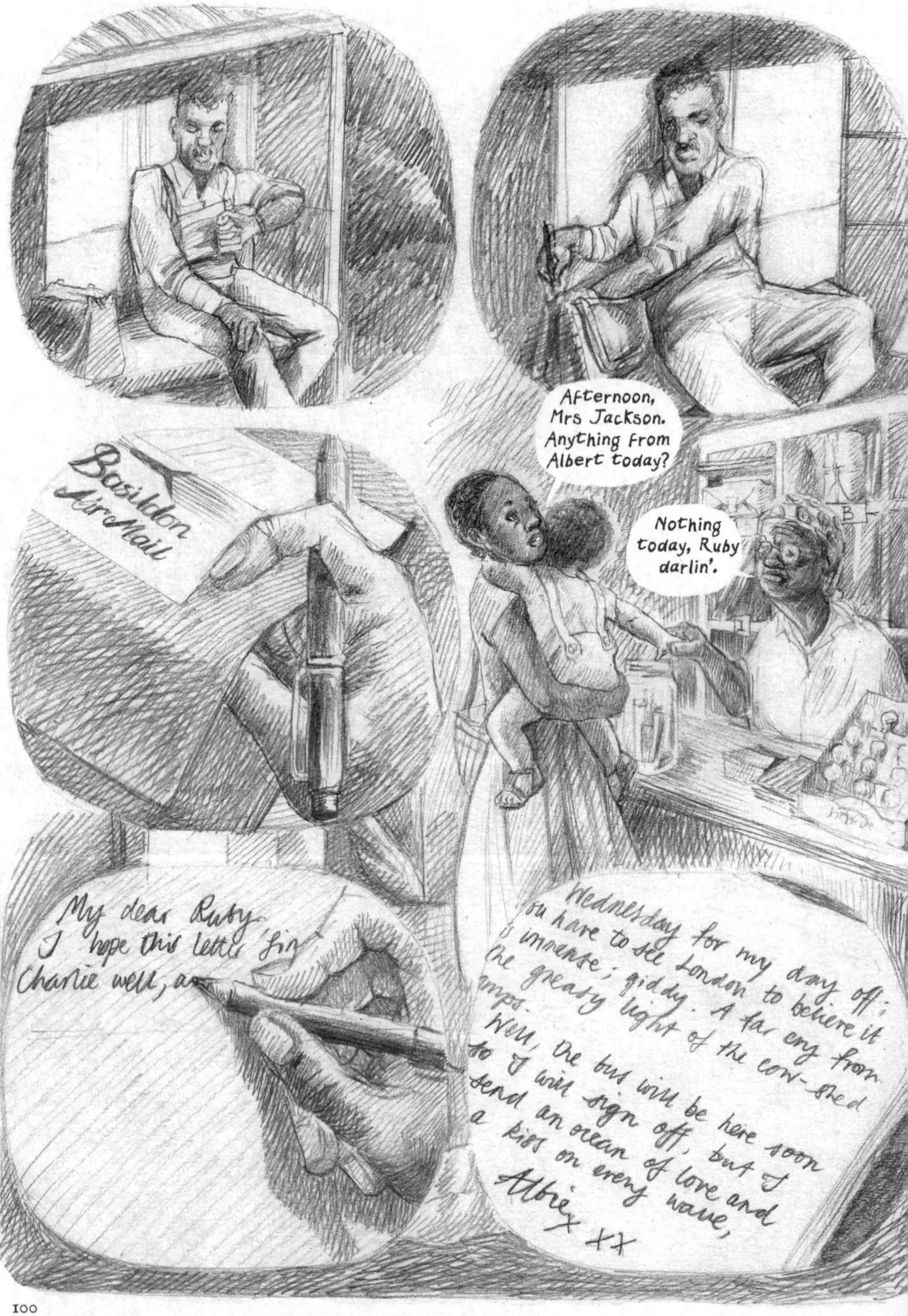

Basildon
Air Mail
Afternoon, Mrs Jackson. Anything from Albert today?
Nothing today, Ruby darlin'.
My dear Ruby
I hope this letter fin
Charlie well, a
Wednesday for my day off;
ou have to see London to believe it
s immense; giddy. A far cry from
he greasy light of the cow-shed
amps.
Well, the bus will be here soon
so I will sign off, but I
send an ocean of love and
a kiss on every wave,
Albie x xx

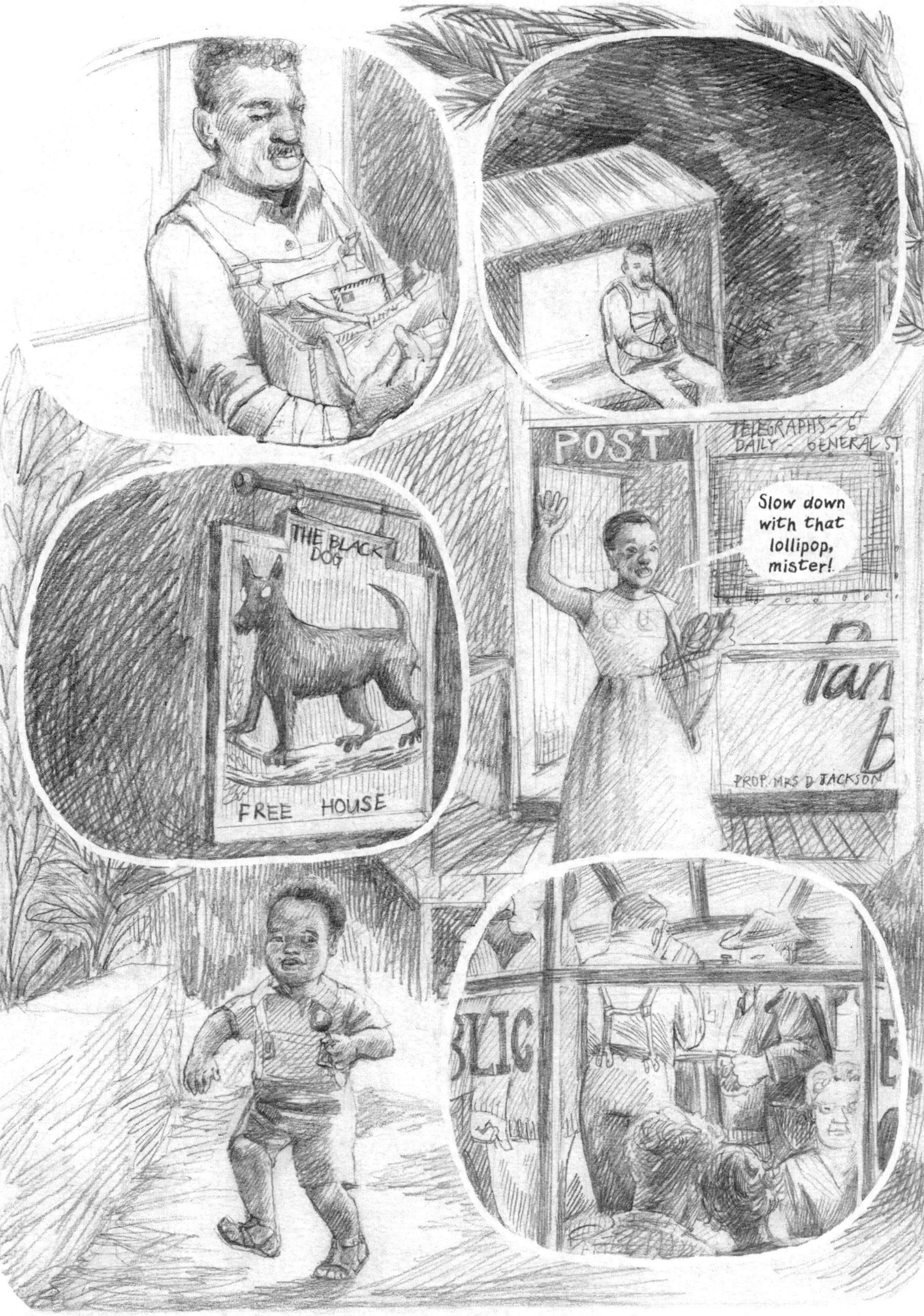
THE BLACK DOG
FREE HOUSE
POST
TELEGRAPHS - 6
DAILY - GENERAL ST
Slow down with that lollipop, mister!
PROP. MRS D JACKSON
BLIC

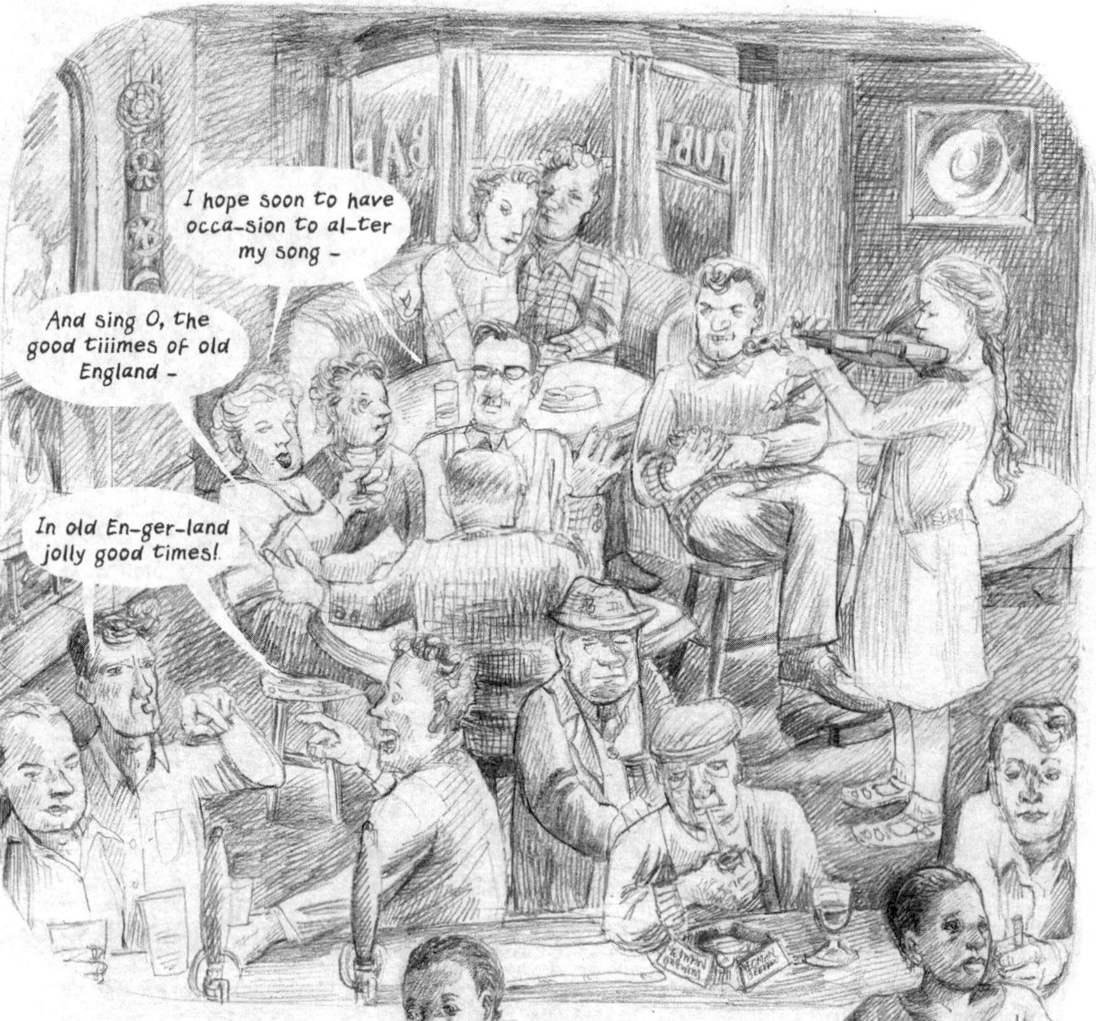
I hope soon to have occa-sion to al-ter my song -
And sing O, the good tiiimes of old England -
In old En-ger-land jolly good times!

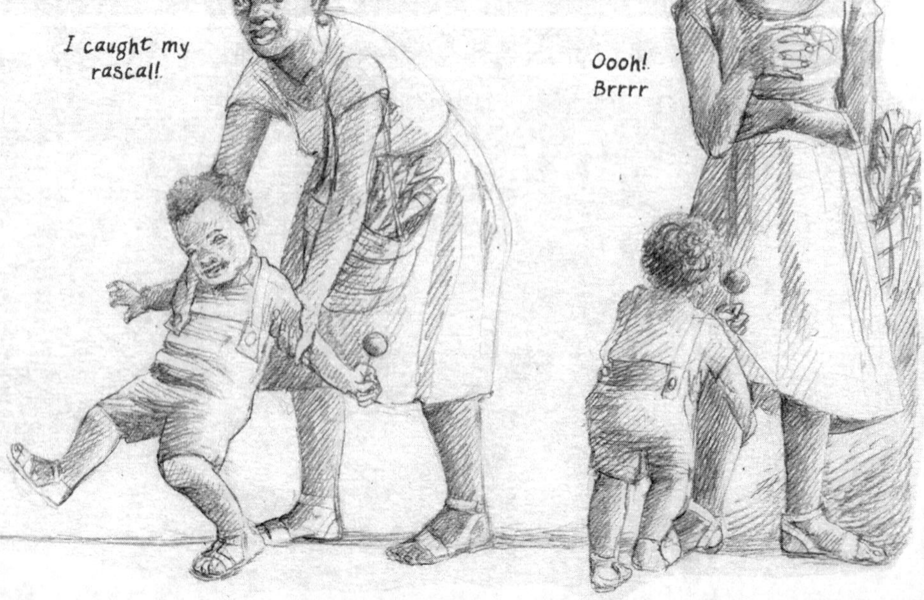
I caught my rascal!
Oooh! Brrrr

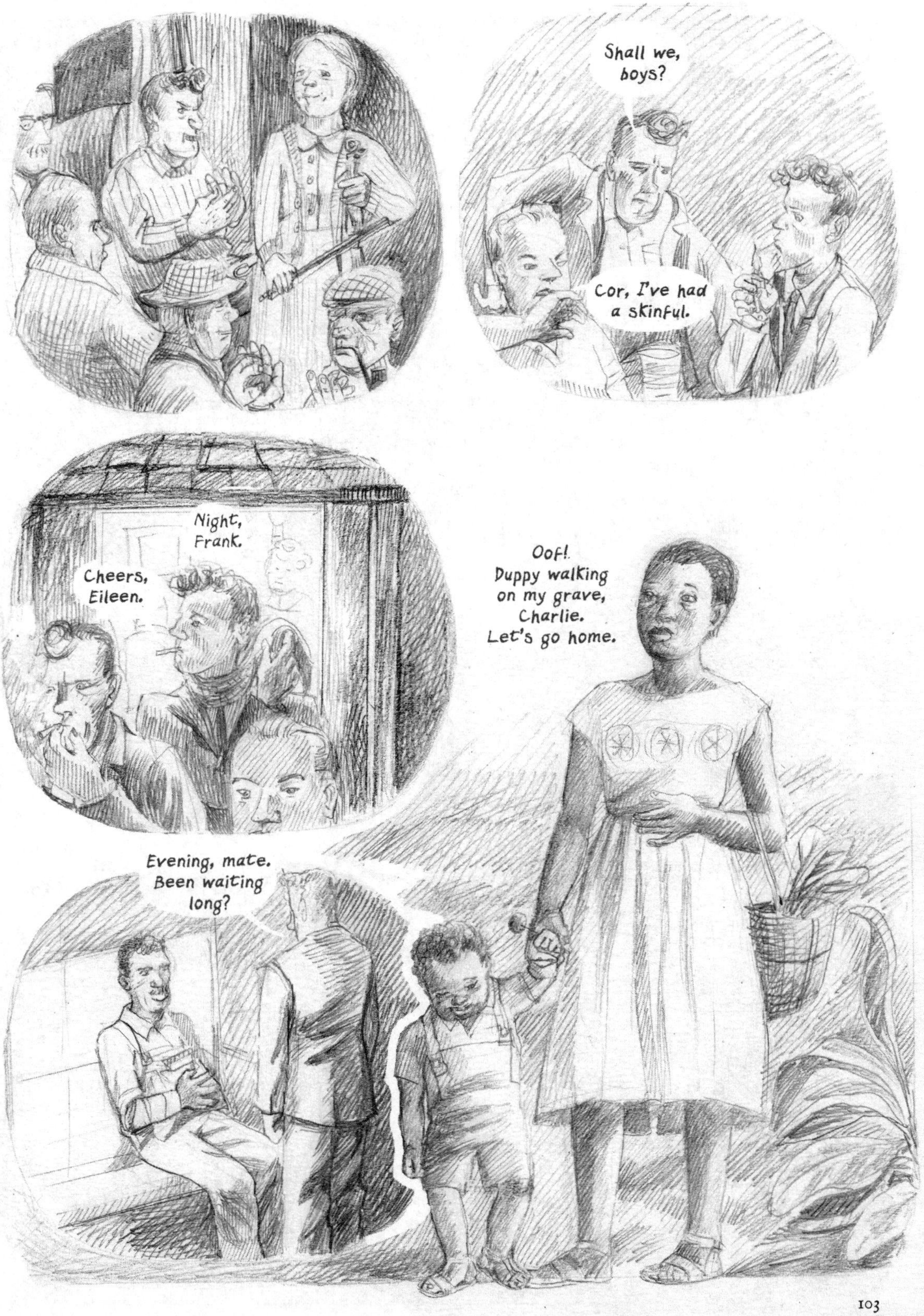
Shall we, boys?
Cor, I've had a skinful.
Night, Frank.
Cheers, Eileen.
Oof! Duppy walking on my grave, Charlie. Let's go home.
Evening, mate. Been waiting long?

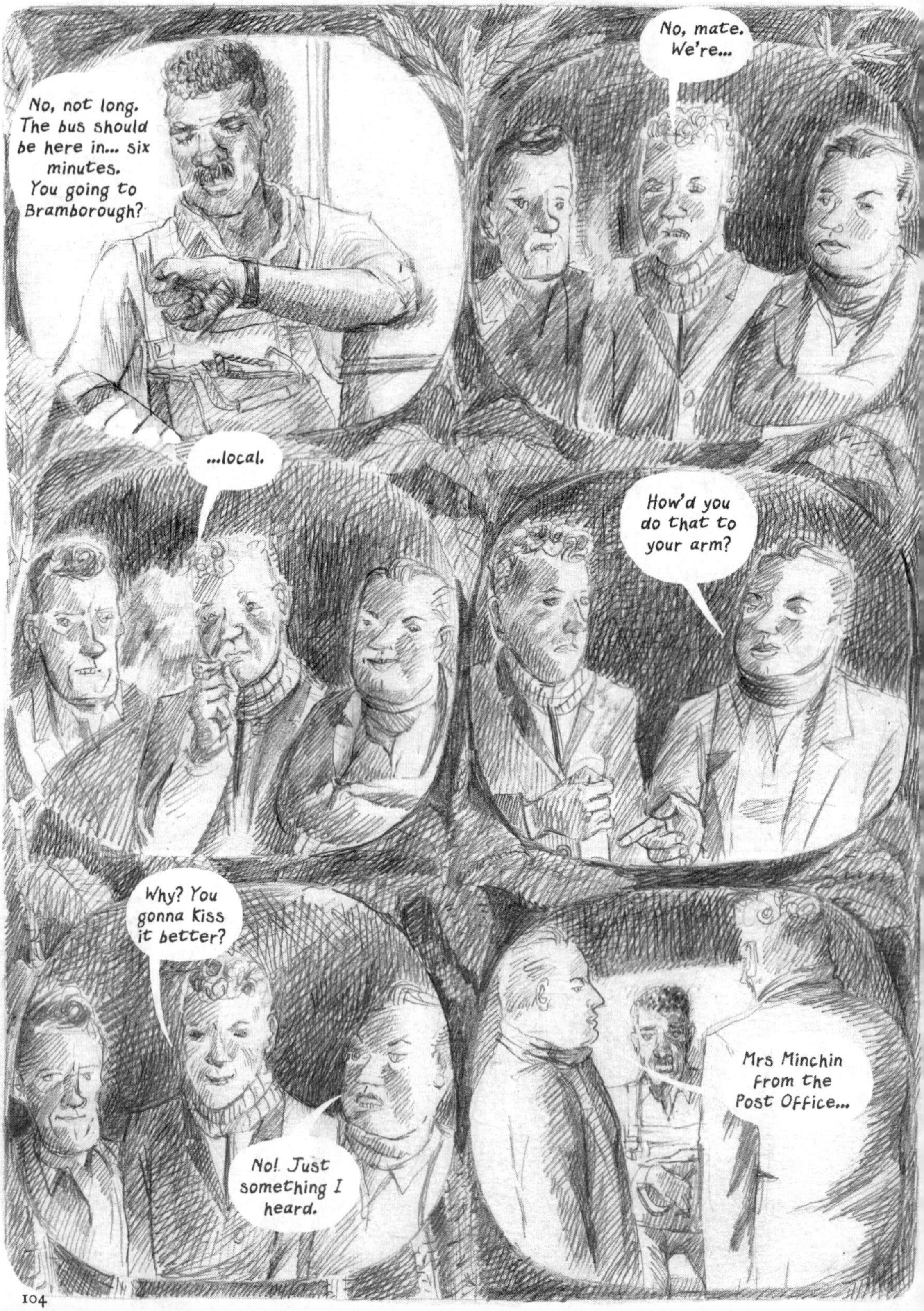
No, not long. The bus should be here in... six minutes. You going to Bramborough?
No, mate. We're...
...local.
How'd you do that to your arm?
Why? You gonna kiss it better?
No! Just something I heard.
Mrs Minchin from the Post Office...

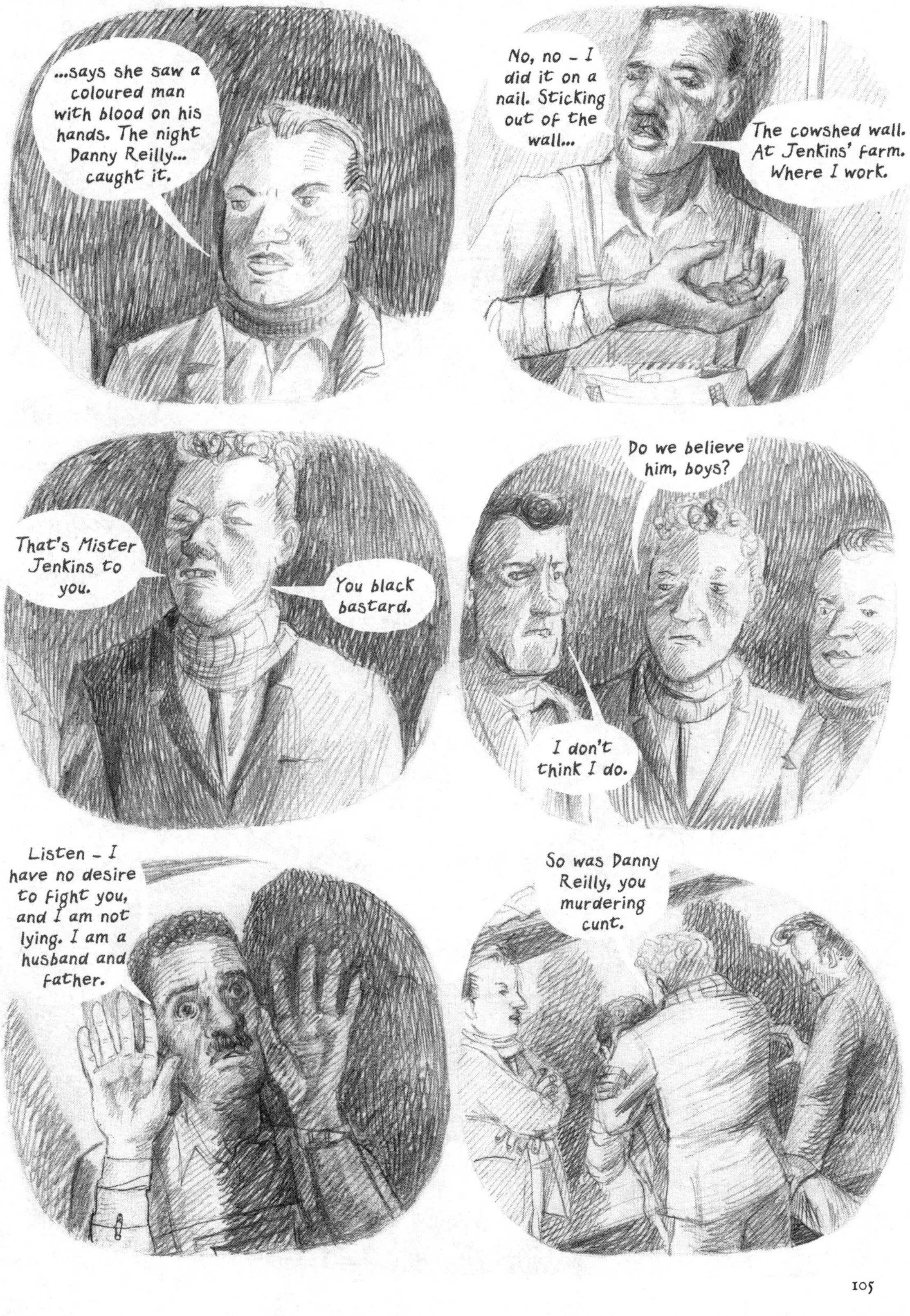
...says she saw a coloured man with blood on his hands. The night Danny Reilly... caught it.
No, no – I did it on a nail. Sticking out of the wall...
The cowshed wall. At Jenkins' farm. Where I work.
That's Mister Jenkins to you.
You black bastard.
Do we believe him, boys?
I don't think I do.
Listen – I have no desire to fight you, and I am not lying. I am a husband and father.
So was Danny Reilly, you murdering cunt.

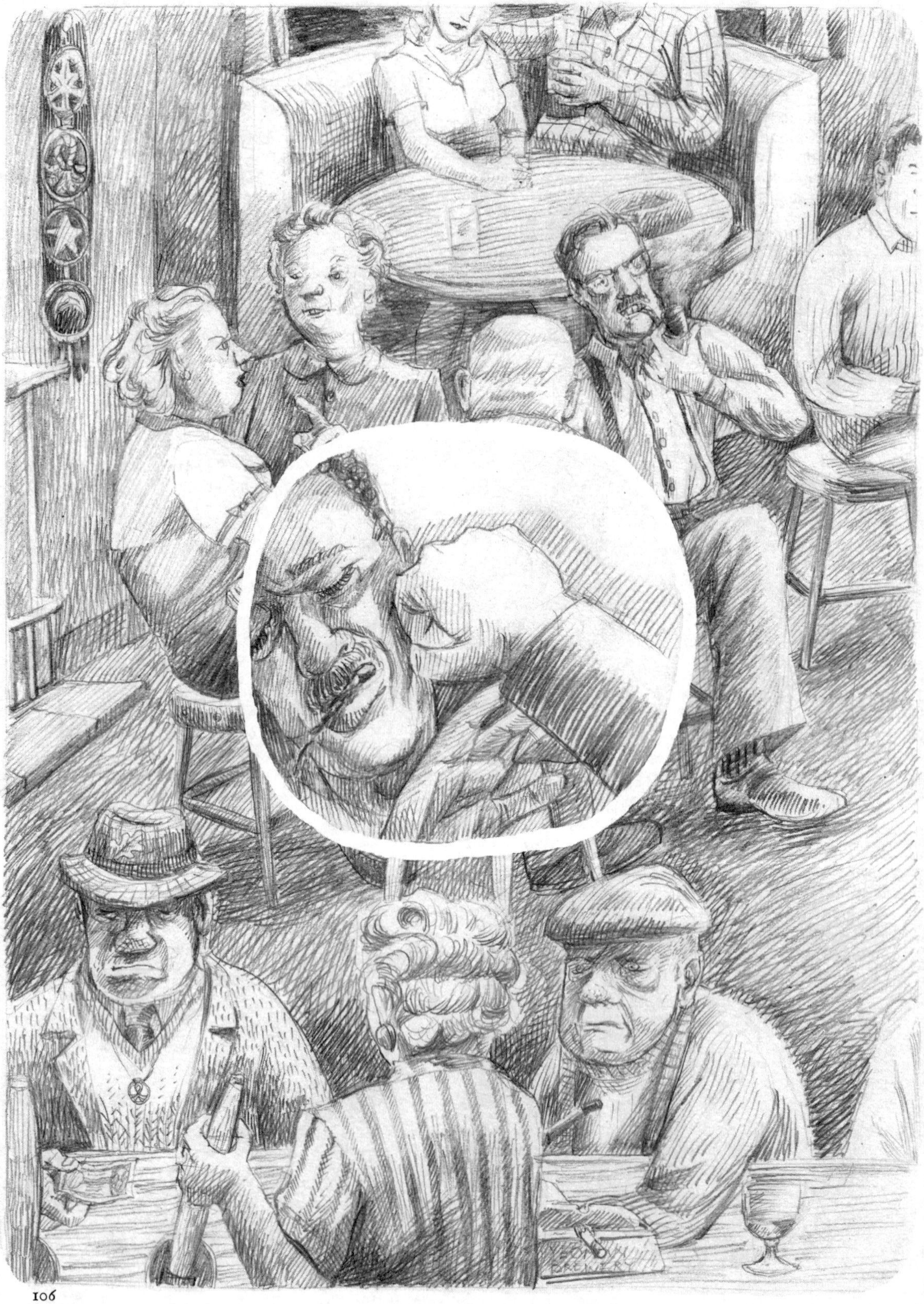
BREWERY

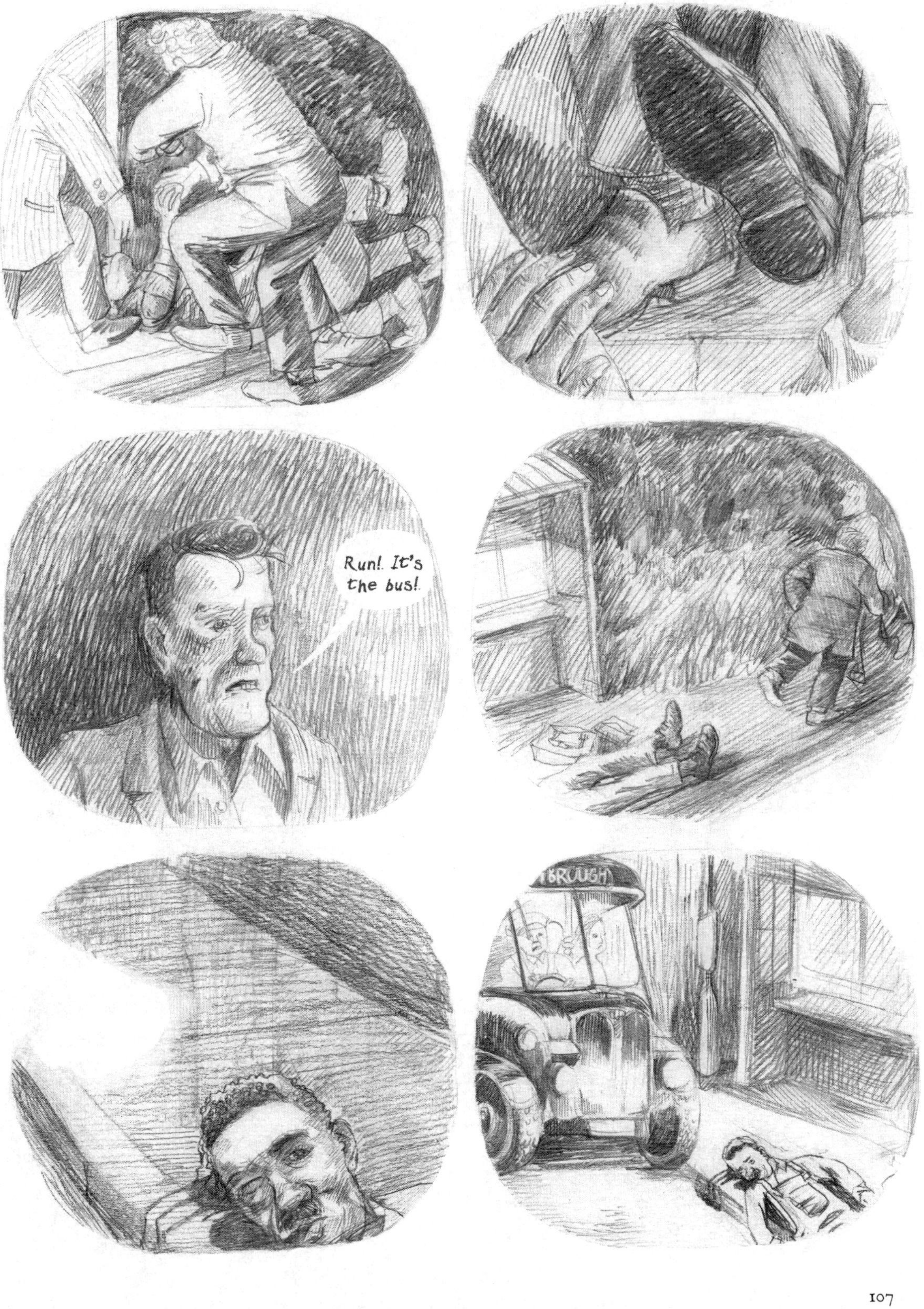
Run!. It's the bus!.
BROUGH

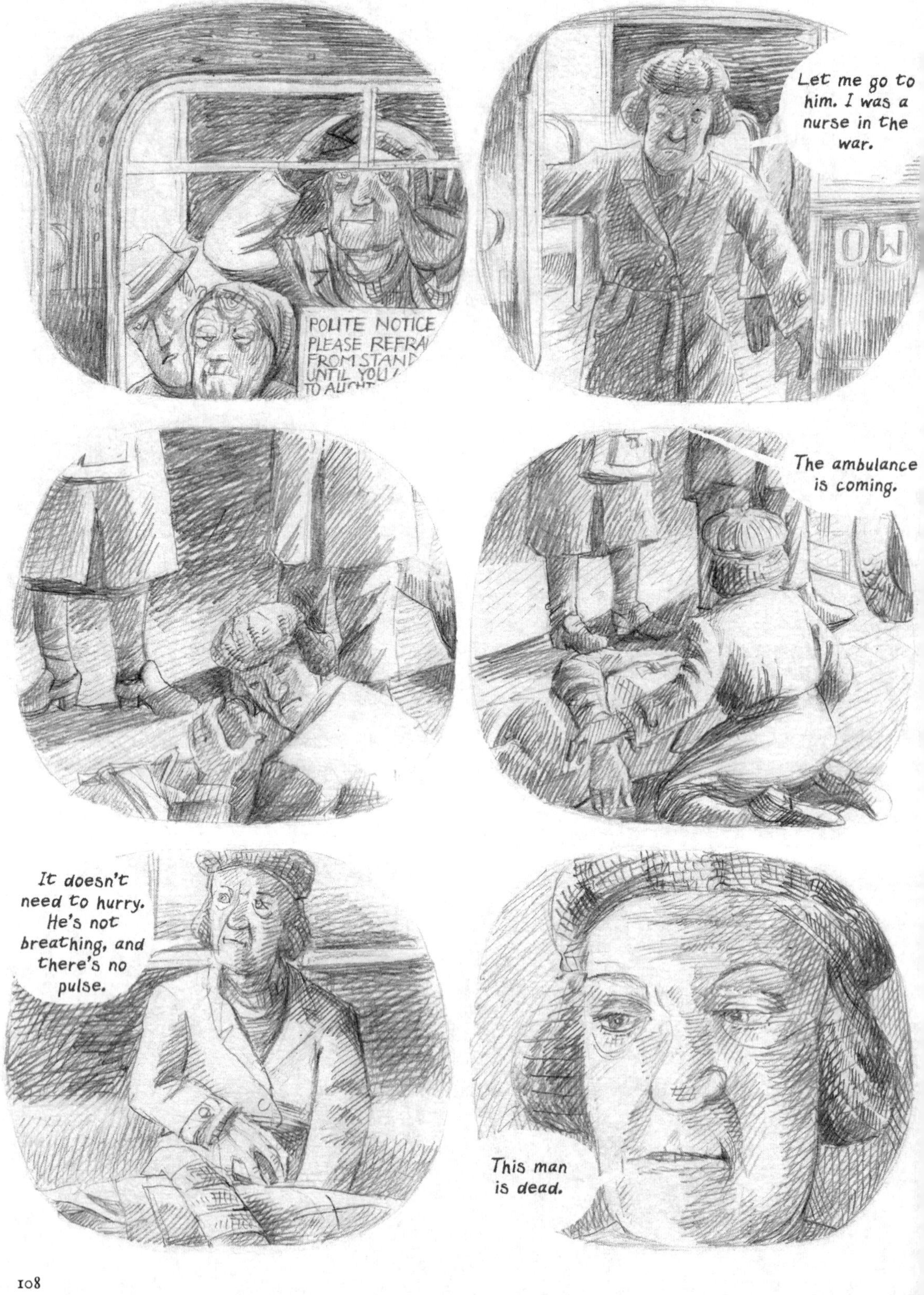
POLITE NOTICE
Let me go to him. I was a nurse in the war.
The ambulance is coming.
It doesn't need to hurry. He's not breathing, and there's no pulse.
This man is dead.

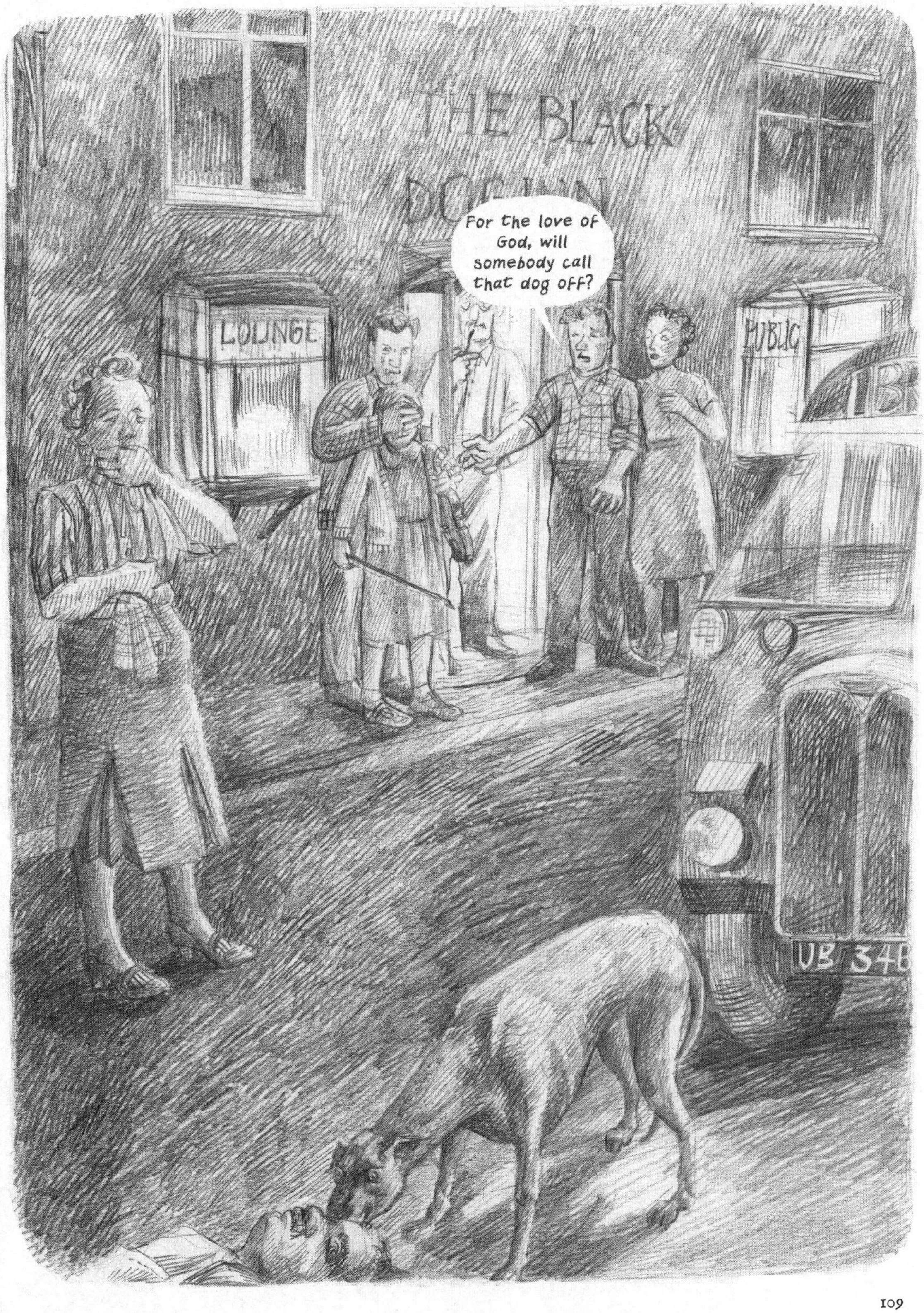
THE BLACK
LOUNGE
For the love of God, will somebody call that dog off?
PUBLIC
UB 34

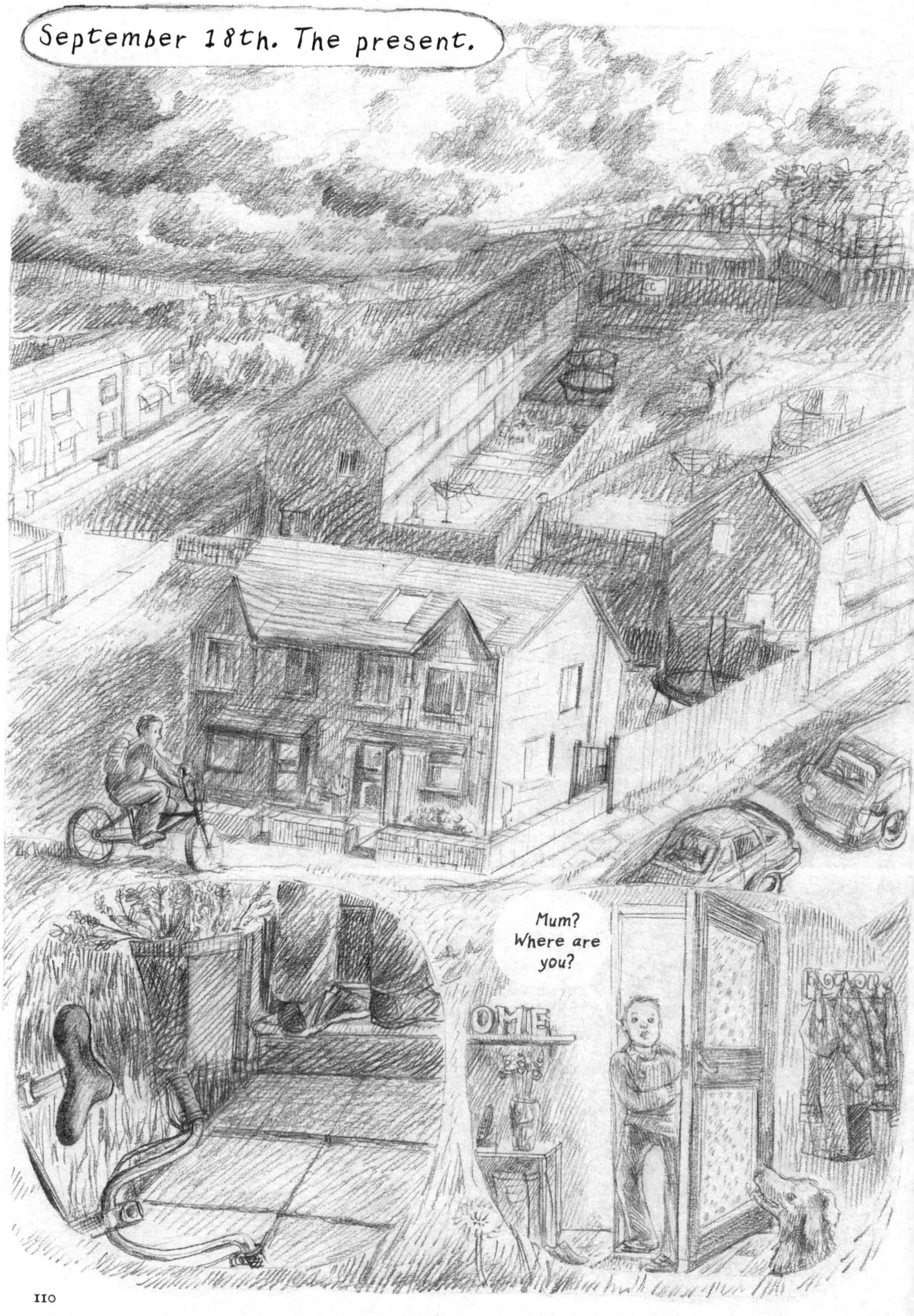
September 18th. The present.
OME
Mum? Where are you?

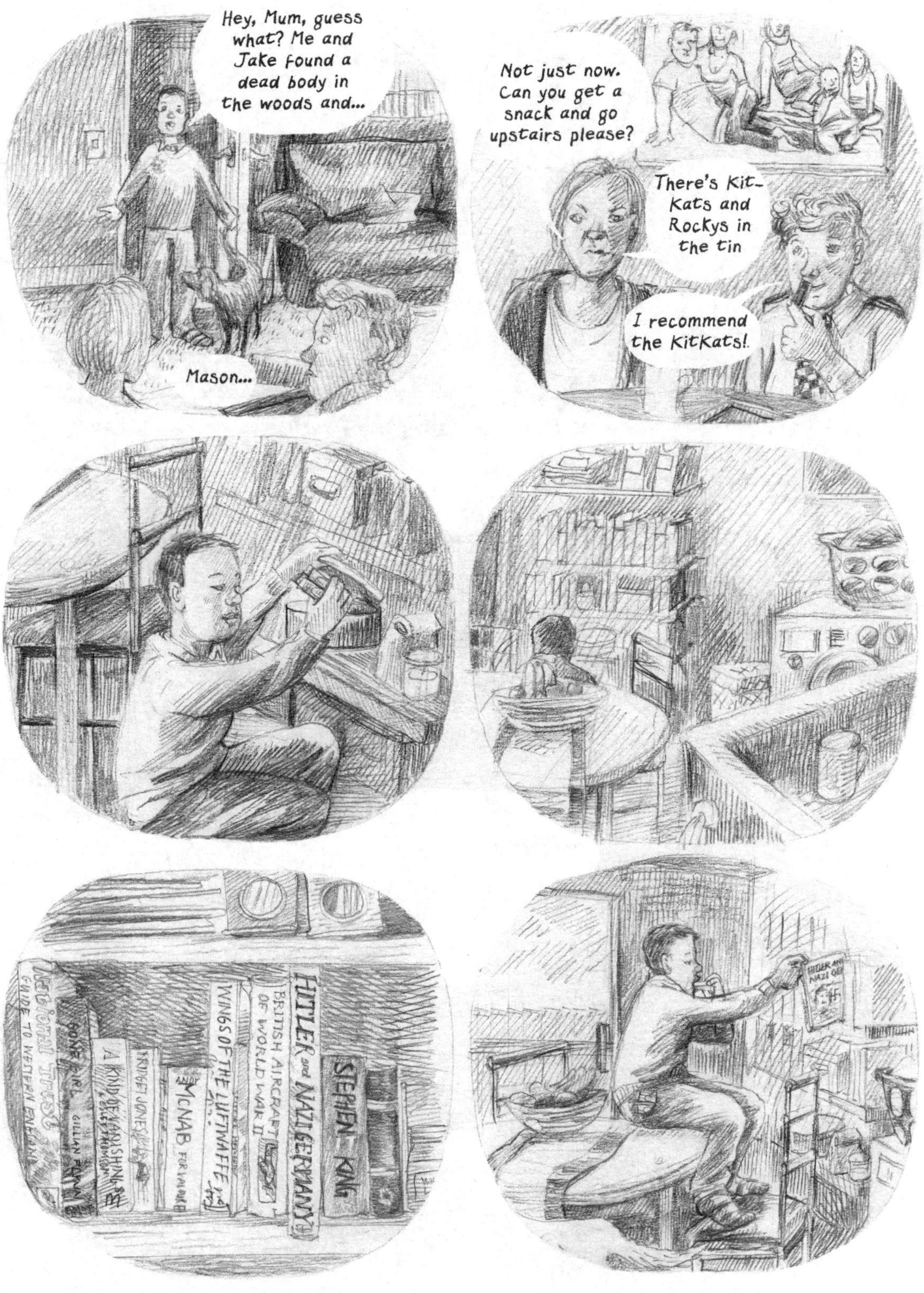
Hey, Mum, guess what? Me and Jake found a dead body in the woods and...
Mason...
Not just now. Can you get a snack and go upstairs please?
There's Kit-Kats and Rockys in the tin
I recommend the KitKats!
HITLER and NAZI GERMANY
BRITISH AIRCRAFT OF WORLD WAR II
WINGS OF THE LUFTWAFFE
STEPHEN KING
GONE GIRL
GILLIAN FLYNN
GUIDE TO WESTERN ENGLAND

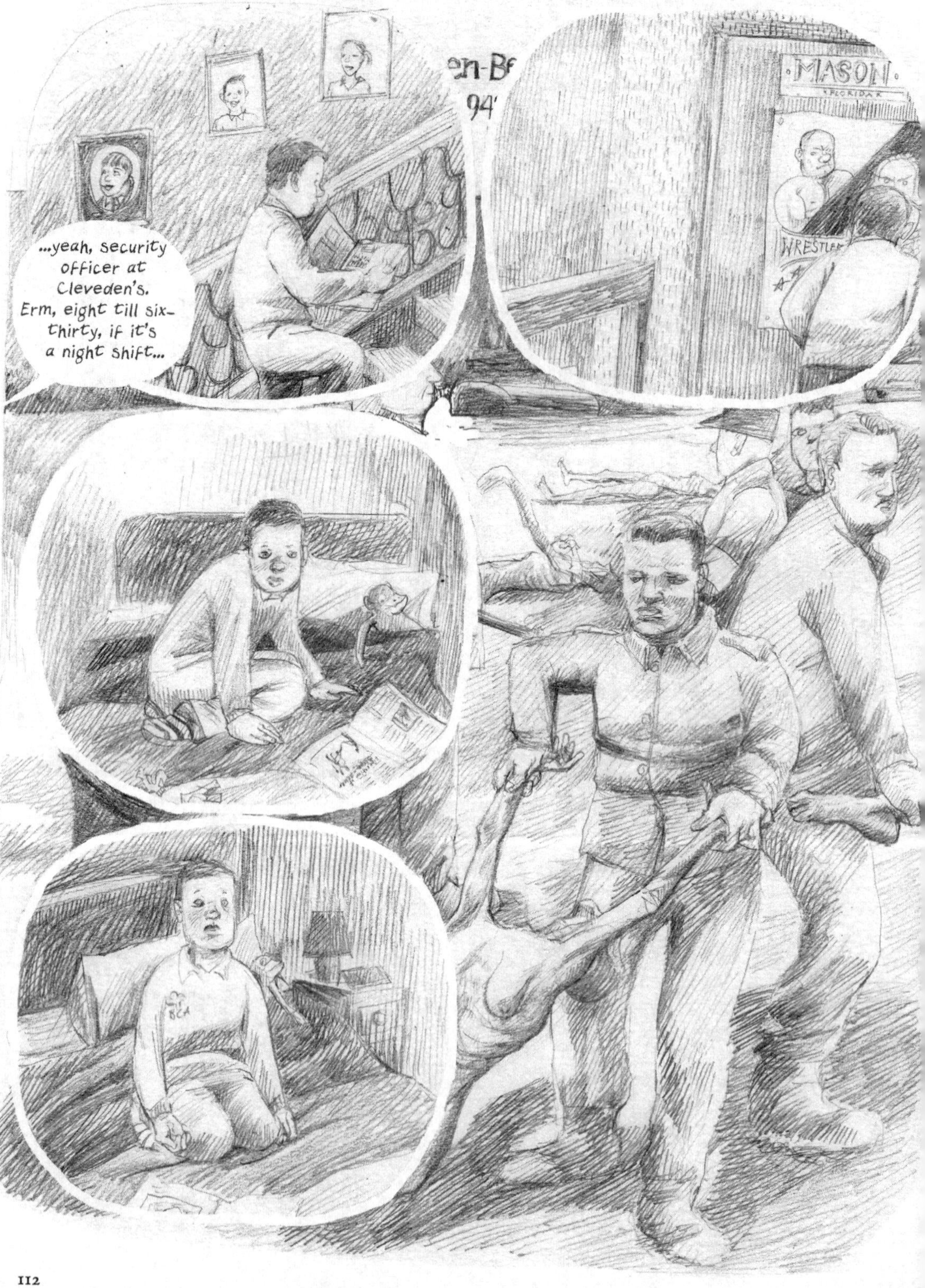
...yeah, security officer at Cleveden's. Erm, eight till six-thirty, if it's a night shift...
MASON
WRESTLE

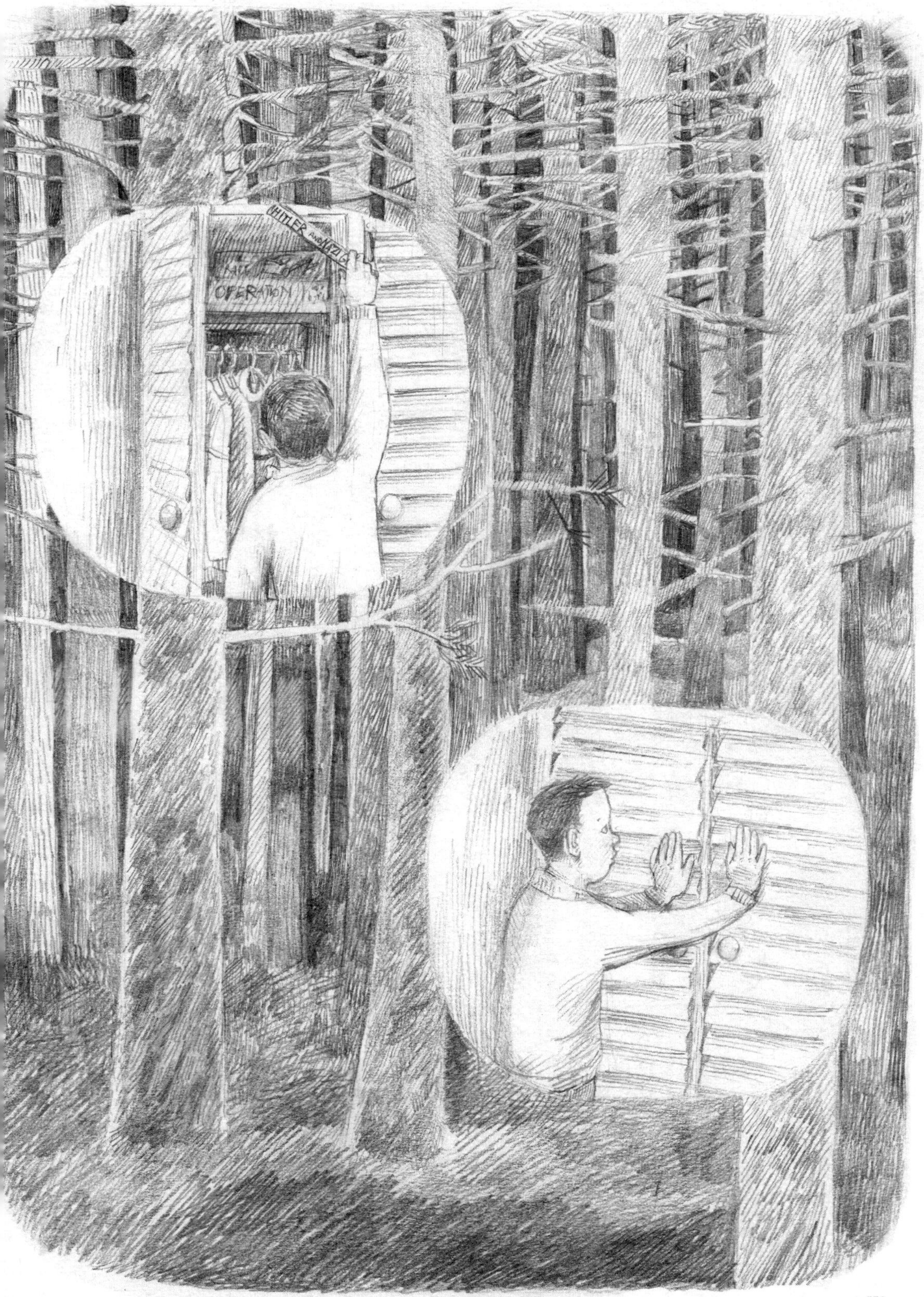
HITLER AND NAZIS
OPERATION

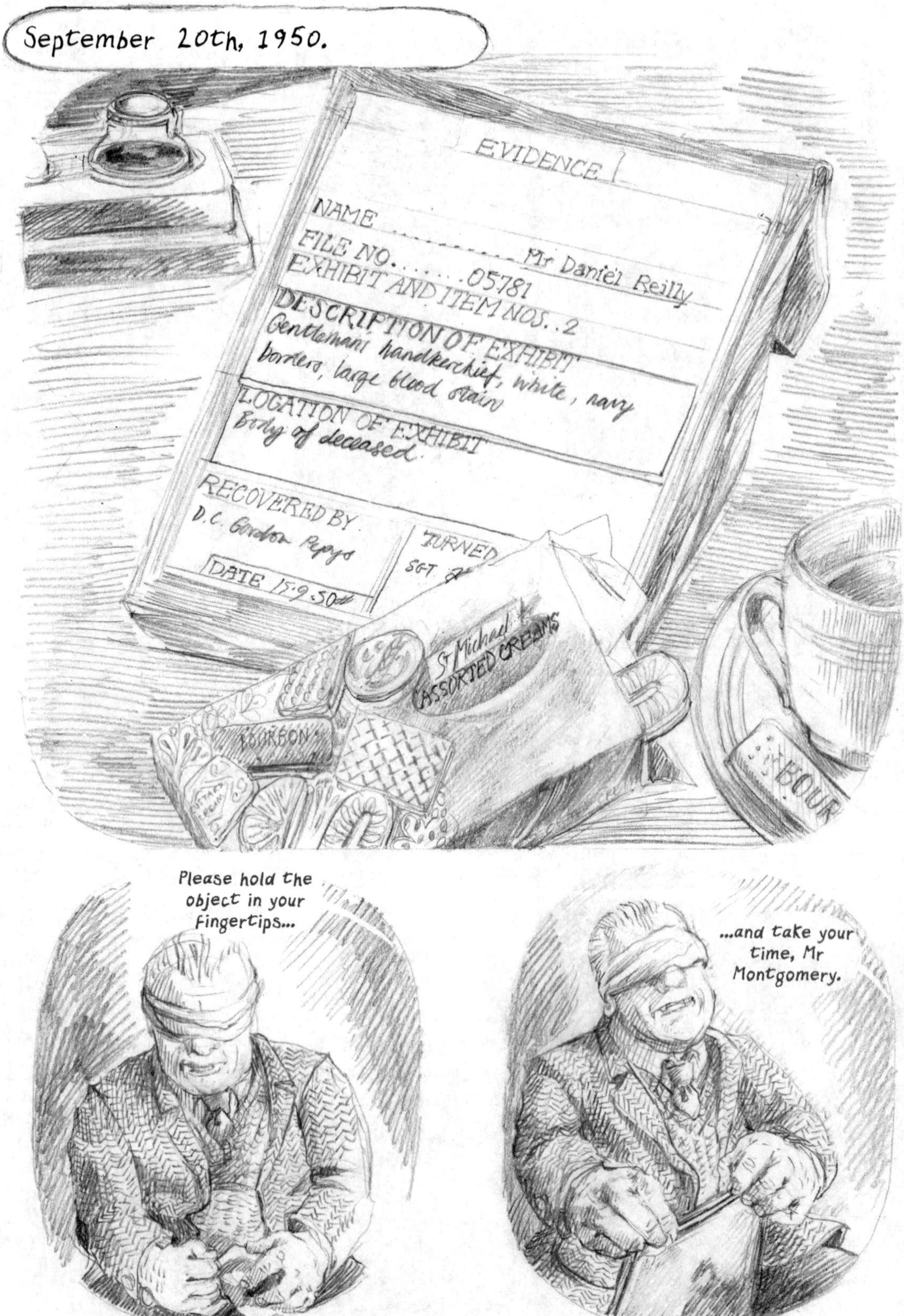
September 20th, 1950.
EVIDENCE
NAME .... Mr Daniel Reilly
FILE NO. 05781
EXHIBIT AND ITEM NOS. .2
DESCRIPTION OF EXHIBIT
Gentleman's handkerchief, white, navy borders, large blood stain
LOCATION OF EXHIBIT
Body of deceased
RECOVERED BY
D.C. Gordon Pepys
DATE 15.9.50
TURNED
St Michael
ASSORTED CREAMS
BOURBON
Please hold the object in your fingertips...
...and take your time, Mr Montgomery.

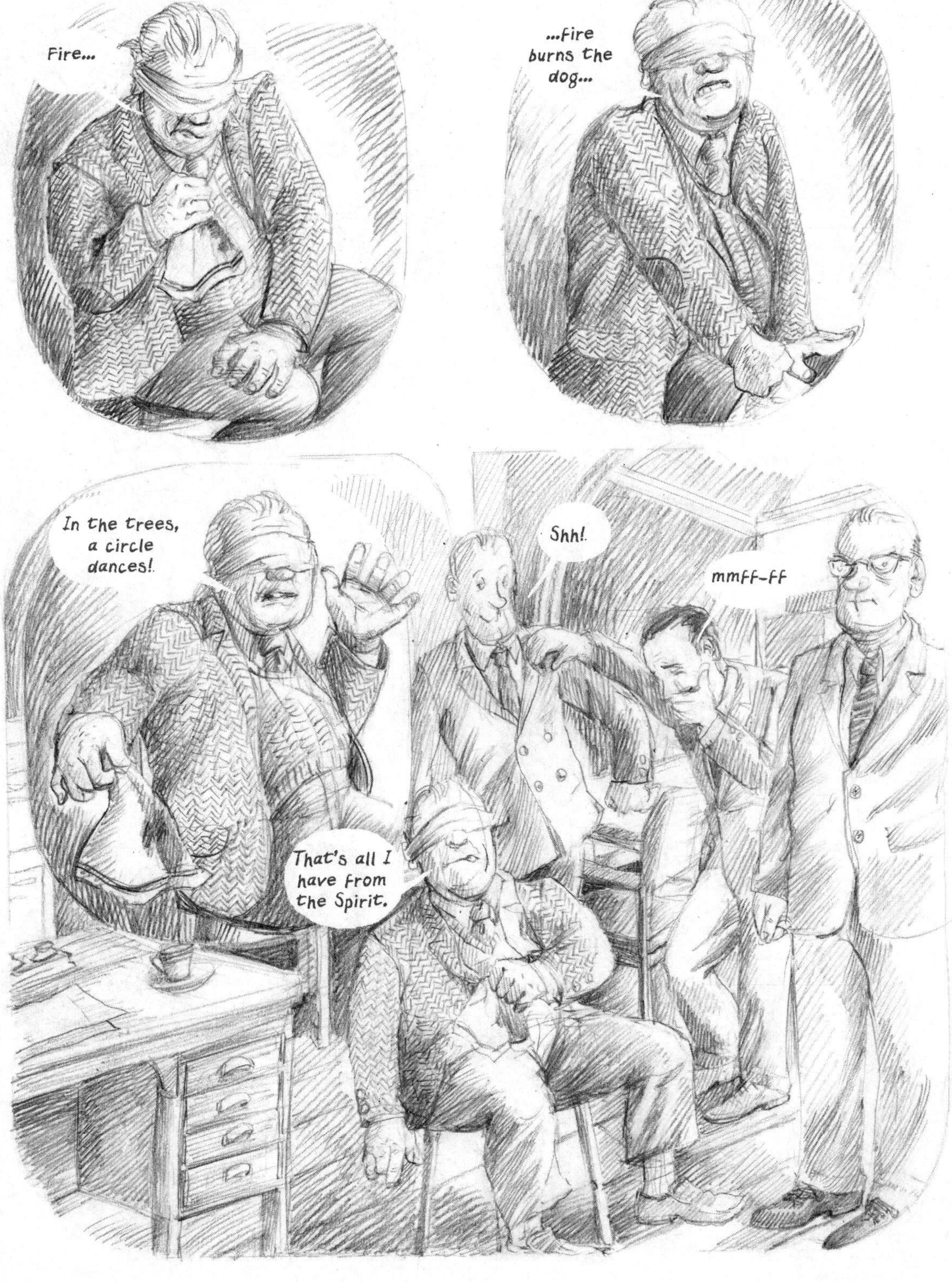
Fire...
...fire burns the dog...
In the trees, a circle dances!.
Shh!.
mmff-ff
That's all I have from the Spirit.

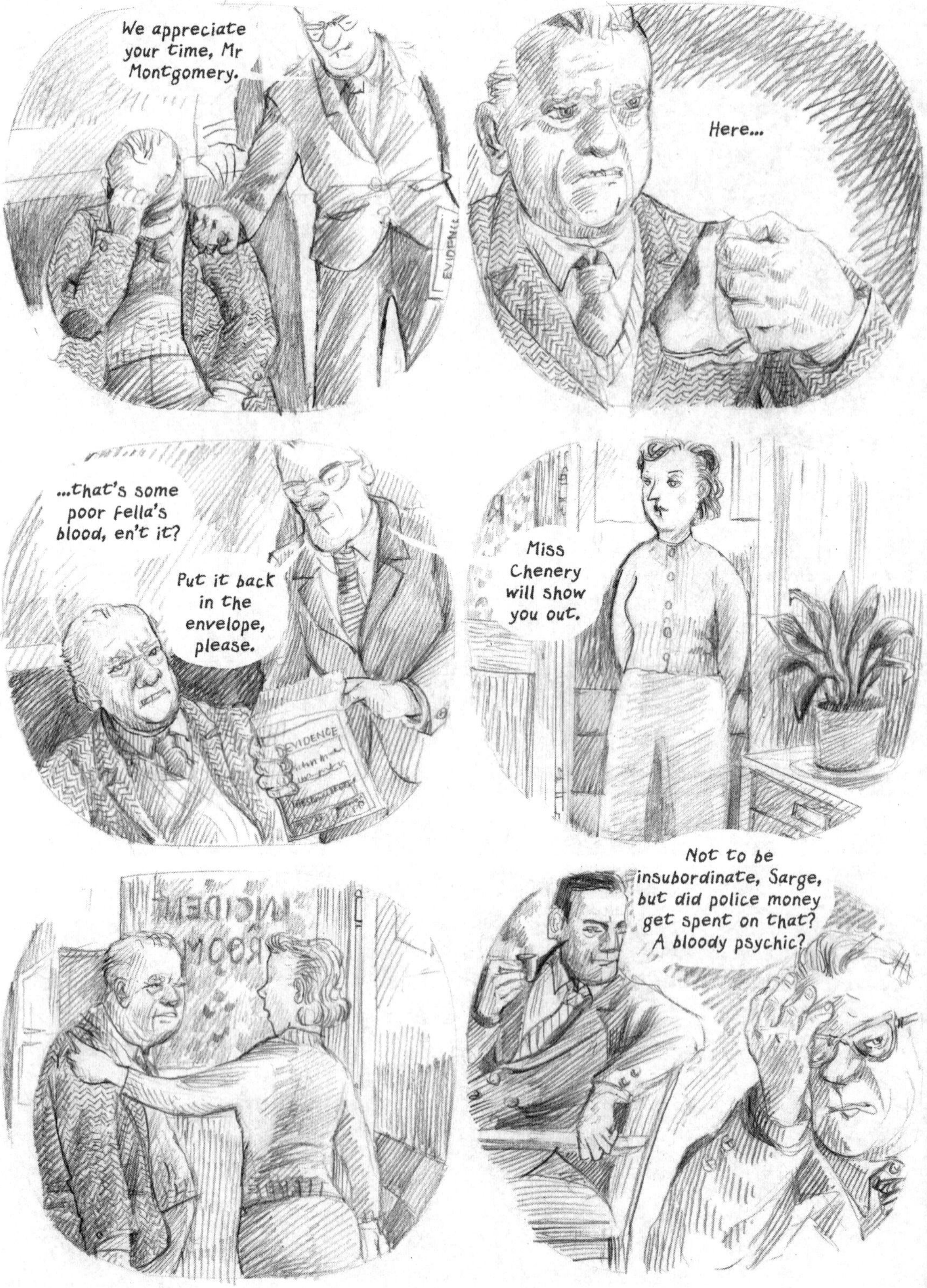
We appreciate your time, Mr Montgomery.
EVIDENCE
Here...
...that's some poor fella's blood, en't it?
Put it back in the envelope, please.
EVIDENCE
Miss Chenery will show you out.
INCIDENT ROOM
Not to be insubordinate, Sarge, but did police money get spent on that? A bloody psychic?

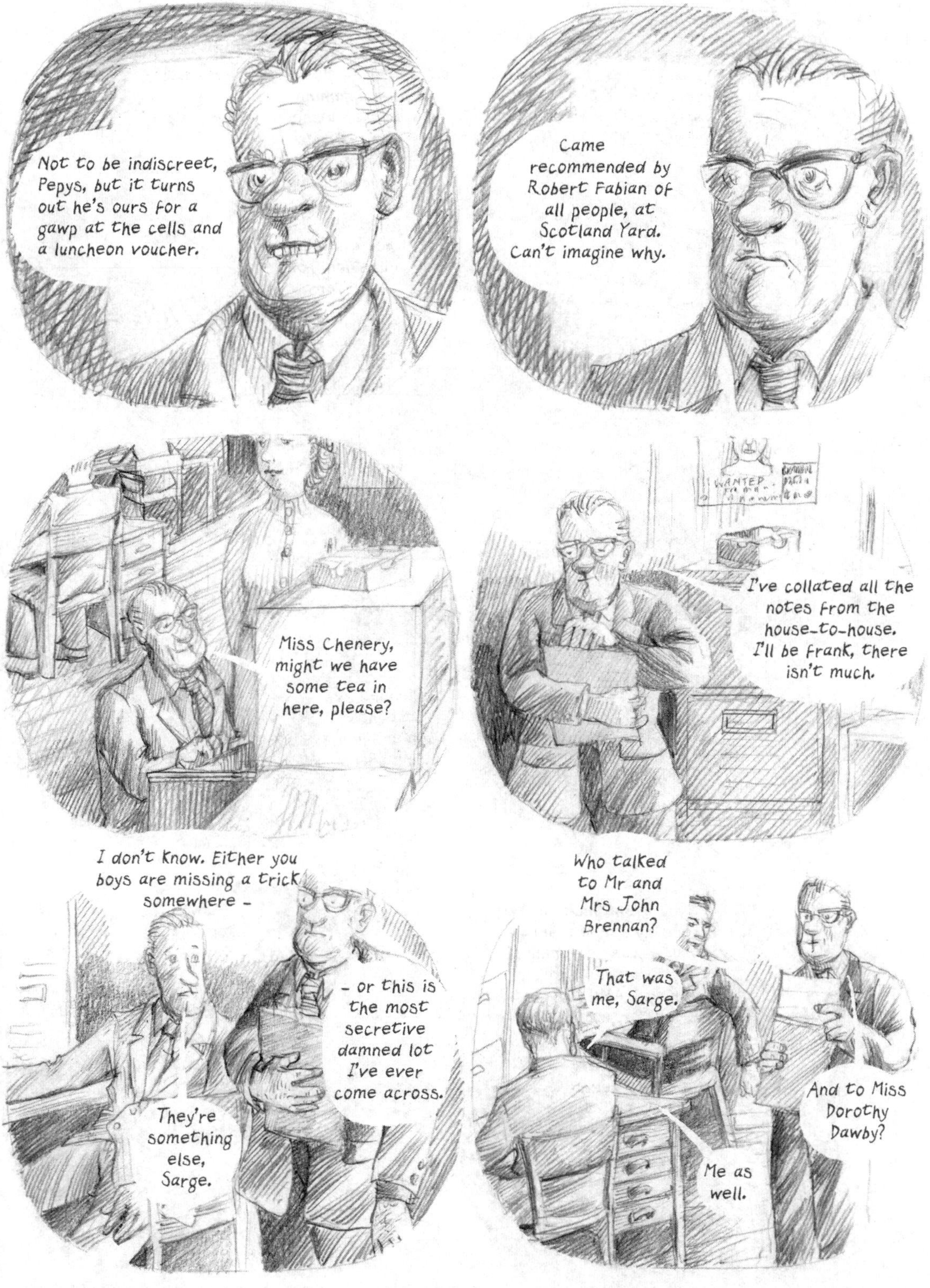
Not to be indiscreet, Pepys, but it turns out he's ours for a gawp at the cells and a luncheon voucher.
Came recommended by Robert Fabian of all people, at Scotland Yard. Can't imagine why.
Miss Chenery, might we have some tea in here, please?
I've collated all the notes from the house-to-house. I'll be frank, there isn't much.
I don't know. Either you boys are missing a trick somewhere –
– or this is the most secretive damned lot I've ever come across.
They're something else, Sarge.
Who talked to Mr and Mrs John Brennan?
That was me, Sarge.
And to Miss Dorothy Dawby?
Me as well.

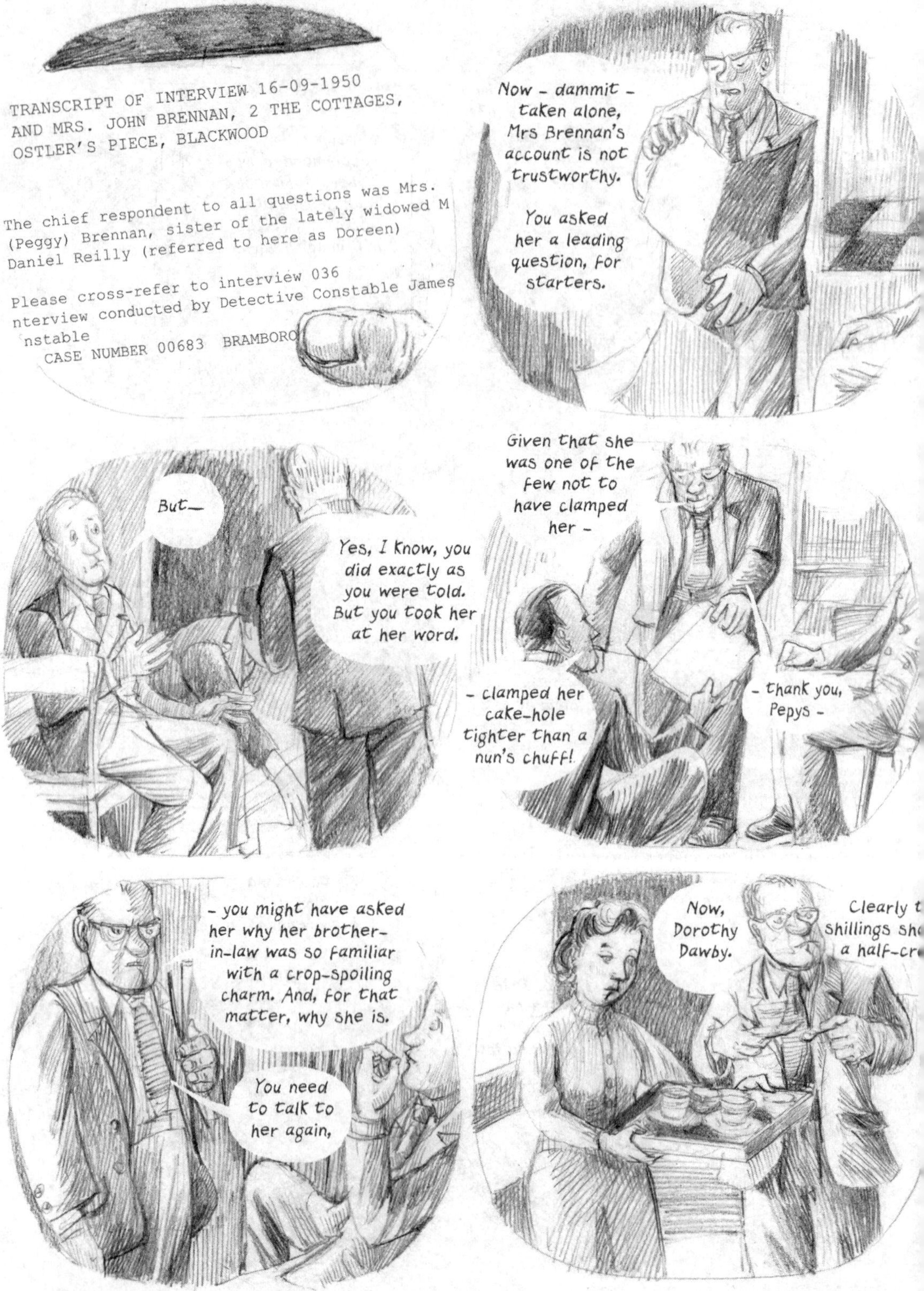
TRANSCRIPT OF INTERVIEW 16-09-1950
AND MRS. JOHN BRENNAN, 2 THE COTTAGES,
OSTLER'S PIECE, BLACKWOOD
The chief respondent to all questions was Mrs.
(Peggy) Brennan, sister of the lately widowed M
Daniel Reilly (referred to here as Doreen)
Please cross-refer to interview 036
nterview conducted by Detective Constable James
nstable
CASE NUMBER 00683 BRAMBORO
Now - dammit - taken alone, Mrs Brennan's account is not trustworthy.
You asked her a leading question, for starters.
But—
Yes, I know, you did exactly as you were told. But you took her at her word.
Given that she was one of the few not to have clamped her -
- clamped her cake-hole tighter than a nun's chuff!
- thank you, Pepys -
- you might have asked her why her brother-in-law was so familiar with a crop-spoiling charm. And, for that matter, why she is.
You need to talk to her again,
Now, Dorothy Dawby.
Clearly t shillings sh a half-cr

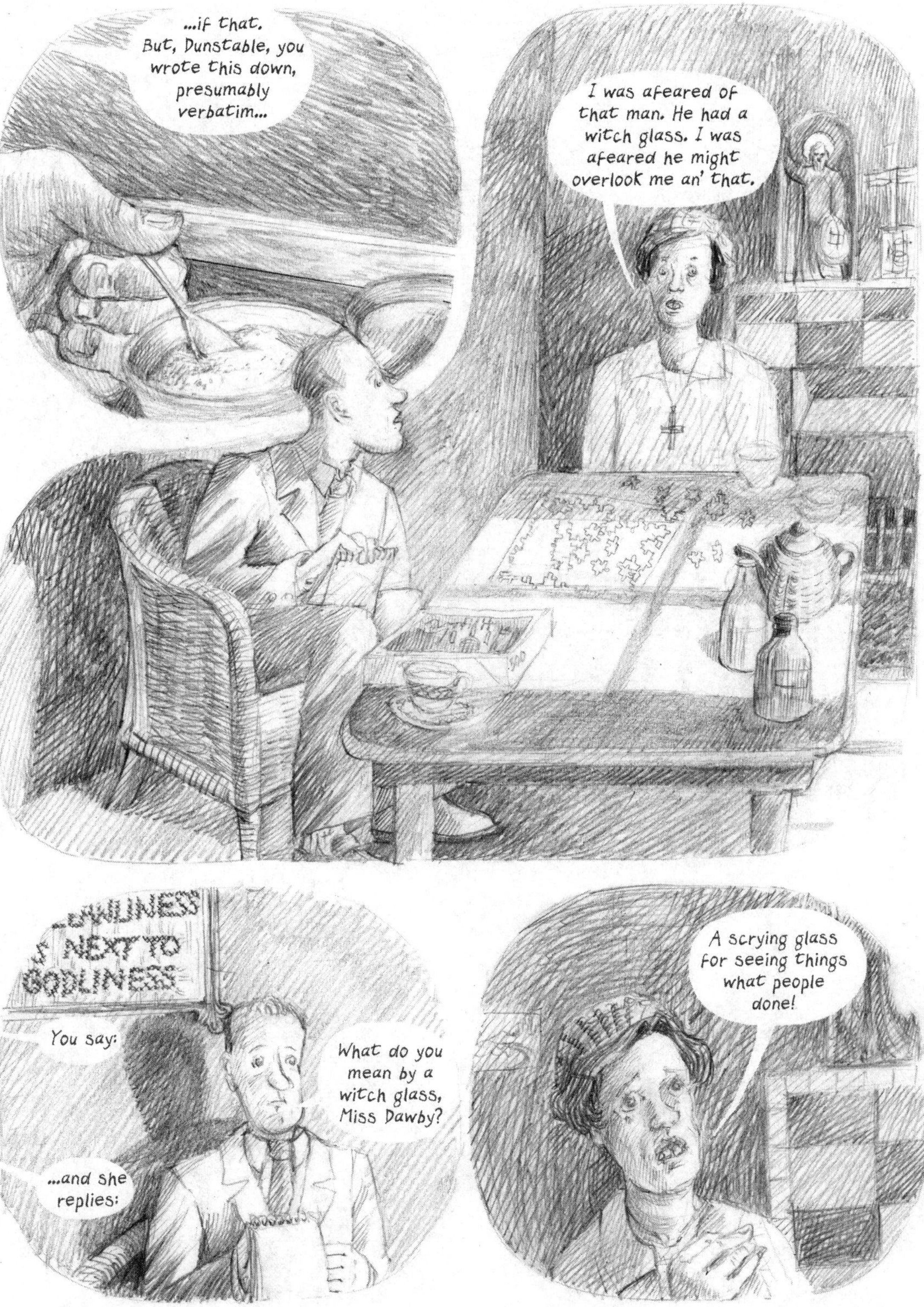
...if that. But, Dunstable, you wrote this down, presumably verbatim...
I was afeared of that man. He had a witch glass. I was afeared he might overlook me an' that.
NEXT TO
GODLINESS
You say:
What do you mean by a witch glass, Miss Dawby?
...and she replies:
A scrying glass for seeing things what people done!

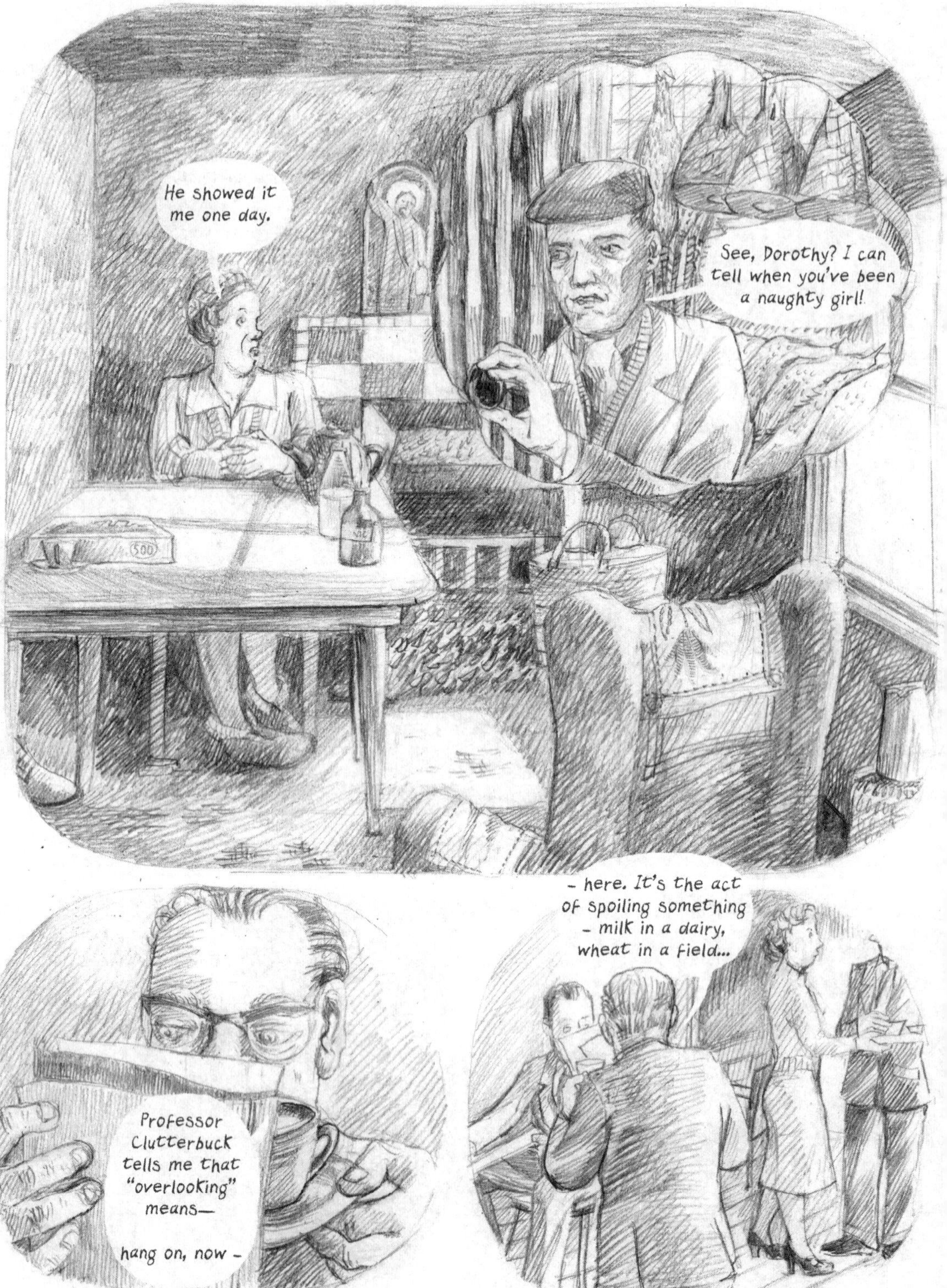
He showed it me one day.
See, Dorothy? I can tell when you've been a naughty girl!
Professor Clutterbuck tells me that "overlooking" means—
hang on, now -
- here. It's the act of spoiling something - milk in a dairy, wheat in a field...

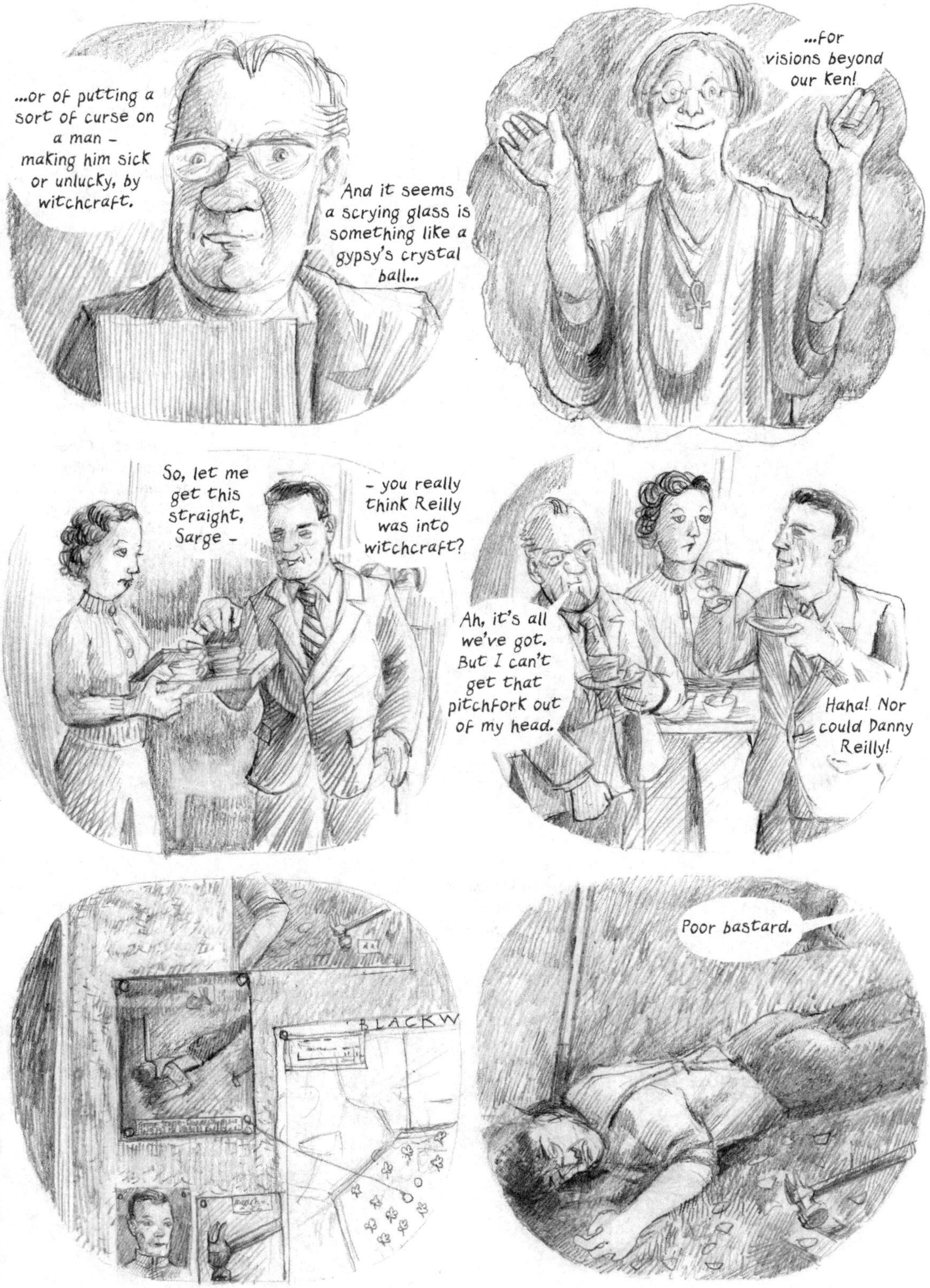
...or of putting a sort of curse on a man – making him sick or unlucky, by witchcraft.
And it seems a scrying glass is something like a gypsy's crystal ball...
...for visions beyond our Ken!
So, let me get this straight, Sarge –
– you really think Reilly was into witchcraft?
Ah, it's all we've got. But I can't get that pitchfork out of my head.
Haha! Nor could Danny Reilly!
BLACKW
Poor bastard.

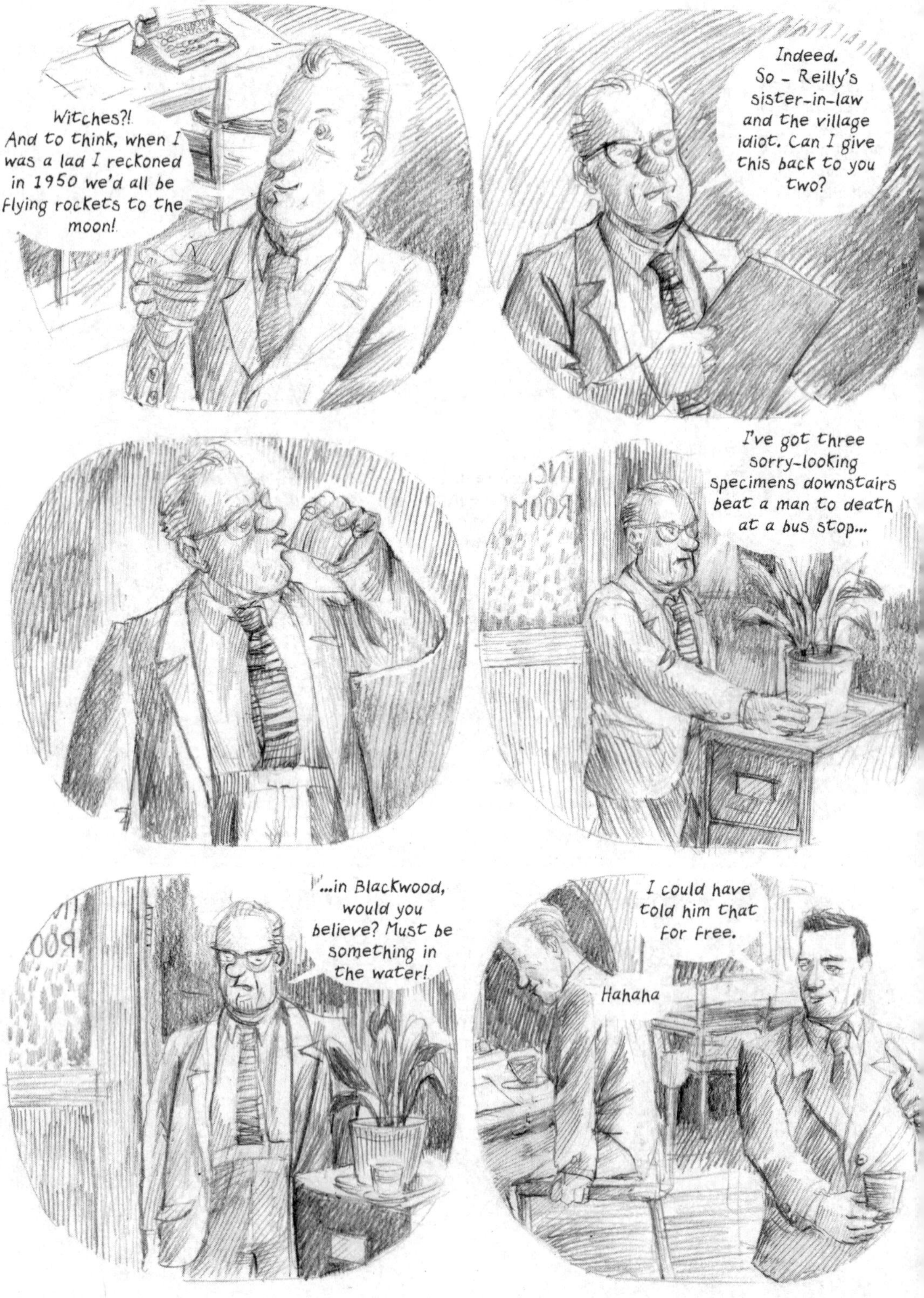
Witches?! And to think, when I was a lad I reckoned in 1950 we'd all be flying rockets to the moon!
Indeed. So - Reilly's sister-in-law and the village idiot. Can I give this back to you two?
I've got three sorry-looking specimens downstairs beat a man to death at a bus stop...
...in Blackwood, would you believe? Must be something in the water!
I could have told him that for free.
Hahaha

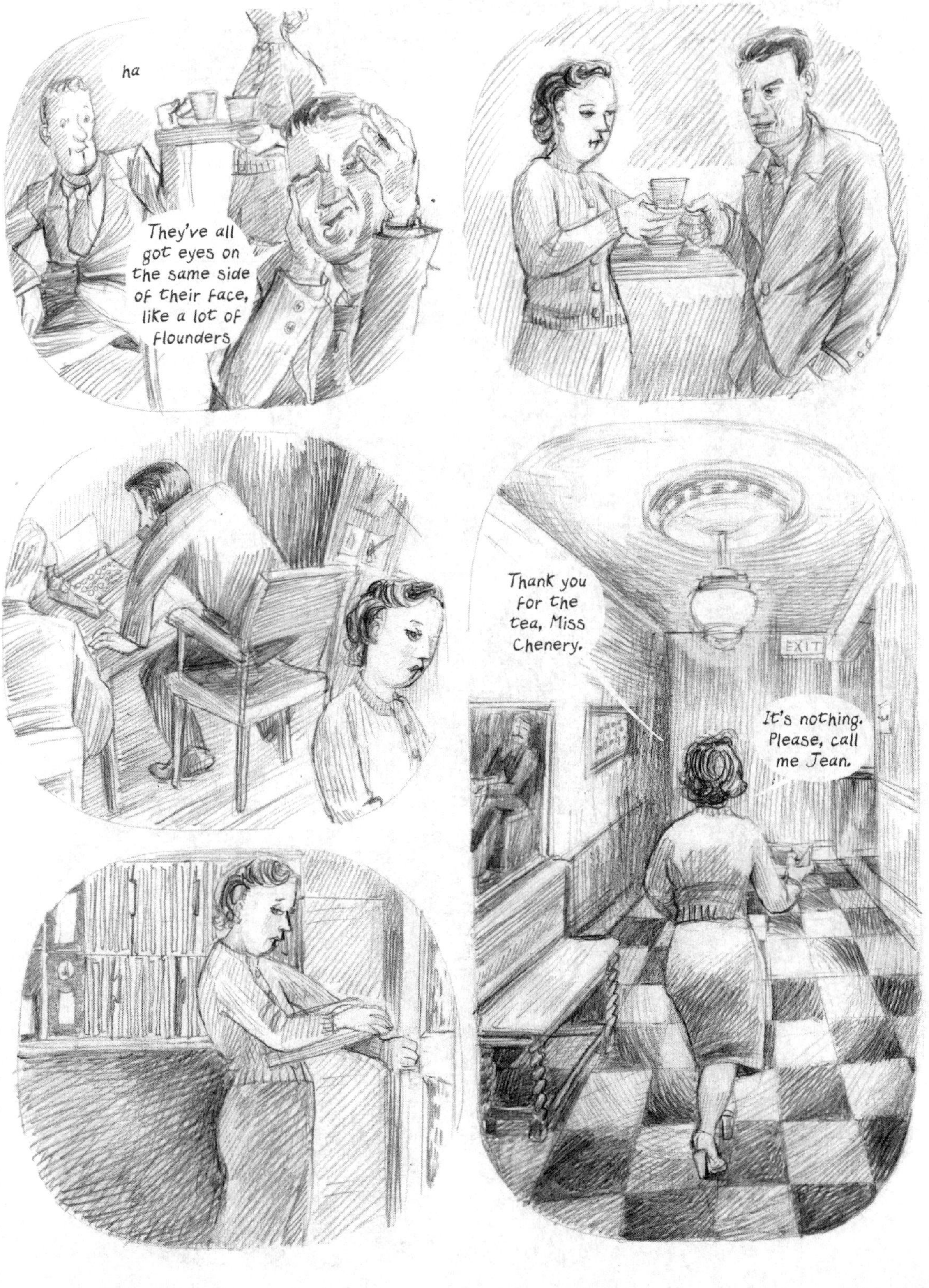
ha
They've all got eyes on the same side of their face, like a lot of flounders
Thank you for the tea, Miss Chenery.
EXIT
It's nothing. Please, call me Jean.

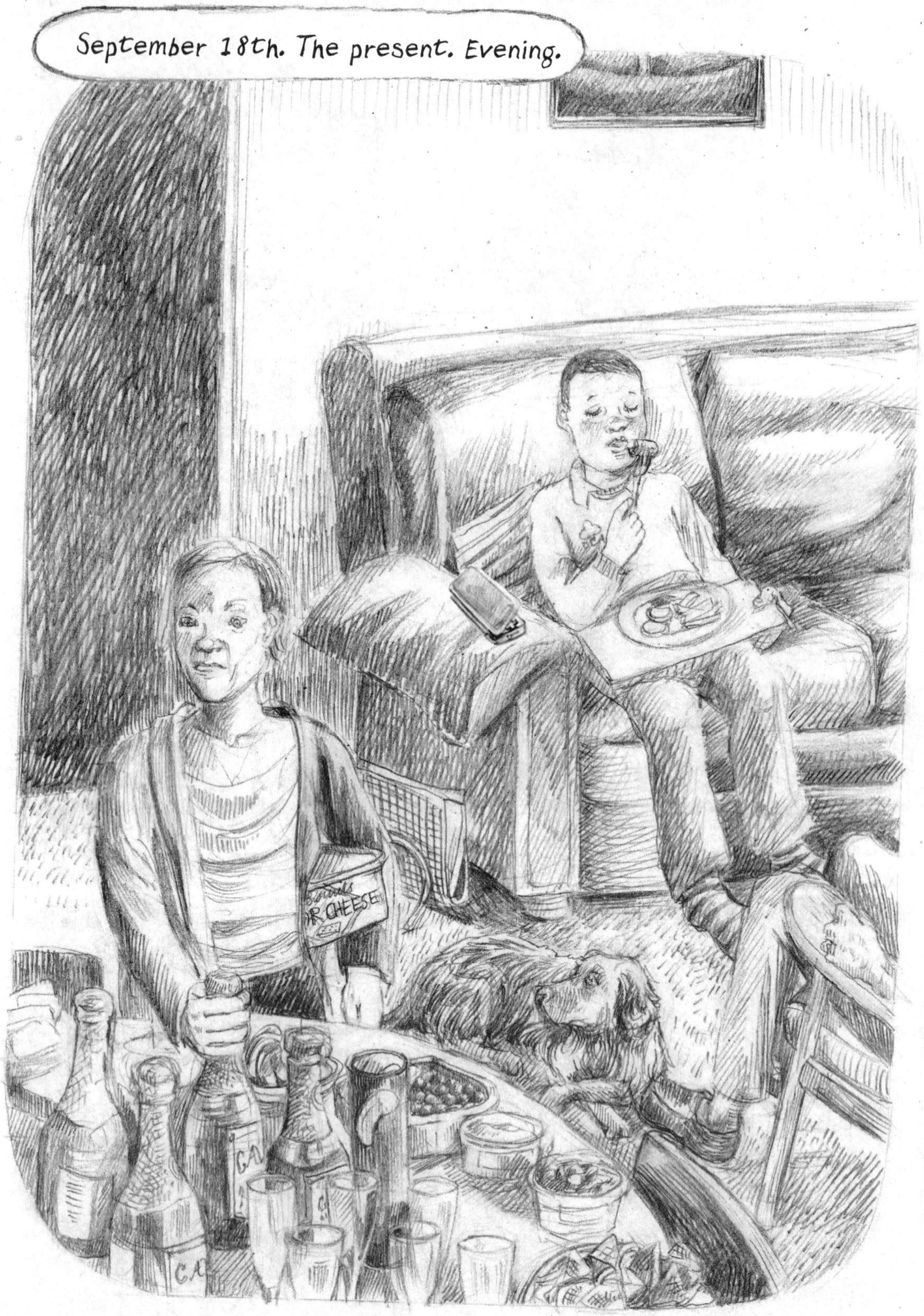
September 18th. The present. Evening.

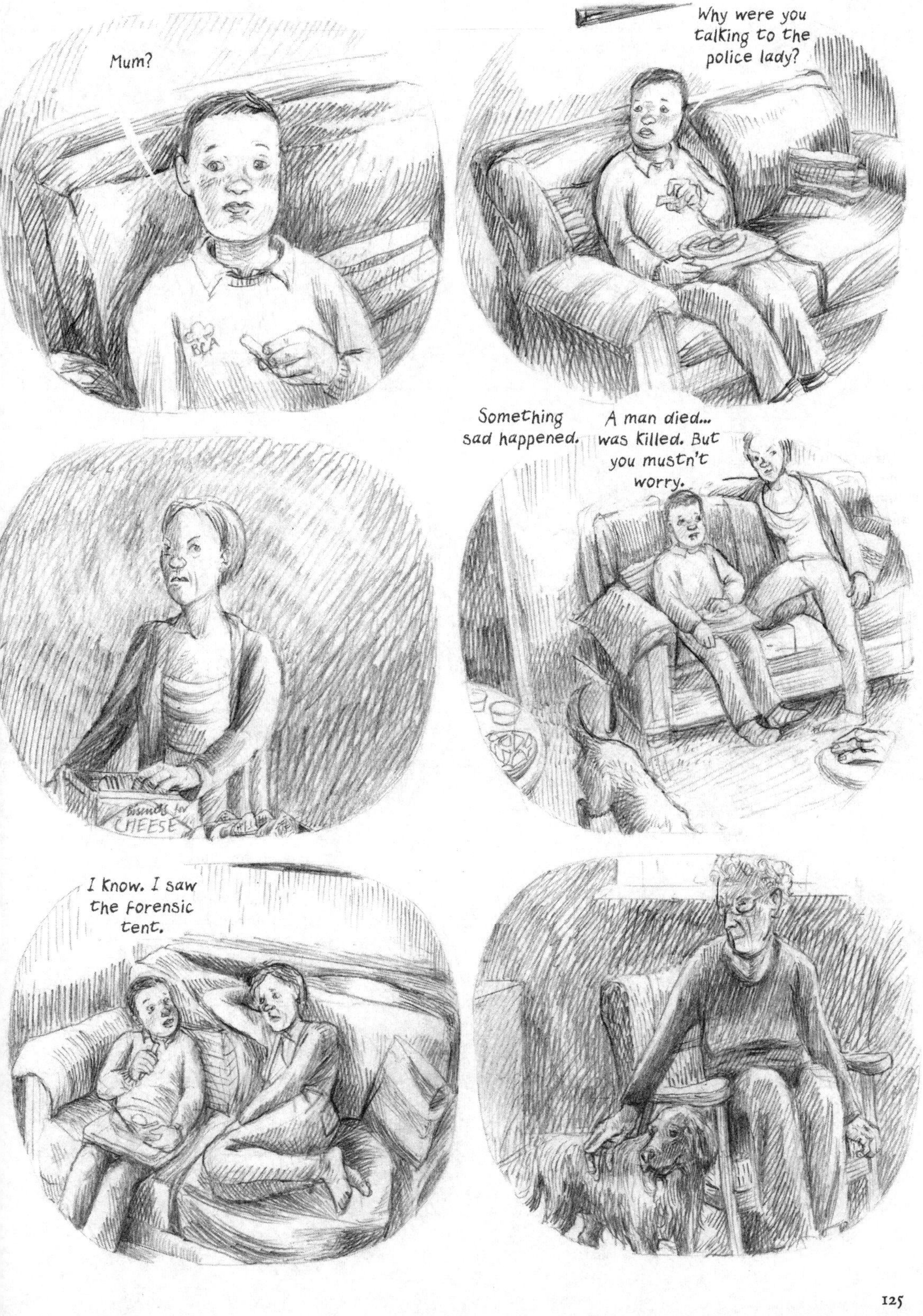
Mum?
Why were you talking to the police lady?
Biscuits for CHEESE
Something sad happened.
A man died... was killed. But you mustn't worry.
I know. I saw the forensic tent.

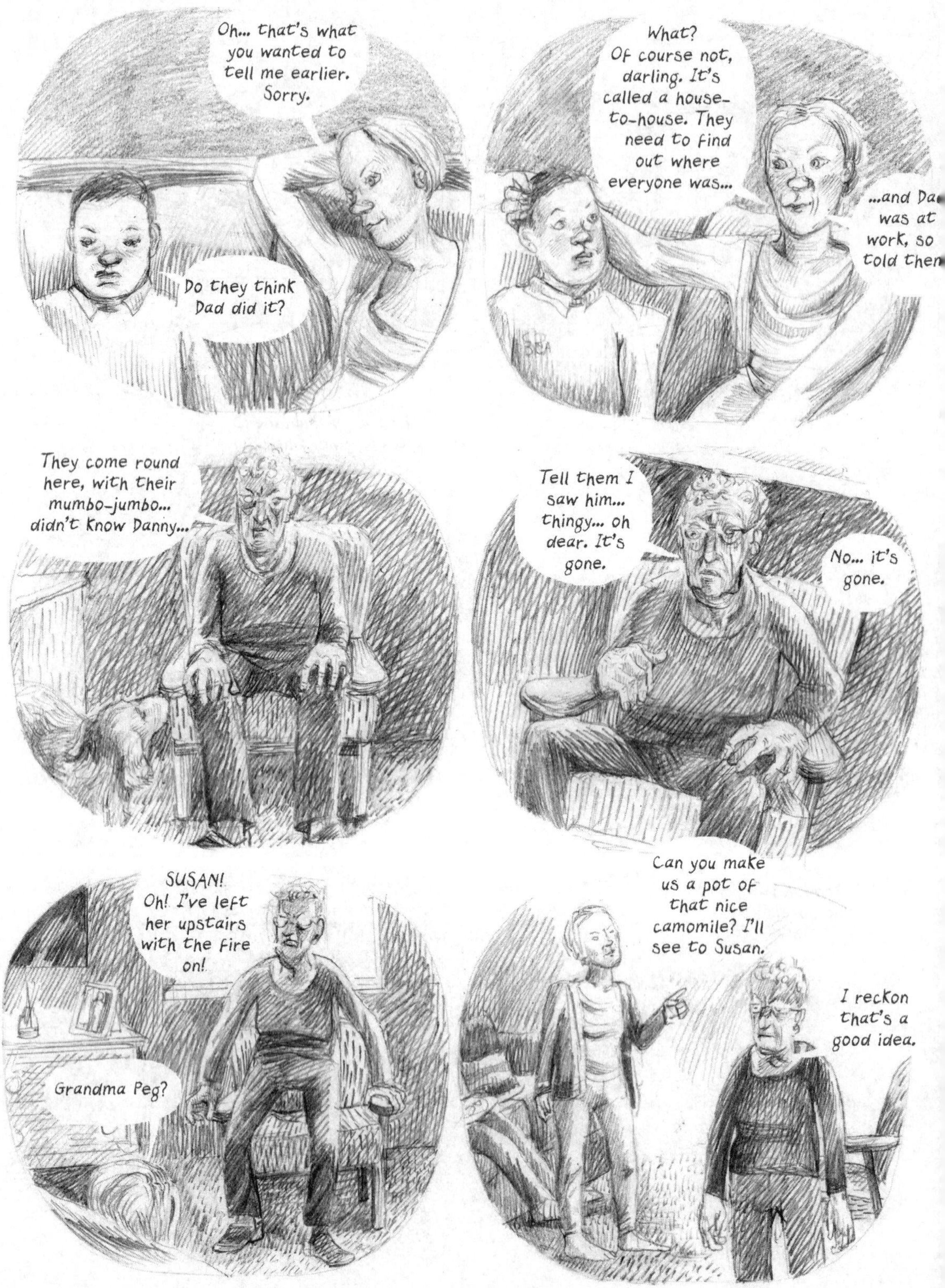

Oh... that's what you wanted to tell me earlier. Sorry.
Do they think Dad did it?
What? Of course not, darling. It's called a house-to-house. They need to find out where everyone was...
...and Da was at work, so told then
They come round here, with their mumbo-jumbo... didn't know Danny...
Tell them I saw him... thingy... oh dear. It's gone.
No... it's gone.
SUSAN! Oh! I've left her upstairs with the fire on!
Grandma Peg?
Can you make us a pot of that nice camomile? I'll see to Susan.
I reckon that's a good idea.

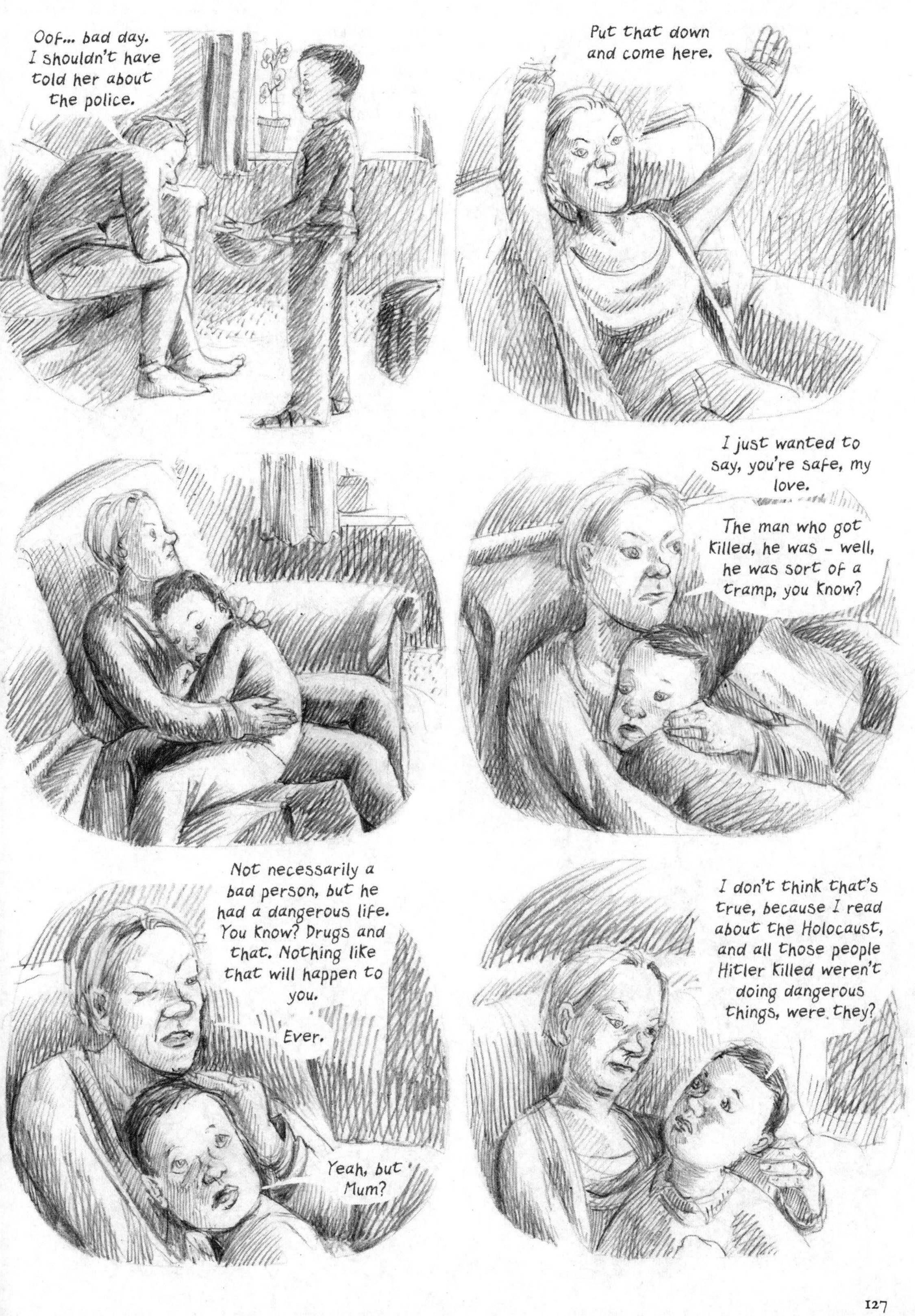
Oof... bad day. I shouldn't have told her about the police.
Put that down and come here.
I just wanted to say, you're safe, my love.
The man who got killed, he was - well, he was sort of a tramp, you know?
Not necessarily a bad person, but he had a dangerous life. You know? Drugs and that. Nothing like that will happen to you.
Ever.
Yeah, but Mum?
I don't think that's true, because I read about the Holocaust, and all those people Hitler killed weren't doing dangerous things, were they?

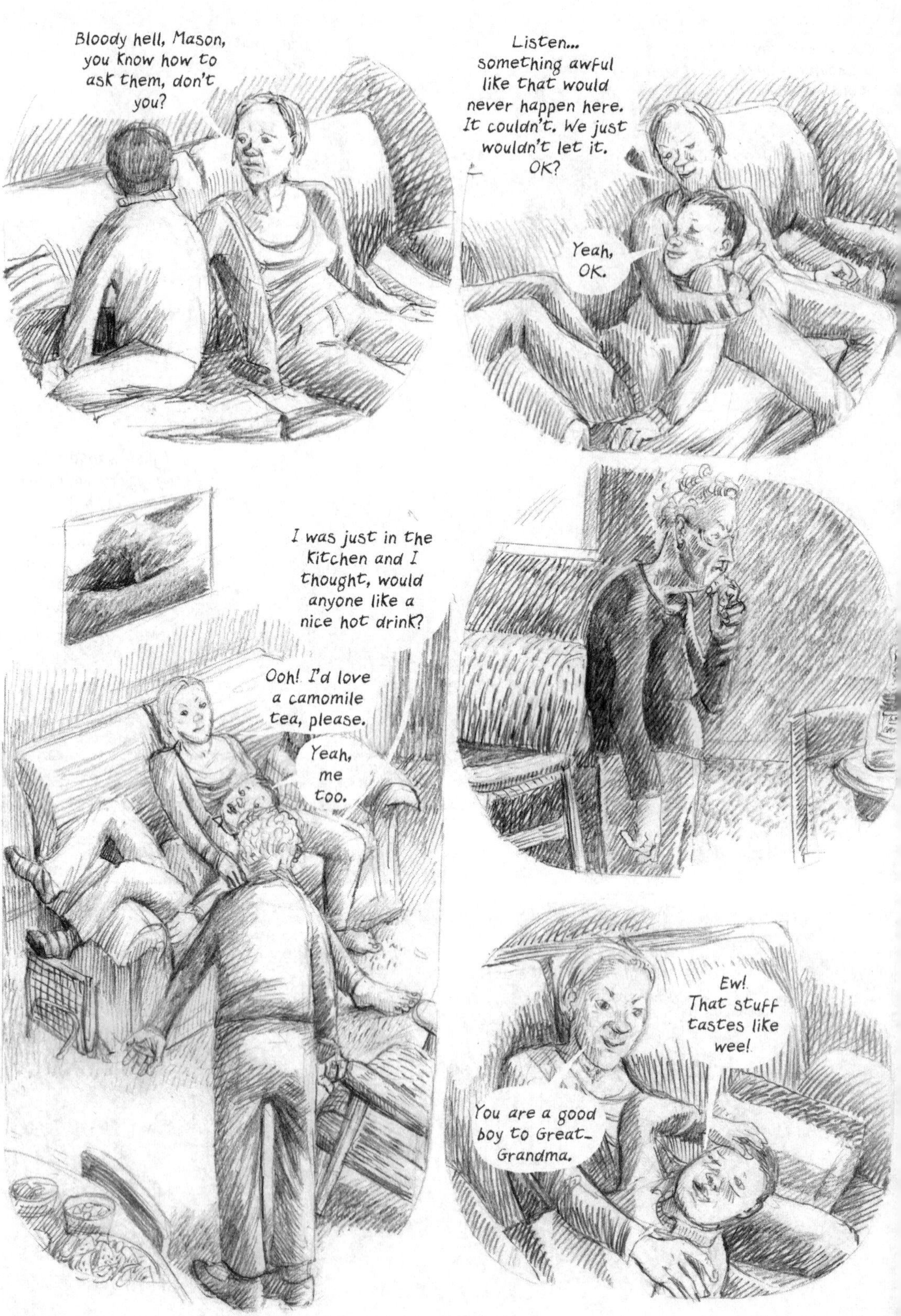
Bloody hell, Mason, you know how to ask them, don't you?
Listen... something awful like that would never happen here. It couldn't. We just wouldn't let it. OK?
Yeah, OK.
I was just in the kitchen and I thought, would anyone like a nice hot drink?
Ooh! I'd love a camomile tea, please.
Yeah, me too.
Ew! That stuff tastes like wee!
You are a good boy to Great-Grandma.

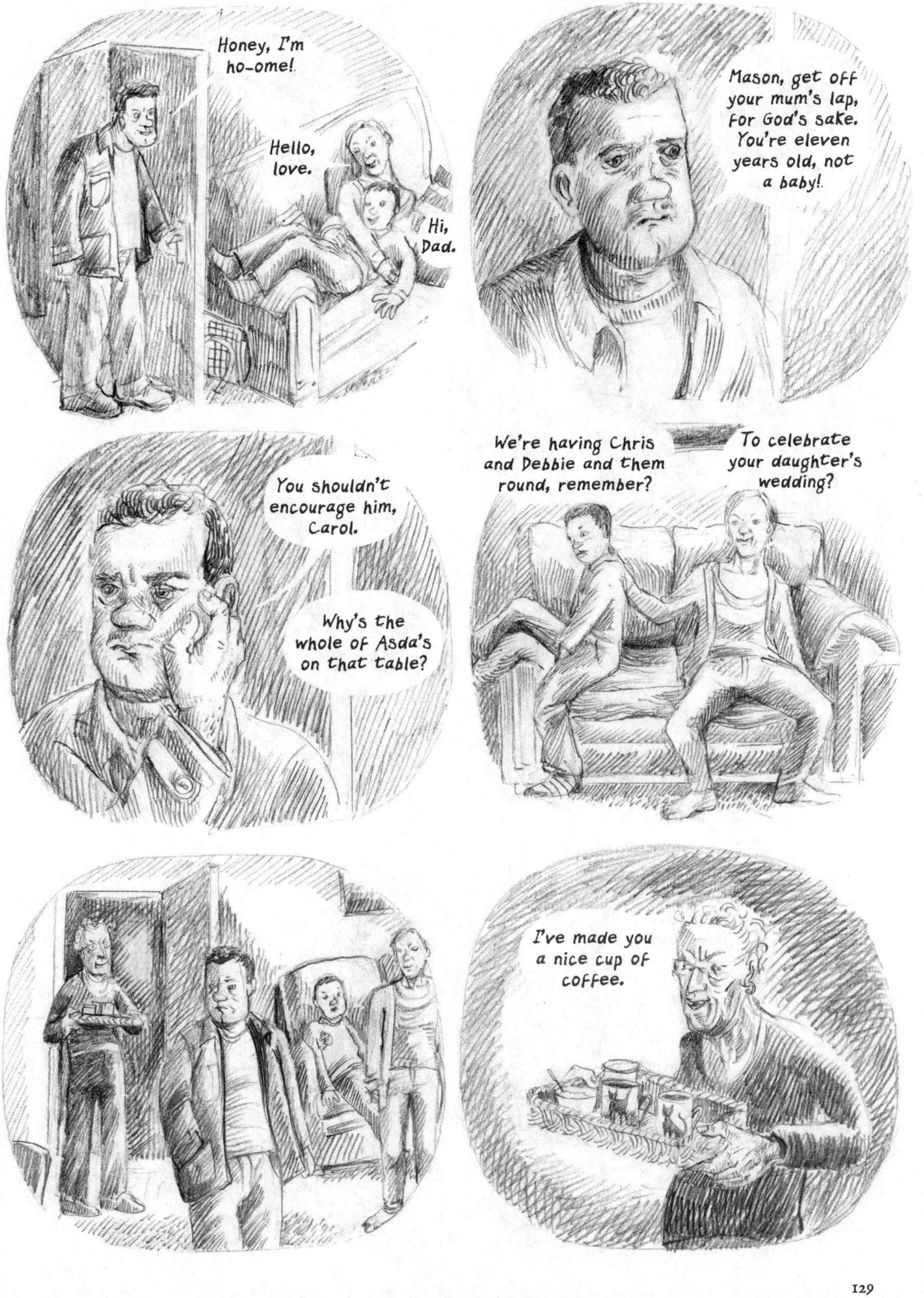
Honey, I'm ho-ome!
Hello, love.
Hi, Dad.
Mason, get off your mum's lap, for God's sake. You're eleven years old, not a baby!
You shouldn't encourage him, Carol.
Why's the whole of Asda's on that table?
We're having Chris and Debbie and them round, remember?
To celebrate your daughter's wedding?
I've made you a nice cup of coffee.

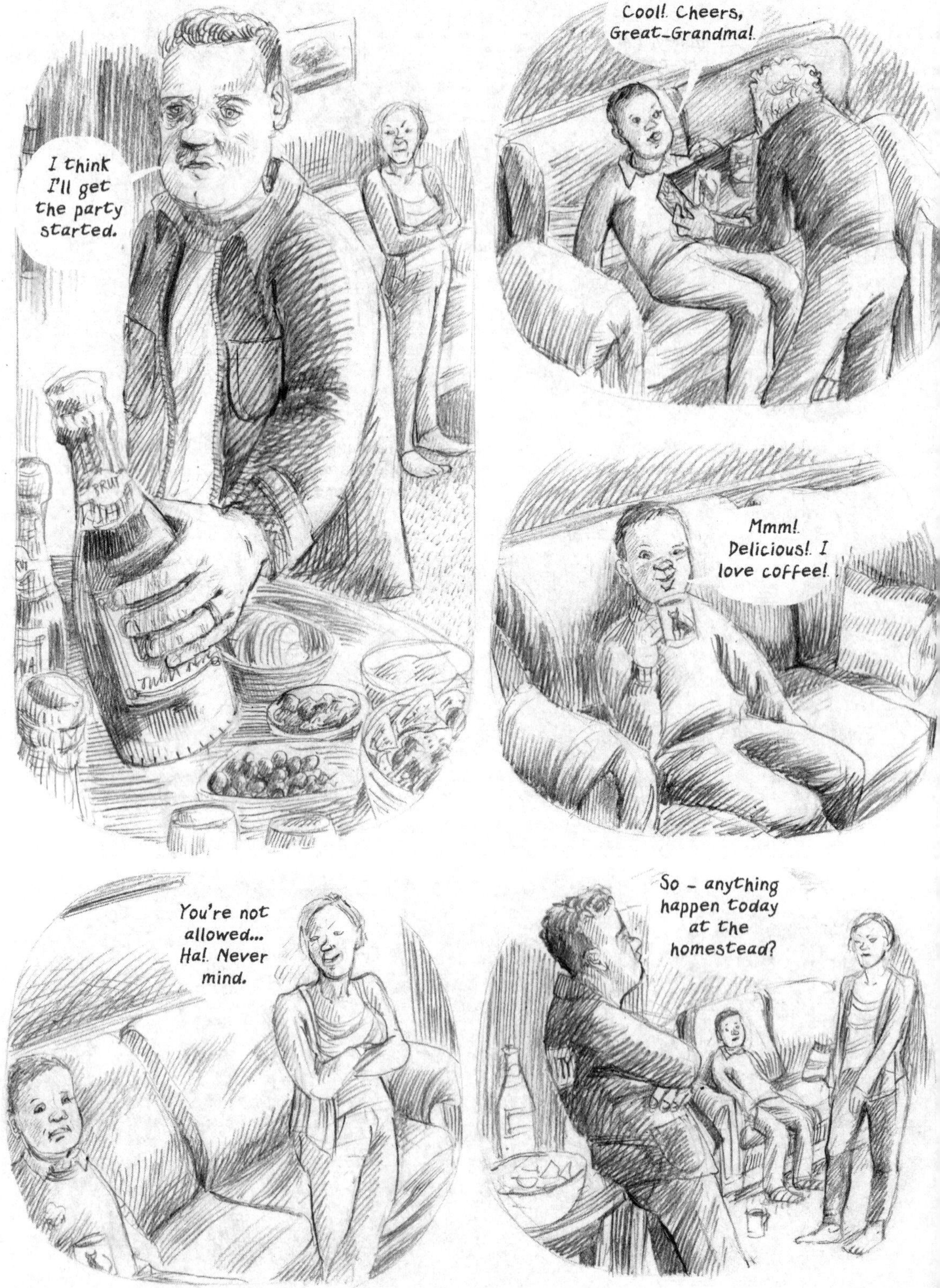
I think I'll get the party started.
Cool!. Cheers, Great-Grandma!.
Mmm!. Delicious!. I love coffee!.
You're not allowed... Ha!. Never mind.
So - anything happen today at the homestead?

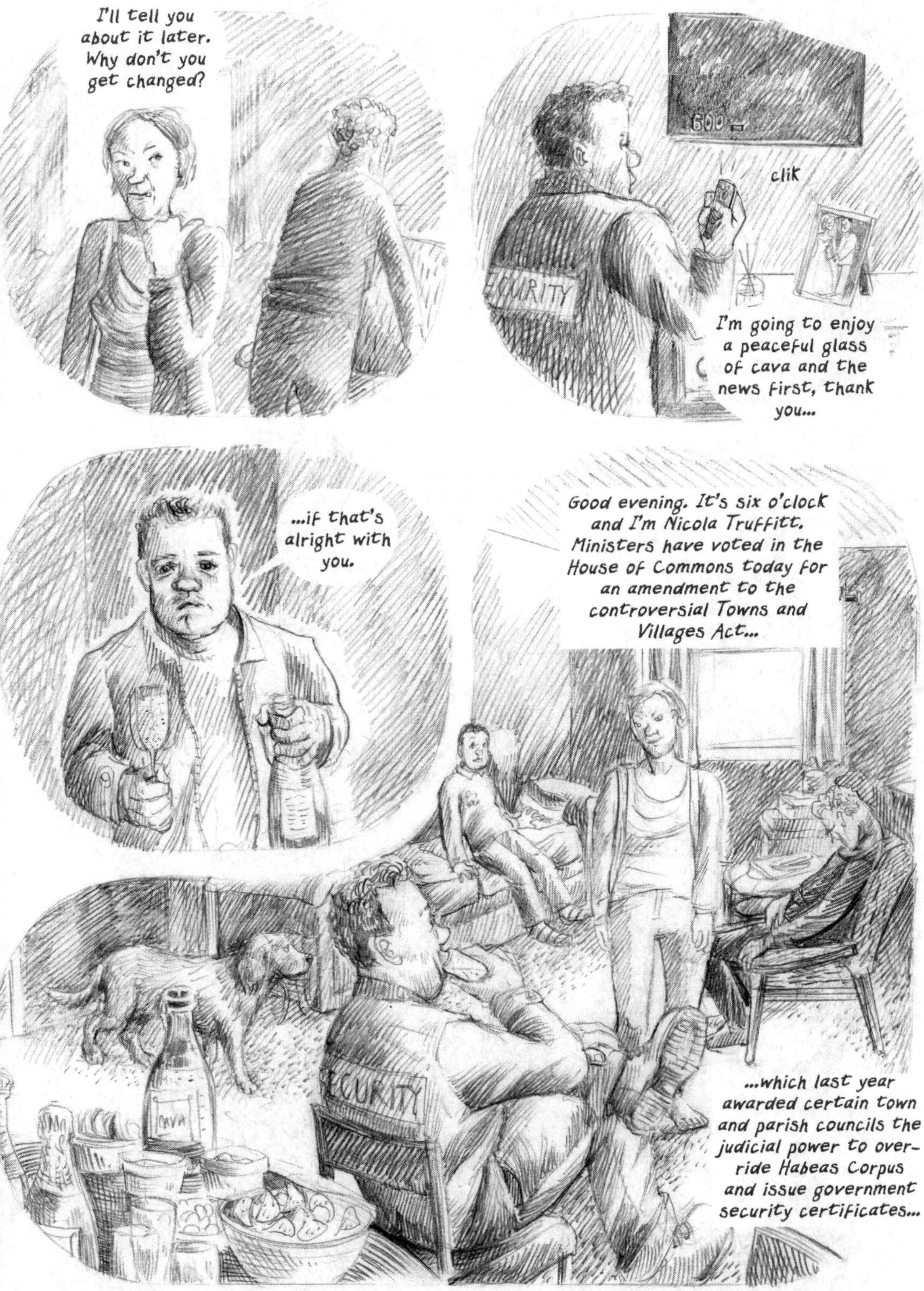
I'll tell you about it later. Why don't you get changed?
clik
I'm going to enjoy a peaceful glass of cava and the news first, thank you...
...if that's alright with you.
Good evening. It's six o'clock and I'm Nicola Truffitt. Ministers have voted in the House of Commons today for an amendment to the controversial Towns and Villages Act...
...which last year awarded certain town and parish councils the judicial power to over-ride Habeas Corpus and issue government security certificates...

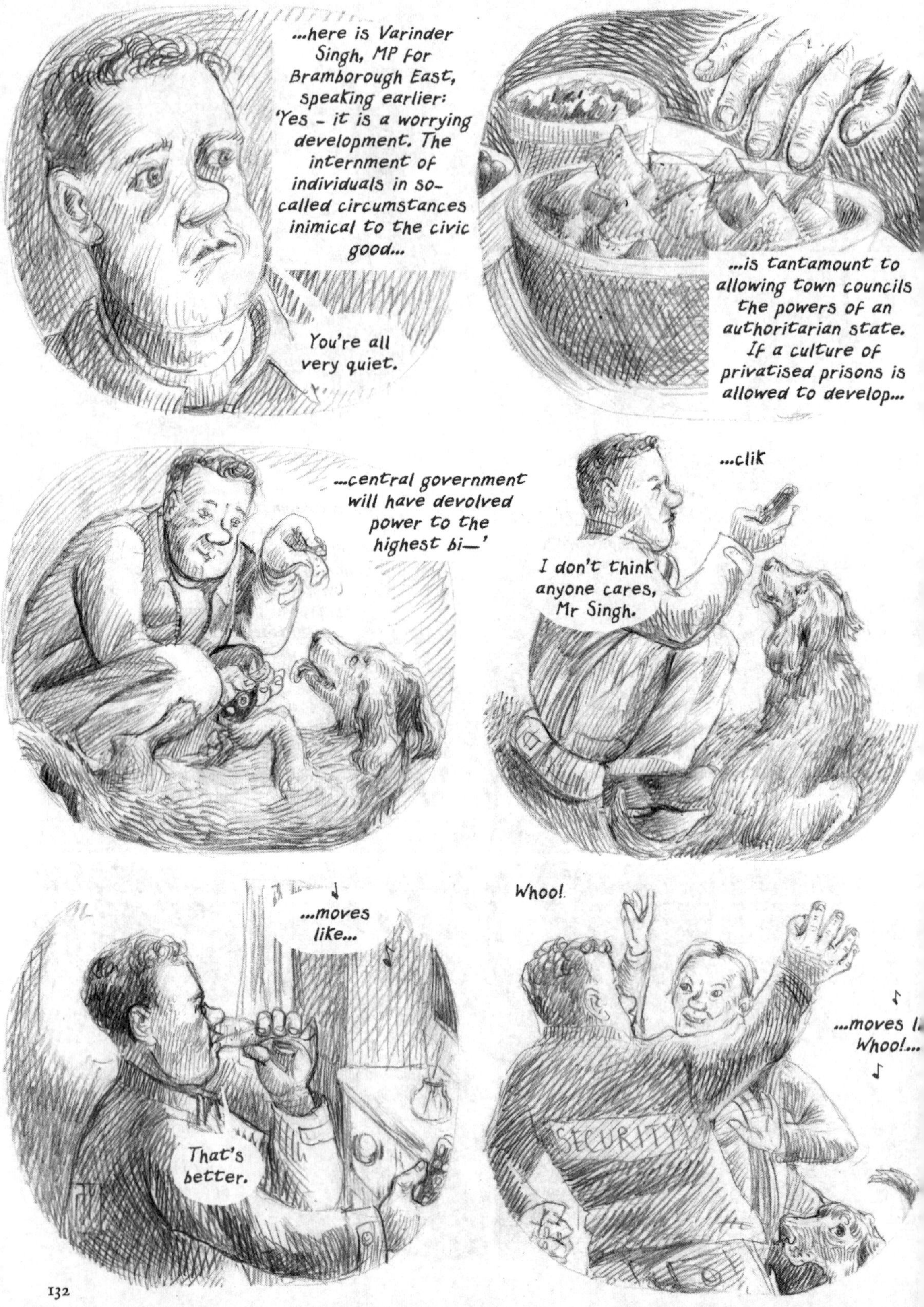
...here is Varinder Singh, MP for Bramborough East, speaking earlier: 'Yes – it is a worrying development. The internment of individuals in so-called circumstances inimical to the civic good...
You're all very quiet.
...is tantamount to allowing town councils the powers of an authoritarian state. If a culture of privatised prisons is allowed to develop...
...central government will have devolved power to the highest bi—'
...clik
I don't think anyone cares, Mr Singh.
...moves like...
That's better.
Whoo!
...moves l
Whoo!...
SECURITY

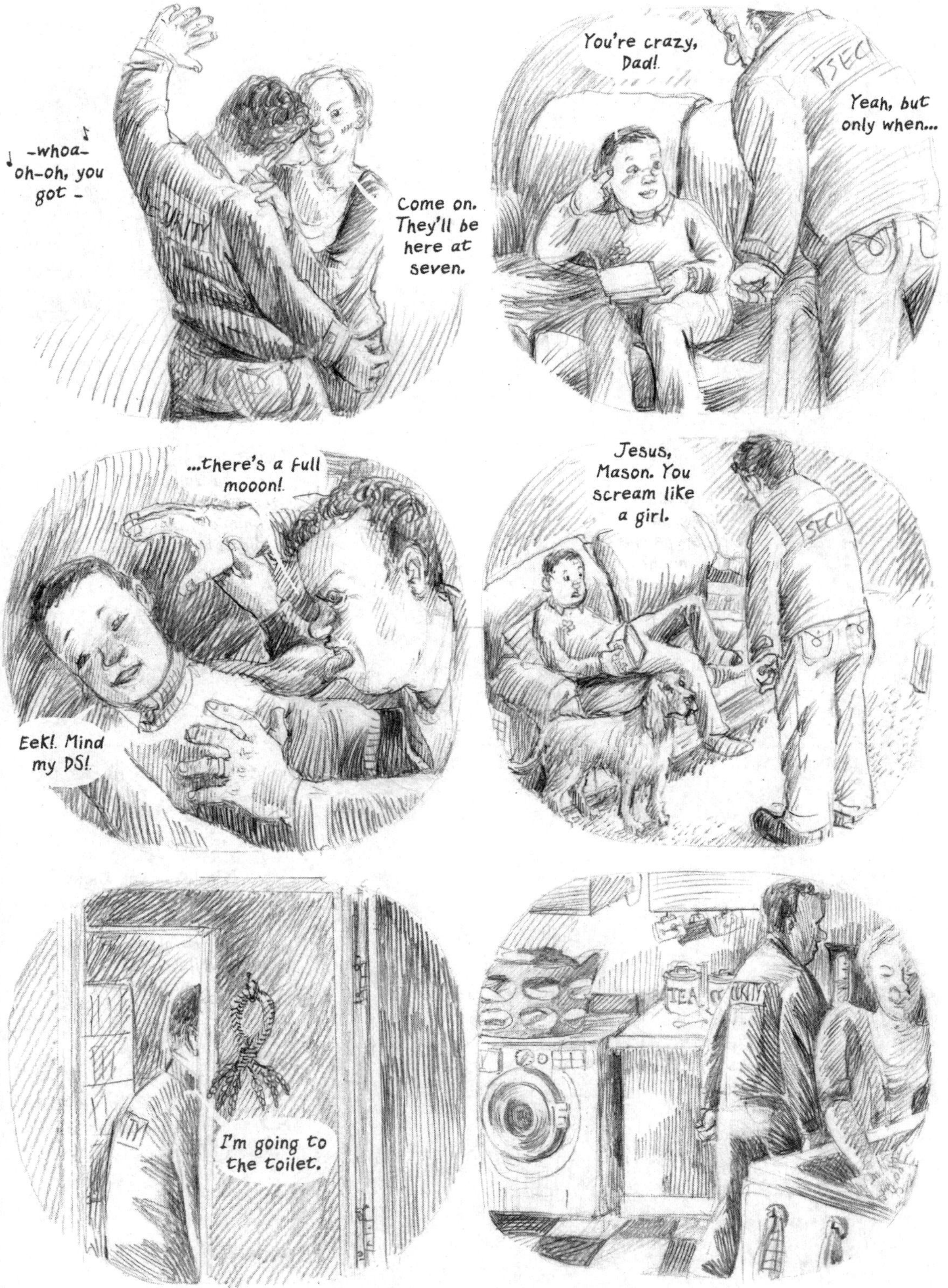
-whoa- oh-oh, you got -
Come on. They'll be here at seven.
You're crazy, Dad!
Yeah, but only when...
...there's a full mooon!
Eek! Mind my DS!
Jesus, Mason. You scream like a girl.
I'm going to the toilet.

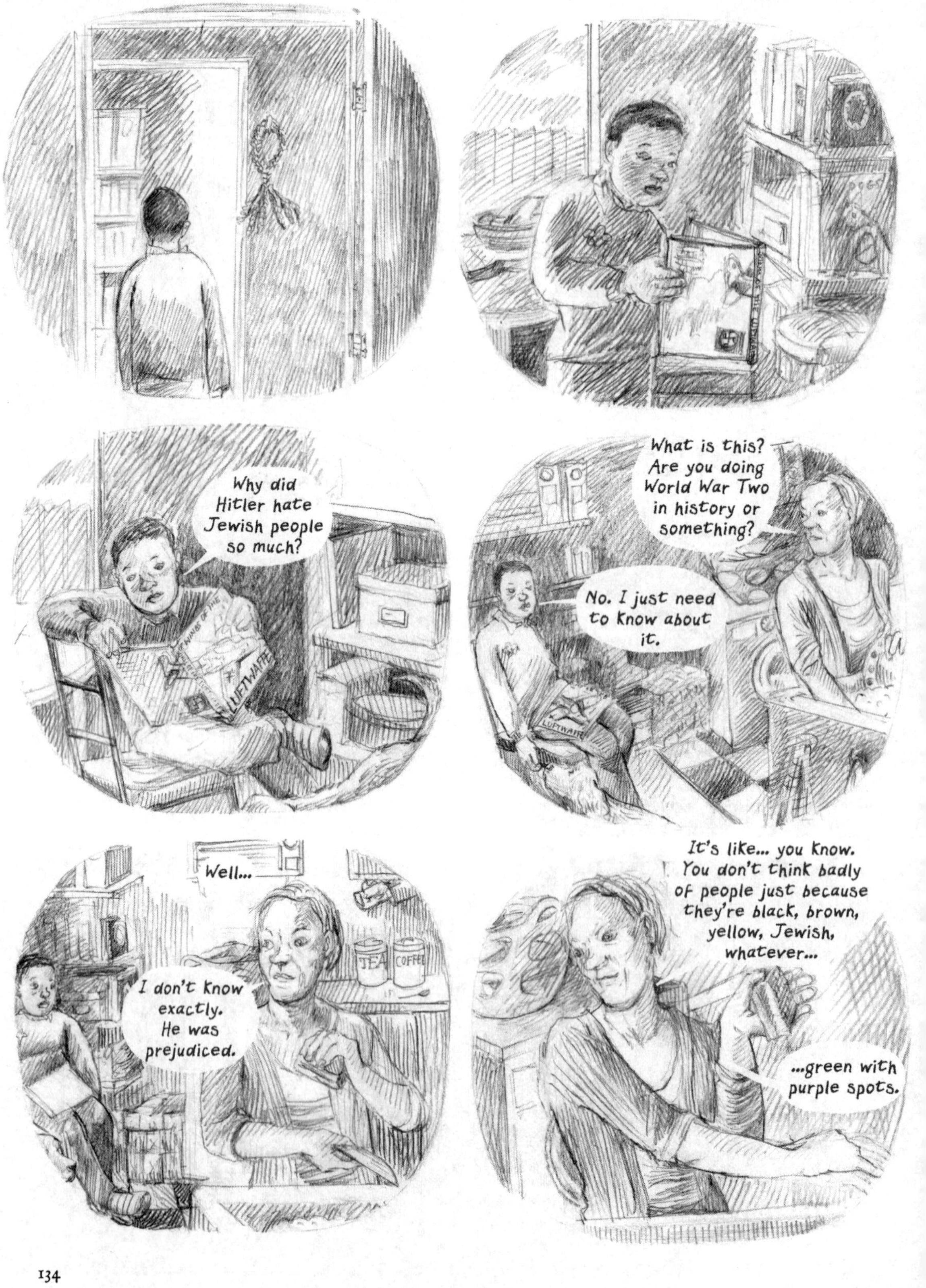
Why did Hitler hate Jewish people so much?
LUFTWAFFE
What is this? Are you doing World War Two in history or something?
No. I just need to know about it.
Well...
TEA
COFFEE
I don't know exactly. He was prejudiced.
It's like... you know. You don't think badly of people just because they're black, brown, yellow, Jewish, whatever...
...green with purple spots.

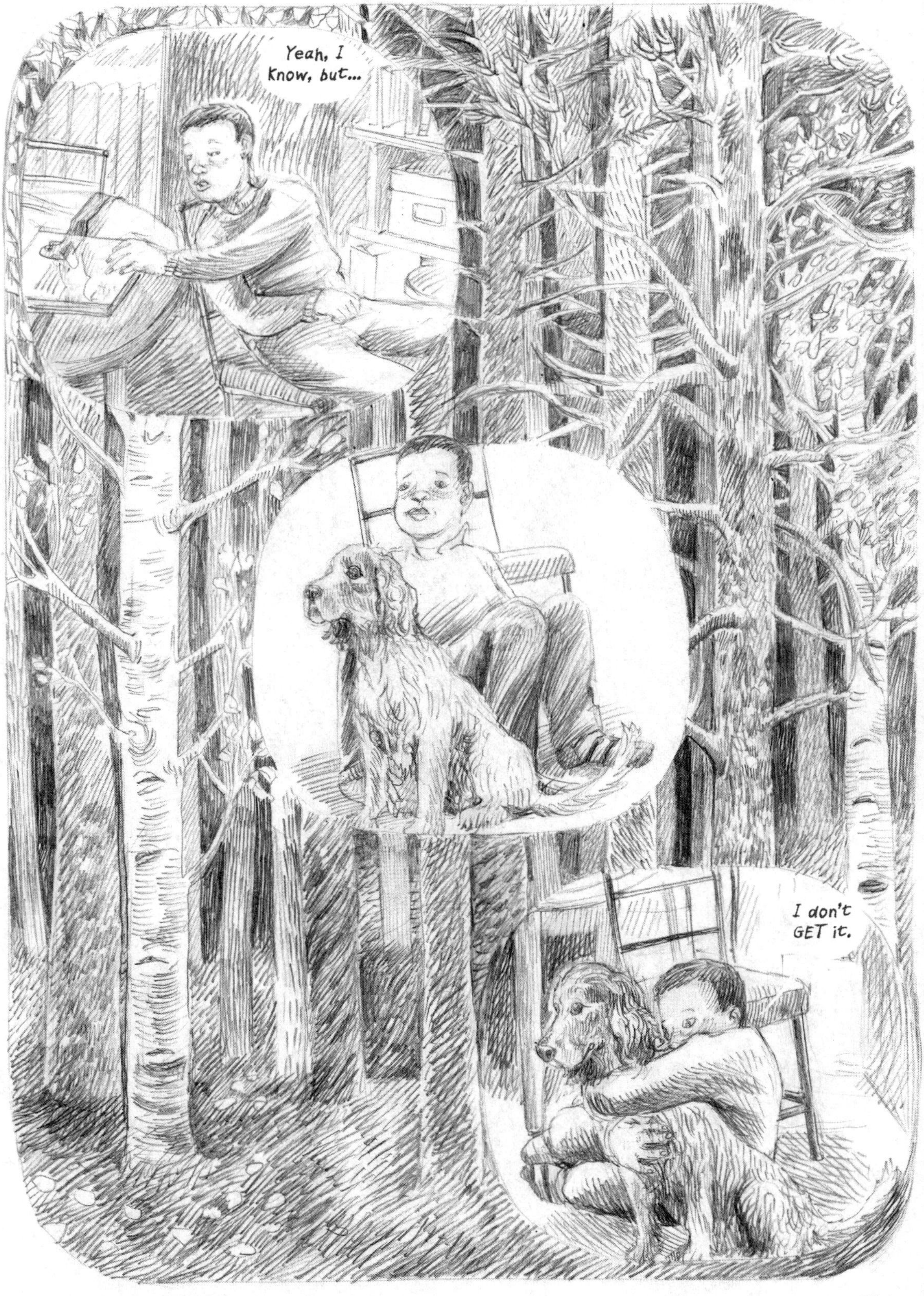
Yeah, I know, but...
I don't GET it.

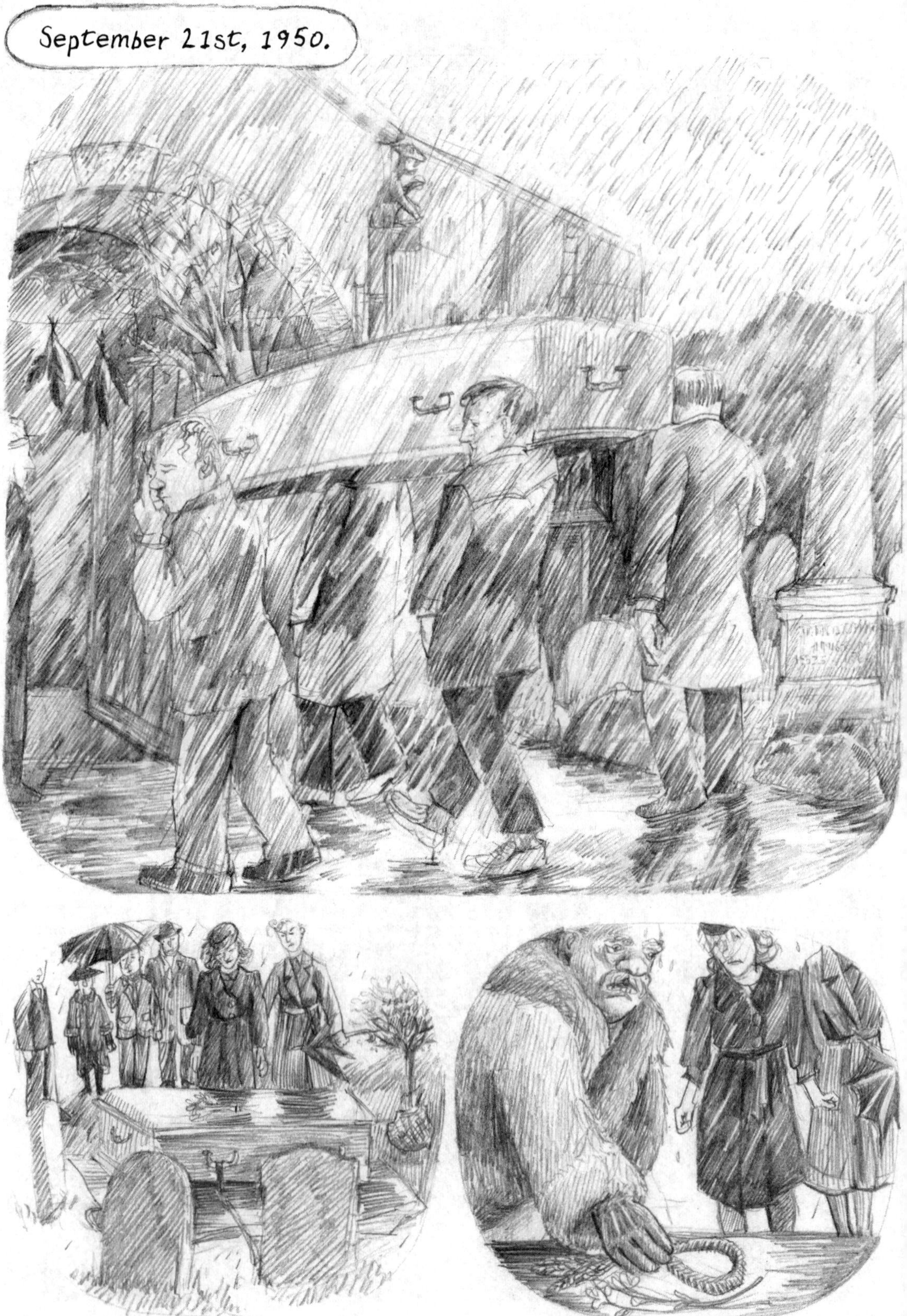
September 21st, 1950.

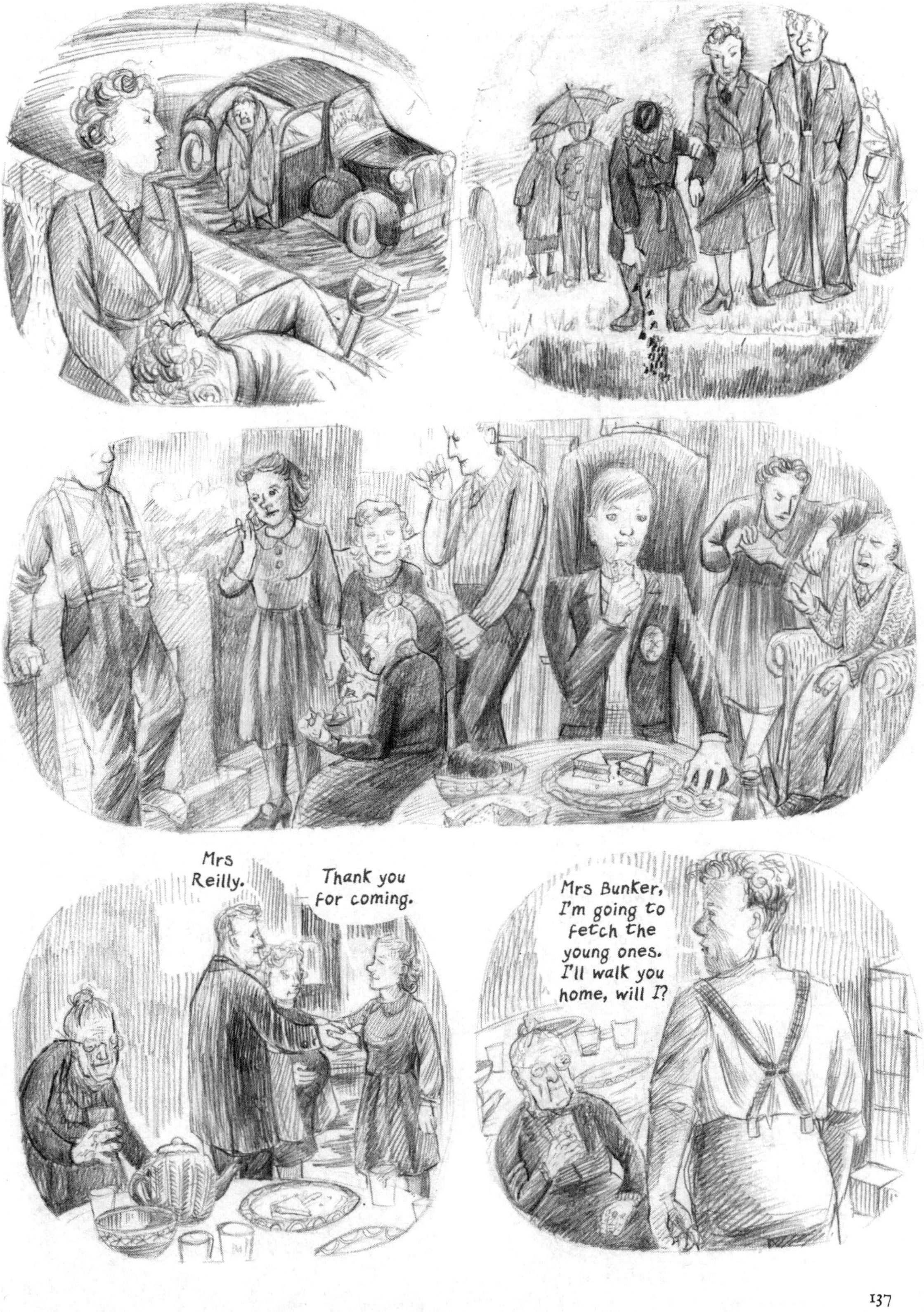
Mrs
Reilly.
Thank you
for coming.
Mrs Bunker,
I'm going to
fetch the
young ones.
I'll walk you
home, will I?

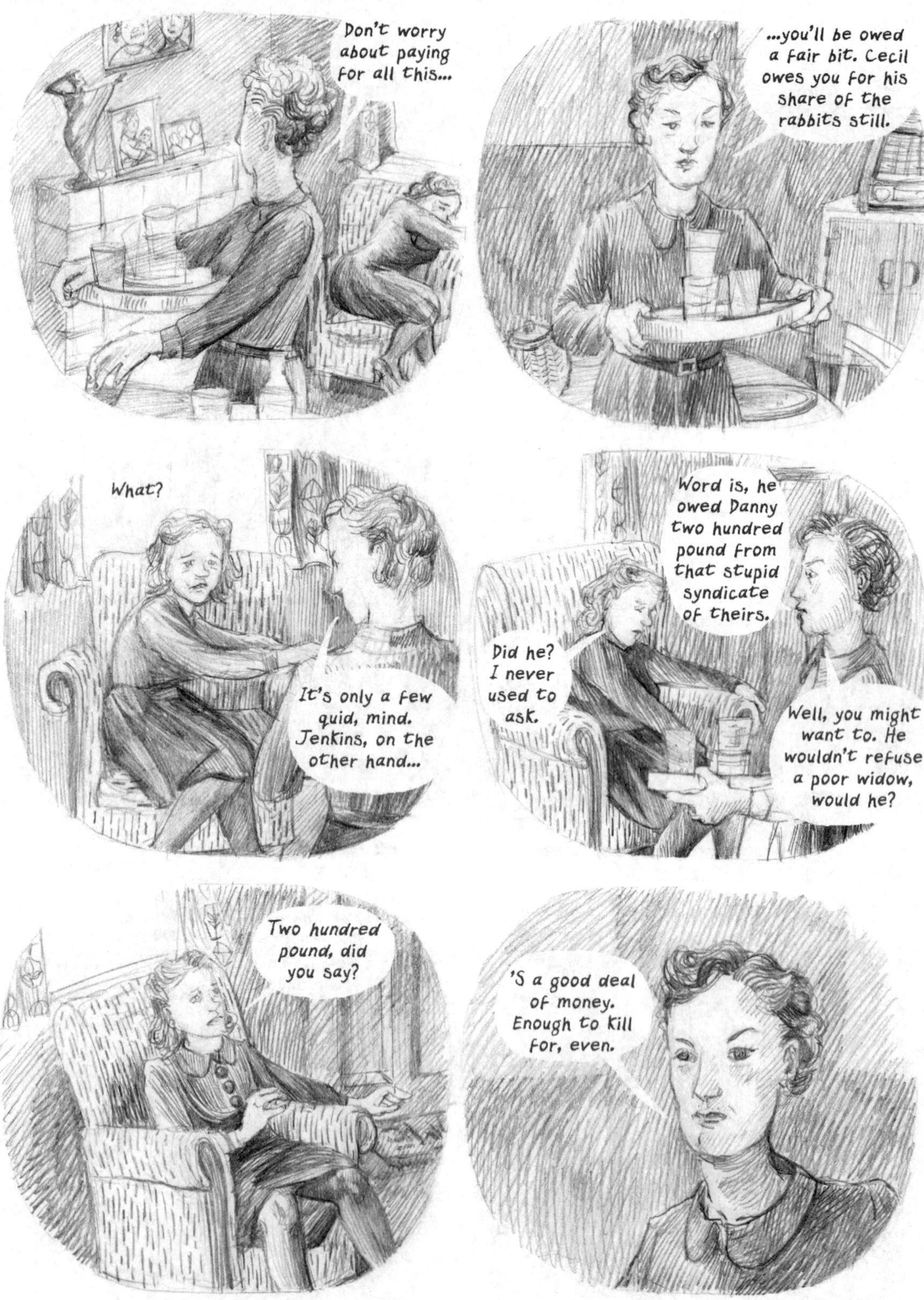
Don't worry about paying for all this...
...you'll be owed a fair bit. Cecil owes you for his share of the rabbits still.
What?
It's only a few quid, mind. Jenkins, on the other hand...
Word is, he owed Danny two hundred pound from that stupid syndicate of theirs.
Did he? I never used to ask.
Well, you might want to. He wouldn't refuse a poor widow, would he?
Two hundred pound, did you say?
'S a good deal of money. Enough to kill for, even.

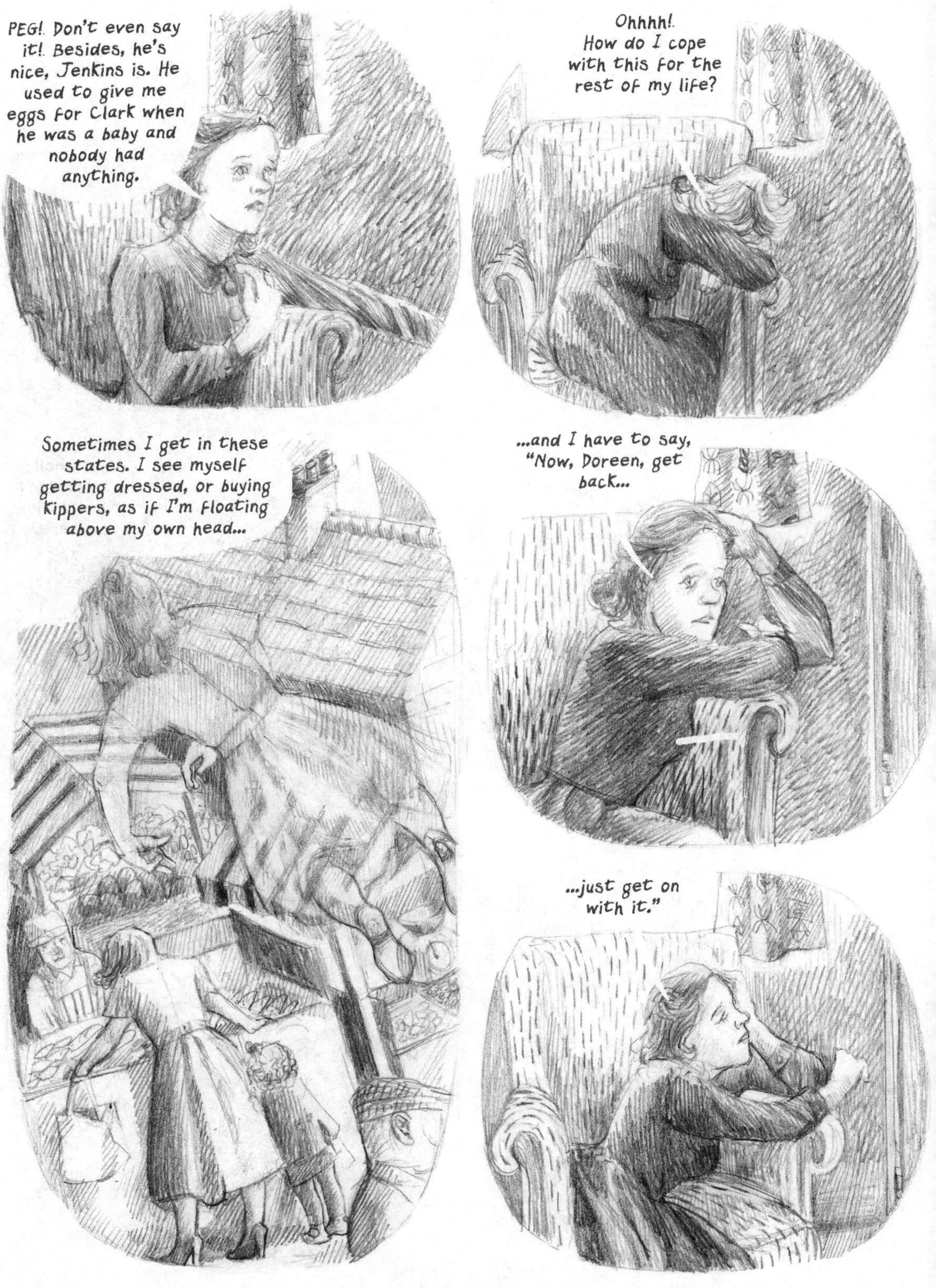
PEG!. Don't even say it!. Besides, he's nice, Jenkins is. He used to give me eggs for Clark when he was a baby and nobody had anything.
Ohhhh!. How do I cope with this for the rest of my life?
Sometimes I get in these states. I see myself getting dressed, or buying kippers, as if I'm floating above my own head...
...and I have to say, "Now, Doreen, get back...
...just get on with it."

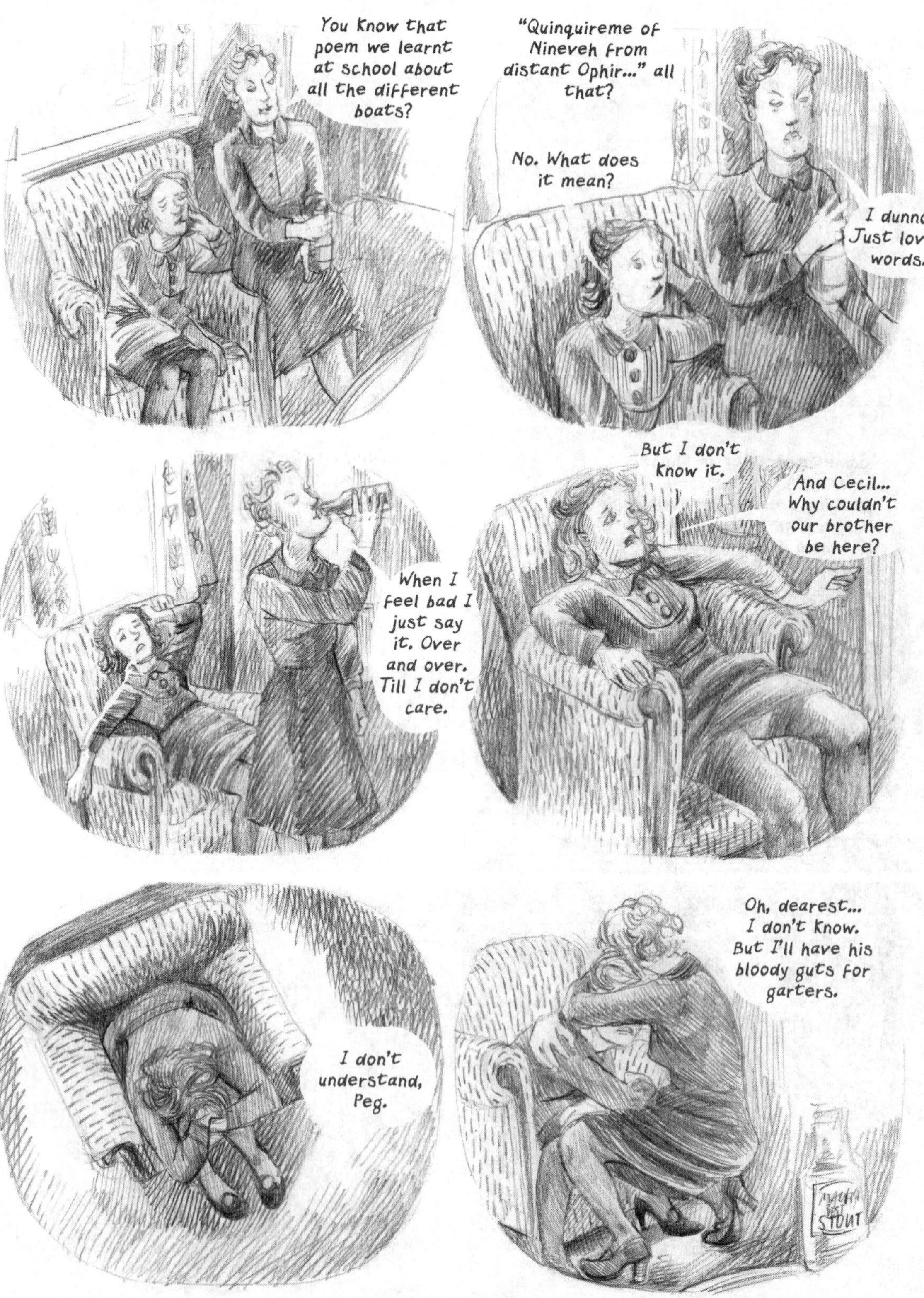
You know that poem we learnt at school about all the different boats?
"Quinquireme of Nineveh from distant Ophir..." all that?
No. What does it mean?
I dunno. Just love words.
When I feel bad I just say it. Over and over. Till I don't care.
But I don't know it.
And Cecil... Why couldn't our brother be here?
I don't understand, Peg.
Oh, dearest... I don't know. But I'll have his bloody guts for garters.
STOUT

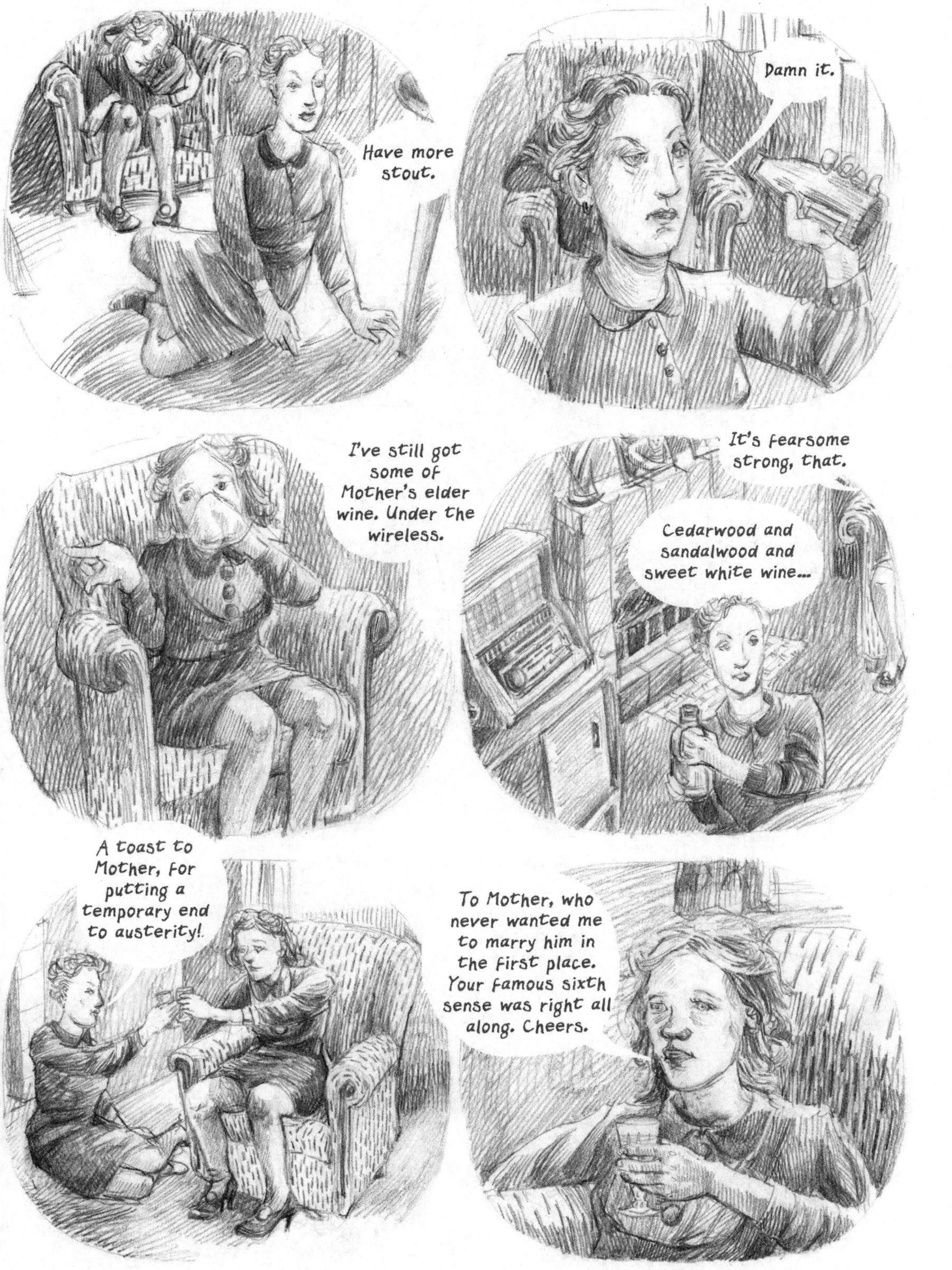
Have more stout.
Damn it.
I've still got some of Mother's elder wine. Under the wireless.
It's fearsome strong, that.
Cedarwood and sandalwood and sweet white wine...
A toast to Mother, for putting a temporary end to austerity!
To Mother, who never wanted me to marry him in the first place. Your famous sixth sense was right all along. Cheers.

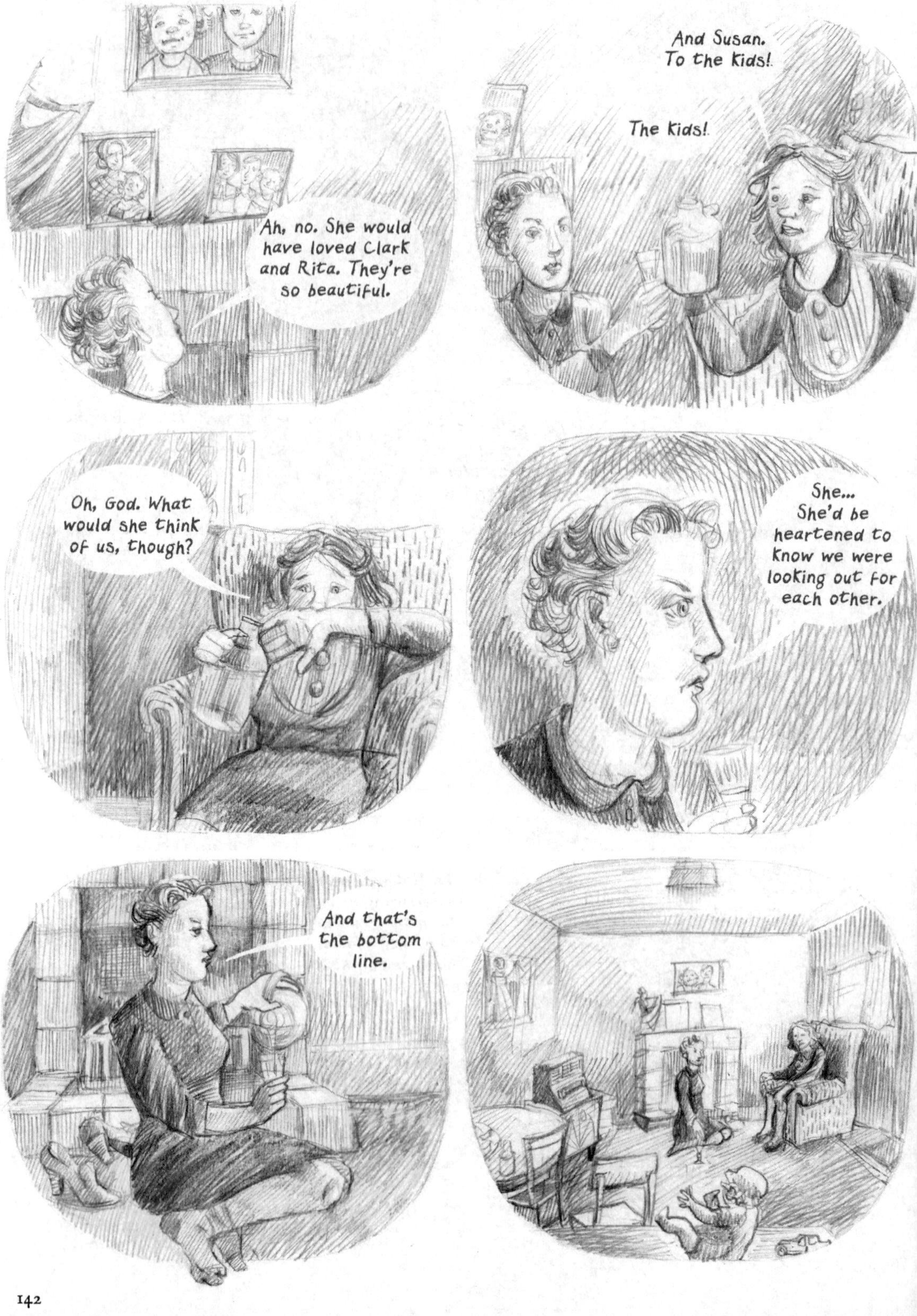
Ah, no. She would have loved Clark and Rita. They're so beautiful.
And Susan. To the kids!.
The kids!.
Oh, God. What would she think of us, though?
She... She'd be heartened to know we were looking out for each other.
And that's the bottom line.

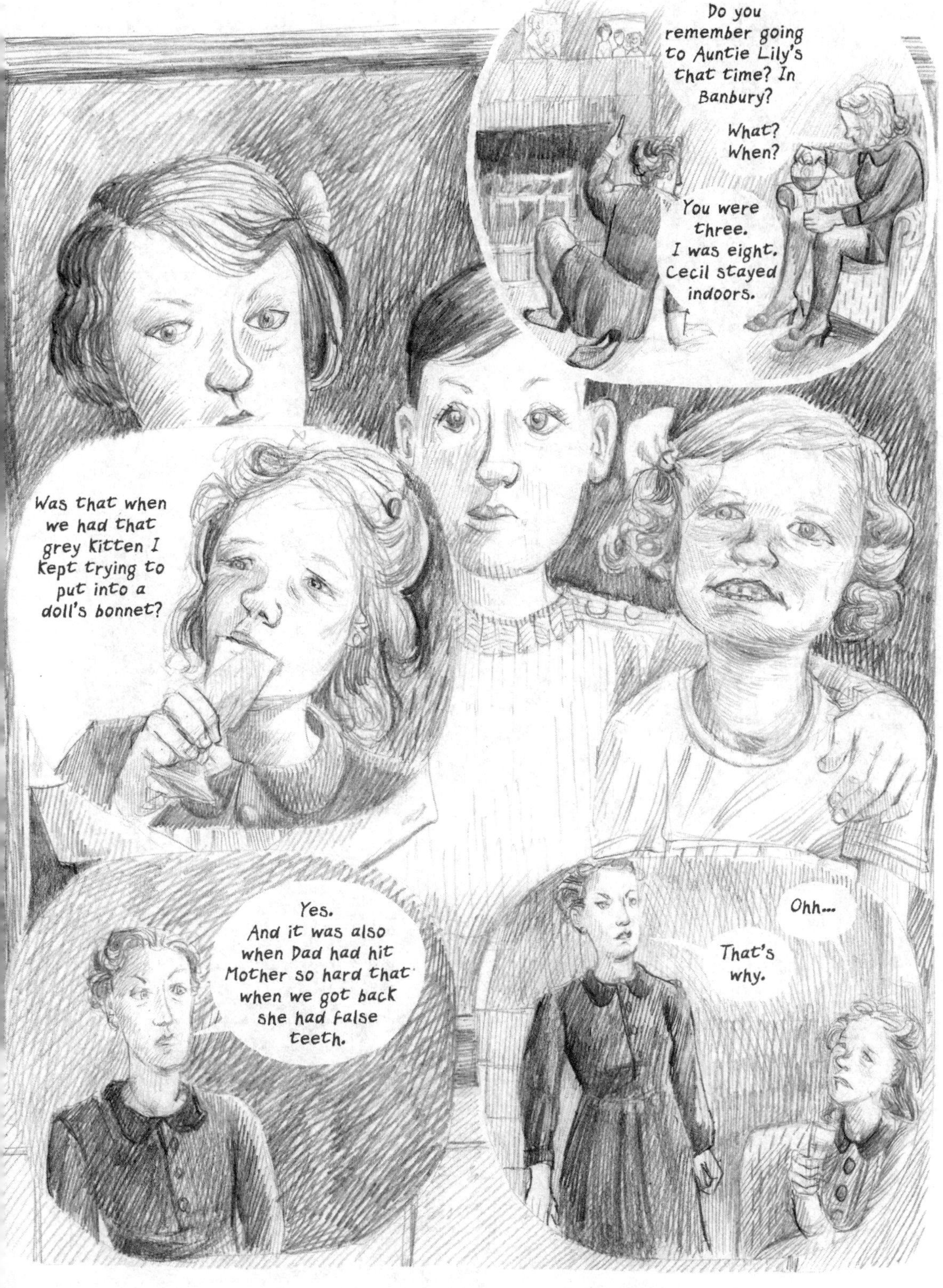
Do you remember going to Auntie Lily's that time? In Banbury?
What? When?
You were three. I was eight. Cecil stayed indoors.
Was that when we had that grey kitten I kept trying to put into a doll's bonnet?
Yes. And it was also when Dad had hit Mother so hard that when we got back she had false teeth.
Ohh...
That's why.

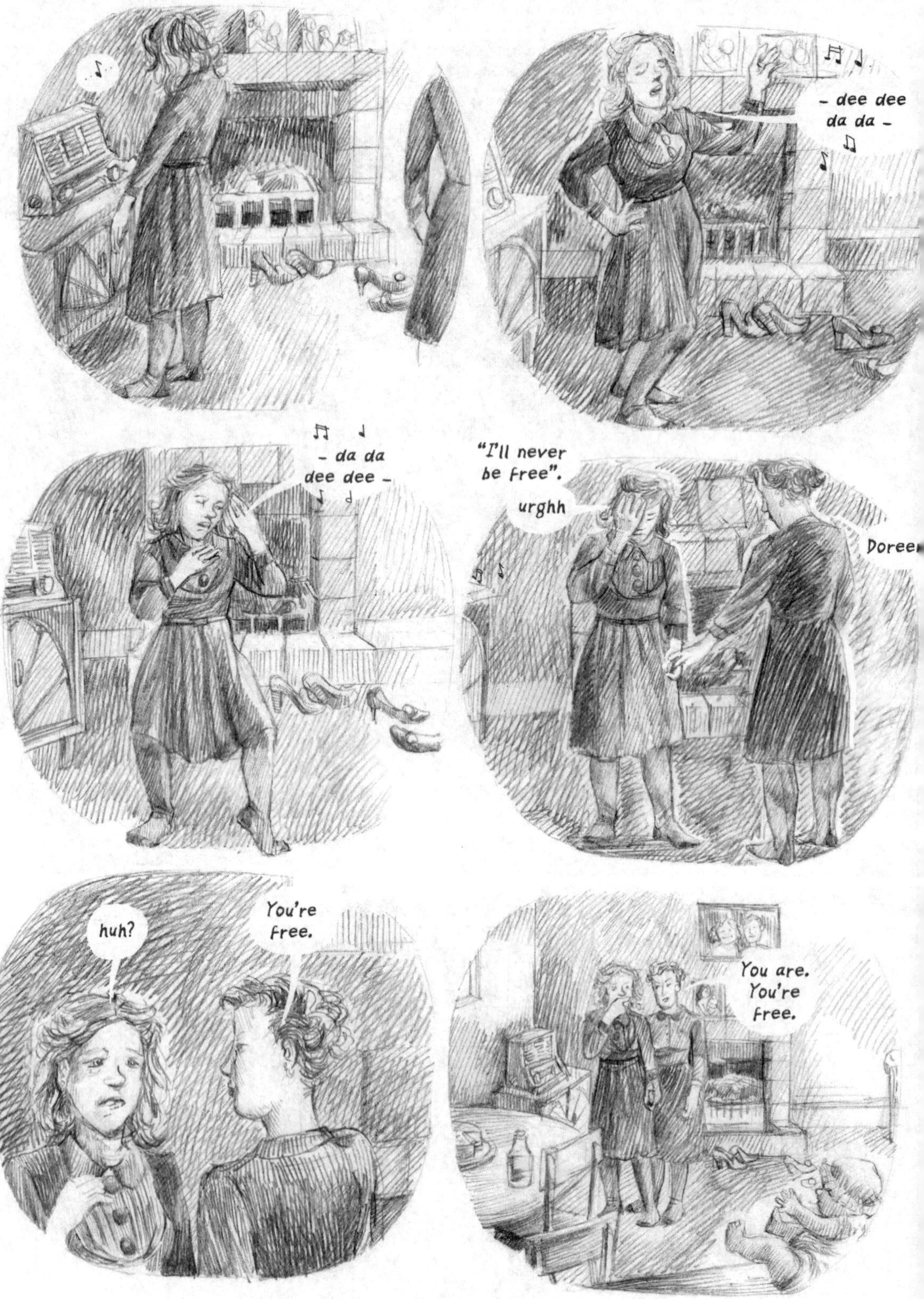
- dee dee
da da -
- da da
dee dee -
"I'll never
be free".
urghh
Doreen
huh?
You're
free.
You are.
You're
free.

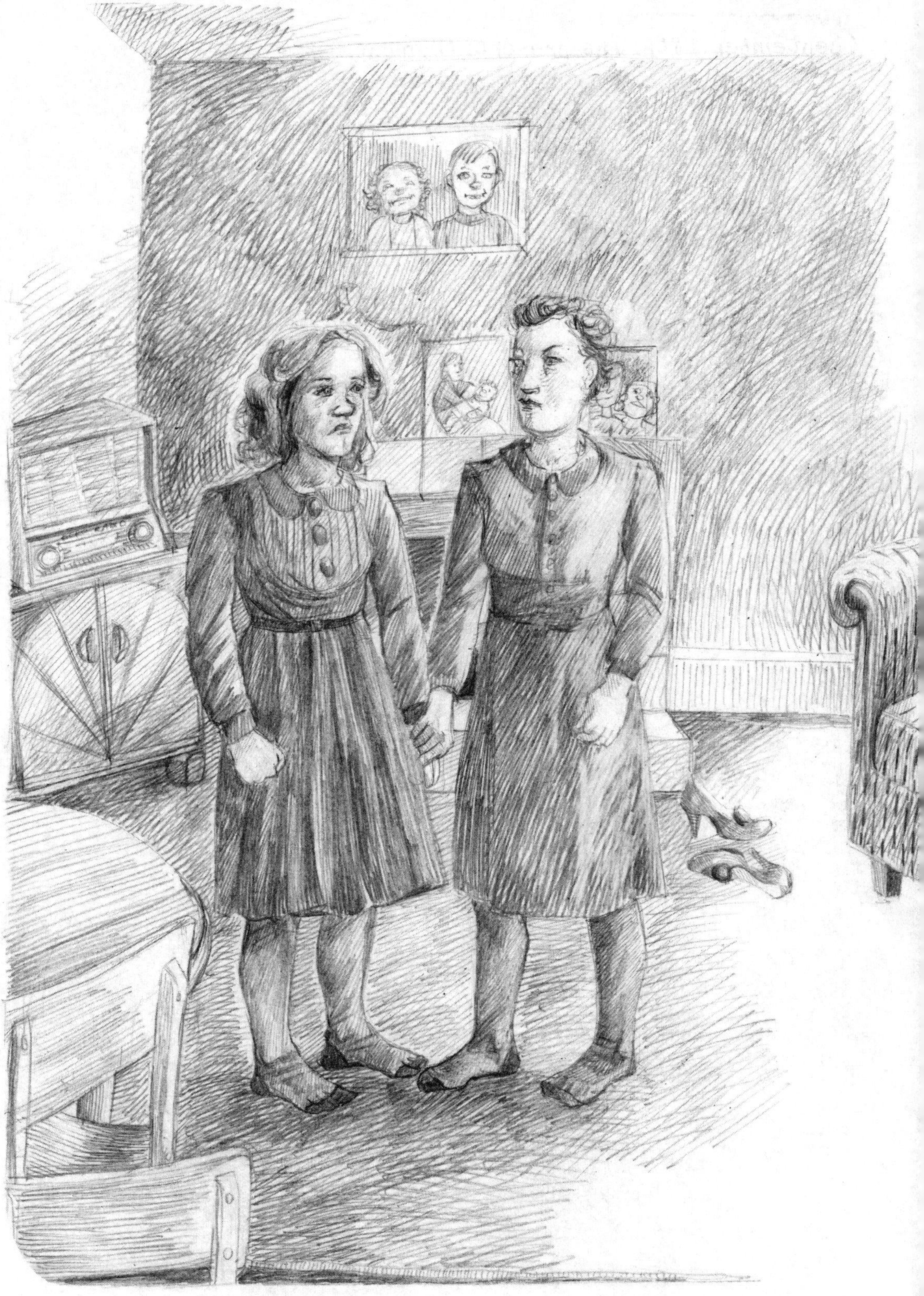

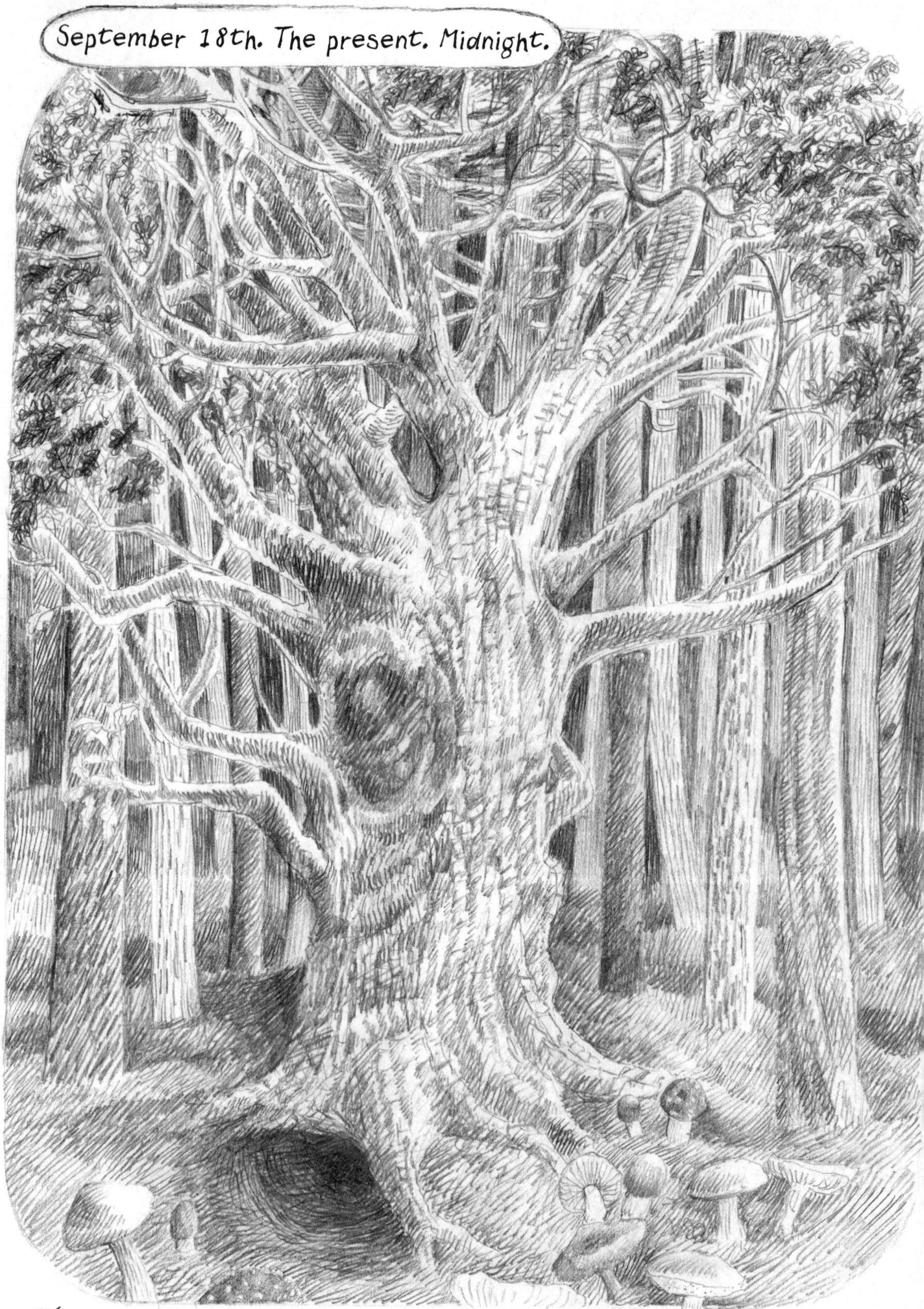
September 18th. The present. Midnight.

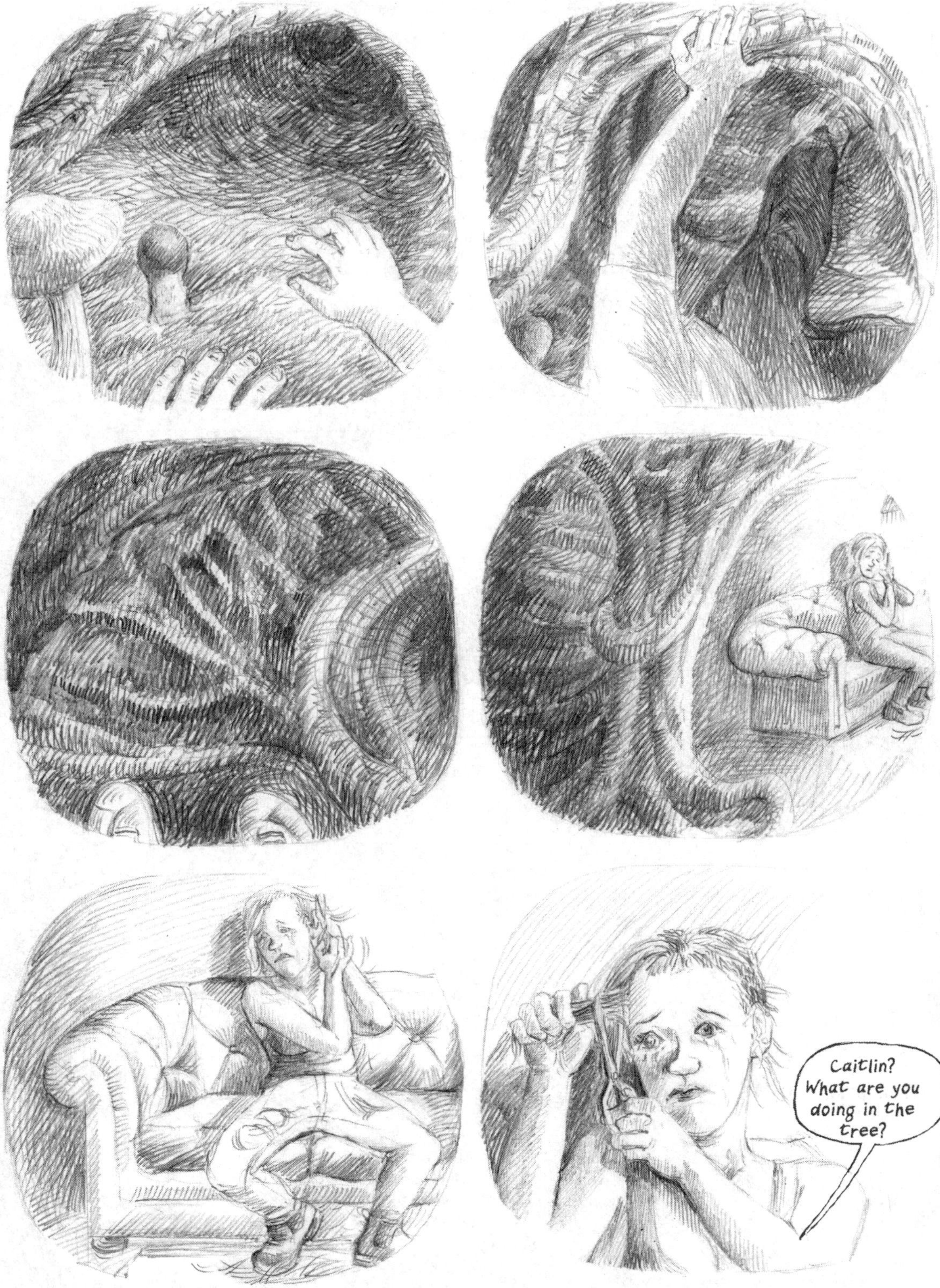
Caitlin? What are you doing in the tree?

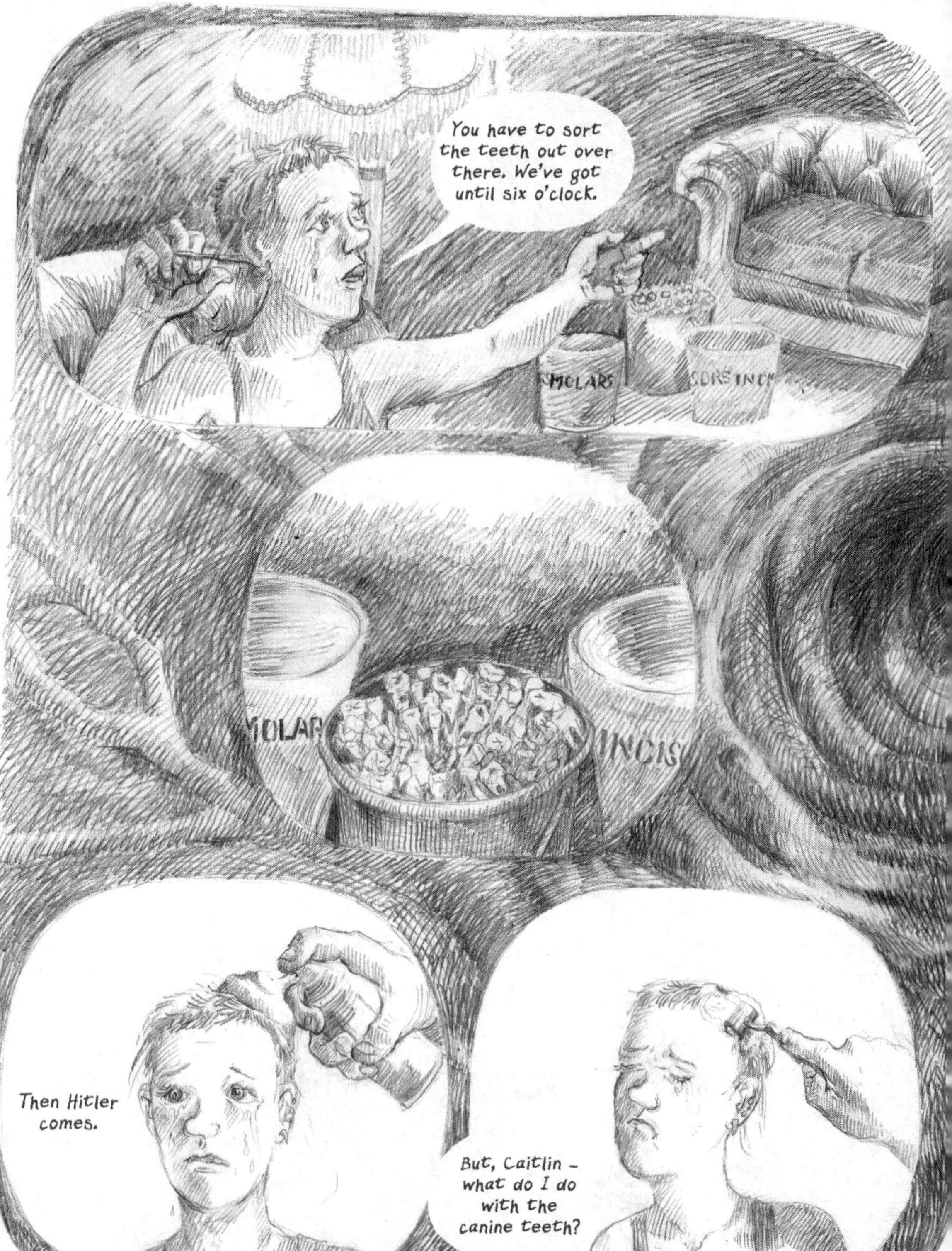
You have to sort the teeth out over there. We've got until six o'clock.
MOLARS
Then Hitler comes.
But, Caitlin - what do I do with the canine teeth?

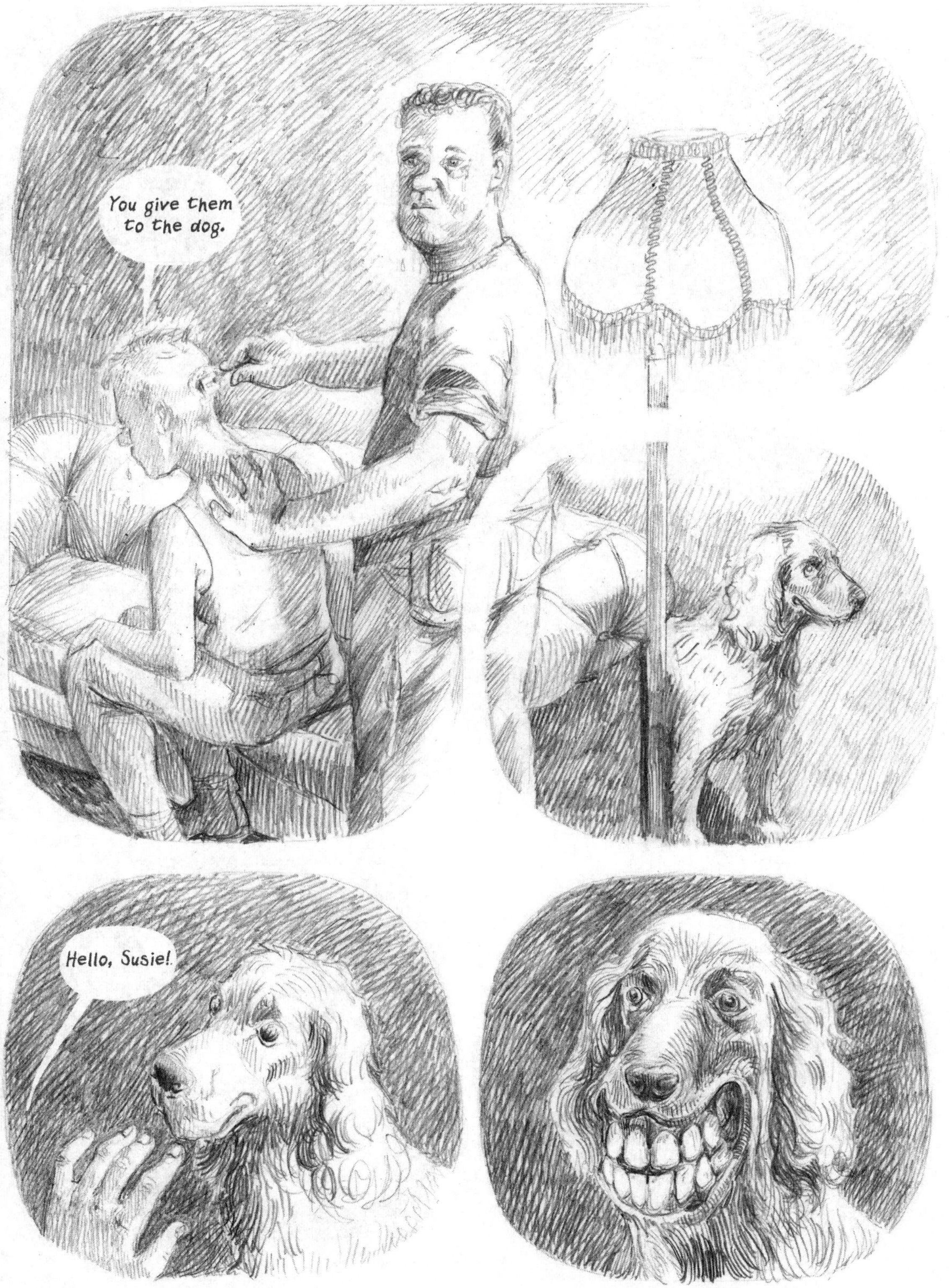
You give them to the dog.
Hello, Susie!

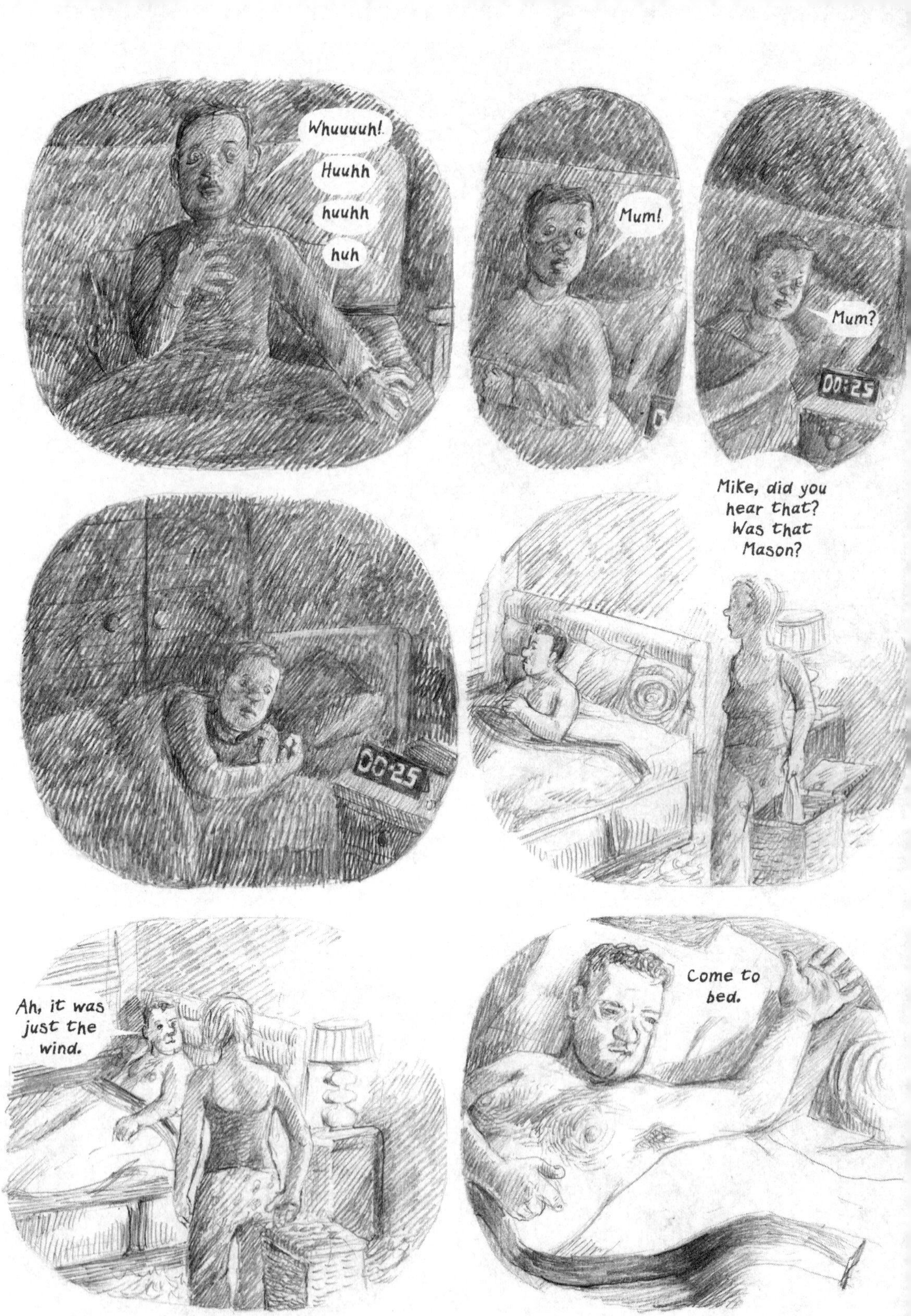
Whuuuuh!.
Huuhh
huuhh
huh
Mum!
Mum?
00:25
00:25
Mike, did you hear that? Was that Mason?
Ah, it was just the wind.
Come to bed.

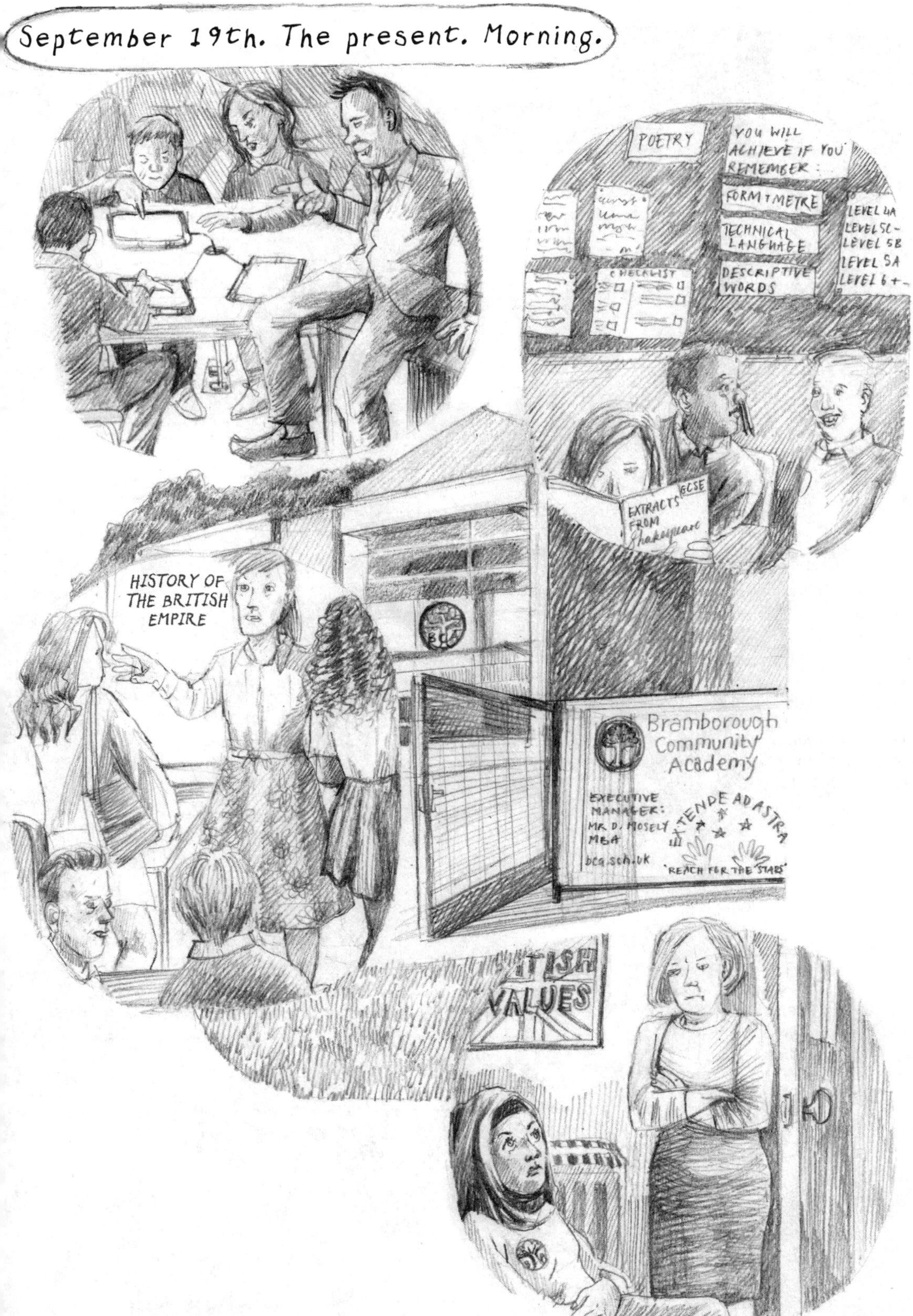
September 19th. The present. Morning.
POETRY
YOU WILL ACHIEVE IF YOU REMEMBER:
FORM + METRE
TECHNICAL LANGUAGE
DESCRIPTIVE WORDS
LEVEL 4A
LEVEL 5C
LEVEL 5B
LEVEL 5A
LEVEL 6+
CHECKLIST
GCSE
EXTRACTS FROM Shakespeare
HISTORY OF THE BRITISH EMPIRE
Bramborough Community Academy
EXECUTIVE MANAGER:
MR D. MOSELY MBA
TENDE AD ASTRA
"REACH FOR THE STARS"
VALUES

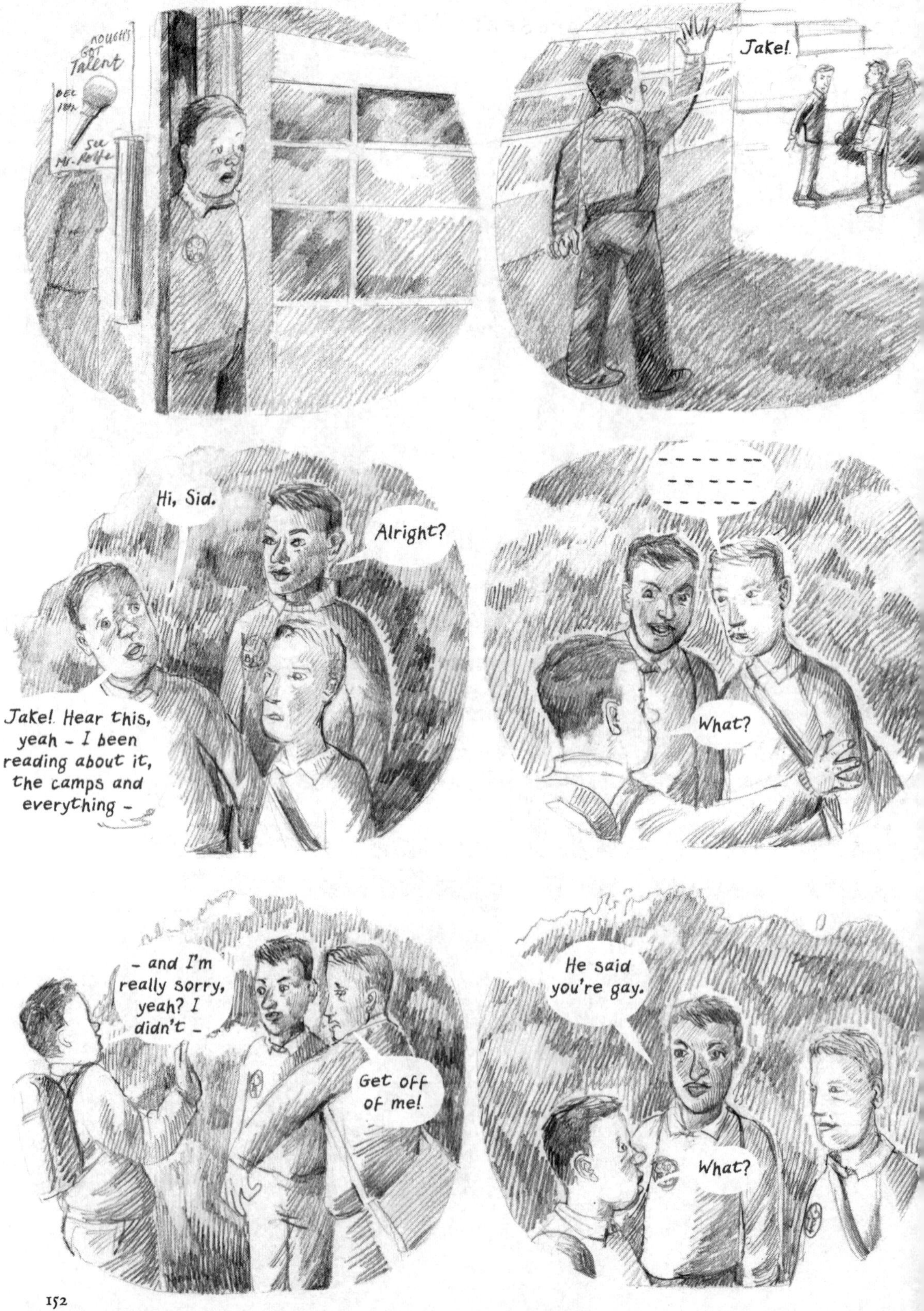
GOT
Talent
See
Jake!
Hi, Sid.
Alright?
Jake! Hear this, yeah - I been reading about it, the camps and everything -
- - - - - - - - - - - - - - - -
What?
- and I'm really sorry, yeah? I didn't -
Get off of me!
He said you're gay.
What?

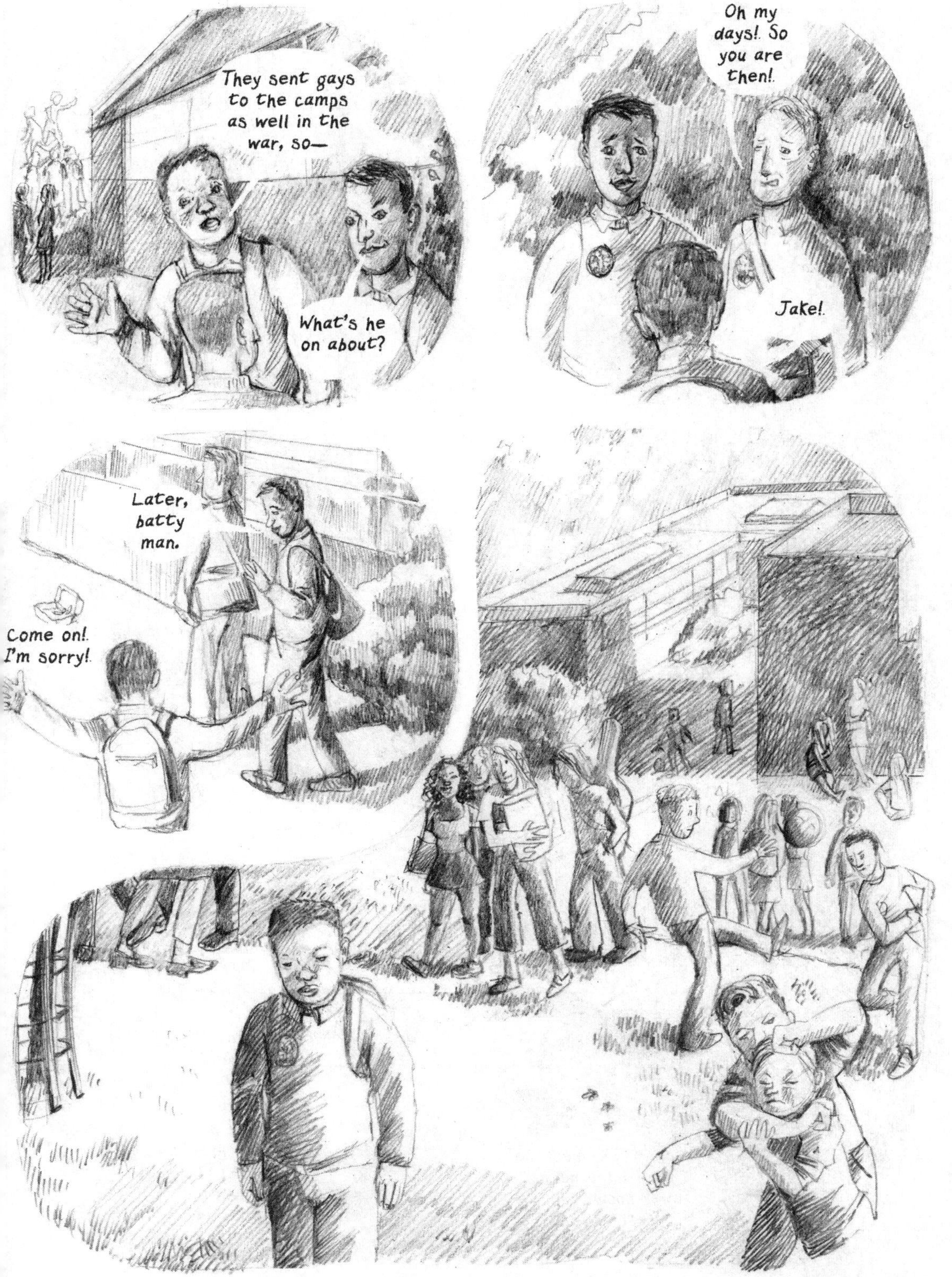
They sent gays to the camps as well in the war, so—
What's he on about?
Oh my days!. So you are then!.
Jake!.
Later, batty man.
Come on!. I'm sorry!.

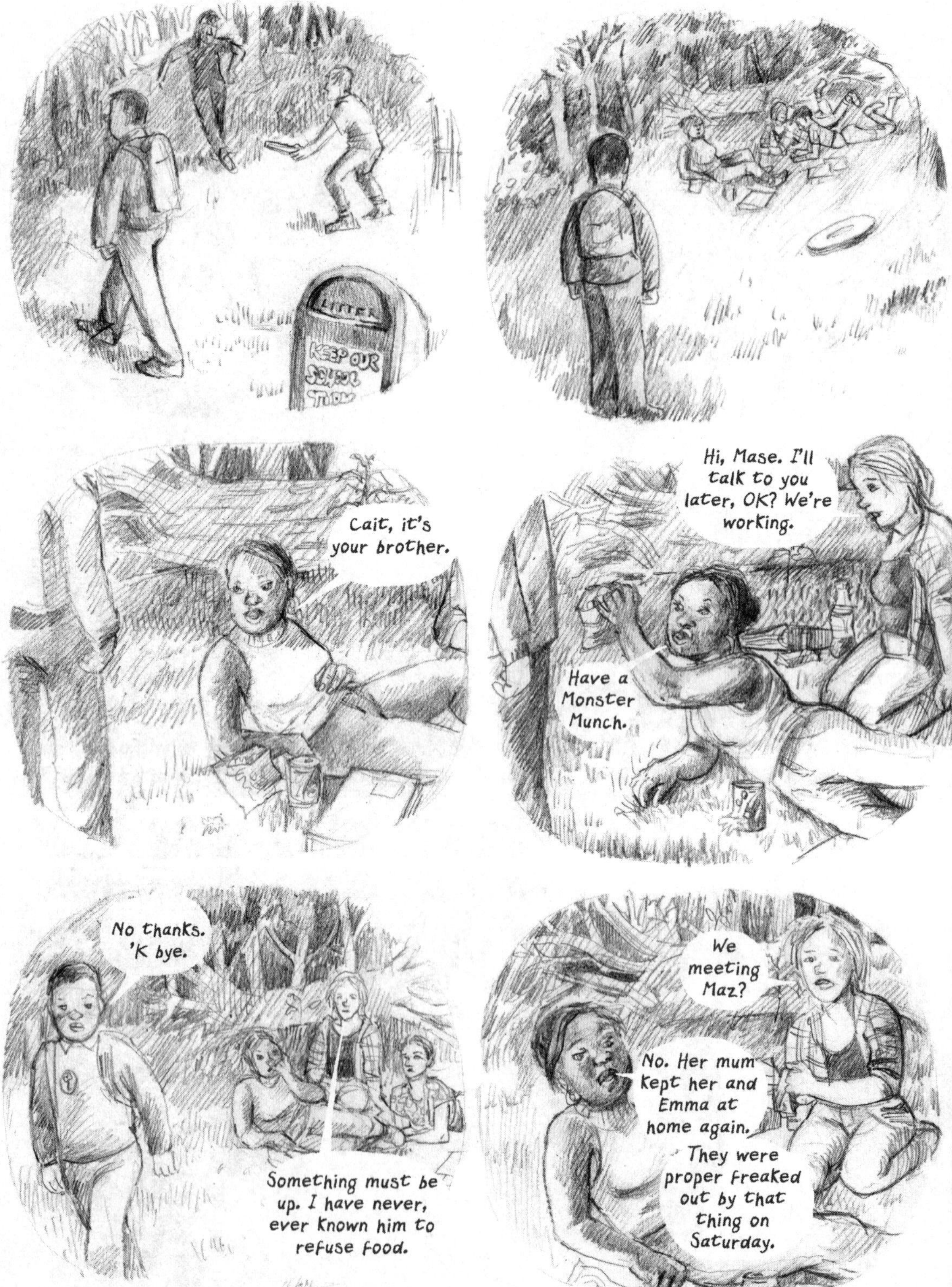

KEEP OUR
Cait, it's your brother.
Hi, Mase. I'll talk to you later, OK? We're working.
Have a Monster Munch.
No thanks. 'K bye.
Something must be up. I have never, ever known him to refuse food.
We meeting Maz?
No. Her mum kept her and Emma at home again.
They were proper freaked out by that thing on Saturday.

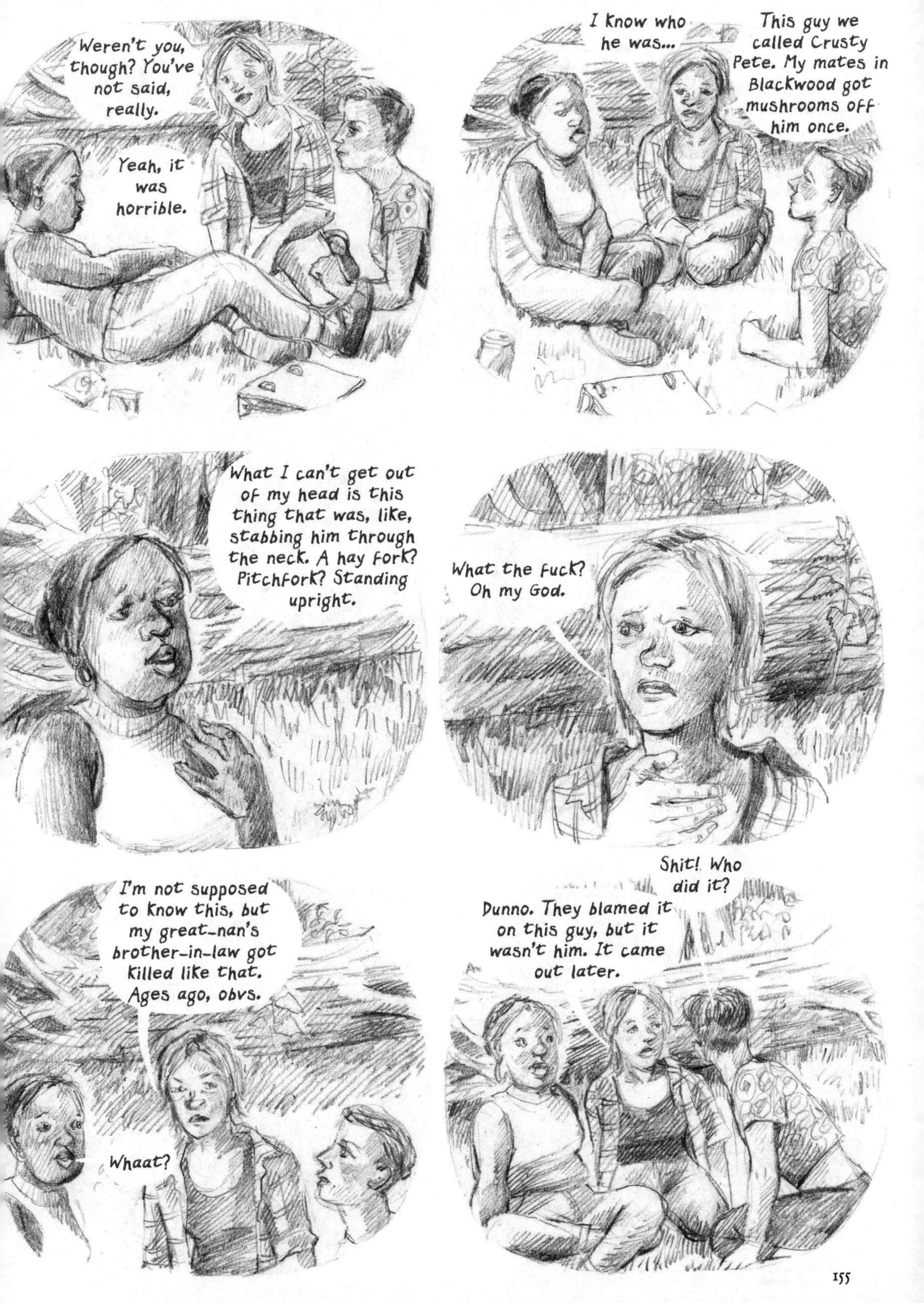
Weren't you, though? You've not said, really.
Yeah, it was horrible.
I know who he was...
This guy we called Crusty Pete. My mates in Blackwood got mushrooms off him once.
What I can't get out of my head is this thing that was, like, stabbing him through the neck. A hay fork? Pitchfork? Standing upright.
What the fuck? Oh my God.
I'm not supposed to know this, but my great-nan's brother-in-law got killed like that. Ages ago, obvs.
Whaat?
Shit! Who did it?
Dunno. They blamed it on this guy, but it wasn't him. It came out later.

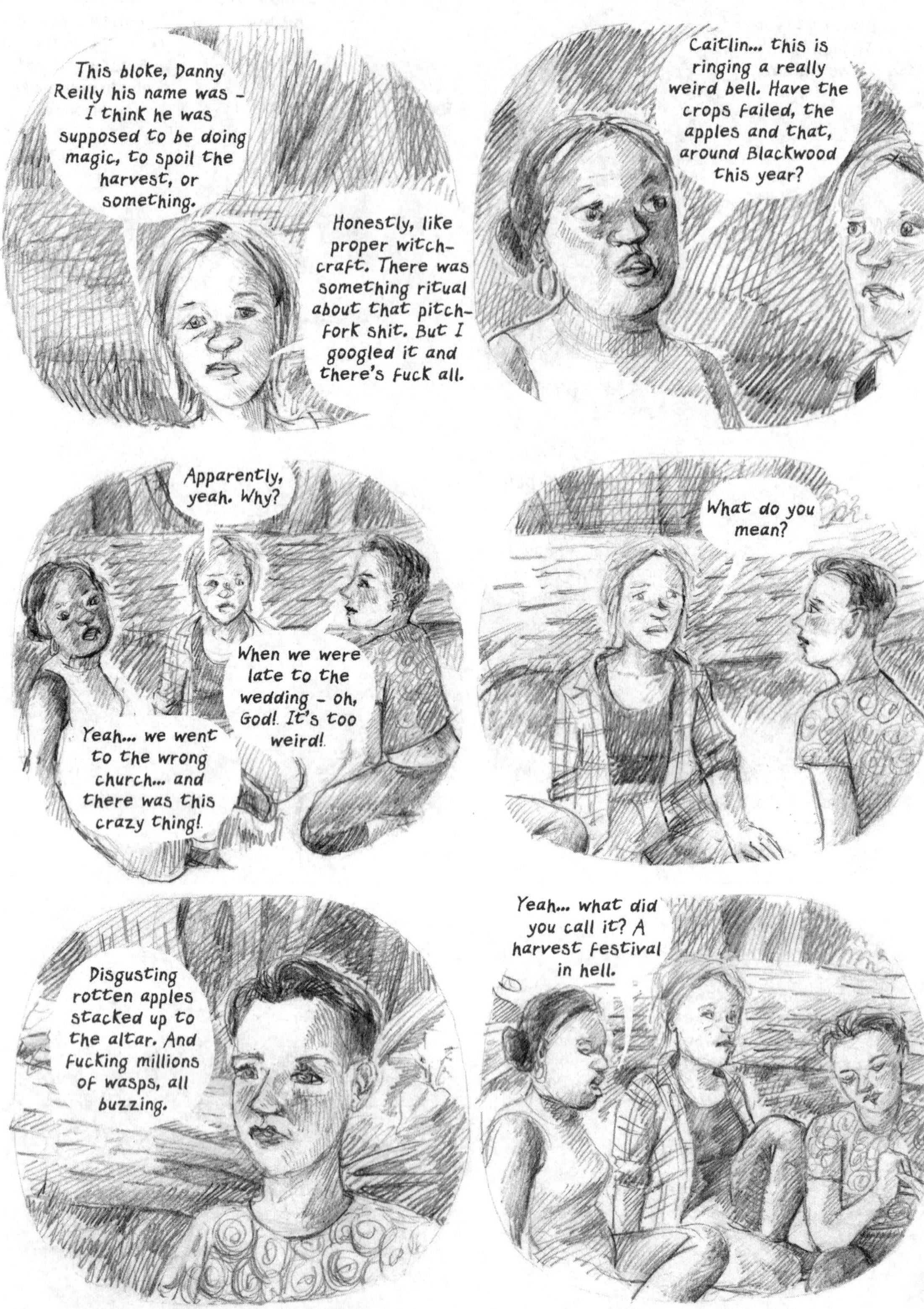
This bloke, Danny Reilly his name was - I think he was supposed to be doing magic, to spoil the harvest, or something.
Honestly, like proper witch-craft. There was something ritual about that pitch-fork shit. But I googled it and there's fuck all.
Caitlin... this is ringing a really weird bell. Have the crops failed, the apples and that, around Blackwood this year?
Apparently, yeah. Why?
When we were late to the wedding - oh, God! It's too weird!
Yeah... we went to the wrong church... and there was this crazy thing!
What do you mean?
Disgusting rotten apples stacked up to the altar. And fucking millions of wasps, all buzzing.
Yeah... what did you call it? A harvest festival in hell.

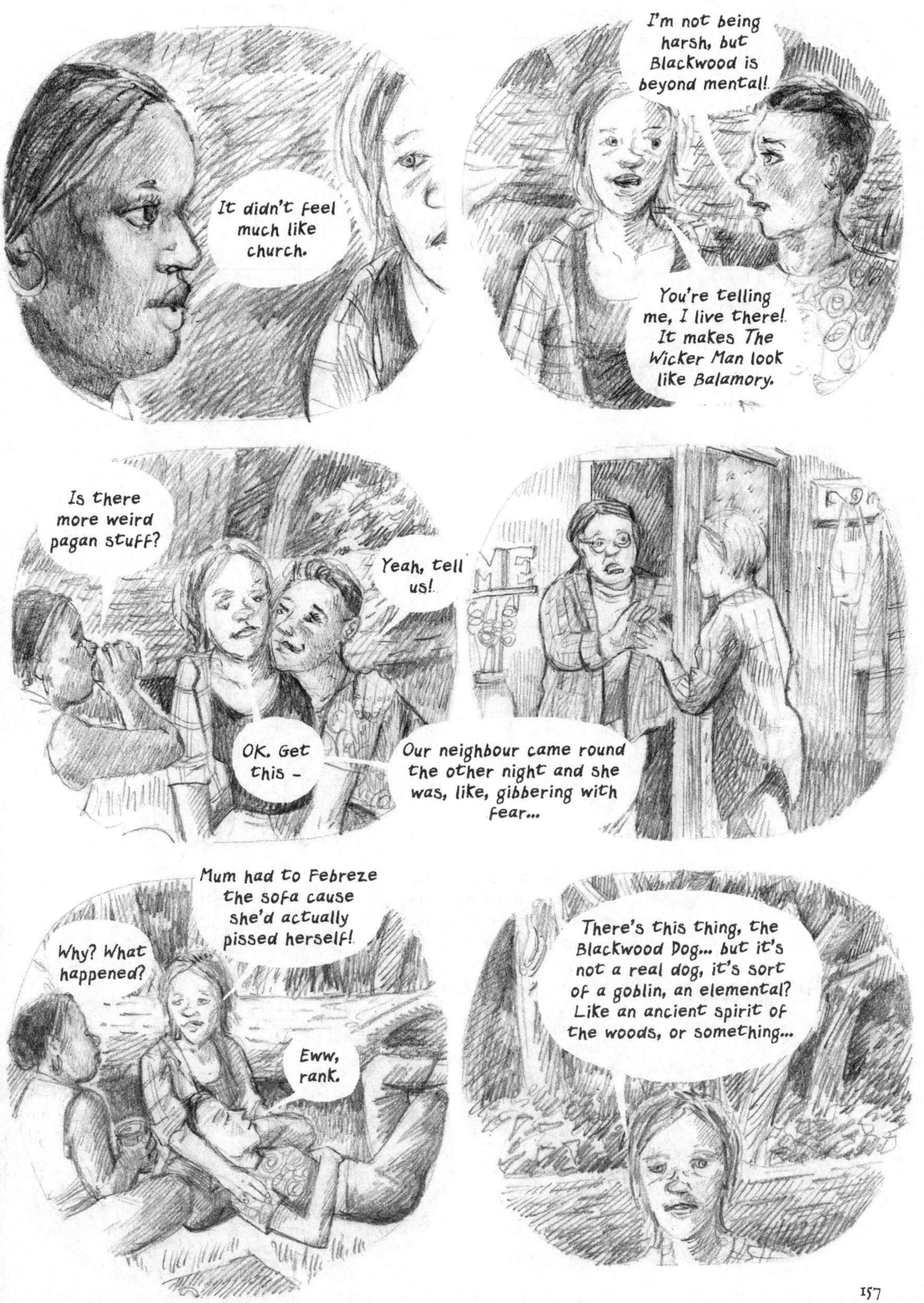
It didn't feel much like church.
I'm not being harsh, but Blackwood is beyond mental!
You're telling me, I live there!. It makes The Wicker Man look like Balamory.
Is there more weird pagan stuff?
Yeah, tell us!.
OK. Get this -
Our neighbour came round the other night and she was, like, gibbering with fear...
Why? What happened?
Mum had to Febreze the sofa cause she'd actually pissed herself!
Eww, rank.
There's this thing, the Blackwood Dog... but it's not a real dog, it's sort of a goblin, an elemental? Like an ancient spirit of the woods, or something...

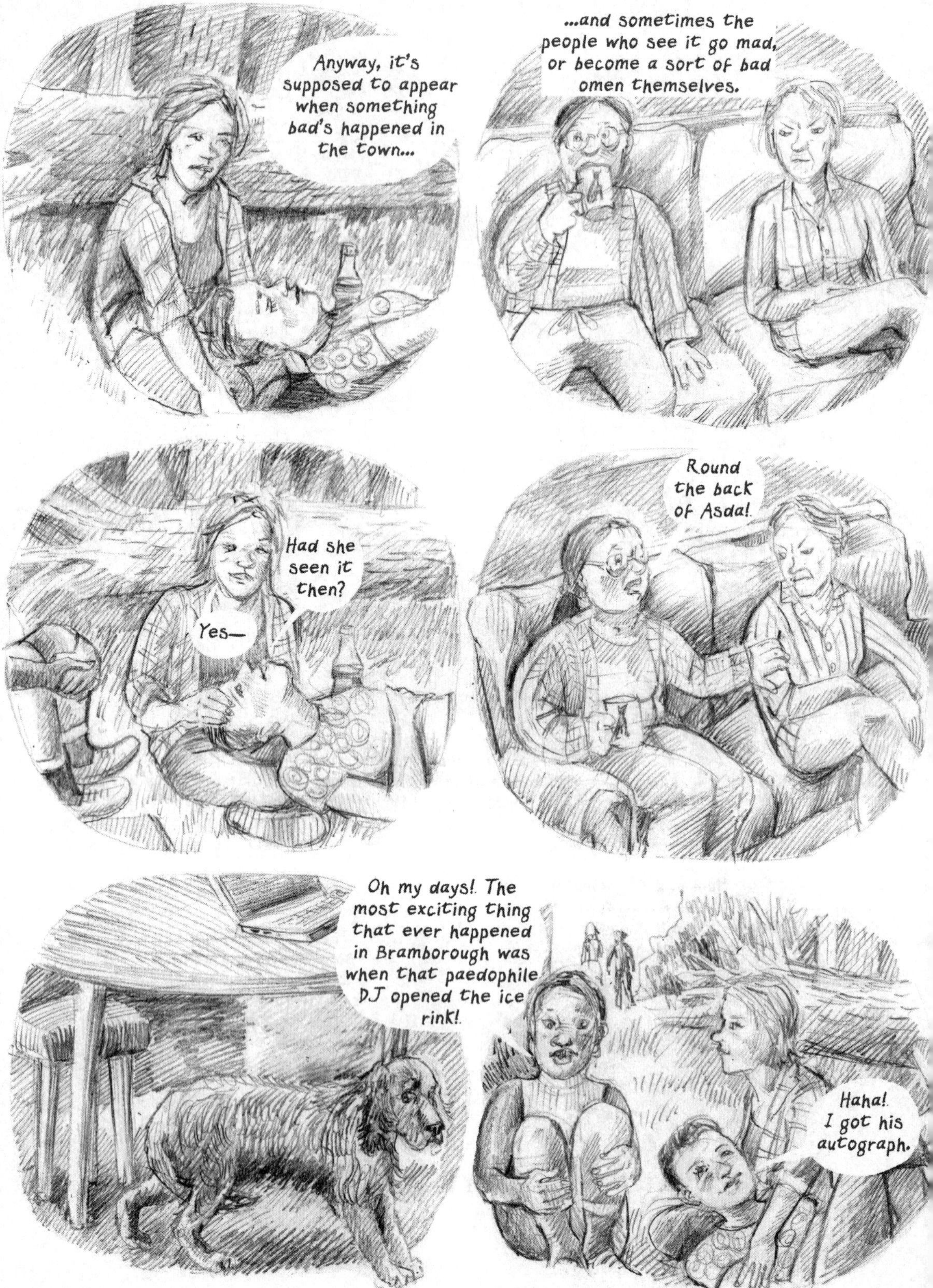

Anyway, it's supposed to appear when something bad's happened in the town...
...and sometimes the people who see it go mad, or become a sort of bad omen themselves.
Had she seen it then?
Yes—
Round the back of Asda!
Oh my days!. The most exciting thing that ever happened in Bramborough was when that paedophile DJ opened the ice rink!.
Haha!. I got his autograph.

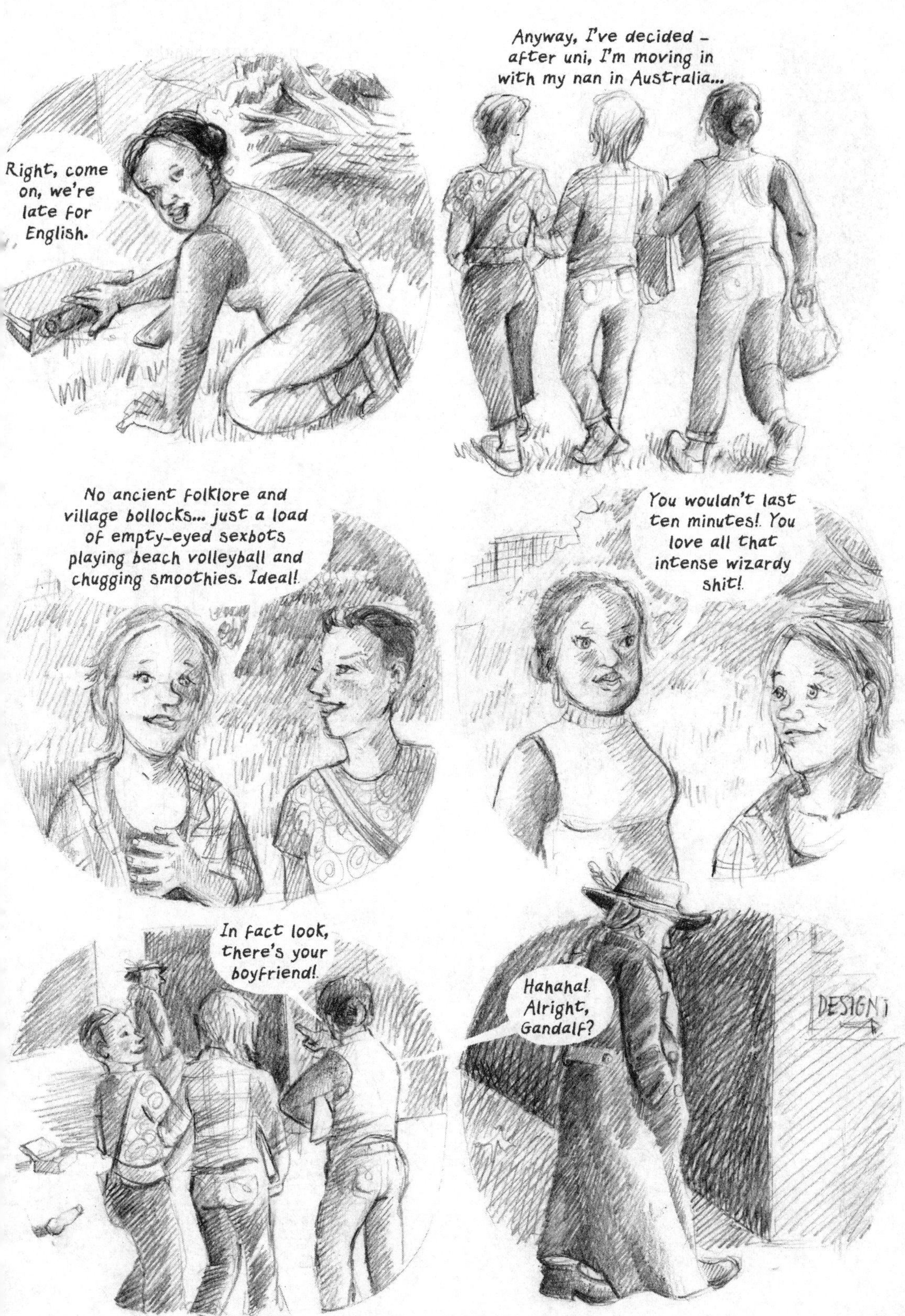
Right, come on, we're late for English.
Anyway, I've decided – after uni, I'm moving in with my nan in Australia...
No ancient folklore and village bollocks... just a load of empty-eyed sexbots playing beach volleyball and chugging smoothies. Ideal!
You wouldn't last ten minutes!. You love all that intense wizardy shit!.
In fact look, there's your boyfriend!.
Hahaha!. Alright, Gandalf?
DESIGN

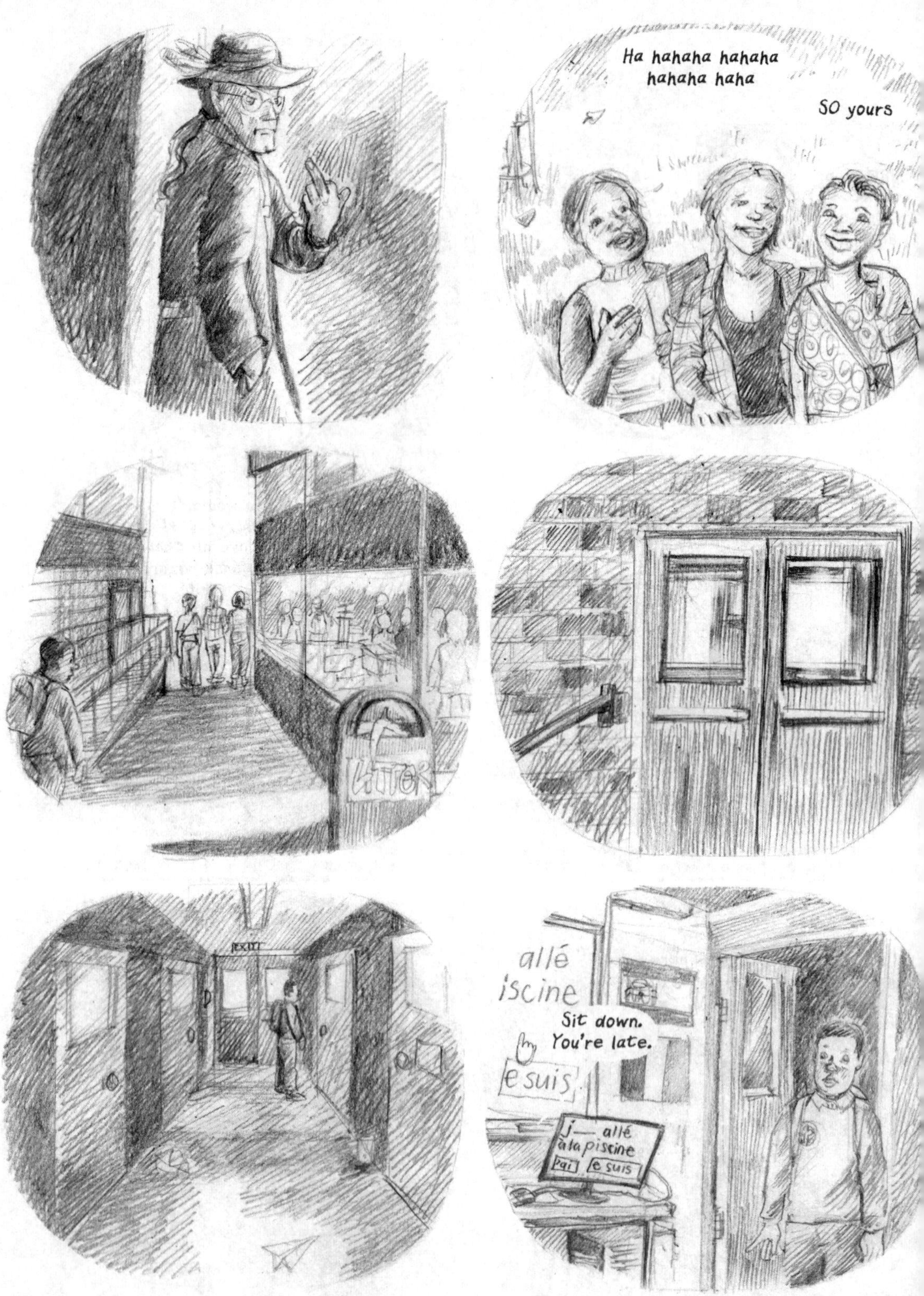
Ha hahaha hahaha
hahaha haha
SO yours
LITTER
EXIT
allé
iscine
Sit down.
You're late.
e suis
j— allé
à la piscine
'ai
e suis

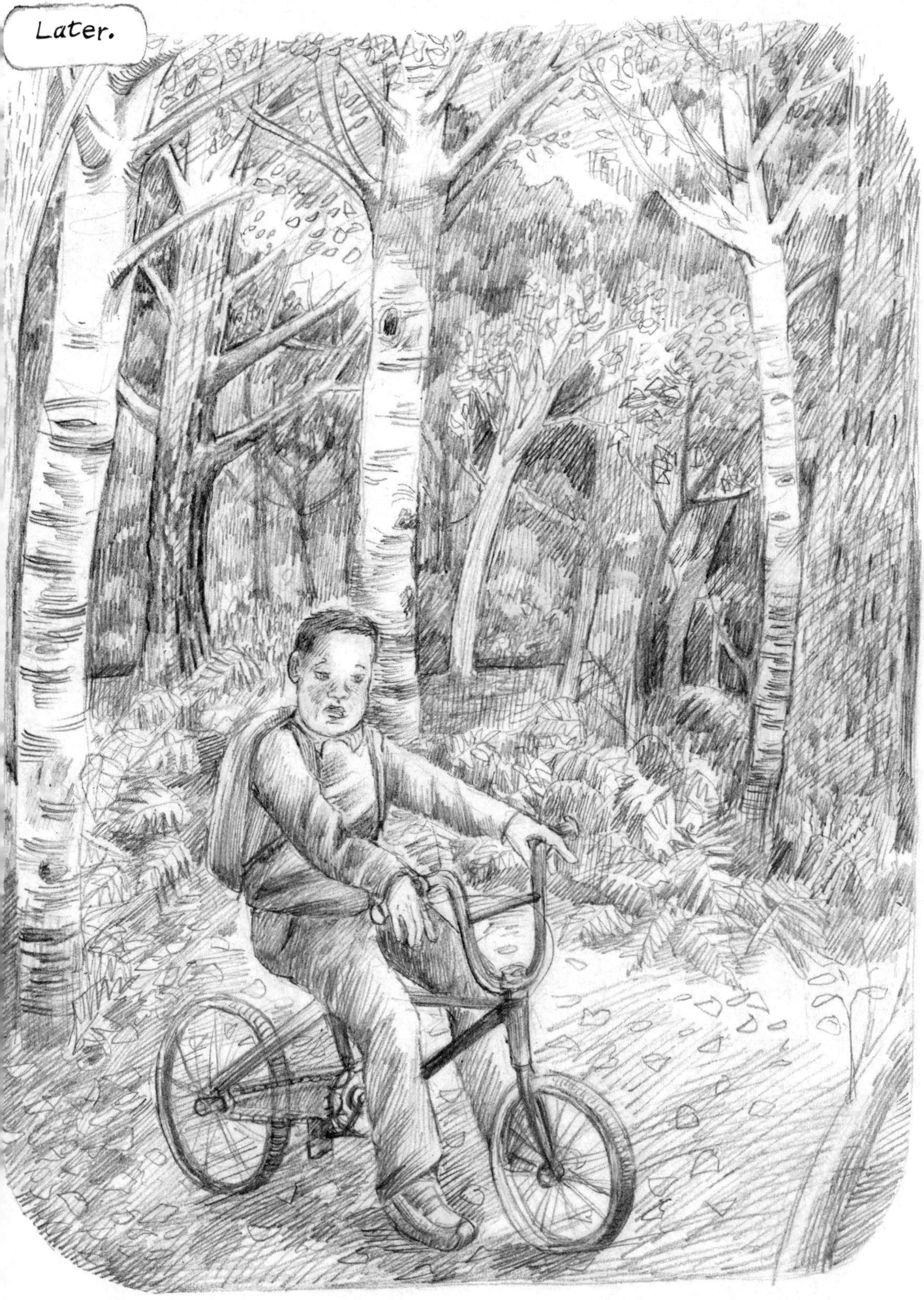
Later.

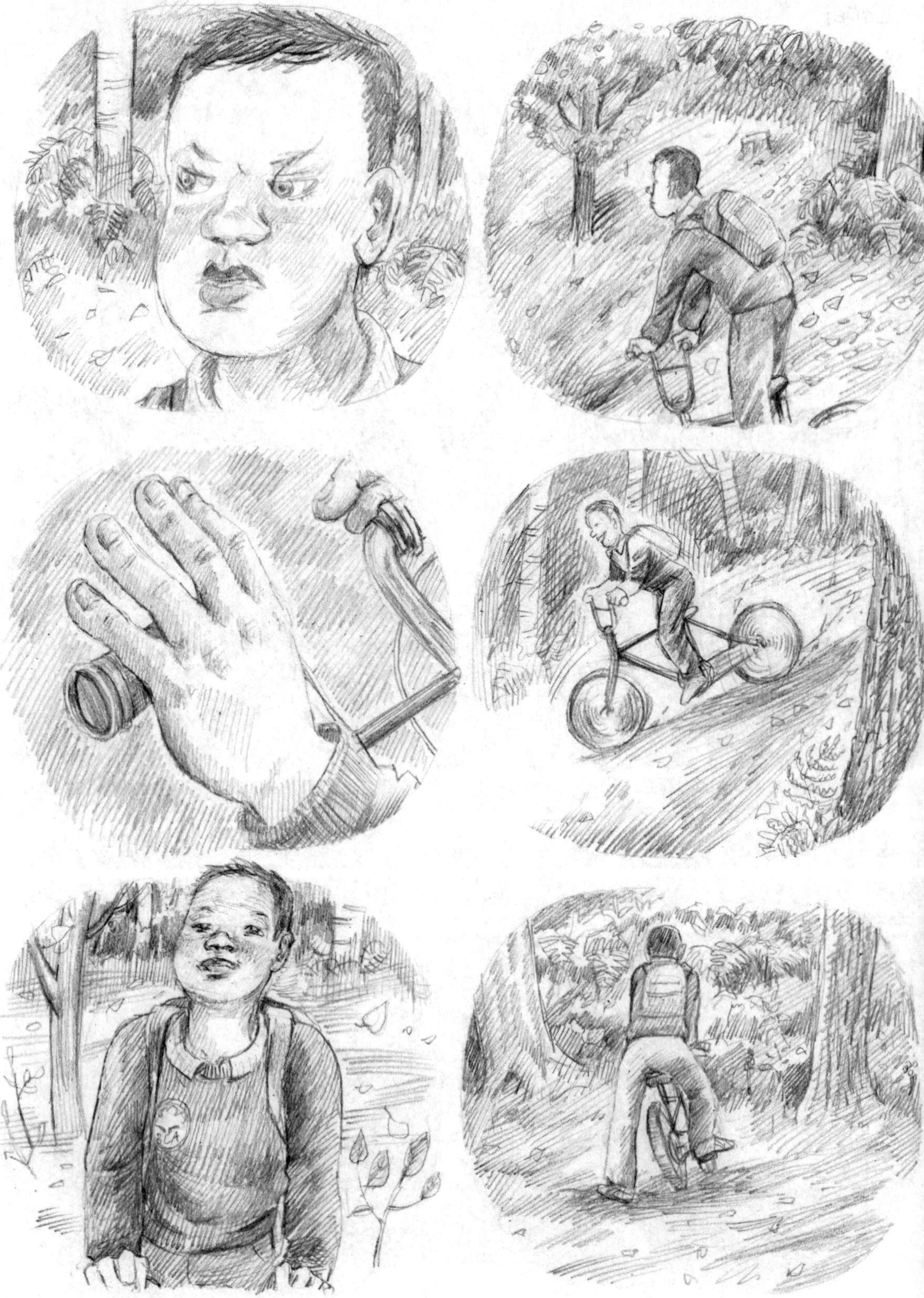

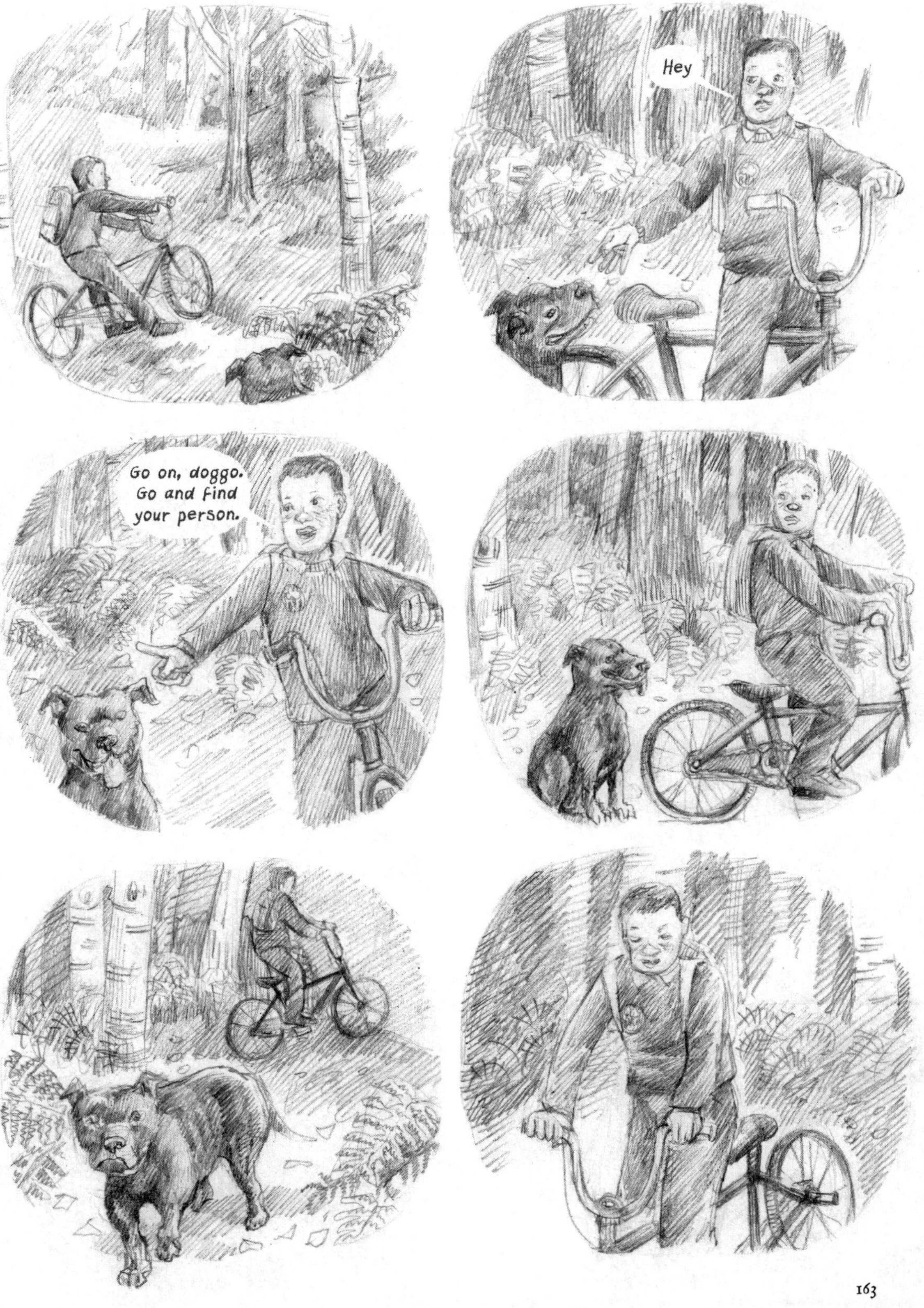
Hey
Go on, doggo. Go and find your person.

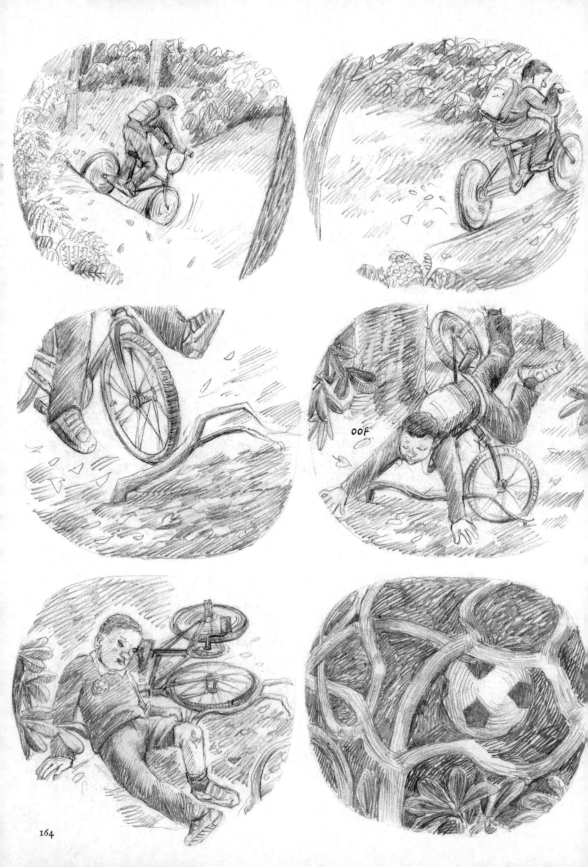

OOF

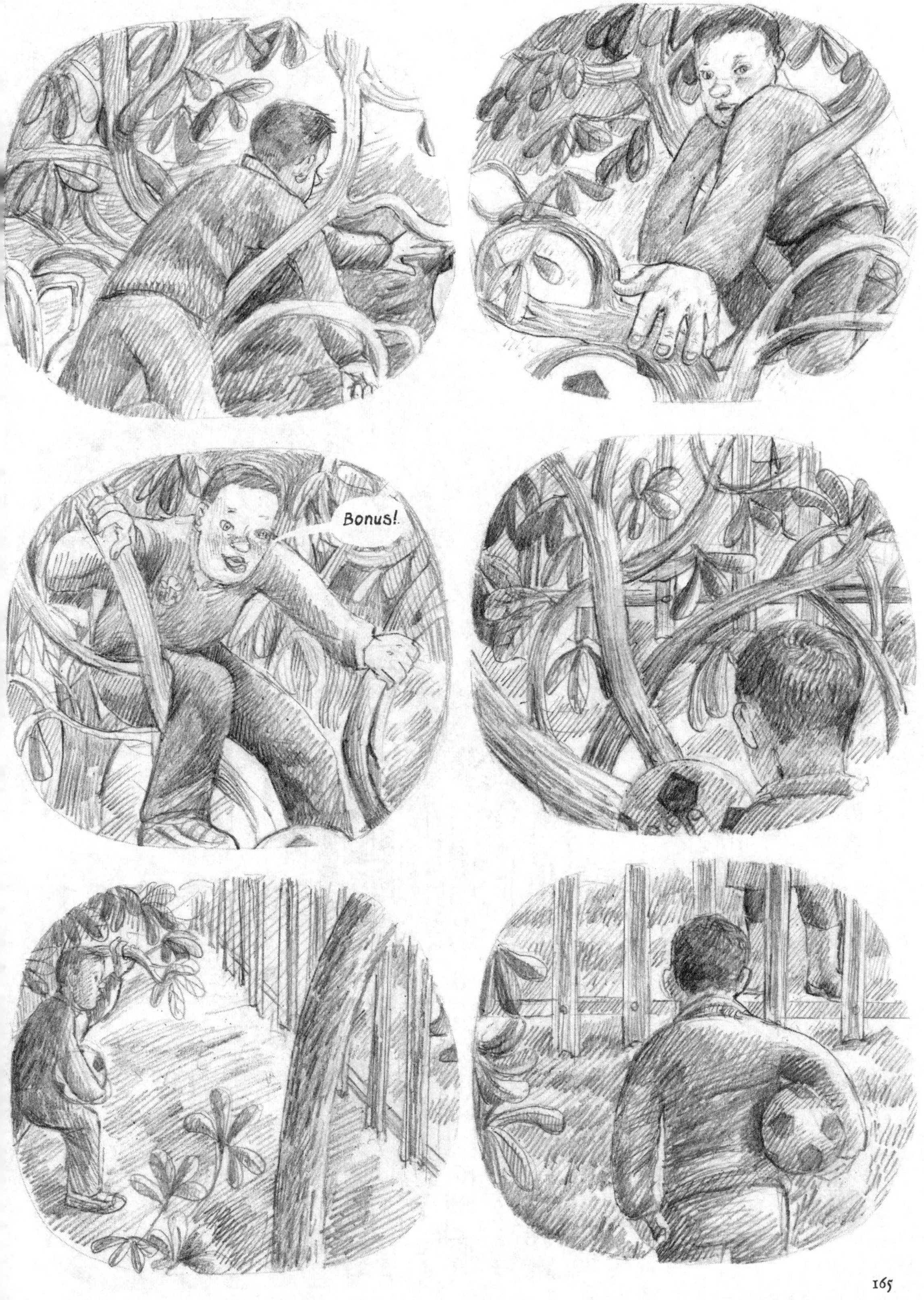
Bonus!

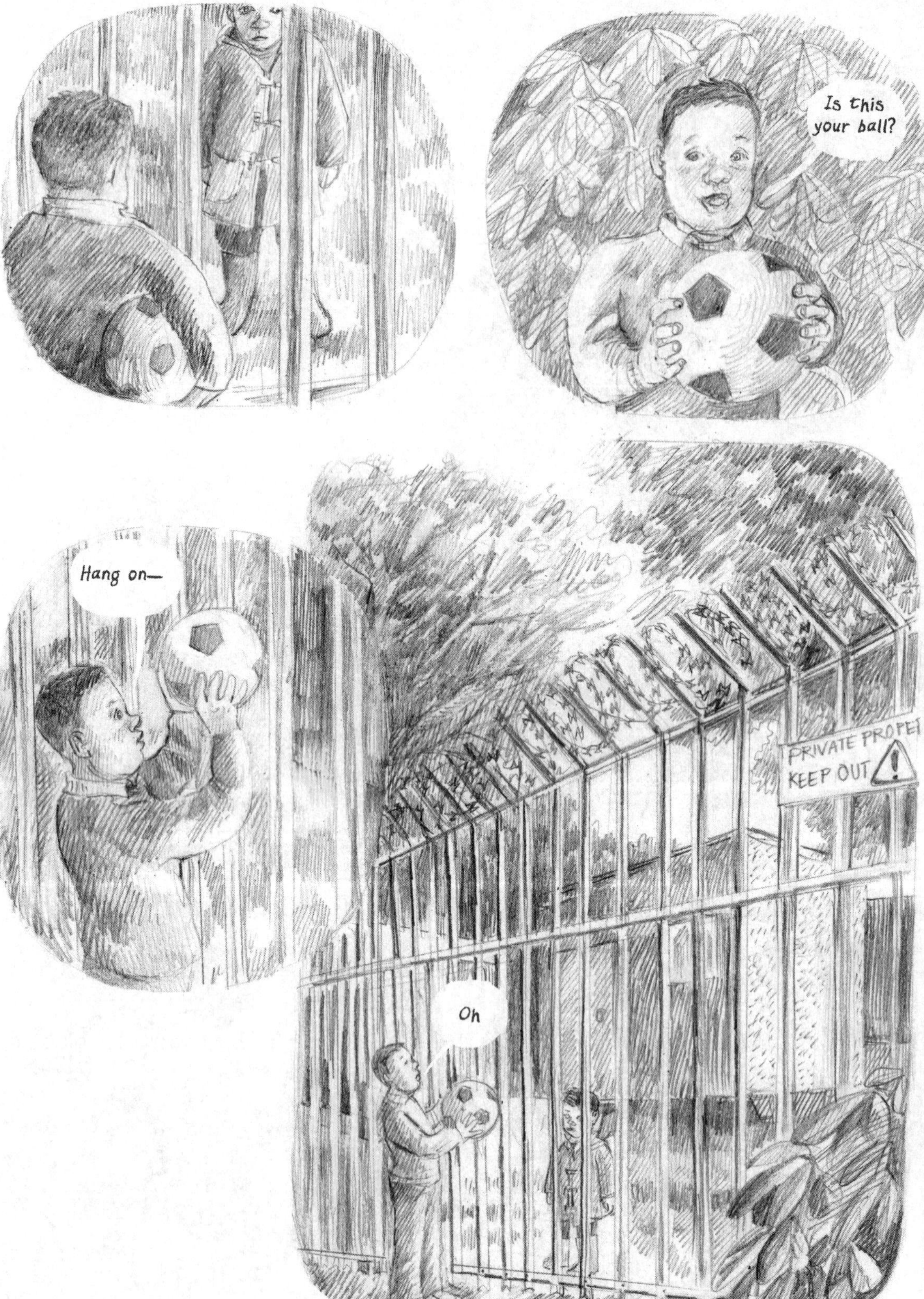

Is this your ball?
Hang on—
PRIVATE PROPE
KEEP OUT
Oh

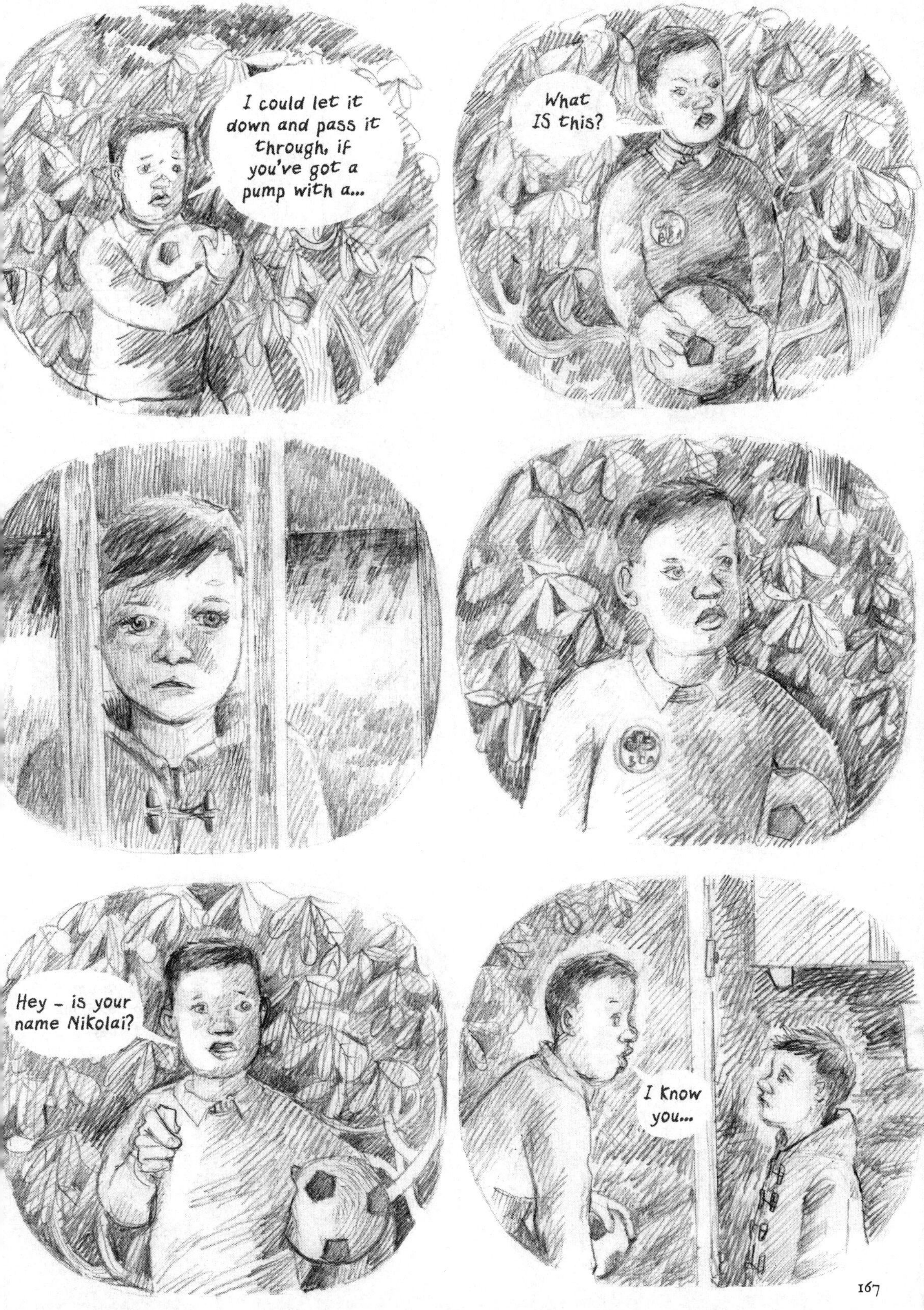
I could let it down and pass it through, if you've got a pump with a...
What IS this?
Hey - is your name Nikolai?
I know you...

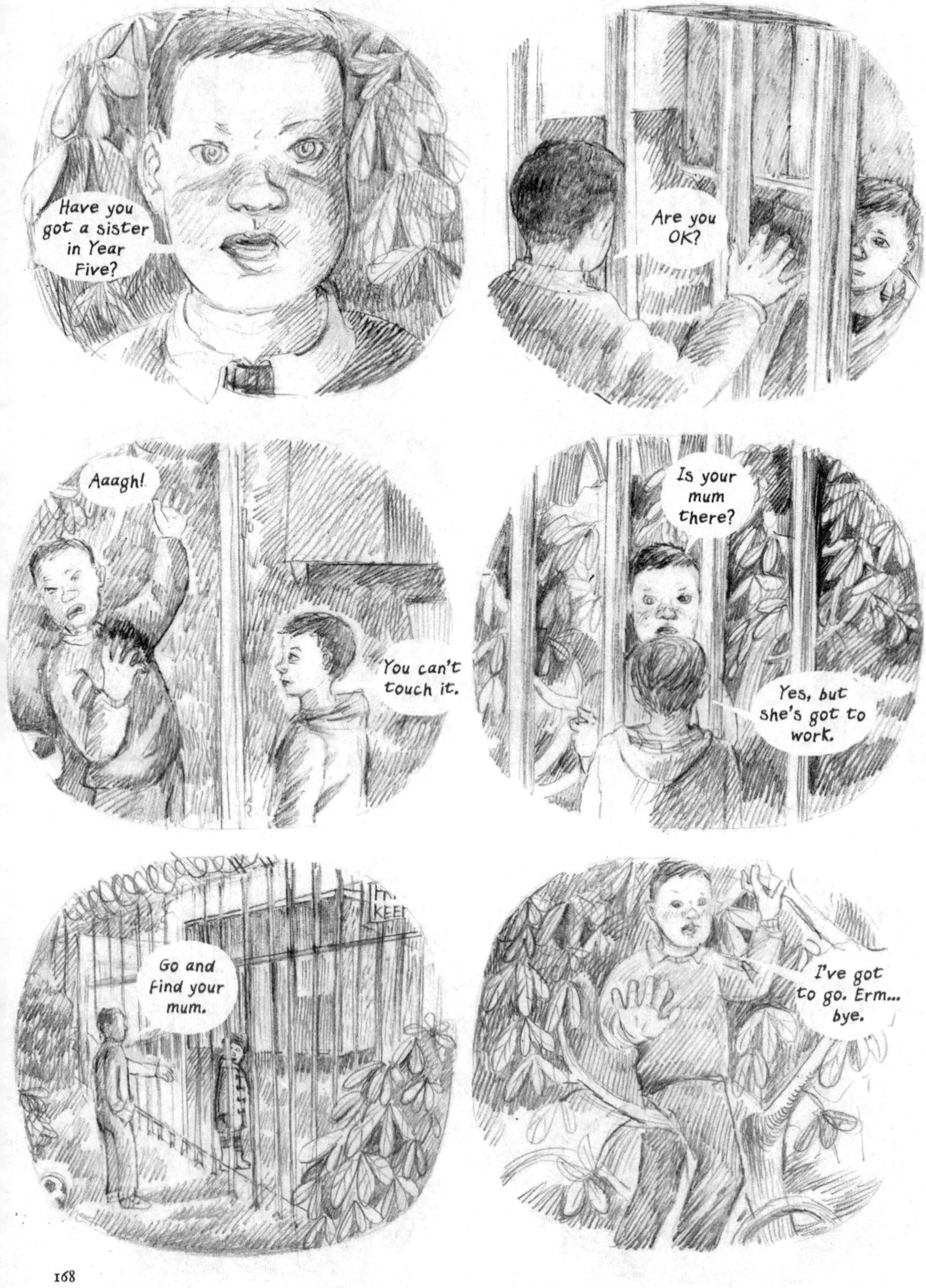
Have you got a sister in Year Five?
Are you OK?
Aaagh!
You can't touch it.
Is your mum there?
Yes, but she's got to work.
Go and find your mum.
I've got to go. Erm... bye.

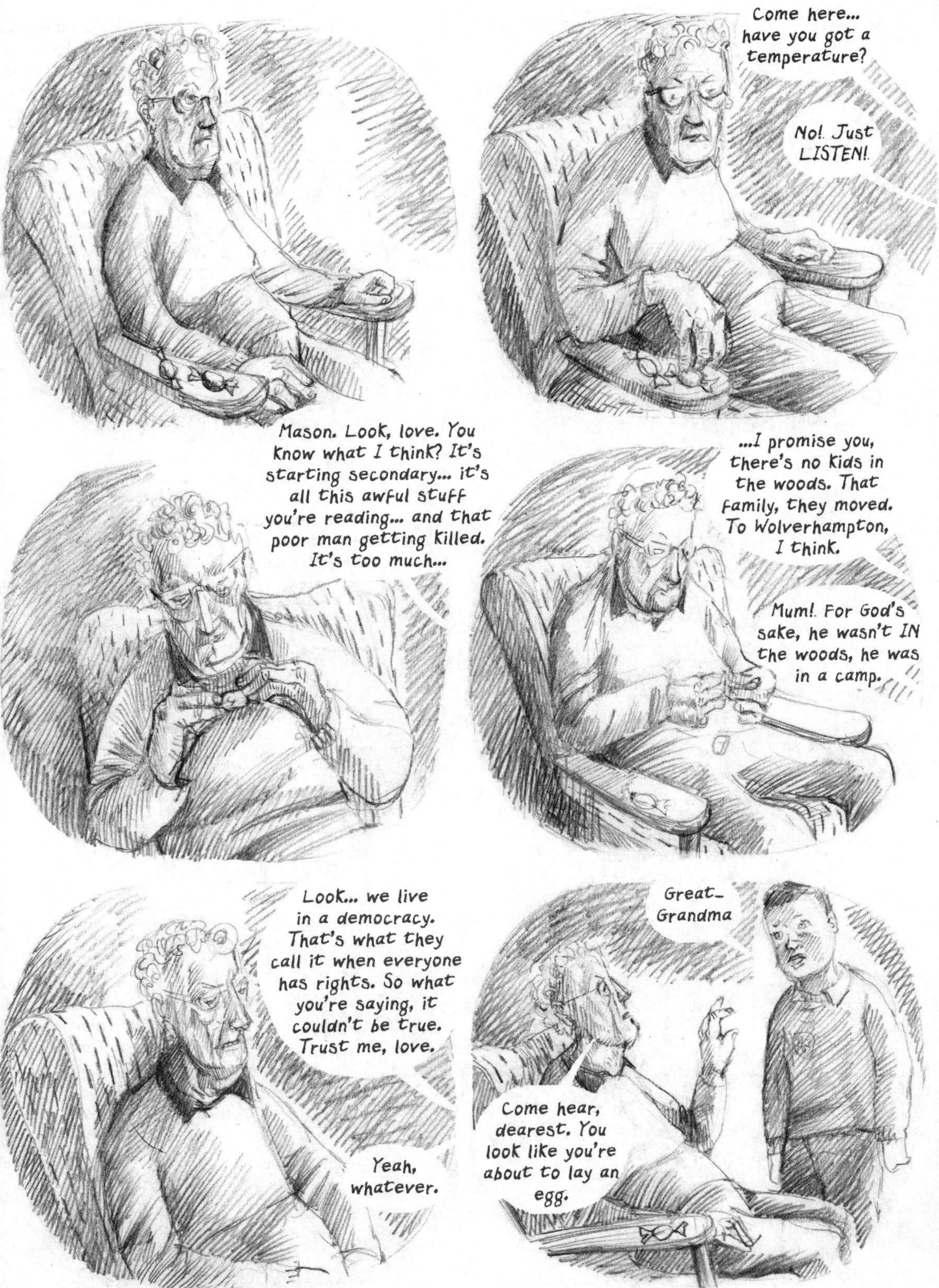
Come here... have you got a temperature?
No!. Just LISTEN!.
Mason. Look, love. You know what I think? It's starting secondary... it's all this awful stuff you're reading... and that poor man getting killed. It's too much...
...I promise you, there's no kids in the woods. That family, they moved. To Wolverhampton, I think.
Mum!. For God's sake, he wasn't IN the woods, he was in a camp.
Look... we live in a democracy. That's what they call it when everyone has rights. So what you're saying, it couldn't be true. Trust me, love.
Yeah, whatever.
Great_ Grandma
Come hear, dearest. You look like you're about to lay an egg.

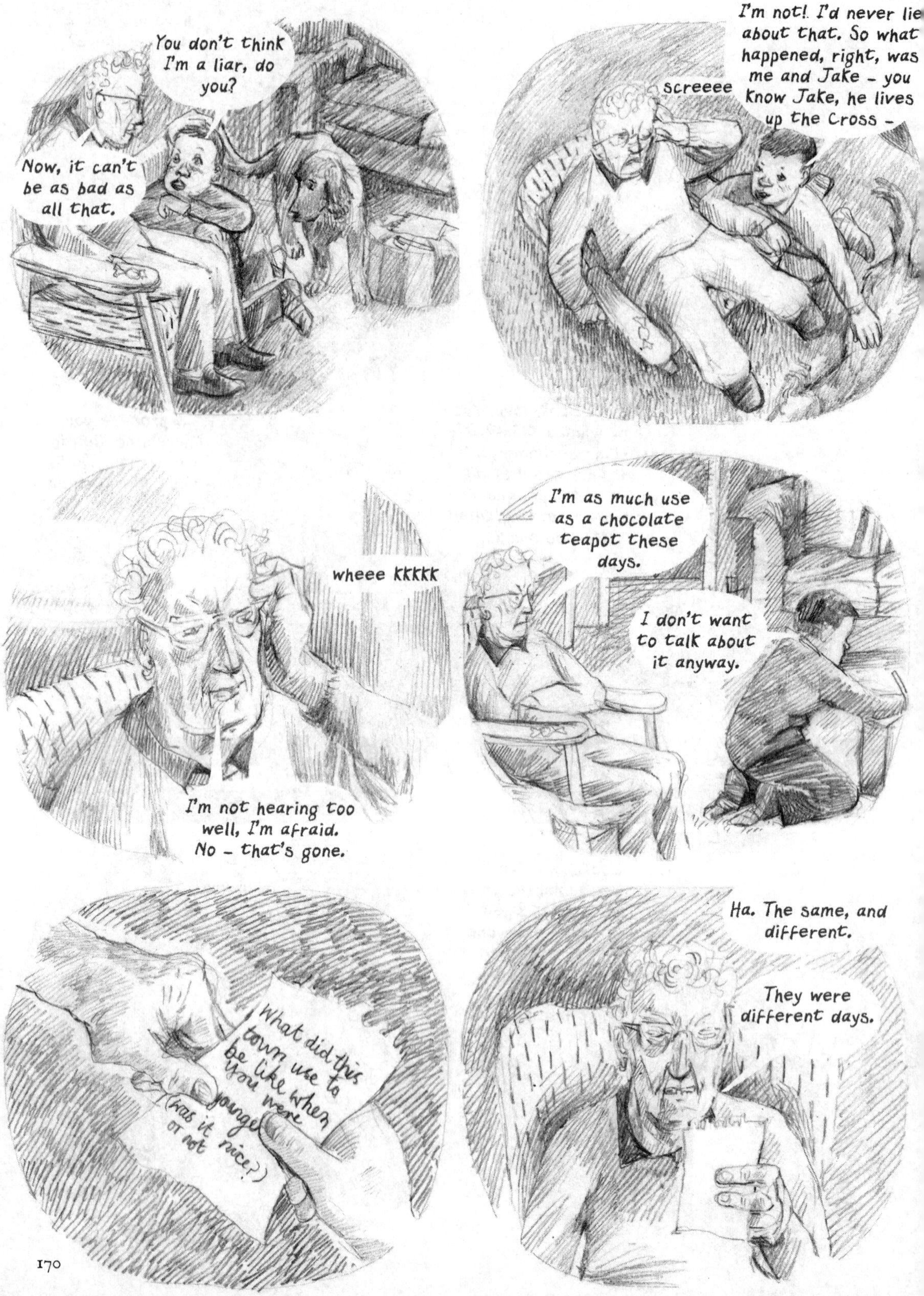
You don't think I'm a liar, do you?
Now, it can't be as bad as all that.
I'm not! I'd never lie about that. So what happened, right, was me and Jake - you know Jake, he lives up the Cross -
screeee
wheee kkkkk
I'm not hearing too well, I'm afraid. No - that's gone.
I'm as much use as a chocolate teapot these days.
I don't want to talk about it anyway.
What did this town use to be like when you were younger
(was it
or not
nice?)
Ha. The same, and different.
They were different days.

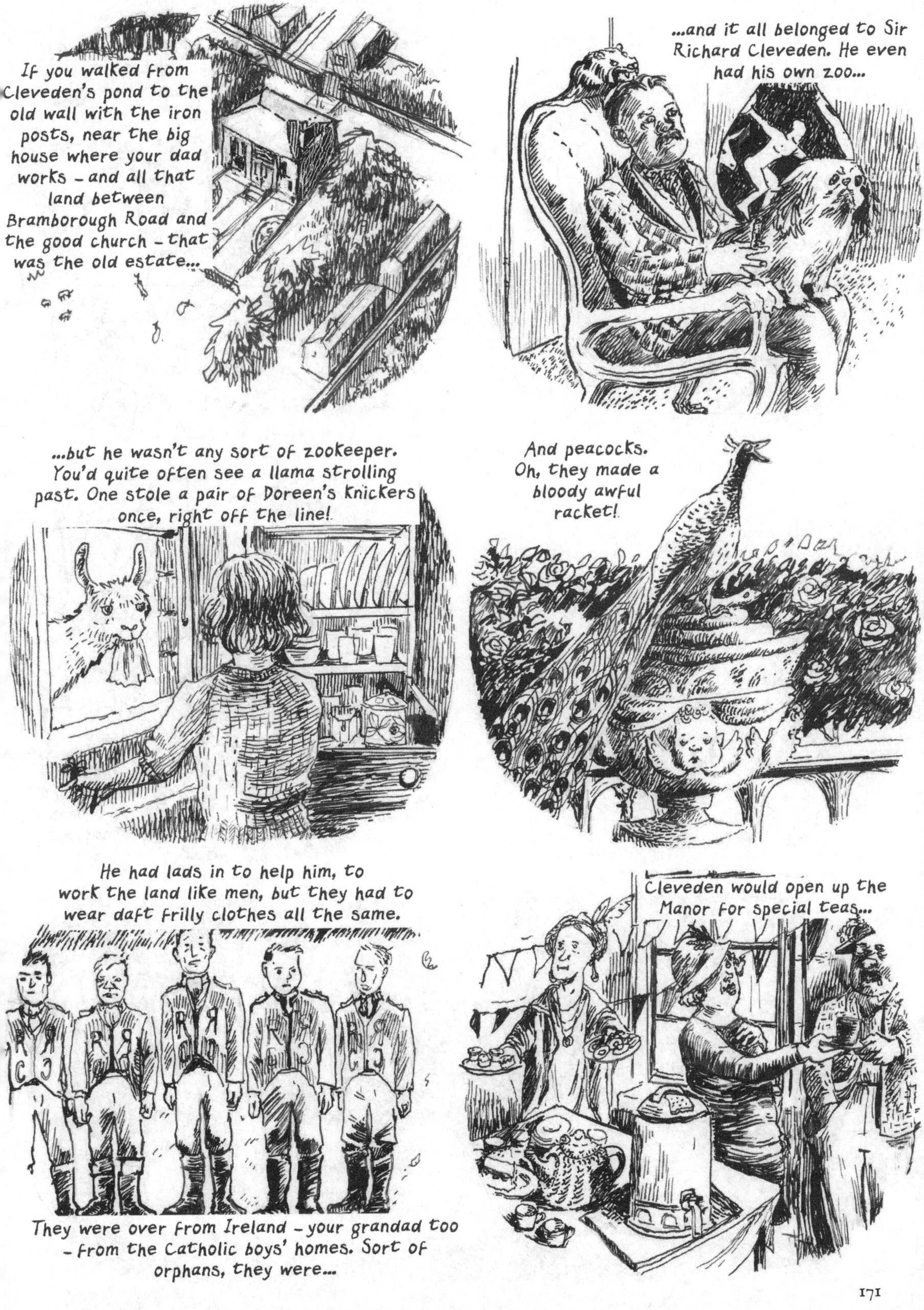
If you walked from Cleveden's pond to the old wall with the iron posts, near the big house where your dad works – and all that land between Bramborough Road and the good church – that was the old estate...
...and it all belonged to Sir Richard Cleveden. He even had his own zoo...
...but he wasn't any sort of zookeeper. You'd quite often see a llama strolling past. One stole a pair of Doreen's knickers once, right off the line!
And peacocks. Oh, they made a bloody awful racket!
He had lads in to help him, to work the land like men, but they had to wear daft frilly clothes all the same.
They were over from Ireland – your grandad too – from the Catholic boys' homes. Sort of orphans, they were...
Cleveden would open up the Manor for special teas...

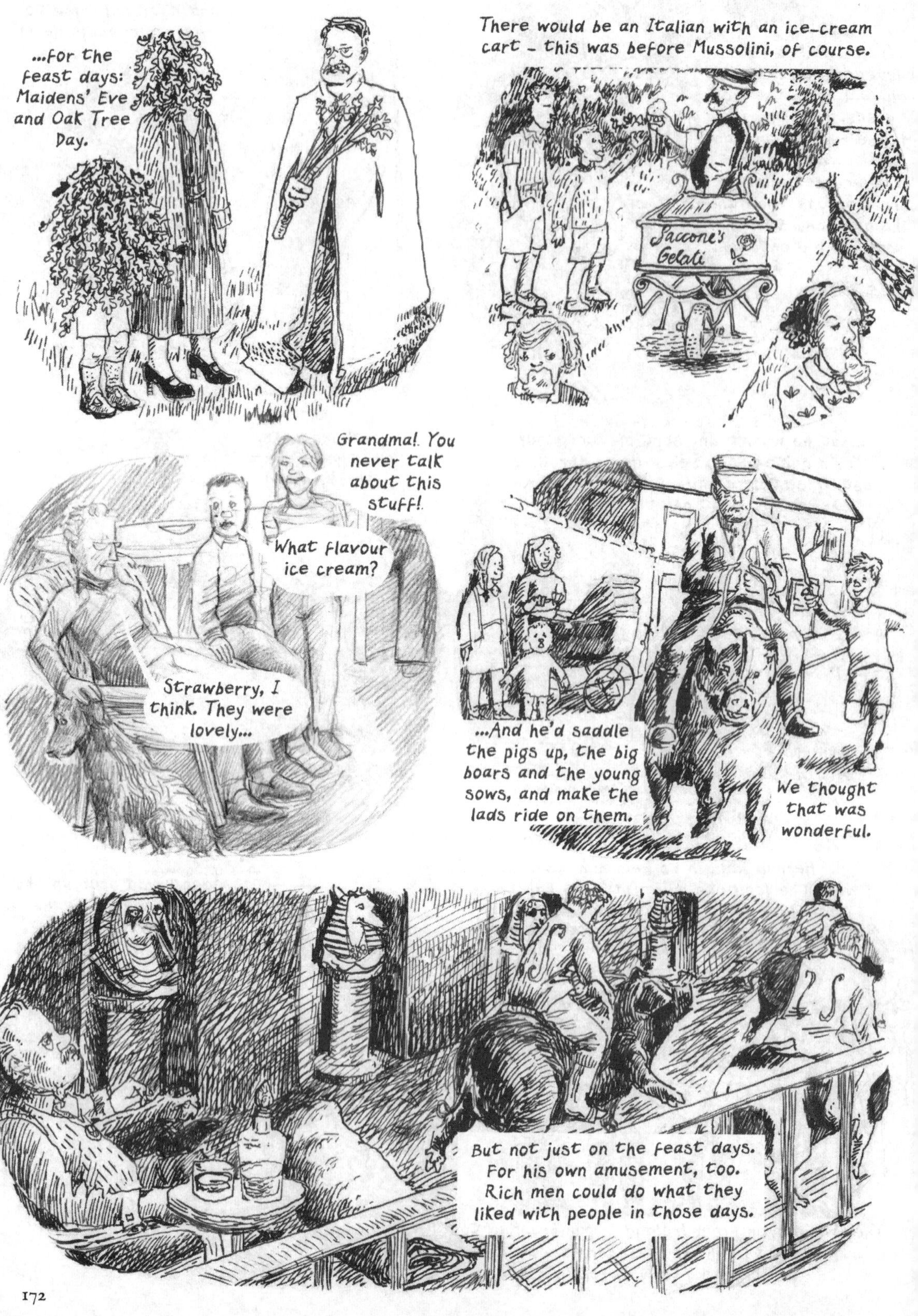
...for the feast days: Maidens' Eve and Oak Tree Day.
There would be an Italian with an ice-cream cart – this was before Mussolini, of course.
Saccone's Gelati
Grandma! You never talk about this stuff!
What flavour ice cream?
Strawberry, I think. They were lovely...
...And he'd saddle the pigs up, the big boars and the young sows, and make the lads ride on them.
We thought that was wonderful.
But not just on the feast days. For his own amusement, too. Rich men could do what they liked with people in those days.

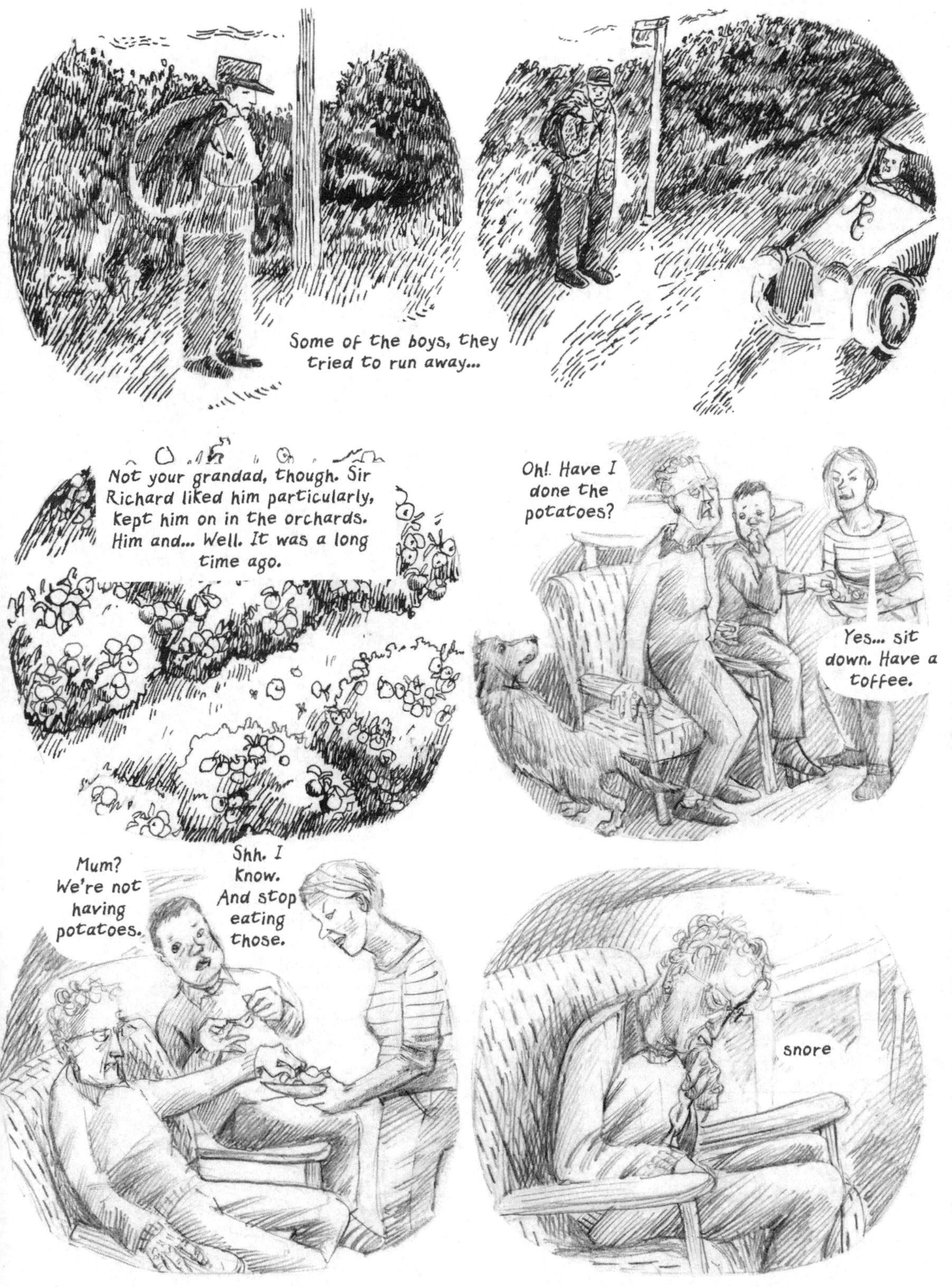
Some of the boys, they tried to run away...
Not your grandad, though. Sir Richard liked him particularly, kept him on in the orchards. Him and... Well. It was a long time ago.
Oh!. Have I done the potatoes?
Yes... sit down. Have a toffee.
Mum? We're not having potatoes.
Shh. I know. And stop eating those.
snore

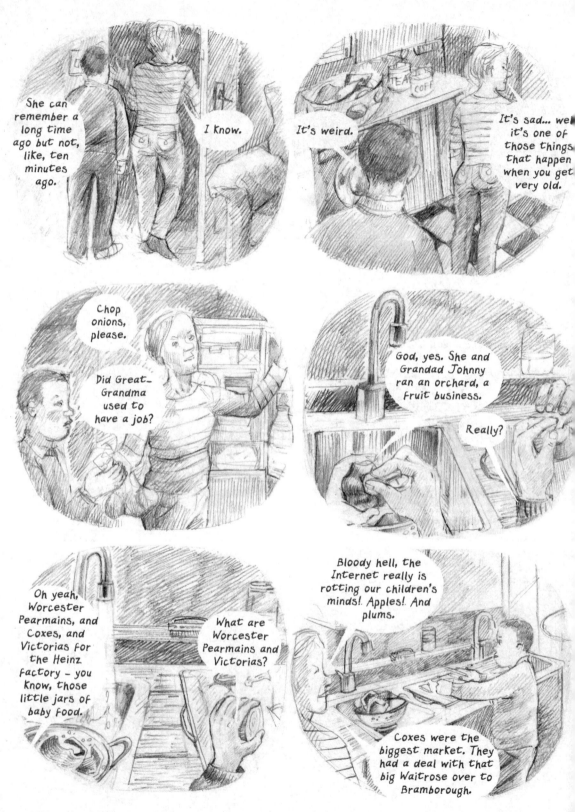

She can remember a long time ago but not, like, ten minutes ago.

I know.

It's weird.

It's sad... well it's one of those things that happen when you get very old.

Chop onions, please.

Did Great-Grandma used to have a job?

God, yes. She and Grandad Johnny ran an orchard, a fruit business.

Really?

Oh yeah, Worcester Pearmains, and Coxes, and Victorias for the Heinz factory - you know, those little jars of baby food.

What are Worcester Pearmains and Victorias?

Bloody hell, the Internet really is rotting our children's minds! Apples! And plums.

Coxes were the biggest market. They had a deal with that big Waitrose over to Bramborough.

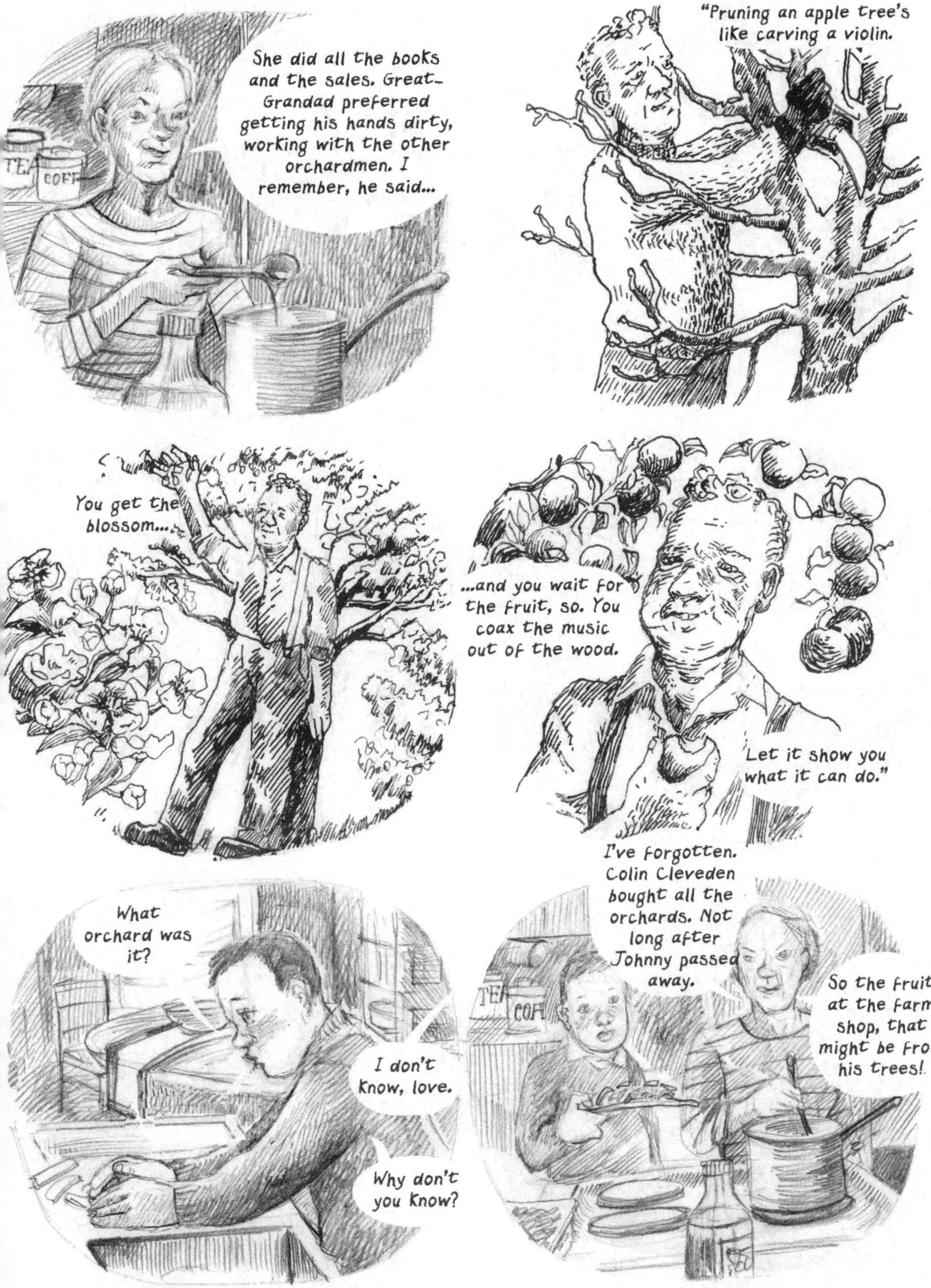

She did all the books and the sales. Great-Grandad preferred getting his hands dirty, working with the other orchardmen. I remember, he said...
"Pruning an apple tree's like carving a violin.
You get the blossom...
...and you wait for the fruit, so. You coax the music out of the wood.
Let it show you what it can do."
What orchard was it?
I don't know, love.
Why don't you know?
I've forgotten. Colin Cleveden bought all the orchards. Not long after Johnny passed away.
So the fruit at the farm shop, that might be from his trees!

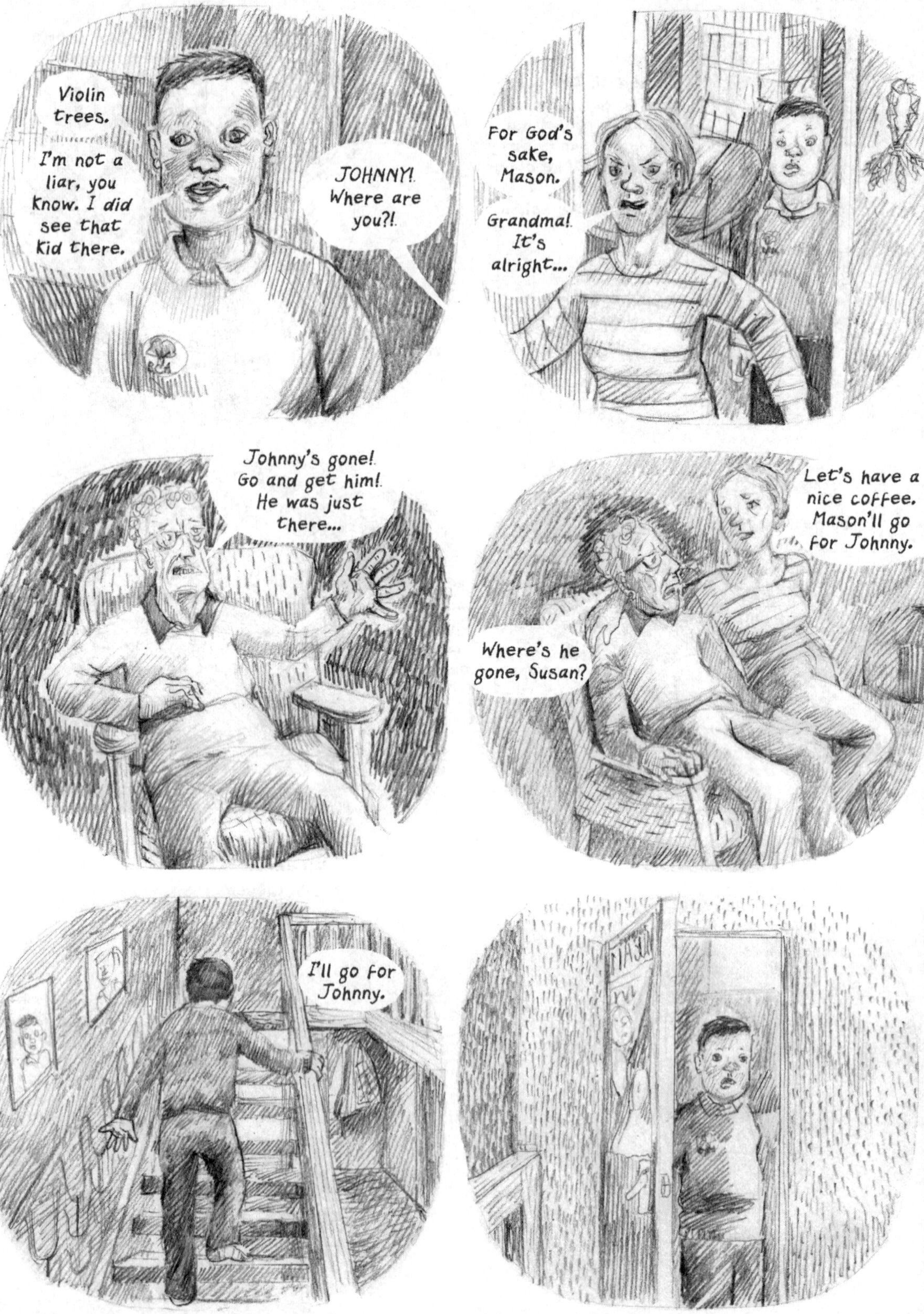
Violin trees.
I'm not a liar, you know. I did see that kid there.
JOHNNY!. Where are you?!.
For God's sake, Mason.
Grandma!. It's alright...
Johnny's gone!. Go and get him!. He was just there...
Let's have a nice coffee. Mason'll go for Johnny.
Where's he gone, Susan?
I'll go for Johnny.

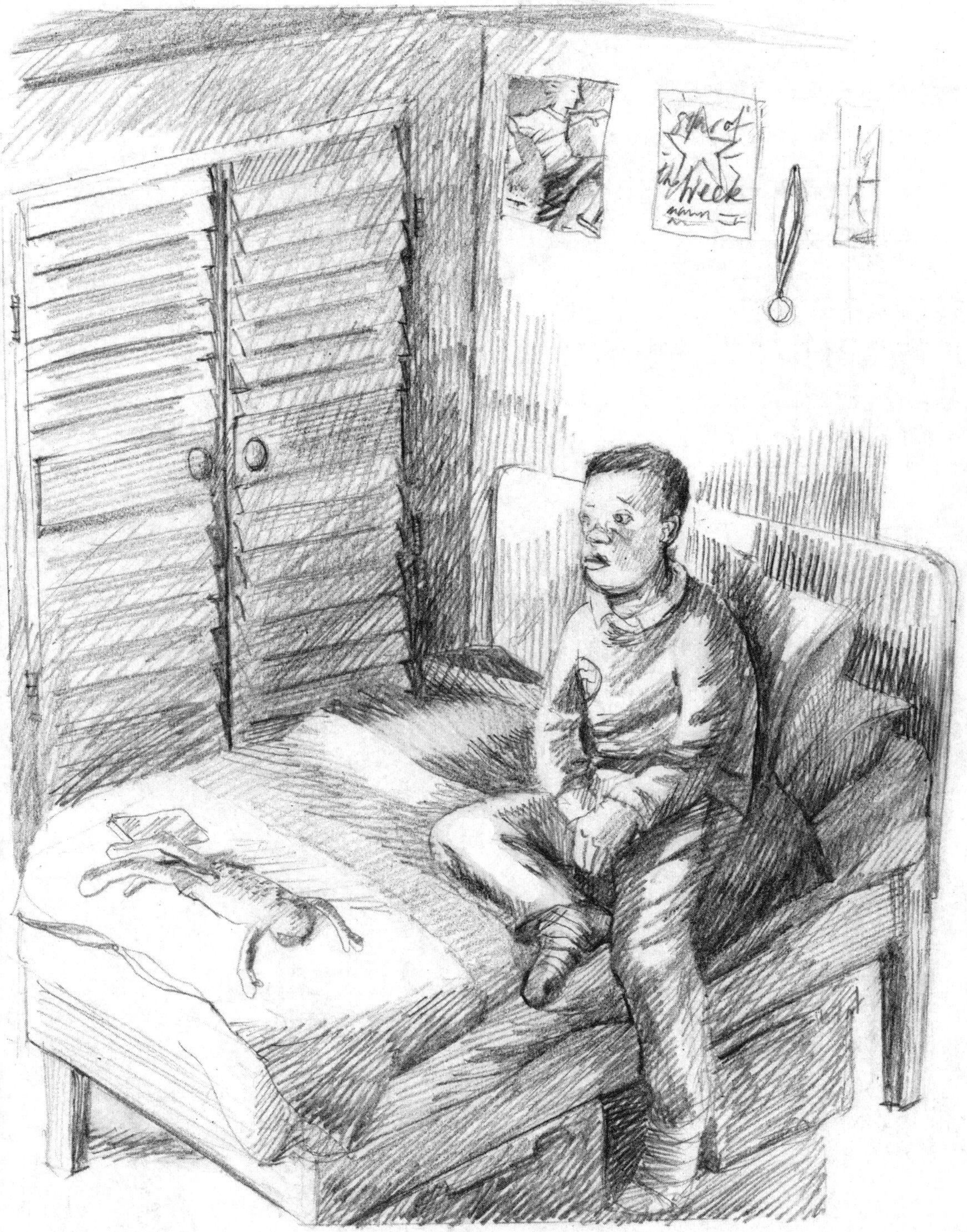

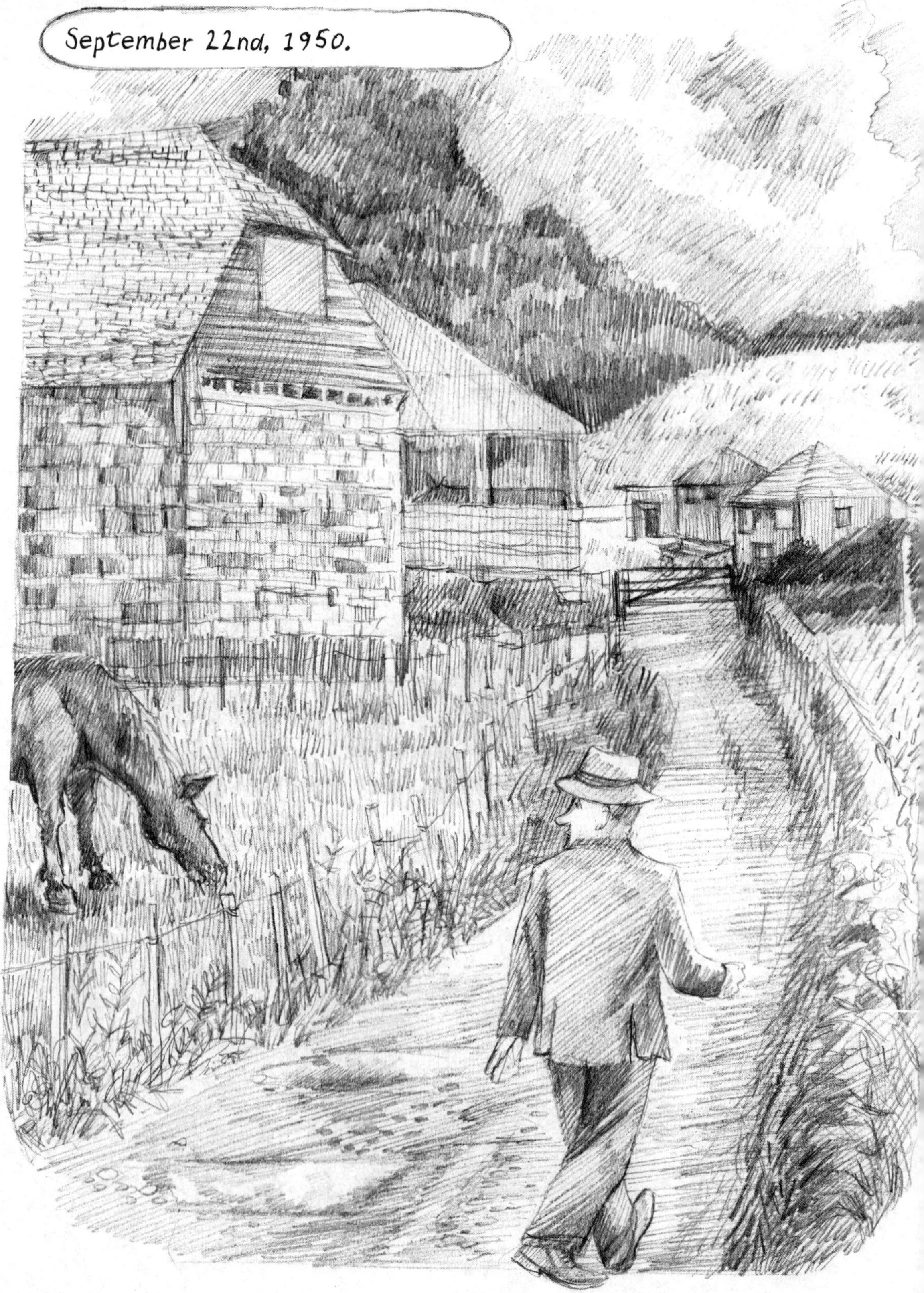
September 22nd, 1950.

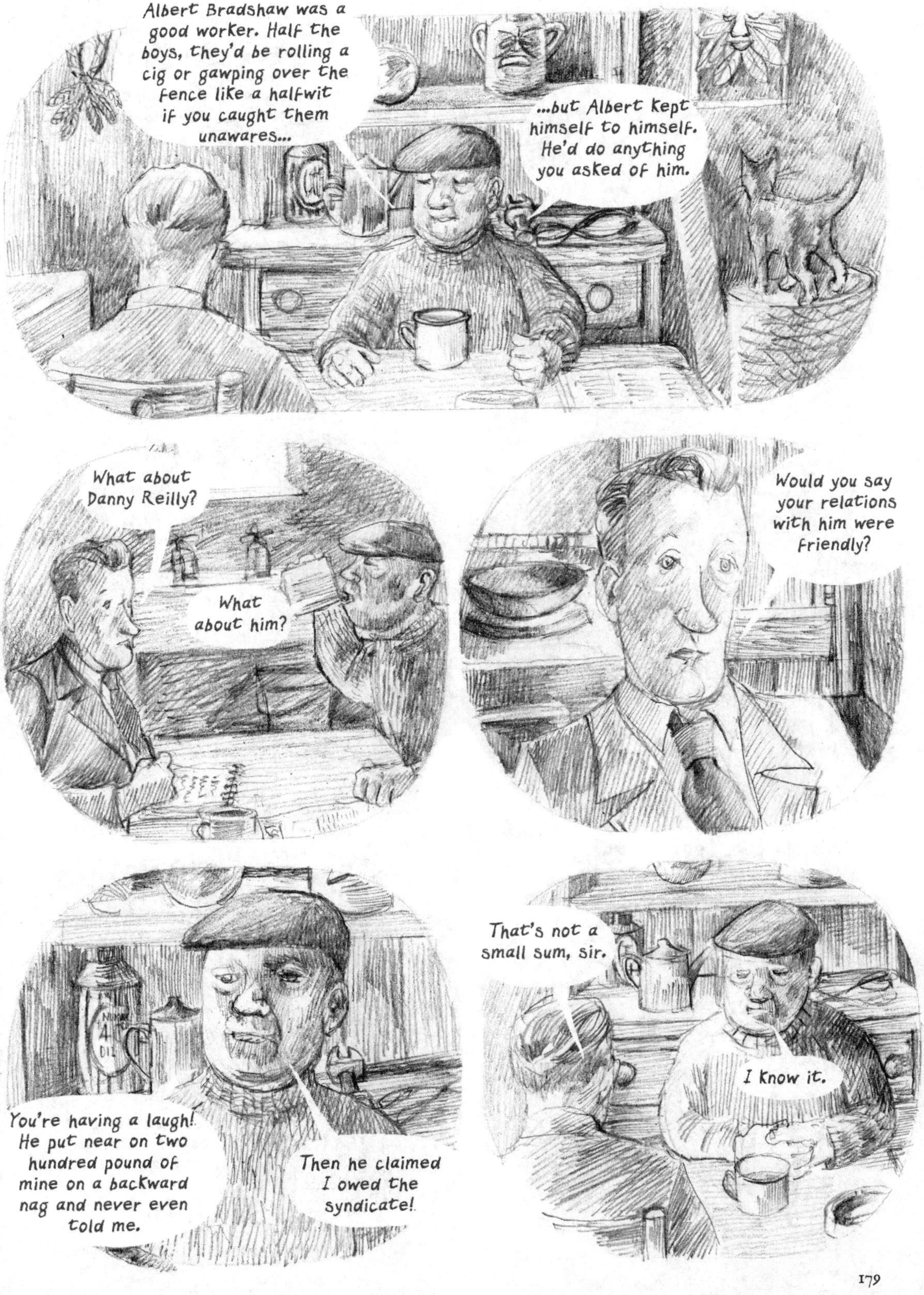
Albert Bradshaw was a good worker. Half the boys, they'd be rolling a cig or gawping over the fence like a halfwit if you caught them unawares...
...but Albert kept himself to himself. He'd do anything you asked of him.
What about Danny Reilly?
What about him?
Would you say your relations with him were friendly?
You're having a laugh! He put near on two hundred pound of mine on a backward nag and never even told me.
Then he claimed I owed the syndicate!
That's not a small sum, sir.
I know it.

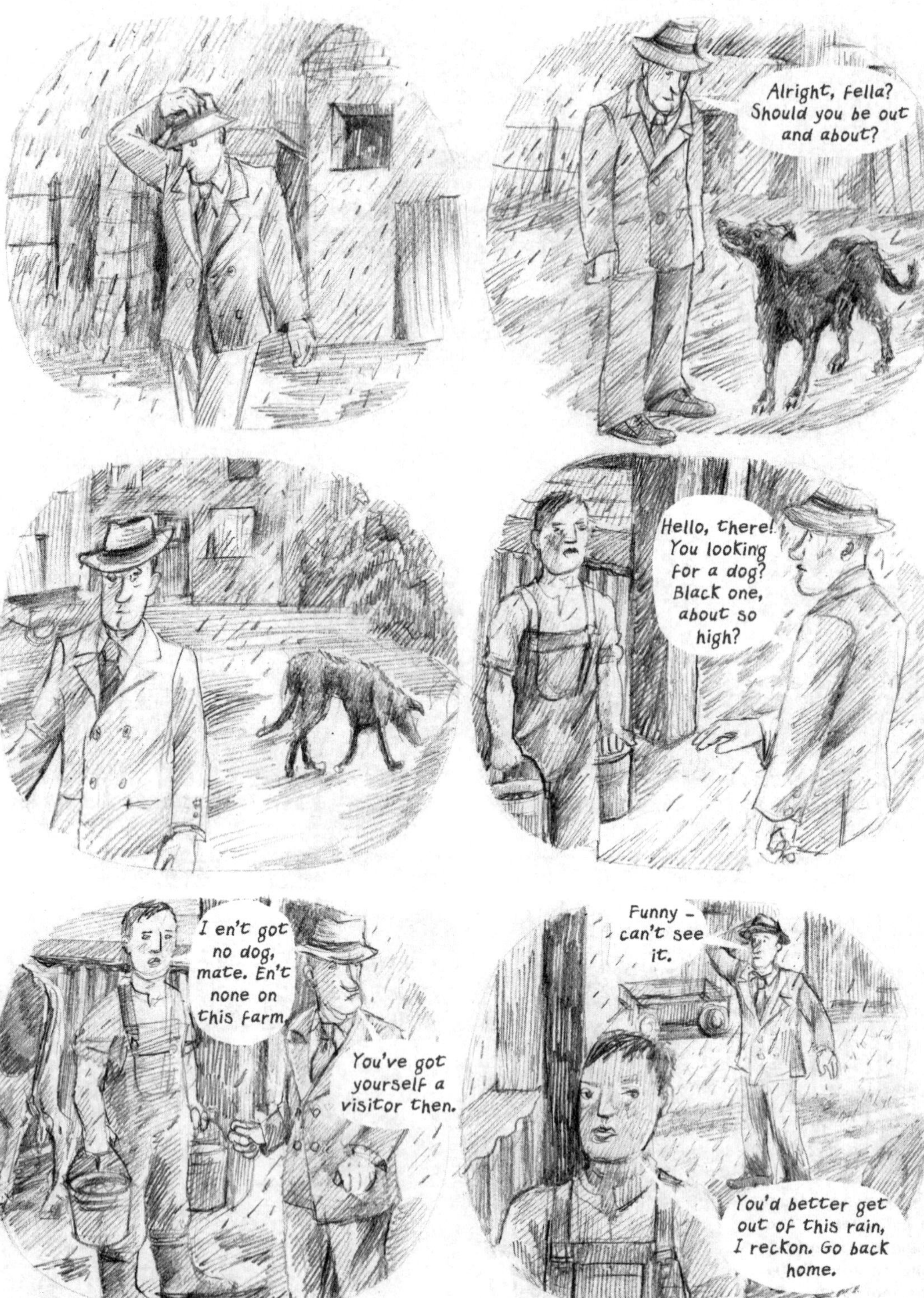
Alright, fella? Should you be out and about?
Hello, there! You looking for a dog? Black one, about so high?
I en't got no dog, mate. En't none on this farm.
You've got yourself a visitor then.
Funny - can't see it.
You'd better get out of this rain, I reckon. Go back home.

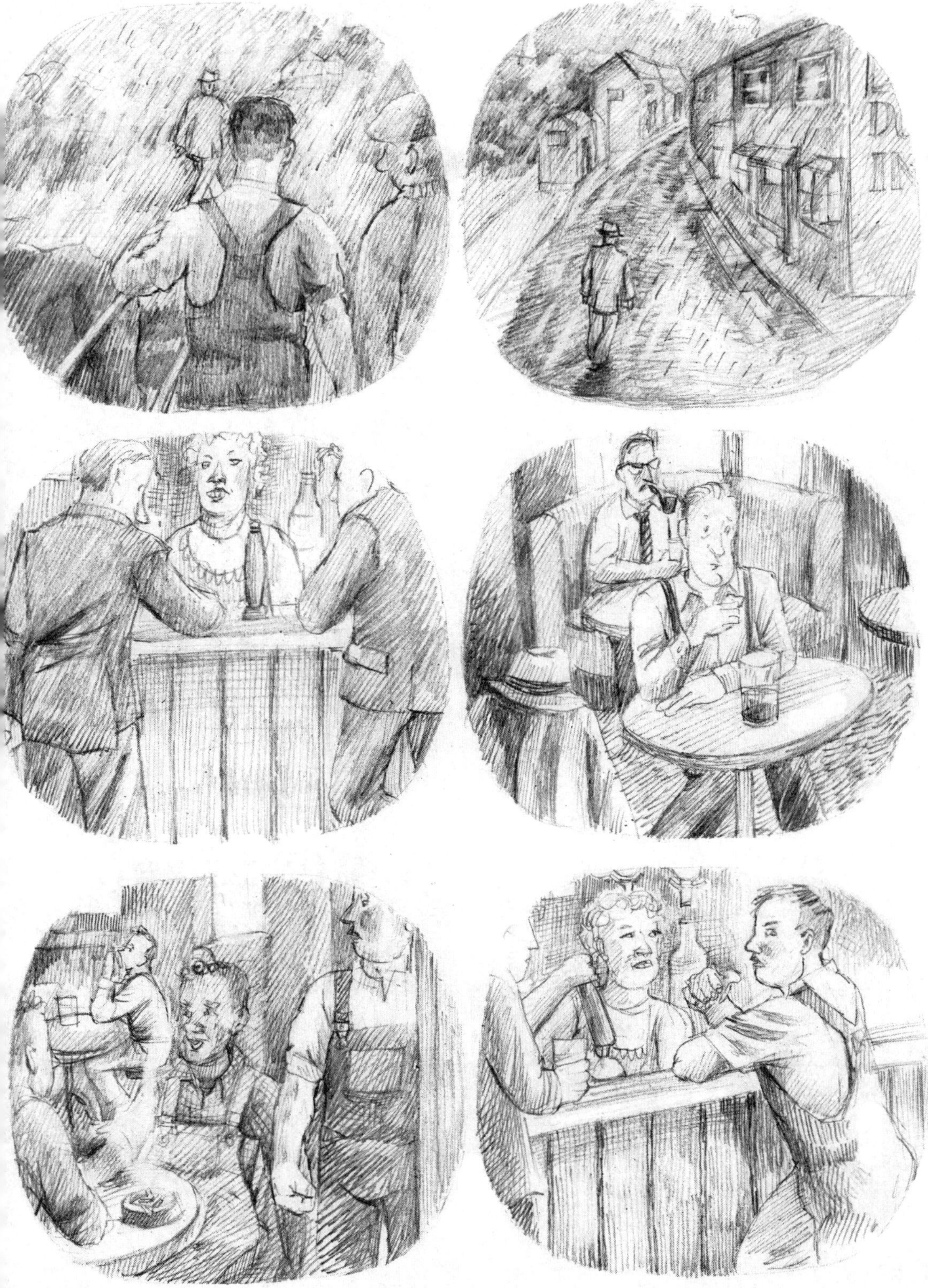

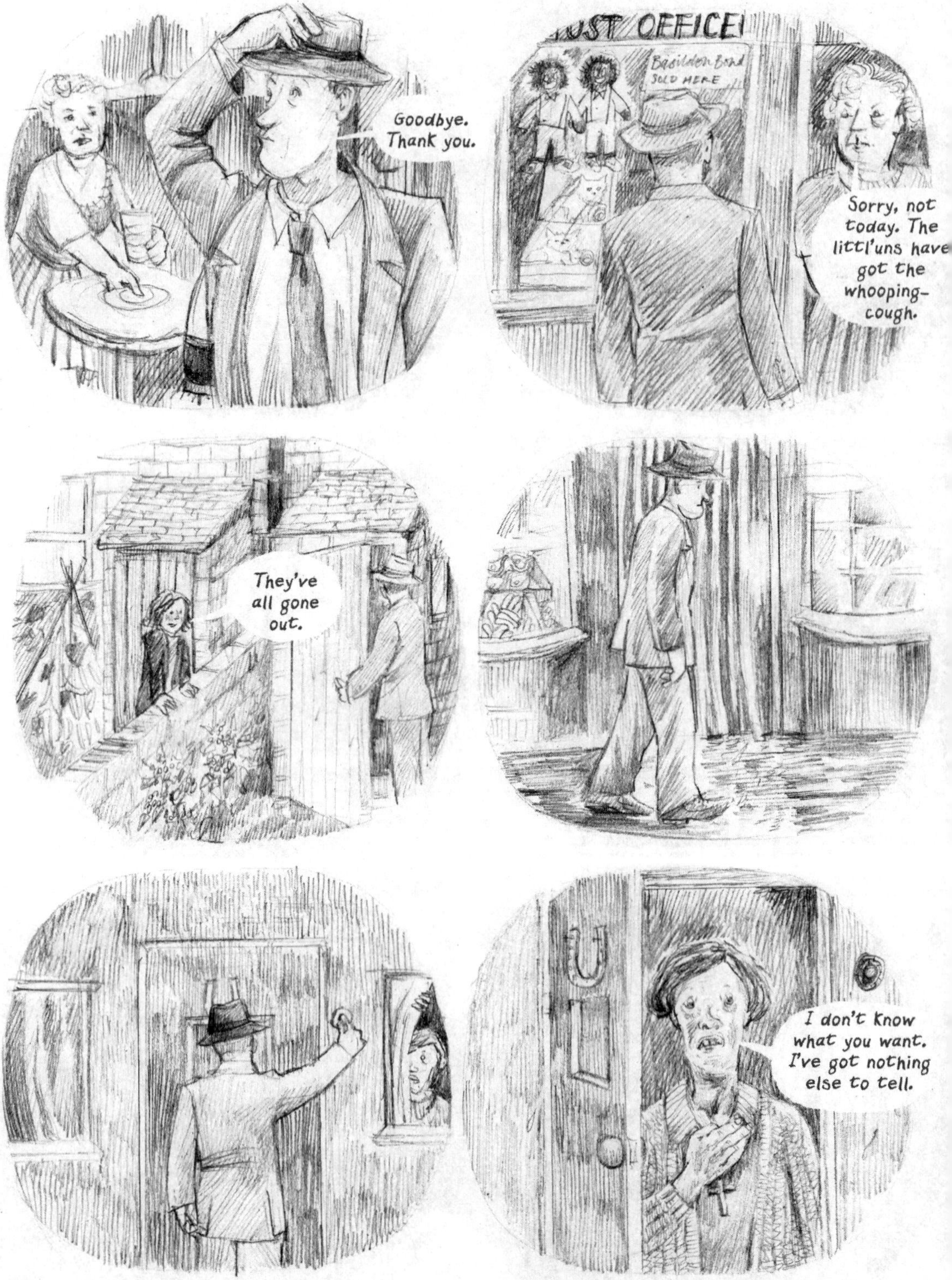
Goodbye. Thank you.
OST OFFICE
Basildon Bond SOLD HERE
Sorry, not today. The littl'uns have got the whooping-cough.
They've all gone out.
I don't know what you want. I've got nothing else to tell.

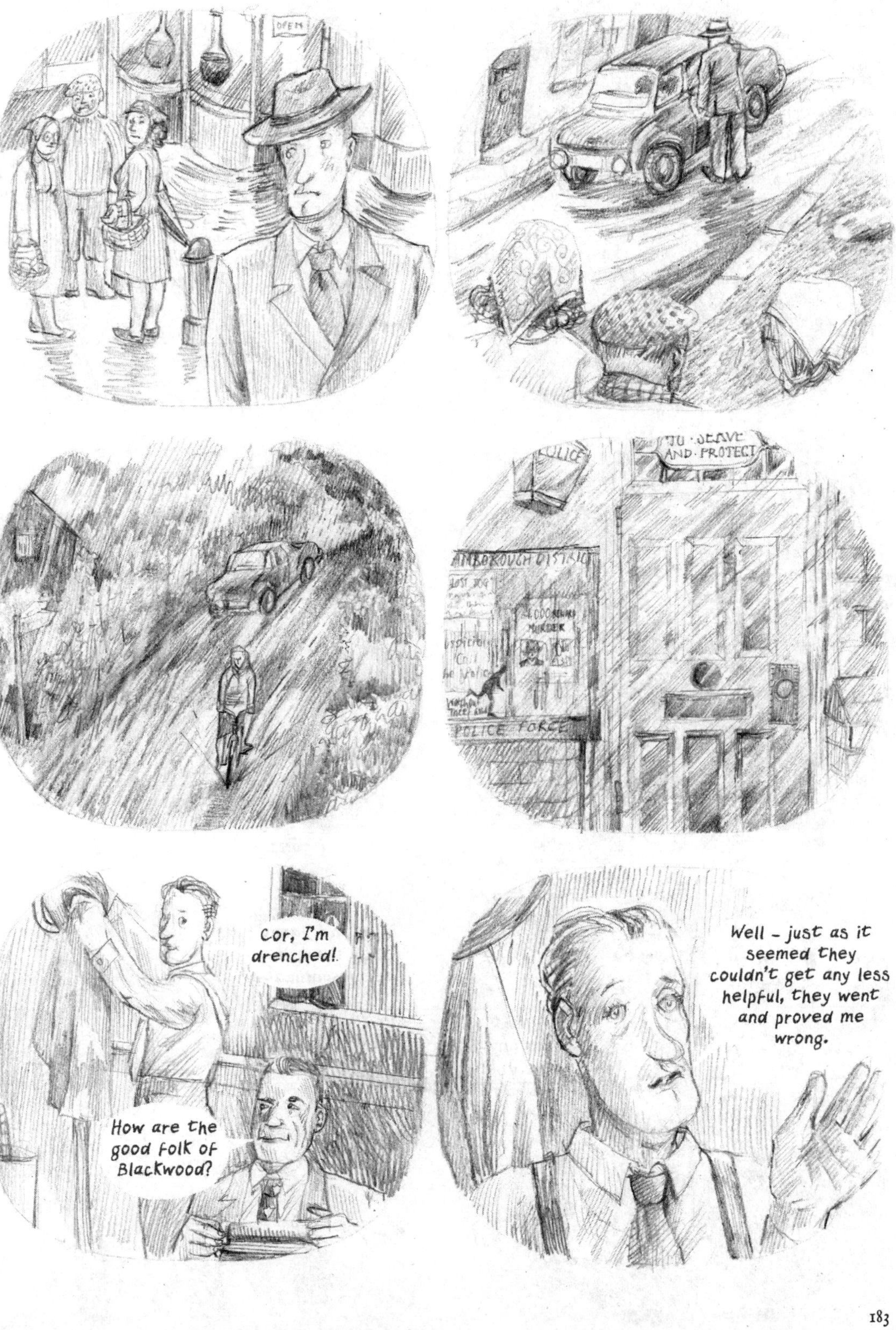
AND PROTECT
POLICE FORCE
Cor, I'm drenched!
How are the good folk of Blackwood?
Well – just as it seemed they couldn't get any less helpful, they went and proved me wrong.

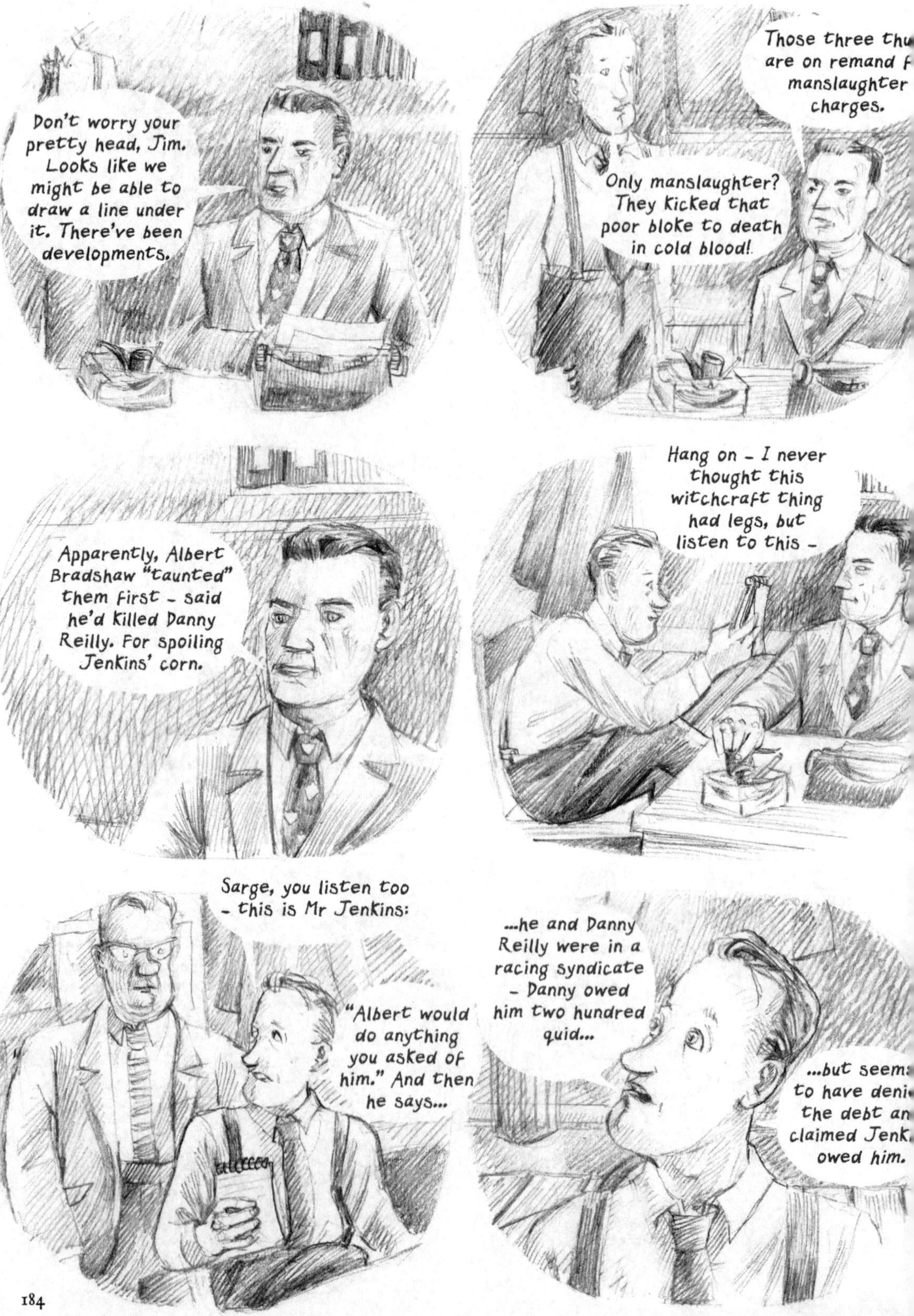
Don't worry your pretty head, Jim. Looks like we might be able to draw a line under it. There've been developments.
Those three thu are on remand f manslaughter charges.
Only manslaughter? They kicked that poor bloke to death in cold blood!
Apparently, Albert Bradshaw "taunted" them first - said he'd killed Danny Reilly. For spoiling Jenkins' corn.
Hang on - I never thought this witchcraft thing had legs, but listen to this -
Sarge, you listen too - this is Mr Jenkins:
"Albert would do anything you asked of him." And then he says...
...he and Danny Reilly were in a racing syndicate - Danny owed him two hundred quid...
...but seem to have deni the debt an claimed Jenk owed him.

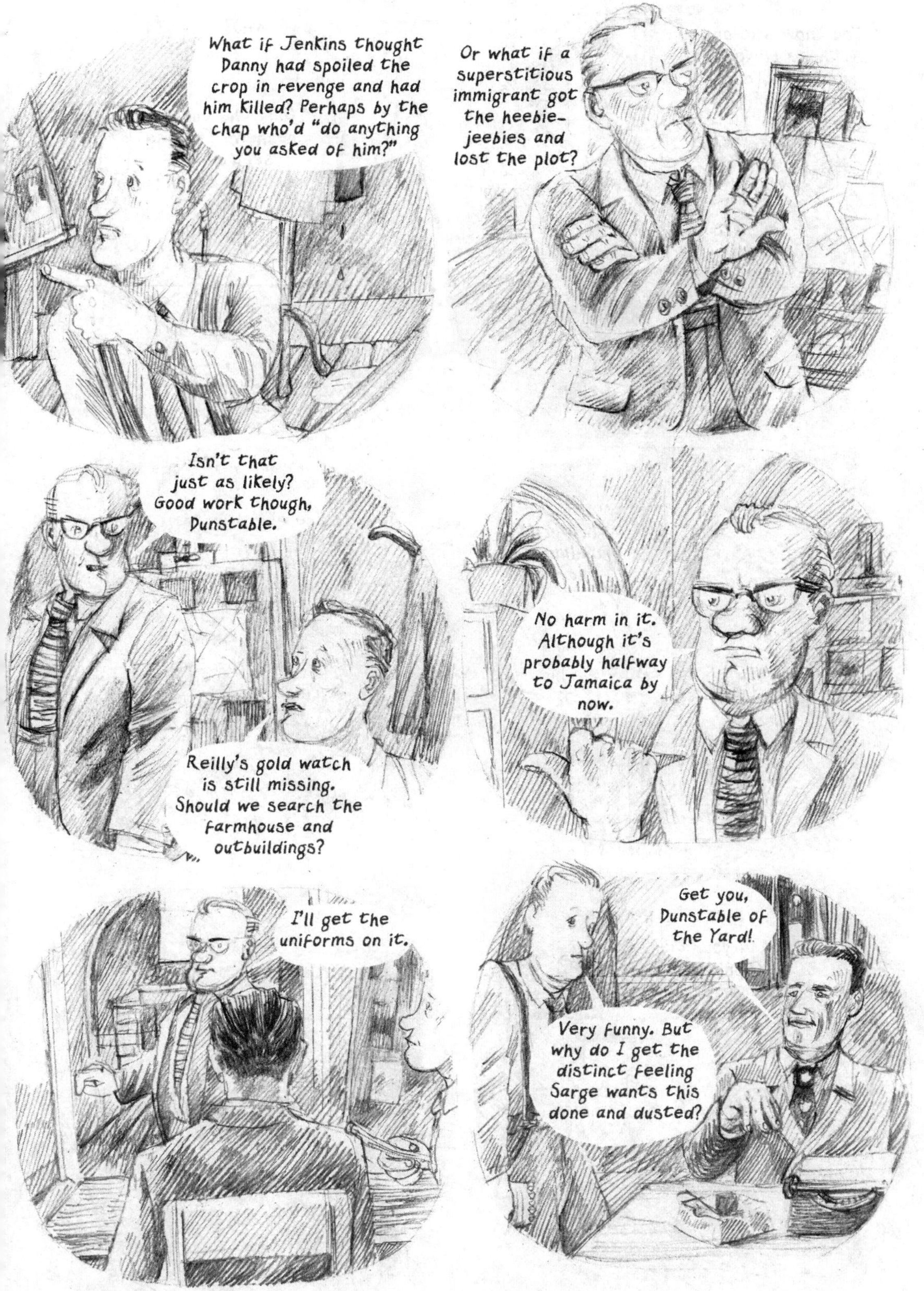
What if Jenkins thought Danny had spoiled the crop in revenge and had him killed? Perhaps by the chap who'd "do anything you asked of him?"
Or what if a superstitious immigrant got the heebie-jeebies and lost the plot?
Isn't that just as likely? Good work though, Dunstable.
Reilly's gold watch is still missing. Should we search the farmhouse and outbuildings?
No harm in it. Although it's probably halfway to Jamaica by now.
I'll get the uniforms on it.
Get you, Dunstable of the Yard!
Very funny. But why do I get the distinct feeling Sarge wants this done and dusted?

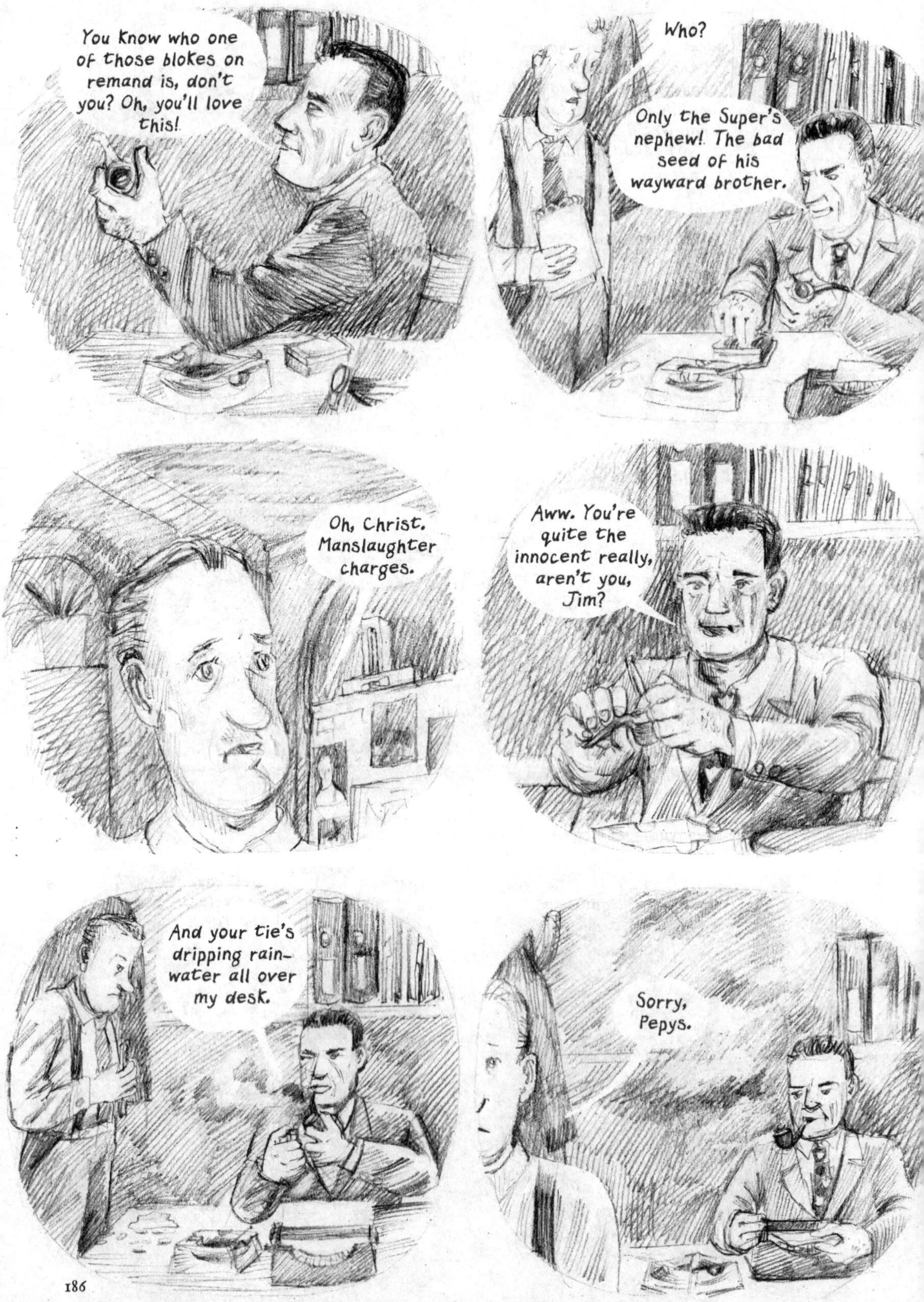
You know who one of those blokes on remand is, don't you? Oh, you'll love this!
Who?
Only the Super's nephew! The bad seed of his wayward brother.
Oh, Christ. Manslaughter charges.
Aww. You're quite the innocent really, aren't you, Jim?
And your tie's dripping rain-water all over my desk.
Sorry, Pepys.

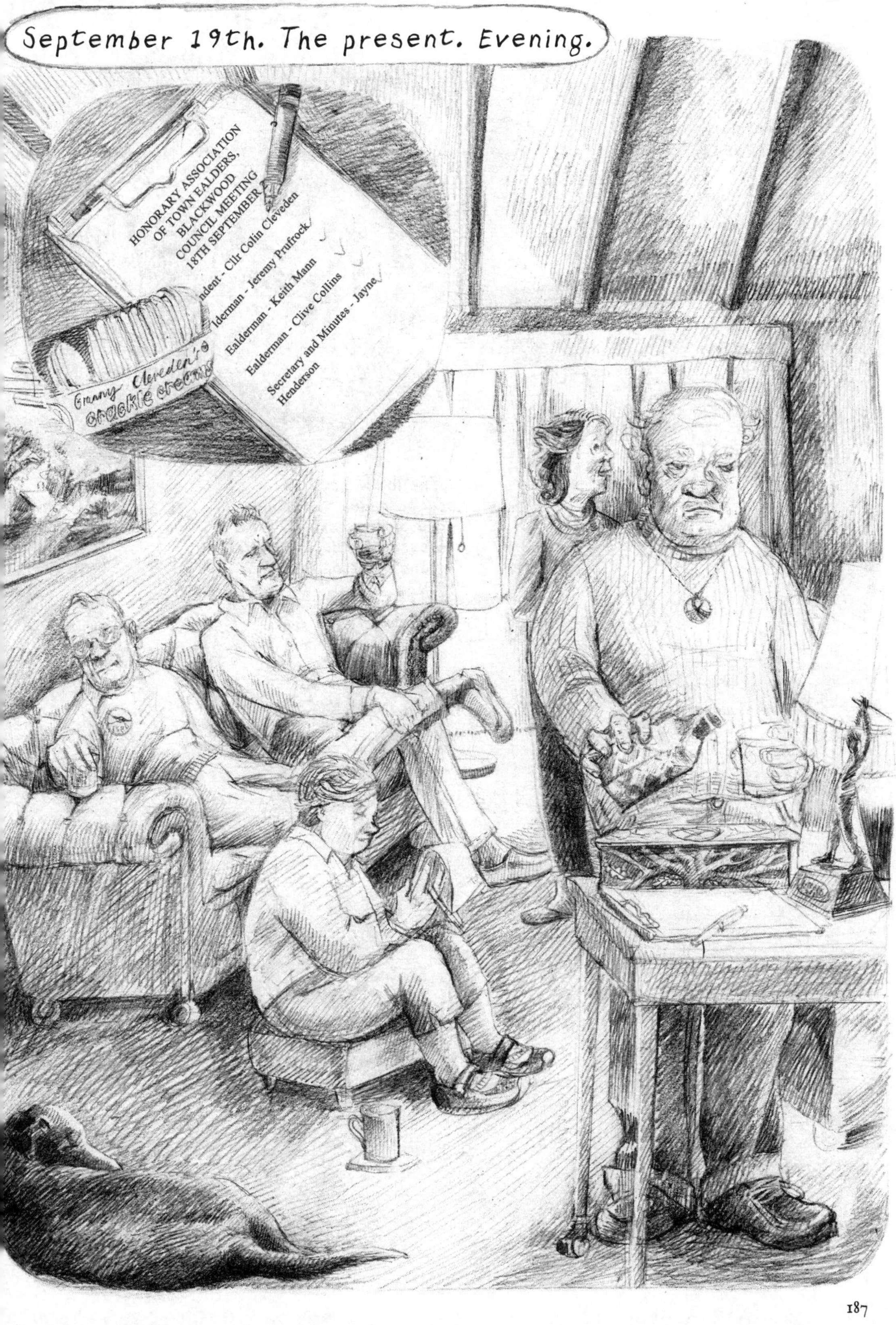
September 19th. The present. Evening.
HONORARY ASSOCIATION
OF TOWN EALDERS,
BLACKWOOD
COUNCIL MEETING
18TH SEPTEMBER
ndent - Cllr Colin Cleveden
lderman - Jeremy Prufrock
Ealderman - Keith Mann
Ealderman - Clive Collins
Secretary and Minutes - Jayne Henderson
Granny Cleveden's crackle

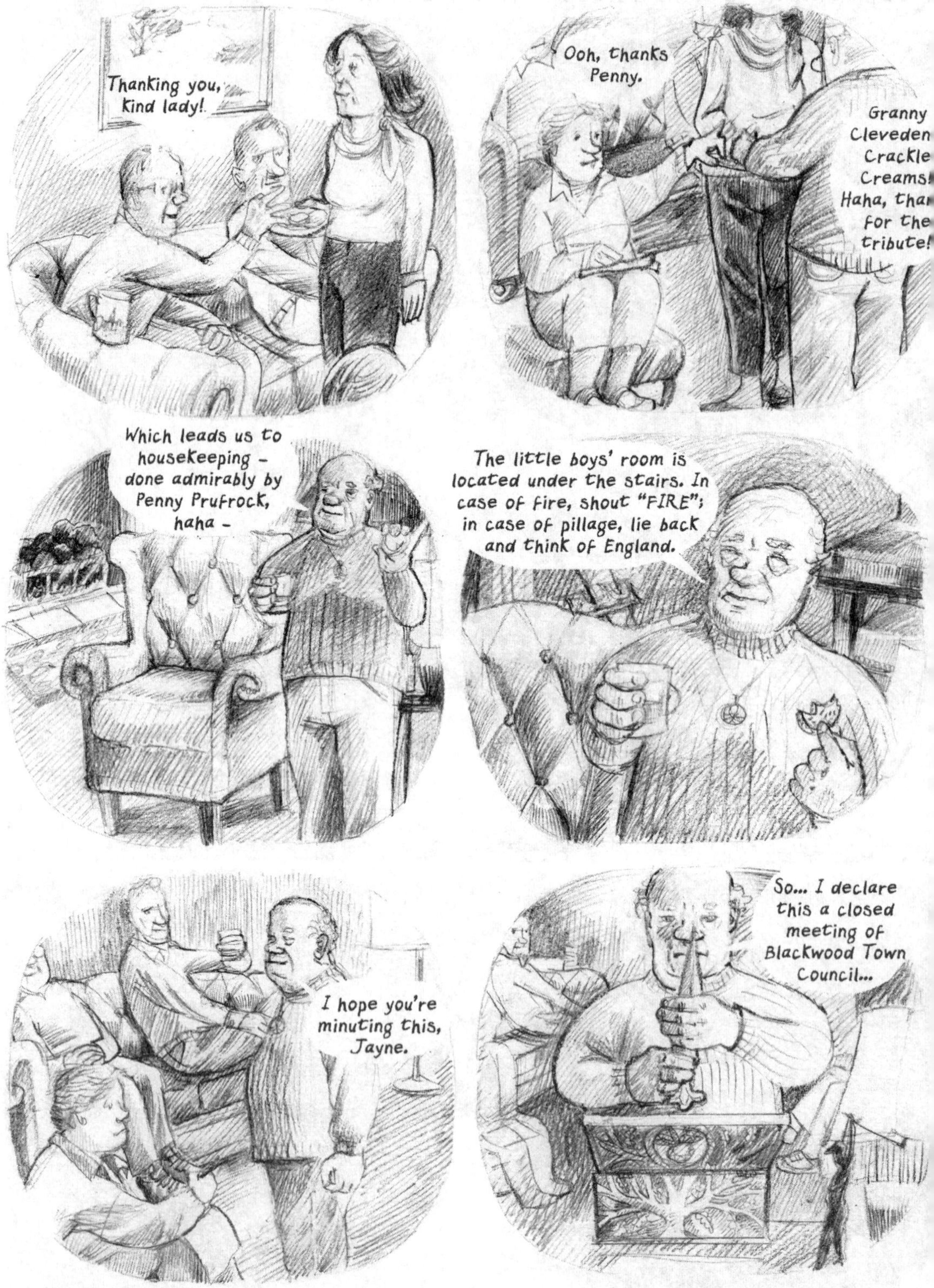

Thanking you, kind lady!
Ooh, thanks Penny.
Granny Cleveden Crackle Creams! Haha, thar for the tribute!
Which leads us to housekeeping - done admirably by Penny Prufrock, haha -
The little boys' room is located under the stairs. In case of fire, shout "FIRE"; in case of pillage, lie back and think of England.
I hope you're minuting this, Jayne.
So... I declare this a closed meeting of Blackwood Town Council...

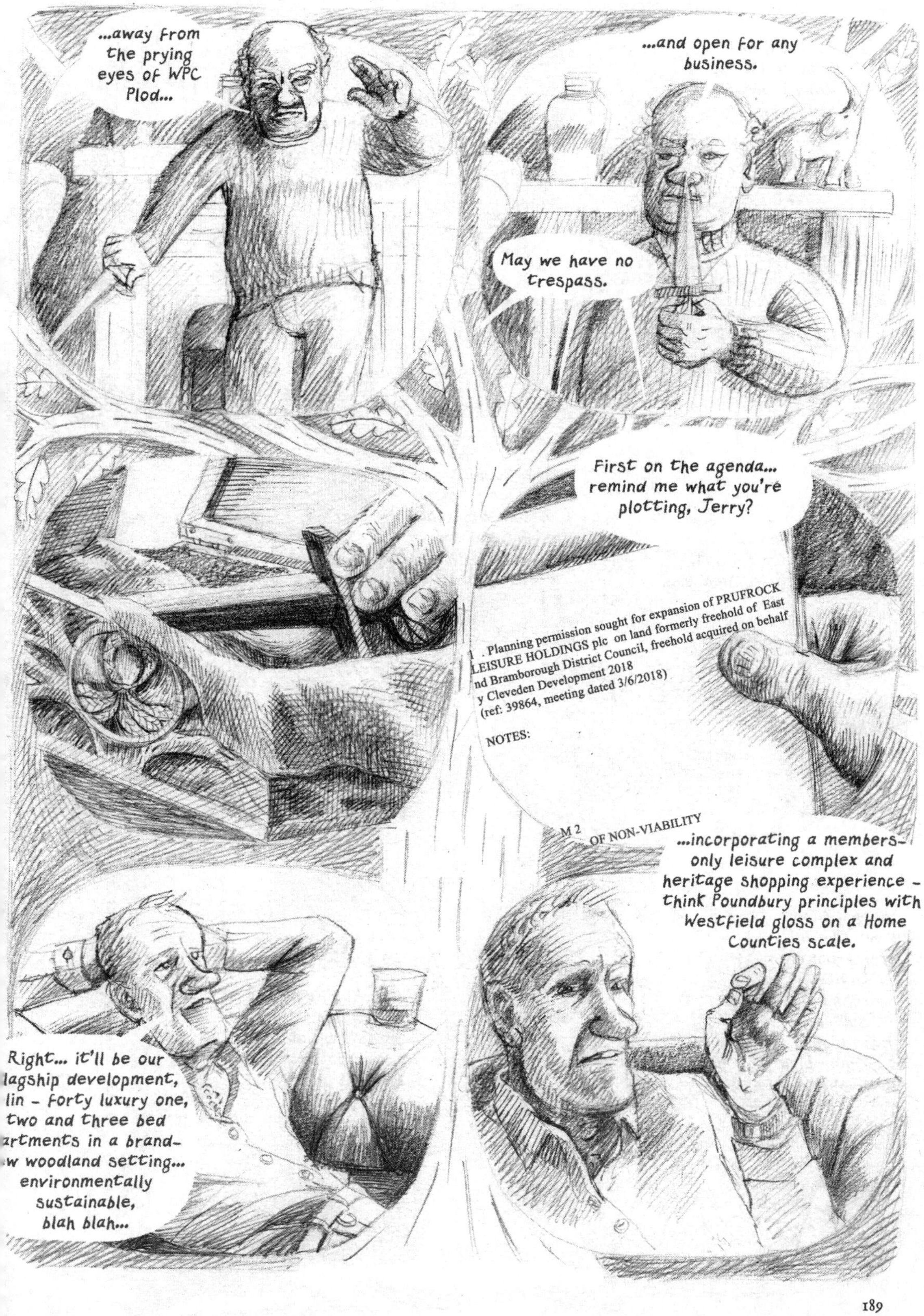

...away from the prying eyes of WPC Plod...
...and open for any business.
May we have no trespass.
First on the agenda... remind me what you're plotting, Jerry?
1 . Planning permission sought for expansion of PRUFROCK LEISURE HOLDINGS plc on land formerly freehold of East nd Bramborough District Council, freehold acquired on behalf y Cleveden Development 2018 (ref: 39864, meeting dated 3/6/2018)
NOTES:
M 2 OF NON-VIABILITY
Right... it'll be our lagship development, lin - forty luxury one, two and three bed artments in a brand- w woodland setting... environmentally sustainable, blah blah...
...incorporating a members-only leisure complex and heritage shopping experience - think Poundbury principles with Westfield gloss on a Home Counties scale.

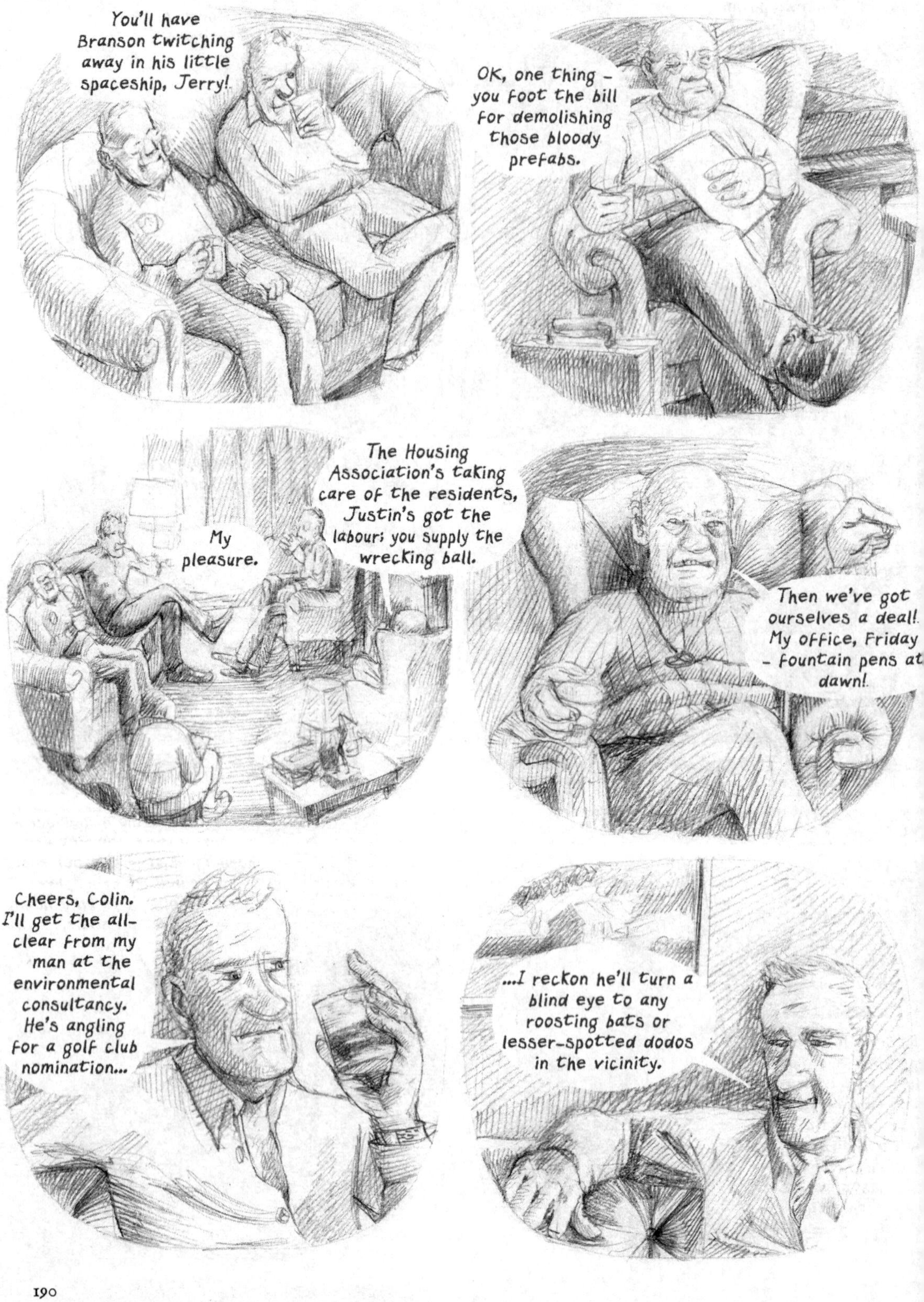
You'll have Branson twitching away in his little spaceship, Jerry!
OK, one thing – you foot the bill for demolishing those bloody prefabs.
The Housing Association's taking care of the residents, Justin's got the labour; you supply the wrecking ball.
My pleasure.
Then we've got ourselves a deal! My office, Friday – fountain pens at dawn!
Cheers, Colin. I'll get the all-clear from my man at the environmental consultancy. He's angling for a golf club nomination...
...I reckon he'll turn a blind eye to any roosting bats or lesser-spotted dodos in the vicinity.

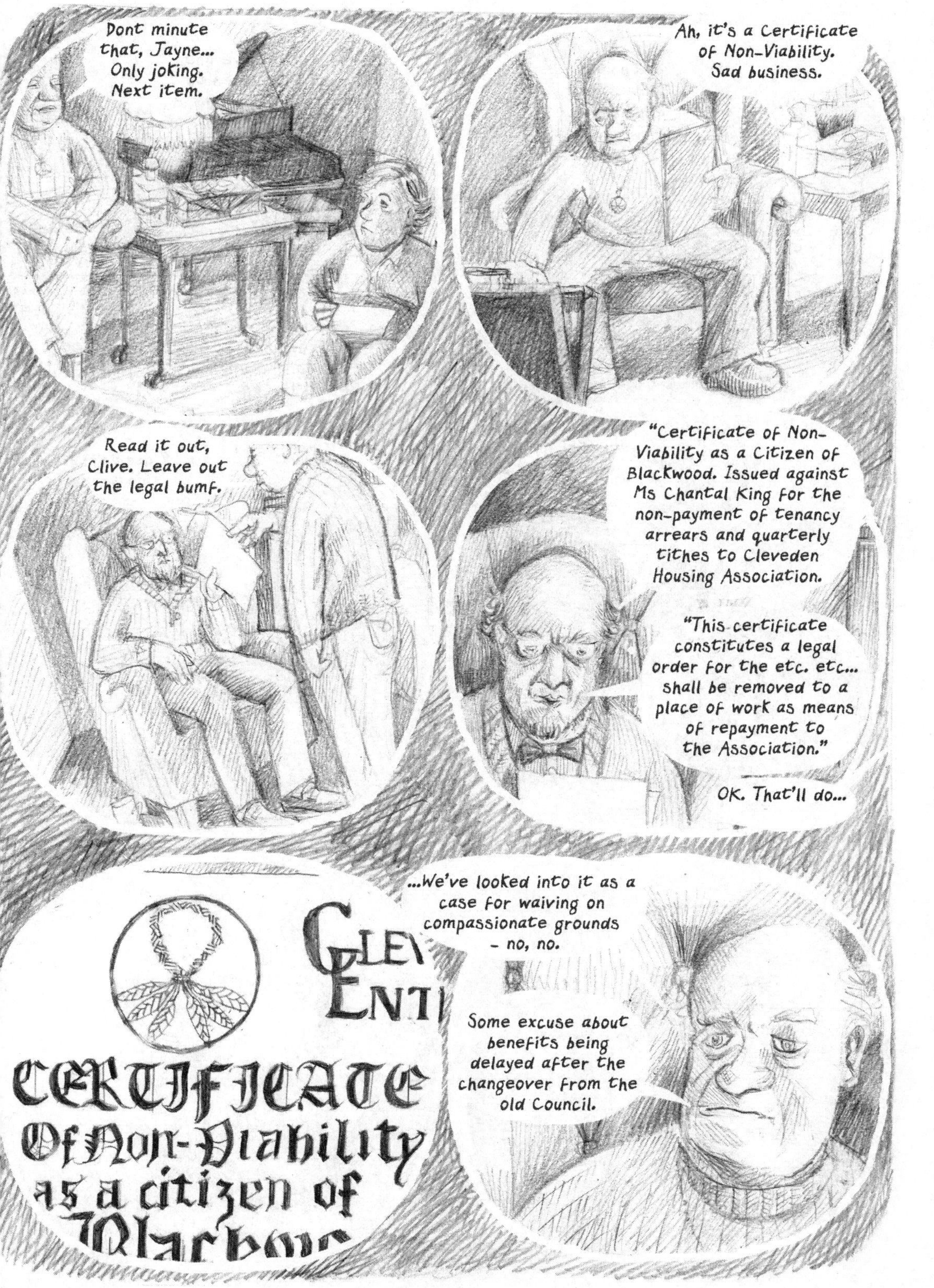
Dont minute that, Jayne... Only joking. Next item.
Ah, it's a Certificate of Non-Viability. Sad business.
Read it out, Clive. Leave out the legal bumf.
"Certificate of Non-Viability as a Citizen of Blackwood. Issued against Ms Chantal King for the non-payment of tenancy arrears and quarterly tithes to Cleveden Housing Association.
"This certificate constitutes a legal order for the etc. etc... shall be removed to a place of work as means of repayment to the Association."
OK. That'll do...
CERTIFICATE
Of Non-Viability
as a citizen of
...We've looked into it as a case for waiving on compassionate grounds - no, no.
Some excuse about benefits being delayed after the changeover from the old Council.

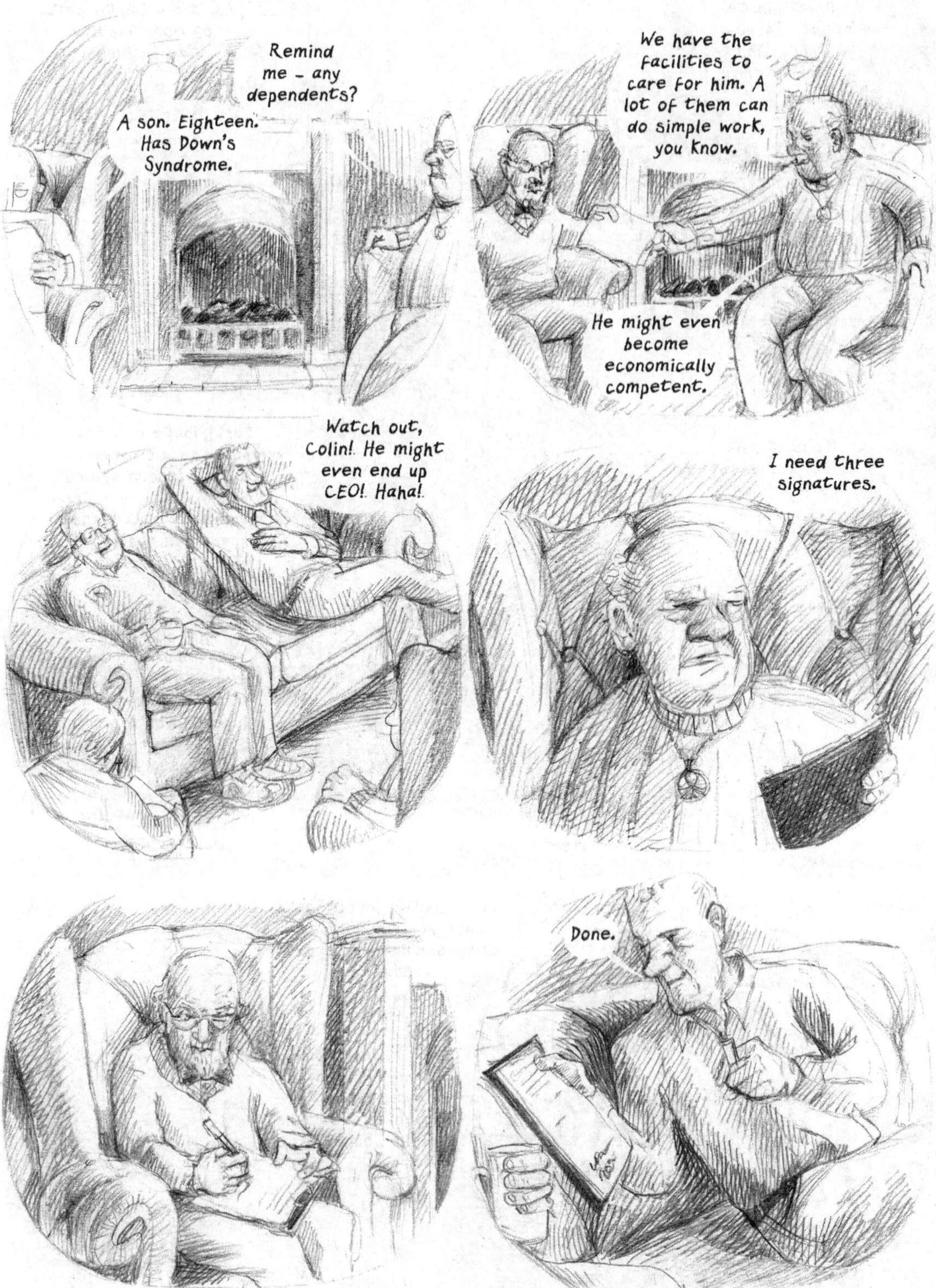
Remind me – any dependents?
A son. Eighteen. Has Down's Syndrome.
We have the facilities to care for him. A lot of them can do simple work, you know.
He might even become economically competent.
Watch out, Colin!. He might even end up CEO!. Haha!.
I need three signatures.
Done.

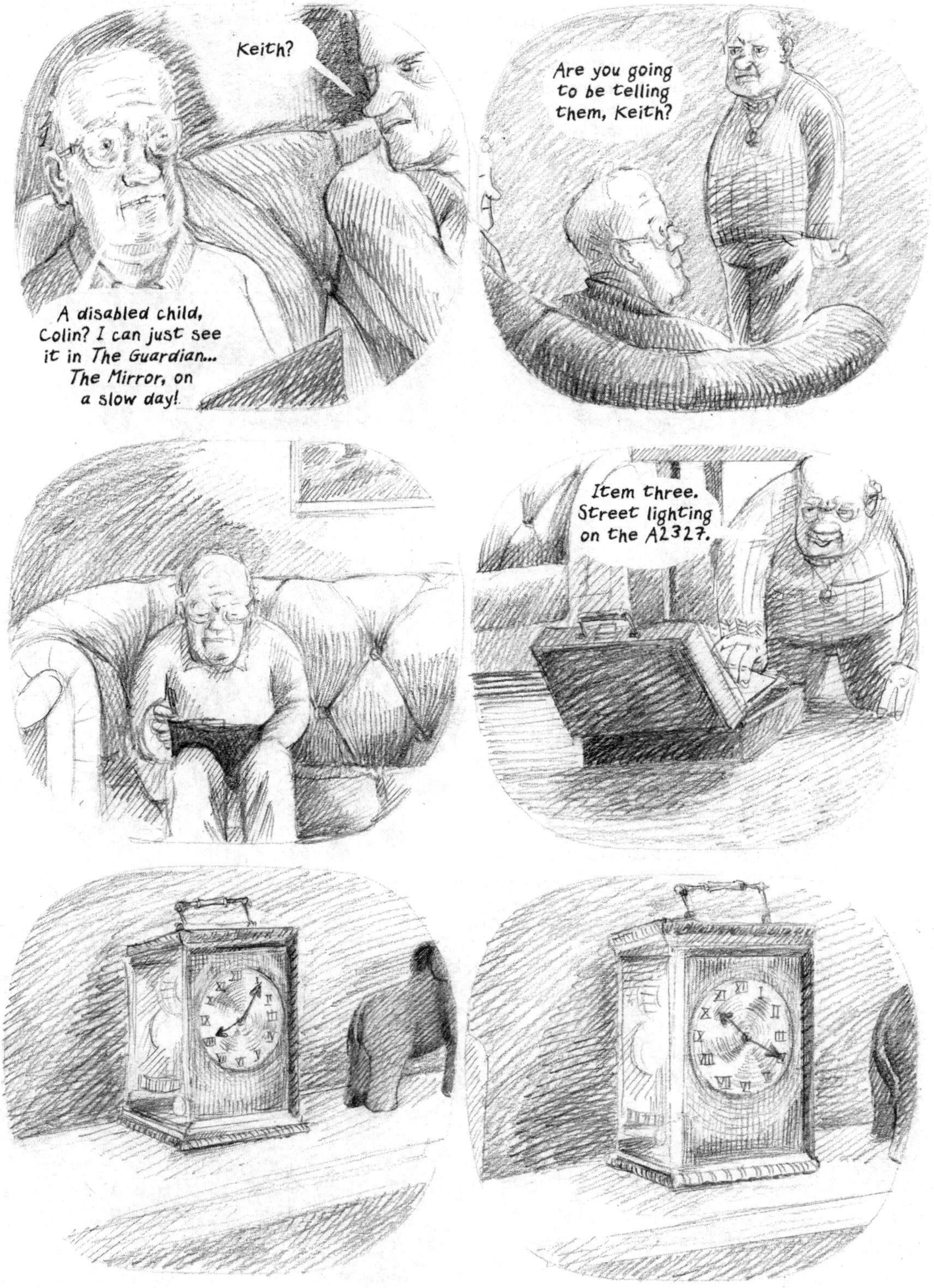
Keith?
A disabled child, Colin? I can just see it in *The Guardian*... *The Mirror*, on a slow day!
Are you going to be telling them, Keith?
Item three. Street lighting on the A2327.

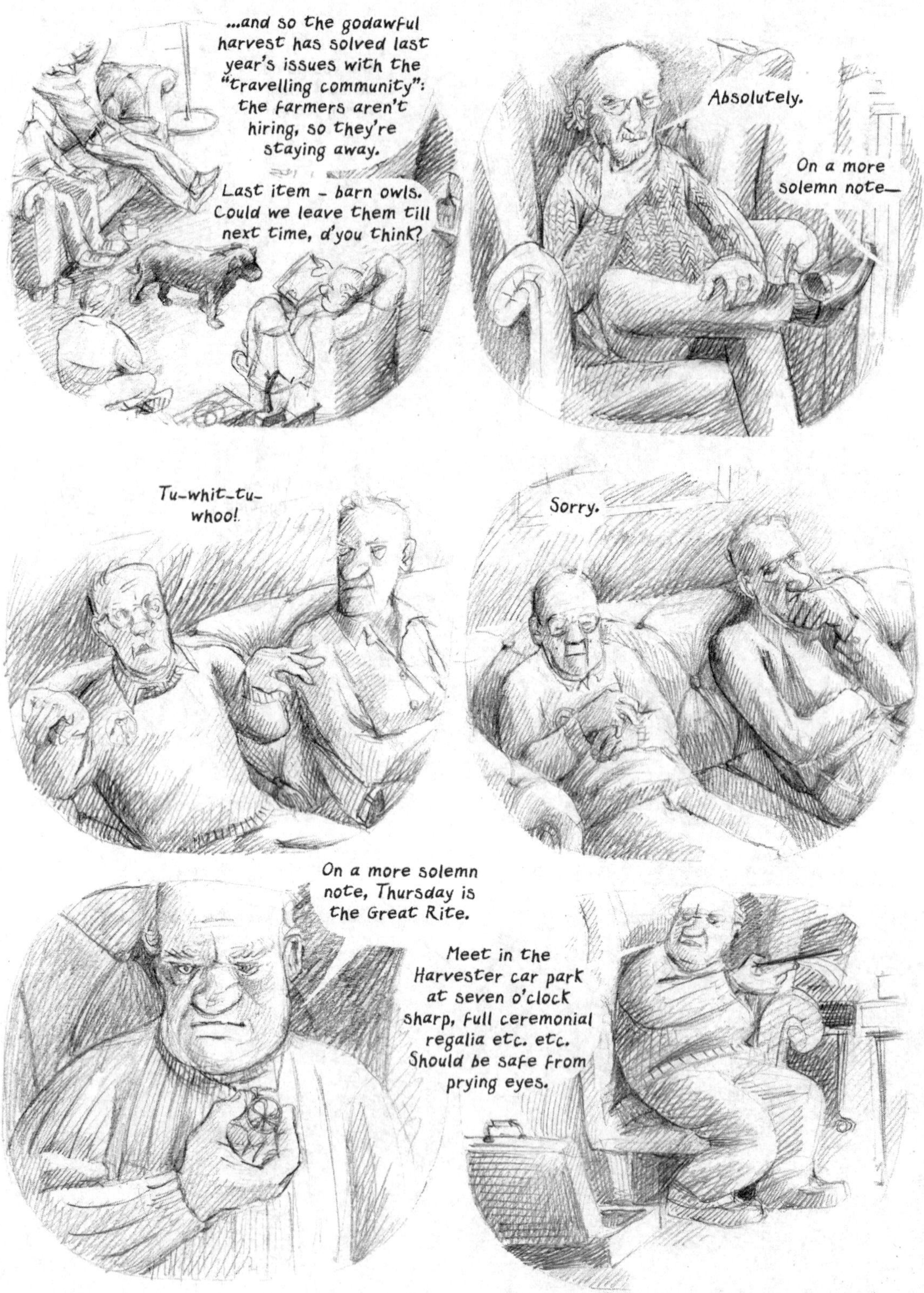
...and so the godawful harvest has solved last year's issues with the "travelling community": the farmers aren't hiring, so they're staying away.
Last item - barn owls. Could we leave them till next time, d'you think?
Absolutely.
On a more solemn note—
Tu-whit-tu-whoo!
Sorry.
On a more solemn note, Thursday is the Great Rite.
Meet in the Harvester car park at seven o'clock sharp, full ceremonial regalia etc. etc. Should be safe from prying eyes.

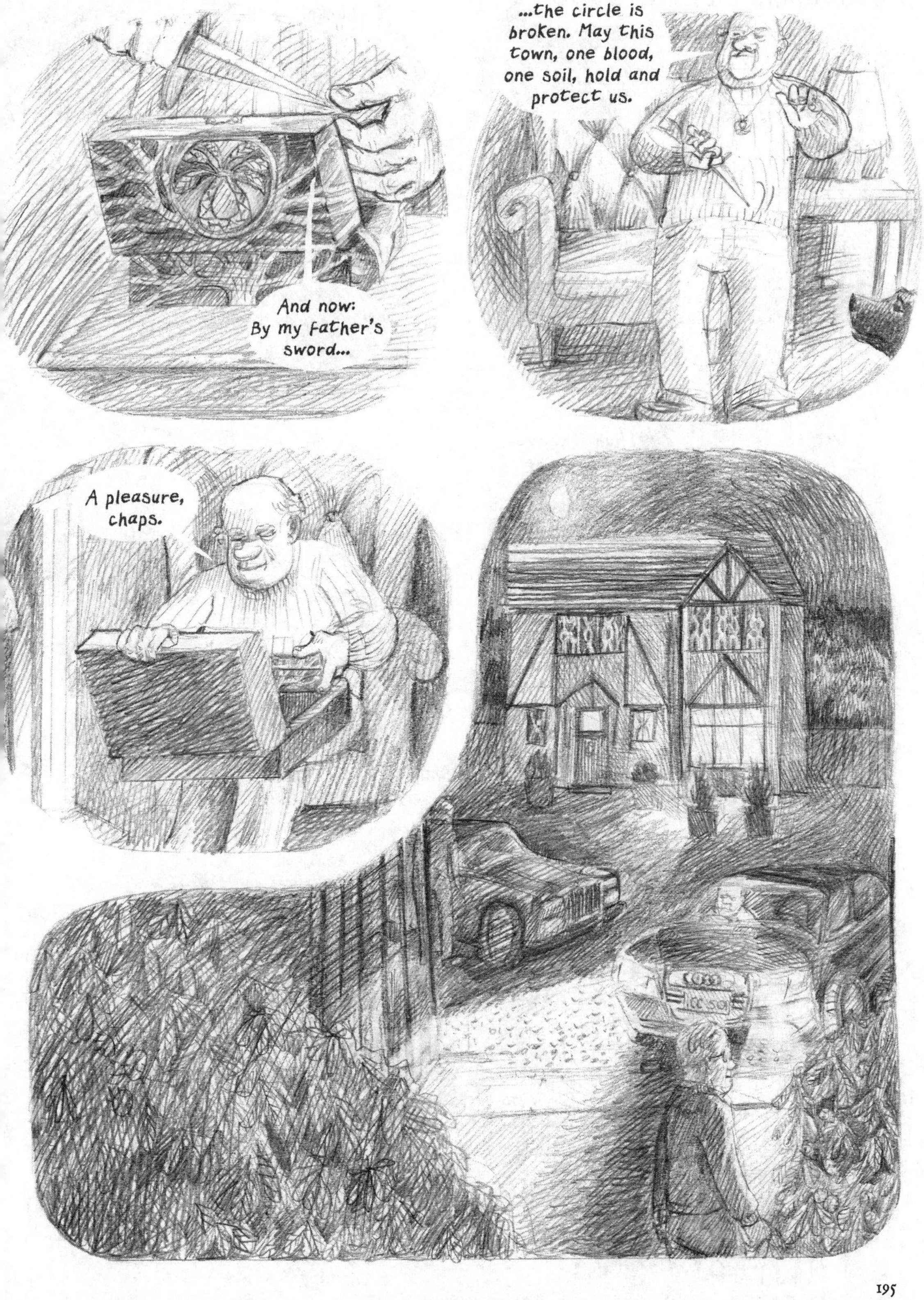
And now: By my father's sword...
...the circle is broken. May this town, one blood, one soil, hold and protect us.
A pleasure, chaps.

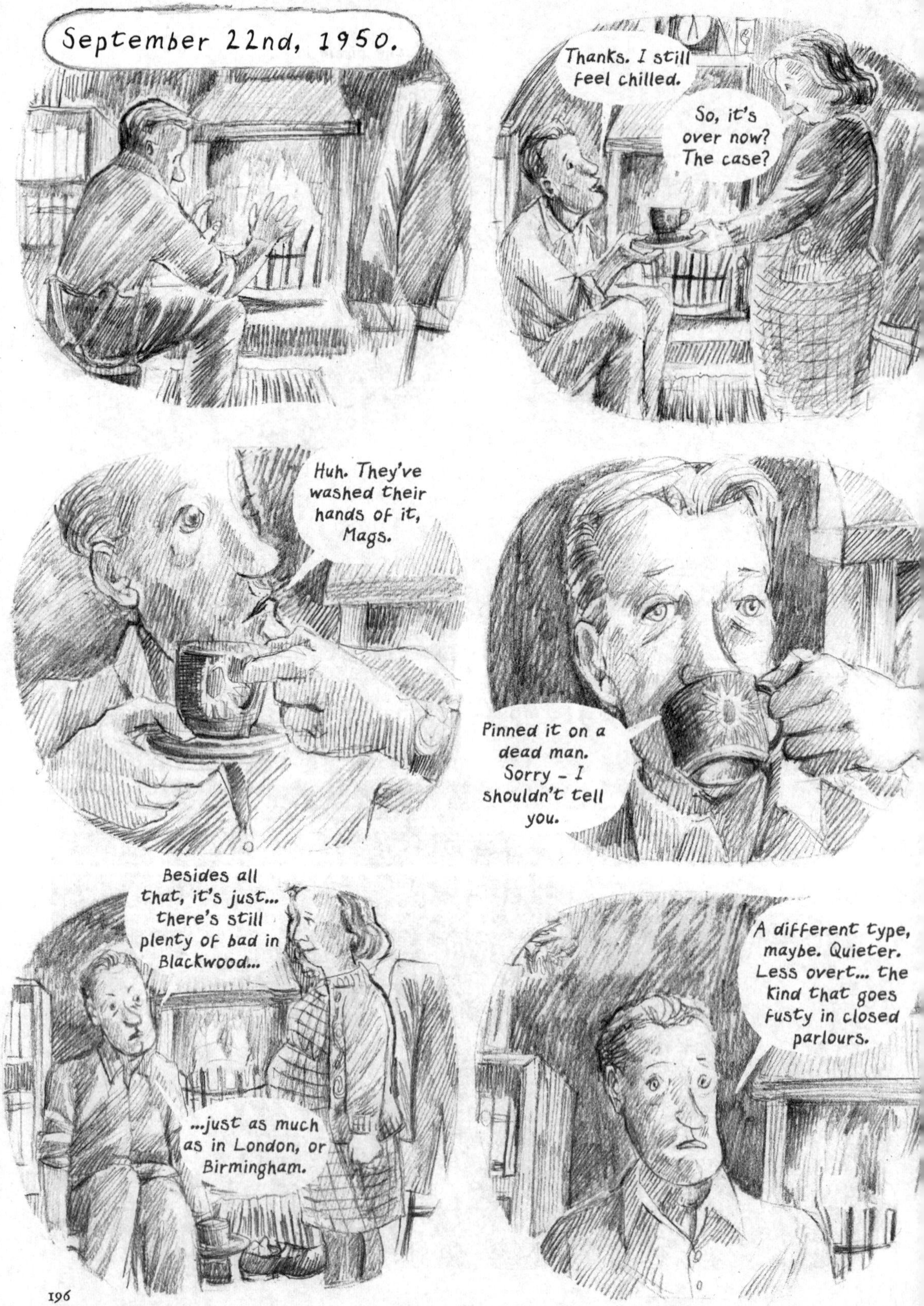
September 22nd, 1950.
Thanks. I still feel chilled.
So, it's over now? The case?
Huh. They've washed their hands of it, Mags.
Pinned it on a dead man. Sorry – I shouldn't tell you.
Besides all that, it's just... there's still plenty of bad in Blackwood...
...just as much as in London, or Birmingham.
A different type, maybe. Quieter. Less overt... the kind that goes fusty in closed parlours.

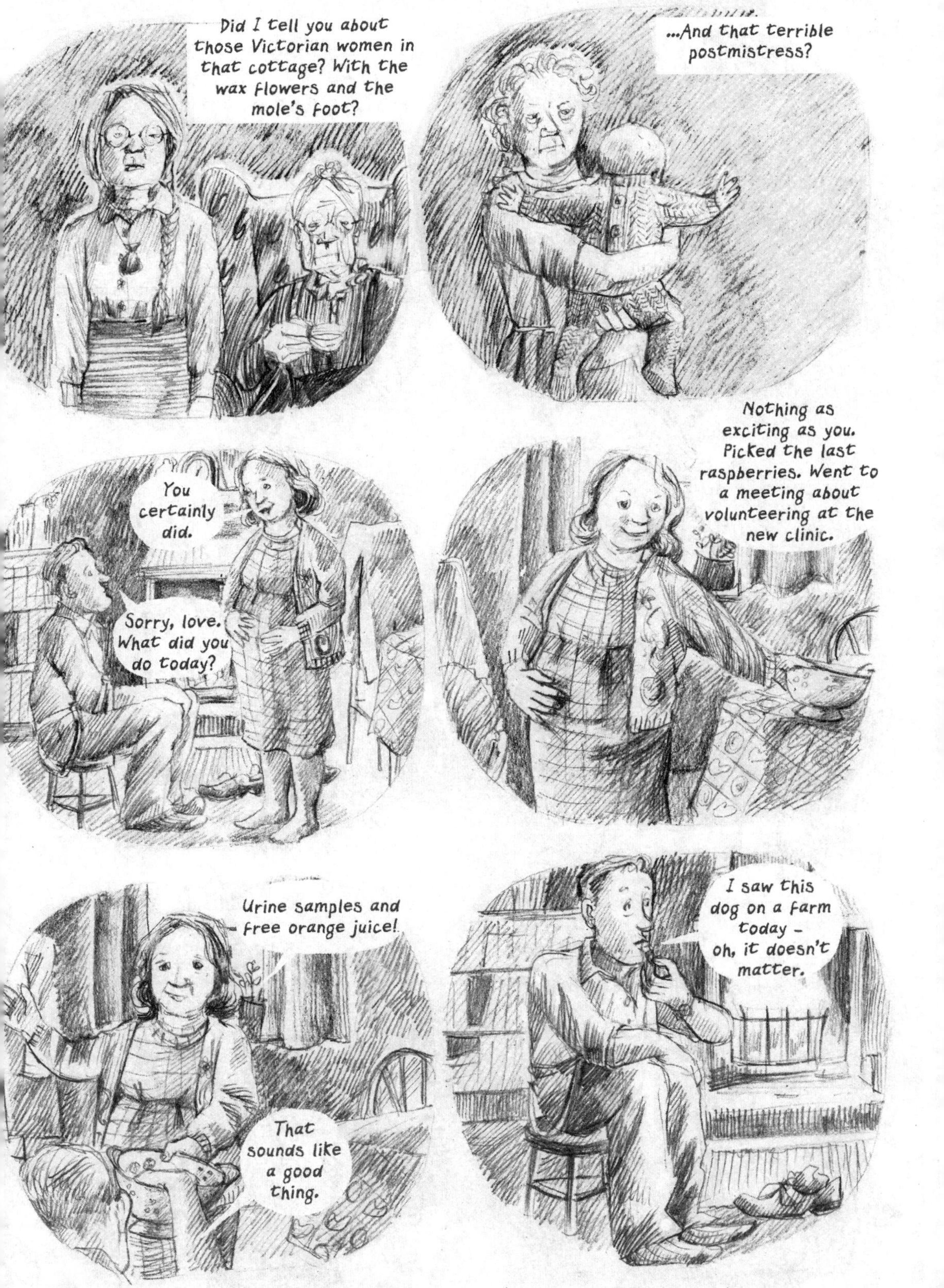
Did I tell you about those Victorian women in that cottage? With the wax flowers and the mole's foot?
...And that terrible postmistress?
You certainly did.
Sorry, love. What did you do today?
Nothing as exciting as you. Picked the last raspberries. Went to a meeting about volunteering at the new clinic.
Urine samples and free orange juice!
That sounds like a good thing.
I saw this dog on a farm today - oh, it doesn't matter.

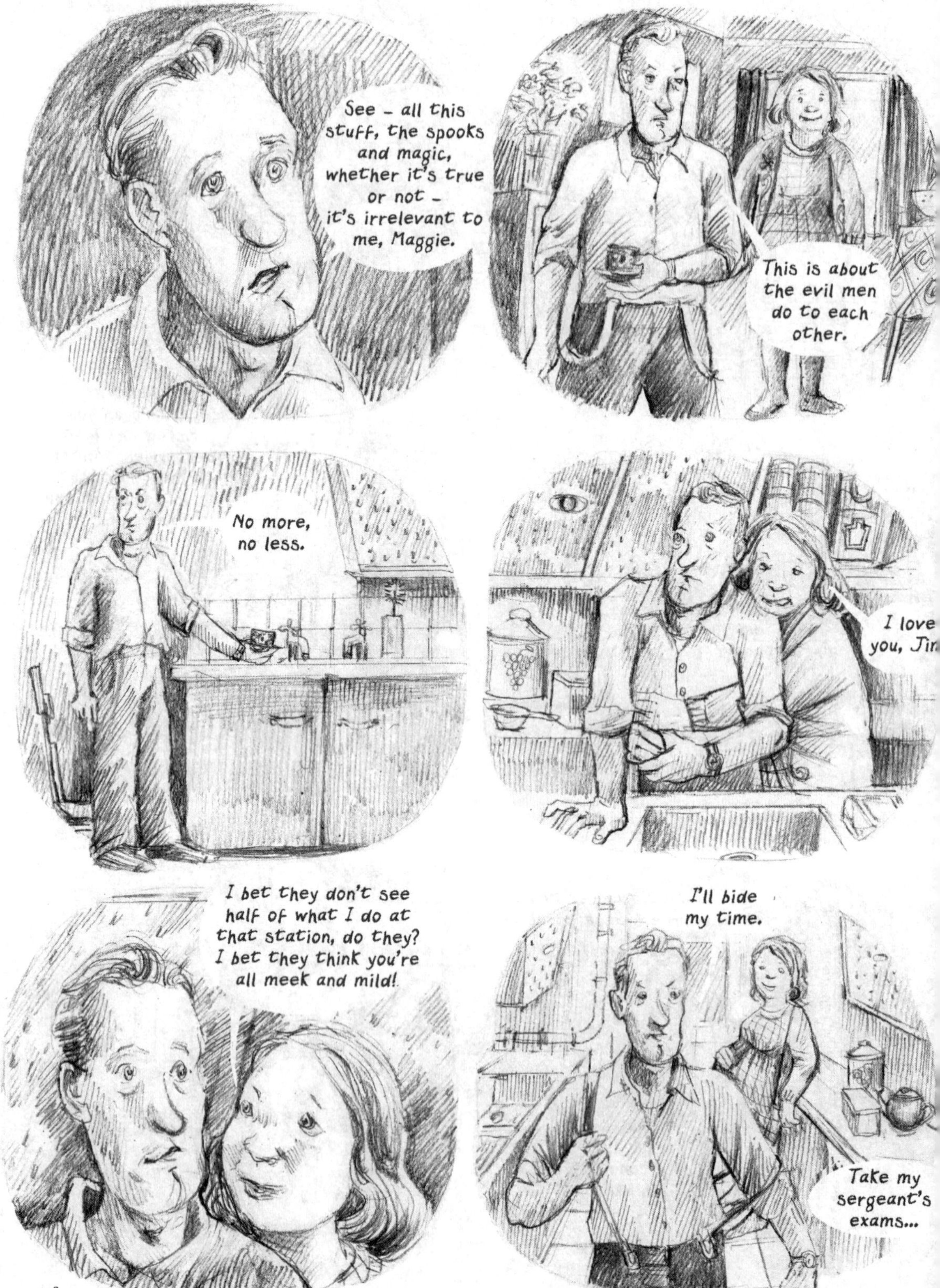
See - all this stuff, the spooks and magic, whether it's true or not - it's irrelevant to me, Maggie.
This is about the evil men do to each other.
No more, no less.
I love you, Jim
I bet they don't see half of what I do at that station, do they? I bet they think you're all meek and mild!
I'll bide my time.
Take my sergeant's exams...

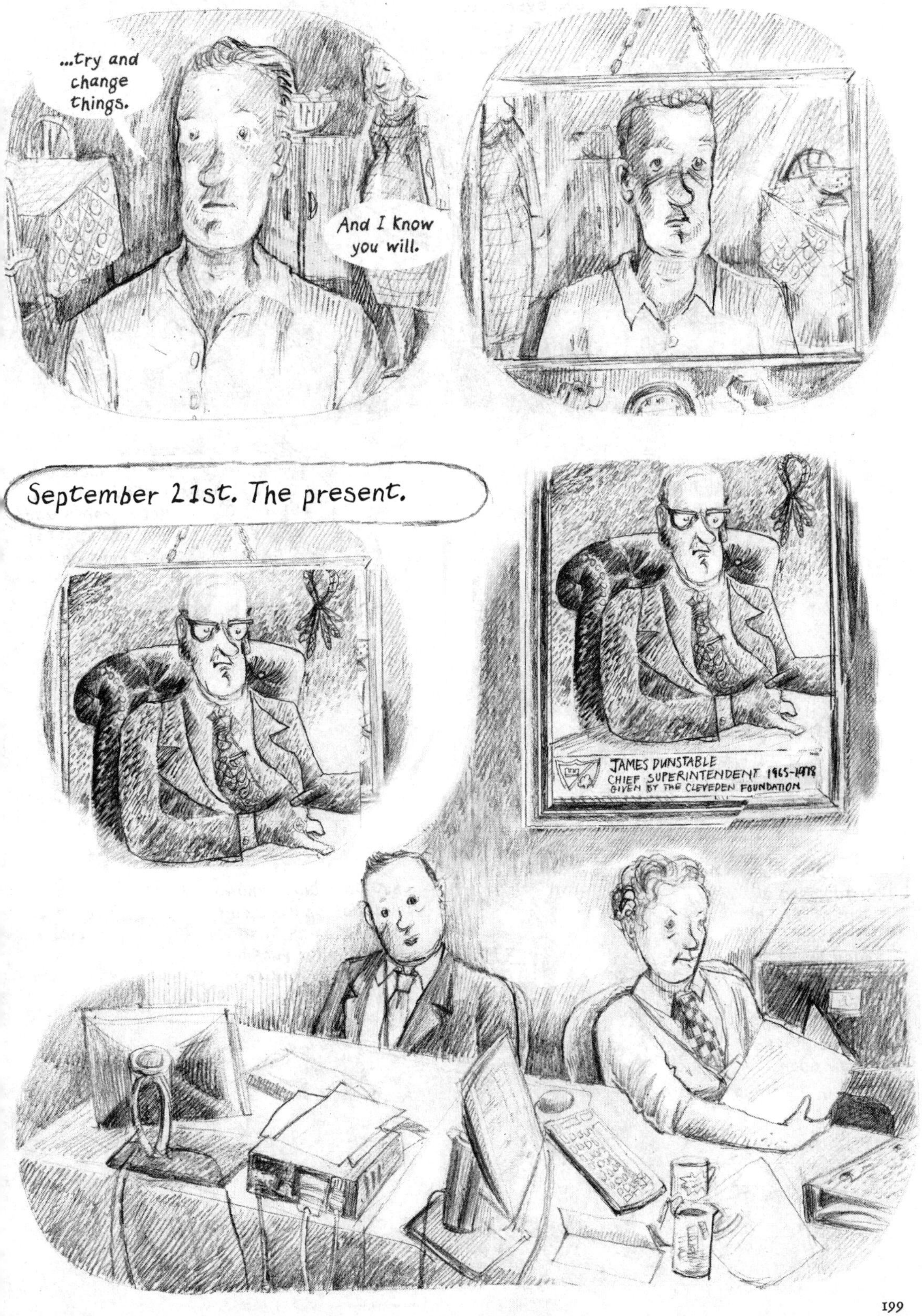
...try and change things.
And I know you will.
September 21st. The present.
JAMES DUNSTABLE
CHIEF SUPERINTENDENT 1965-1978
GIVEN BY THE CLEVEDEN FOUNDATION

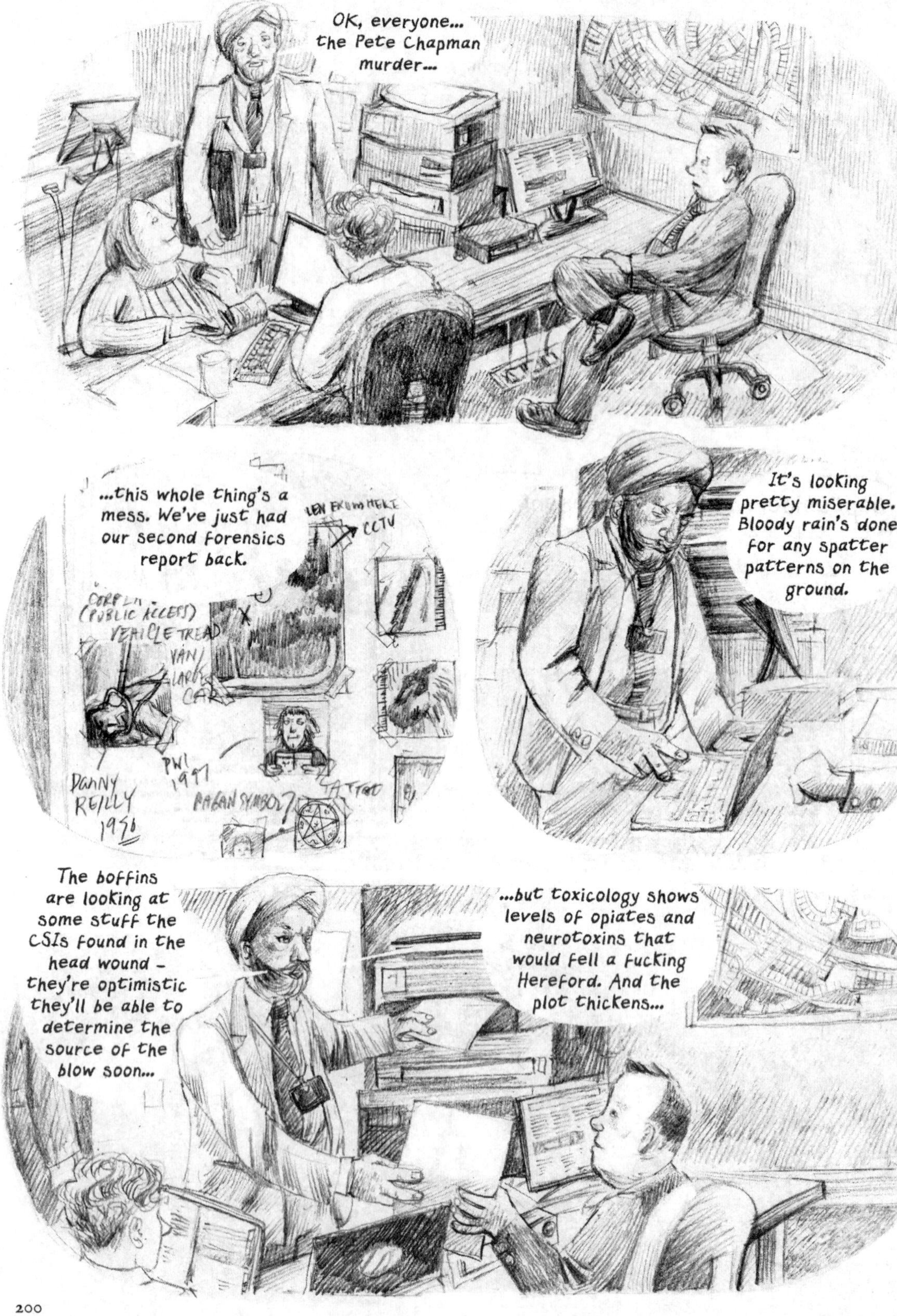
OK, everyone... the Pete Chapman murder...
...this whole thing's a mess. We've just had our second forensics report back.
CCTV
(PUBLIC ACCESS)
VEHICLE TREAD
DANNY REILLY
PWI 1997
PAGAN SYMBOL?
It's looking pretty miserable. Bloody rain's done for any spatter patterns on the ground.
The boffins are looking at some stuff the CSIs found in the head wound – they're optimistic they'll be able to determine the source of the blow soon...
...but toxicology shows levels of opiates and neurotoxins that would fell a fucking Hereford. And the plot thickens...

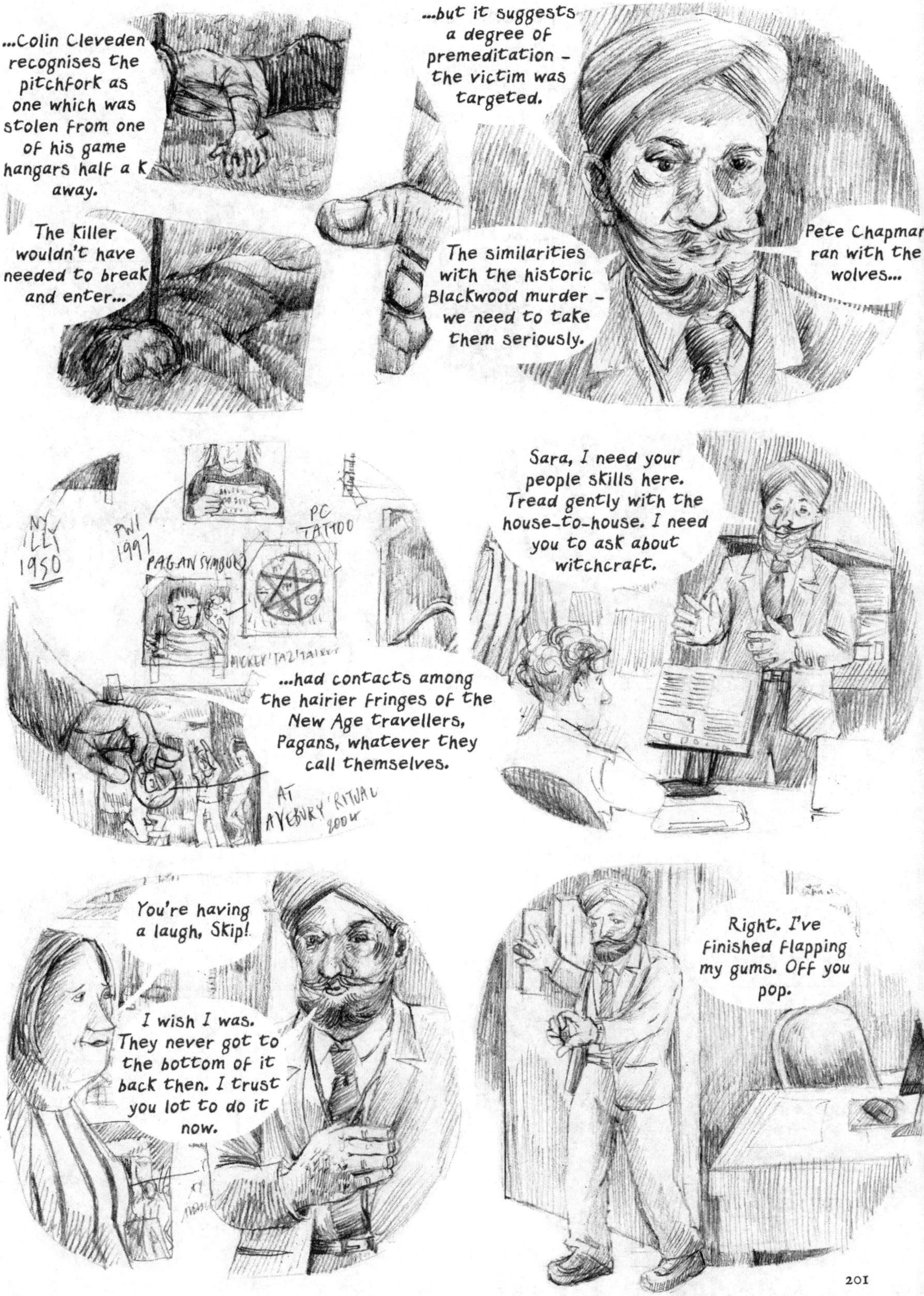
...Colin Cleveden recognises the pitchfork as one which was stolen from one of his game hangars half a K away.
The Killer wouldn't have needed to break and enter...
...but it suggests a degree of premeditation - the victim was targeted.
The similarities with the historic Blackwood murder - we need to take them seriously.
Pete Chapman ran with the wolves...
PC TATTOO
PAGAN SYMBOL
...had contacts among the hairier fringes of the New Age travellers, Pagans, whatever they call themselves.
Sara, I need your people skills here. Tread gently with the house-to-house. I need you to ask about witchcraft.
You're having a laugh, Skip!
I wish I was. They never got to the bottom of it back then. I trust you lot to do it now.
Right. I've finished flapping my gums. Off you pop.

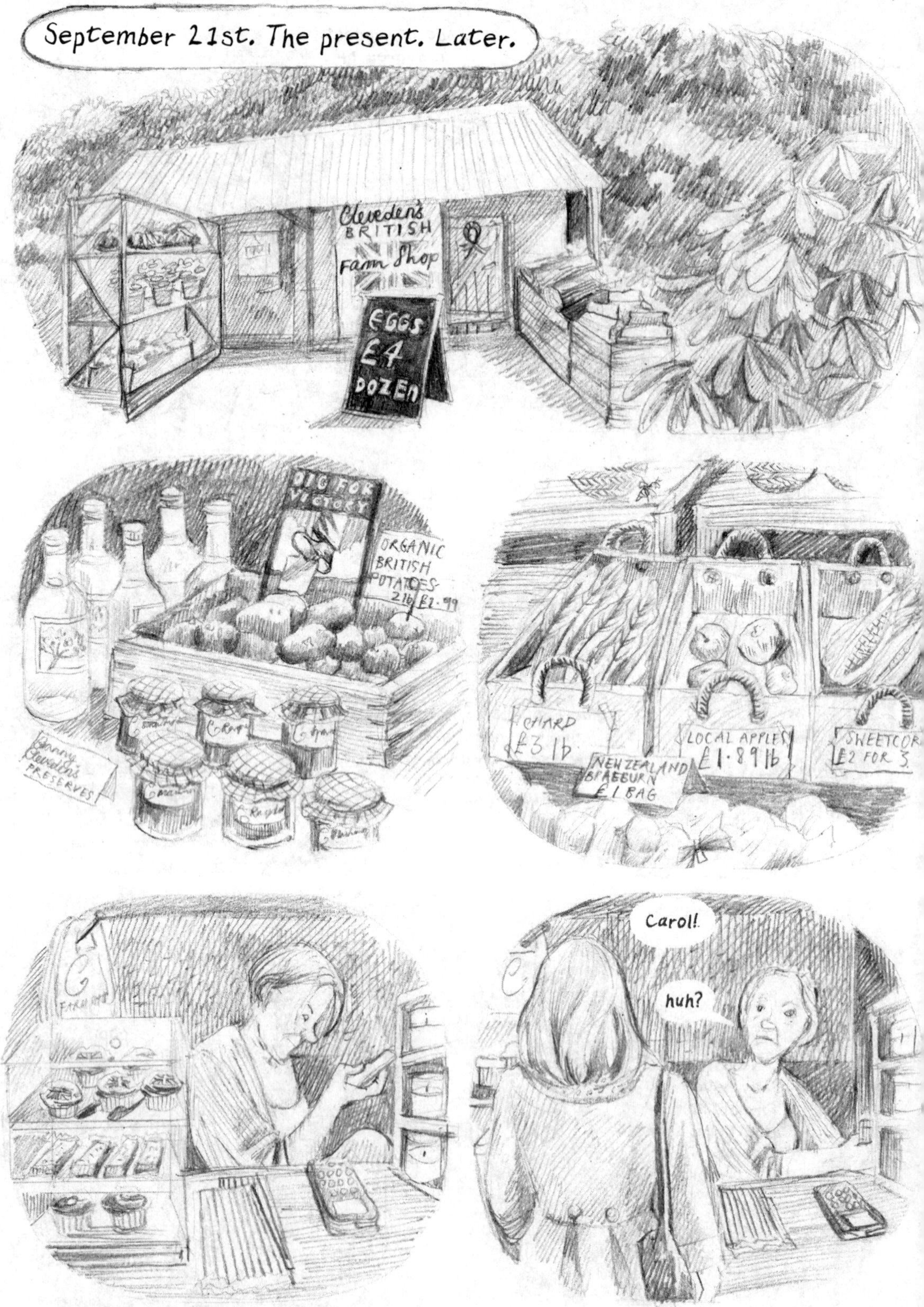
September 21st. The present. Later.
Cleveden's BRITISH Farm Shop
EGGS £4 DOZEN
DIG FOR VICTORY
ORGANIC BRITISH POTATOES 2lb £2.99
PRESERVES
CHARD £3 lb
LOCAL APPLES £1.89 lb
NEW ZEALAND BRAEBURN £1 BAG
SWEETCOR £2 FOR 3
Carol!
huh?

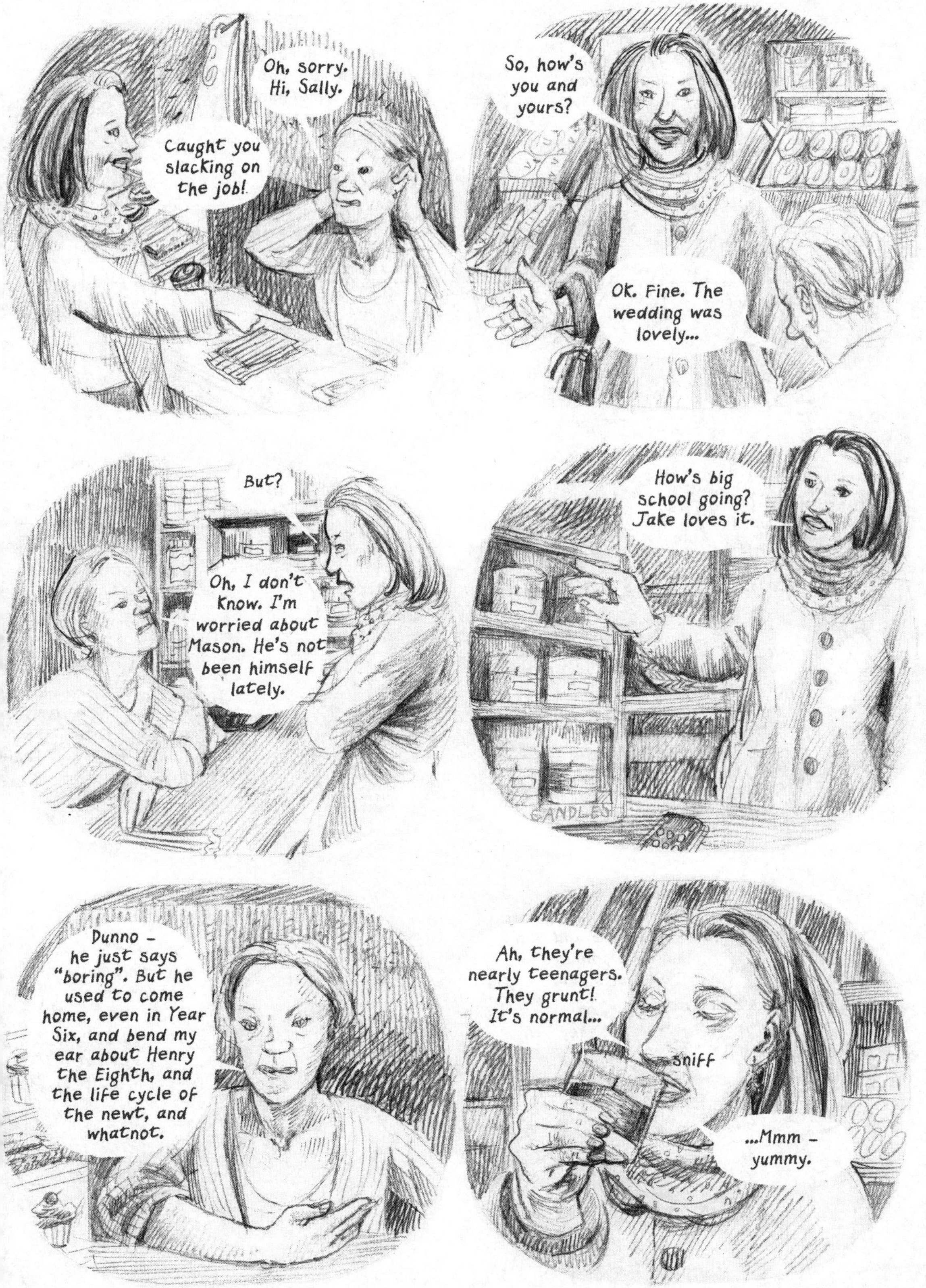
Caught you slacking on the job!
Oh, sorry. Hi, Sally.
So, how's you and yours?
Ok. Fine. The wedding was lovely...
But?
Oh, I don't know. I'm worried about Mason. He's not been himself lately.
How's big school going? Jake loves it.
CANDLES
Dunno – he just says "boring". But he used to come home, even in Year Six, and bend my ear about Henry the Eighth, and the life cycle of the newt, and whatnot.
Ah, they're nearly teenagers. They grunt! It's normal...
sniff
...Mmm – yummy.

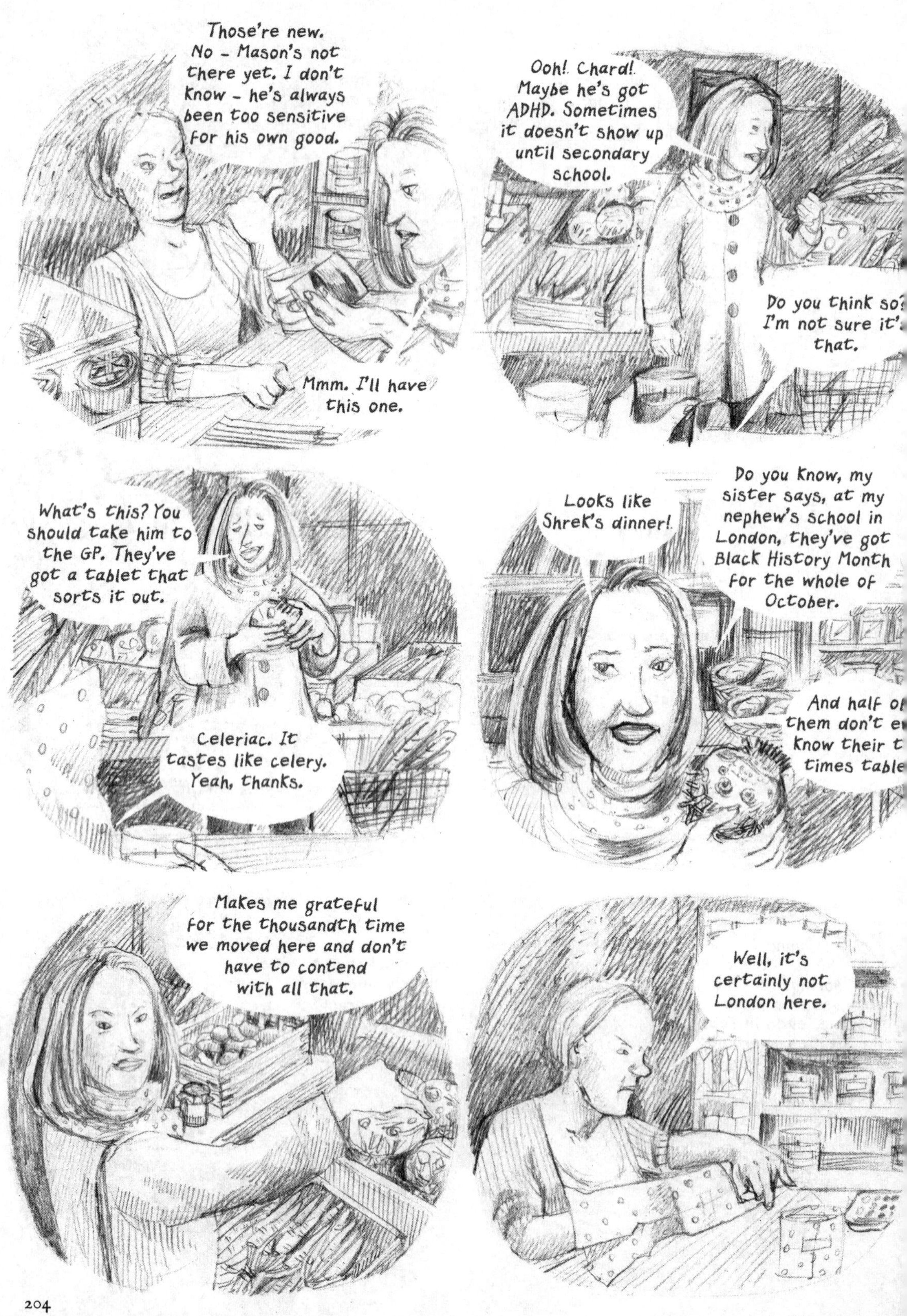
Those're new. No – Mason's not there yet. I don't know – he's always been too sensitive for his own good.
Mmm. I'll have this one.
Ooh! Chard! Maybe he's got ADHD. Sometimes it doesn't show up until secondary school.
Do you think so? I'm not sure it's that.
What's this? You should take him to the GP. They've got a tablet that sorts it out.
Celeriac. It tastes like celery. Yeah, thanks.
Looks like Shrek's dinner!
Do you know, my sister says, at my nephew's school in London, they've got Black History Month for the whole of October.
And half of them don't e know their t times table
Makes me grateful for the thousandth time we moved here and don't have to contend with all that.
Well, it's certainly not London here.

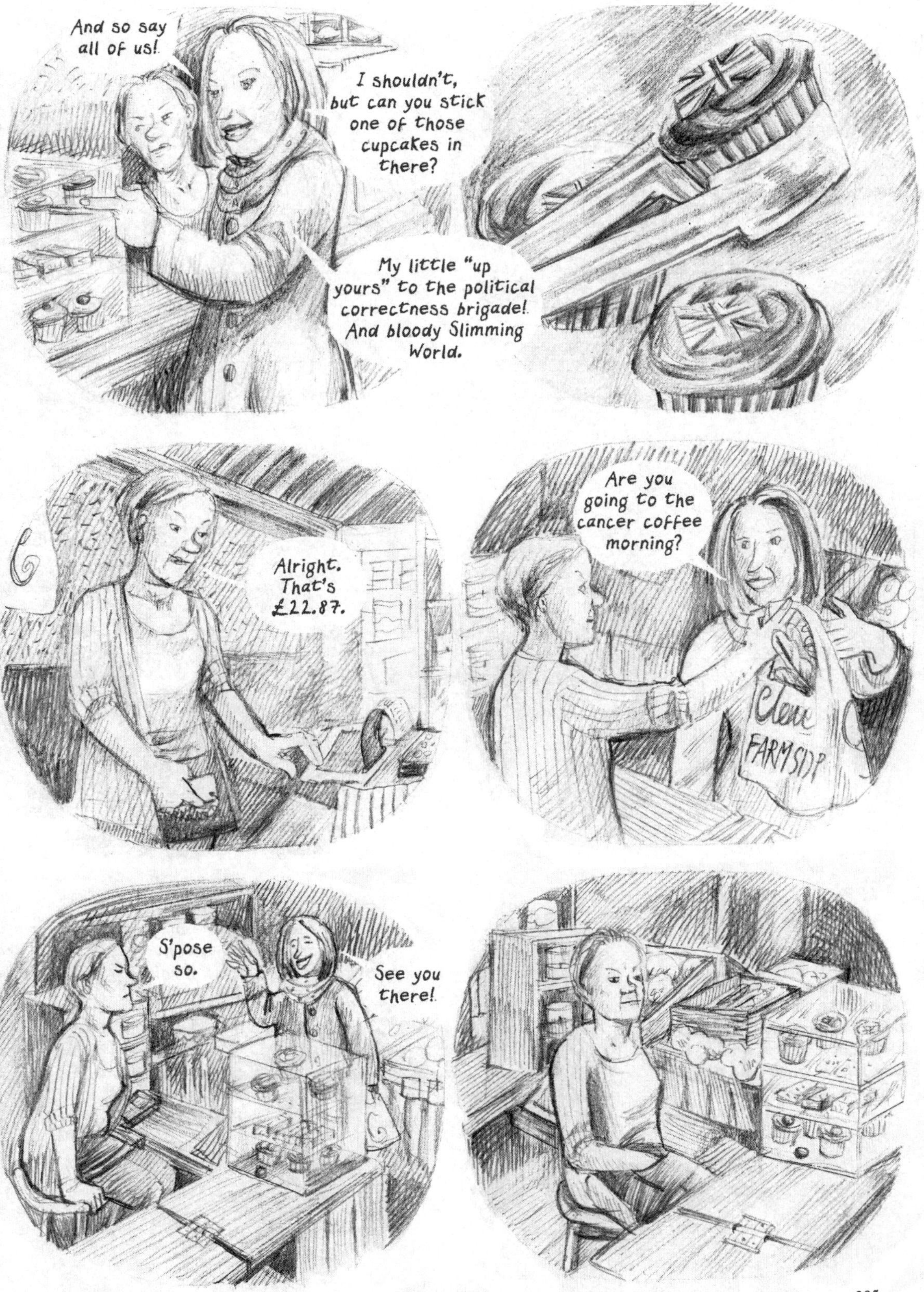
And so say all of us!
I shouldn't, but can you stick one of those cupcakes in there?
My little "up yours" to the political correctness brigade! And bloody Slimming World.
Alright. That's £22.87.
Are you going to the cancer coffee morning?
S'pose so.
See you there!

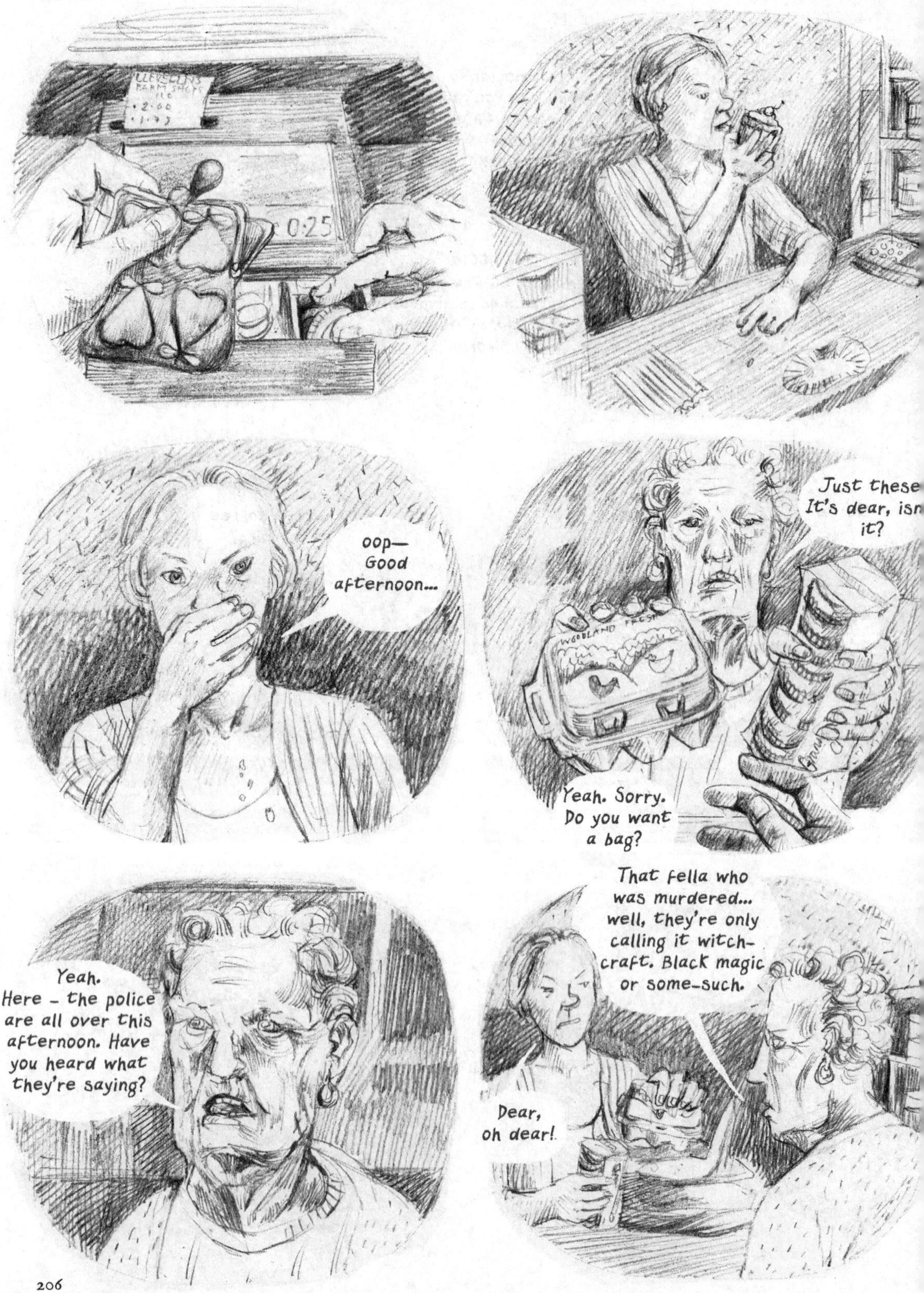
0:25
oop— Good afternoon...
Just these It's dear, isn it?
Yeah. Sorry. Do you want a bag?
Yeah. Here - the police are all over this afternoon. Have you heard what they're saying?
That fella who was murdered... well, they're only calling it witchcraft. Black magic or some-such.
Dear, oh dear!

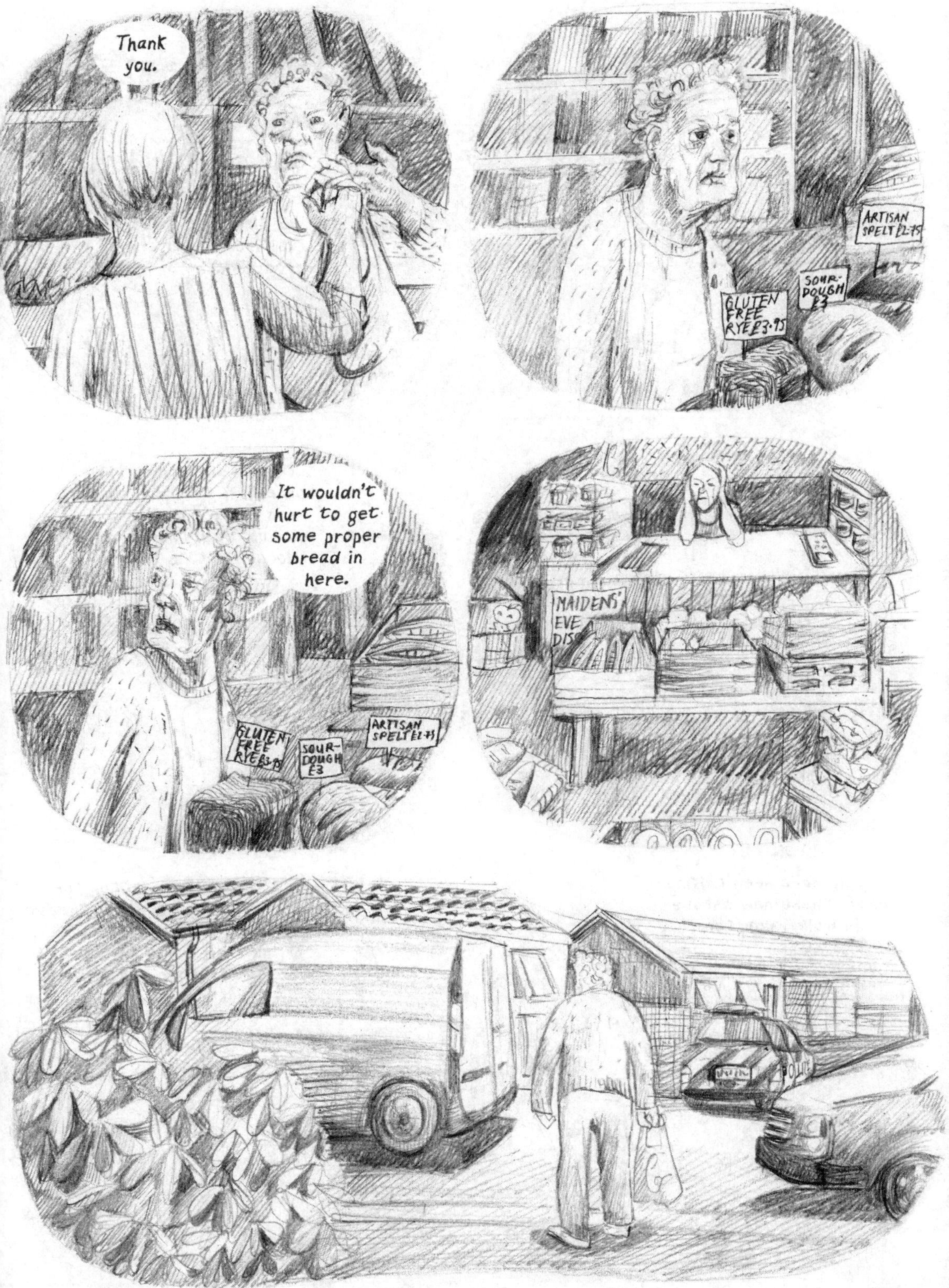
Thank you.
ARTISAN SPELT £2·75
GLUTEN FREE RYE £3·95
SOUR-DOUGH £3
It wouldn't hurt to get some proper bread in here.
MAIDENS' EVE

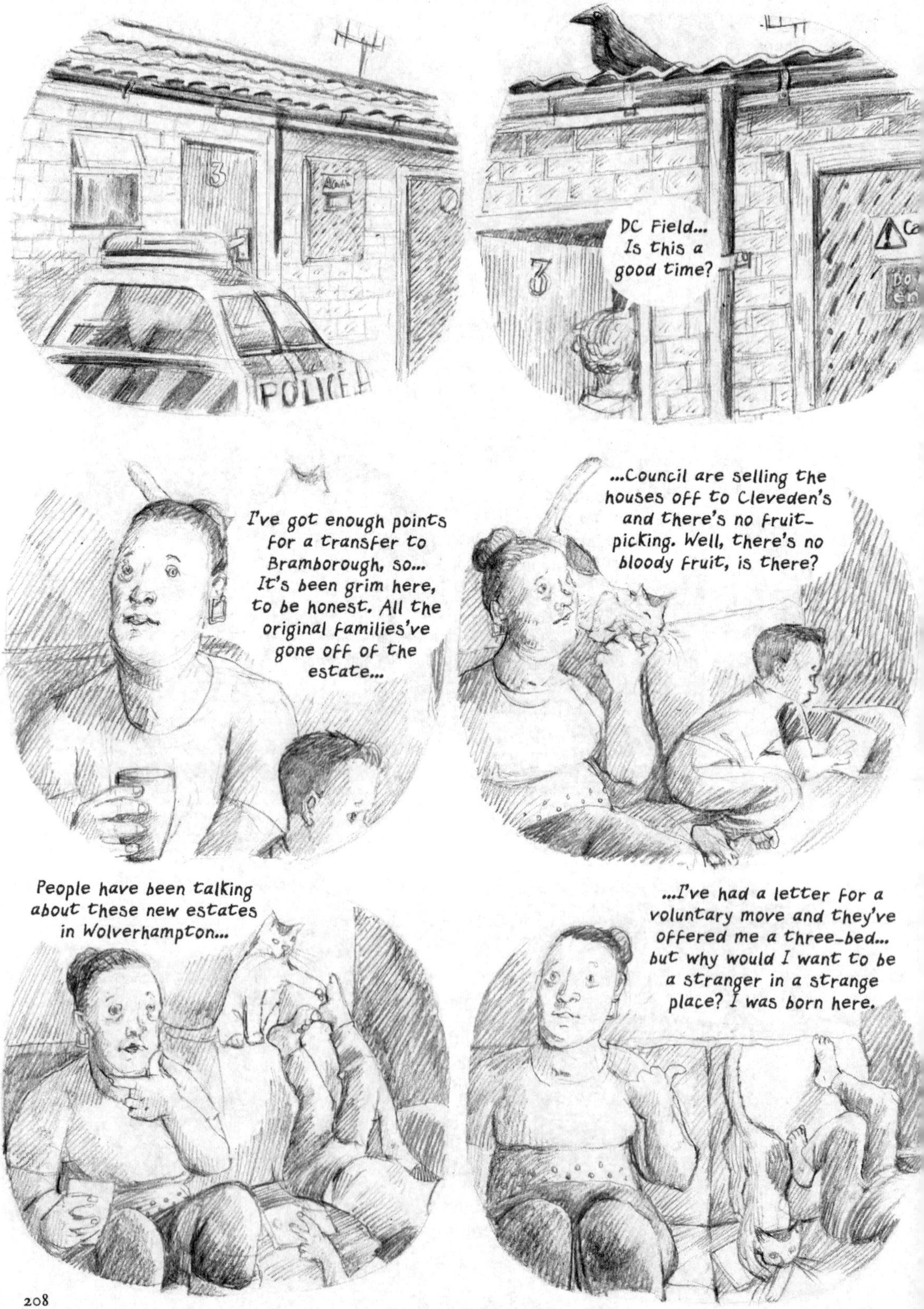
POLICE
DC Field... Is this a good time?
I've got enough points for a transfer to Bramborough, so... It's been grim here, to be honest. All the original families've gone off of the estate...
...Council are selling the houses off to Cleveden's and there's no fruit-picking. Well, there's no bloody fruit, is there?
People have been talking about these new estates in Wolverhampton...
...I've had a letter for a voluntary move and they've offered me a three-bed... but why would I want to be a stranger in a strange place? I was born here.

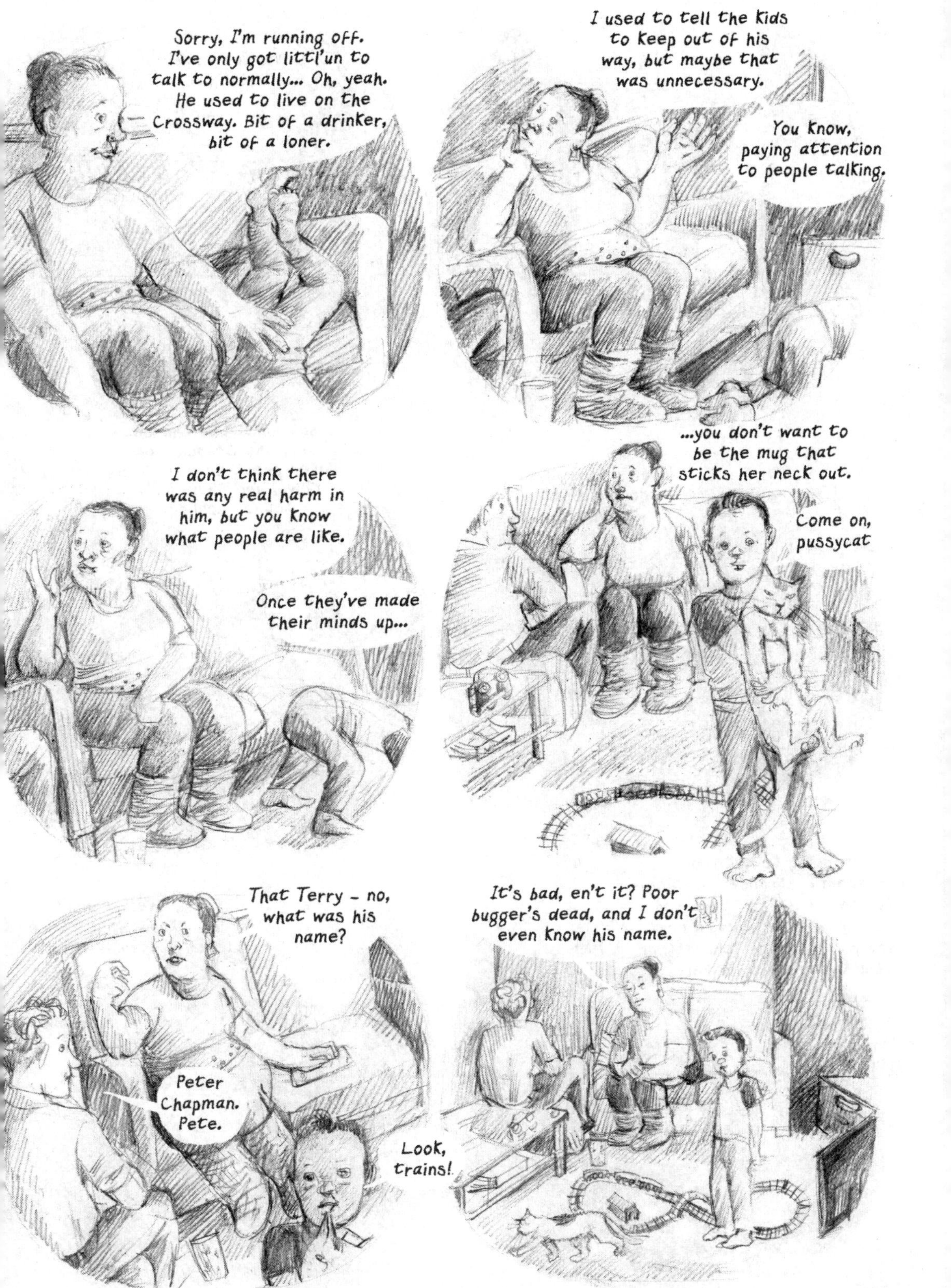
Sorry, I'm running off. I've only got littl'un to talk to normally... Oh, yeah. He used to live on the Crossway. Bit of a drinker, bit of a loner.
I used to tell the kids to keep out of his way, but maybe that was unnecessary.
You know, paying attention to people talking.
I don't think there was any real harm in him, but you know what people are like.
Once they've made their minds up...
...you don't want to be the mug that sticks her neck out.
Come on, pussycat
That Terry – no, what was his name?
Peter Chapman. Pete.
Look, trains!
It's bad, en't it? Poor bugger's dead, and I don't even know his name.

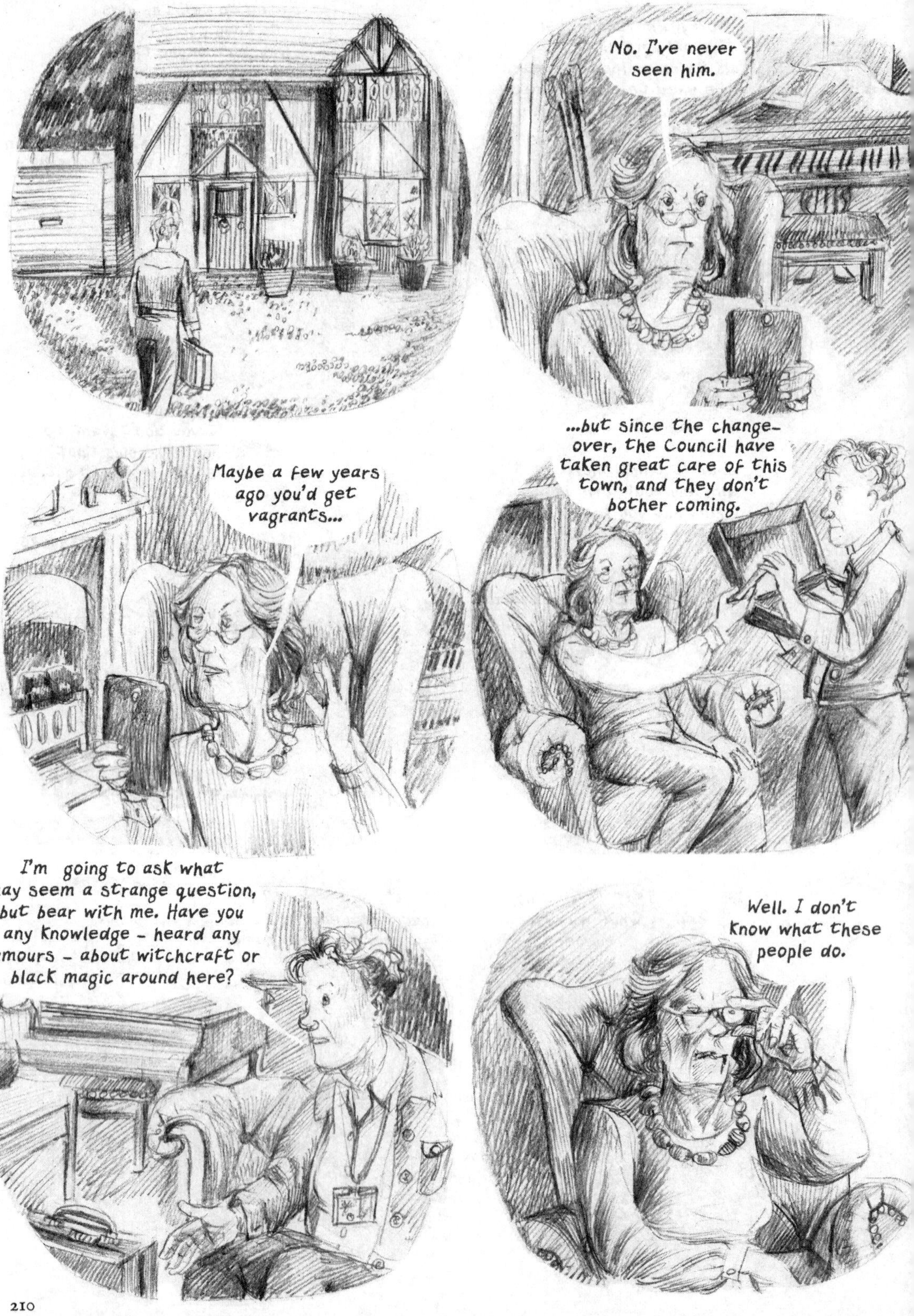
No. I've never seen him.
Maybe a few years ago you'd get vagrants...
...but since the change-over, the Council have taken great care of this town, and they don't bother coming.
I'm going to ask what may seem a strange question, but bear with me. Have you any knowledge - heard any rumours - about witchcraft or black magic around here?
Well. I don't know what these people do.

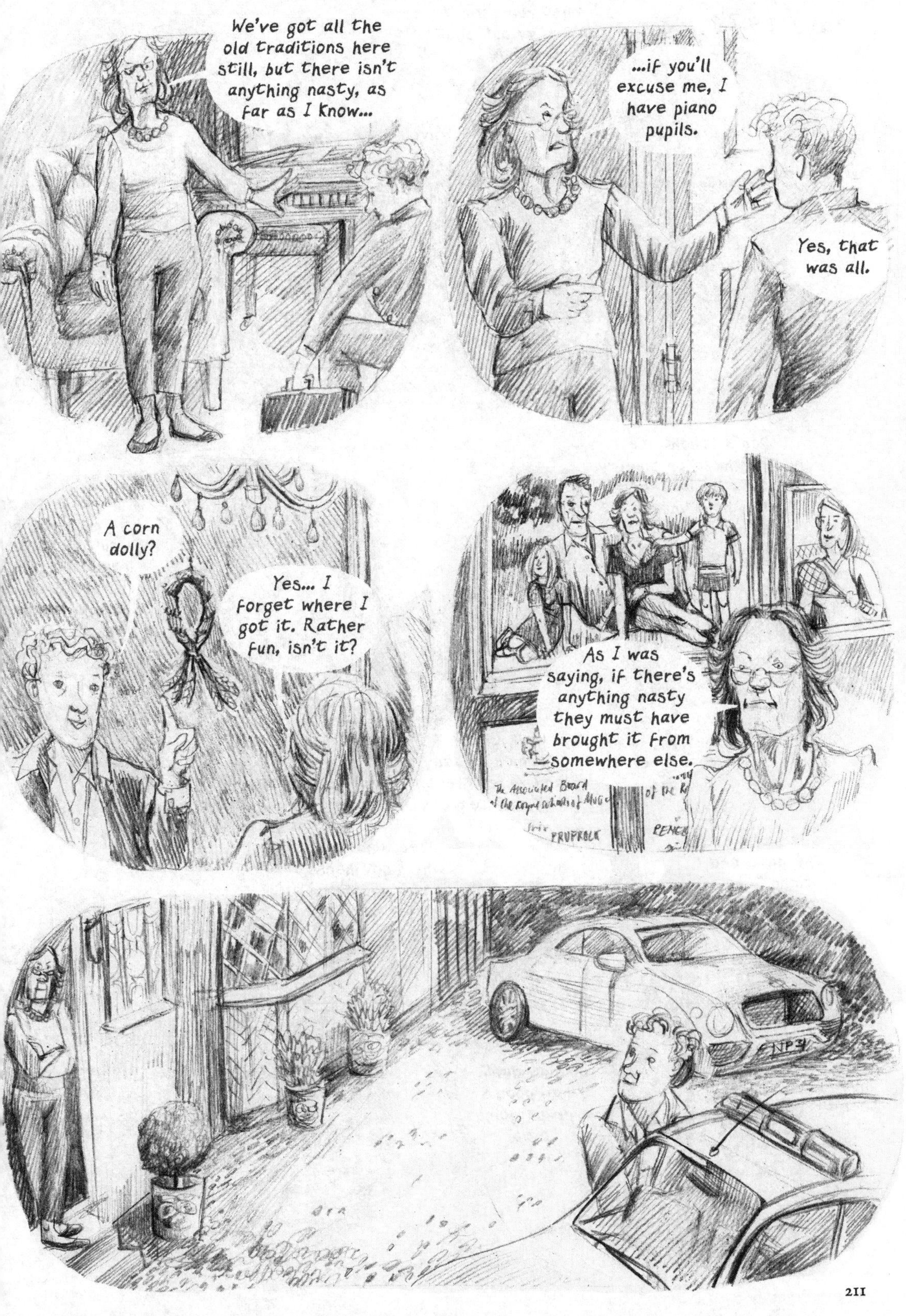
We've got all the old traditions here still, but there isn't anything nasty, as far as I know...
...if you'll excuse me, I have piano pupils.
Yes, that was all.
A corn dolly?
Yes... I forget where I got it. Rather fun, isn't it?
As I was saying, if there's anything nasty they must have brought it from somewhere else.

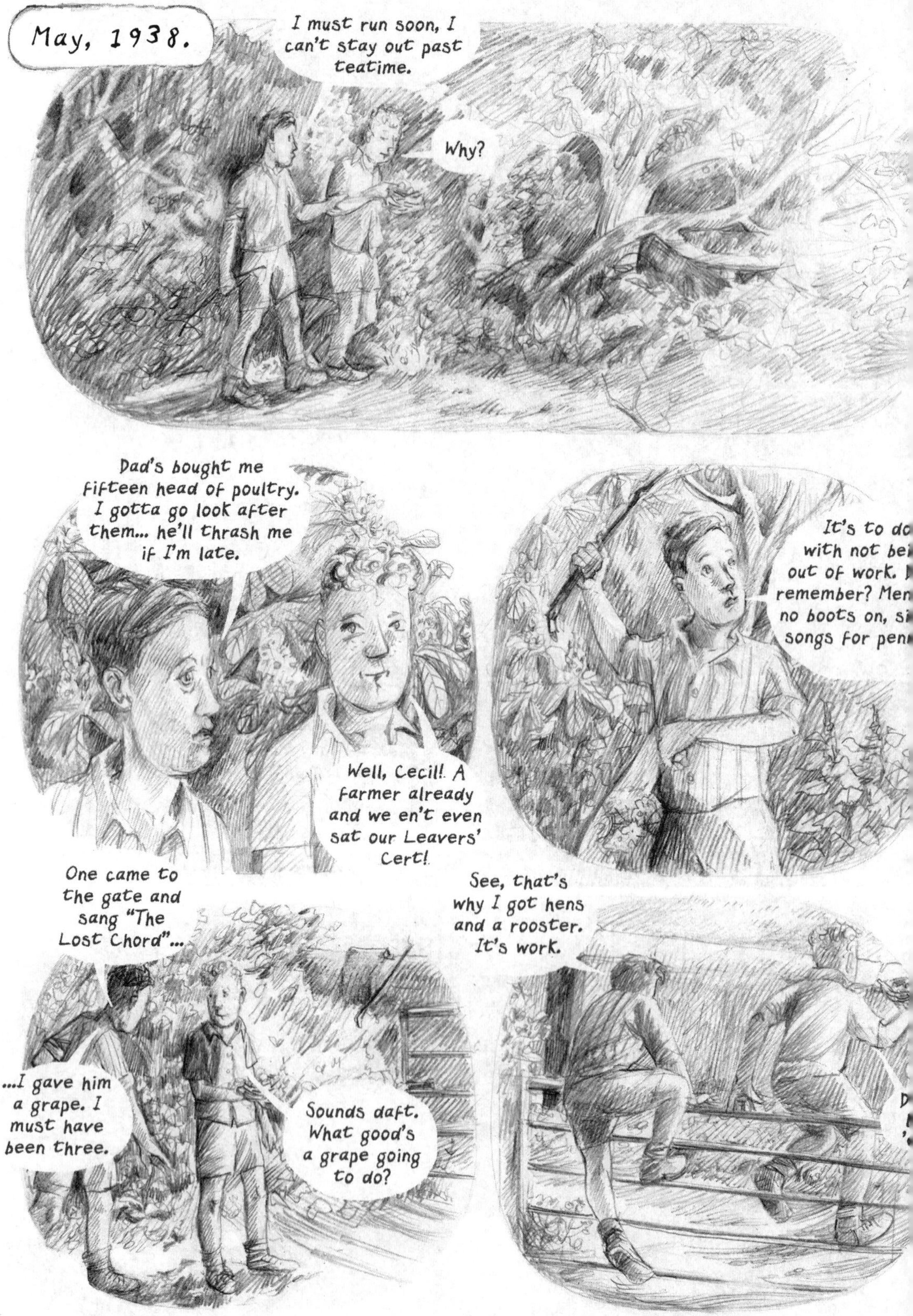
May, 1938.
I must run soon, I can't stay out past teatime.
Why?
Dad's bought me fifteen head of poultry. I gotta go look after them... he'll thrash me if I'm late.
Well, Cecil! A farmer already and we en't even sat our Leavers' Cert!
It's to d
with not be
out of work.
remember? Men
no boots on, s
songs for pen
One came to the gate and sang "The Lost Chord"...
...I gave him a grape. I must have been three.
Sounds daft. What good's a grape going to do?
See, that's why I got hens and a rooster. It's work.

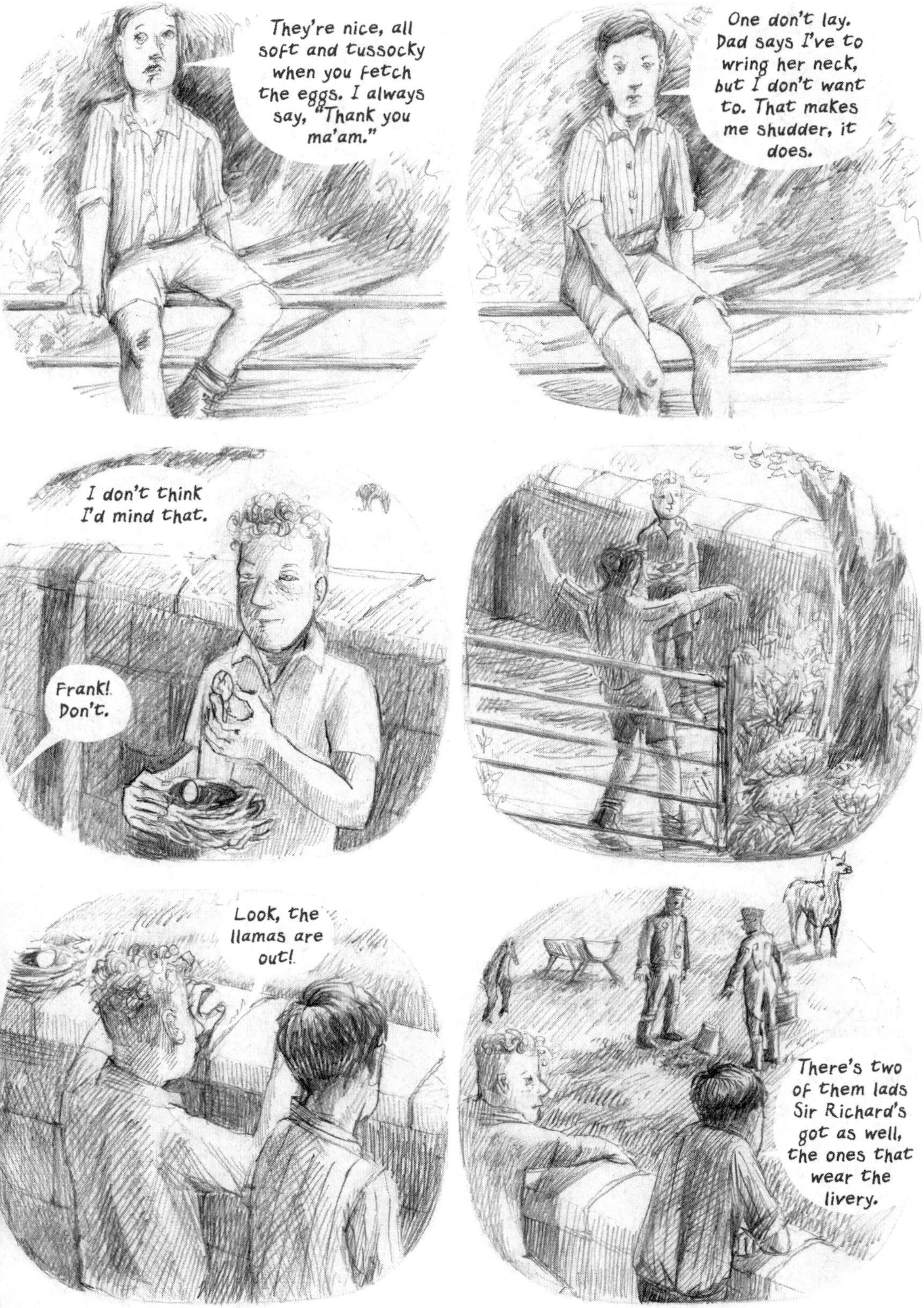
They're nice, all soft and tussocky when you fetch the eggs. I always say, "Thank you ma'am."
One don't lay. Dad says I've to wring her neck, but I don't want to. That makes me shudder, it does.
I don't think I'd mind that.
Frank!. Don't.
Look, the llamas are out!.
There's two of them lads Sir Richard's got as well, the ones that wear the livery.

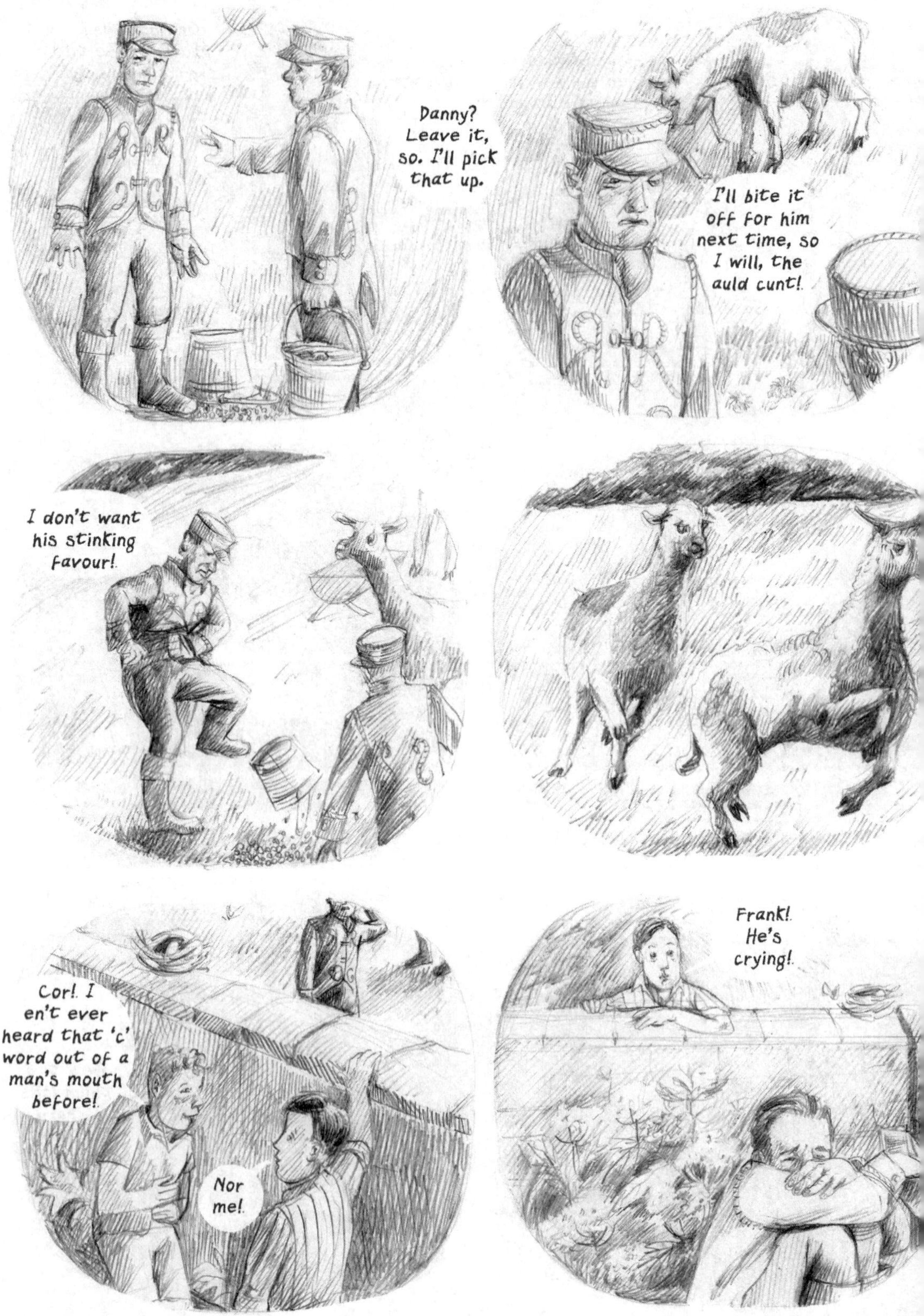
Danny? Leave it, so. I'll pick that up.
I'll bite it off for him next time, so I will, the auld cunt!.
I don't want his stinking favour!.
Cor!. I en't ever heard that 'c' word out of a man's mouth before!.
Nor me!.
Frank!. He's crying!.

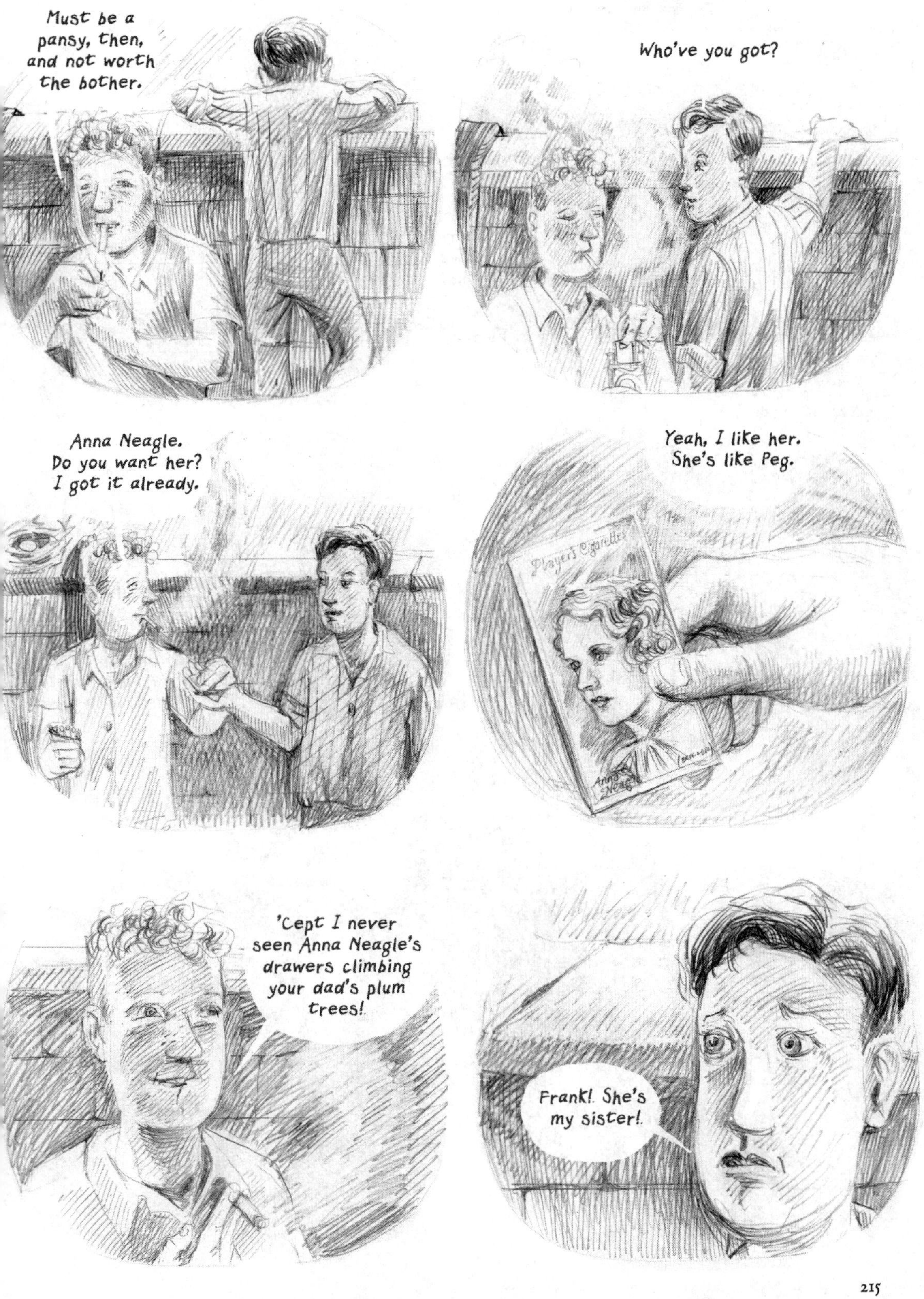
Must be a pansy, then, and not worth the bother.
Who've you got?
Anna Neagle. Do you want her? I got it already.
Yeah, I like her. She's like Peg.
Player's Cigarettes
'Cept I never seen Anna Neagle's drawers climbing your dad's plum trees!.
Frank!. She's my sister!.

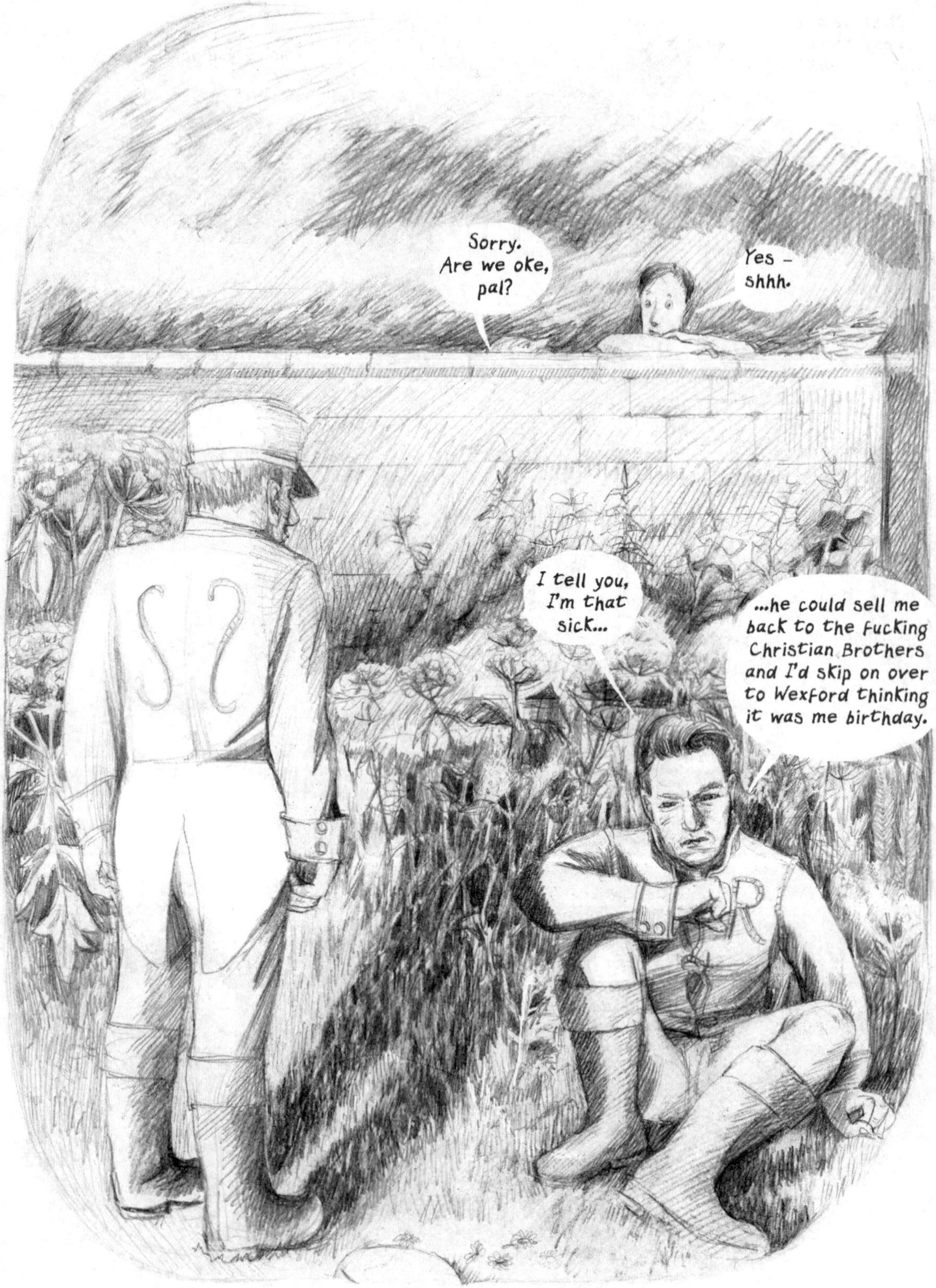
Sorry. Are we oke, pal?
Yes – shhh.
I tell you, I'm that sick...
...he could sell me back to the fucking Christian Brothers and I'd skip on over to Wexford thinking it was me birthday.

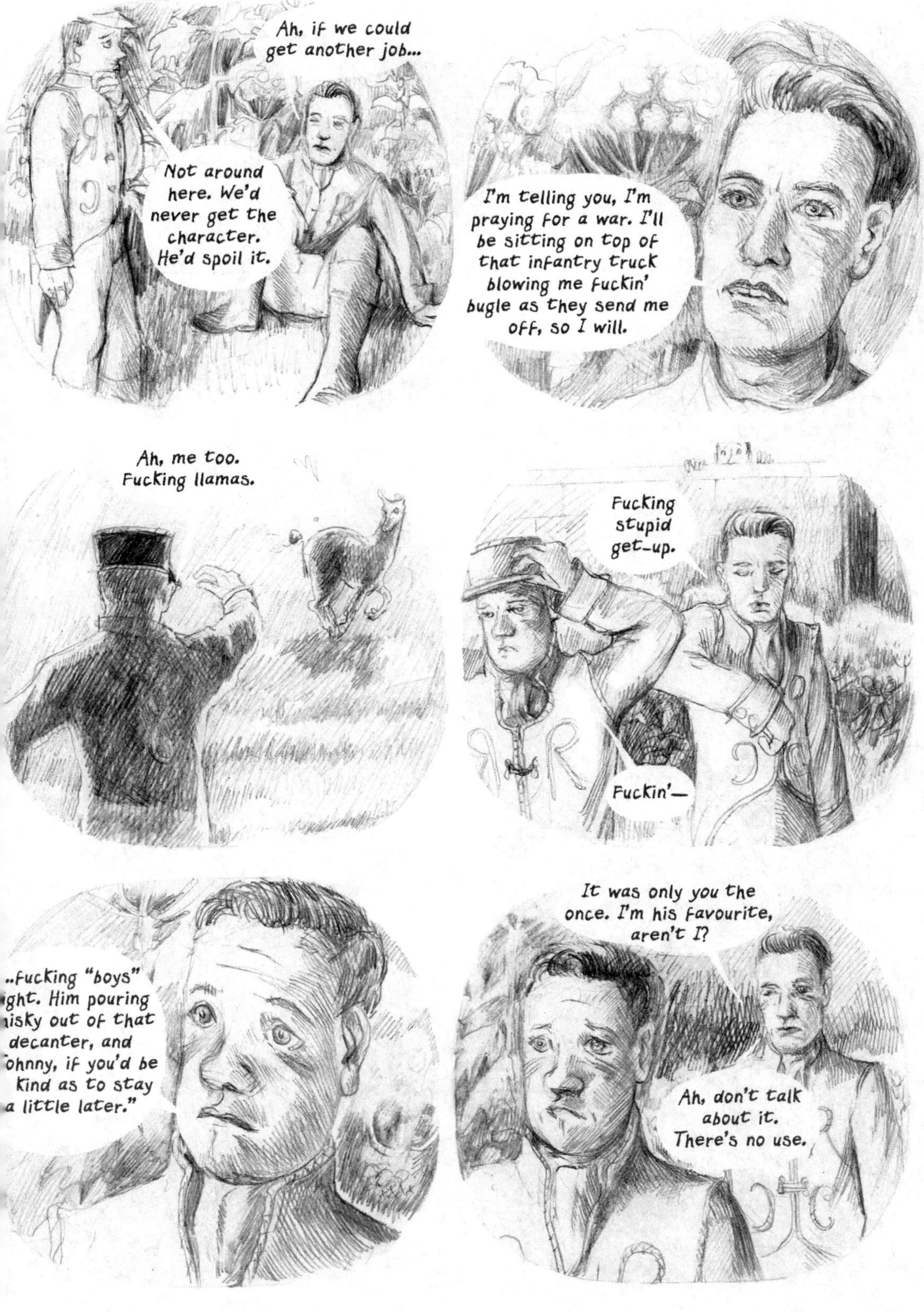

Ah, if we could get another job...
Not around here. We'd never get the character. He'd spoil it.
I'm telling you, I'm praying for a war. I'll be sitting on top of that infantry truck blowing me fuckin' bugle as they send me off, so I will.
Ah, me too. Fucking llamas.
Fucking stupid get-up.
Fuckin'—
..fucking "boys" ight. Him pouring isky out of that decanter, and ohnny, if you'd be kind as to stay a little later."
It was only you the once. I'm his favourite, aren't I?
Ah, don't talk about it. There's no use.

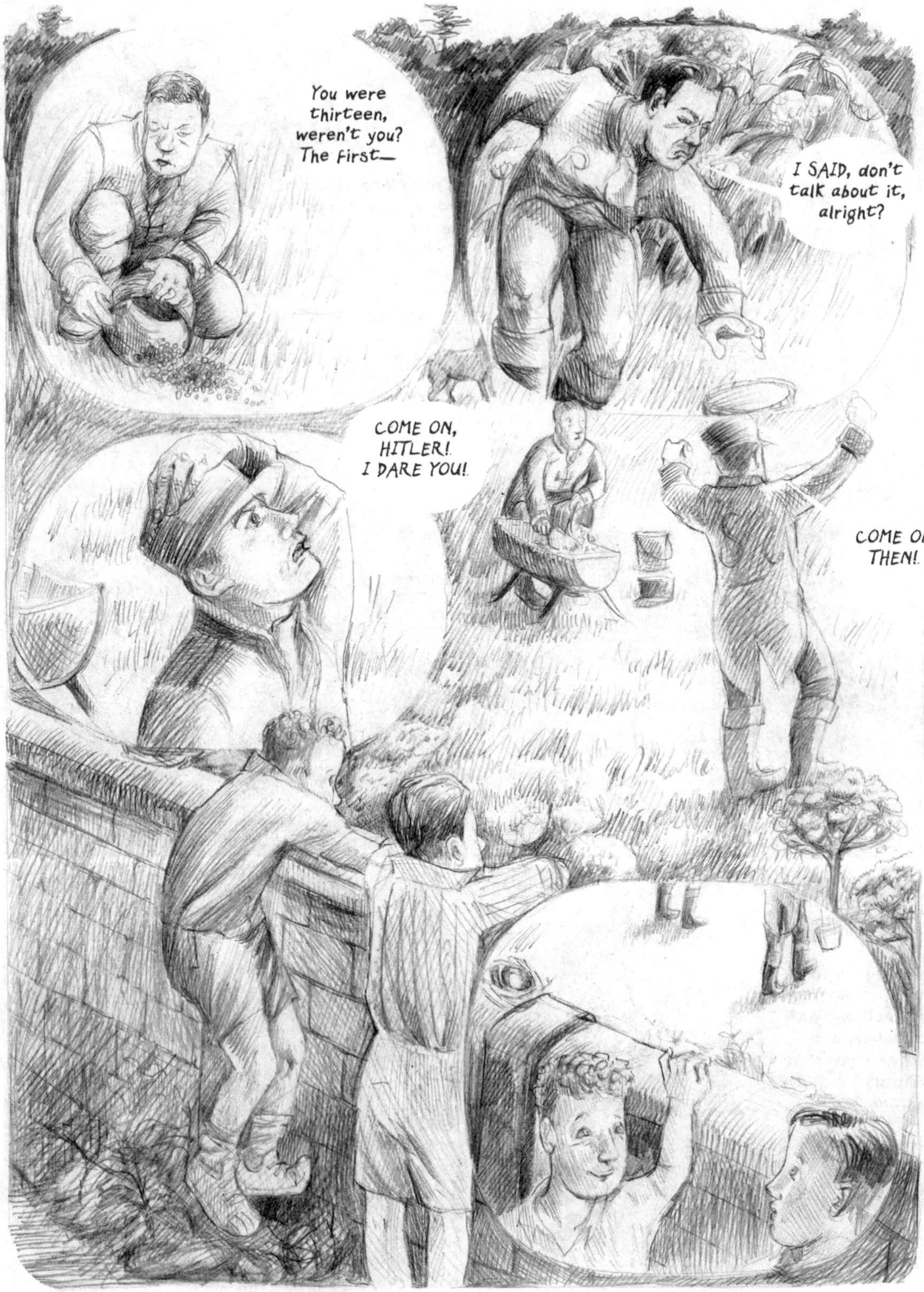
You were thirteen, weren't you? The first—
I SAID, don't talk about it, alright?
COME ON, HITLER! I DARE YOU!
COME ON THEN!

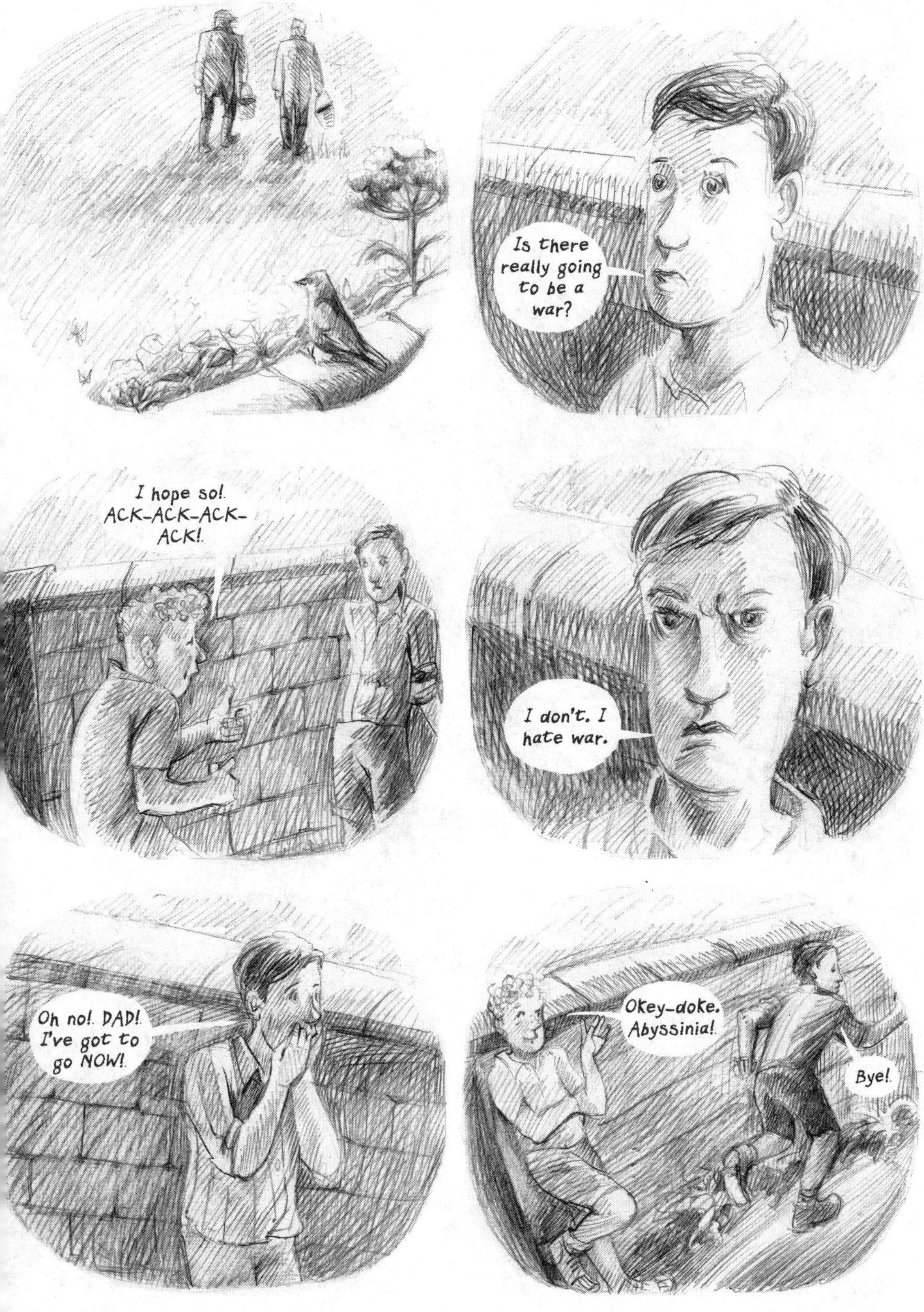
Is there really going to be a war?
I hope so! ACK-ACK-ACK-ACK!
I don't. I hate war.
Oh no!. DAD!. I've got to go NOW!.
Okey-doke. Abyssinia!.
Bye!.

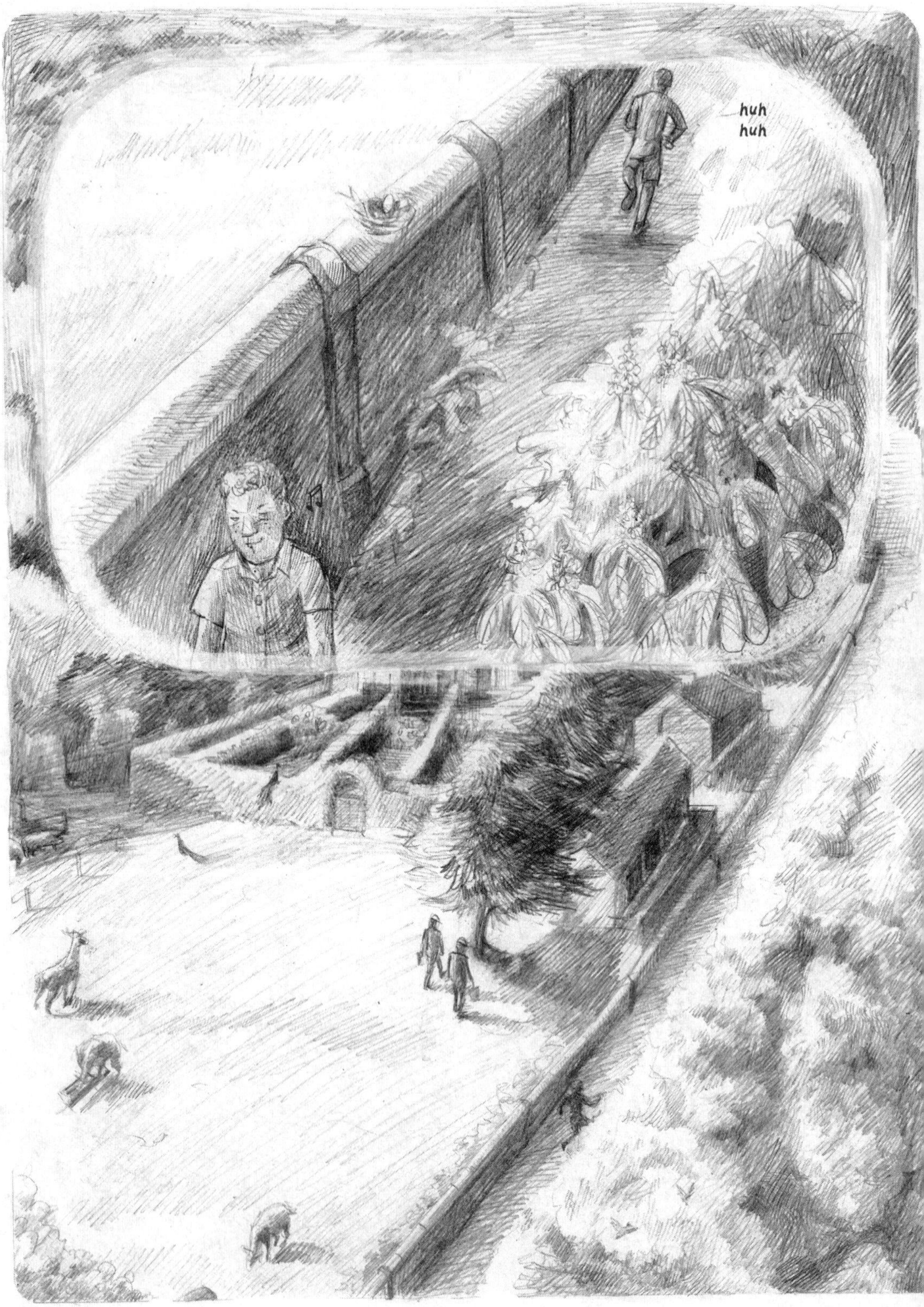
huh
huh

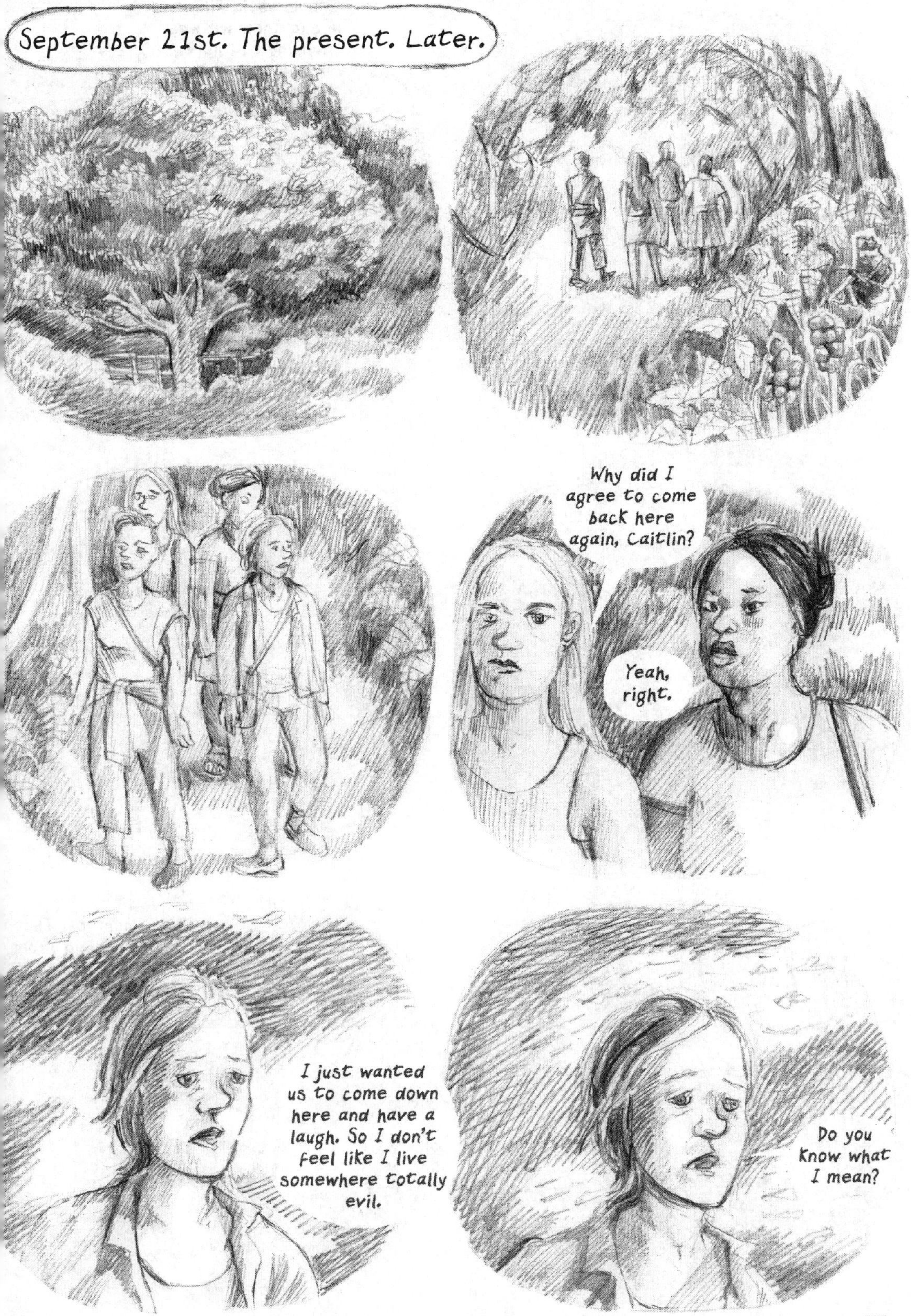
September 21st. The present. Later.
Why did I agree to come back here again, Caitlin?
Yeah, right.
I just wanted us to come down here and have a laugh. So I don't feel like I live somewhere totally evil.
Do you know what I mean?

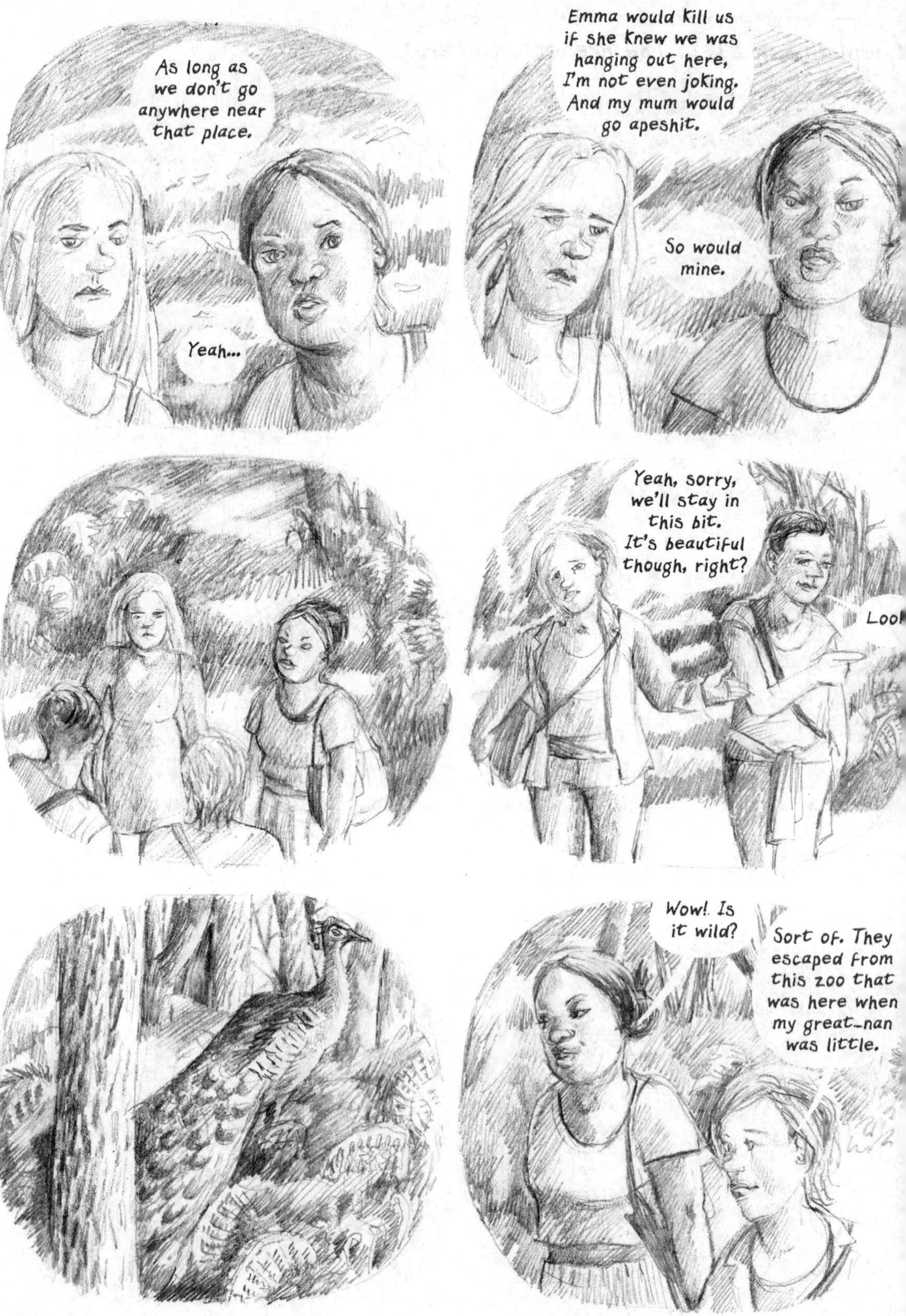
As long as we don't go anywhere near that place.
Yeah...
Emma would kill us if she knew we was hanging out here, I'm not even joking. And my mum would go apeshit.
So would mine.
Yeah, sorry, we'll stay in this bit. It's beautiful though, right?
Loo
Wow!. Is it wild?
Sort of. They escaped from this zoo that was here when my great-nan was little.

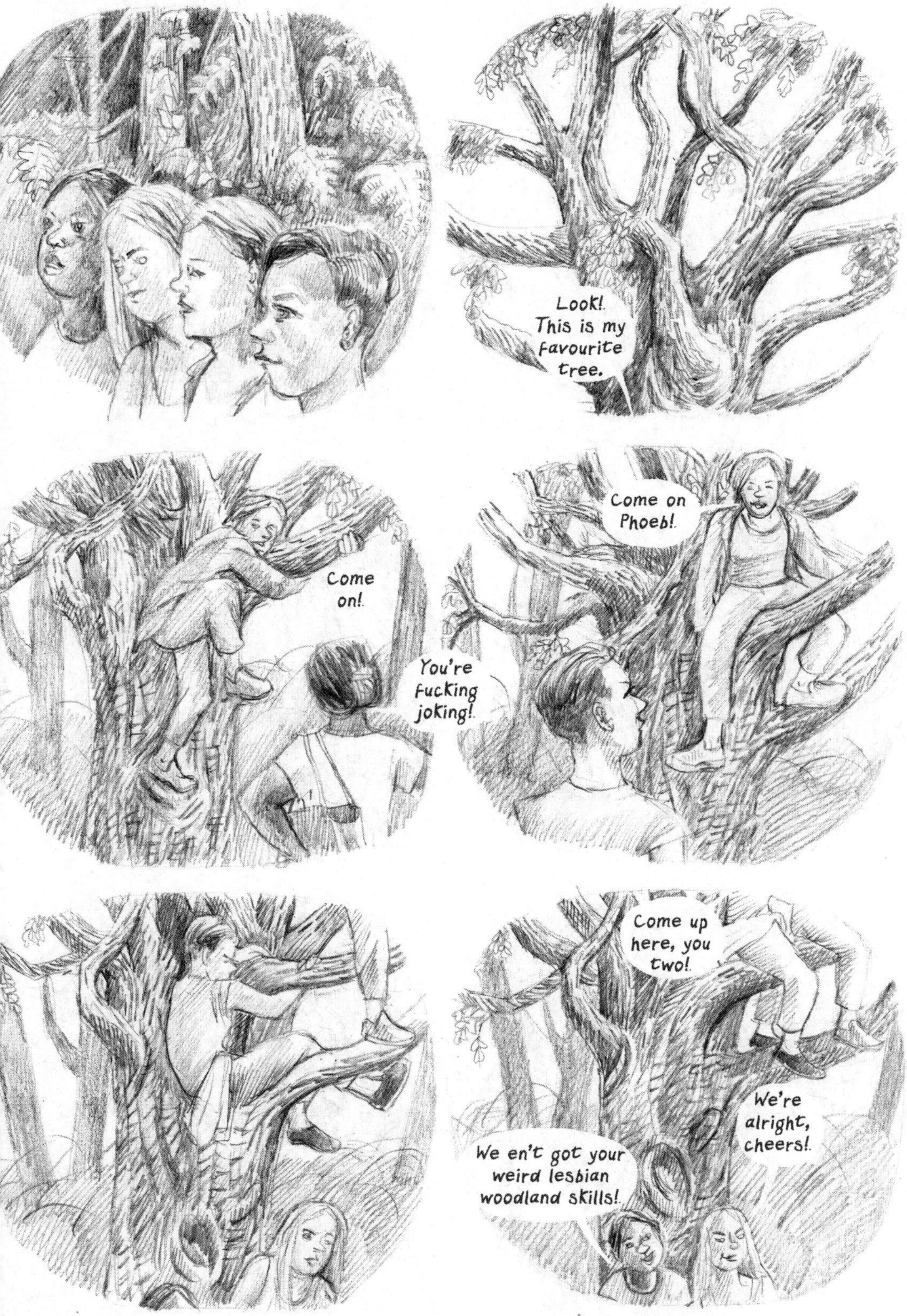
Look!. This is my favourite tree.
Come on!.
You're fucking joking!.
Come on Phoeb!.
Come up here, you two!.
We're alright, cheers!.
We en't got your weird lesbian woodland skills!.

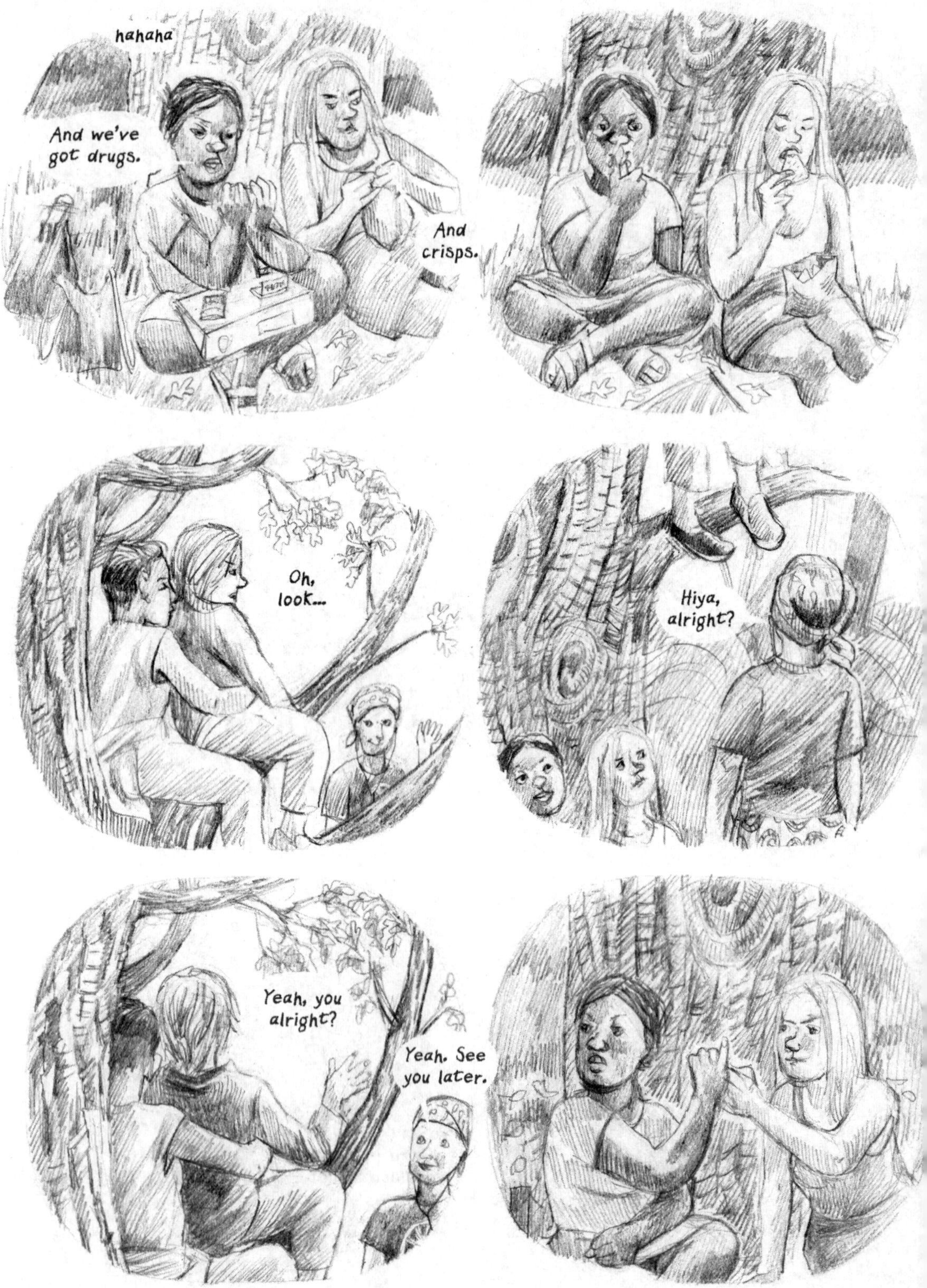
hahaha
And we've got drugs.
And crisps.
Oh, look...
Hiya, alright?
Yeah, you alright?
Yeah. See you later.

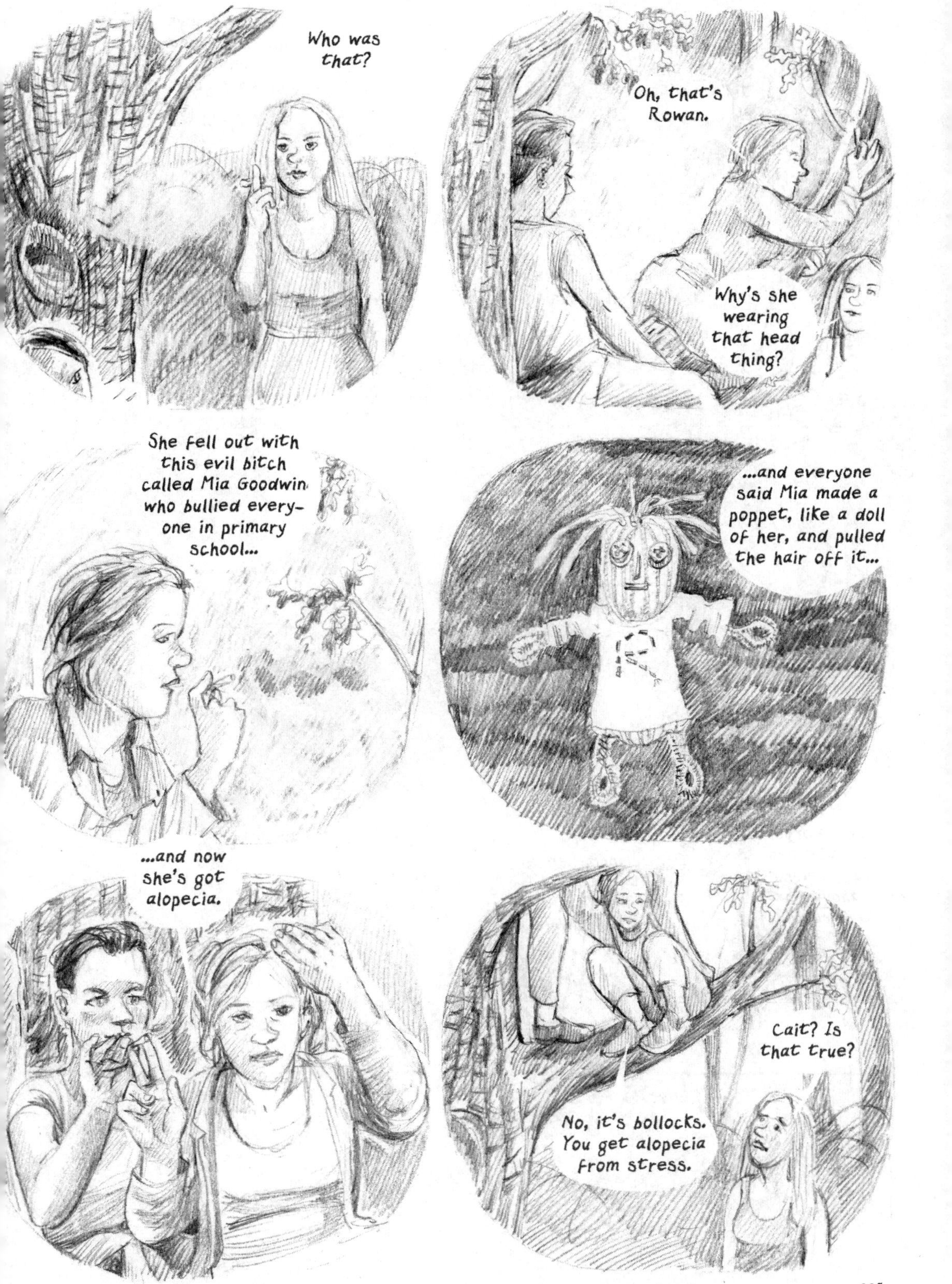
Who was that?
Oh, that's Rowan.
Why's she wearing that head thing?
She fell out with this evil bitch called Mia Goodwin who bullied every-one in primary school...
...and everyone said Mia made a poppet, like a doll of her, and pulled the hair off it...
...and now she's got alopecia.
Cait? Is that true?
No, it's bollocks. You get alopecia from stress.

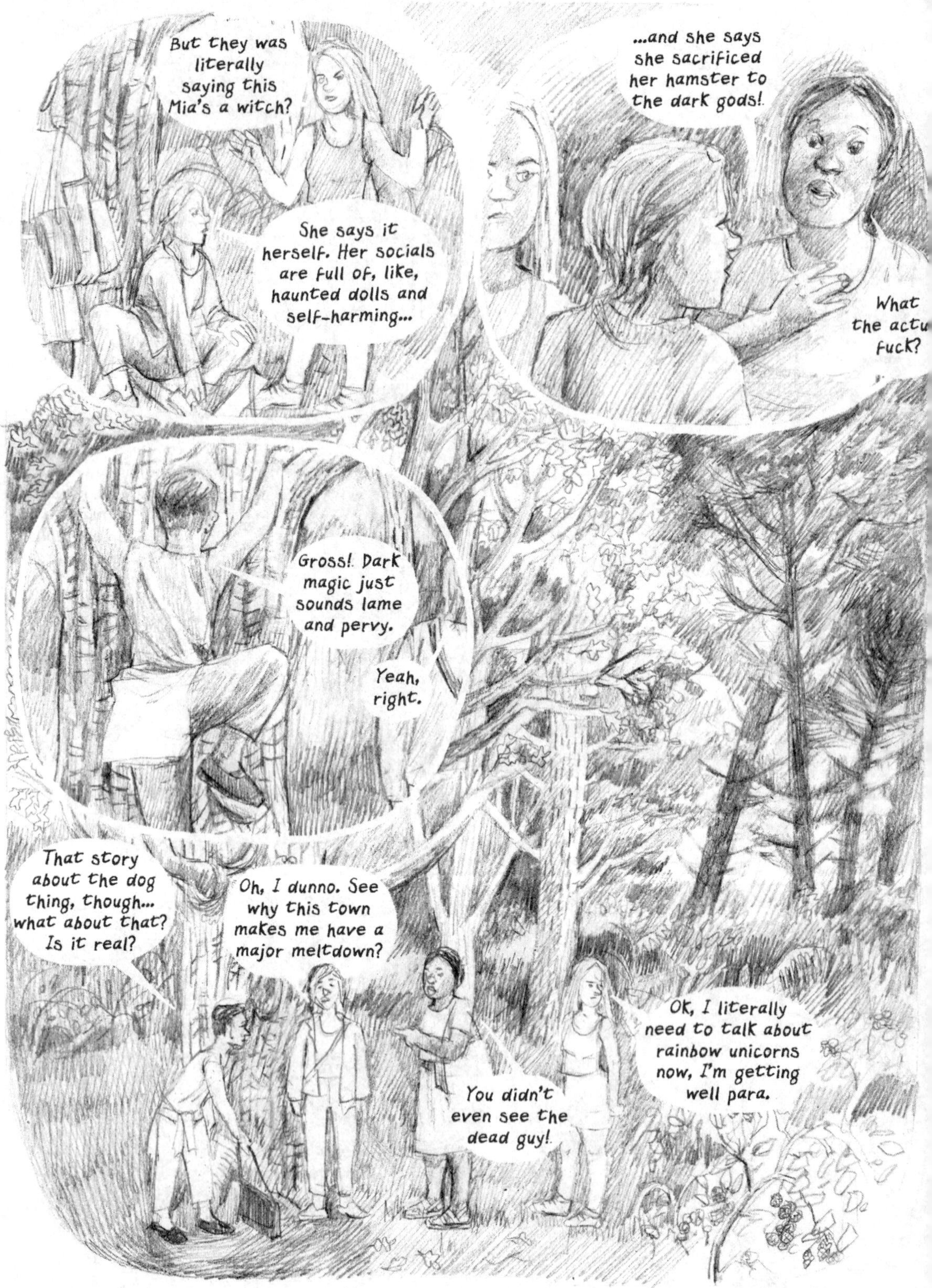
But they was literally saying this Mia's a witch?
She says it herself. Her socials are full of, like, haunted dolls and self-harming...
...and she says she sacrificed her hamster to the dark gods!.
What the actu fuck?
Gross!. Dark magic just sounds lame and pervy.
Yeah, right.
That story about the dog thing, though... what about that? Is it real?
Oh, I dunno. See why this town makes me have a major meltdown?
You didn't even see the dead guy!.
Ok, I literally need to talk about rainbow unicorns now, I'm getting well para.

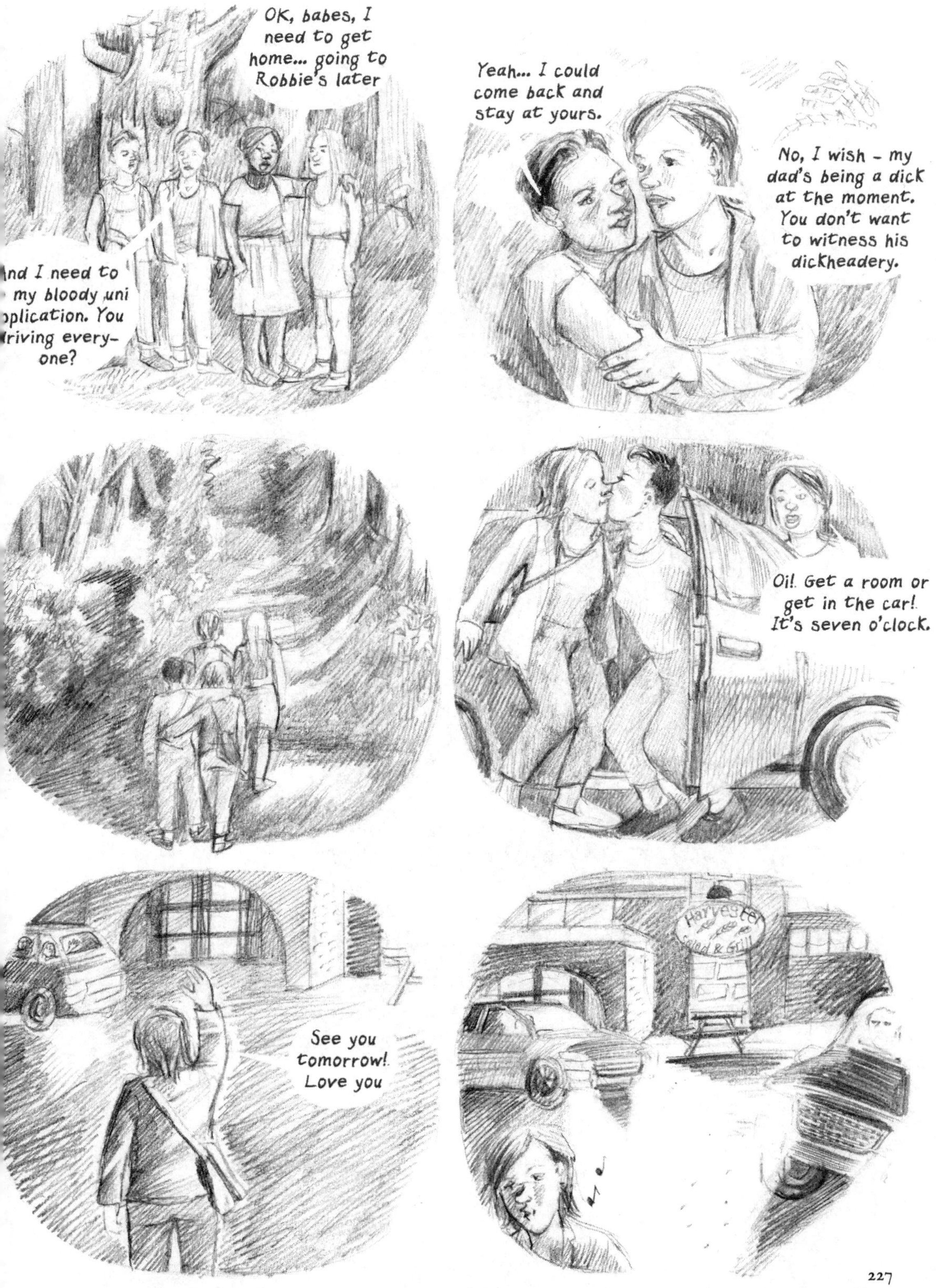
OK, babes, I need to get home... going to Robbie's later
nd I need to my bloody uni plication. You riving every-one?
Yeah... I could come back and stay at yours.
No, I wish - my dad's being a dick at the moment. You don't want to witness his dickheadery.
Oi! Get a room or get in the car! It's seven o'clock.
See you tomorrow! Love you
Harvester
Salad & Grill

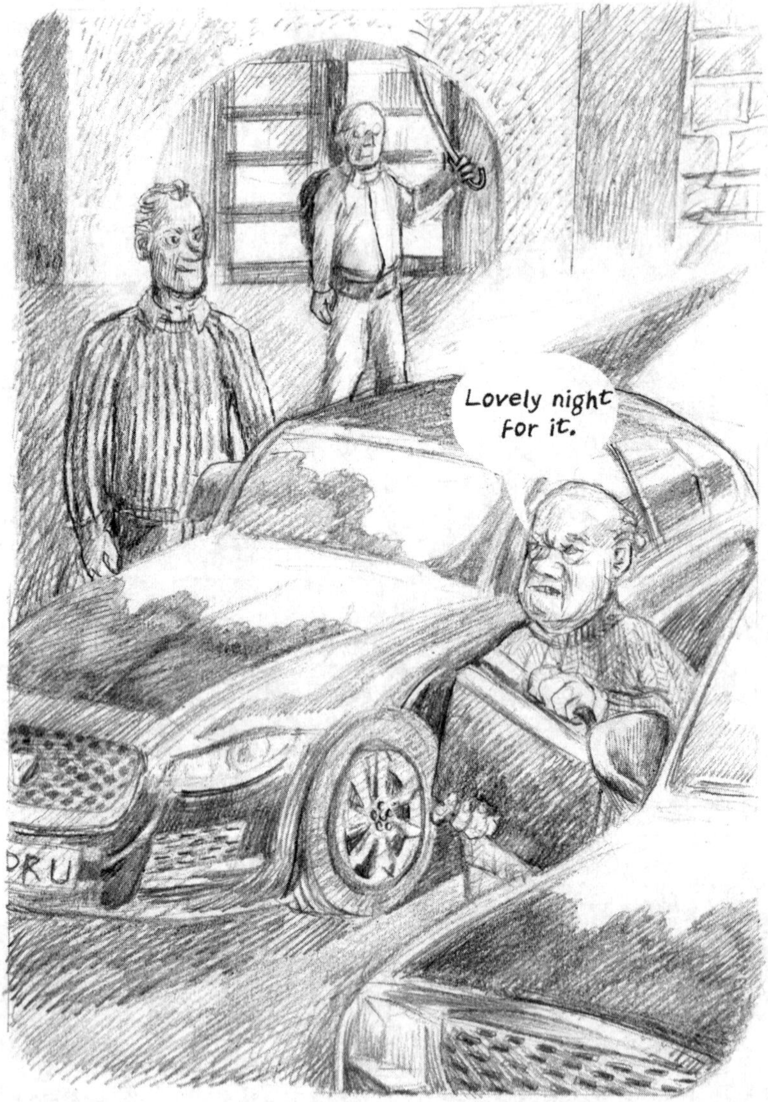
Lovely night for it.
DRU

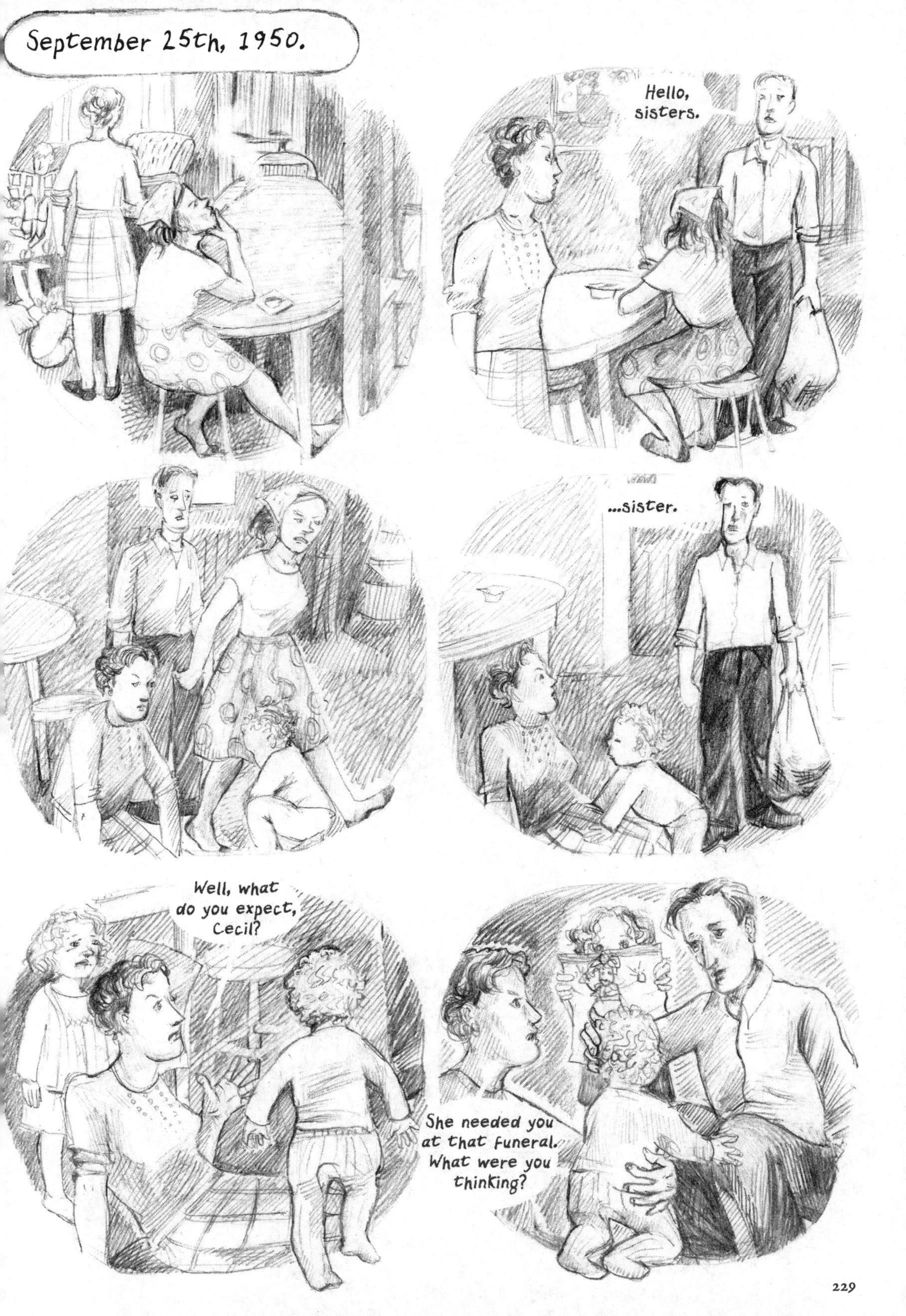
September 25th, 1950.
Hello, sisters.
...sister.
Well, what do you expect, Cecil?
She needed you at that funeral. What were you thinking?

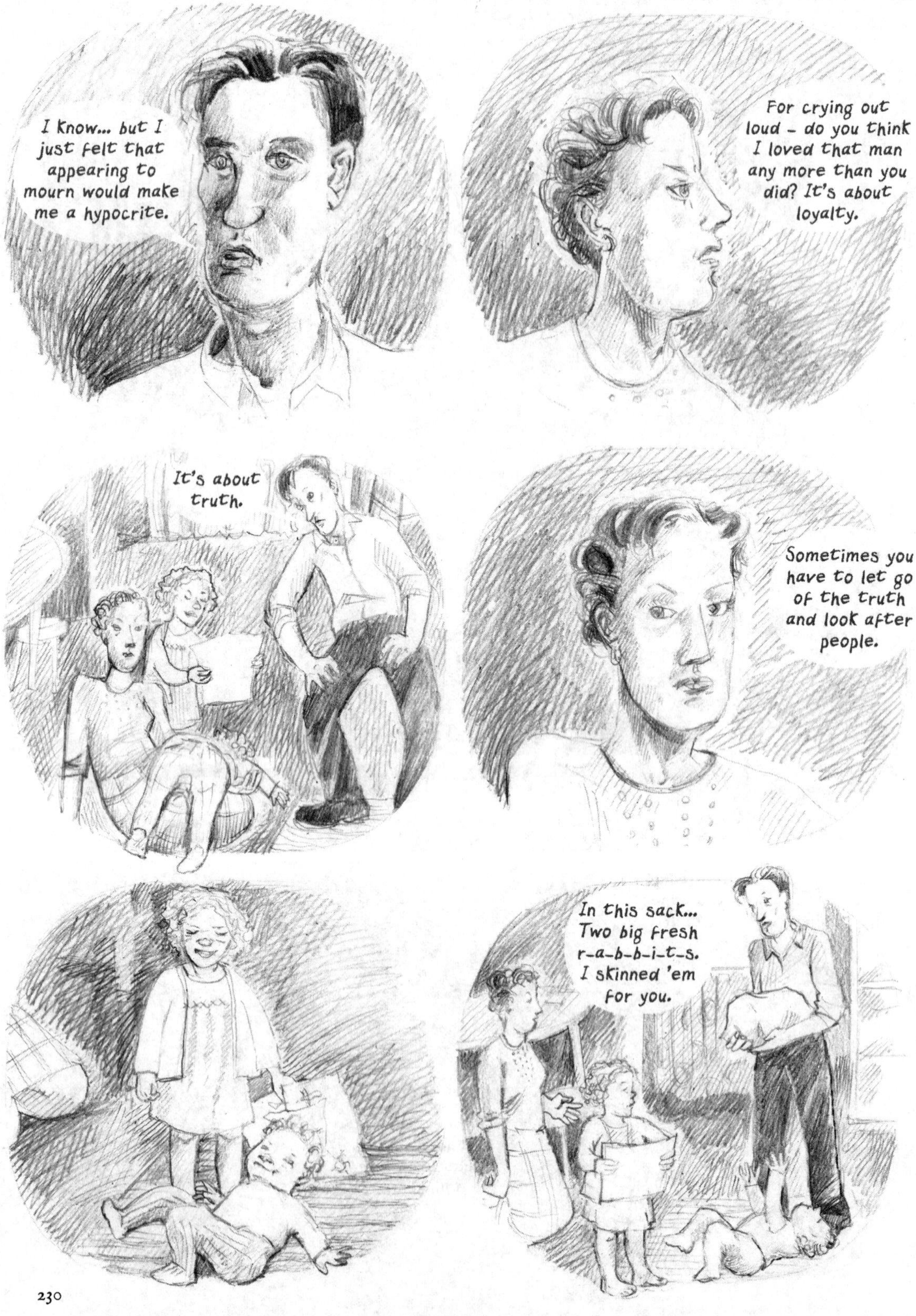
I know... but I just felt that appearing to mourn would make me a hypocrite.
For crying out loud - do you think I loved that man any more than you did? It's about loyalty.
It's about truth.
Sometimes you have to let go of the truth and look after people.
In this sack... Two big fresh r-a-b-b-i-t-s. I skinned 'em for you.

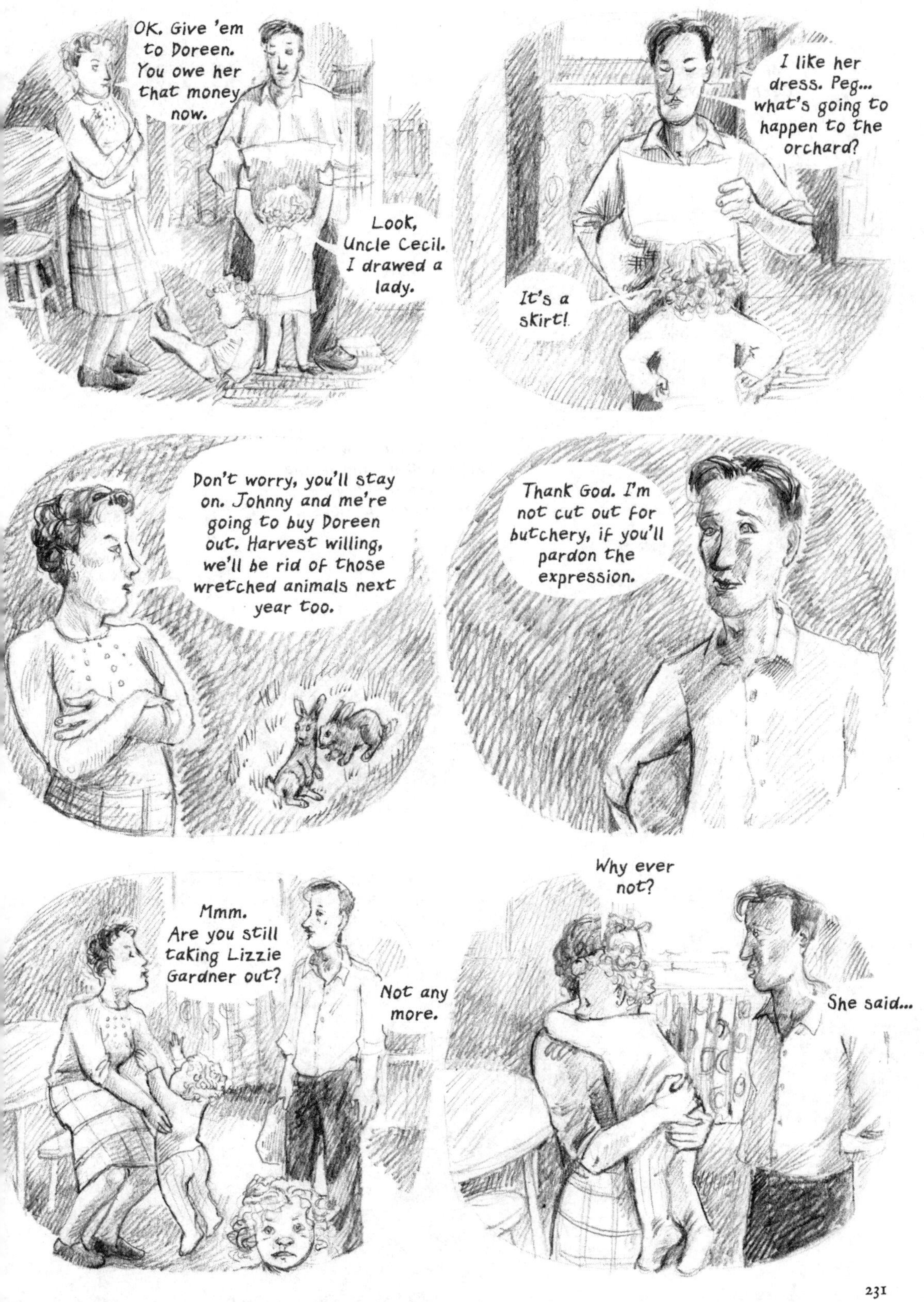
OK. Give 'em to Doreen. You owe her that money now.
Look, Uncle Cecil. I drawed a lady.
I like her dress. Peg... what's going to happen to the orchard?
It's a skirt!
Don't worry, you'll stay on. Johnny and me're going to buy Doreen out. Harvest willing, we'll be rid of those wretched animals next year too.
Thank God. I'm not cut out for butchery, if you'll pardon the expression.
Mmm. Are you still taking Lizzie Gardner out?
Not any more.
Why ever not?
She said...

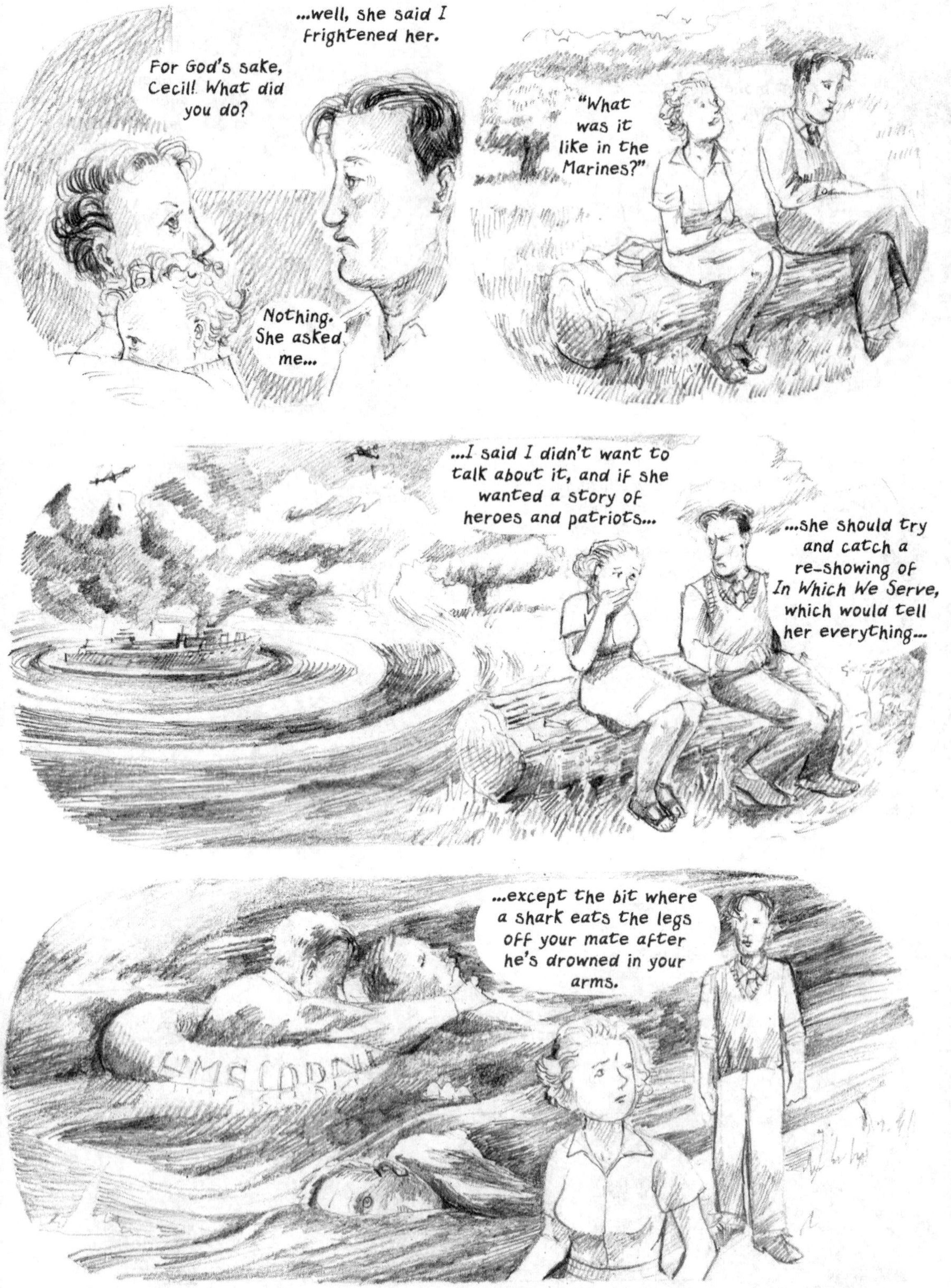
For God's sake, Cecil! What did you do?
...well, she said I frightened her.
Nothing. She asked me...
"What was it like in the Marines?"
...I said I didn't want to talk about it, and if she wanted a story of heroes and patriots...
...she should try and catch a re-showing of *In Which We Serve*, which would tell her everything...
...except the bit where a shark eats the legs off your mate after he's drowned in your arms.

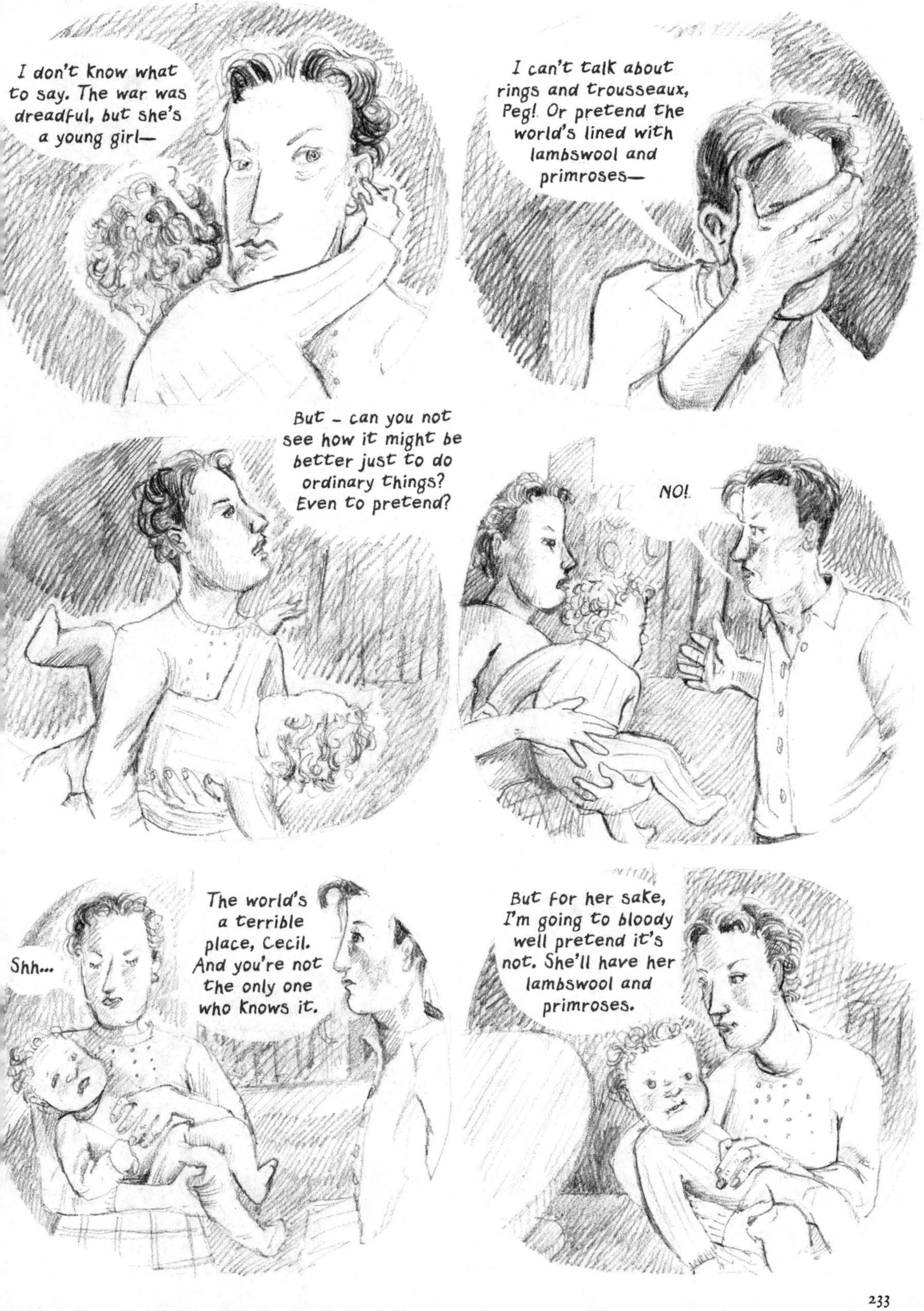
I don't know what to say. The war was dreadful, but she's a young girl—
I can't talk about rings and trousseaux, Peg!. Or pretend the world's lined with lambswool and primroses—
But – can you not see how it might be better just to do ordinary things? Even to pretend?
NO!.
Shh...
The world's a terrible place, Cecil. And you're not the only one who knows it.
But for her sake, I'm going to bloody well pretend it's not. She'll have her lambswool and primroses.

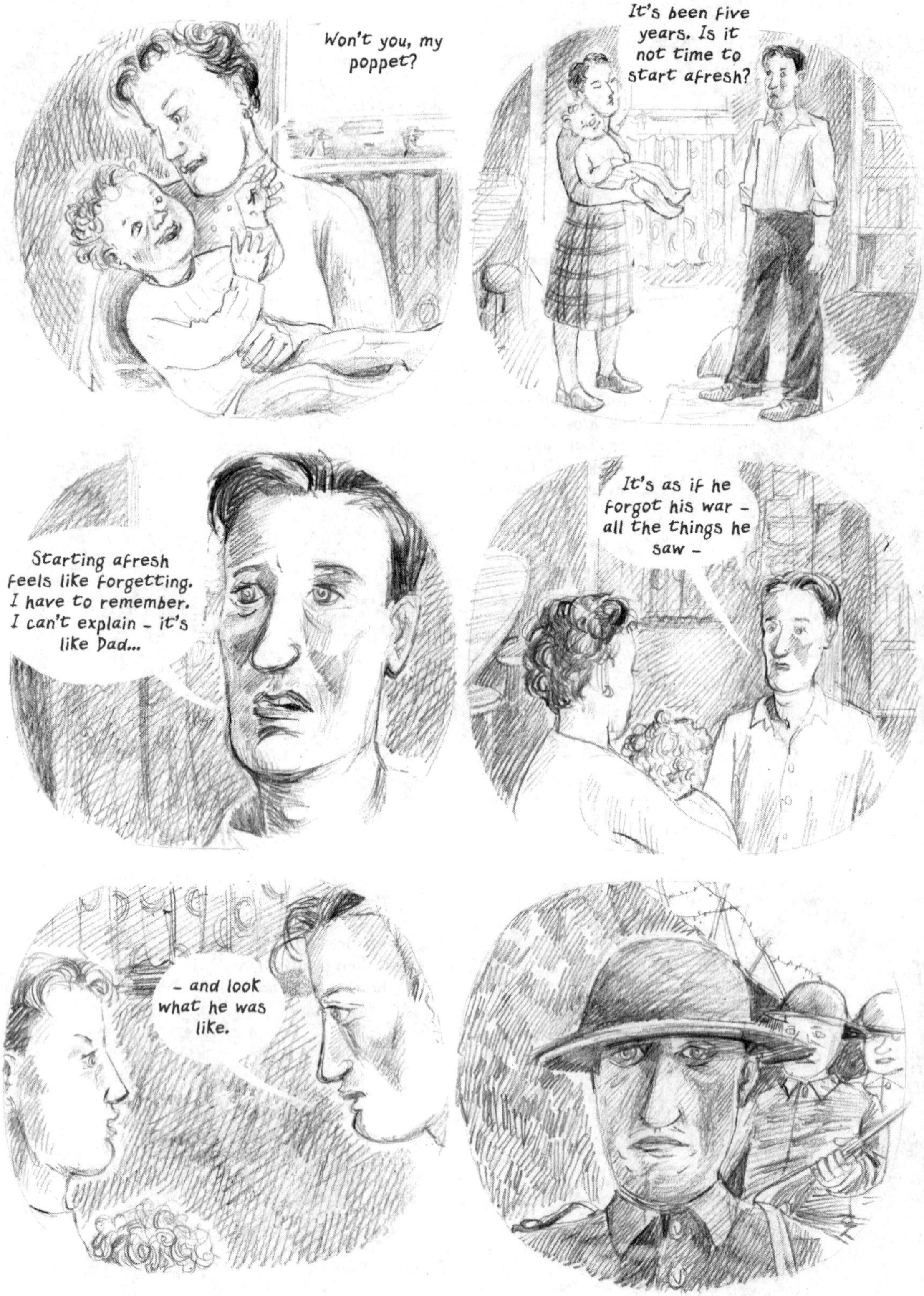
Won't you, my poppet?
It's been five years. Is it not time to start afresh?
Starting afresh feels like forgetting. I have to remember. I can't explain – it's like Dad...
It's as if he forgot his war – all the things he saw –
– and look what he was like.

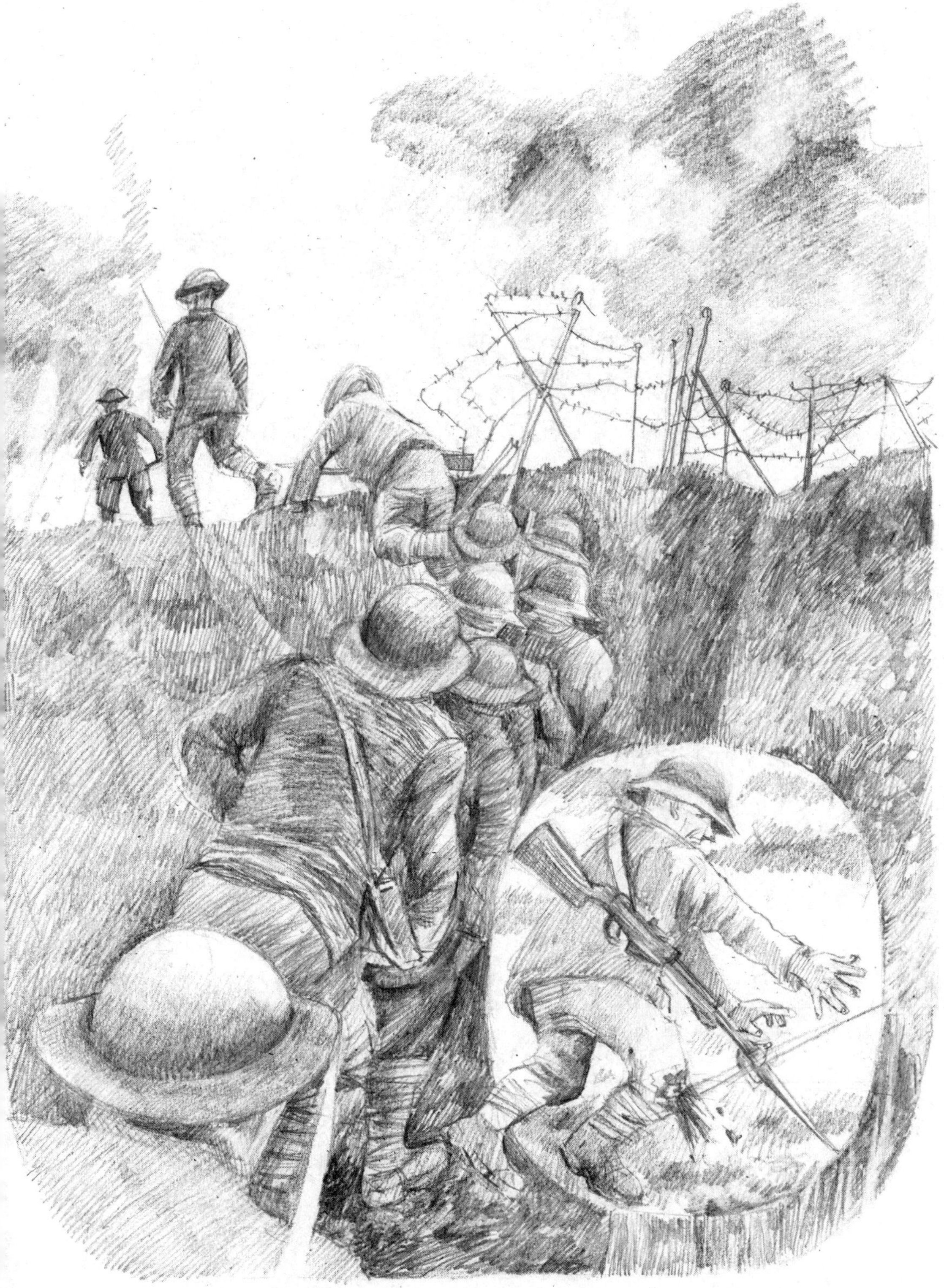

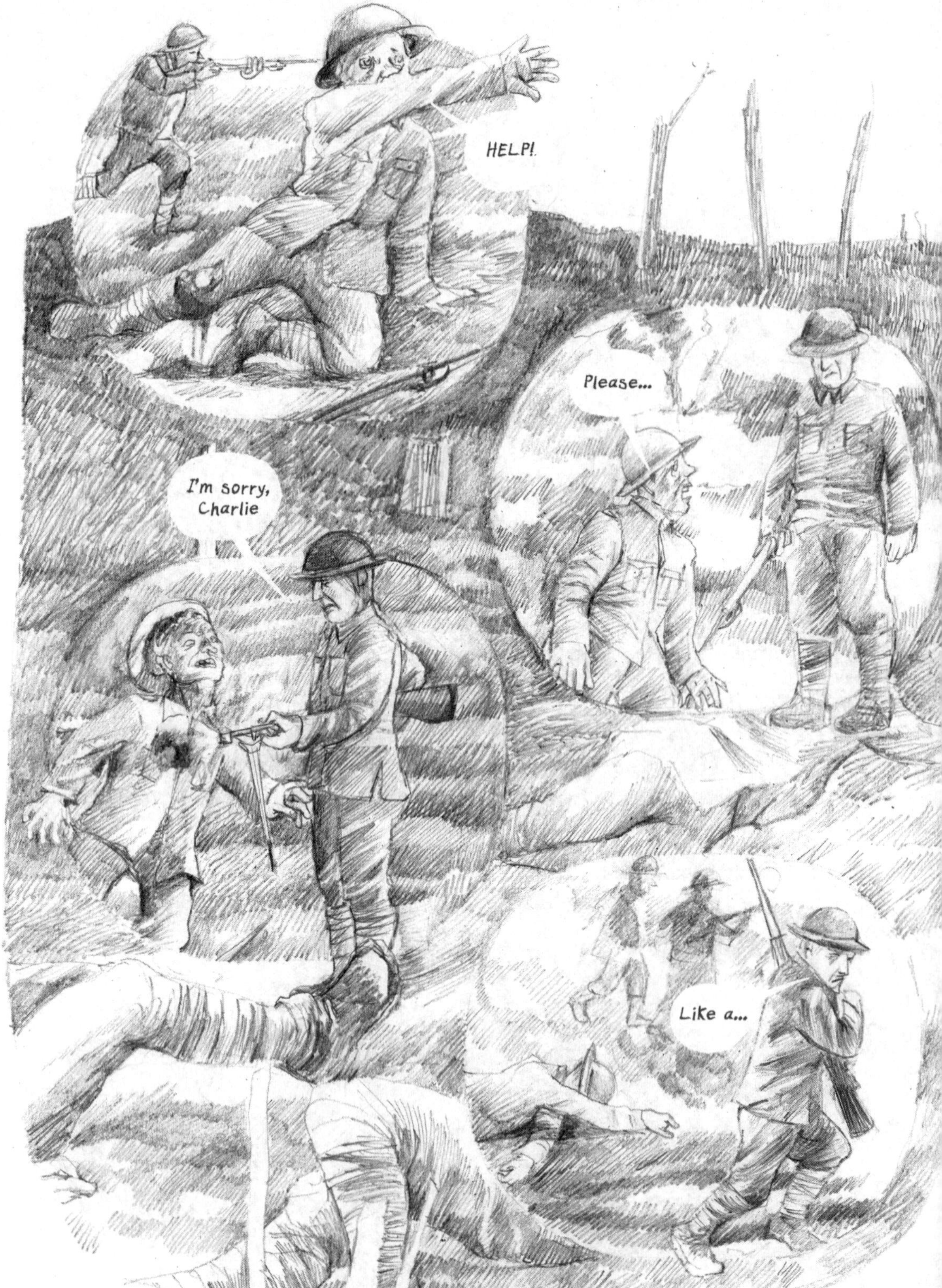
HELP!
Please...
I'm sorry, Charlie
Like a...

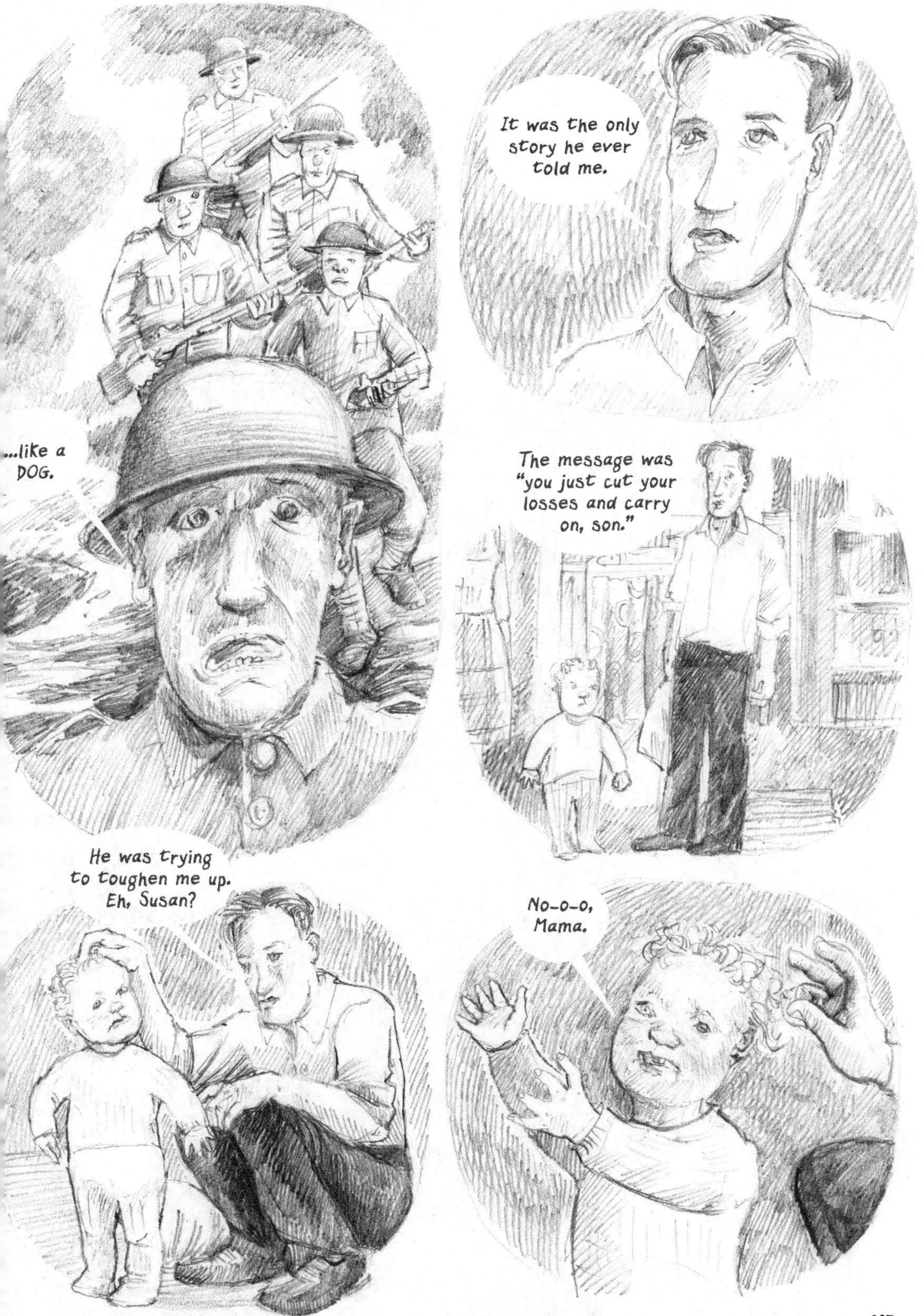
...like a DOG.
It was the only story he ever told me.
The message was "you just cut your losses and carry on, son."
He was trying to toughen me up. Eh, Susan?
No-o-o, Mama.

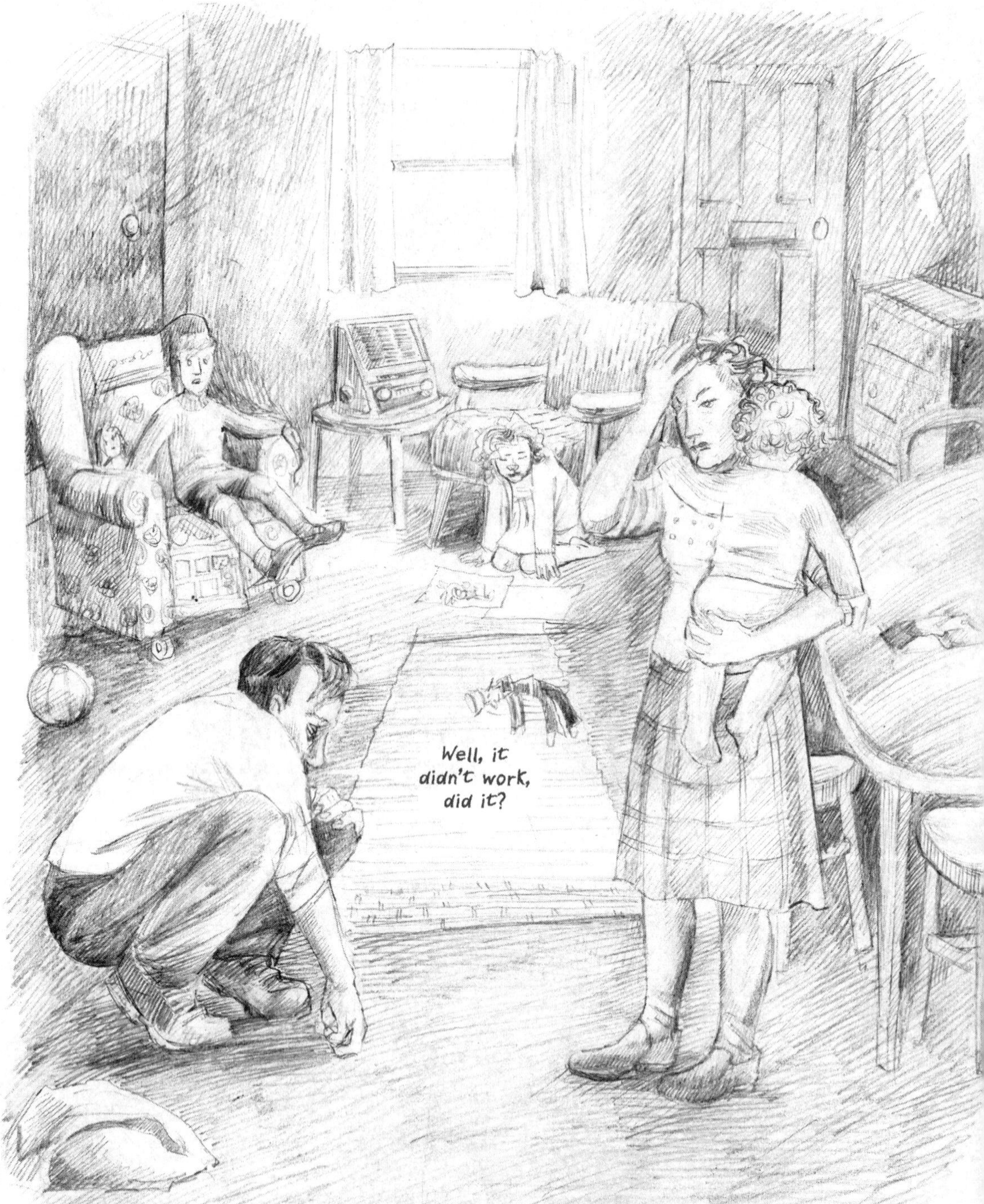
Well, it
didn't work,
did it?

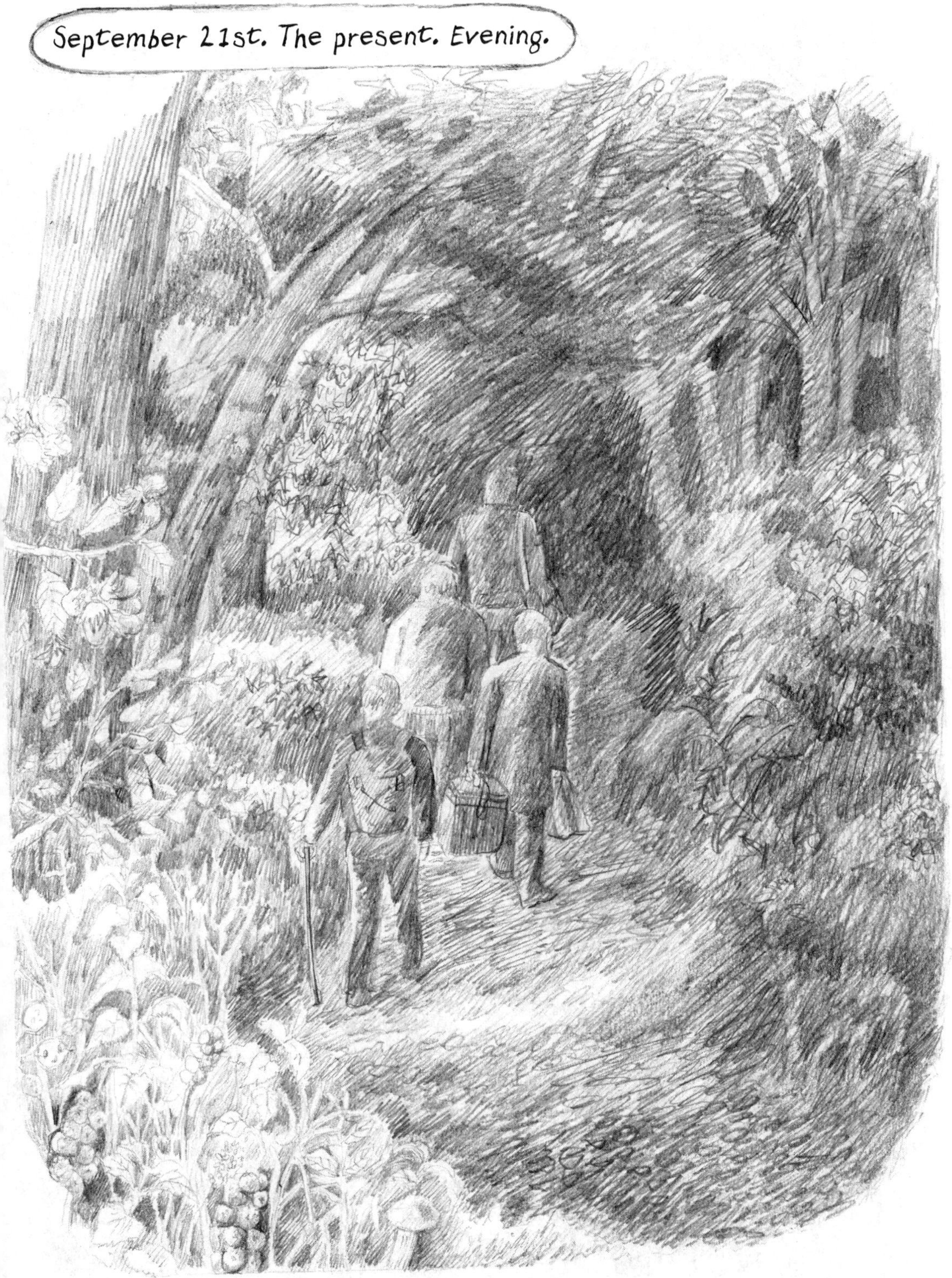
September 21st. The present. Evening.

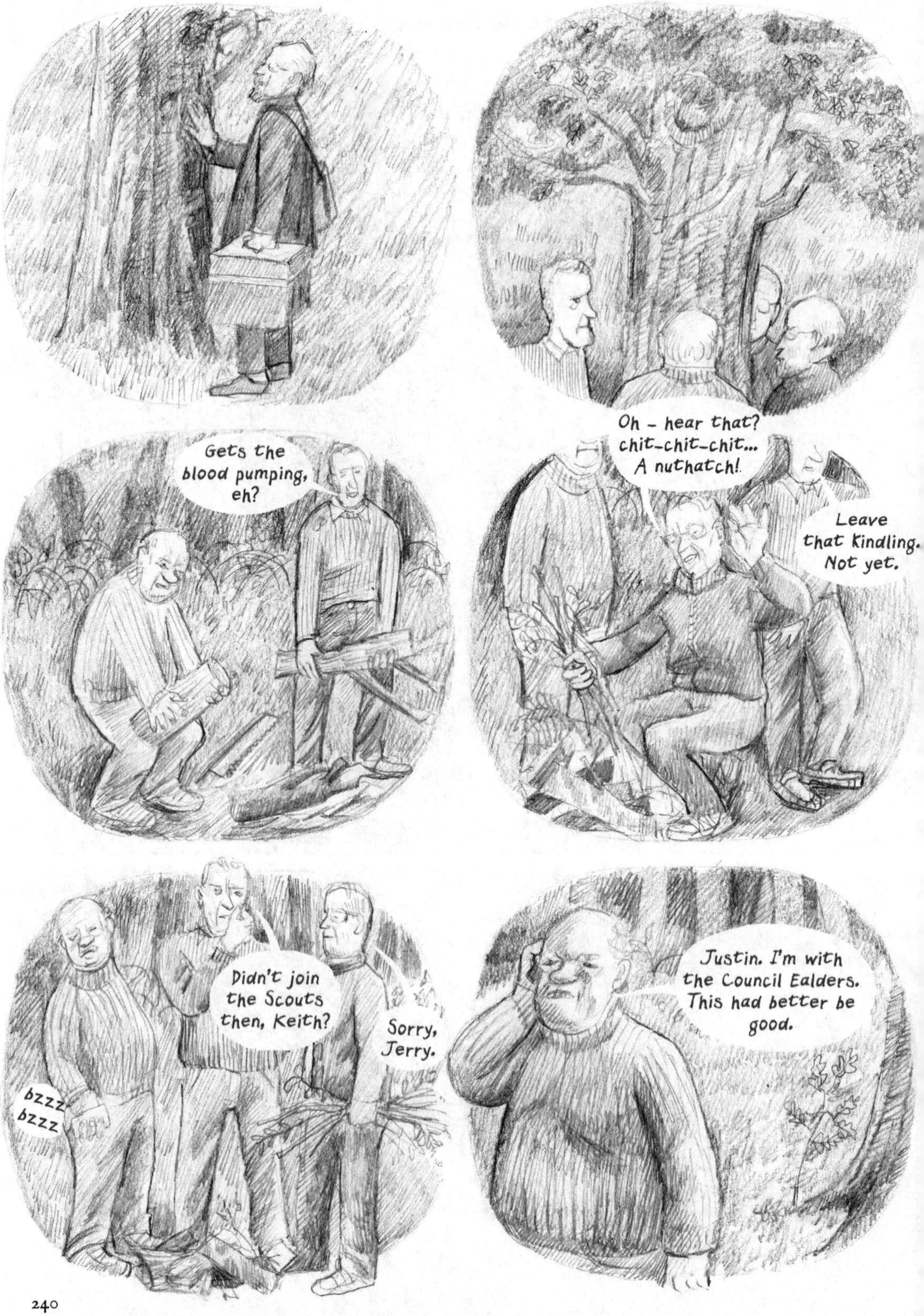
Gets the blood pumping, eh?
Oh - hear that? chit-chit-chit... A nuthatch!
Leave that kindling. Not yet.
Didn't join the Scouts then, Keith?
Sorry, Jerry.
bzzz bzzz
Justin. I'm with the Council Ealders. This had better be good.

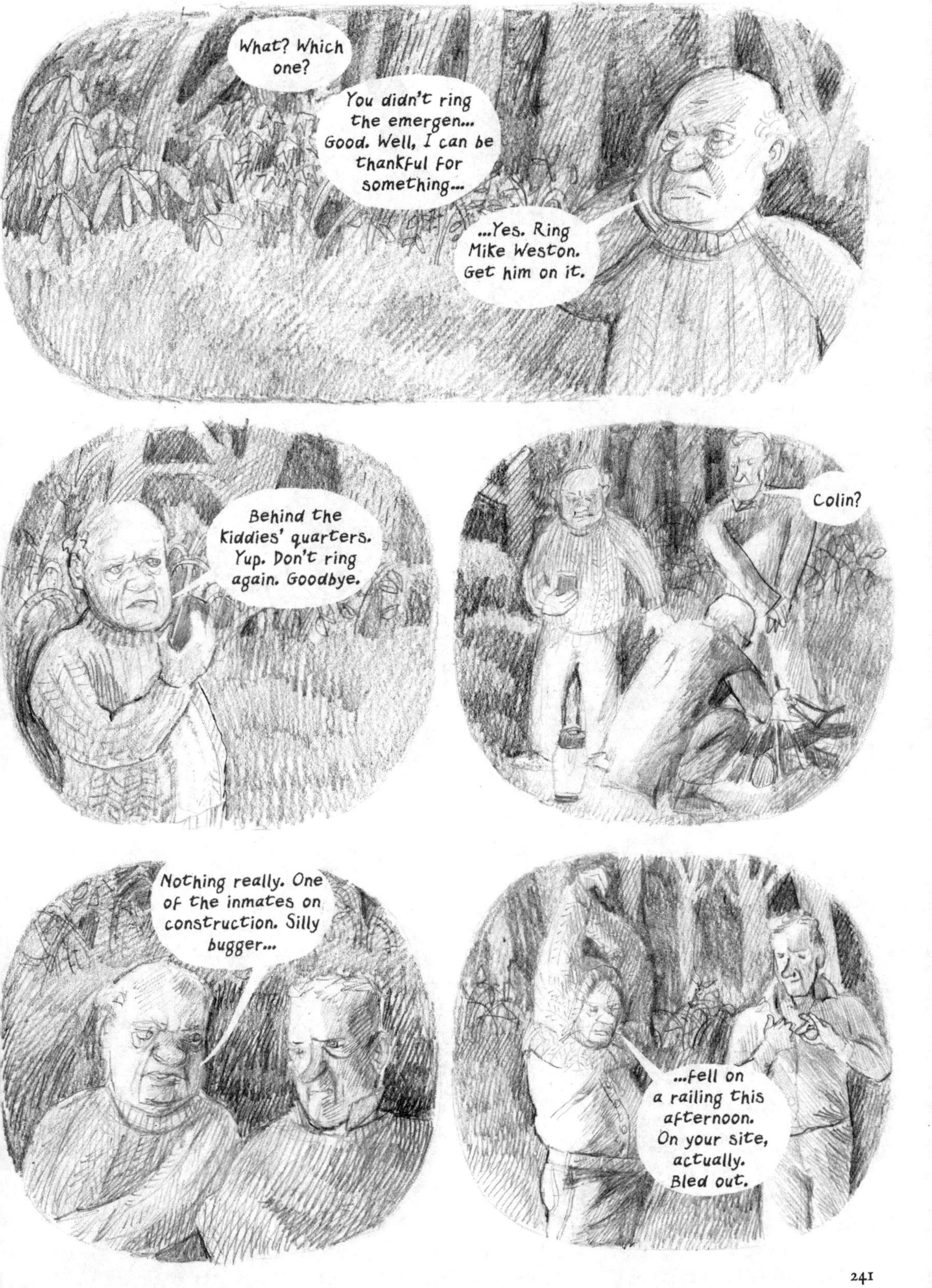
What? Which one?
You didn't ring the emergen... Good. Well, I can be thankful for something...
...Yes. Ring Mike Weston. Get him on it.
Behind the kiddies' quarters. Yup. Don't ring again. Goodbye.
Colin?
Nothing really. One of the inmates on construction. Silly bugger...
...fell on a railing this afternoon. On your site, actually. Bled out.

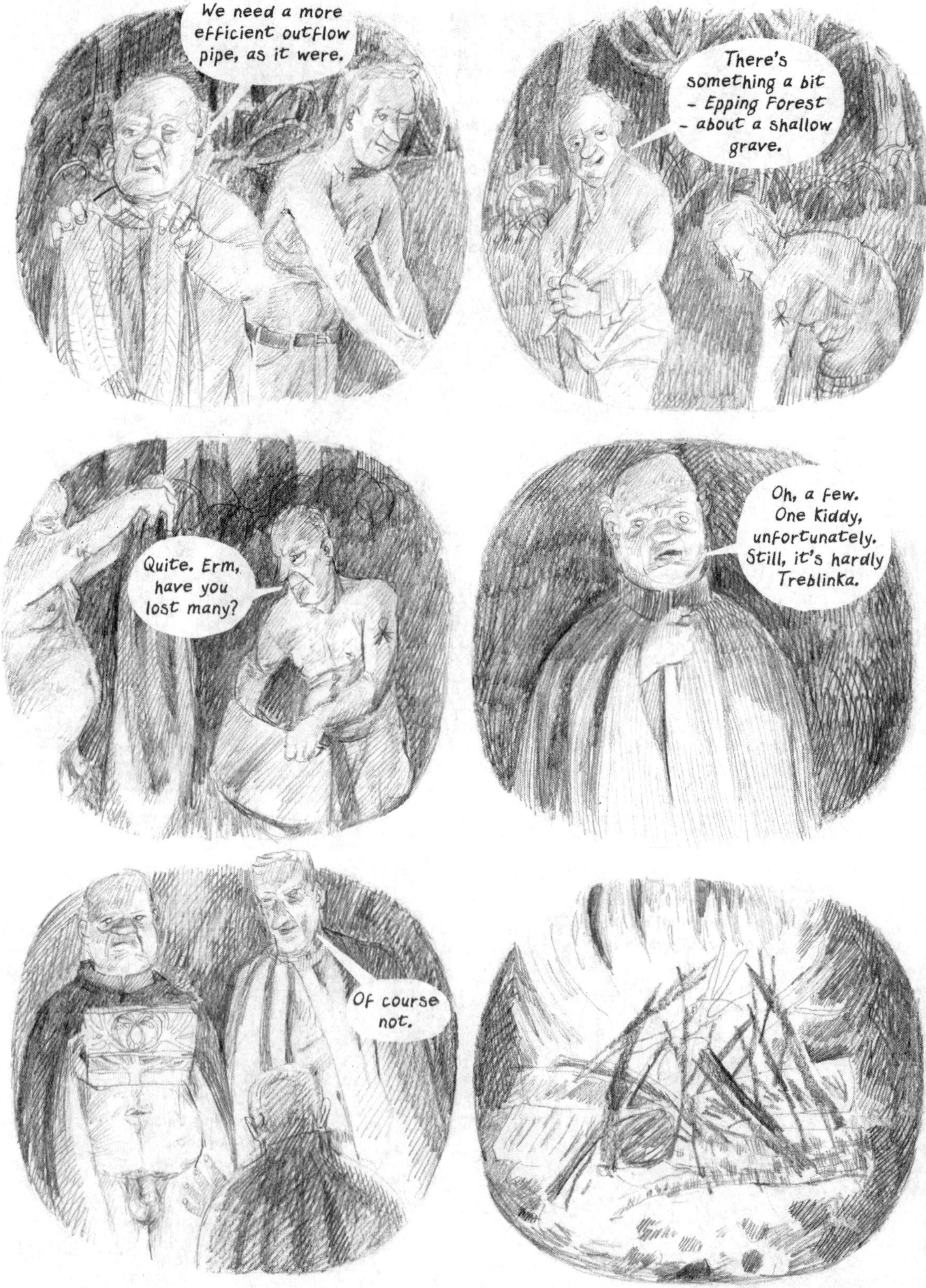
We need a more efficient outflow pipe, as it were.
There's something a bit - Epping Forest - about a shallow grave.
Quite. Erm, have you lost many?
Oh, a few. One kiddy, unfortunately. Still, it's hardly Treblinka.
Of course not.

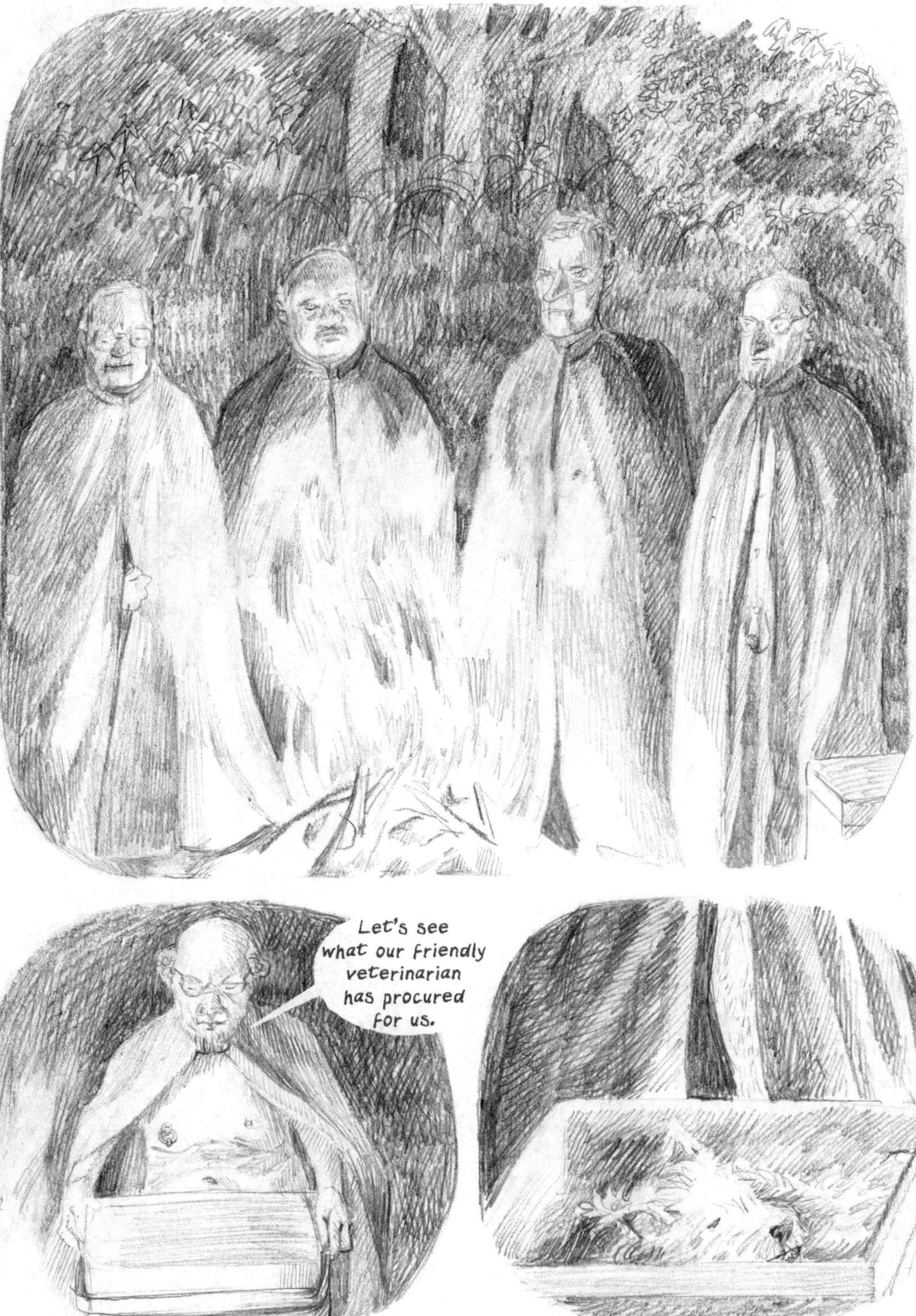
Let's see what our friendly veterinarian has procured for us.

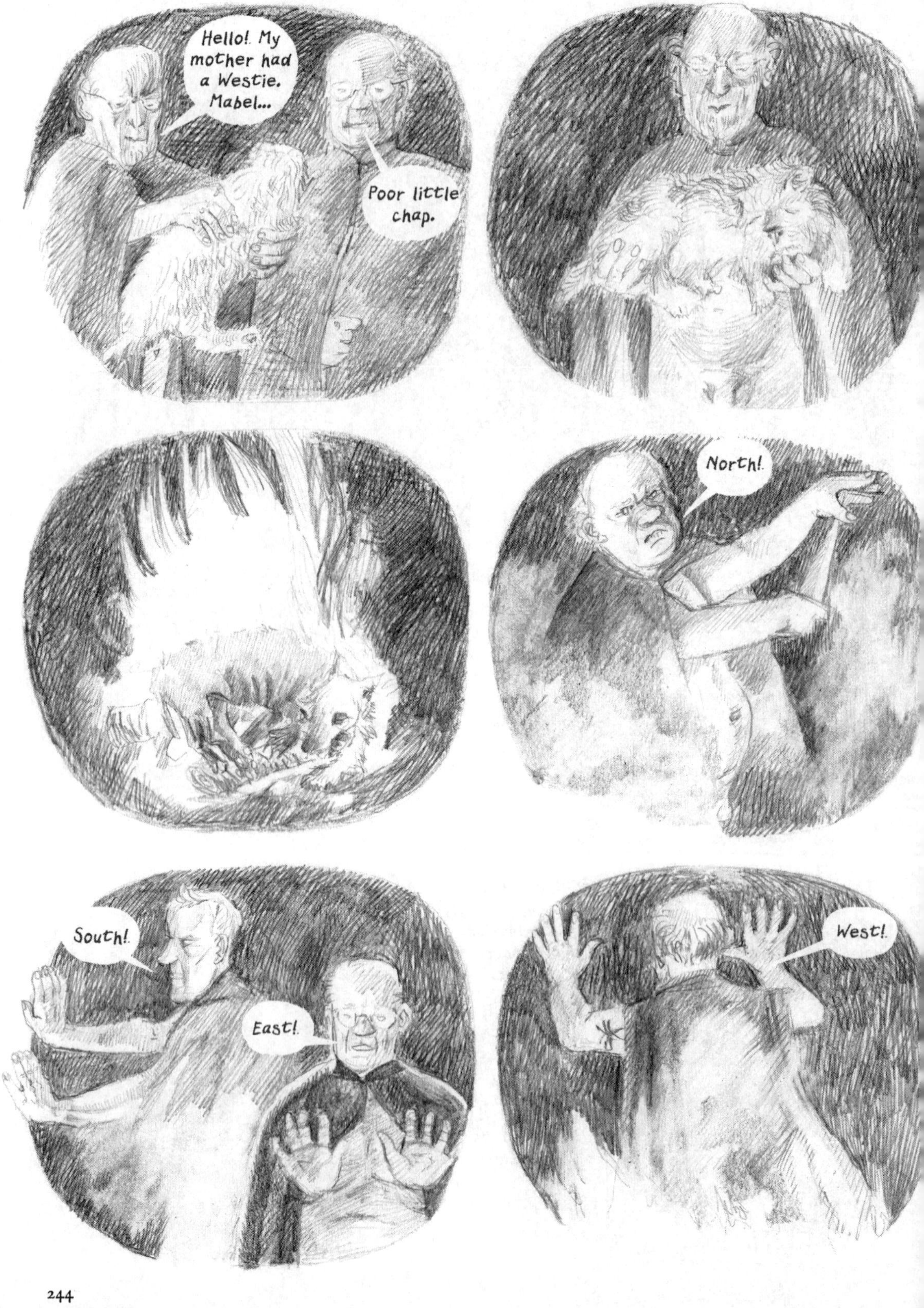
Hello!. My mother had a Westie. Mabel...
Poor little chap.
North!.
South!.
East!.
West!.

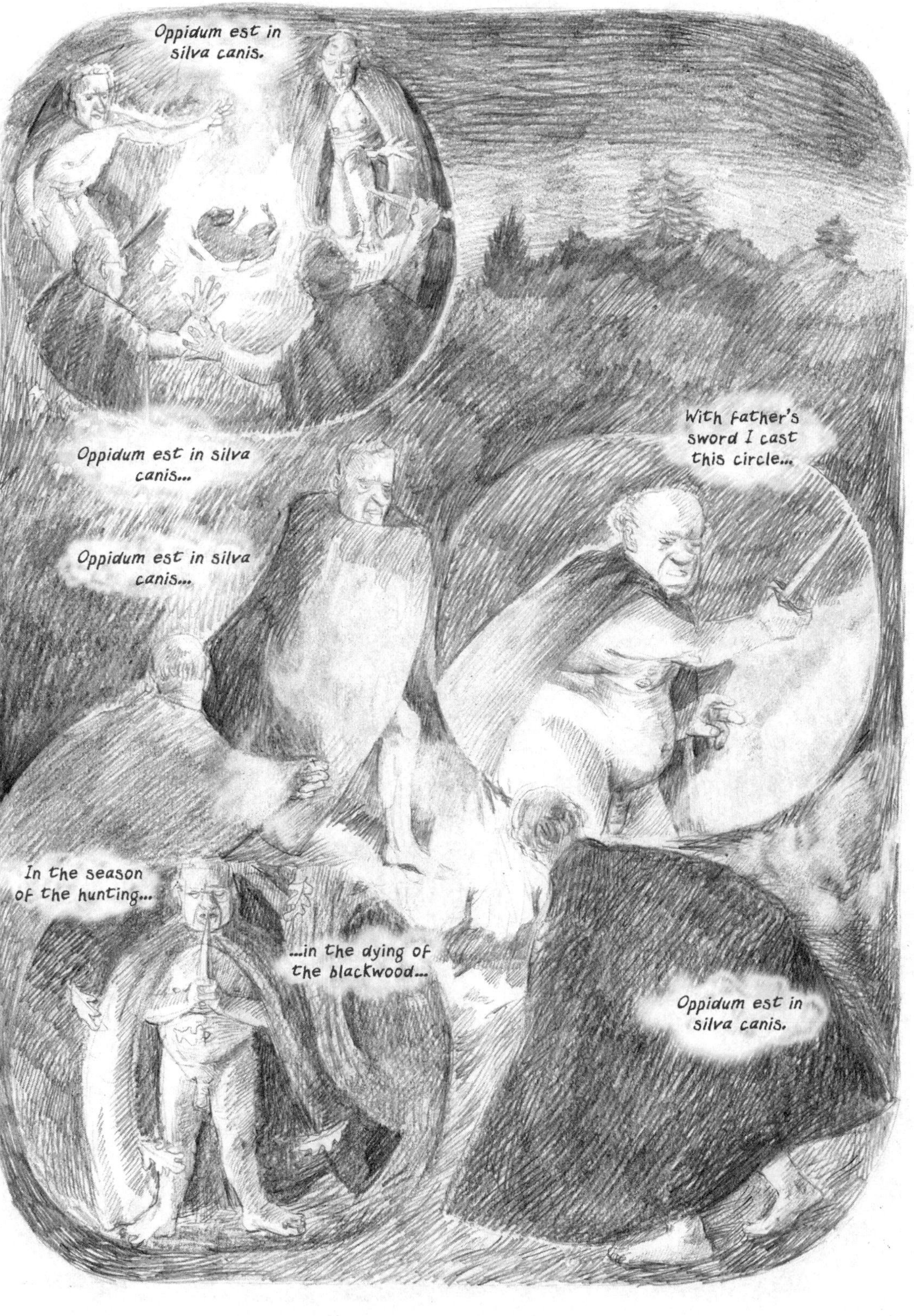

Oppidum est in silva canis.
With father's sword I cast this circle...
Oppidum est in silva canis...
Oppidum est in silva canis...
In the season of the hunting...
...in the dying of the blackwood...
Oppidum est in silva canis.

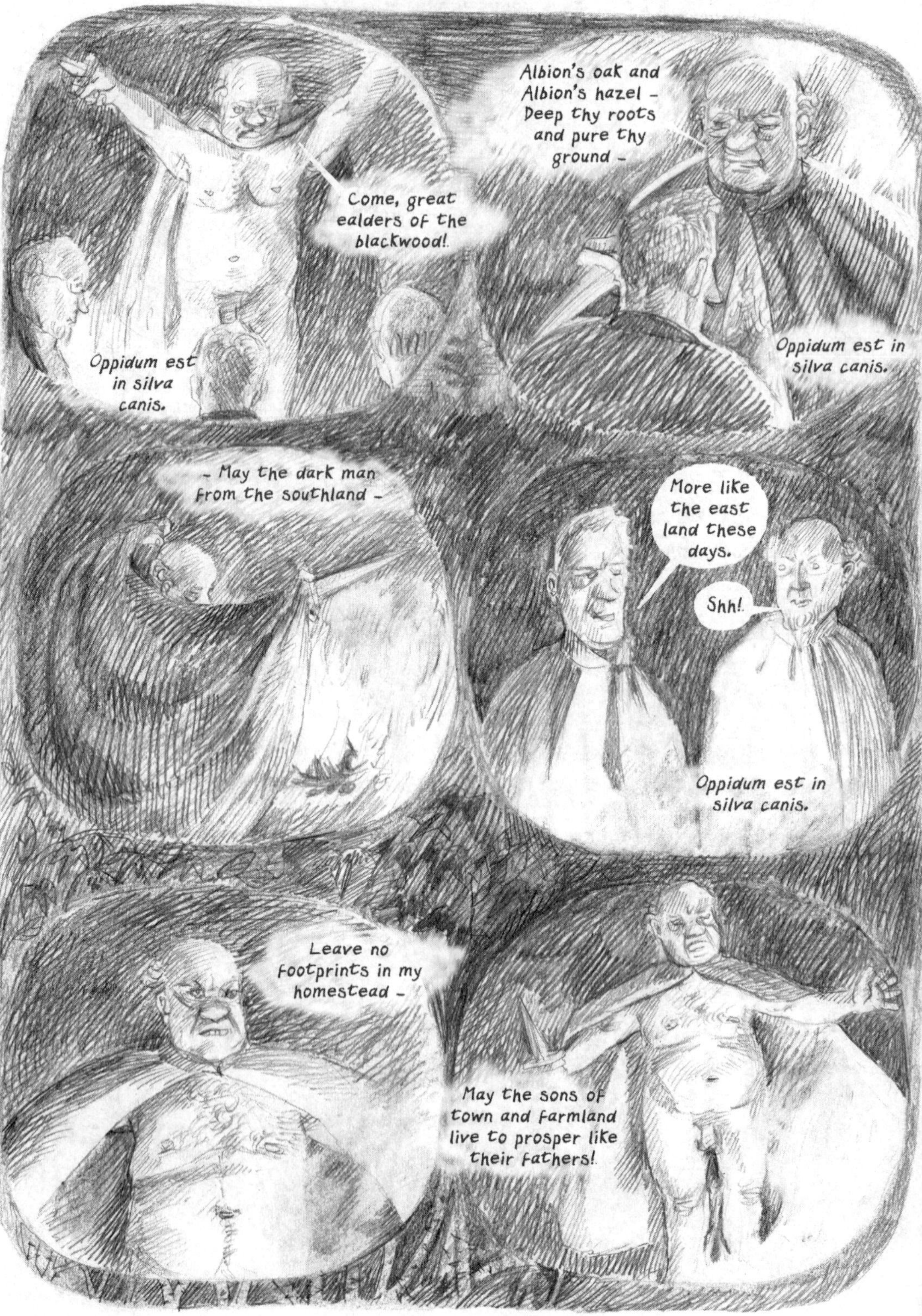
Come, great ealders of the blackwood!
Oppidum est in silva canis.
Albion's oak and Albion's hazel - Deep thy roots and pure thy ground -
Oppidum est in silva canis.
- May the dark man from the southland -
More like the east land these days.
Shh!
Oppidum est in silva canis.
Leave no footprints in my homestead -
May the sons of town and farmland live to prosper like their fathers!

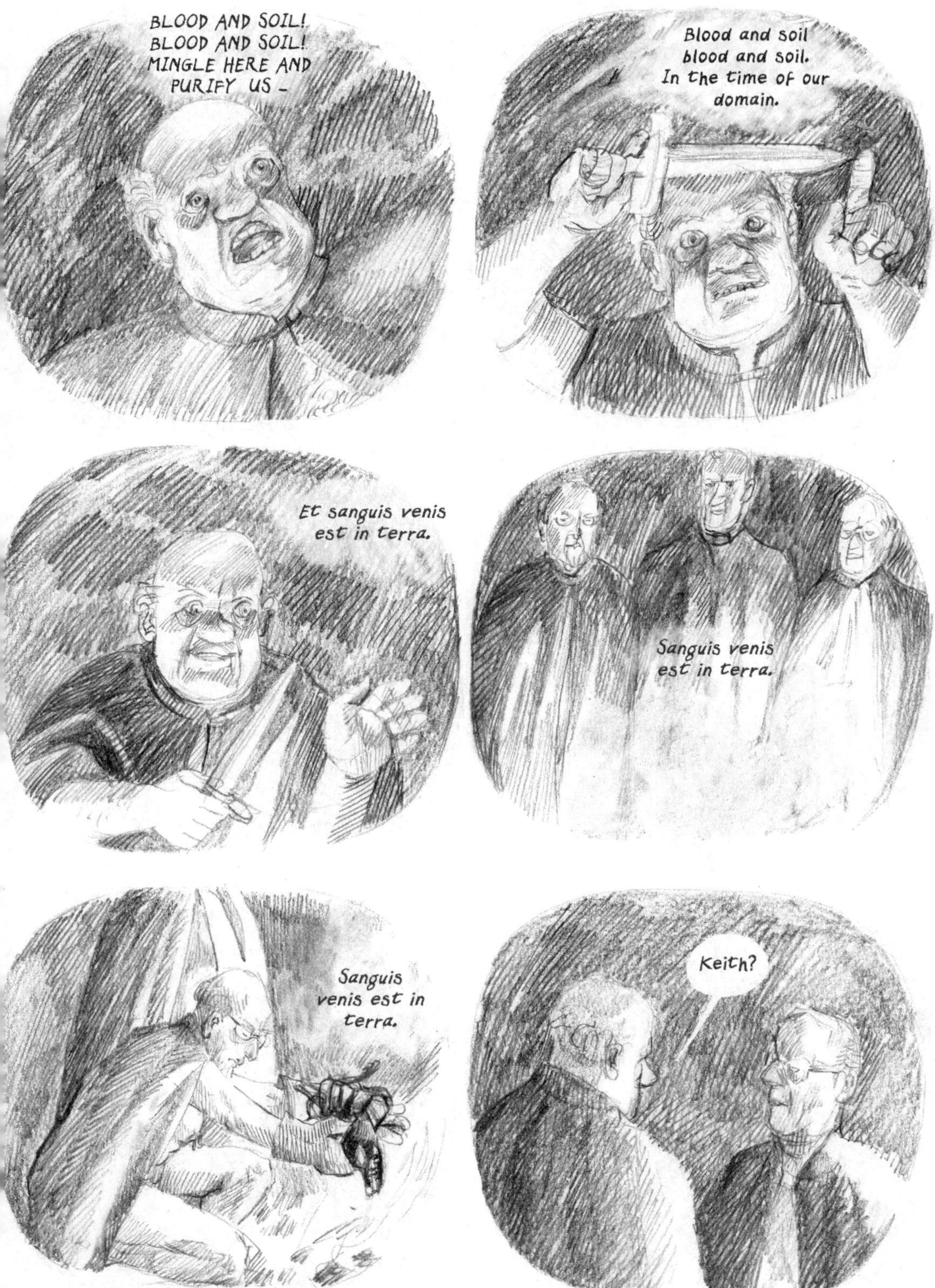
BLOOD AND SOIL! BLOOD AND SOIL! MINGLE HERE AND PURIFY US –
Blood and soil blood and soil. In the time of our domain.
Et sanguis venis est in terra.
Sanguis venis est in terra.
Sanguis venis est in terra.
Keith?

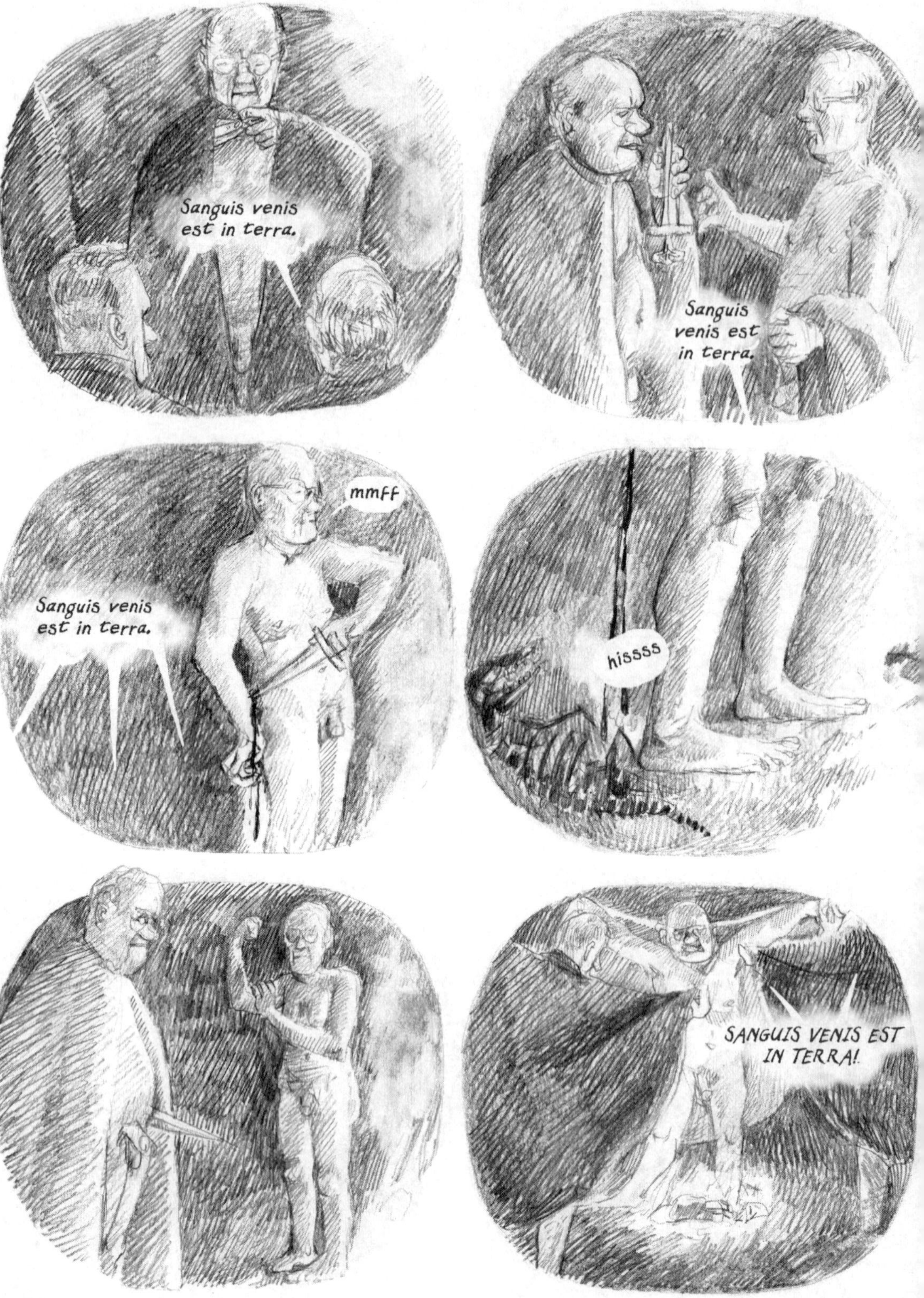

Sanguis venis est in terra.
Sanguis venis est in terra.
mmff
Sanguis venis est in terra.
hissss
SANGUIS VENIS EST IN TERRA!

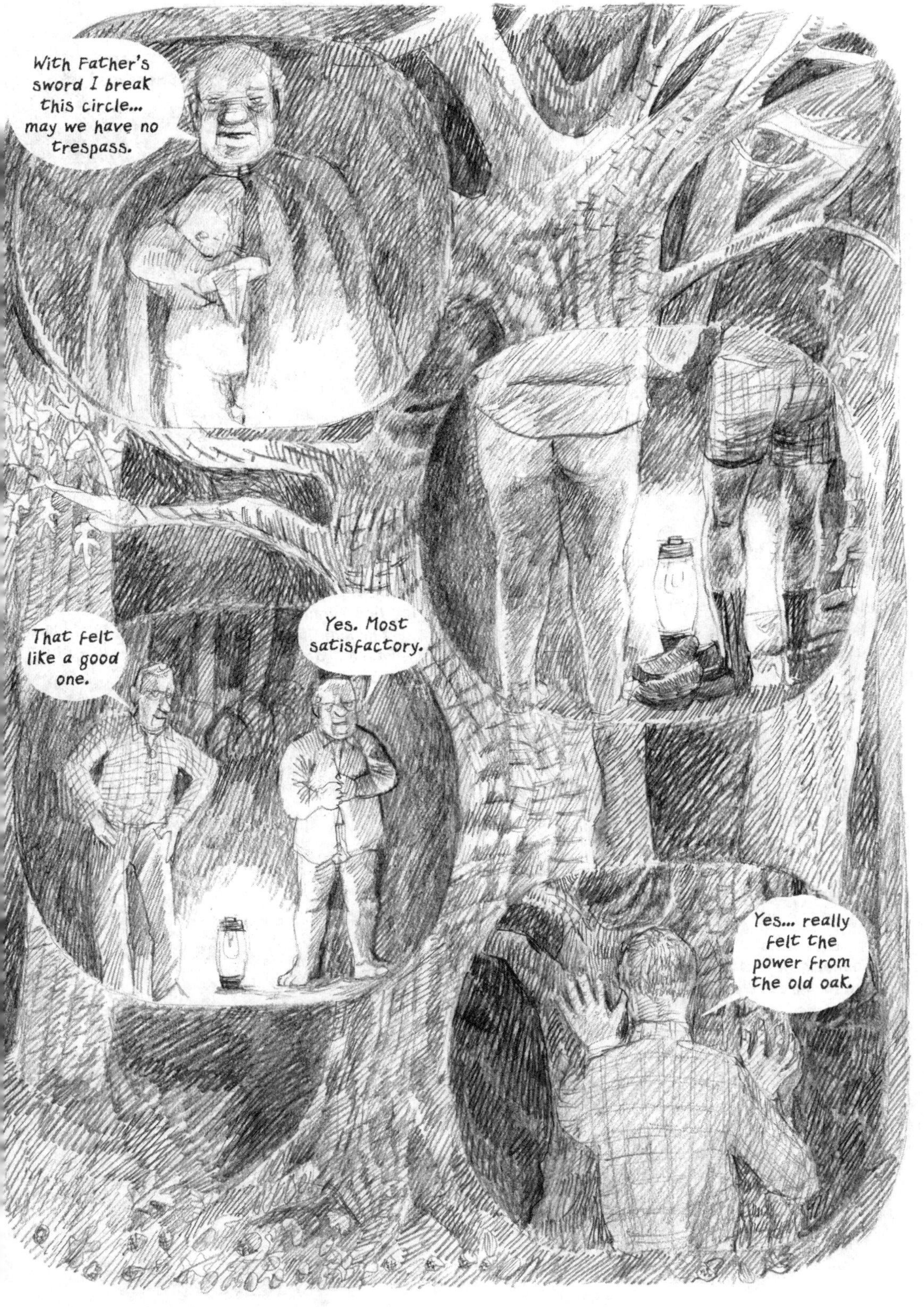
With Father's sword I break this circle... may we have no trespass.
That felt like a good one.
Yes. Most satisfactory.
Yes... really felt the power from the old oak.

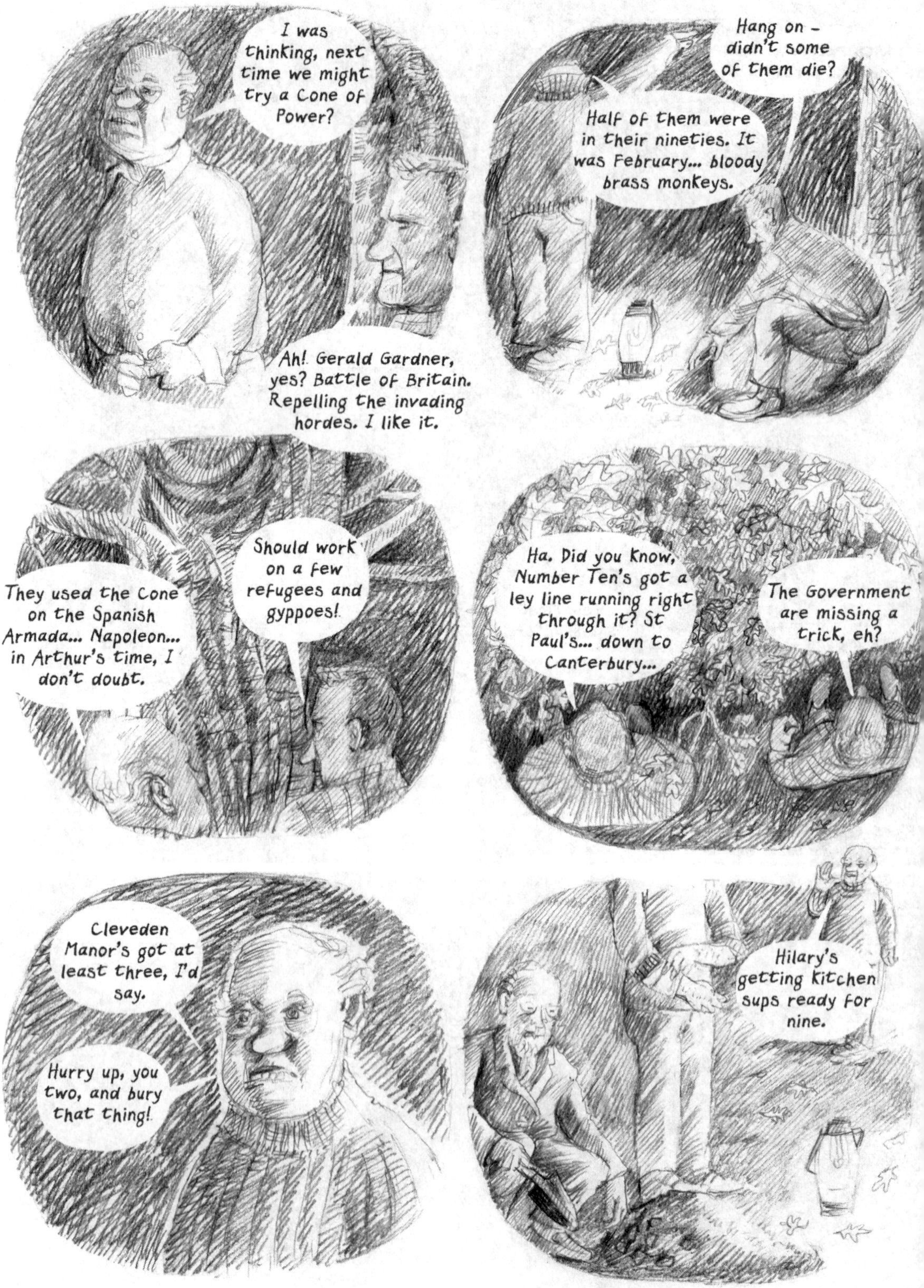
I was thinking, next time we might try a Cone of Power?
Ah! Gerald Gardner, yes? Battle of Britain. Repelling the invading hordes. I like it.
Hang on - didn't some of them die?
Half of them were in their nineties. It was February... bloody brass monkeys.
They used the Cone on the Spanish Armada... Napoleon... in Arthur's time, I don't doubt.
Should work on a few refugees and gyppoes!
Ha. Did you know, Number Ten's got a ley line running right through it? St Paul's... down to Canterbury...
The Government are missing a trick, eh?
Cleveden Manor's got at least three, I'd say.
Hurry up, you two, and bury that thing!
Hilary's getting kitchen sups ready for nine.

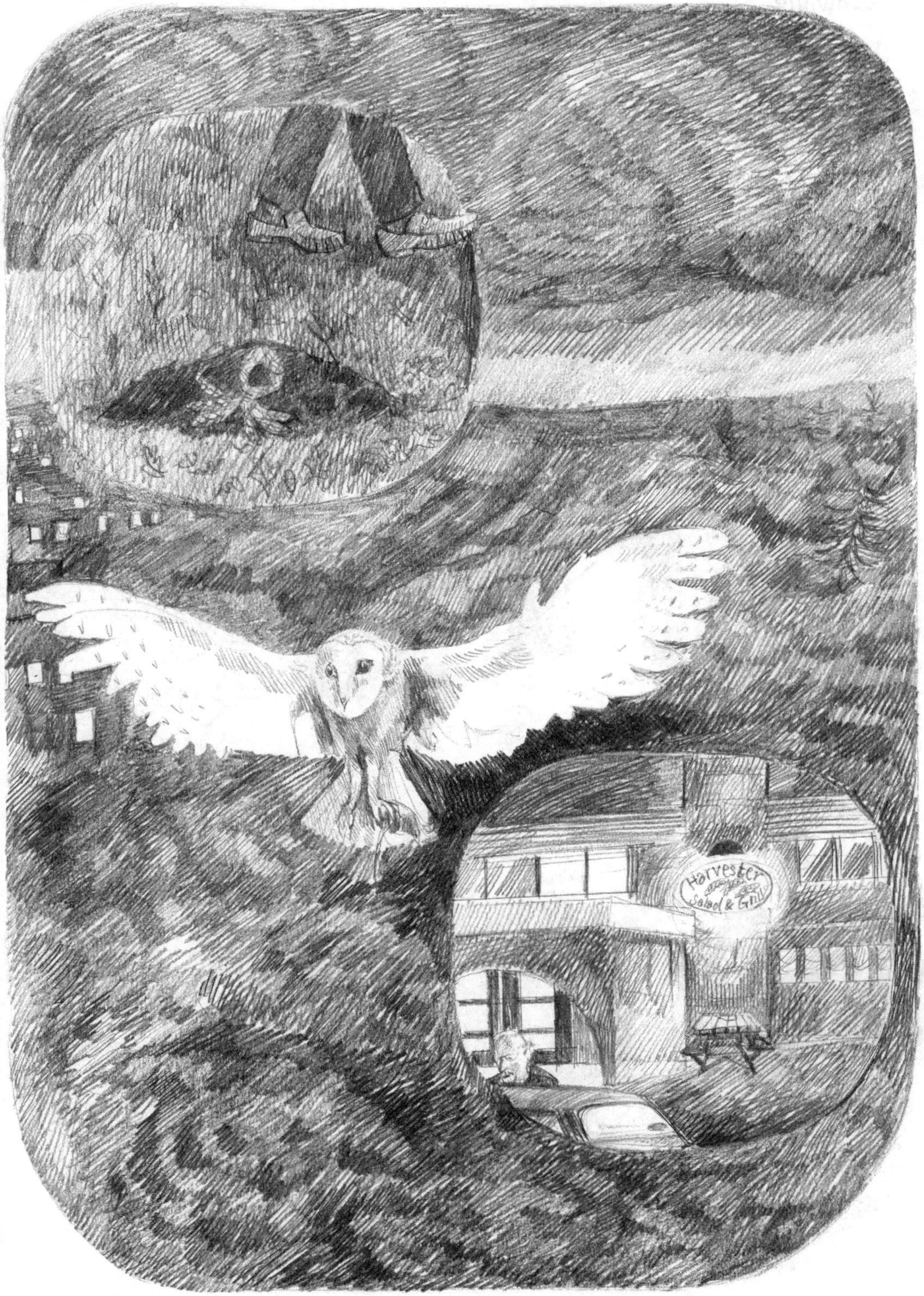
Harvester
Salad & Grill

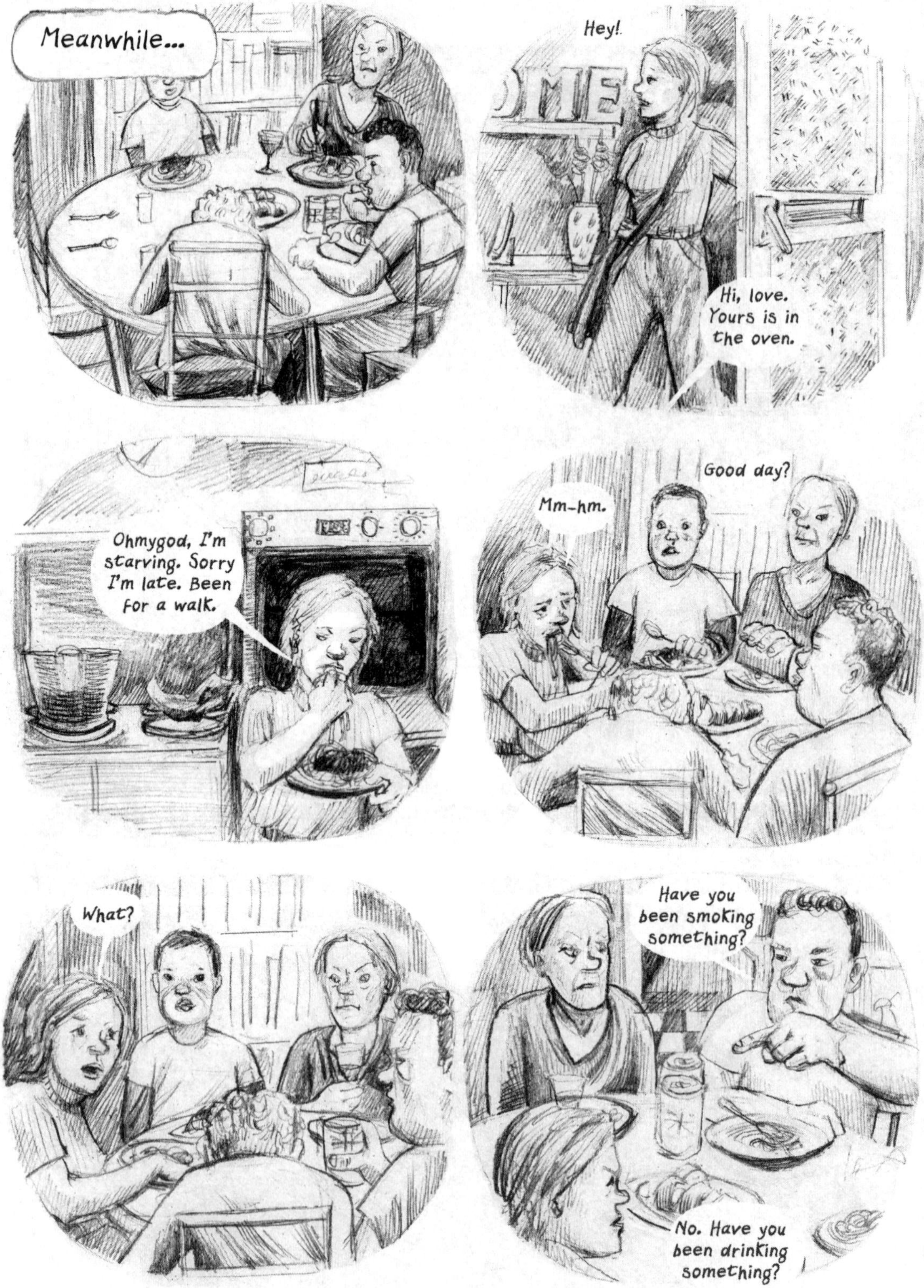
Meanwhile...
Hey!.
Hi, love. Yours is in the oven.
Ohmygod, I'm starving. Sorry I'm late. Been for a walk.
Good day?
Mm-hm.
What?
Have you been smoking something?
No. Have you been drinking something?

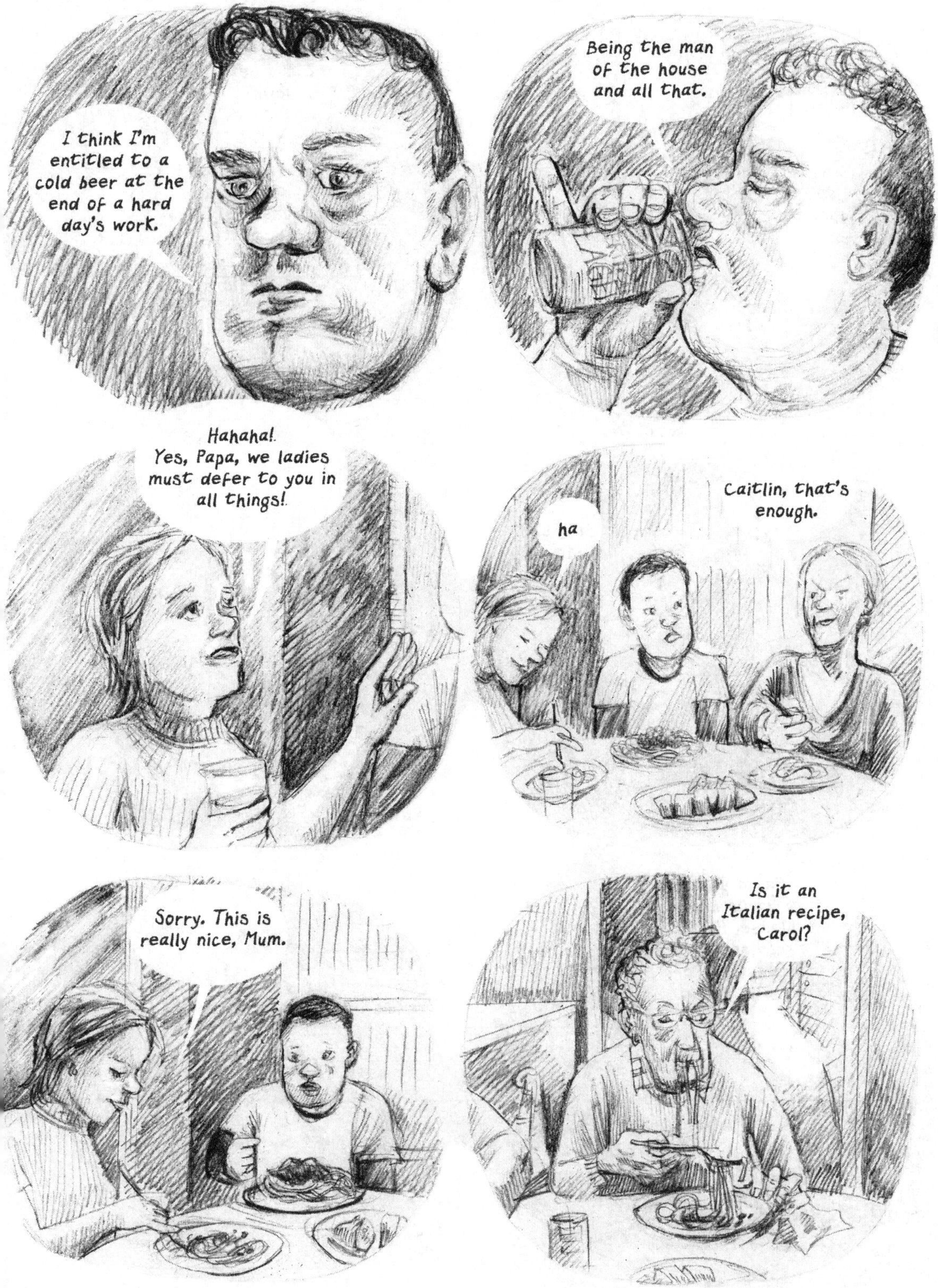
I think I'm entitled to a cold beer at the end of a hard day's work.
Being the man of the house and all that.
Hahaha! Yes, Papa, we ladies must defer to you in all things!
ha
Caitlin, that's enough.
Sorry. This is really nice, Mum.
Is it an Italian recipe, Carol?

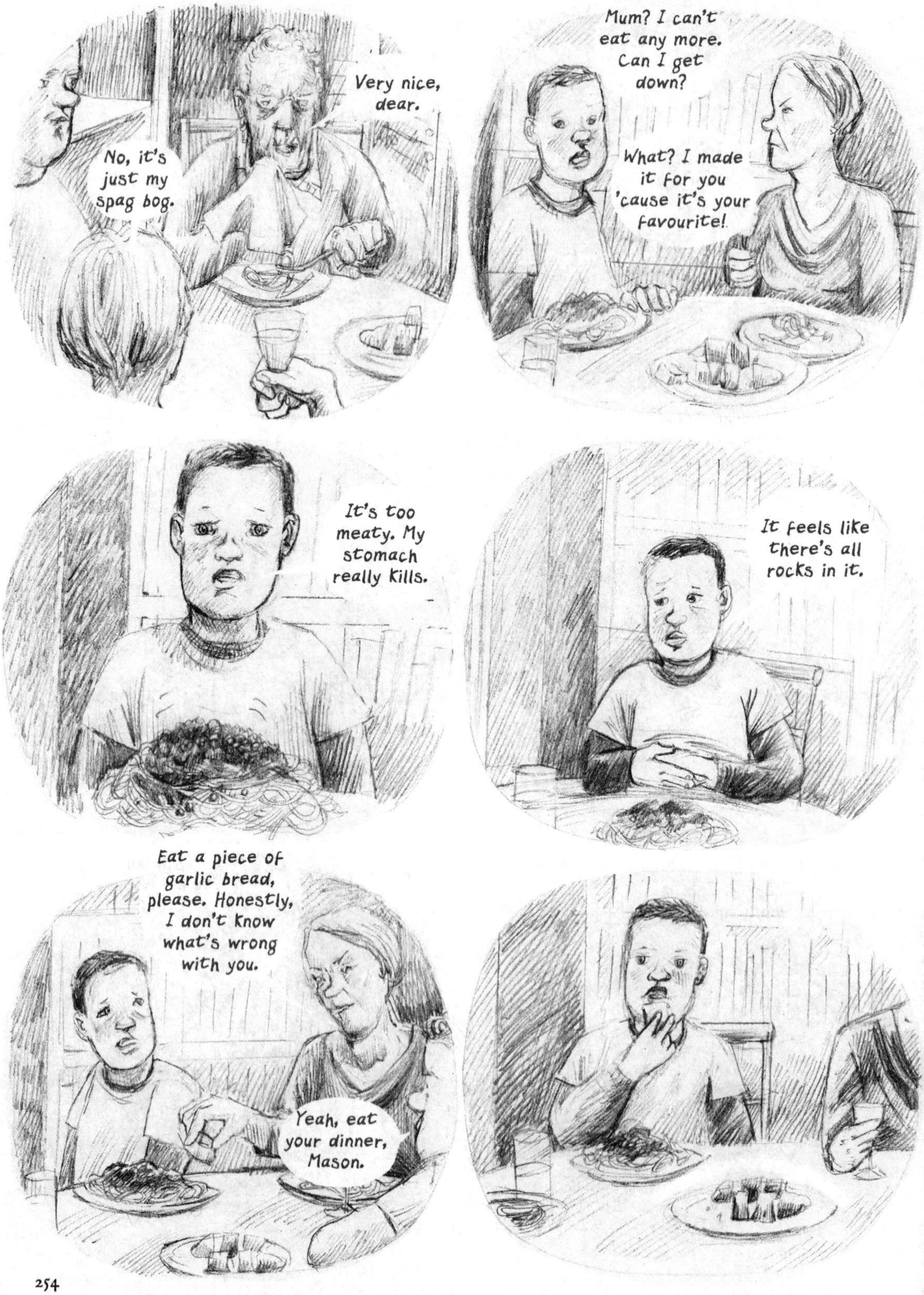

Very nice, dear.
No, it's just my spag bog.
Mum? I can't eat any more. Can I get down?
What? I made it for you 'cause it's your favourite!
It's too meaty. My stomach really kills.
It feels like there's all rocks in it.
Eat a piece of garlic bread, please. Honestly, I don't know what's wrong with you.
Yeah, eat your dinner, Mason.

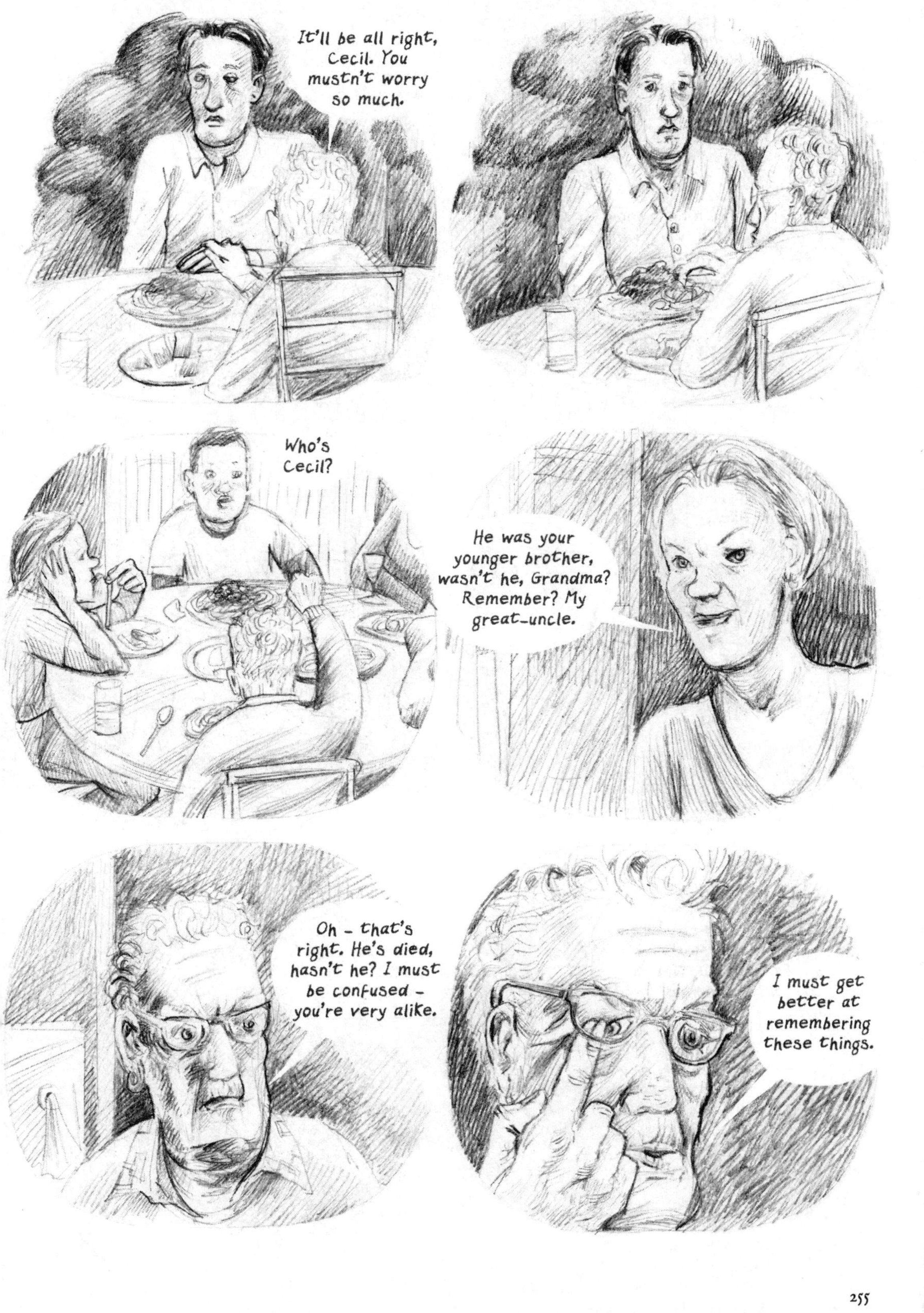
It'll be all right, Cecil. You mustn't worry so much.
Who's Cecil?
He was your younger brother, wasn't he, Grandma? Remember? My great-uncle.
Oh - that's right. He's died, hasn't he? I must be confused - you're very alike.
I must get better at remembering these things.

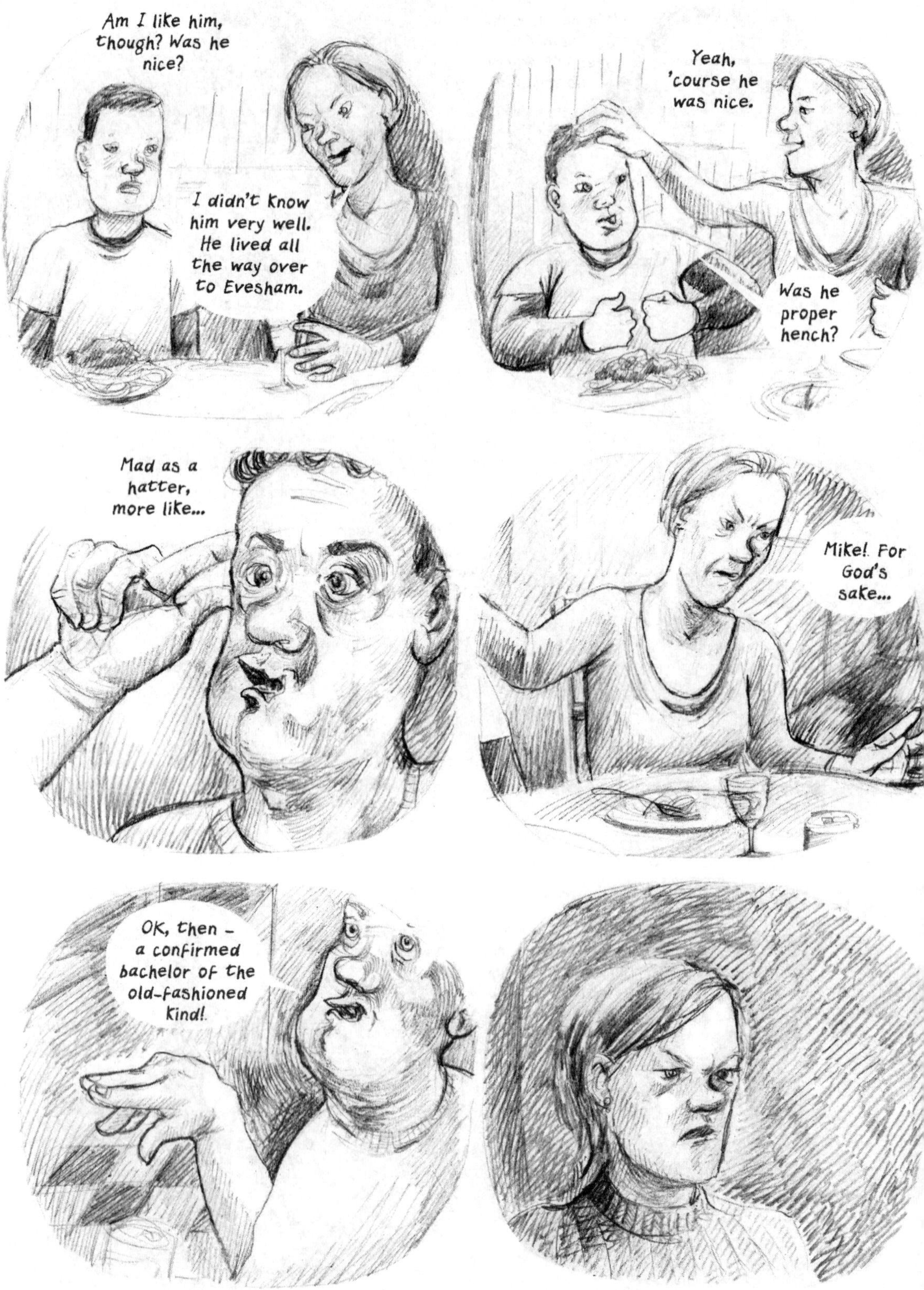
Am I like him, though? Was he nice?
I didn't know him very well. He lived all the way over to Evesham.
Yeah, 'course he was nice.
Was he proper hench?
Mad as a hatter, more like...
Mike!. For God's sake...
OK, then – a confirmed bachelor of the old-fashioned kind!.

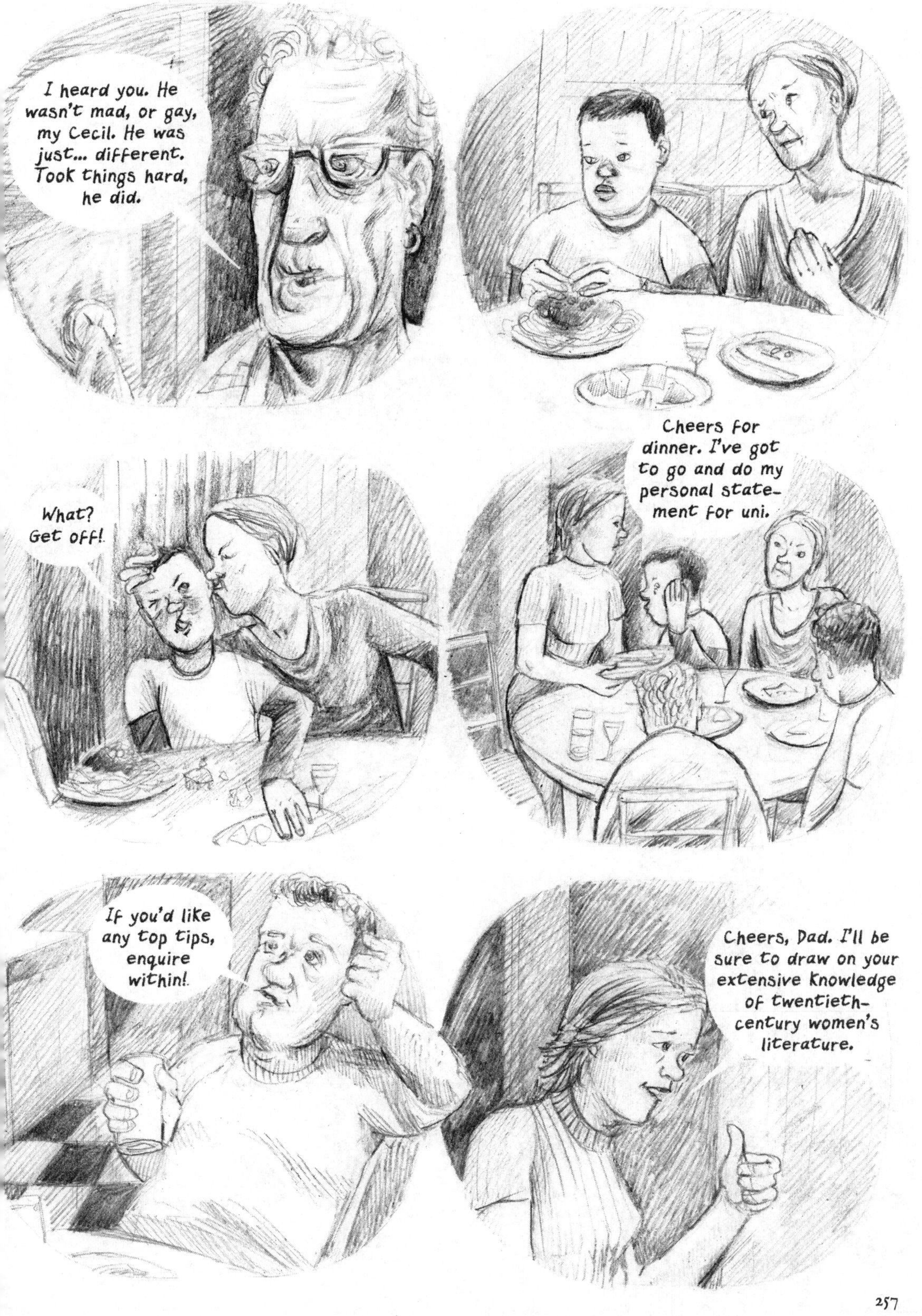
I heard you. He wasn't mad, or gay, my Cecil. He was just... different. Took things hard, he did.
What? Get off!
Cheers for dinner. I've got to go and do my personal statement for uni.
If you'd like any top tips, enquire within!
Cheers, Dad. I'll be sure to draw on your extensive knowledge of twentieth-century women's literature.

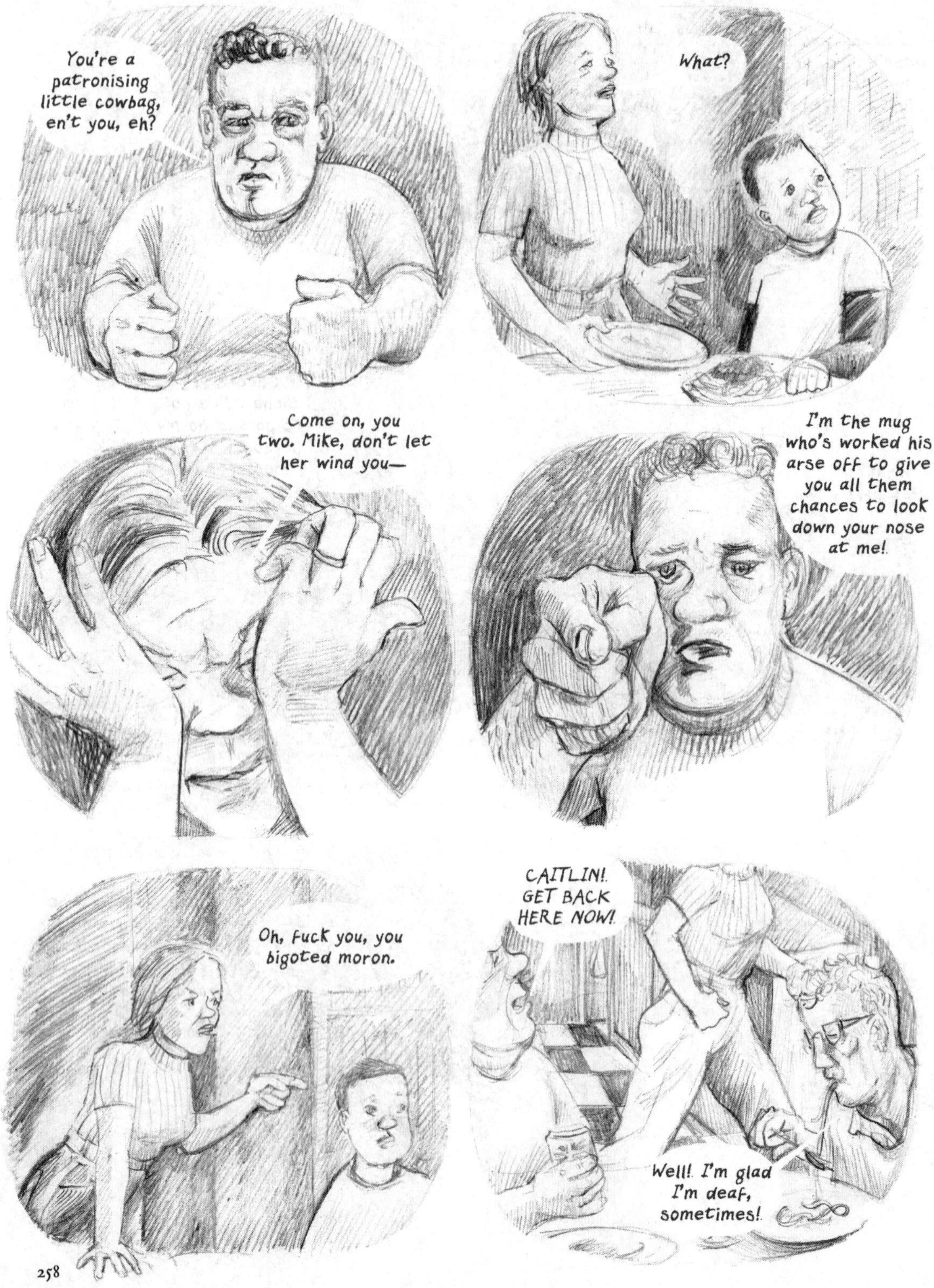
You're a patronising little cowbag, en't you, eh?
What?
Come on, you two. Mike, don't let her wind you—
I'm the mug who's worked his arse off to give you all them chances to look down your nose at me!.
Oh, fuck you, you bigoted moron.
CAITLIN!. GET BACK HERE NOW!.
Well!. I'm glad I'm deaf, sometimes!.

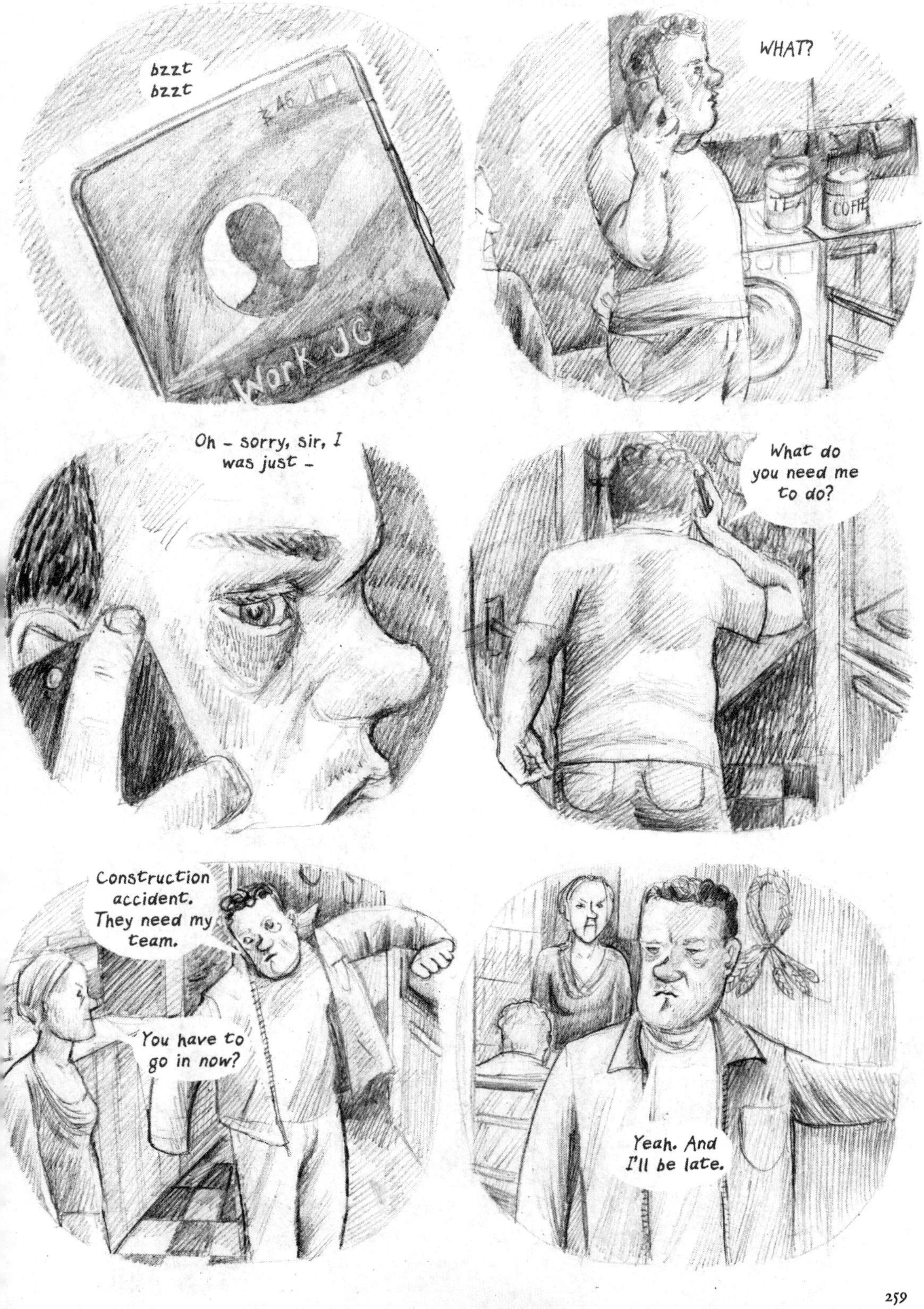
bzzt
bzzt
Work JC
WHAT?
TEA
COFFE
Oh – sorry, sir, I was just –
What do you need me to do?
Construction accident. They need my team.
You have to go in now?
Yeah. And I'll be late.

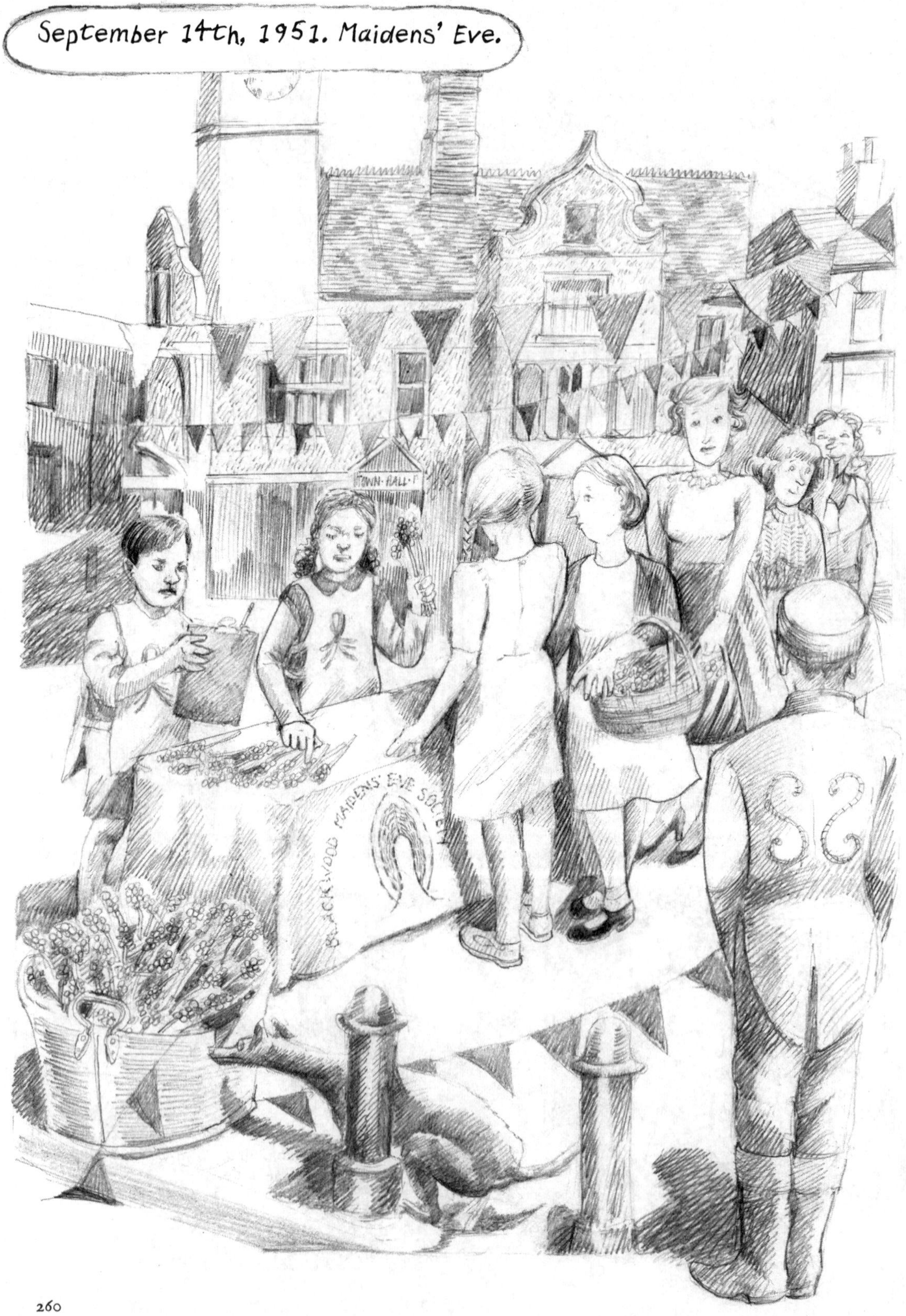
September 14th, 1951. Maidens' Eve.
TOWN HALL

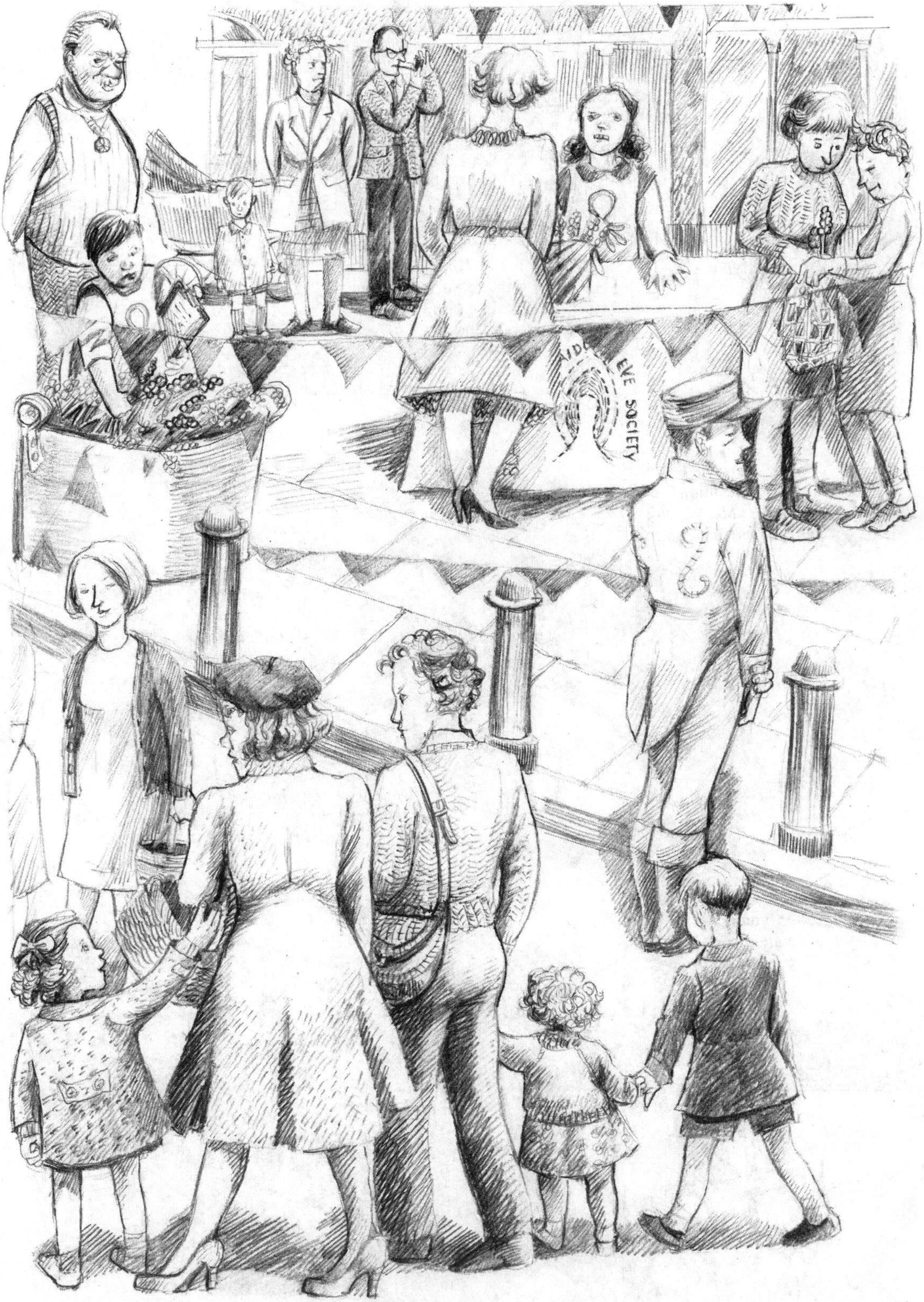
EVE SOCIETY

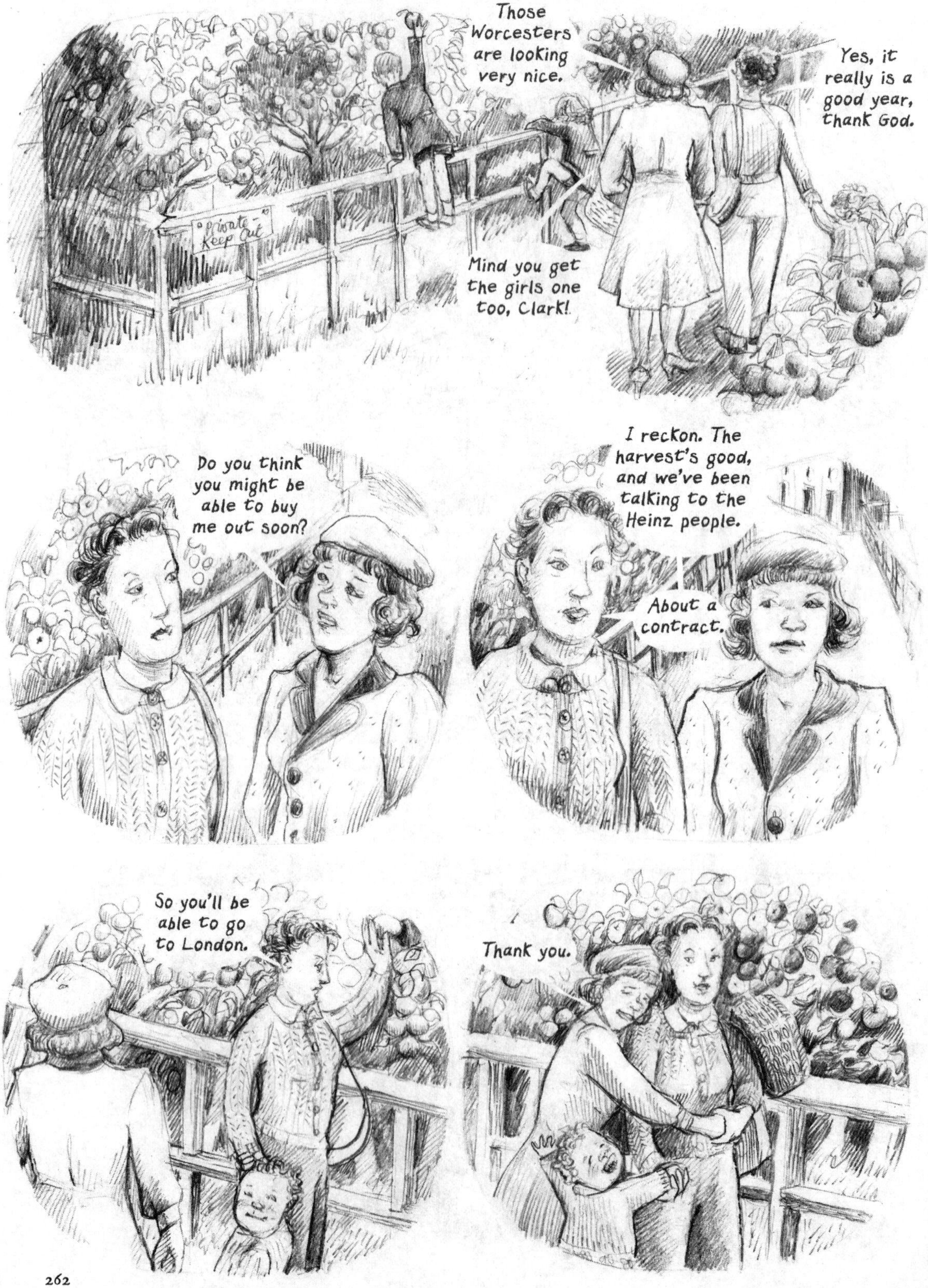
Private – Keep Out
Those Worcesters are looking very nice.
Yes, it really is a good year, thank God.
Mind you get the girls one too, Clark!
Do you think you might be able to buy me out soon?
I reckon. The harvest's good, and we've been talking to the Heinz people.
About a contract.
So you'll be able to go to London.
Thank you.

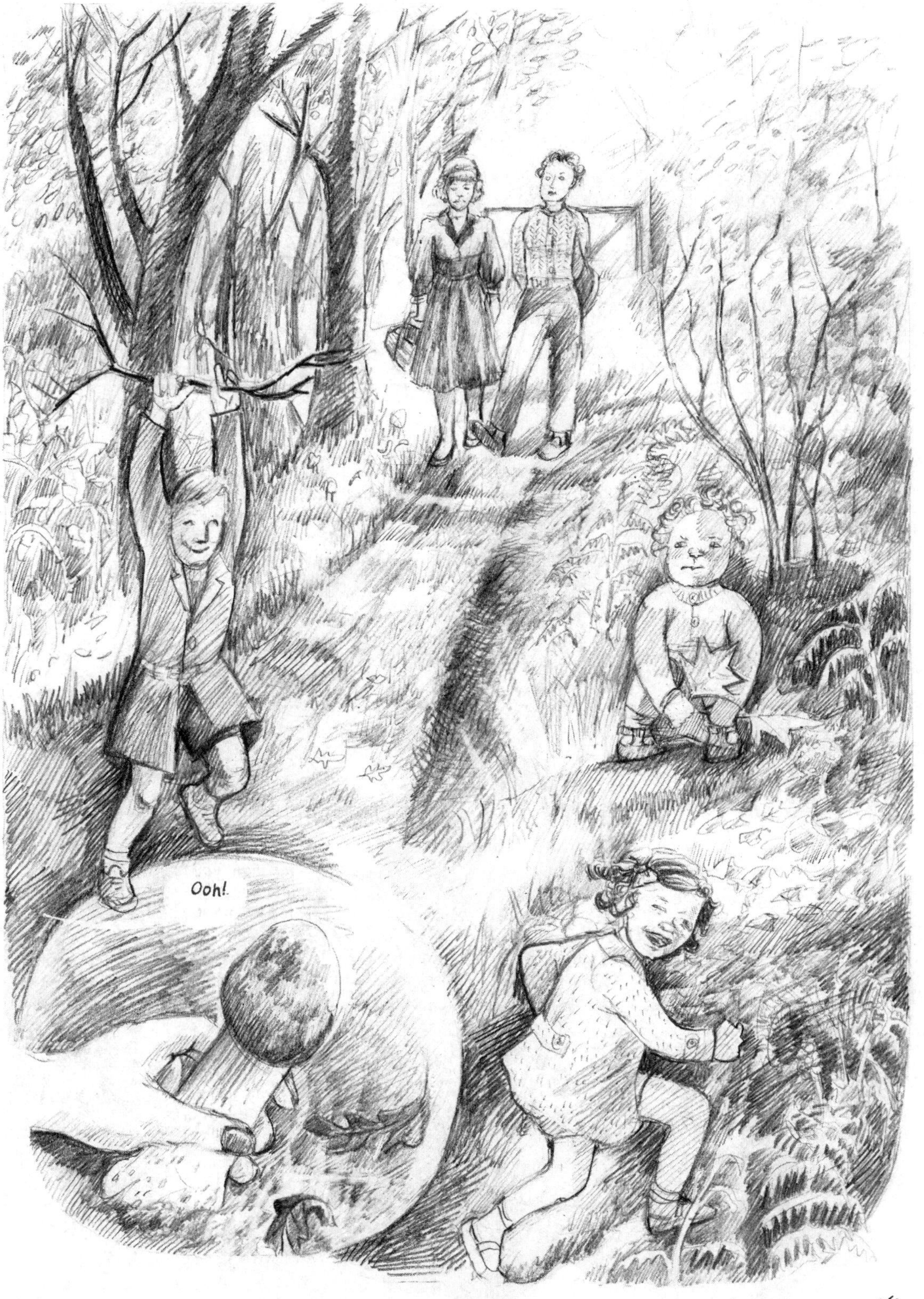
Ooh!

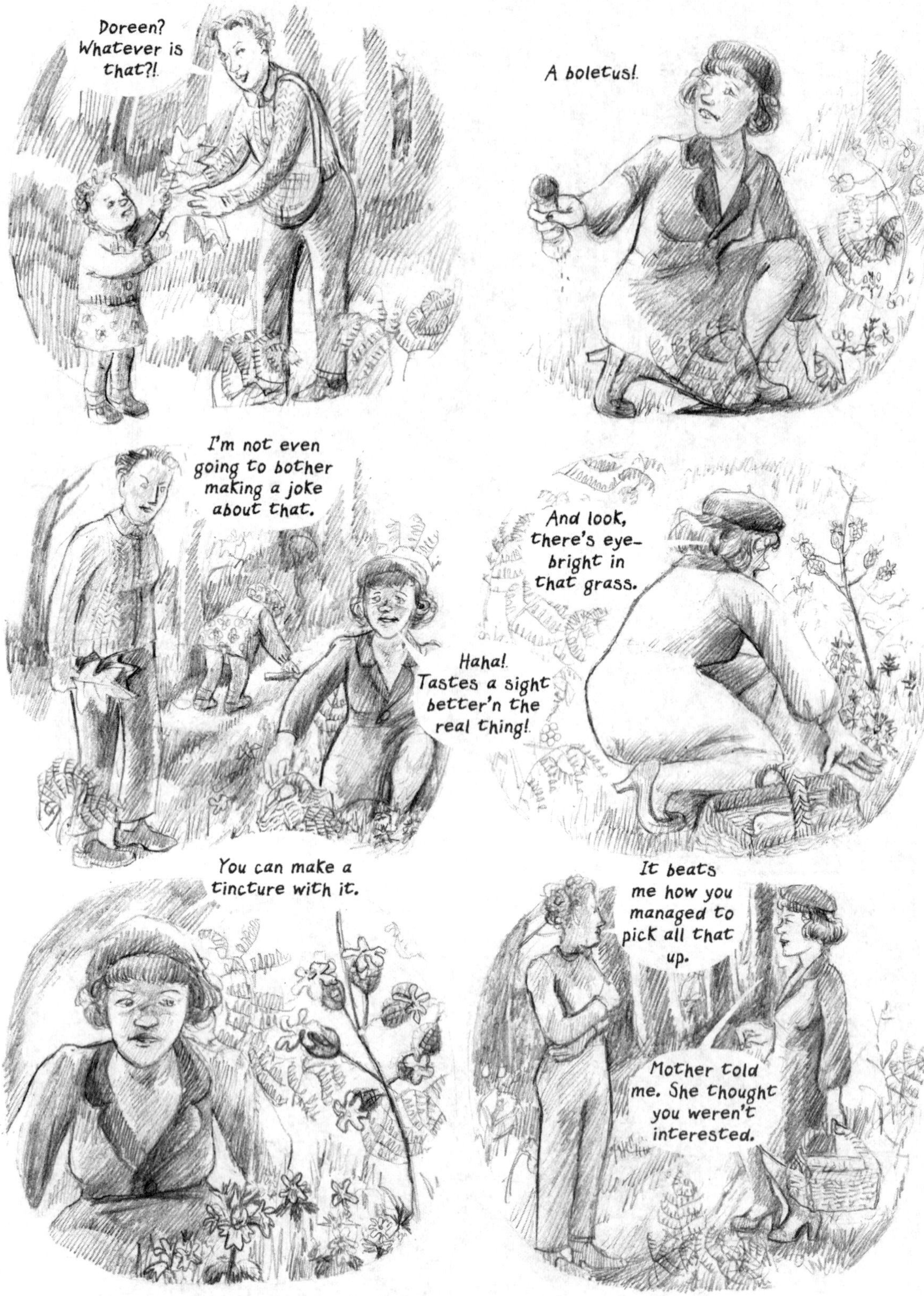
Doreen? Whatever is that?!.
A boletus!.
I'm not even going to bother making a joke about that.
Haha!. Tastes a sight better'n the real thing!.
And look, there's eye-bright in that grass.
You can make a tincture with it.
It beats me how you managed to pick all that up.
Mother told me. She thought you weren't interested.

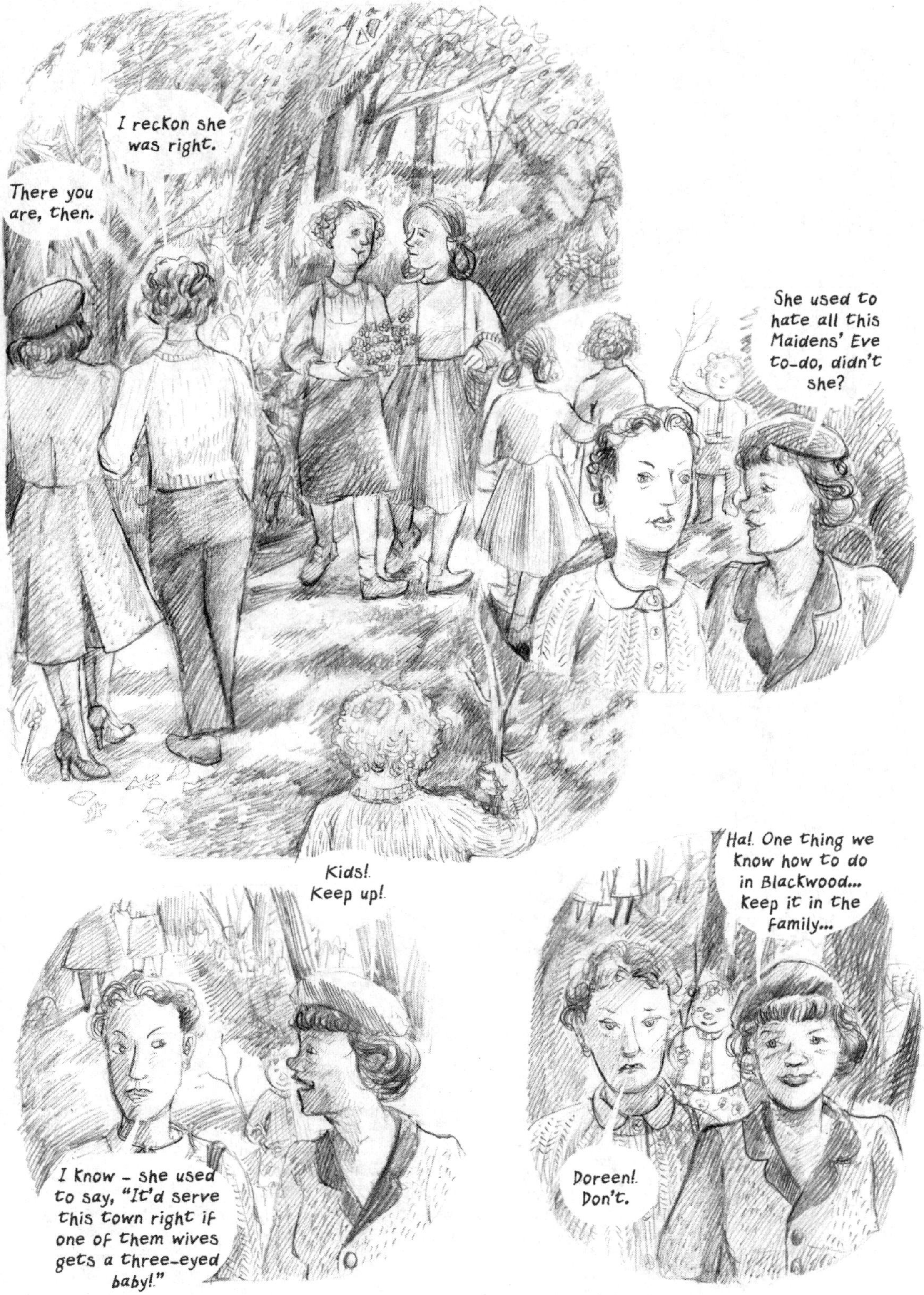

I reckon she was right.
There you are, then.
She used to hate all this Maidens' Eve to-do, didn't she?
Kids! Keep up!
I know - she used to say, "It'd serve this town right if one of them wives gets a three-eyed baby!"
Ha! One thing we know how to do in Blackwood... Keep it in the family...
Doreen! Don't.

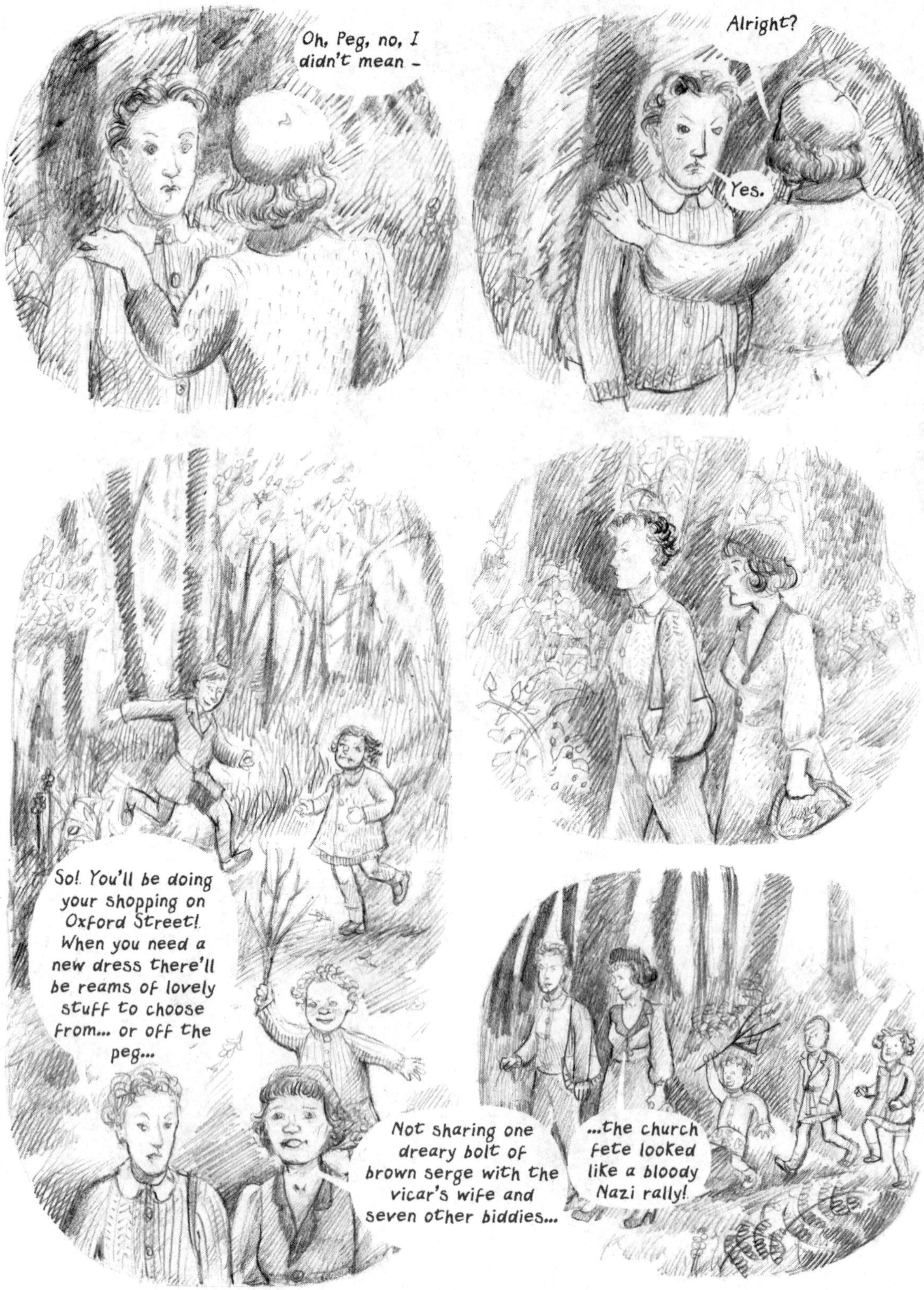

Oh, Peg, no, I didn't mean -
Alright?
Yes.
So!. You'll be doing your shopping on Oxford Street!. When you need a new dress there'll be reams of lovely stuff to choose from... or off the peg...
Not sharing one dreary bolt of brown serge with the vicar's wife and seven other biddies...
...the church fete looked like a bloody Nazi rally!

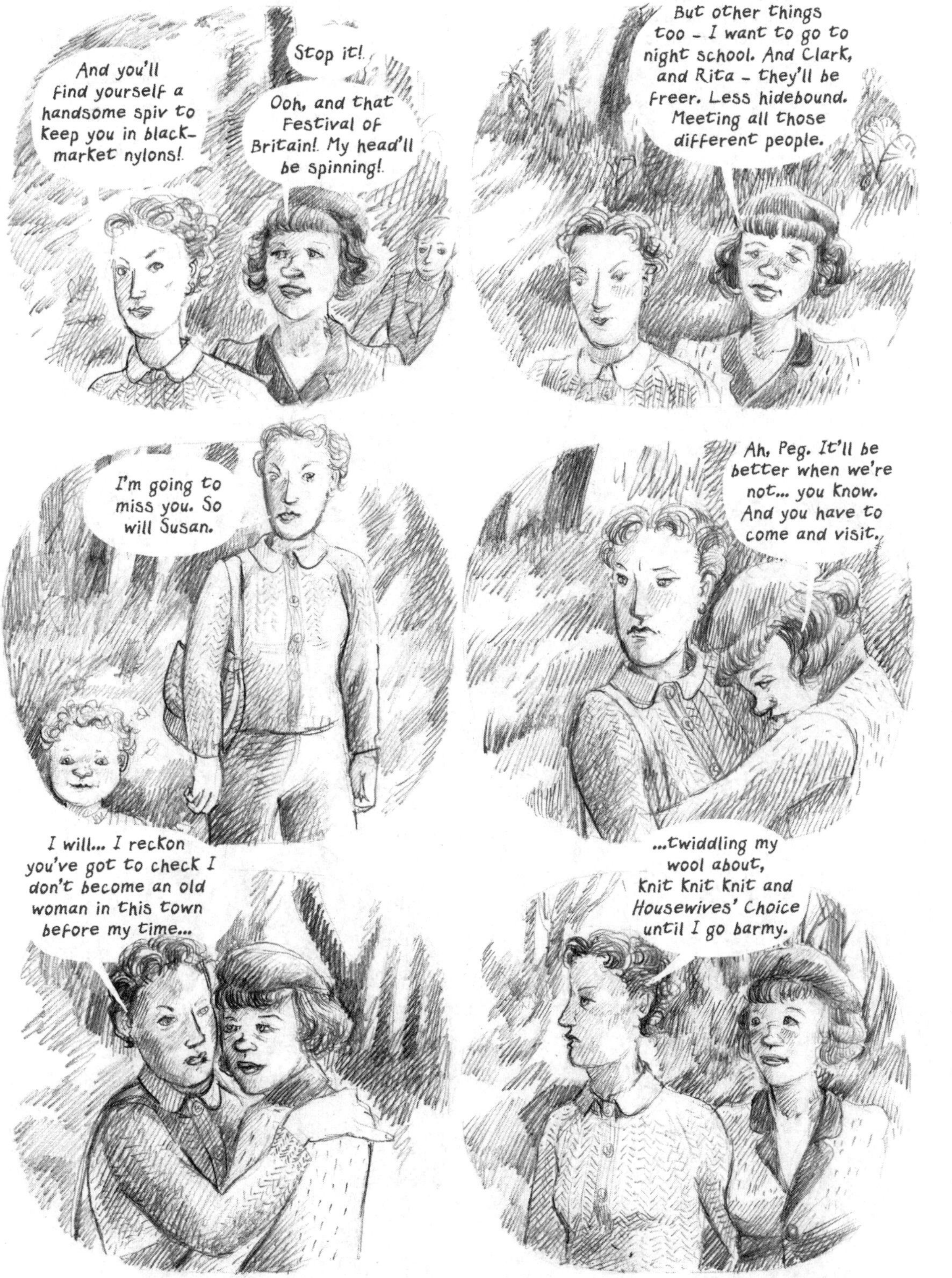
And you'll find yourself a handsome spiv to keep you in black-market nylons!.
Stop it!.
Ooh, and that Festival of Britain!. My head'll be spinning!.
But other things too - I want to go to night school. And Clark, and Rita - they'll be freer. Less hidebound. Meeting all those different people.
I'm going to miss you. So will Susan.
Ah, Peg. It'll be better when we're not... you know. And you have to come and visit.
I will... I reckon you've got to check I don't become an old woman in this town before my time...
...twiddling my wool about, Knit Knit Knit and Housewives' Choice until I go barmy.

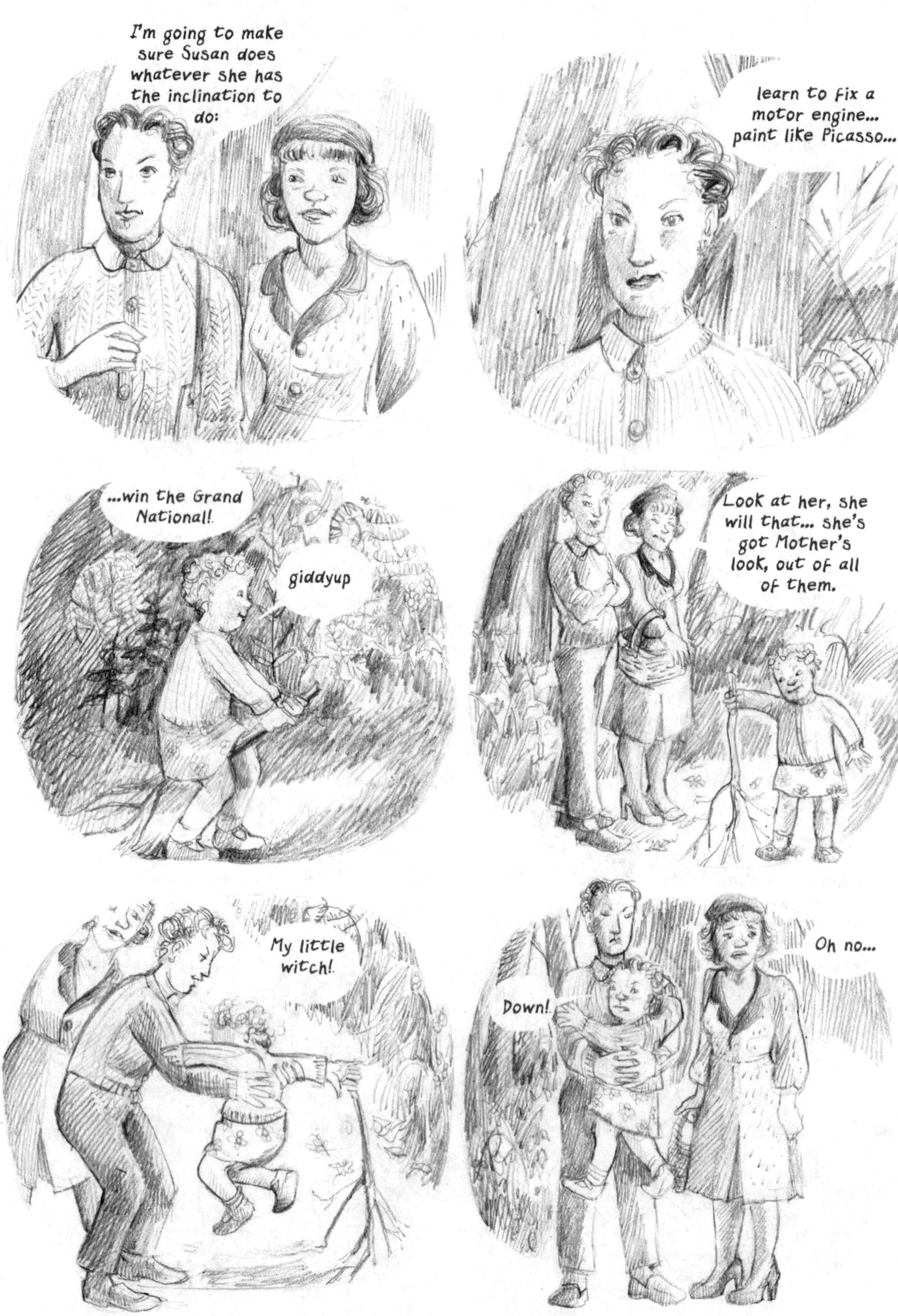

I'm going to make sure Susan does whatever she has the inclination to do:
learn to fix a motor engine... paint like Picasso...
...win the Grand National!
giddyup
Look at her, she will that... she's got Mother's look, out of all of them.
My little witch!
Oh no...
Down!

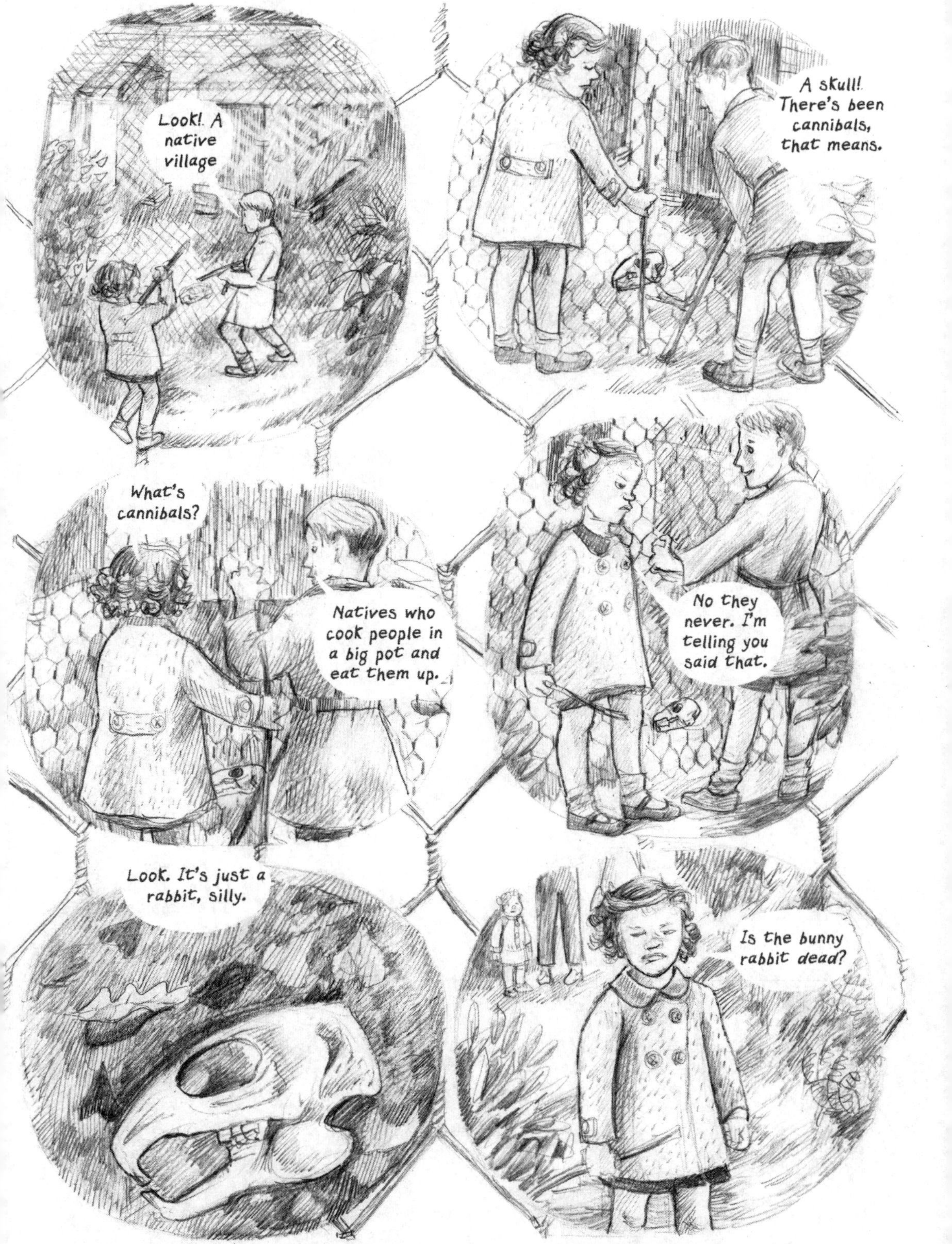
Look!. A native village
A skull!. There's been cannibals, that means.
What's cannibals?
Natives who cook people in a big pot and eat them up.
No they never. I'm telling you said that.
Look. It's just a rabbit, silly.
Is the bunny rabbit dead?

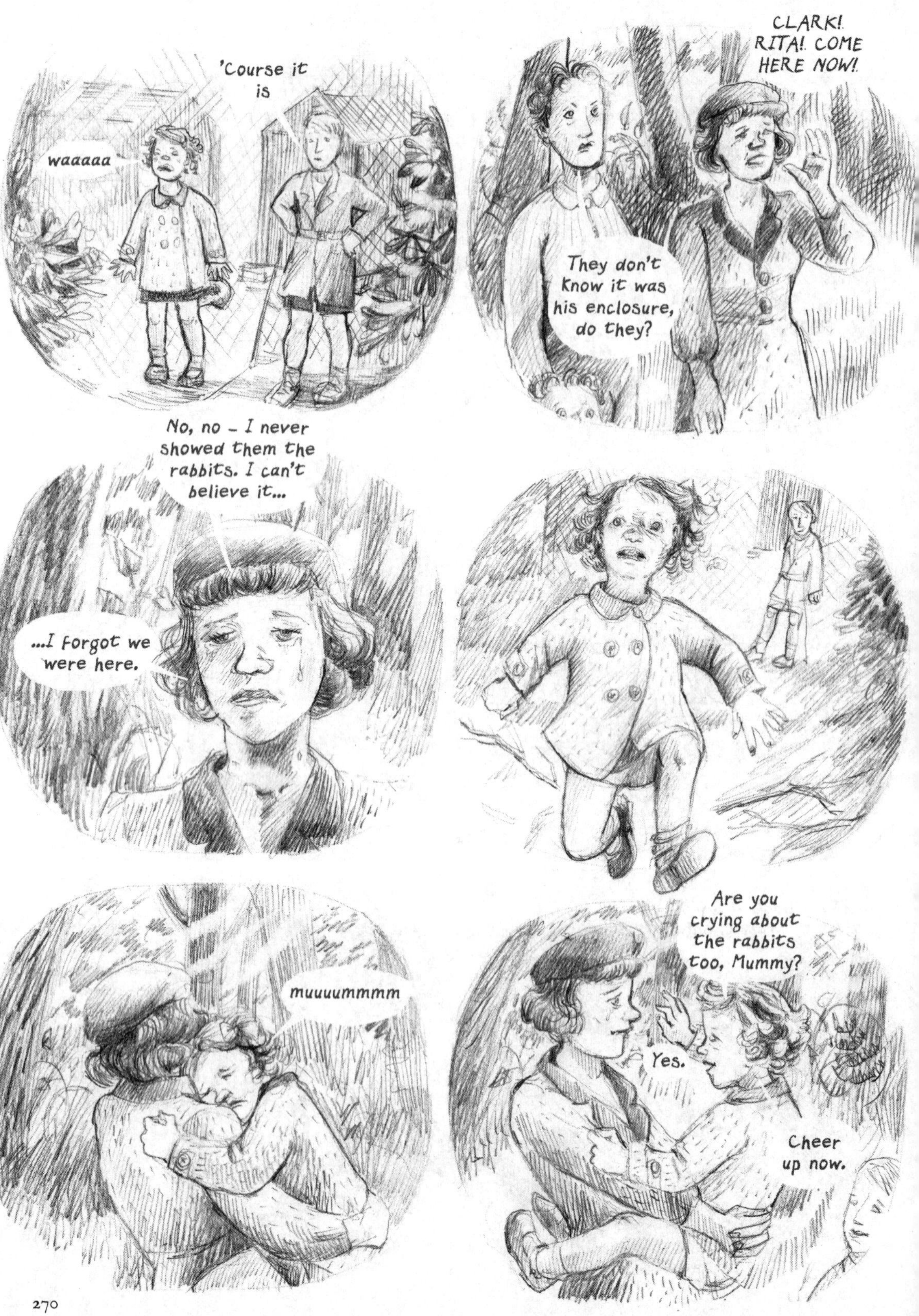

'Course it is
waaaaa
CLARK! RITA! COME HERE NOW!
They don't know it was his enclosure, do they?
No, no – I never showed them the rabbits. I can't believe it...
...I forgot we were here.
muuuummmm
Are you crying about the rabbits too, Mummy?
Yes.
Cheer up now.

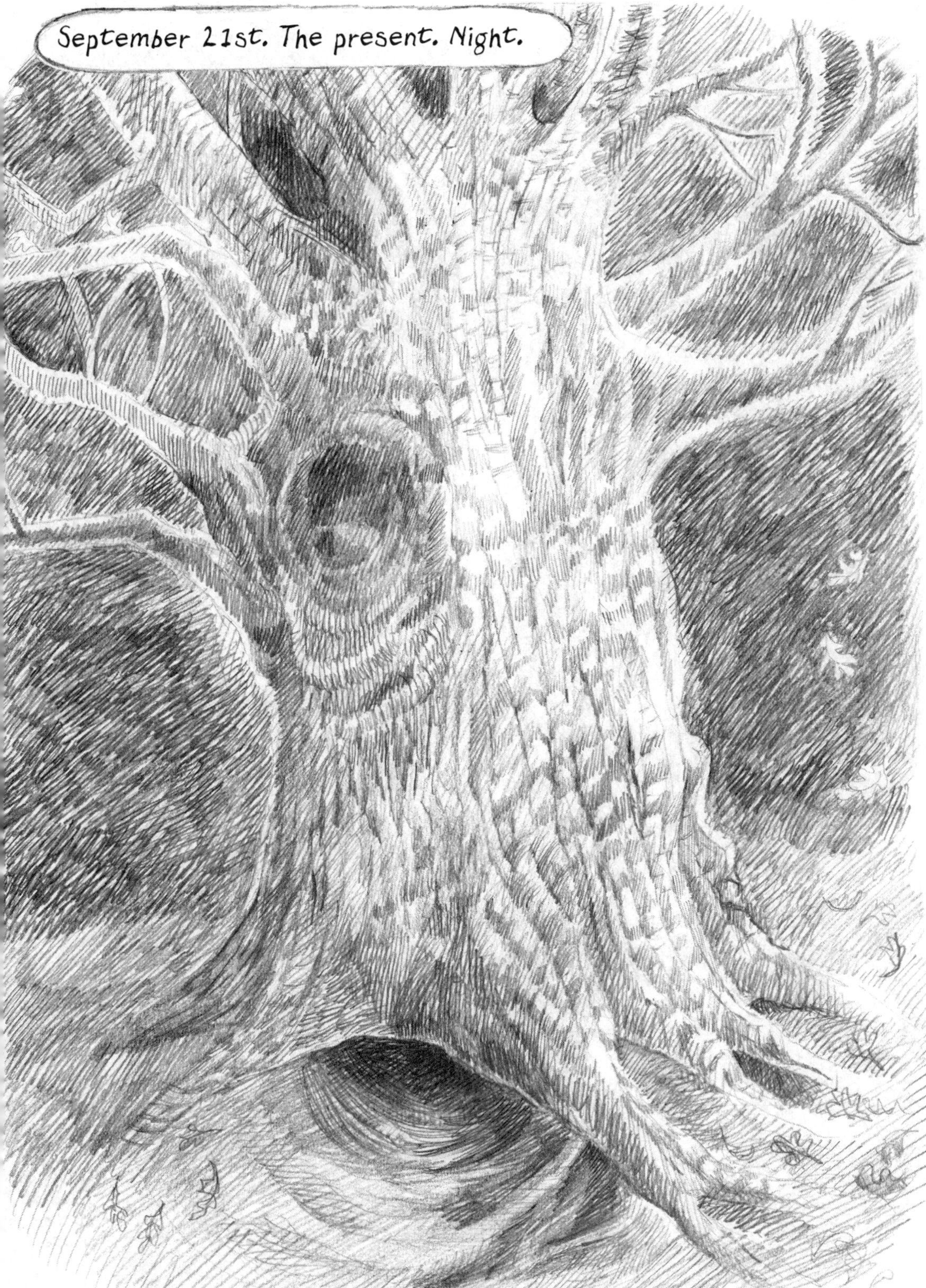
September 21st. The present. Night.

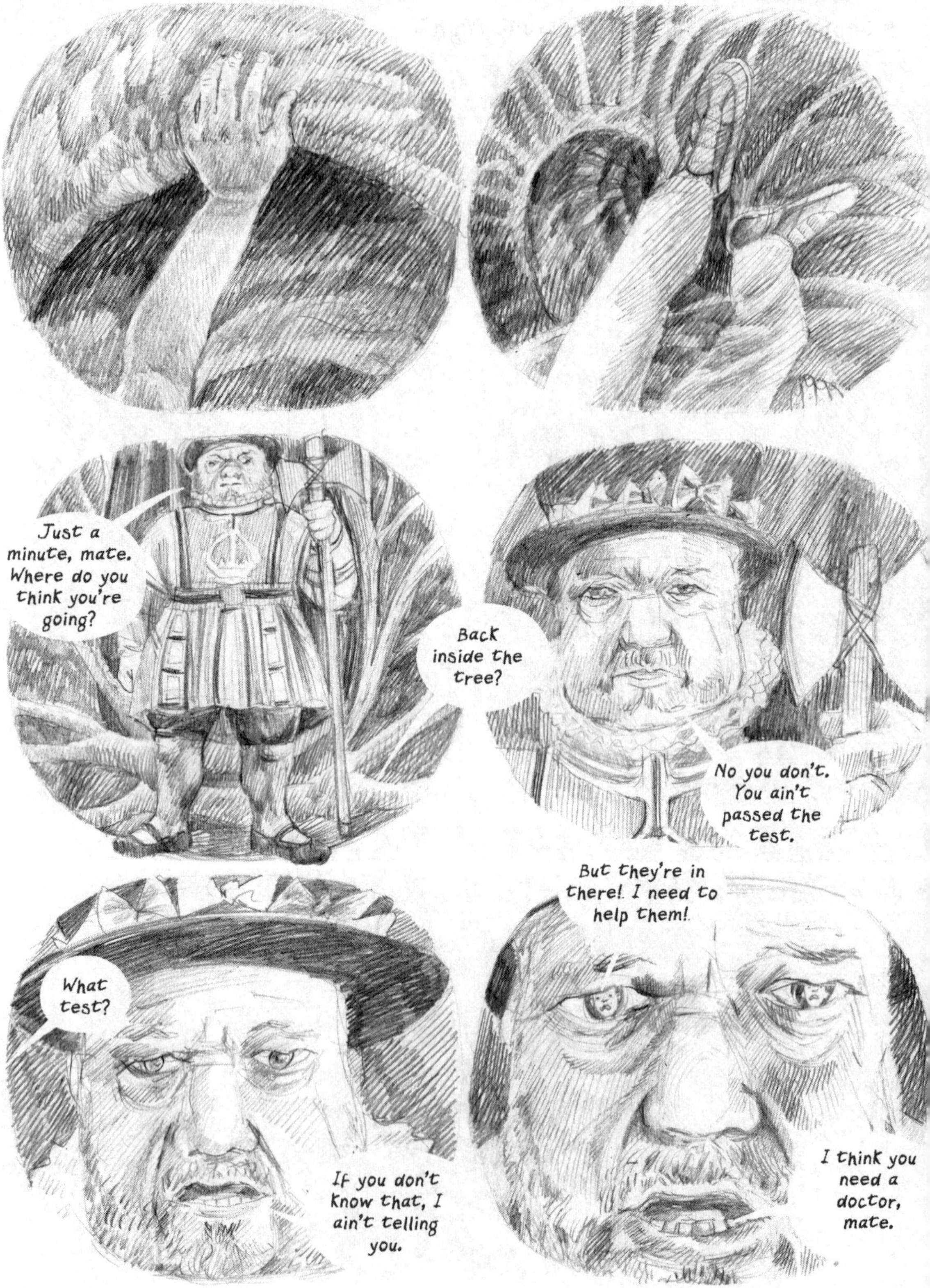
Just a minute, mate. Where do you think you're going?
Back inside the tree?
No you don't. You ain't passed the test.
What test?
If you don't know that, I ain't telling you.
But they're in there!. I need to help them!.
I think you need a doctor, mate.

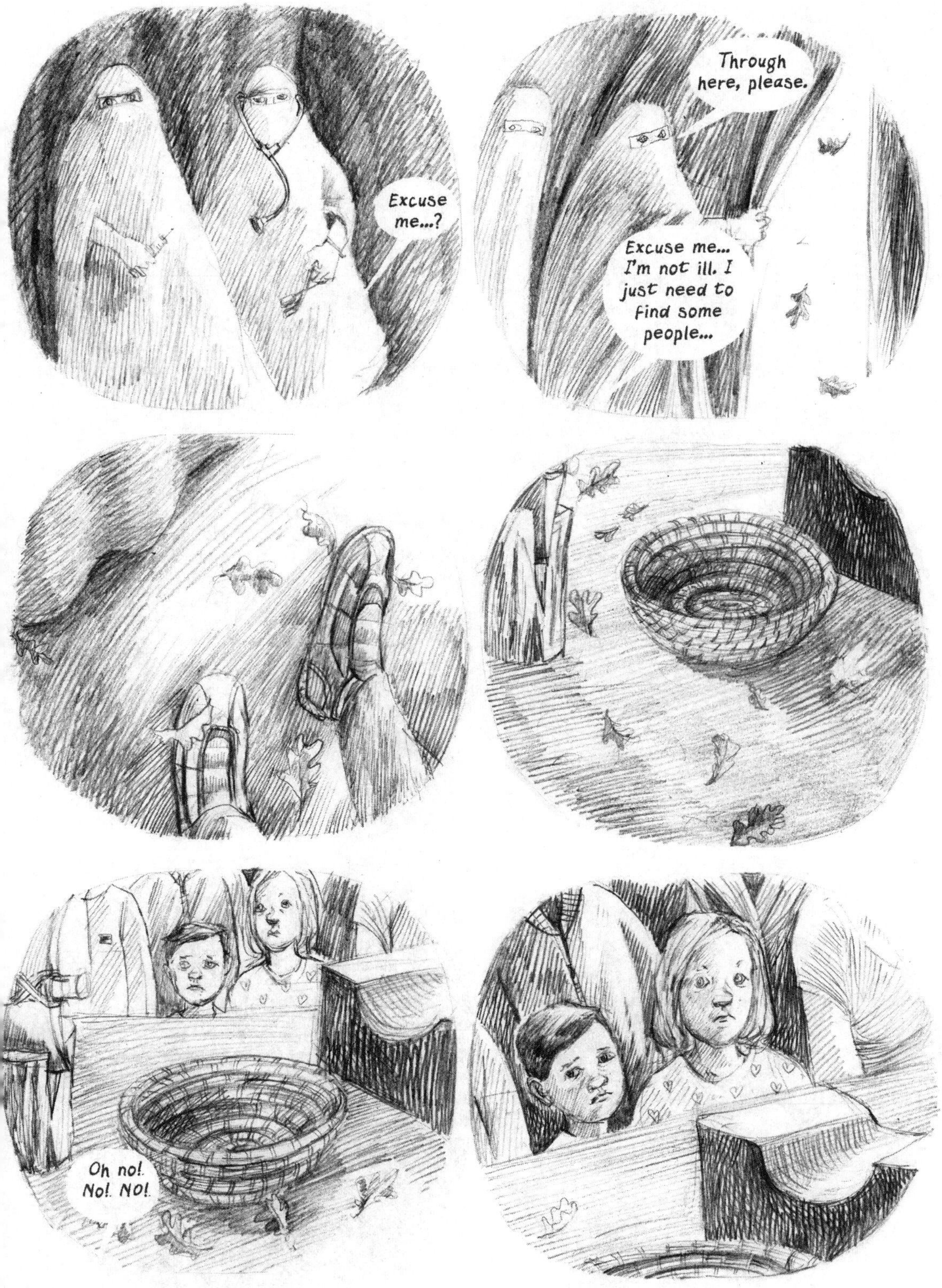
Excuse me...?
Through here, please.
Excuse me... I'm not ill. I just need to find some people...
Oh no!. No!. NO!.

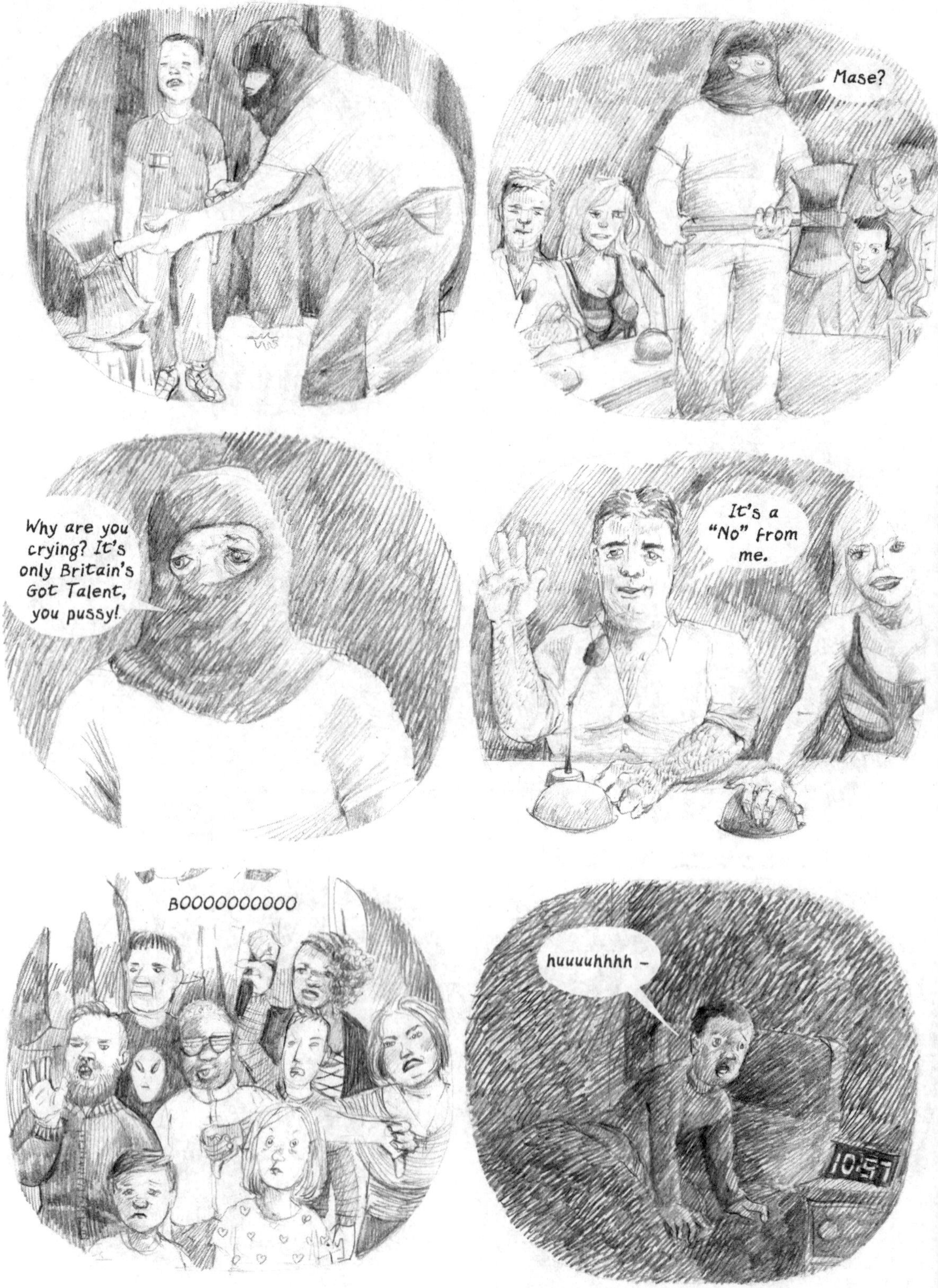
Mase?
Why are you crying? It's only Britain's Got Talent, you pussy!
It's a "No" from me.
BOOOOOOOOOO
huuuuhhhh –
10:57

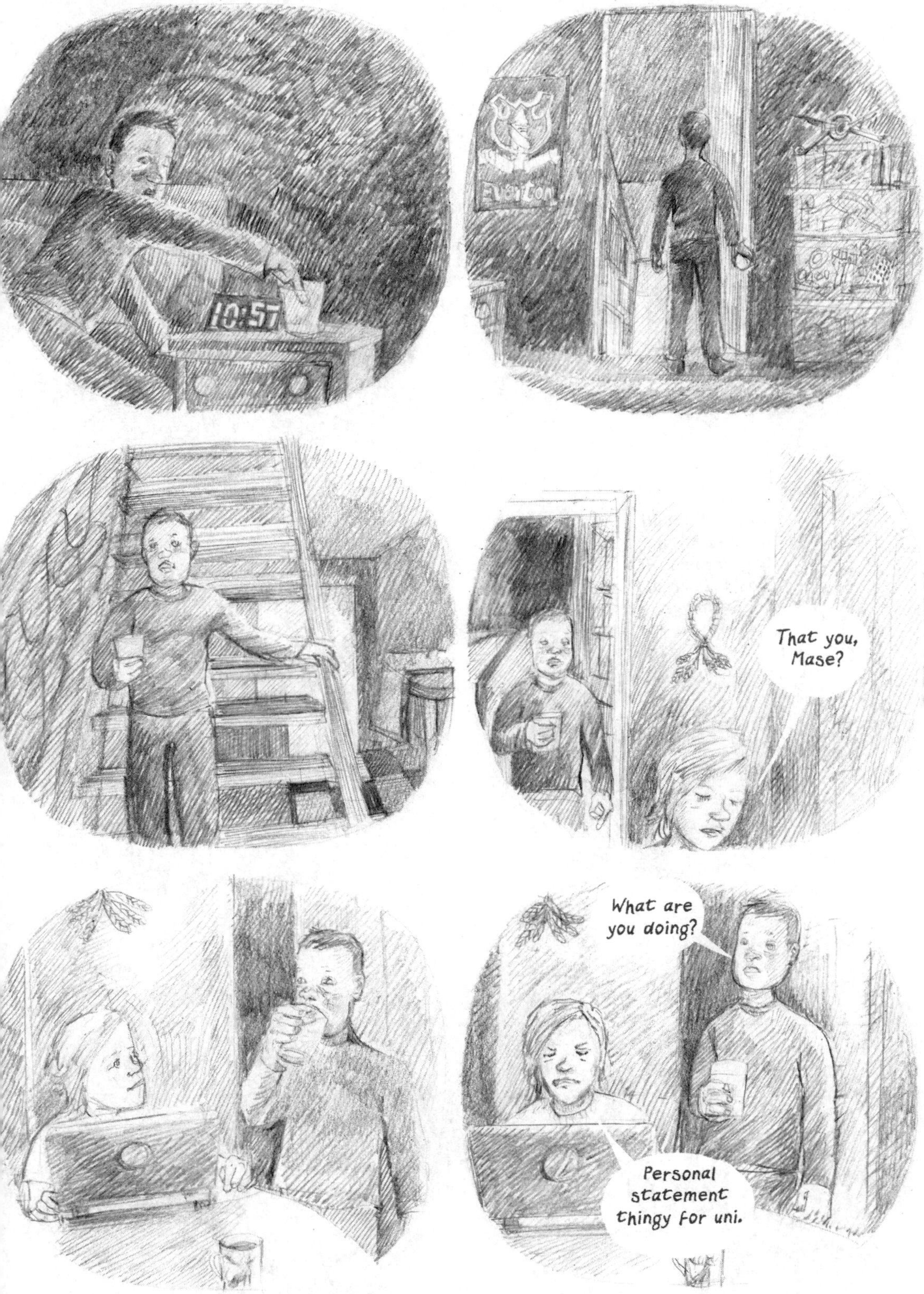
10:57
That you, Mase?
What are you doing?
Personal statement thingy for uni.

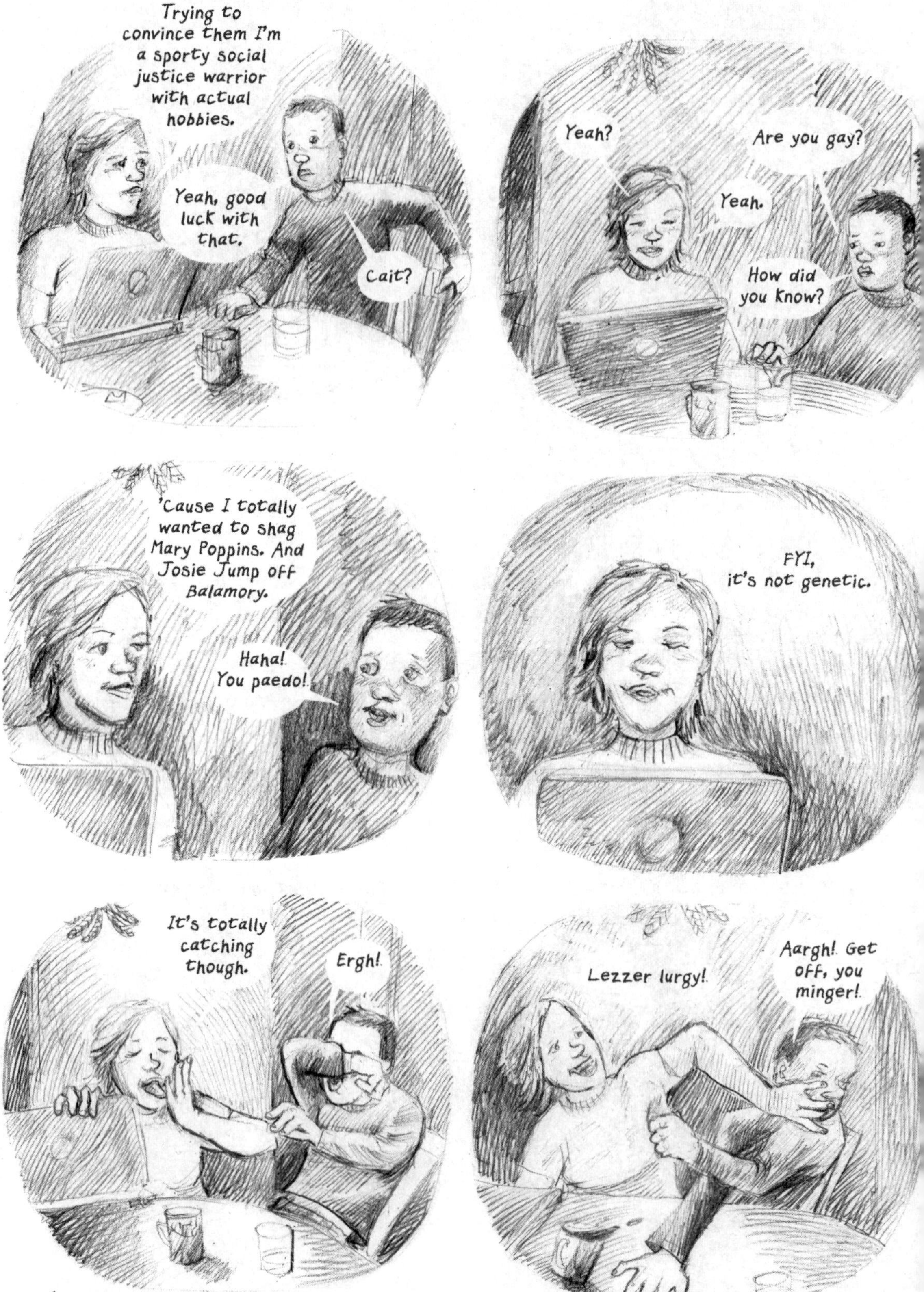
Trying to convince them I'm a sporty social justice warrior with actual hobbies.
Yeah, good luck with that.
Cait?
Yeah?
Are you gay?
Yeah.
How did you know?
'Cause I totally wanted to shag Mary Poppins. And Josie Jump off Balamory.
Haha! You paedo!
FYI, it's not genetic.
It's totally catching though.
Ergh!
Lezzer lurgy!
Aargh! Get off, you minger!

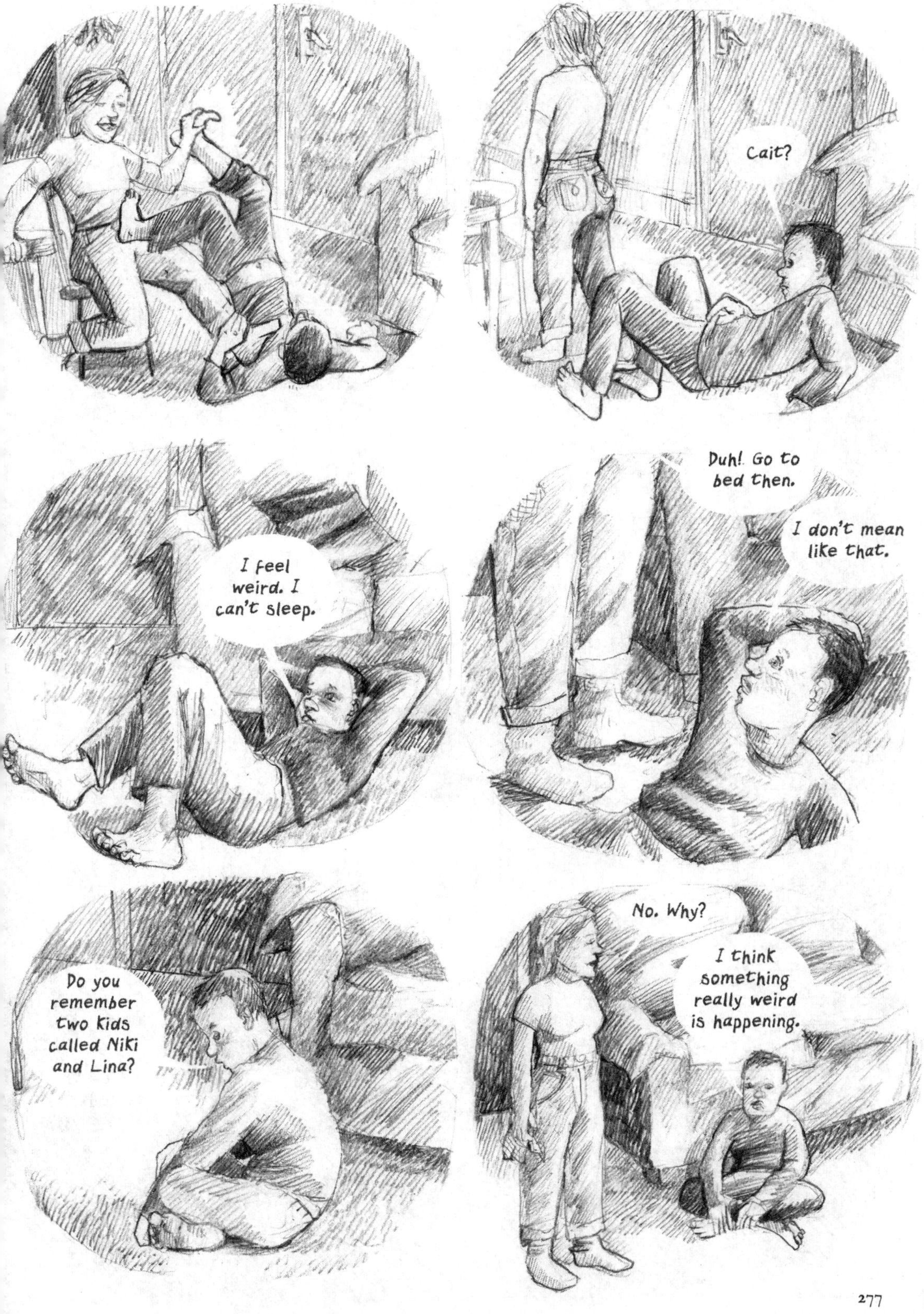
Cait?
I feel weird. I can't sleep.
Duh! Go to bed then.
I don't mean like that.
Do you remember two kids called Niki and Lina?
No. Why?
I think something really weird is happening.

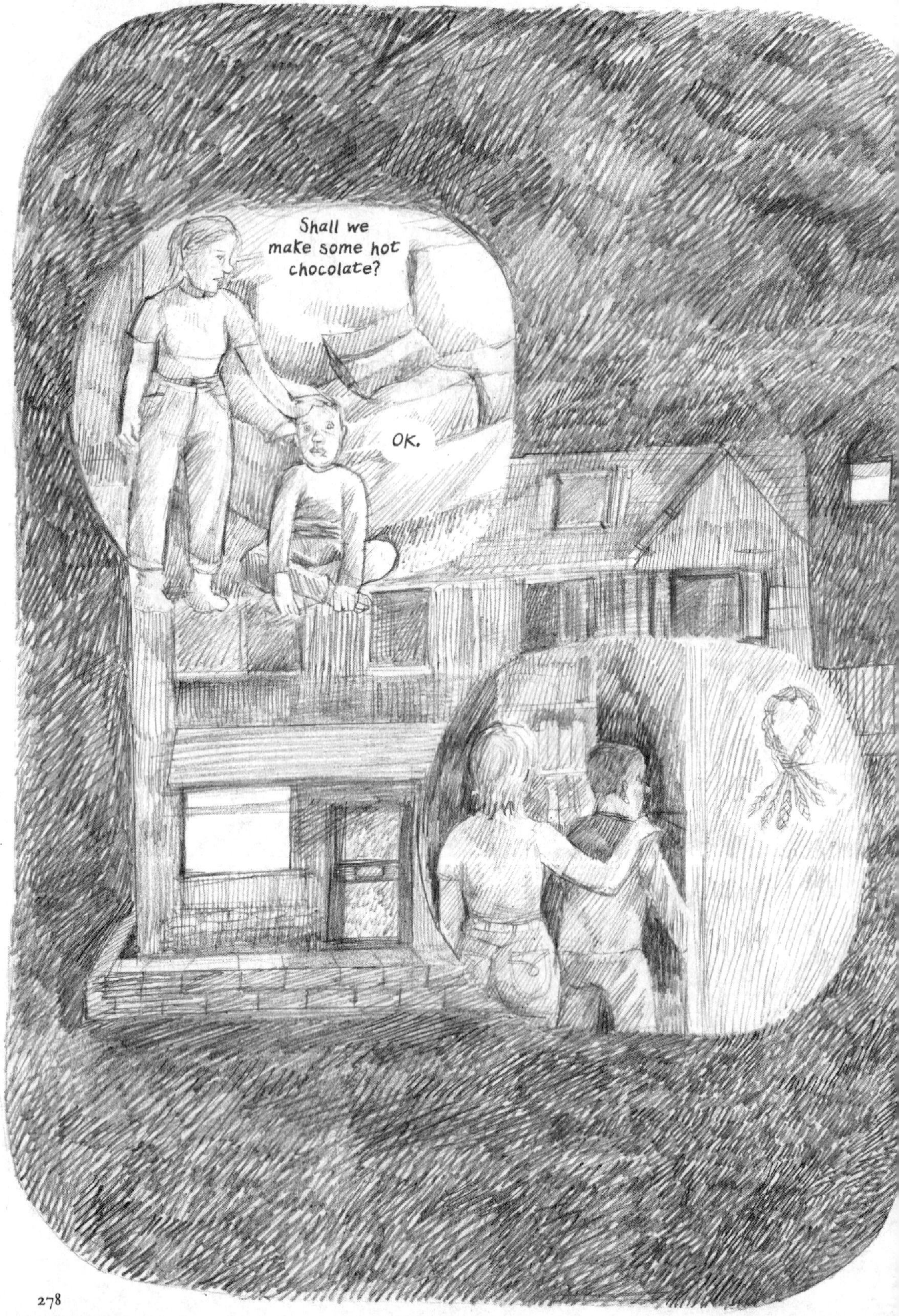
Shall we make some hot chocolate?
OK.

September 22nd. The present.

Knock Knock

Justin Cleveden
naging Director

Come in.

Justin Cleveden
naging Director

Yeah.
Mike, hi.

SE

tin Cleveden
ng Director

Listen – I'm gonna keep it short – just a chat, yeah?

I see you haven't brought a union rep – good call, dude.

FYI, they're not allowed anyway.

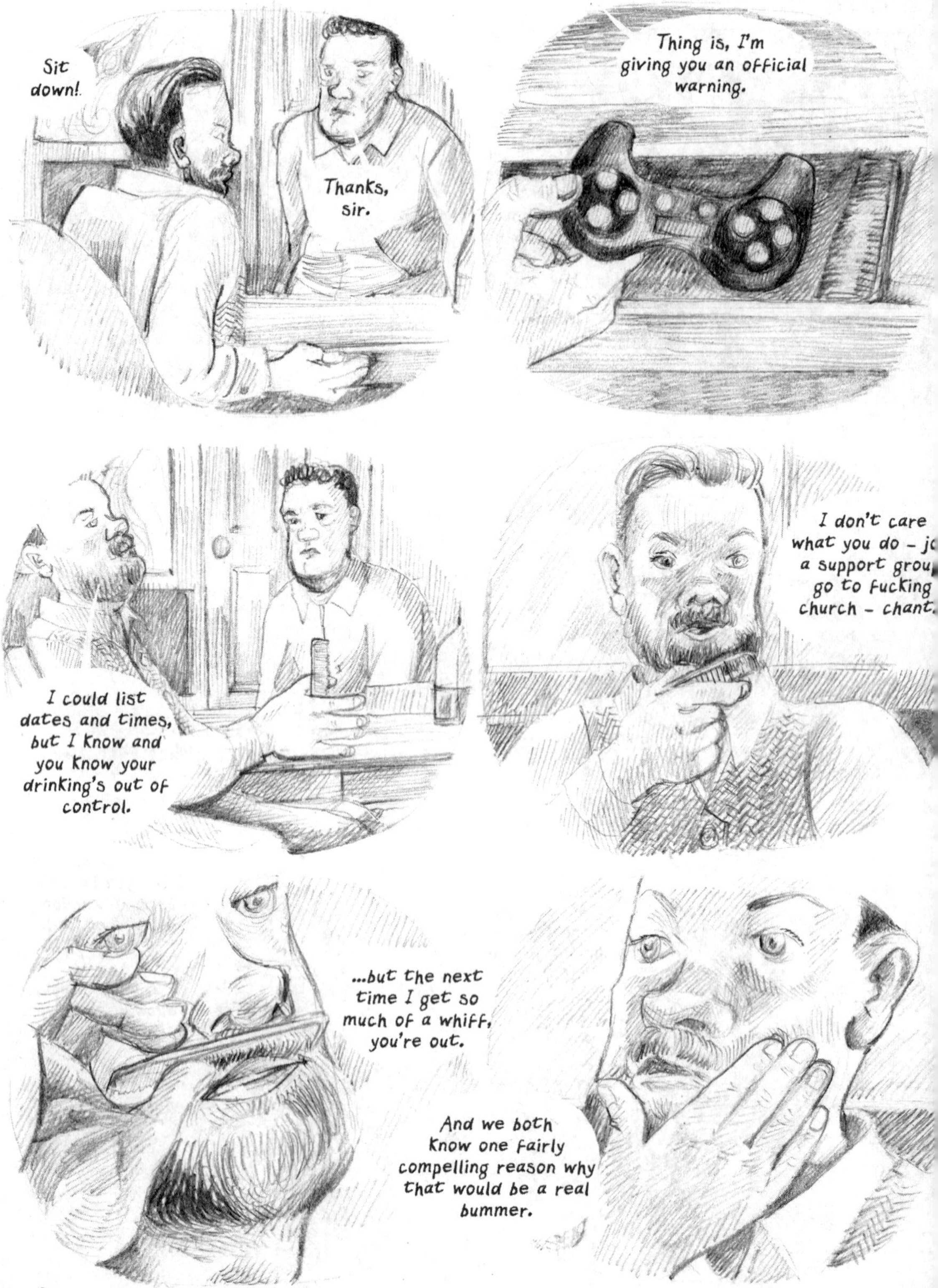
Sit down!.
Thanks, sir.
Thing is, I'm giving you an official warning.
I could list dates and times, but I know and you know your drinking's out of control.
I don't care what you do – jo a support grou go to fucking church – chant.
...but the next time I get so much of a whiff, you're out.
And we both know one fairly compelling reason why that would be a real bummer.

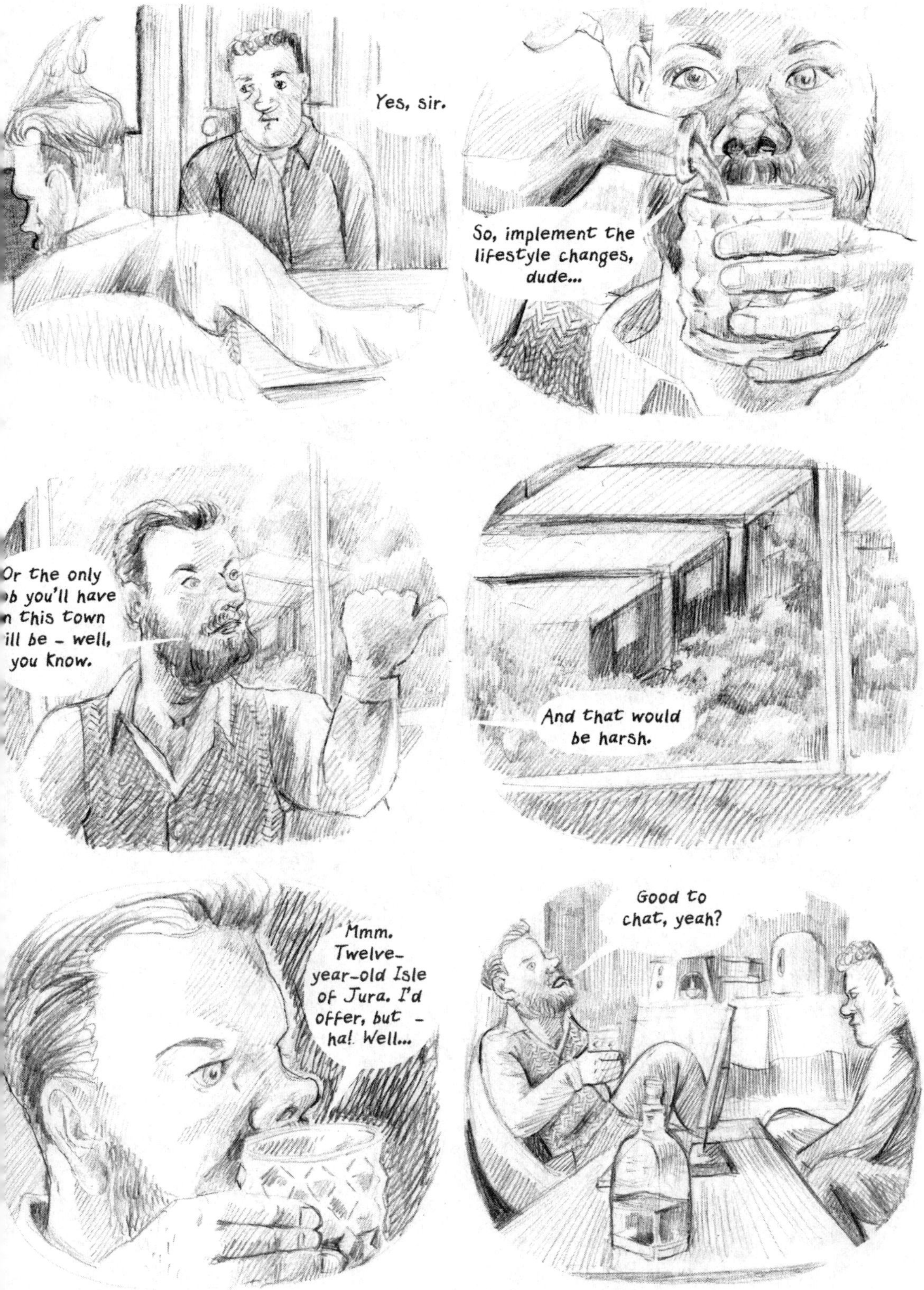
Yes, sir.
So, implement the lifestyle changes, dude...
Or the only
b you'll have
n this town
ill be - well,
you know.
And that would be harsh.
Mmm. Twelve-year-old Isle of Jura. I'd offer, but - ha! Well...
Good to chat, yeah?

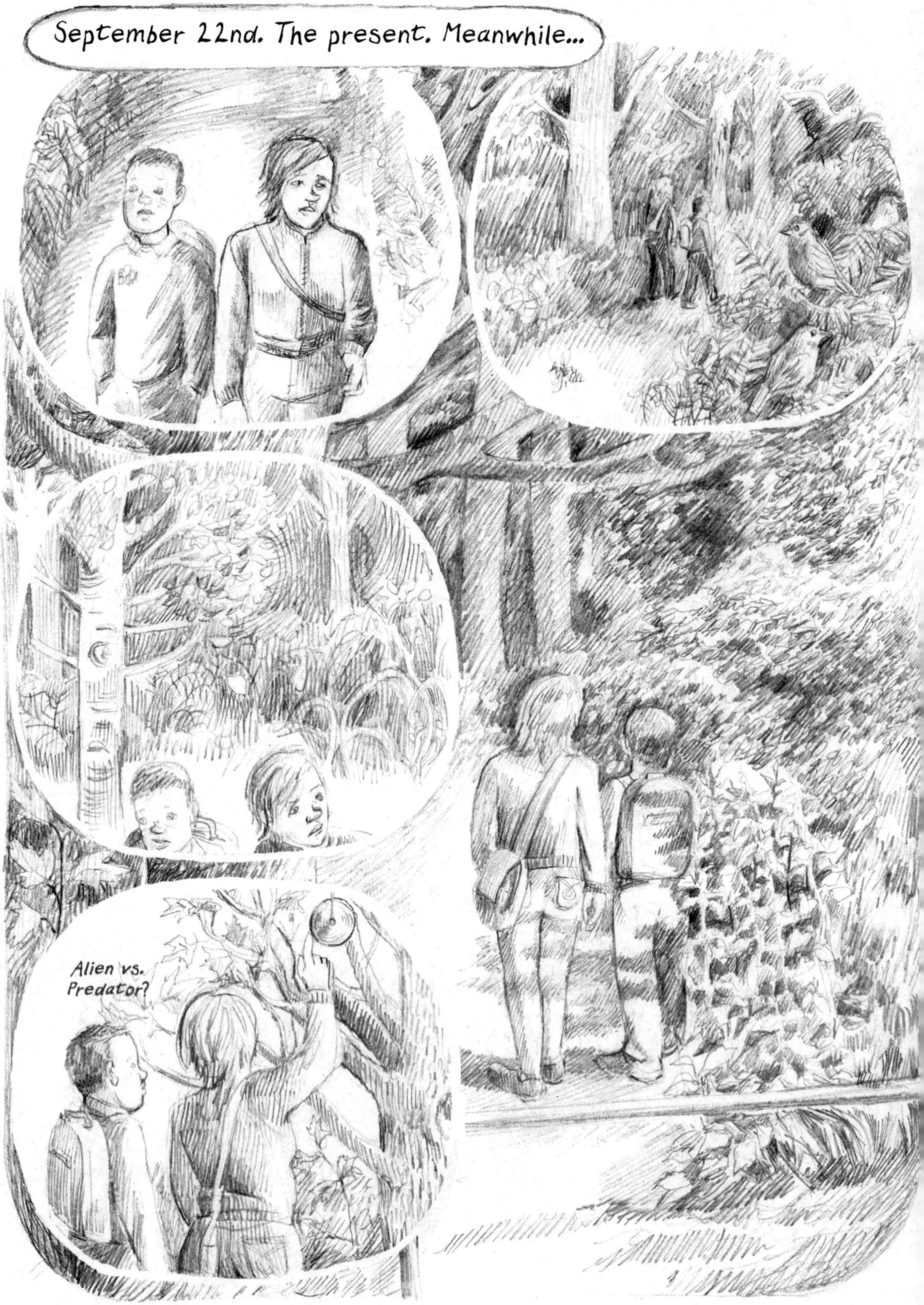
September 22nd. The present. Meanwhile...
Alien vs. Predator?

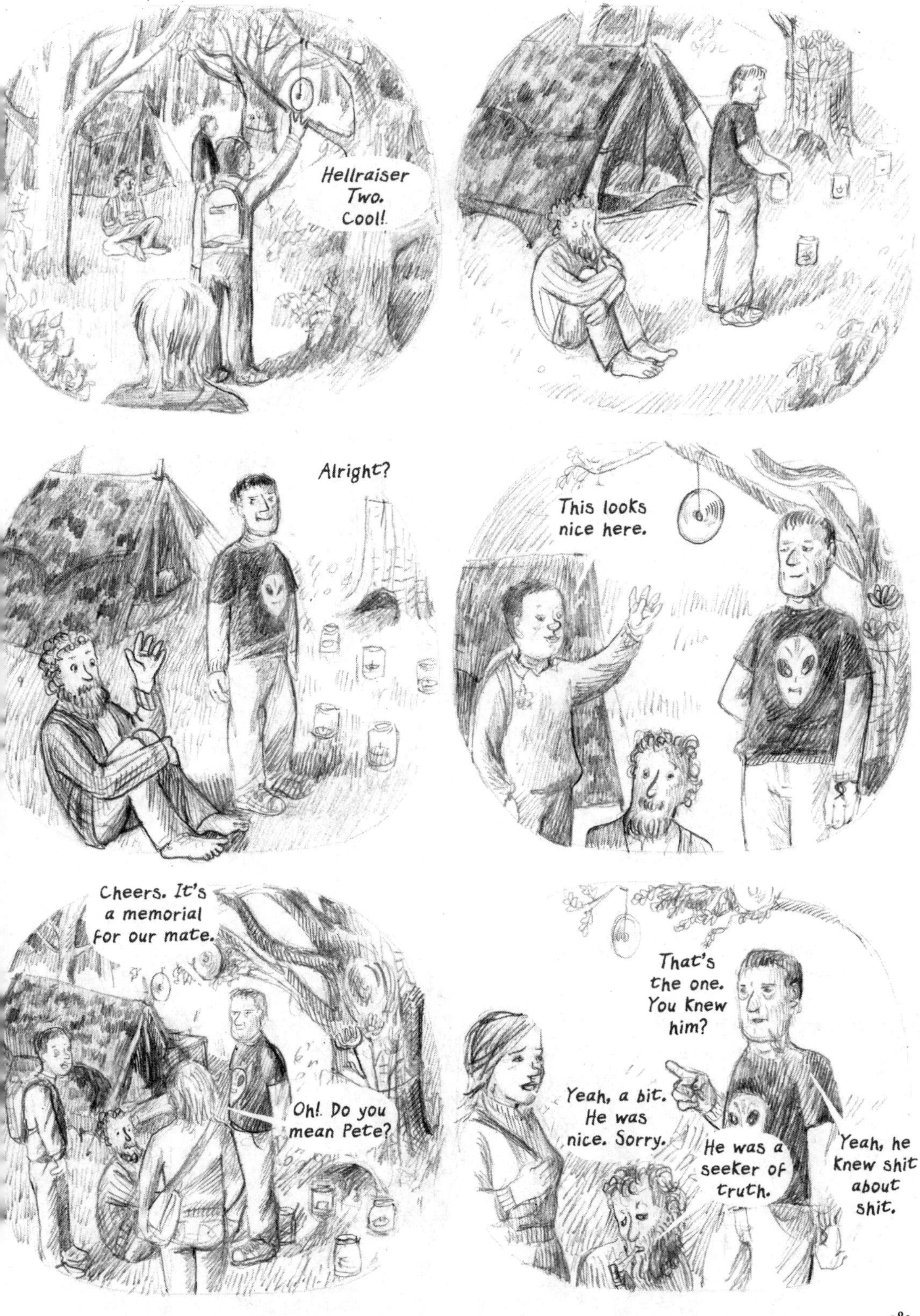
Hellraiser Two. Cool!
Alright?
This looks nice here.
Cheers. It's a memorial for our mate.
Oh!. Do you mean Pete?
That's the one. You knew him?
Yeah, a bit. He was nice. Sorry.
He was a seeker of truth.
Yeah, he knew shit about shit.

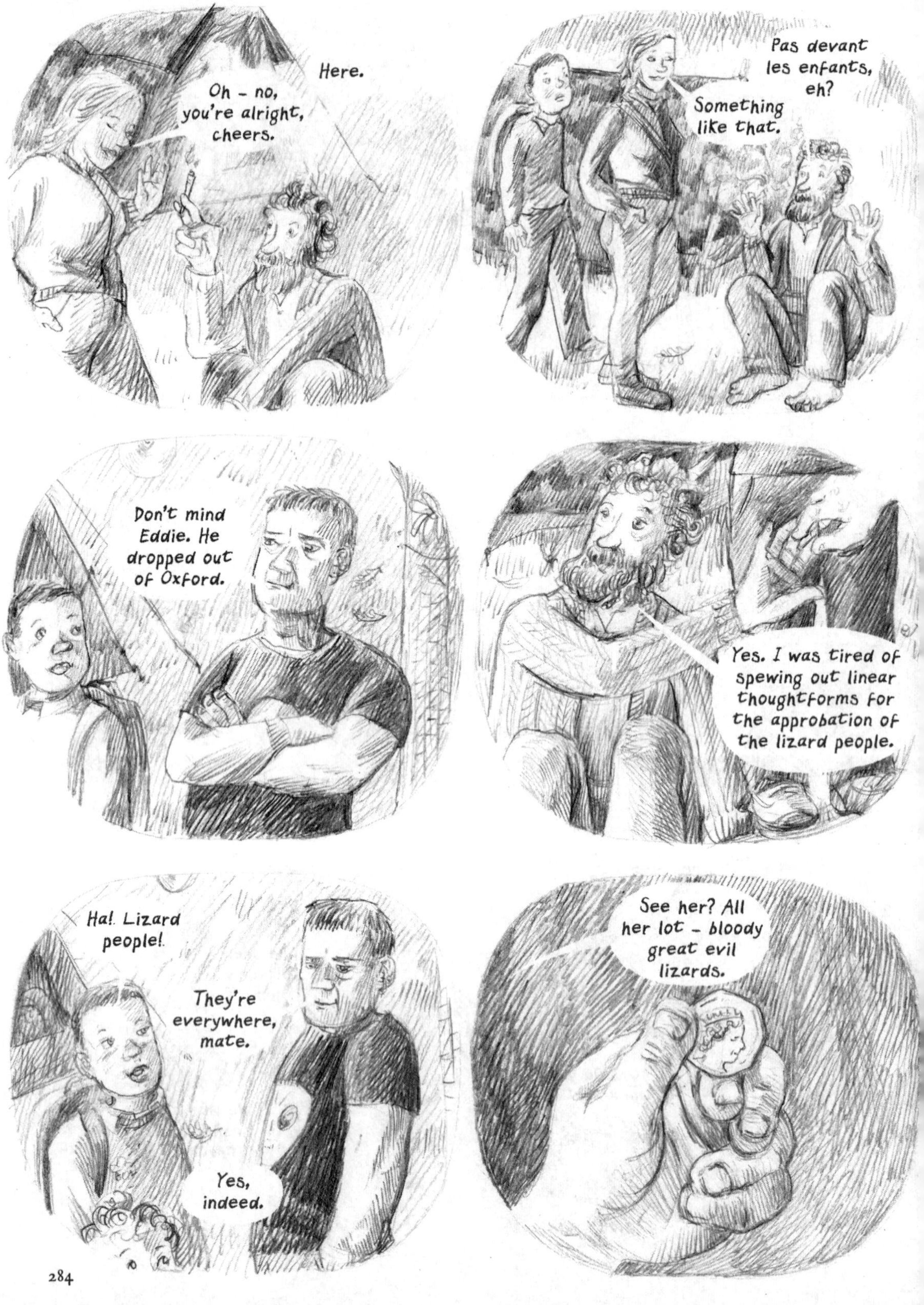
Here.
Oh – no, you're alright, cheers.
Pas devant les enfants, eh?
Something like that.
Don't mind Eddie. He dropped out of Oxford.
Yes. I was tired of spewing out linear thoughtforms for the approbation of the lizard people.
Ha!. Lizard people!.
They're everywhere, mate.
Yes, indeed.
See her? All her lot – bloody great evil lizards.

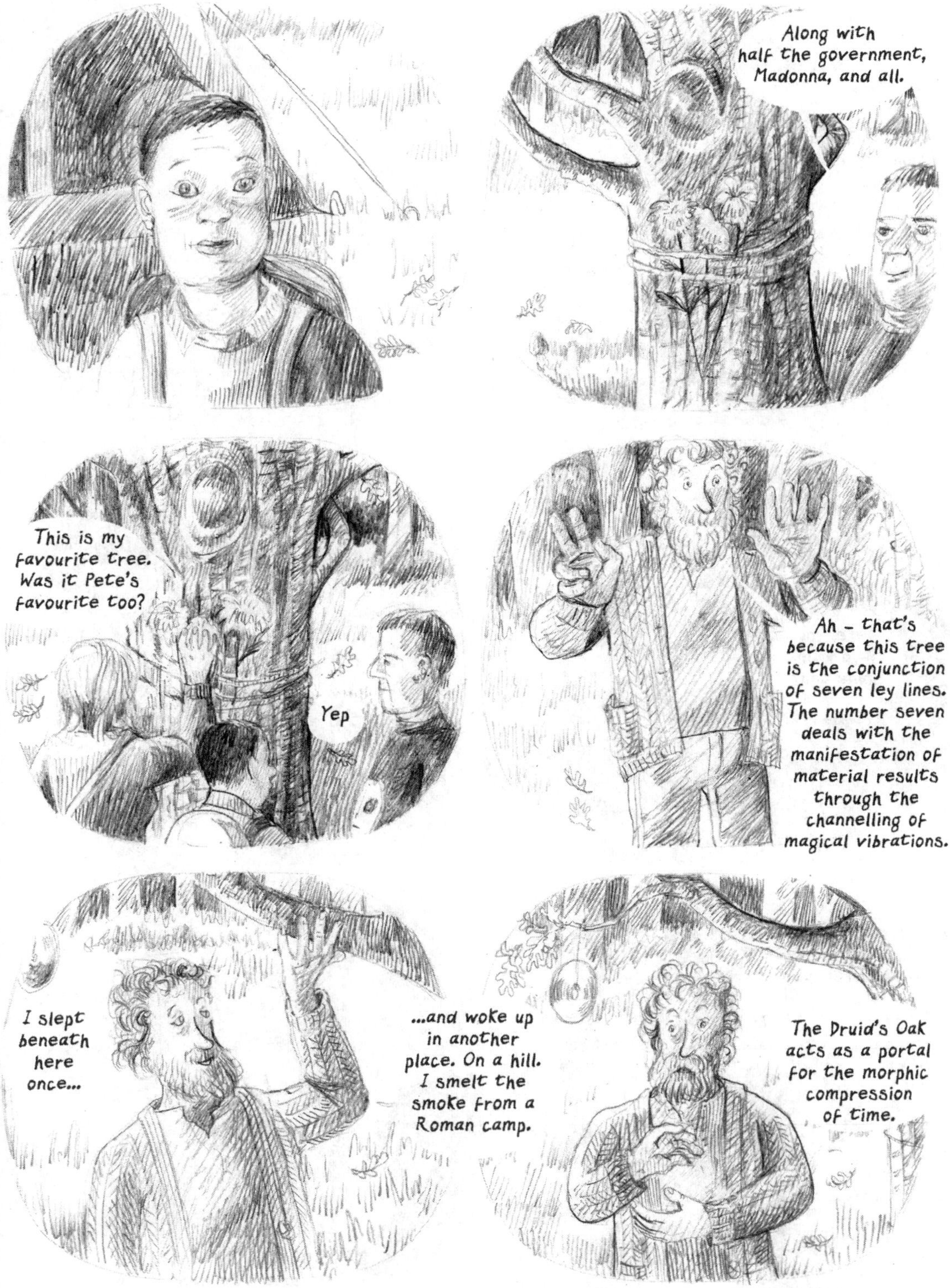
Along with half the government, Madonna, and all.
This is my favourite tree. Was it Pete's favourite too?
Yep
Ah – that's because this tree is the conjunction of seven ley lines. The number seven deals with the manifestation of material results through the channelling of magical vibrations.
I slept beneath here once...
...and woke up in another place. On a hill. I smelt the smoke from a Roman camp.
The Druid's Oak acts as a portal for the morphic compression of time.

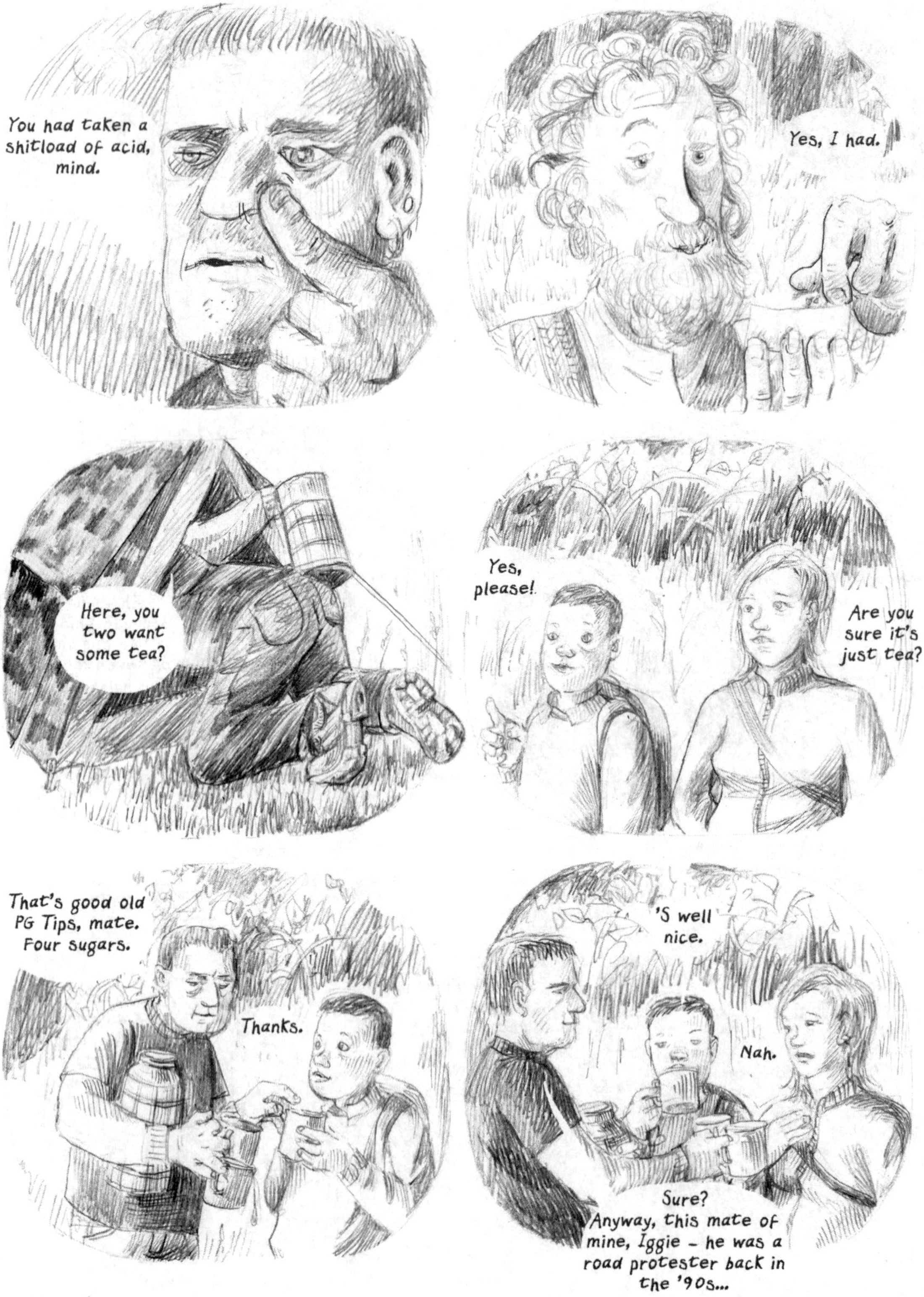
You had taken a shitload of acid, mind.
Yes, I had.
Here, you two want some tea?
Yes, please!
Are you sure it's just tea?
That's good old PG Tips, mate. Four sugars.
Thanks.
'S well nice.
Nah.
Sure?
Anyway, this mate of mine, Iggie – he was a road protester back in the '90s...

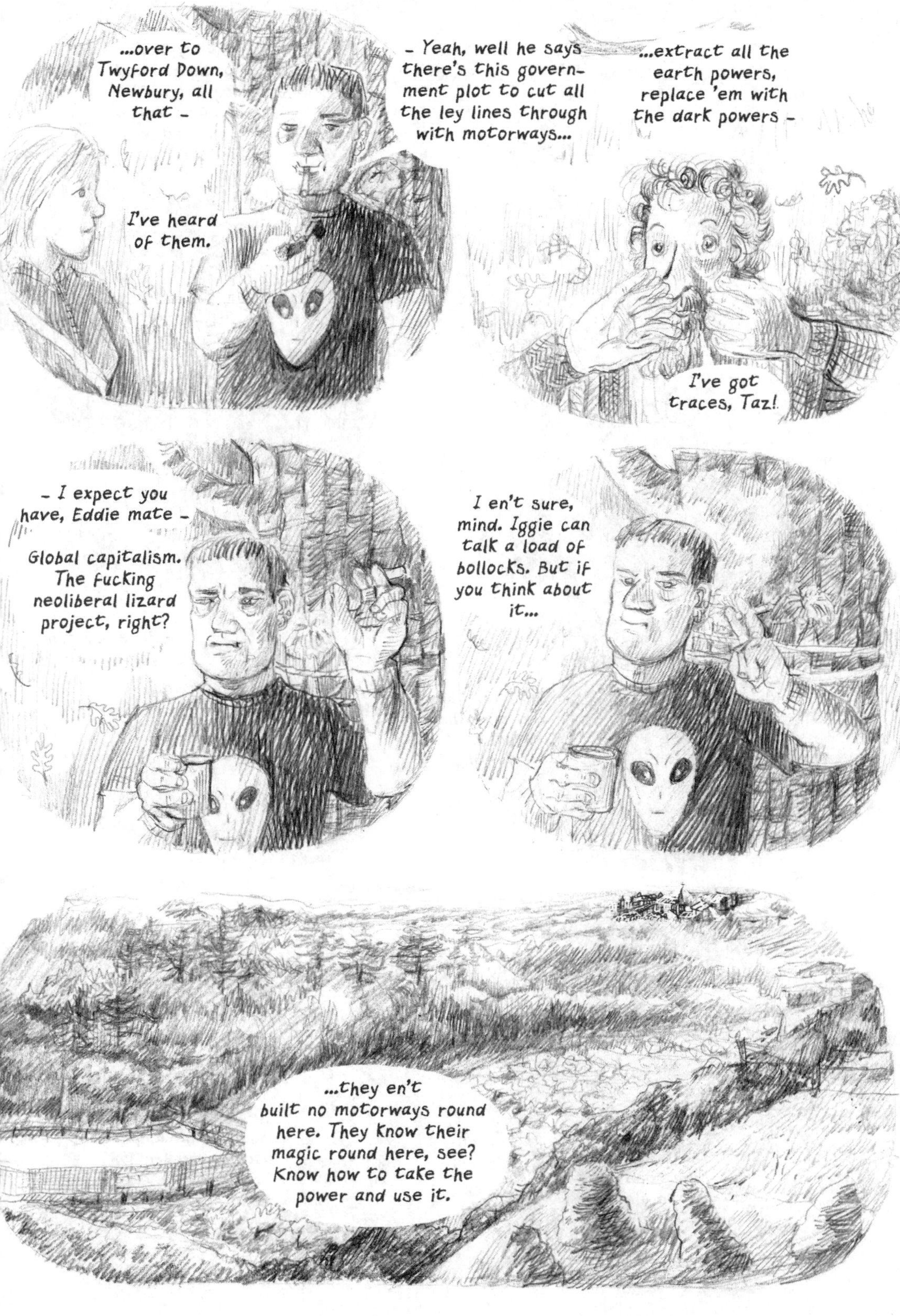

...over to Twyford Down, Newbury, all that –
I've heard of them.
– Yeah, well he says there's this govern-ment plot to cut all the ley lines through with motorways...
...extract all the earth powers, replace 'em with the dark powers –
I've got traces, Taz!
– I expect you have, Eddie mate –
Global capitalism. The fucking neoliberal lizard project, right?
I en't sure, mind. Iggie can talk a load of bollocks. But if you think about it...
...they en't built no motorways round here. They know their magic round here, see? Know how to take the power and use it.

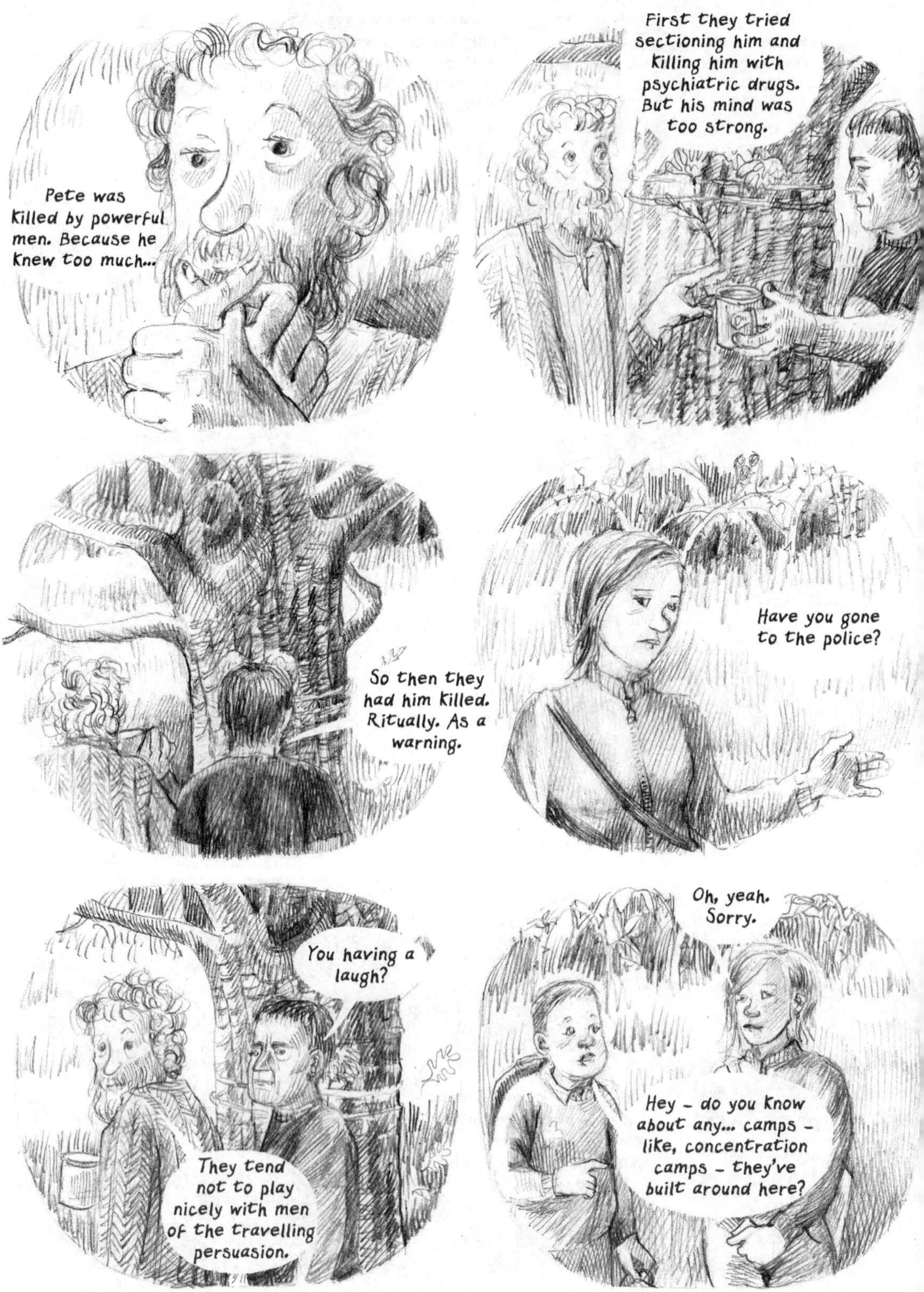
Pete was killed by powerful men. Because he knew too much...
First they tried sectioning him and killing him with psychiatric drugs. But his mind was too strong.
So then they had him killed. Ritually. As a warning.
Have you gone to the police?
You having a laugh?
They tend not to play nicely with men of the travelling persuasion.
Oh, yeah. Sorry.
Hey - do you know about any... camps - like, concentration camps - they've built around here?

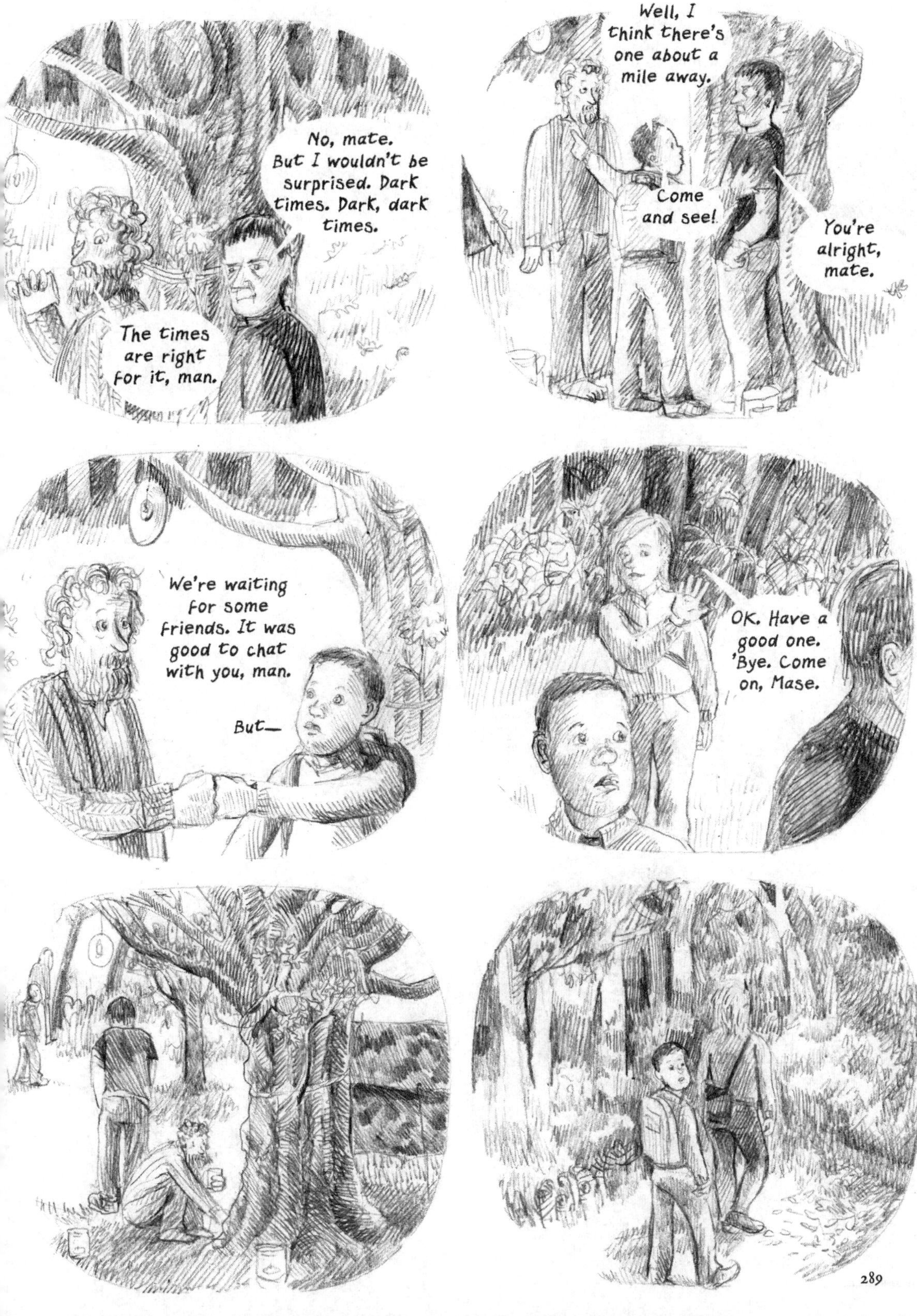

No, mate. But I wouldn't be surprised. Dark times. Dark, dark times.
The times are right for it, man.
Well, I think there's one about a mile away.
Come and see!
You're alright, mate.
We're waiting for some friends. It was good to chat with you, man.
But—
OK. Have a good one. 'Bye. Come on, Mase.

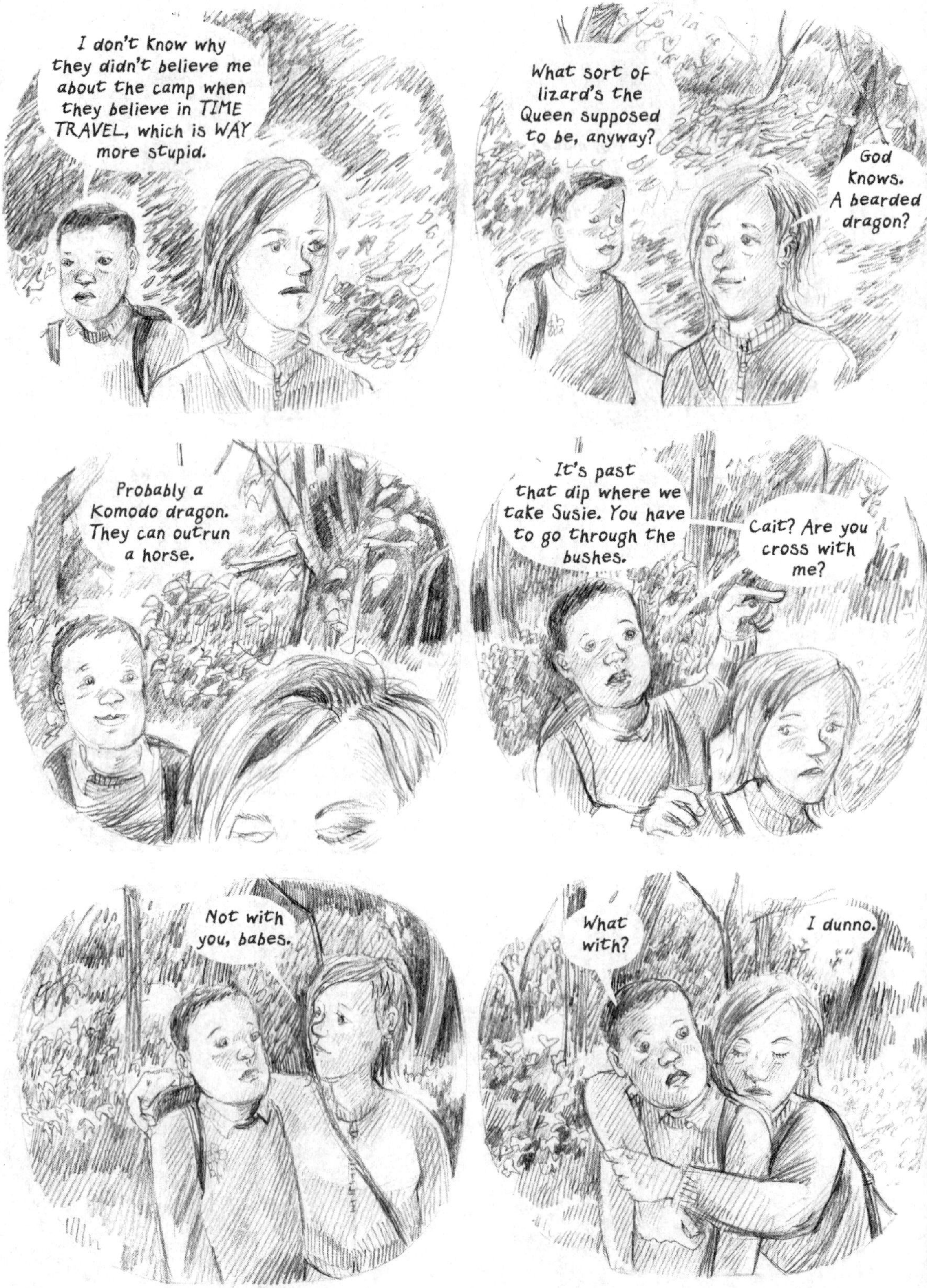
I don't know why they didn't believe me about the camp when they believe in TIME TRAVEL, which is WAY more stupid.
What sort of lizard's the Queen supposed to be, anyway?
God knows. A bearded dragon?
Probably a Komodo dragon. They can outrun a horse.
It's past that dip where we take Susie. You have to go through the bushes.
Cait? Are you cross with me?
Not with you, babes.
What with?
I dunno.

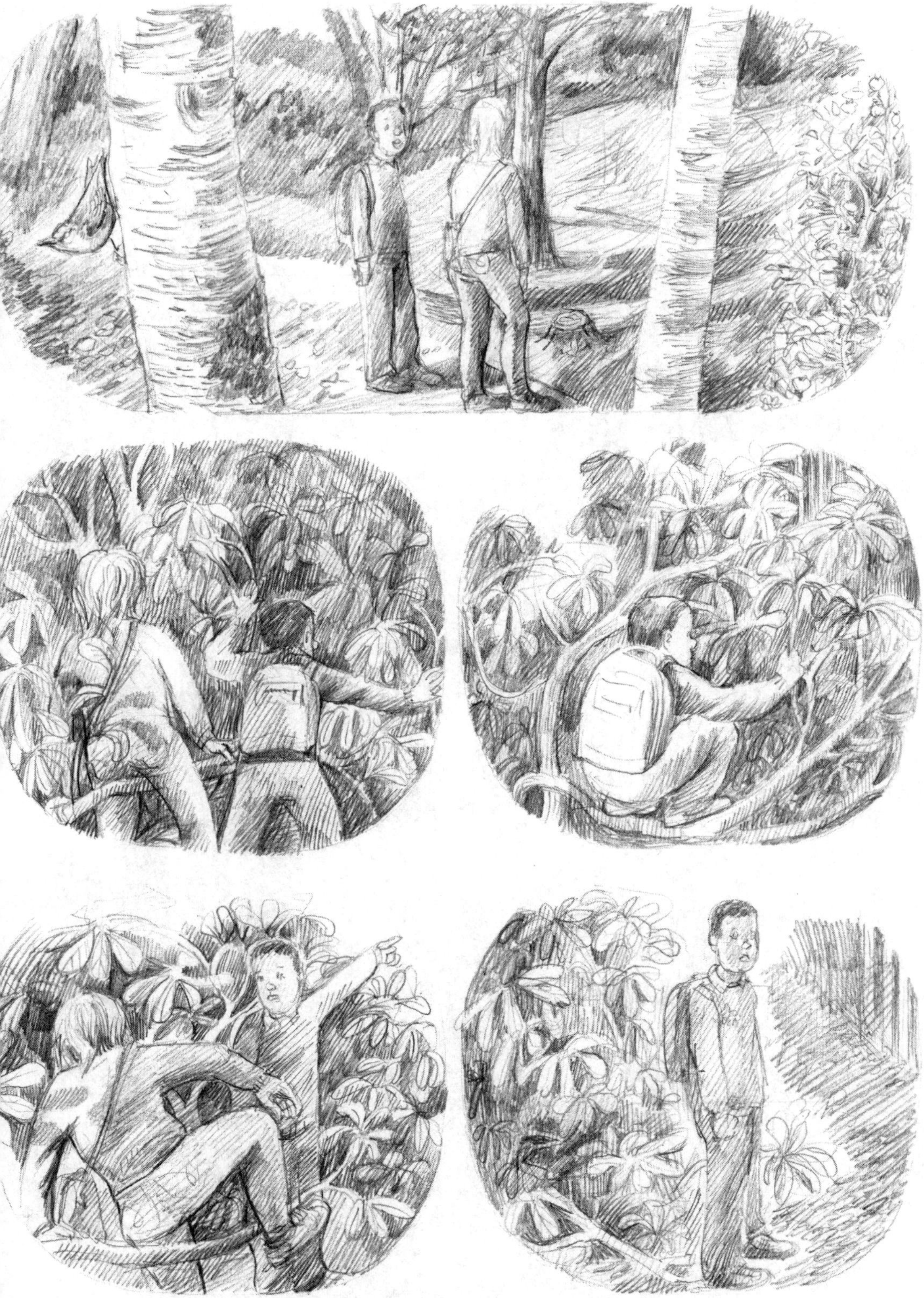

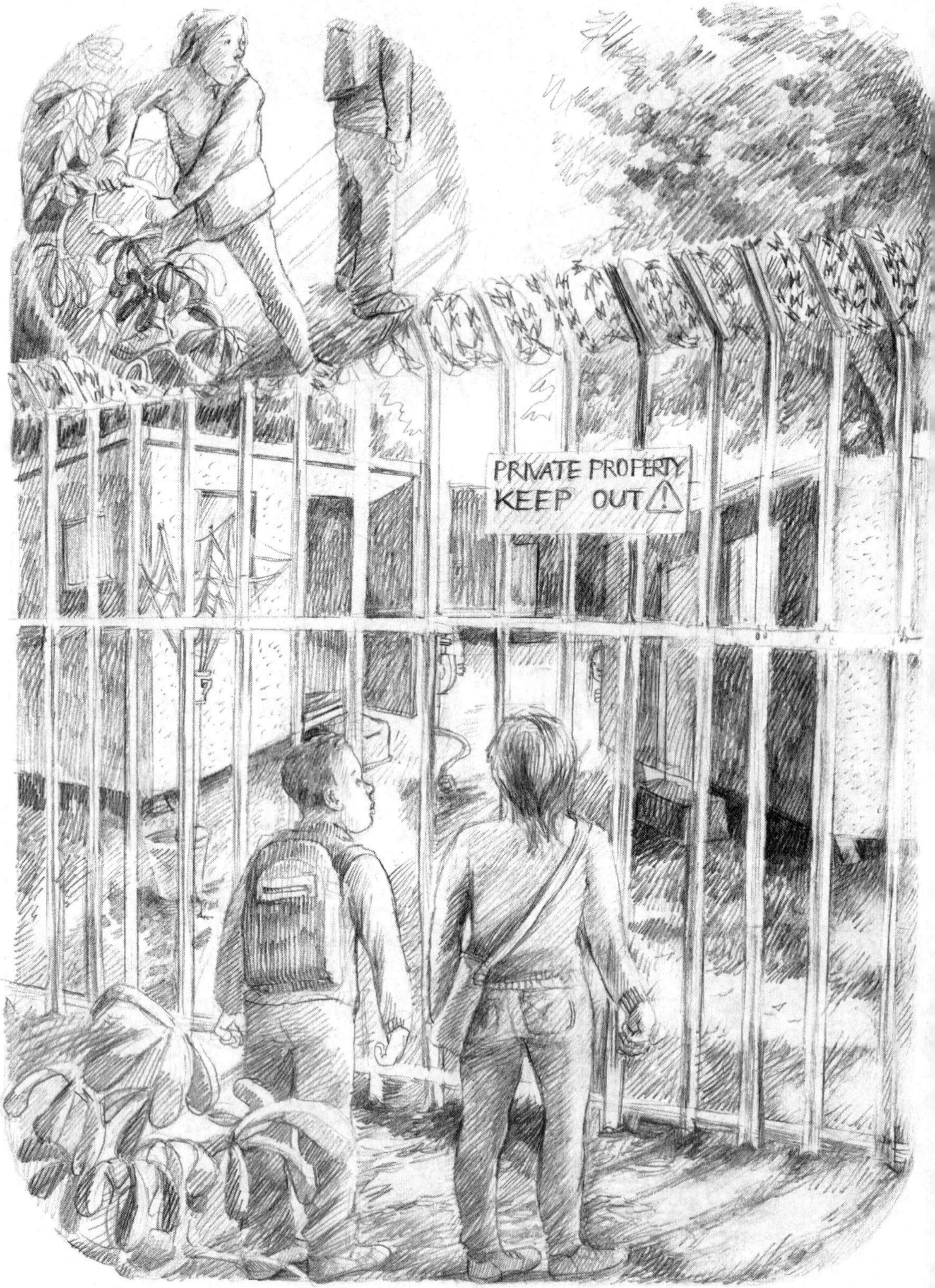
PRIVATE PROPERTY
KEEP OUT

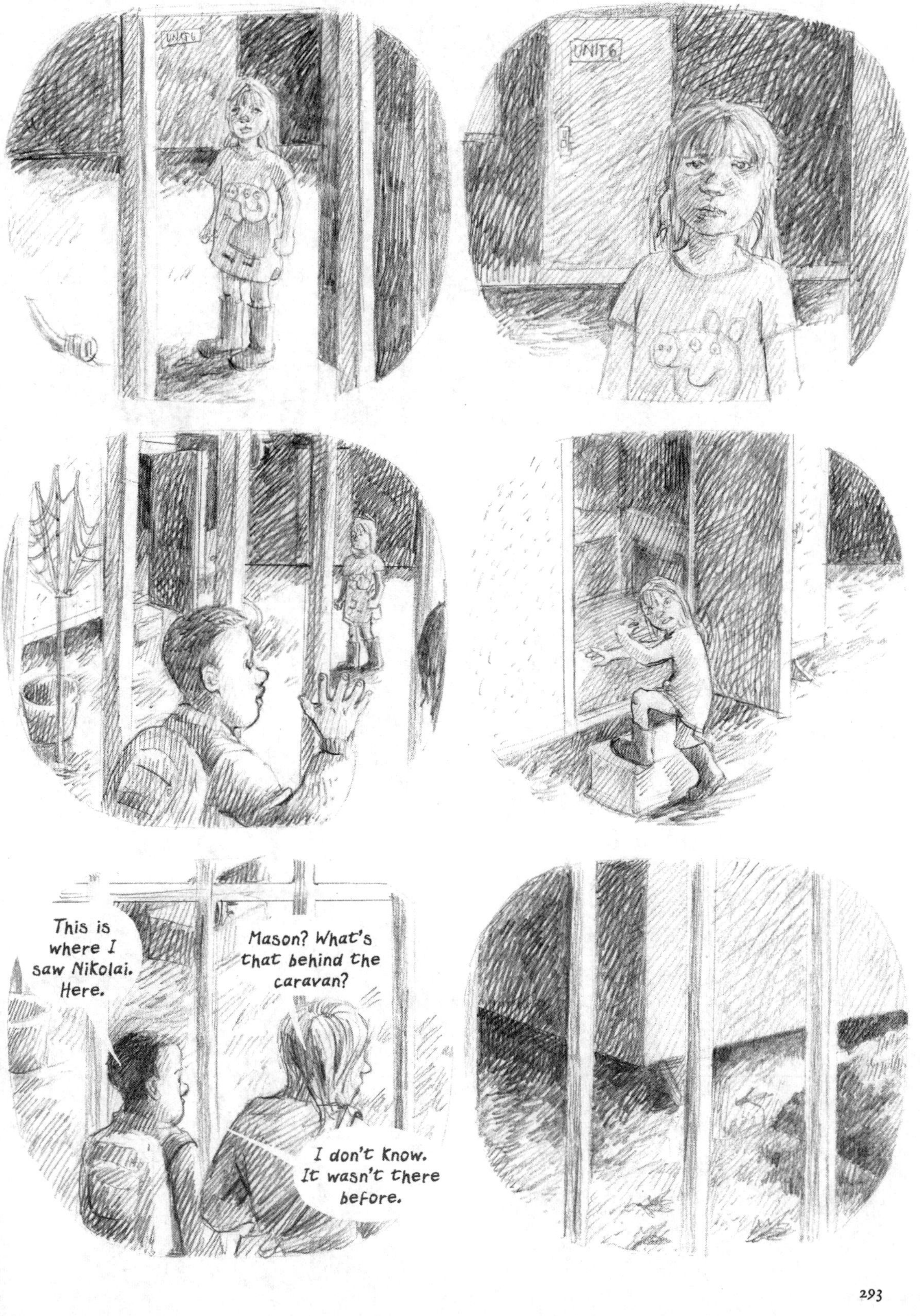
UNIT 6
UNIT 6
This is where I saw Nikolai. Here.
Mason? What's that behind the caravan?
I don't know. It wasn't there before.

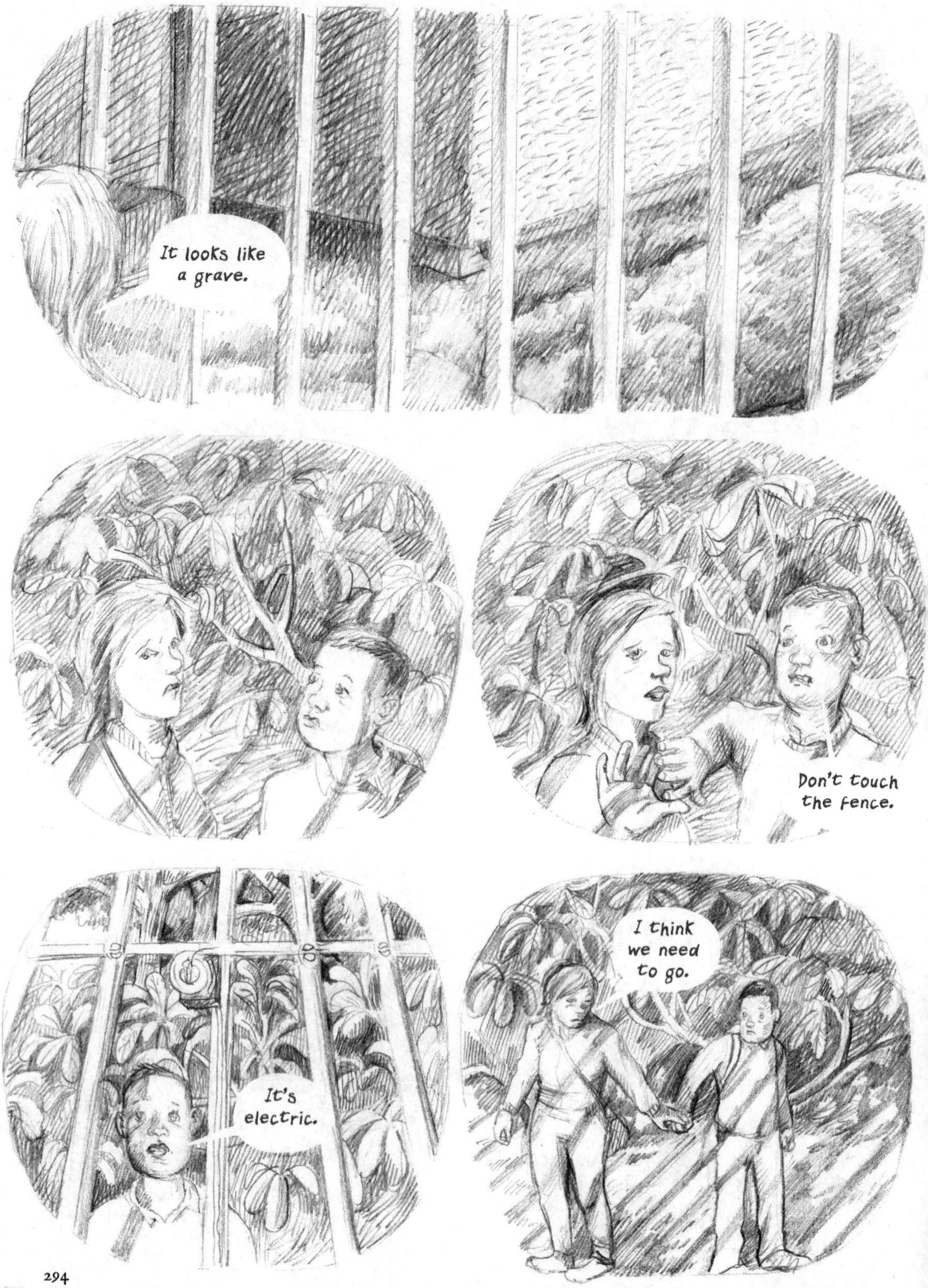
It looks like a grave.
Don't touch the fence.
It's electric.
I think we need to go.

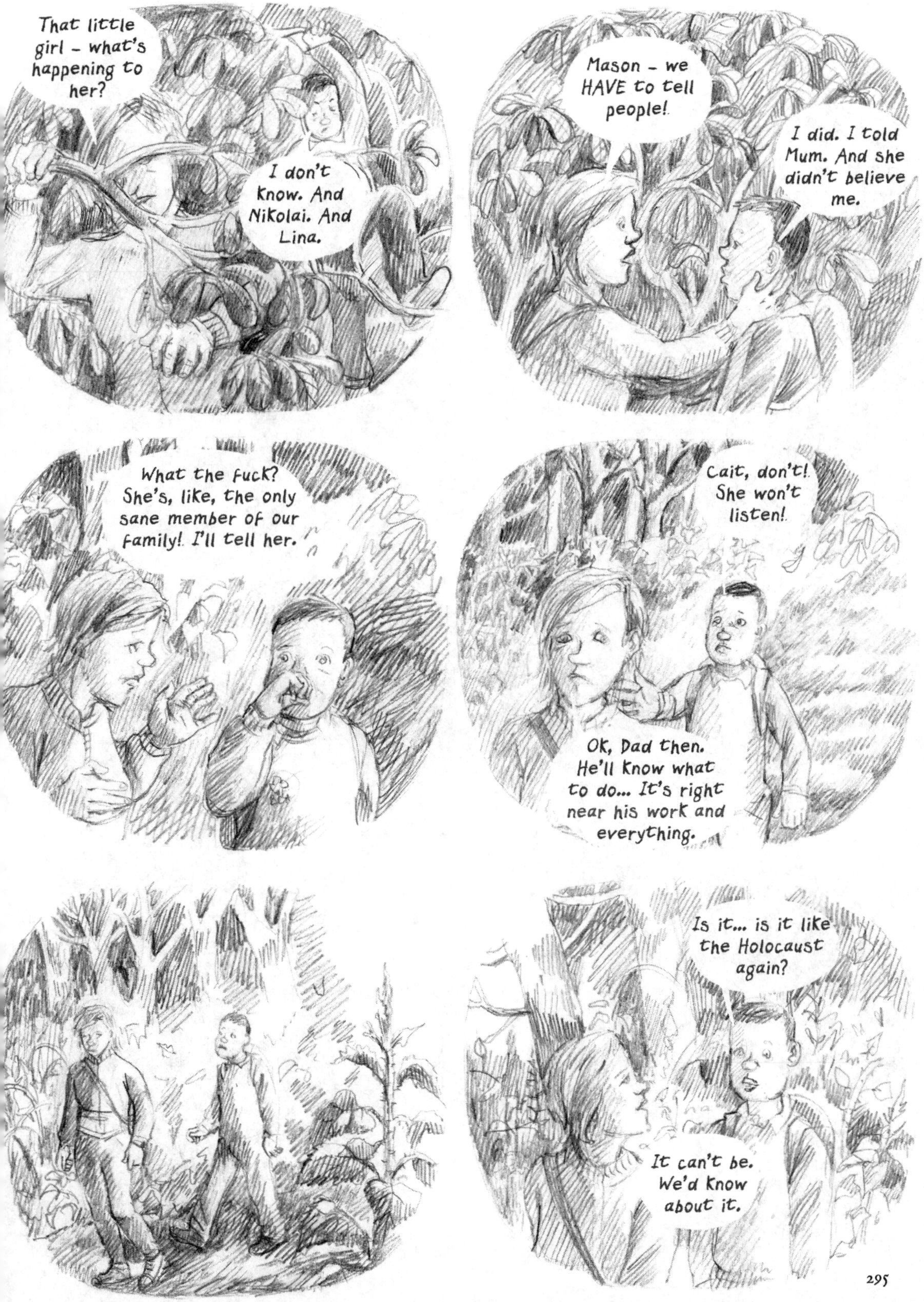
That little girl - what's happening to her?
I don't know. And Nikolai. And Lina.
Mason - we HAVE to tell people!
I did. I told Mum. And she didn't believe me.
What the fuck? She's, like, the only sane member of our family! I'll tell her.
Cait, don't! She won't listen!
Ok, Dad then. He'll know what to do... It's right near his work and everything.
Is it... is it like the Holocaust again?
It can't be. We'd know about it.

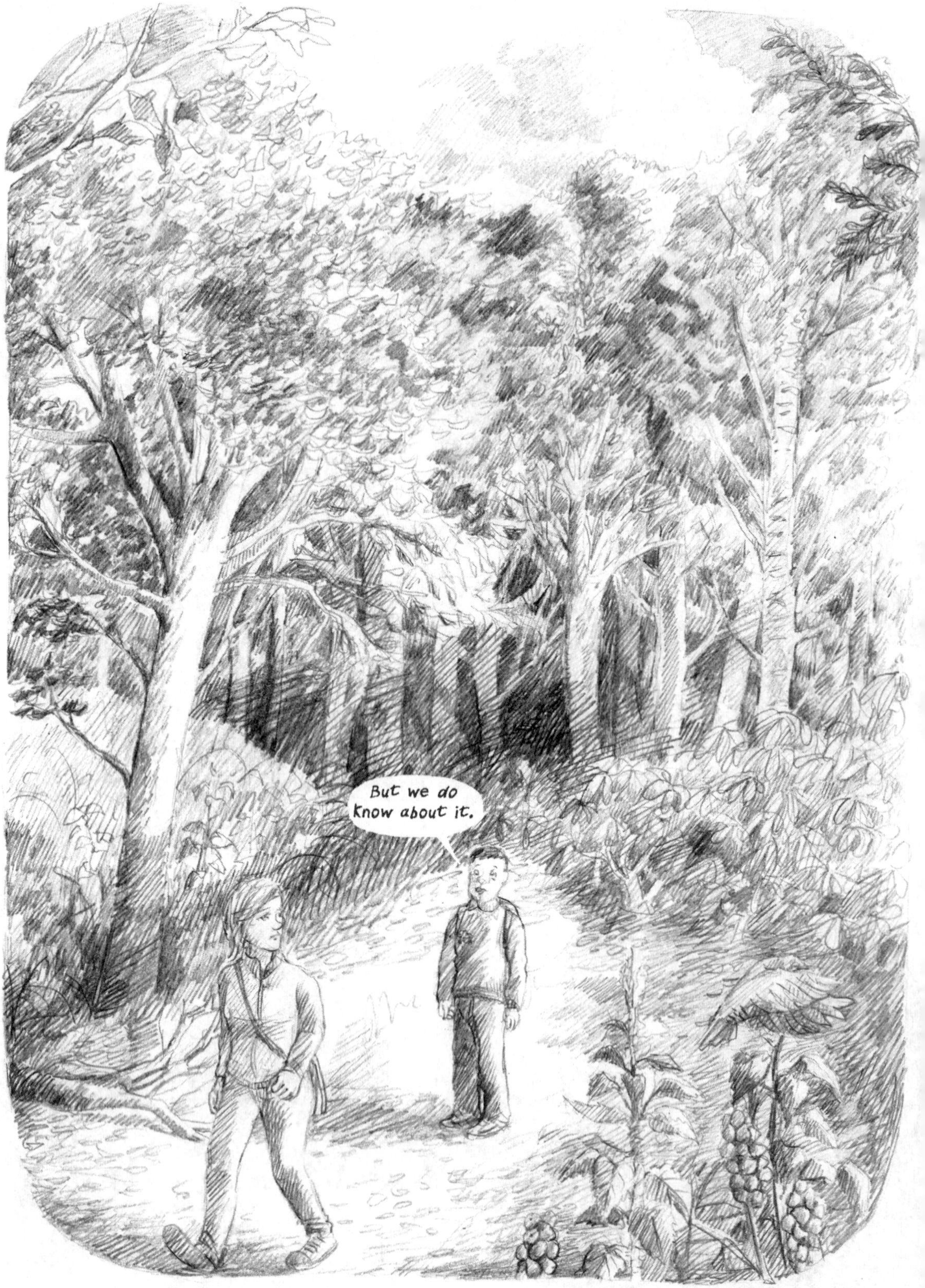
But we do
know about it.

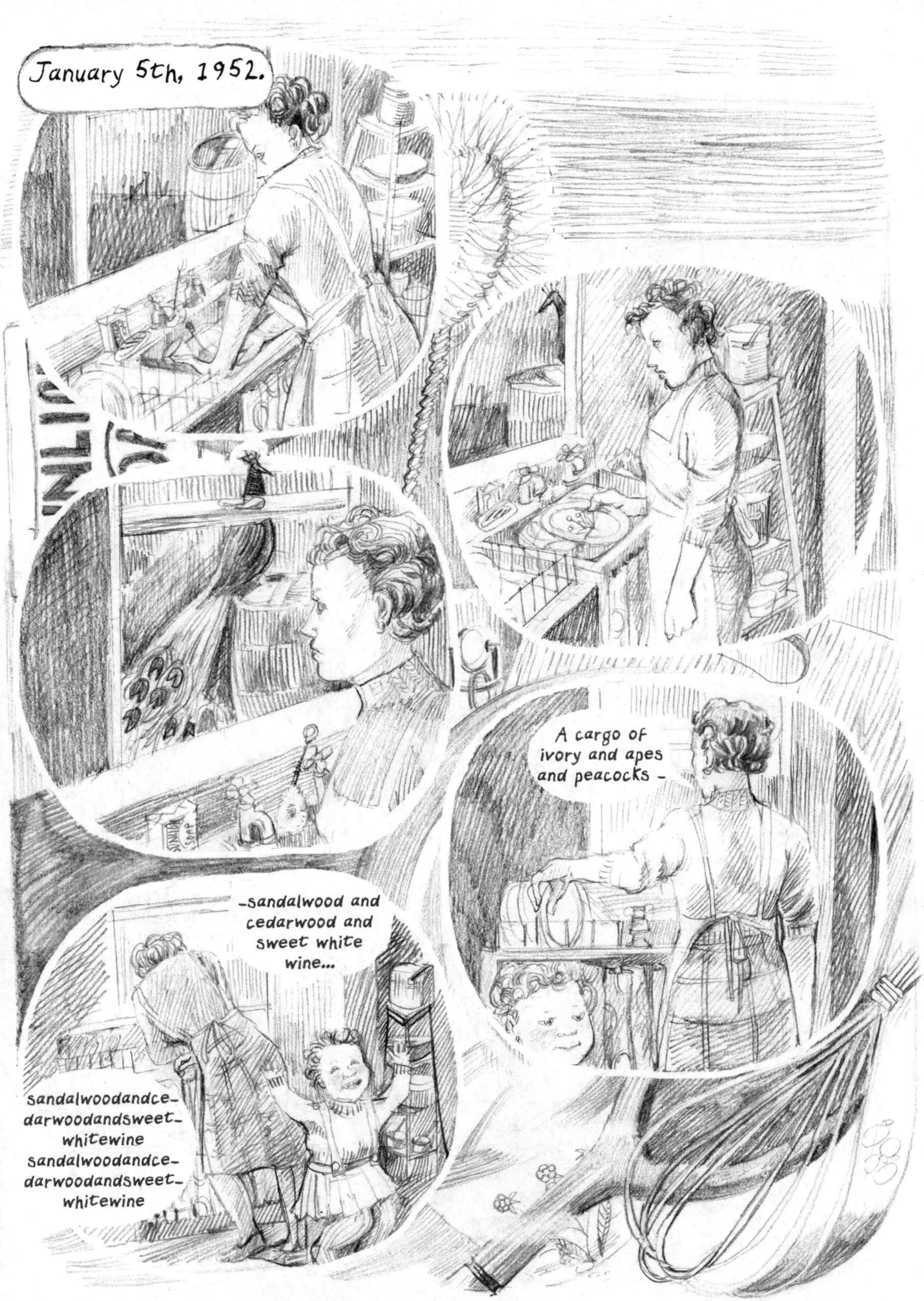
January 5th, 1952.
A cargo of ivory and apes and peacocks –
–sandalwood and cedarwood and sweet white wine...
sandalwoodandce-darwoodandsweet-whitewine sandalwoodandce-darwoodandsweet-whitewine

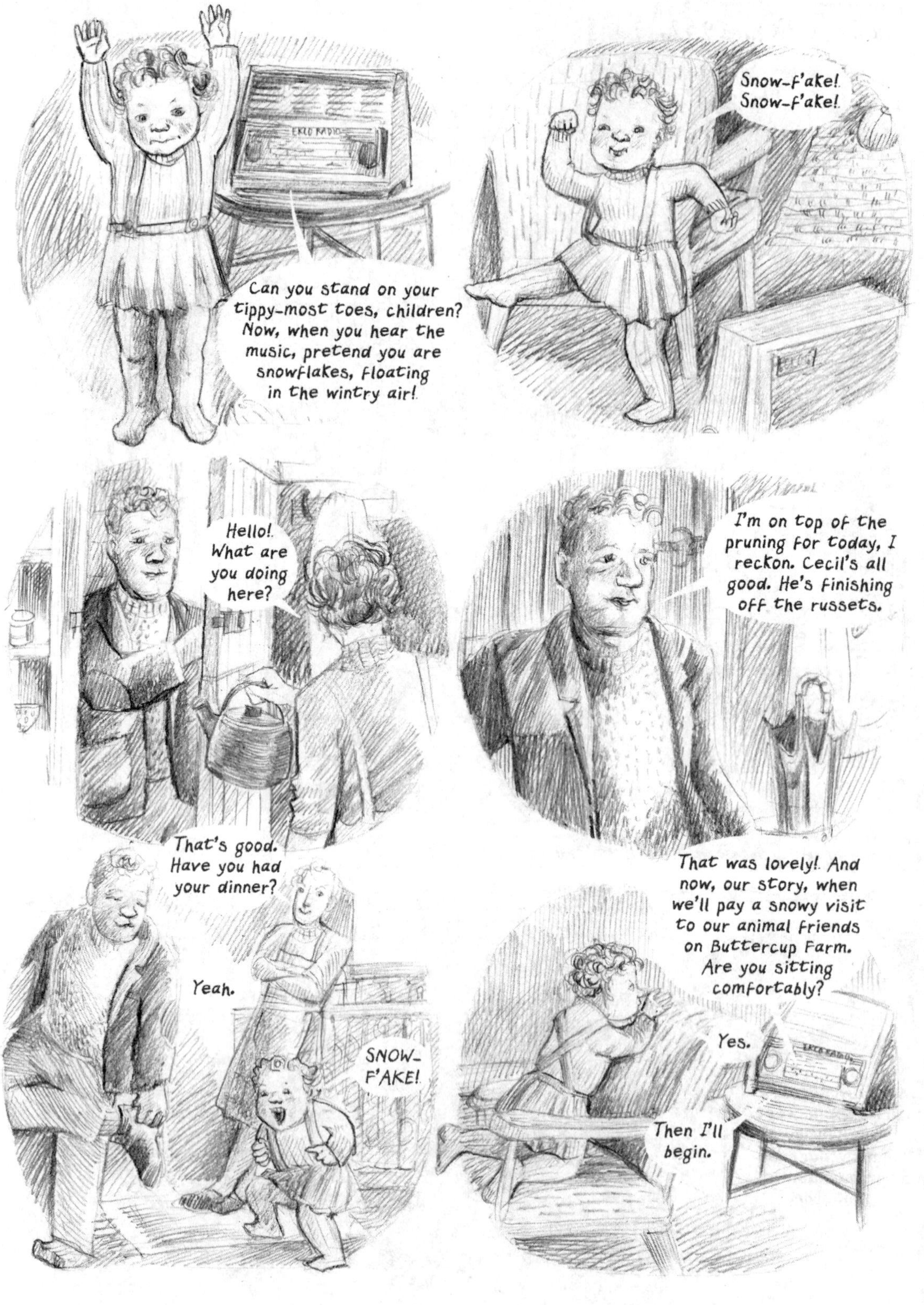
Can you stand on your tippy-most toes, children? Now, when you hear the music, pretend you are snowflakes, floating in the wintry air!
Snow-f'ake! Snow-f'ake!
Hello! What are you doing here?
I'm on top of the pruning for today, I reckon. Cecil's all good. He's finishing off the russets.
That's good. Have you had your dinner?
Yeah.
SNOW-F'AKE!
That was lovely! And now, our story, when we'll pay a snowy visit to our animal friends on Buttercup Farm. Are you sitting comfortably?
Yes.
Then I'll begin.

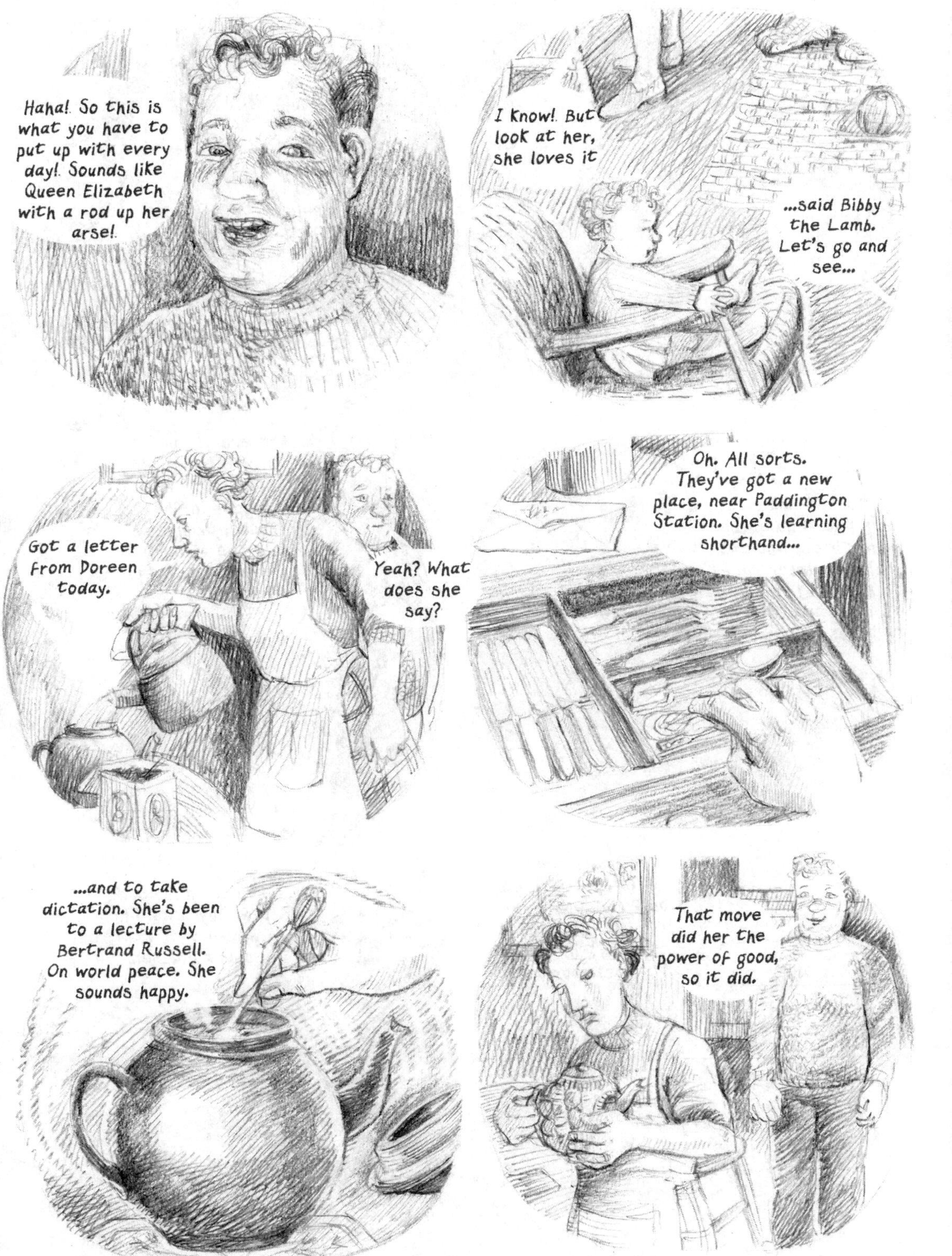
Haha!. So this is what you have to put up with every day!. Sounds like Queen Elizabeth with a rod up her arse!.
I know!. But look at her, she loves it
...said Bibby the Lamb. Let's go and see...
Got a letter from Doreen today.
Yeah? What does she say?
Oh. All sorts. They've got a new place, near Paddington Station. She's learning shorthand...
...and to take dictation. She's been to a lecture by Bertrand Russell. On world peace. She sounds happy.
That move did her the power of good, so it did.

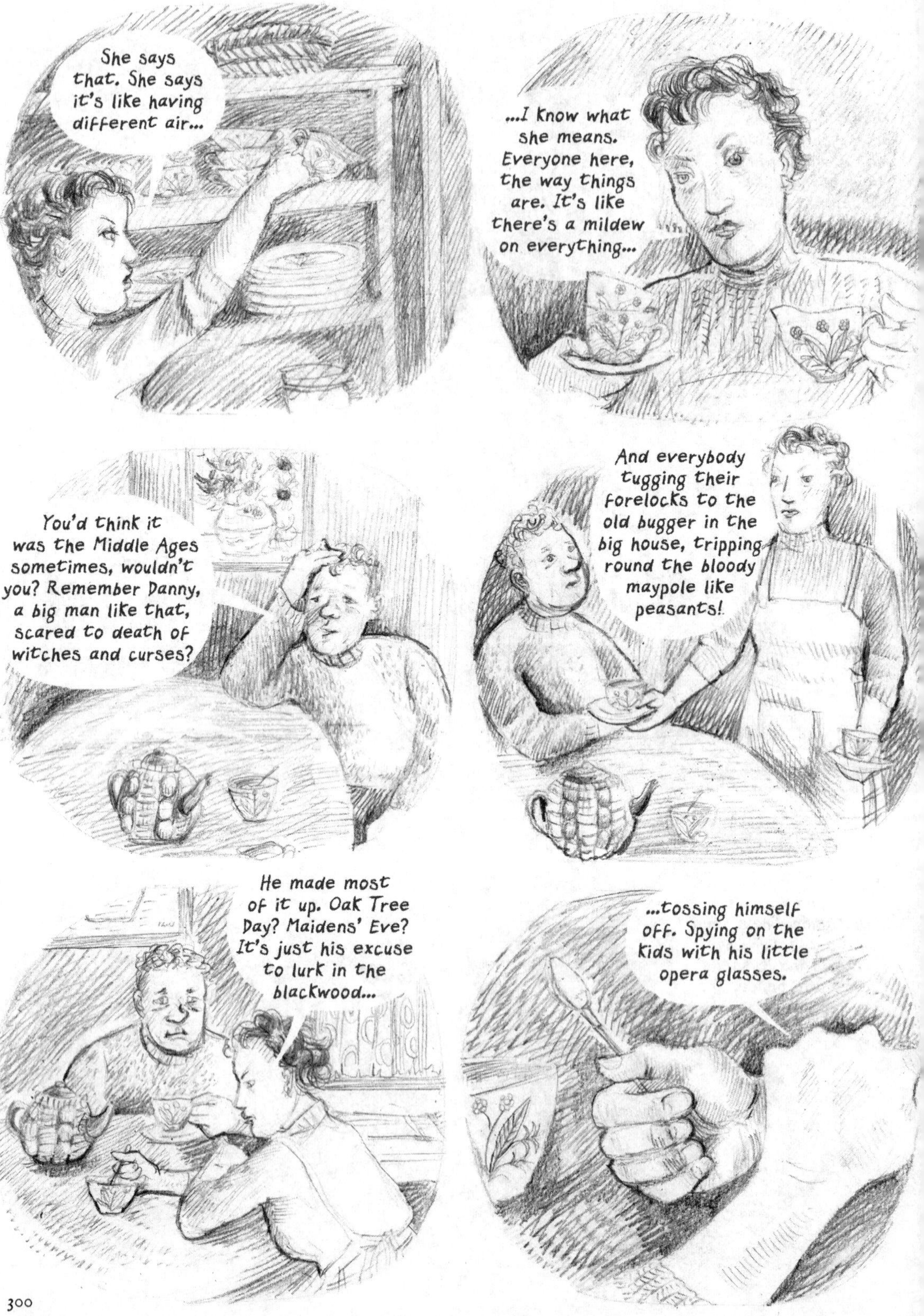
She says that. She says it's like having different air...
...I know what she means. Everyone here, the way things are. It's like there's a mildew on everything...
You'd think it was the Middle Ages sometimes, wouldn't you? Remember Danny, a big man like that, scared to death of witches and curses?
And everybody tugging their forelocks to the old bugger in the big house, tripping round the bloody maypole like peasants!
He made most of it up. Oak Tree Day? Maidens' Eve? It's just his excuse to lurk in the blackwood...
...tossing himself off. Spying on the kids with his little opera glasses.

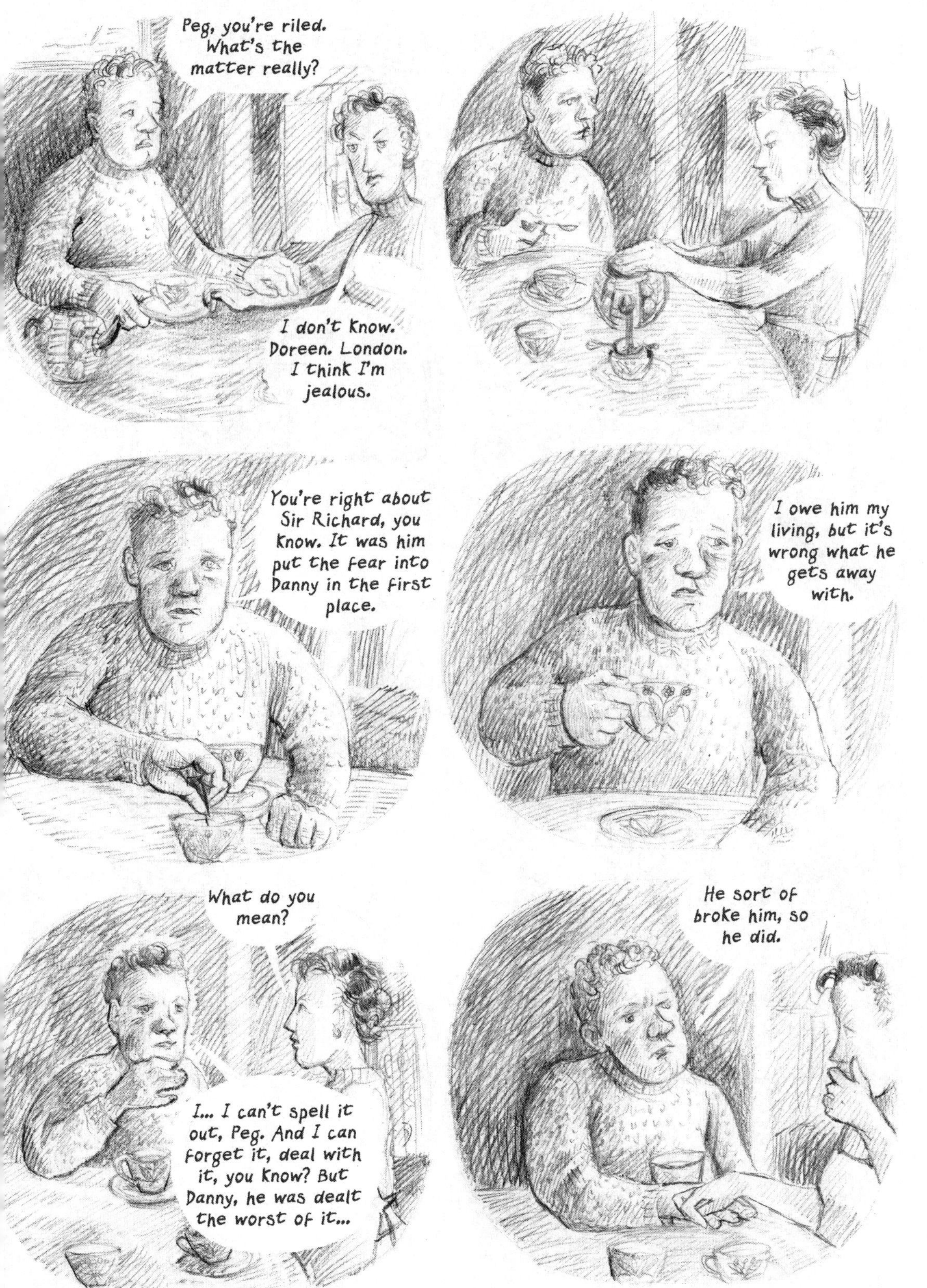
Peg, you're riled. What's the matter really?
I don't know. Doreen. London. I think I'm jealous.
You're right about Sir Richard, you know. It was him put the fear into Danny in the first place.
I owe him my living, but it's wrong what he gets away with.
What do you mean?
I... I can't spell it out, Peg. And I can forget it, deal with it, you know? But Danny, he was dealt the worst of it...
He sort of broke him, so he did.

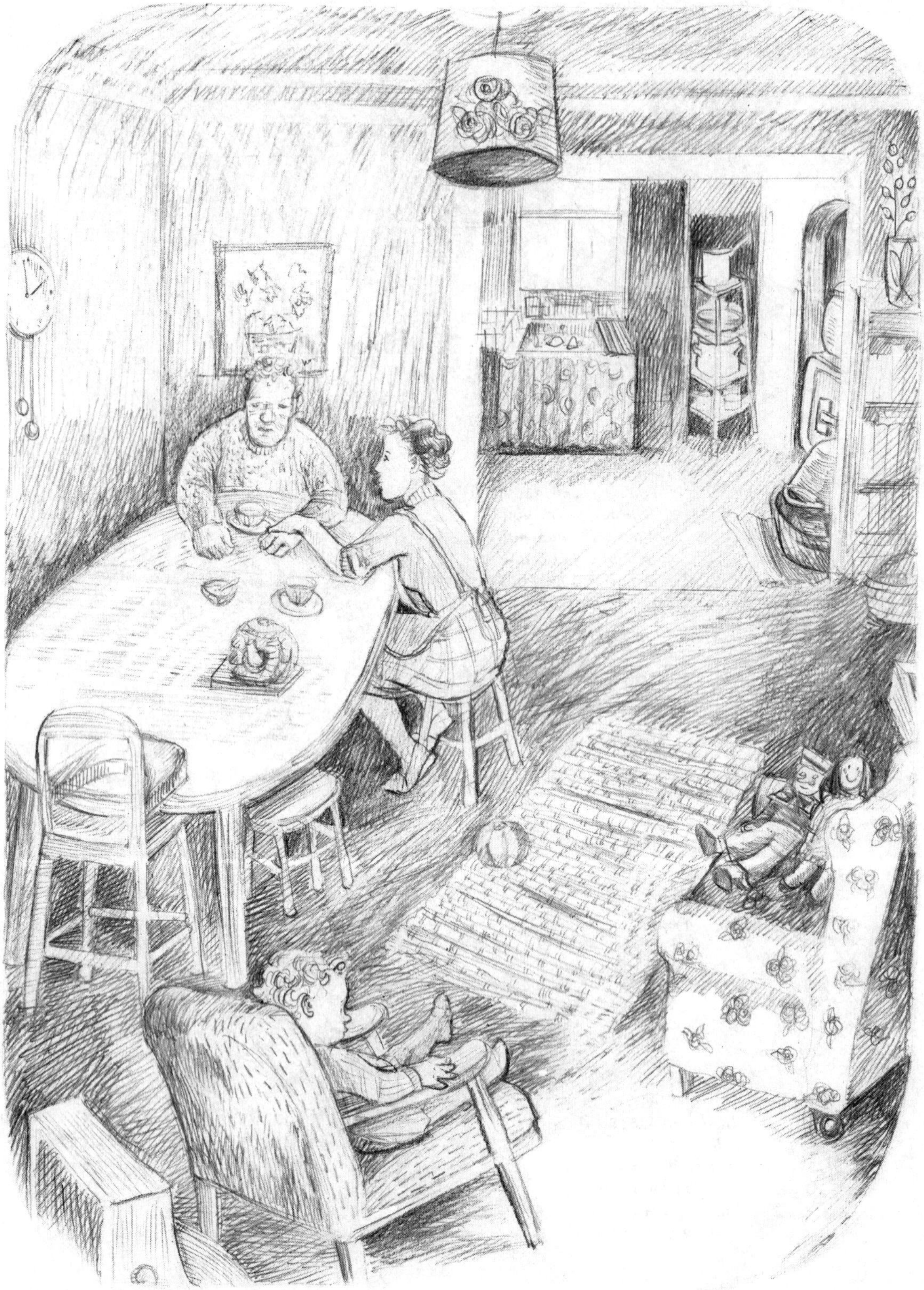

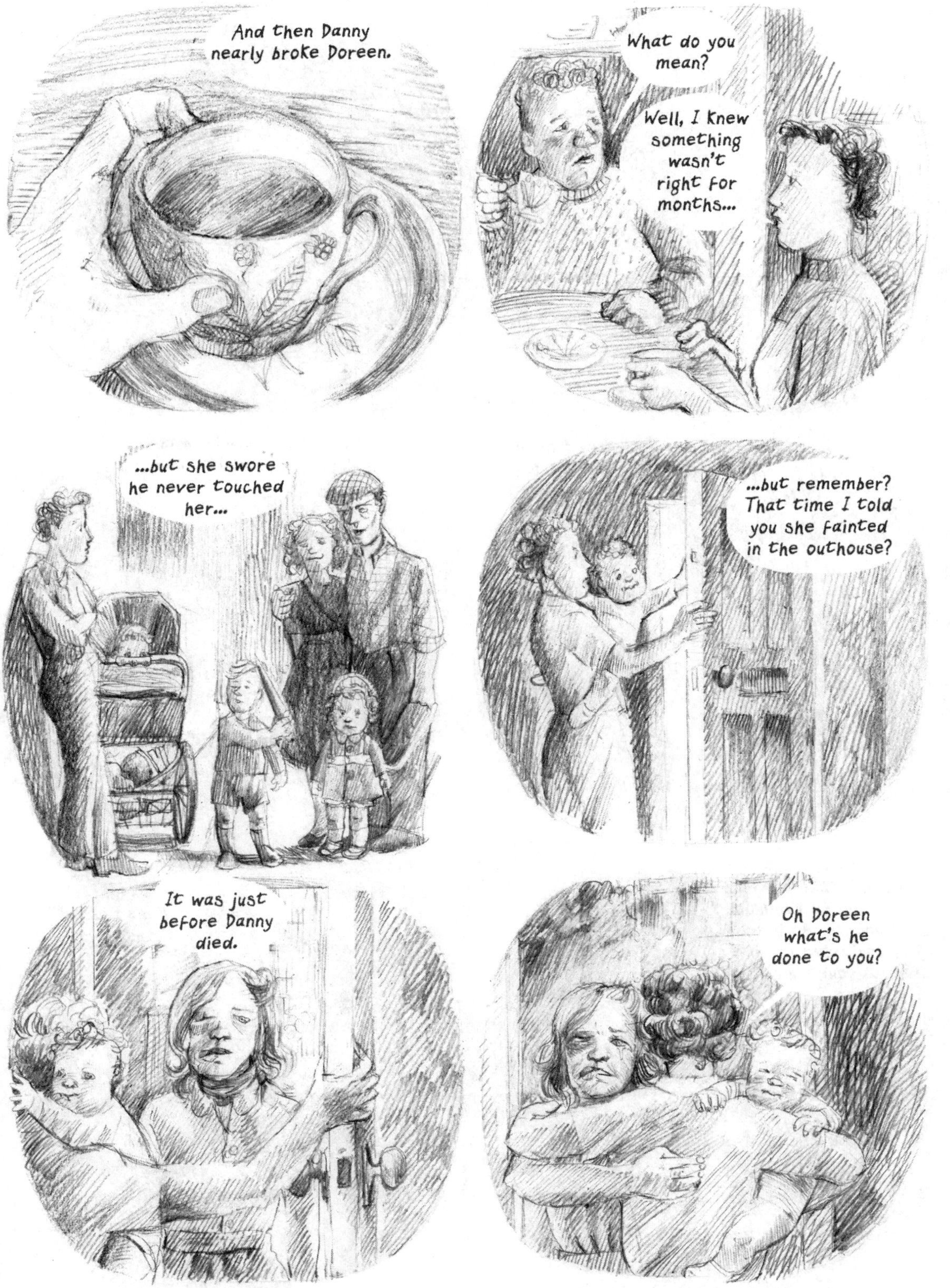
And then Danny nearly broke Doreen.
What do you mean?
Well, I knew something wasn't right for months...
...but she swore he never touched her...
...but remember? That time I told you she fainted in the outhouse?
It was just before Danny died.
Oh Doreen what's he done to you?

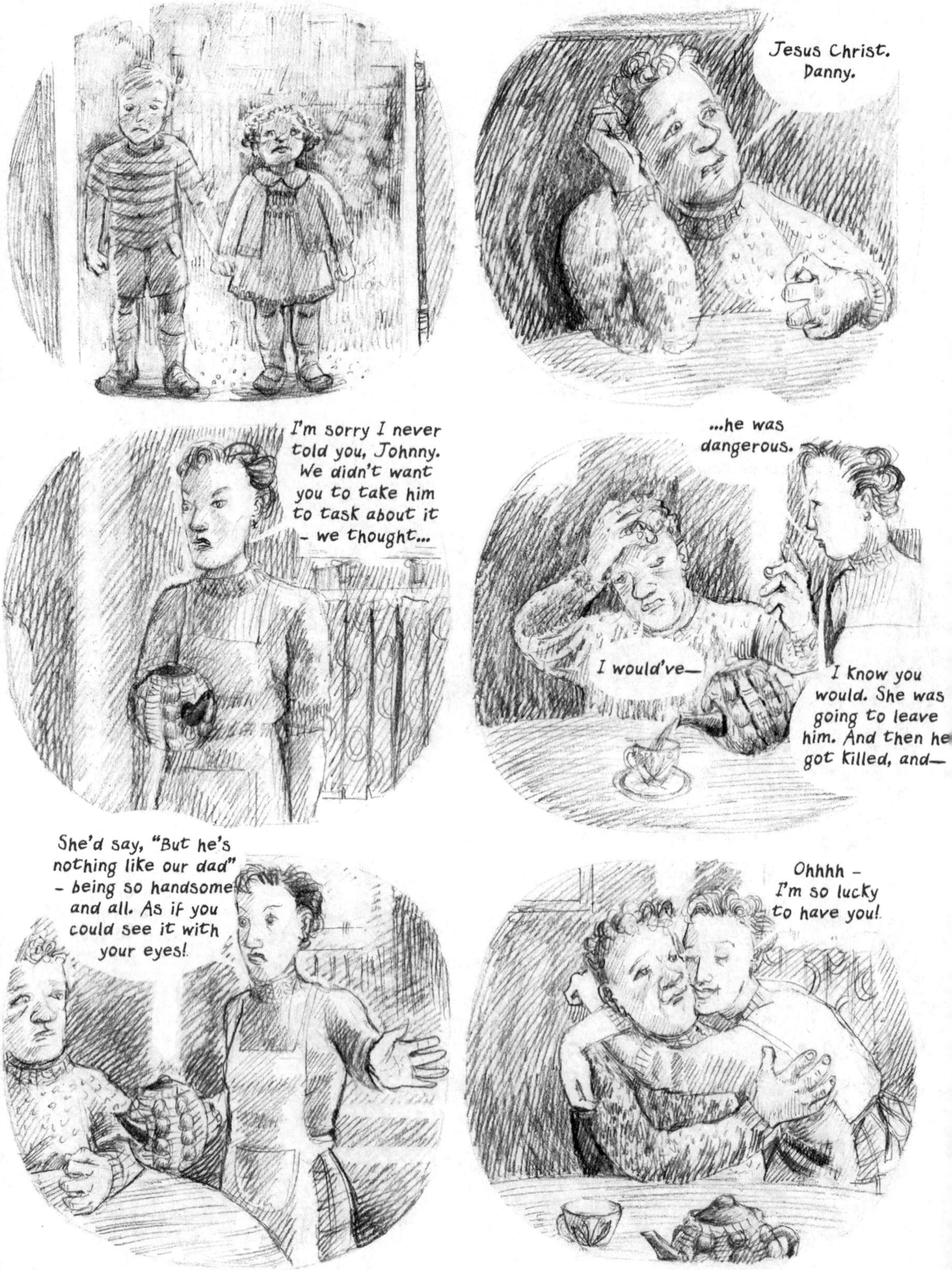

Jesus Christ. Danny.
I'm sorry I never told you, Johnny. We didn't want you to take him to task about it - we thought...
...he was dangerous.
I would've—
I know you would. She was going to leave him. And then he got killed, and—
She'd say, "But he's nothing like our dad" - being so handsome and all. As if you could see it with your eyes!
Ohhhh - I'm so lucky to have you!

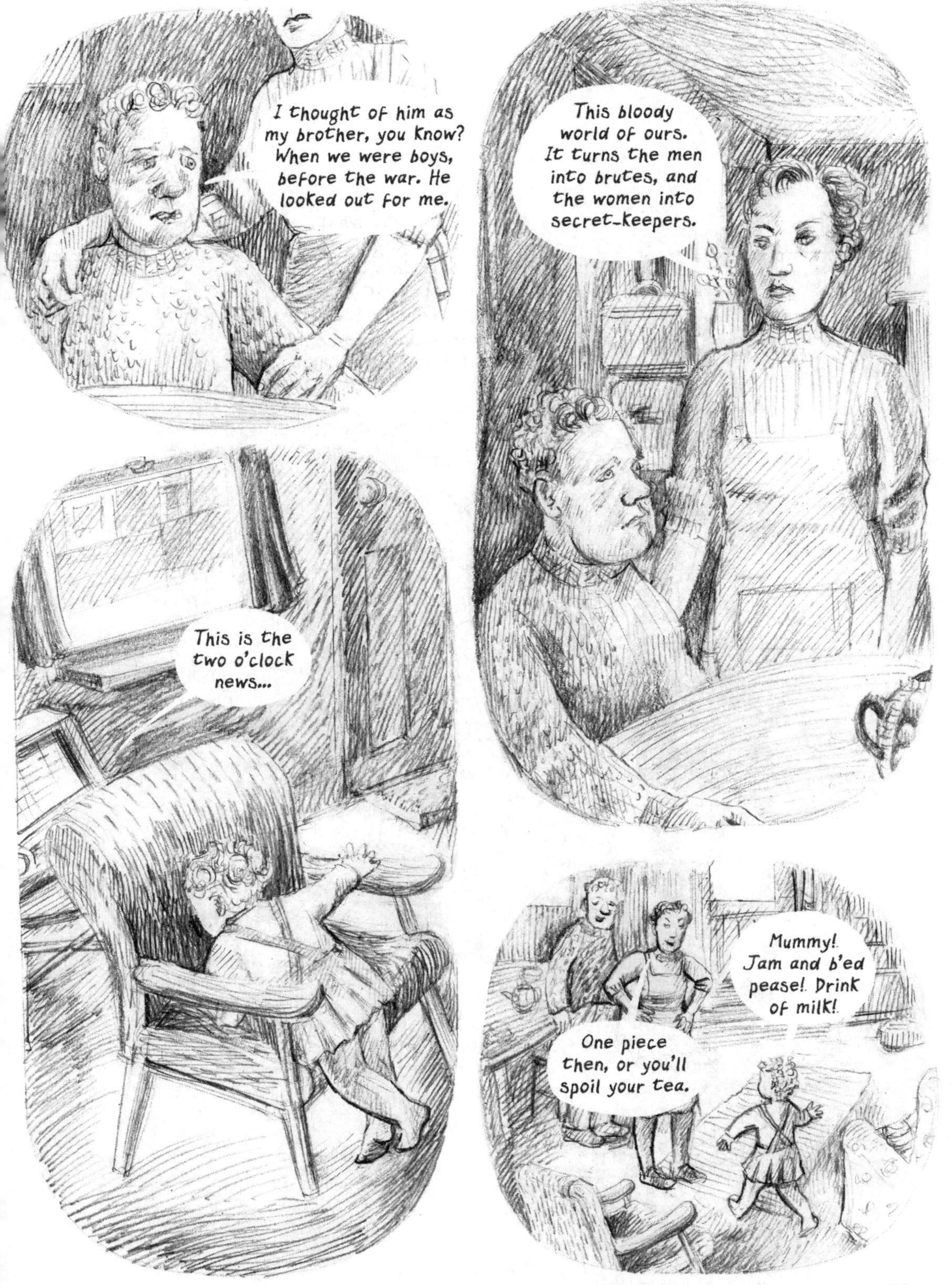
I thought of him as my brother, you know? When we were boys, before the war. He looked out for me.
This bloody world of ours. It turns the men into brutes, and the women into secret-keepers.
This is the two o'clock news...
Mummy!. Jam and b'ed pease!. Drink of milk!.
One piece then, or you'll spoil your tea.

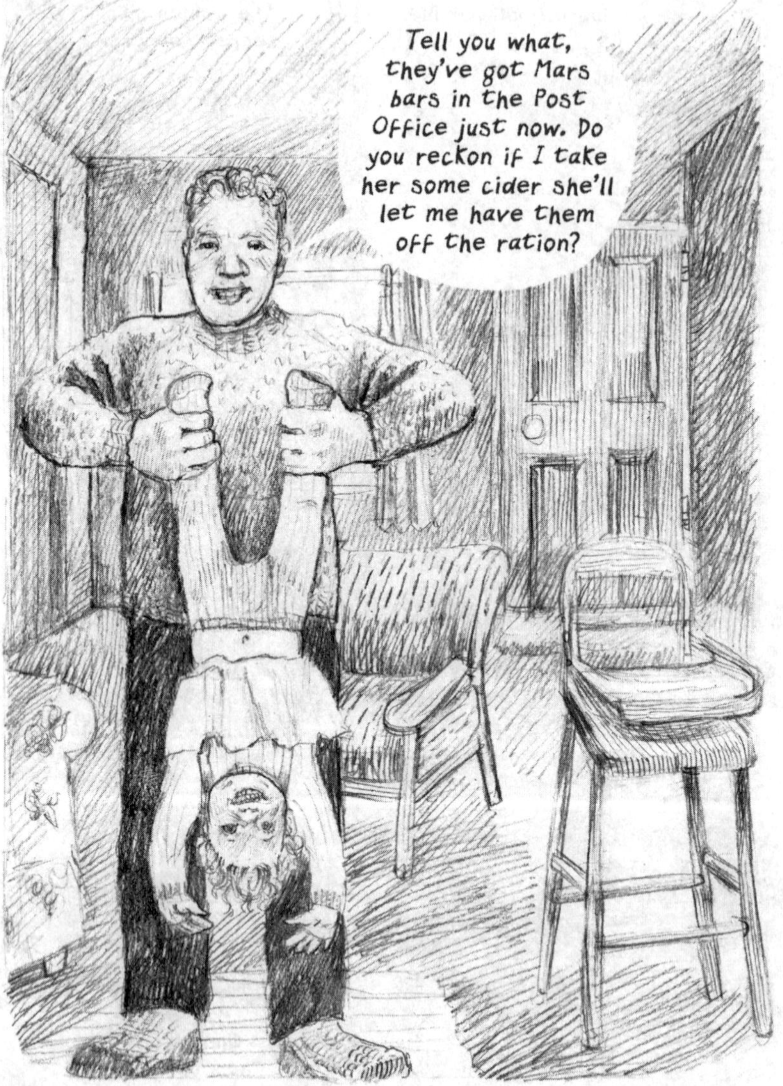
Tell you what, they've got Mars bars in the Post Office just now. Do you reckon if I take her some cider she'll let me have them off the ration?

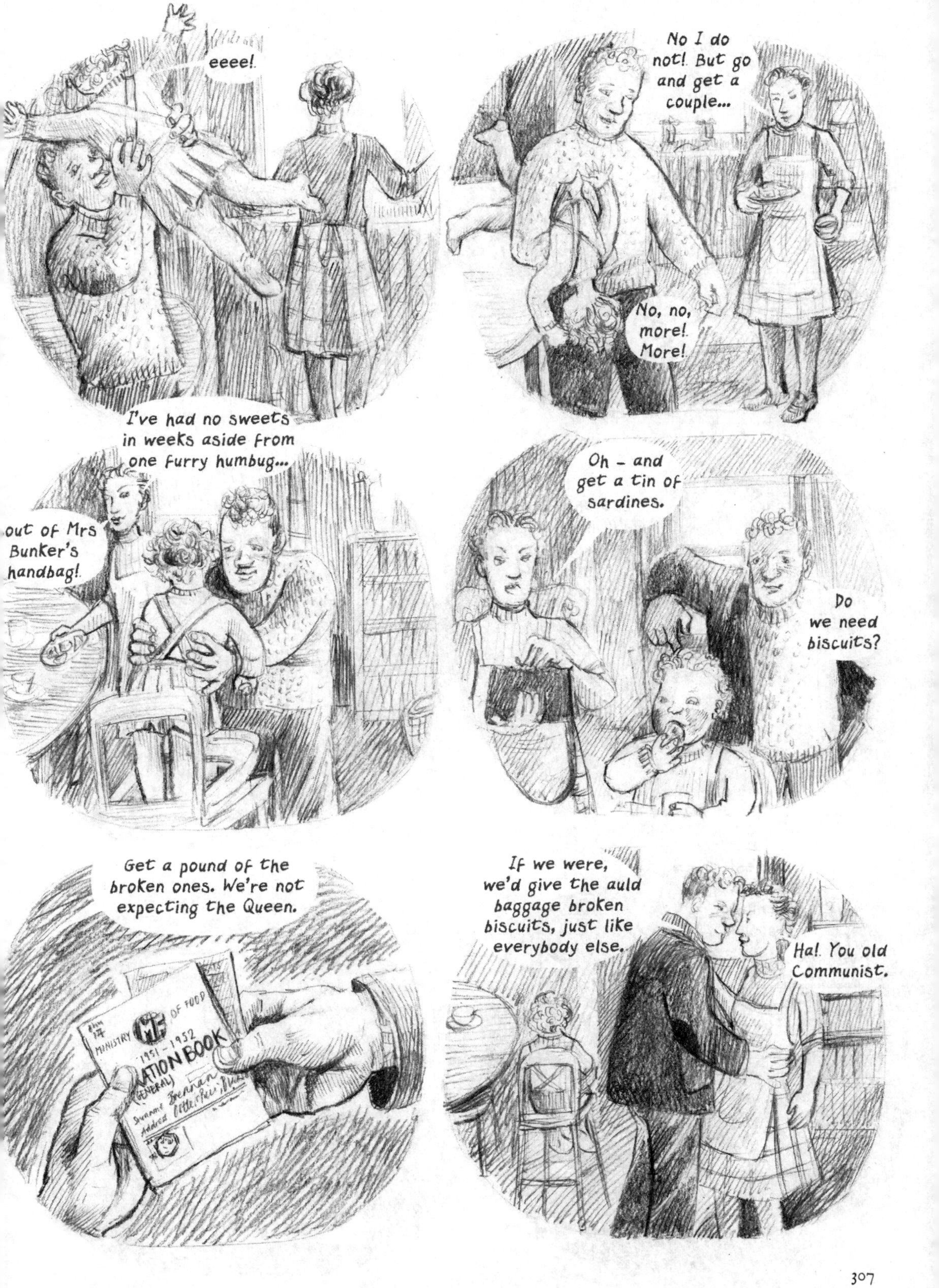
eeee!.
No I do not!. But go and get a couple...
No, no, more!. More!
I've had no sweets in weeks aside from one furry humbug...
out of Mrs Bunker's handbag!.
Oh - and get a tin of sardines.
Do we need biscuits?
Get a pound of the broken ones. We're not expecting the Queen.
MINISTRY OF FOOD
1951 - 1952
RATION BOOK
(GENERAL)
Surname Brennan
Address
If we were, we'd give the auld baggage broken biscuits, just like everybody else.
Ha!. You old Communist.

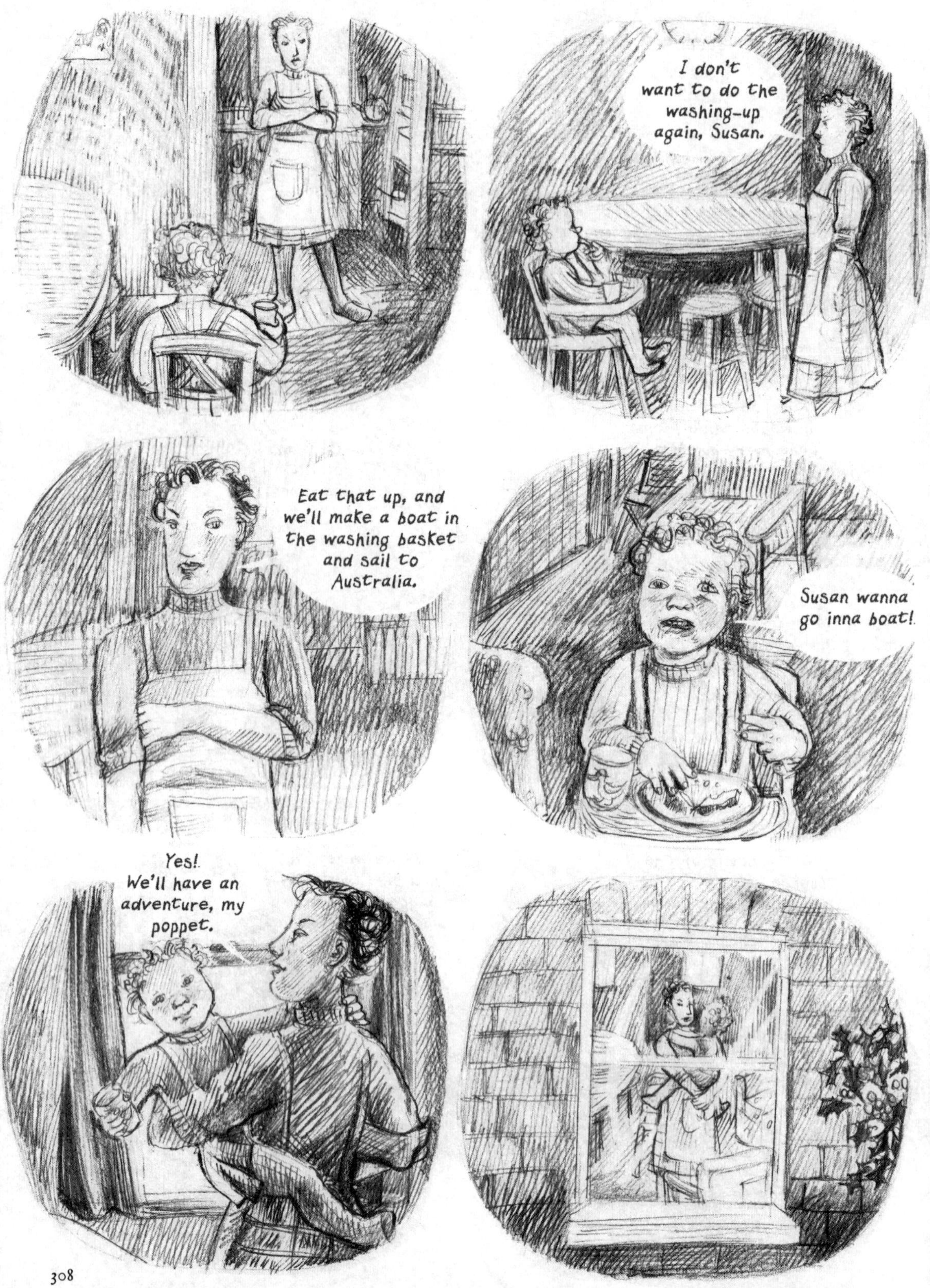
I don't want to do the washing-up again, Susan.
Eat that up, and we'll make a boat in the washing basket and sail to Australia.
Susan wanna go inna boat!
Yes! We'll have an adventure, my poppet.

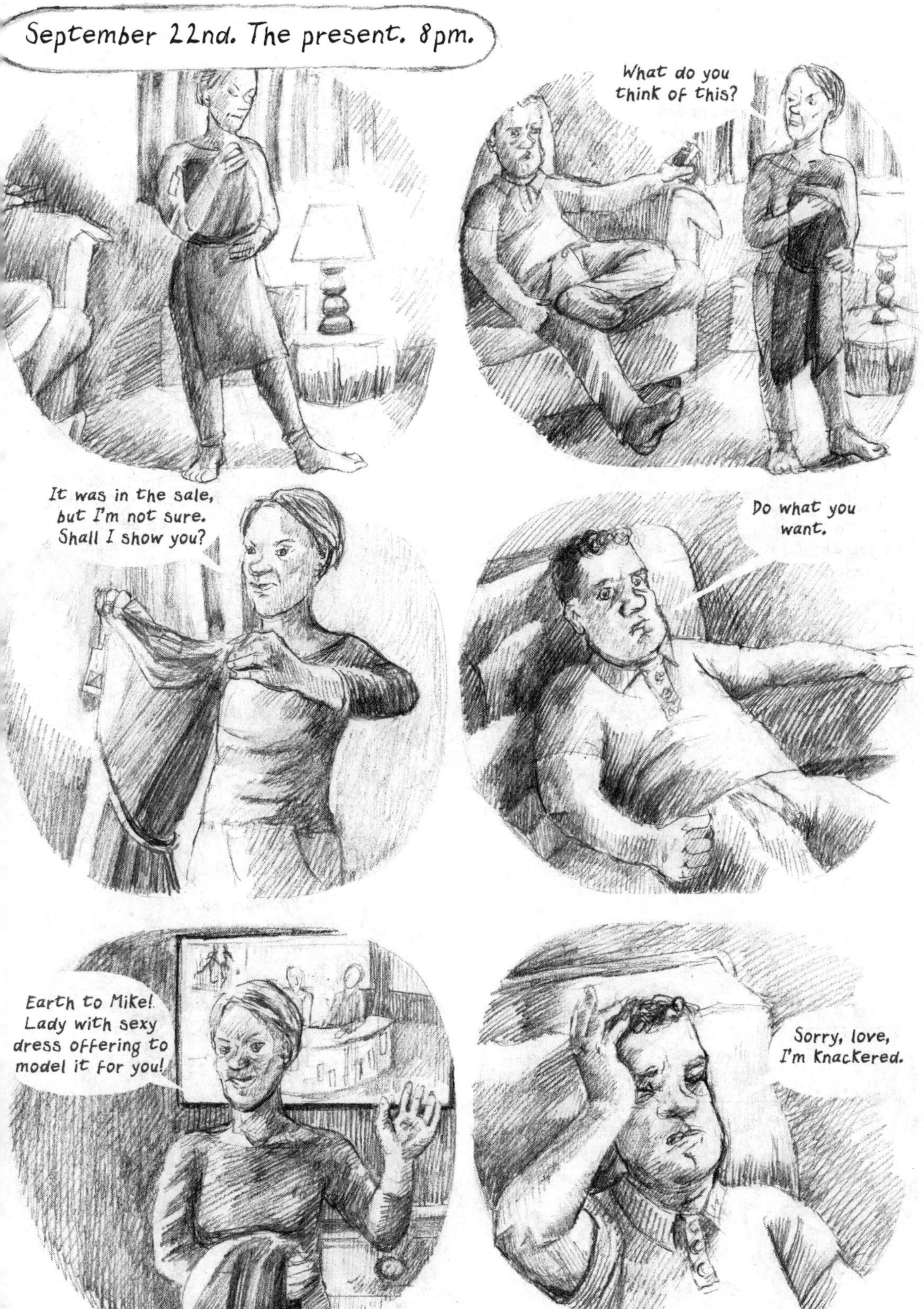
September 22nd. The present. 8pm.
What do you think of this?
It was in the sale, but I'm not sure. Shall I show you?
Do what you want.
Earth to Mike! Lady with sexy dress offering to model it for you!
Sorry, love, I'm knackered.

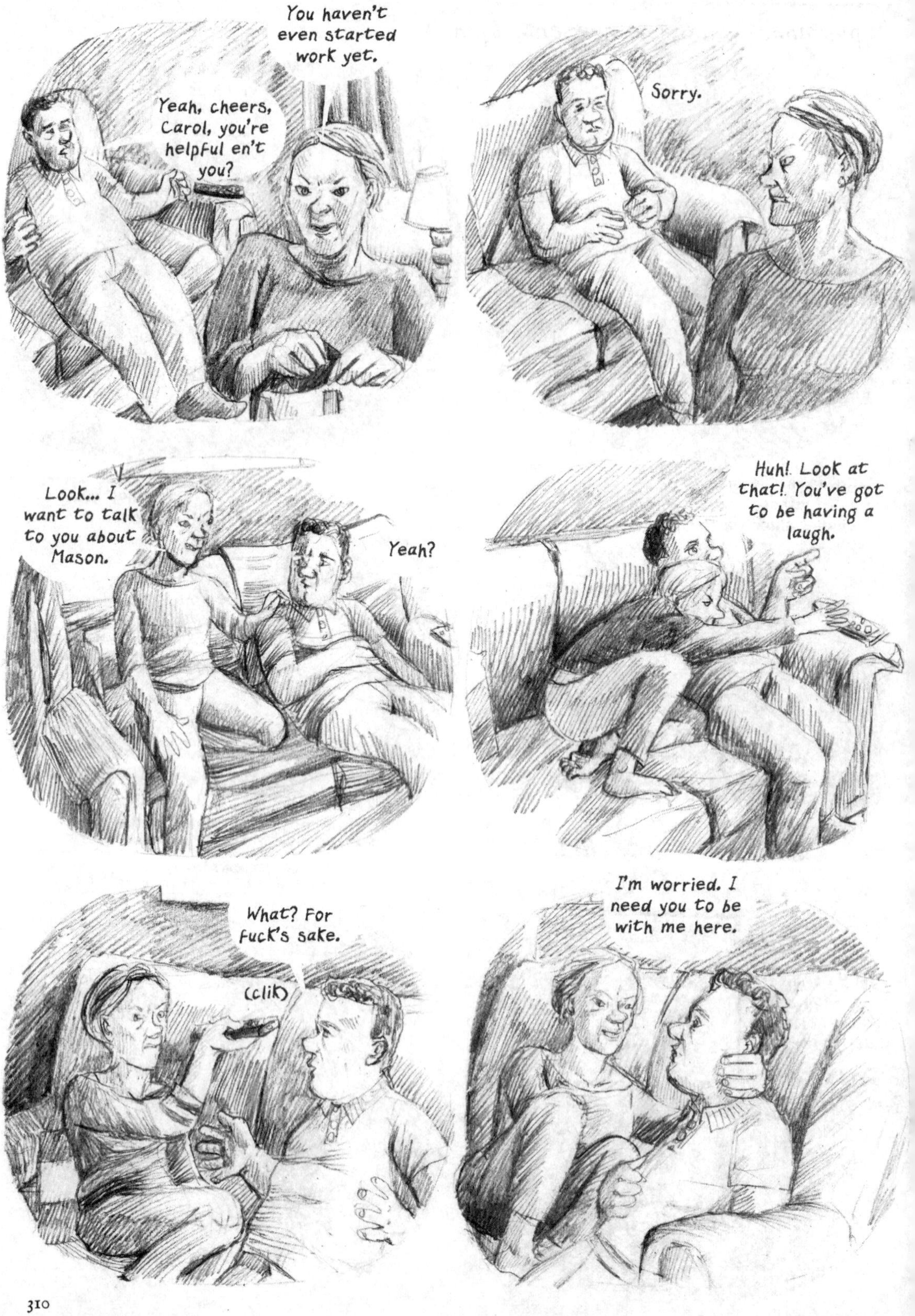
You haven't even started work yet.
Yeah, cheers, Carol, you're helpful en't you?
Sorry.
Look... I want to talk to you about Mason.
Yeah?
Huh! Look at that!. You've got to be having a laugh.
What? For fuck's sake.
(clik)
I'm worried. I need you to be with me here.

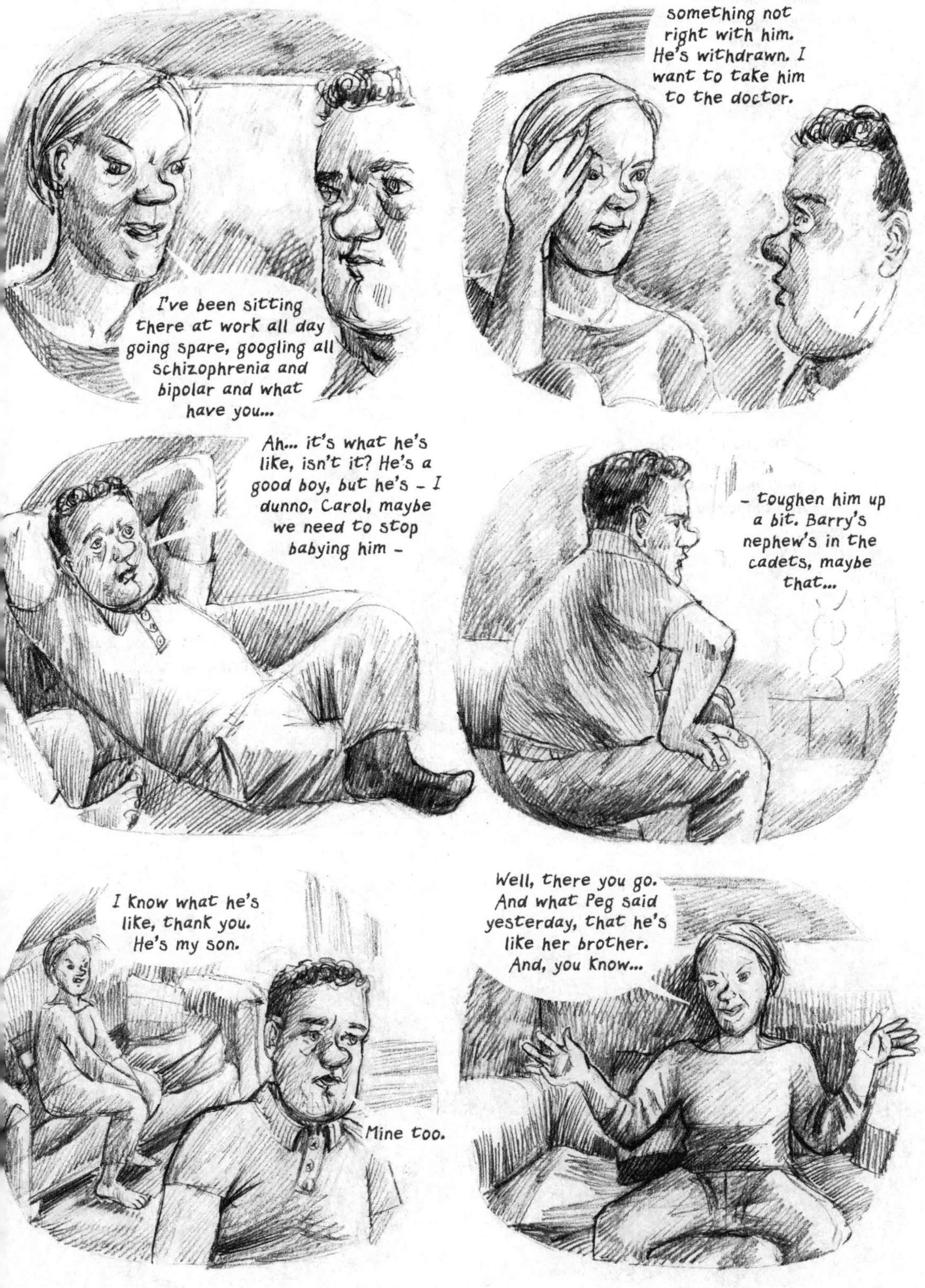
I've been sitting there at work all day going spare, googling all schizophrenia and bipolar and what have you...
...there's something not right with him. He's withdrawn. I want to take him to the doctor.
Ah... it's what he's like, isn't it? He's a good boy, but he's – I dunno, Carol, maybe we need to stop babying him –
– toughen him up a bit. Barry's nephew's in the cadets, maybe that...
I know what he's like, thank you. He's my son.
Mine too.
Well, there you go. And what Peg said yesterday, that he's like her brother. And, you know...

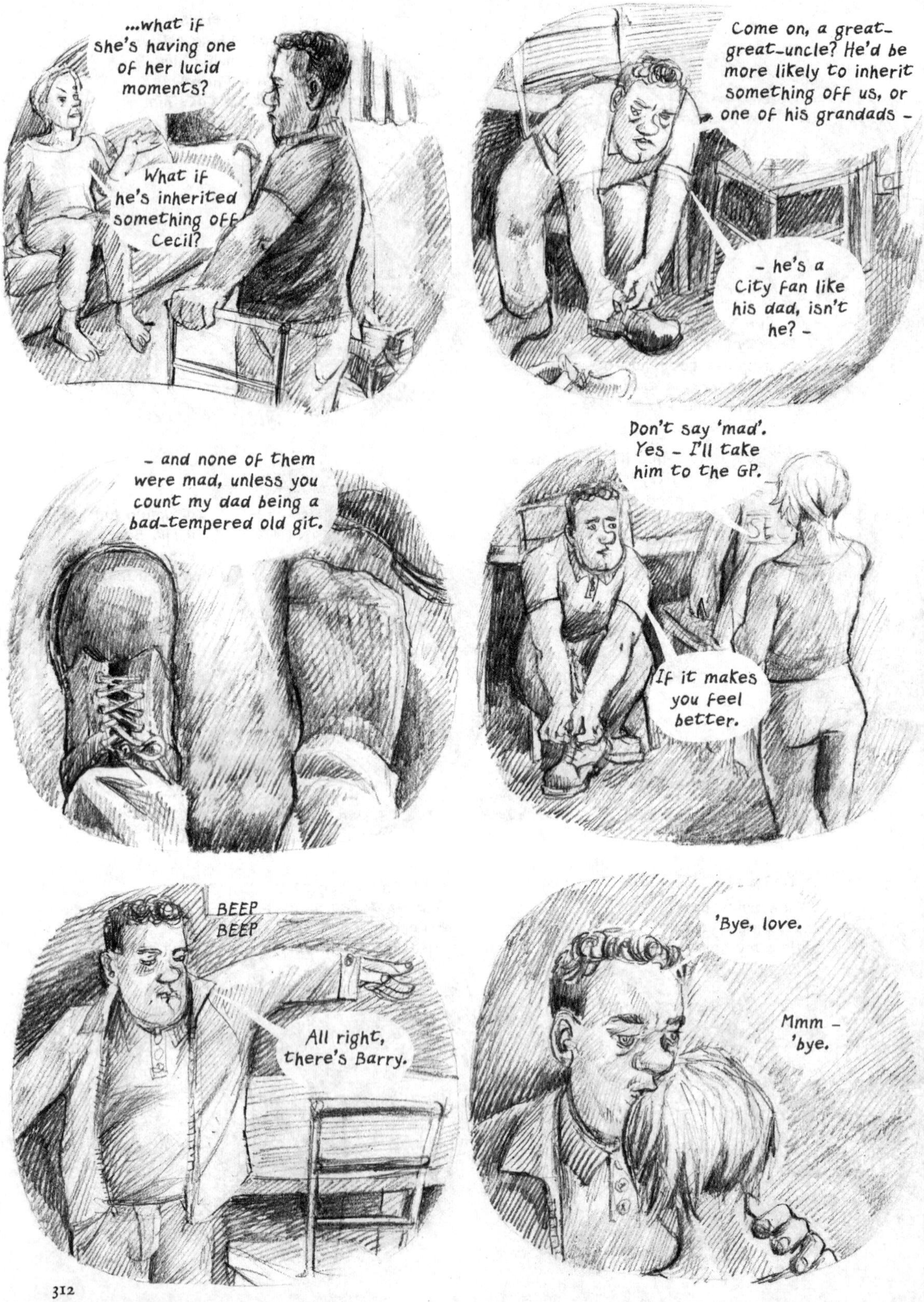
...what if she's having one of her lucid moments?
What if he's inherited something off Cecil?
Come on, a great-great-uncle? He'd be more likely to inherit something off us, or one of his grandads -
- he's a City fan like his dad, isn't he? -
- and none of them were mad, unless you count my dad being a bad-tempered old git.
Don't say 'mad'. Yes - I'll take him to the GP.
If it makes you feel better.
BEEP BEEP
All right, there's Barry.
'Bye, love.
Mmm - 'bye.

nex

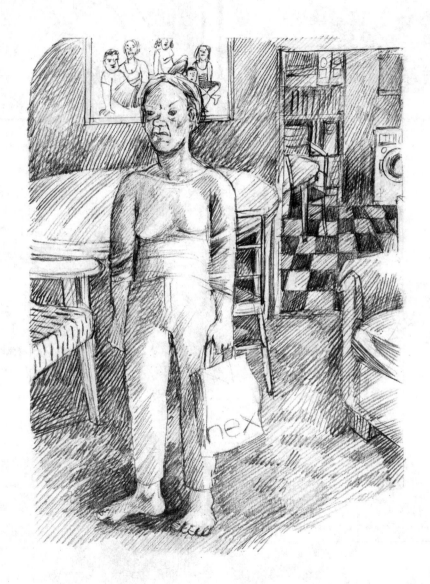

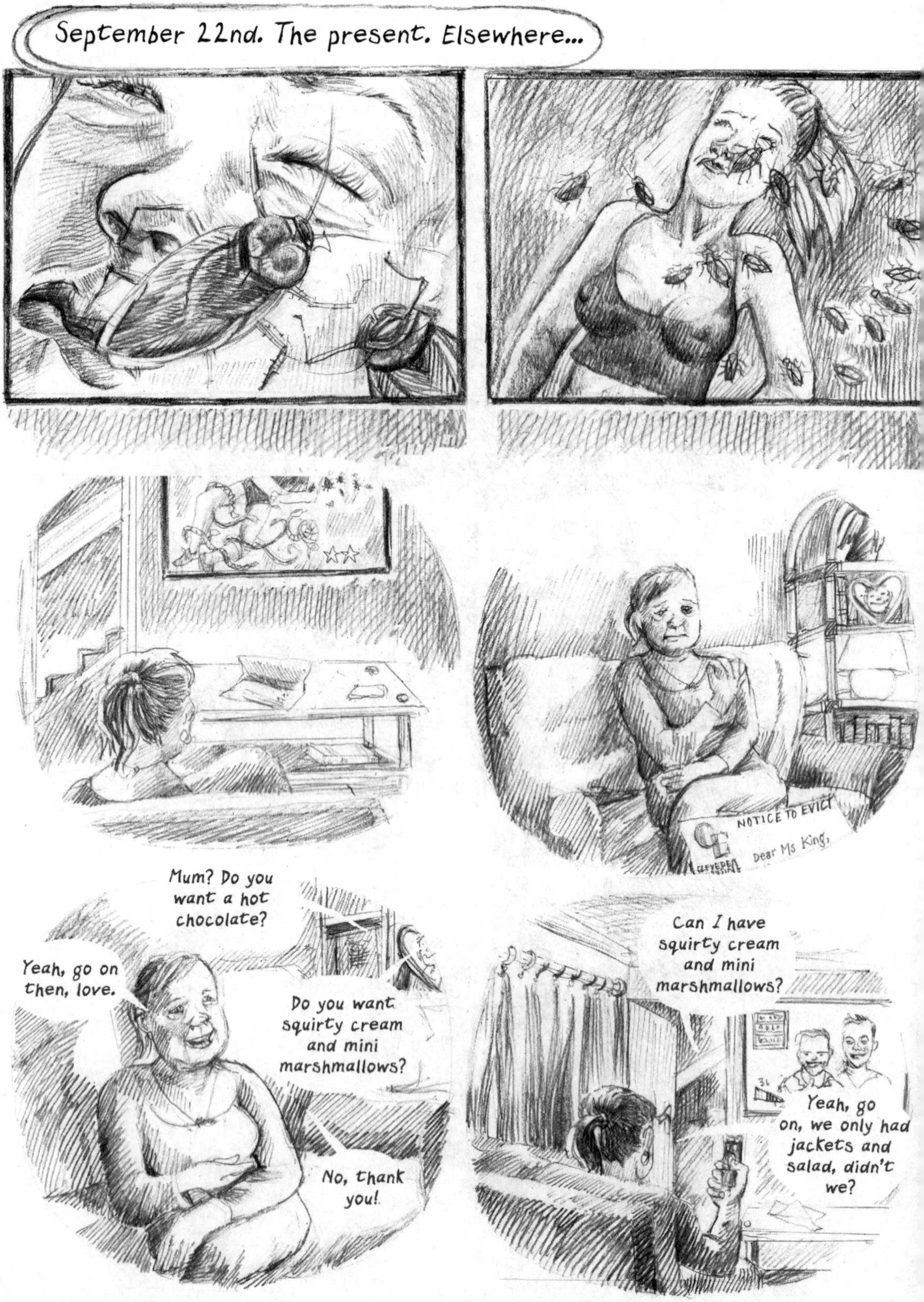
September 22nd. The present. Elsewhere...
NOTICE TO EVICT
Dear Ms King,
Mum? Do you want a hot chocolate?
Yeah, go on then, love.
Do you want squirty cream and mini marshmallows?
No, thank you!
Can I have squirty cream and mini marshmallows?
Yeah, go on, we only had jackets and salad, didn't we?

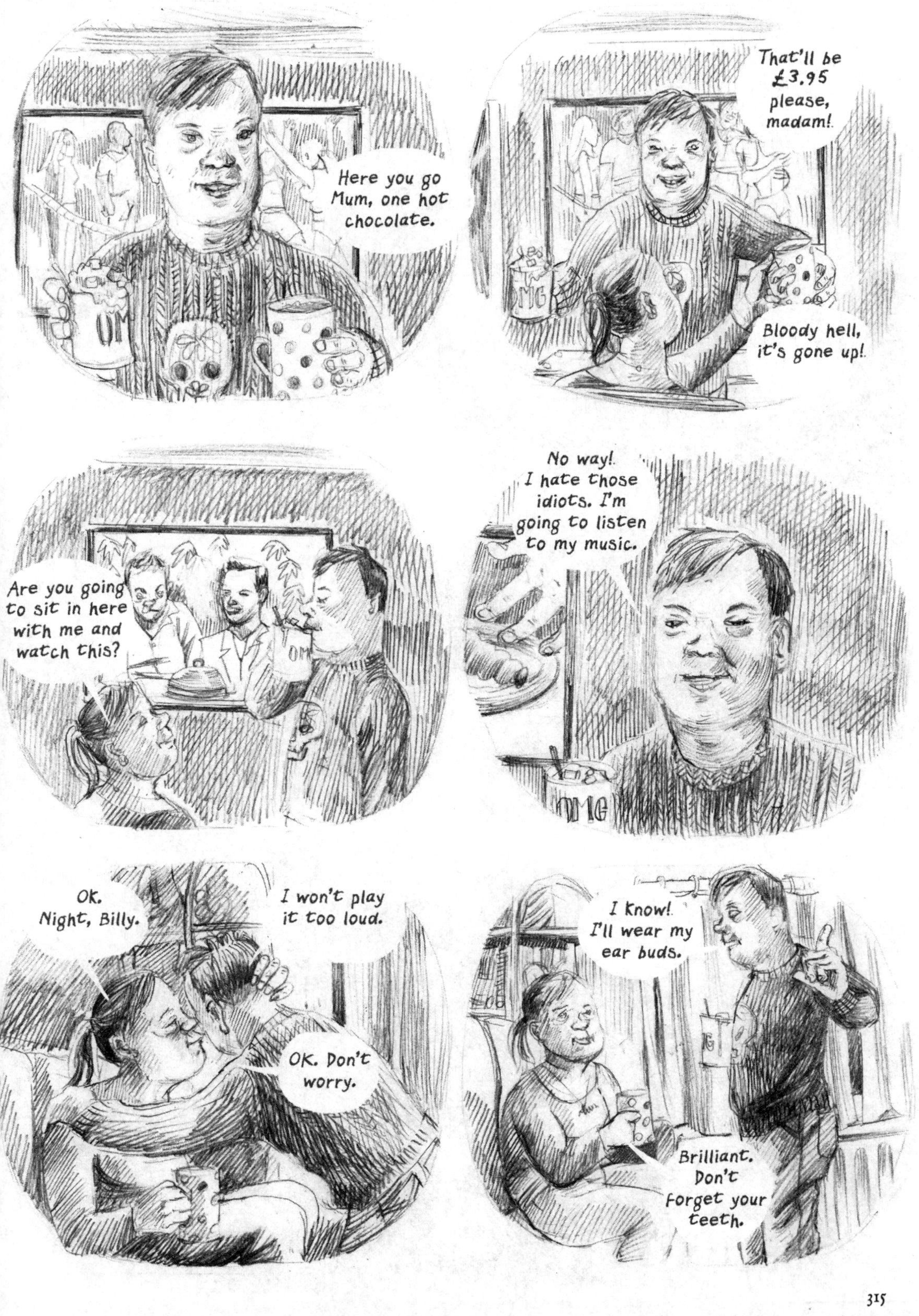
Here you go Mum, one hot chocolate.
OM
That'll be £3.95 please, madam!.
OMG
Bloody hell, it's gone up!.
Are you going to sit in here with me and watch this?
No way!. I hate those idiots. I'm going to listen to my music.
OMG
OK. Night, Billy.
I won't play it too loud.
OK. Don't worry.
I know!. I'll wear my ear buds.
Brilliant. Don't forget your teeth.

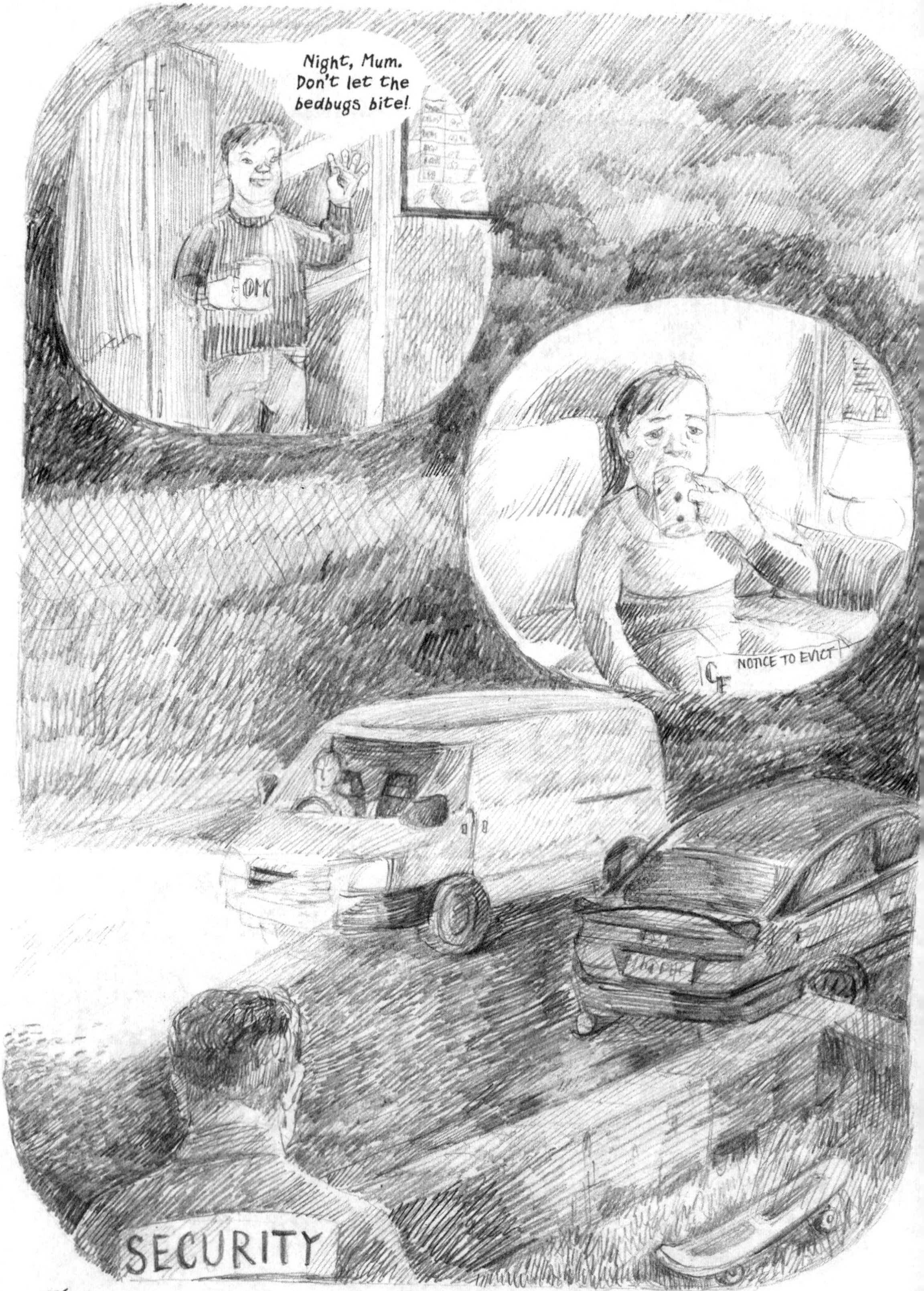
Night, Mum. Don't let the bedbugs bite!
NOTICE TO EVICT
SECURITY

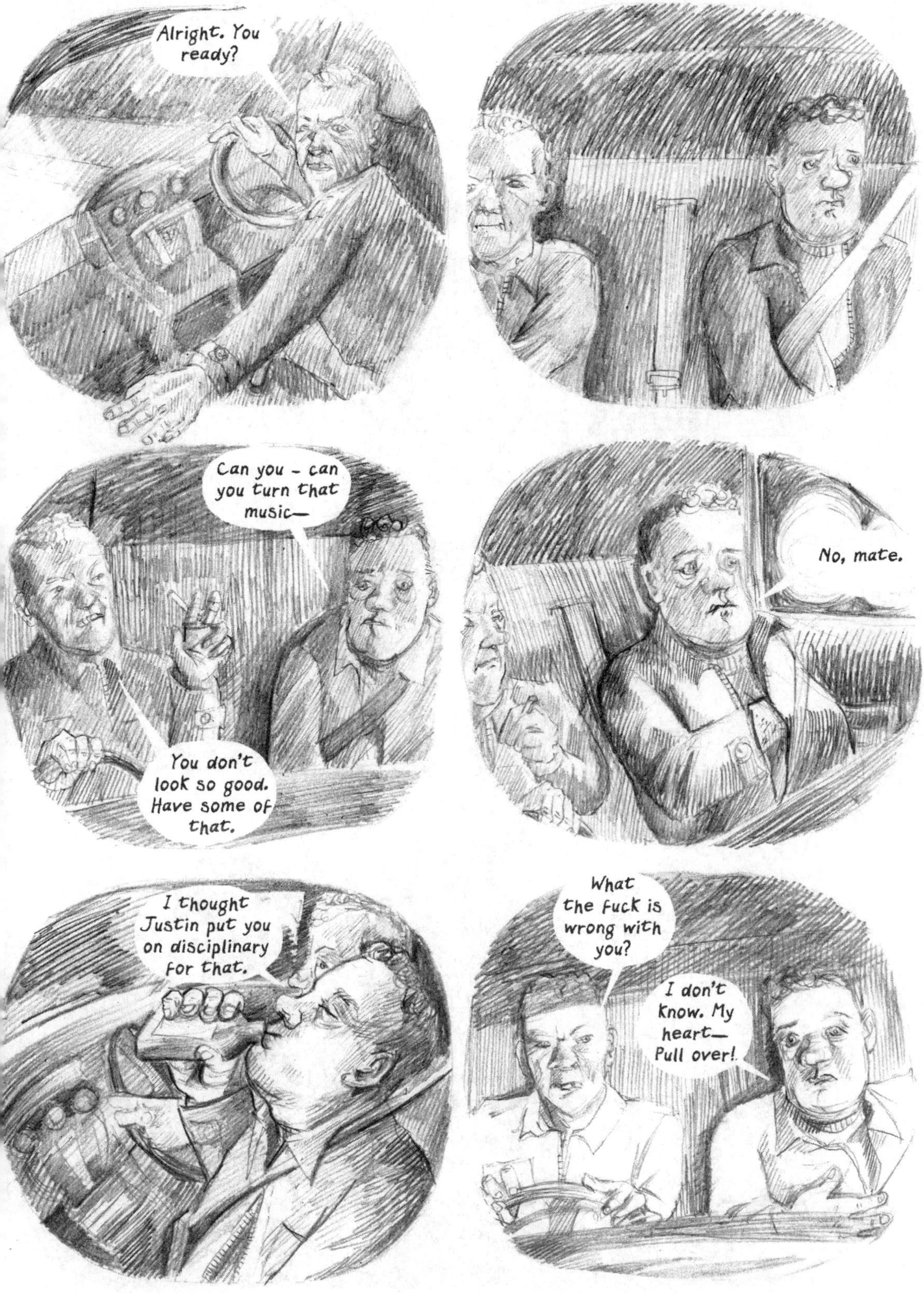
Alright. You ready?
Can you - can you turn that music—
You don't look so good. Have some of that.
No, mate.
I thought Justin put you on disciplinary for that.
What the fuck is wrong with you?
I don't know. My heart— Pull over!

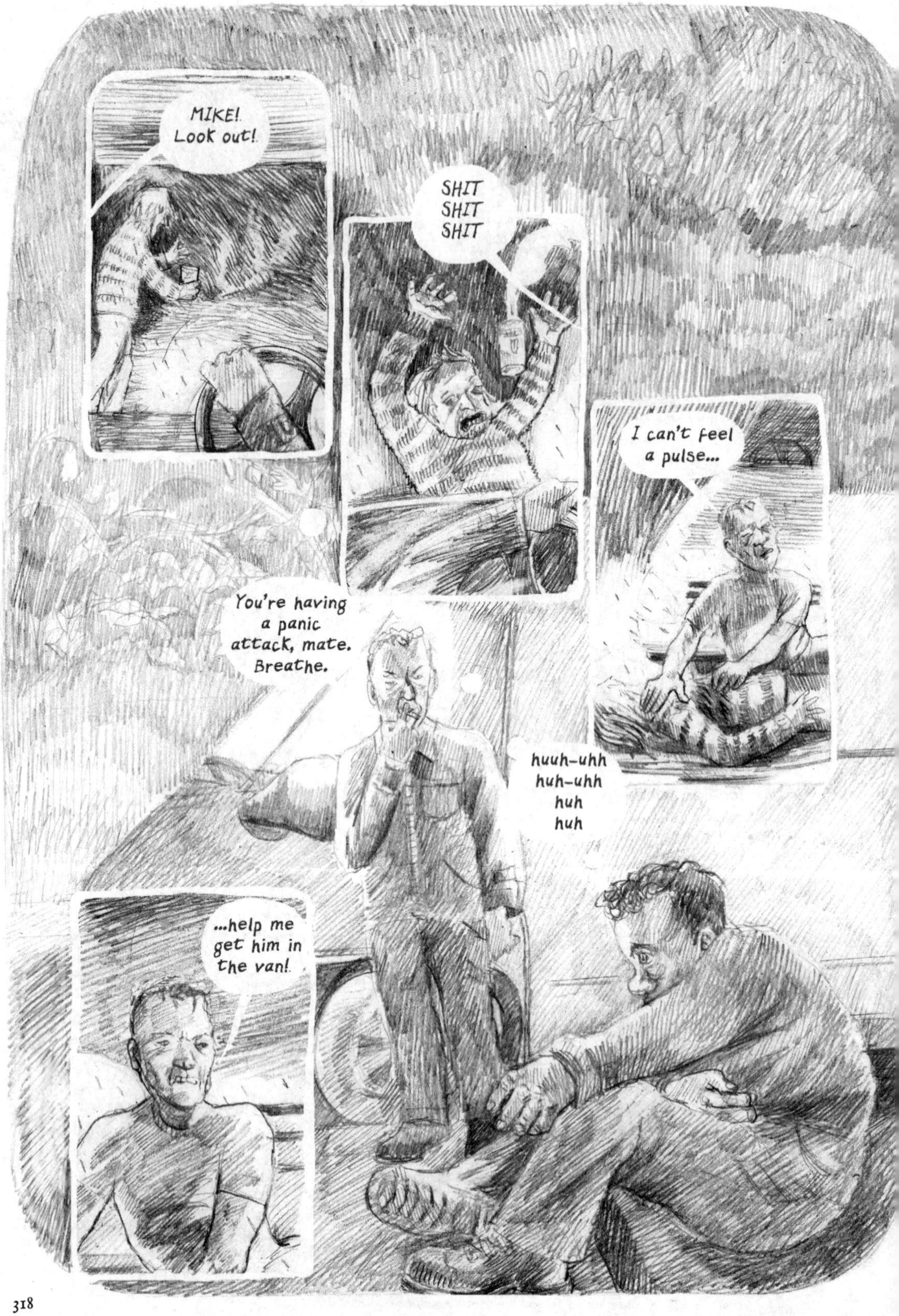
MIKE! Look out!
SHIT SHIT SHIT
I can't feel a pulse...
You're having a panic attack, mate. Breathe.
huuh-uhh huh-uhh huh huh
...help me get him in the van!

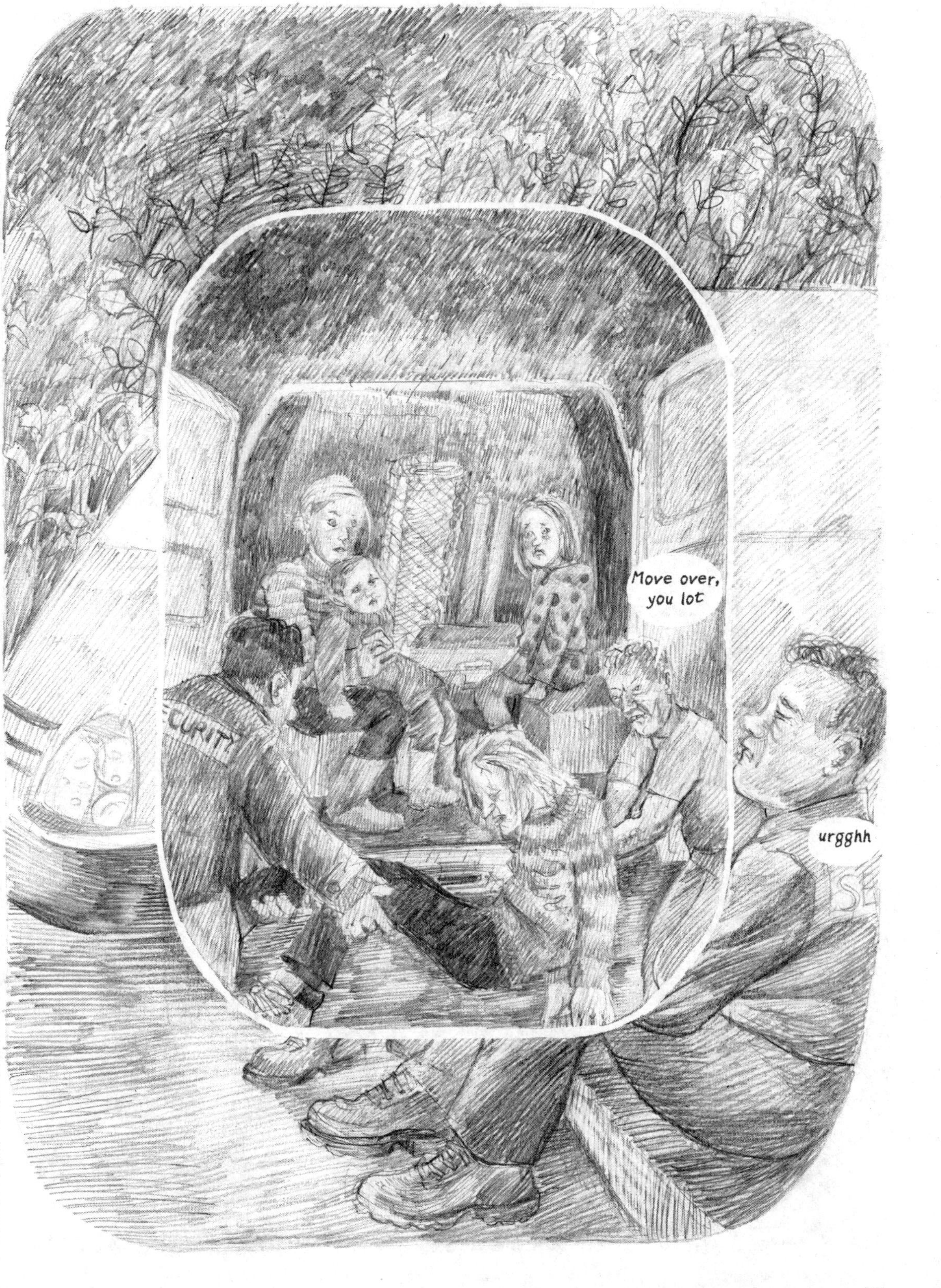
Move over, you lot
urgghh

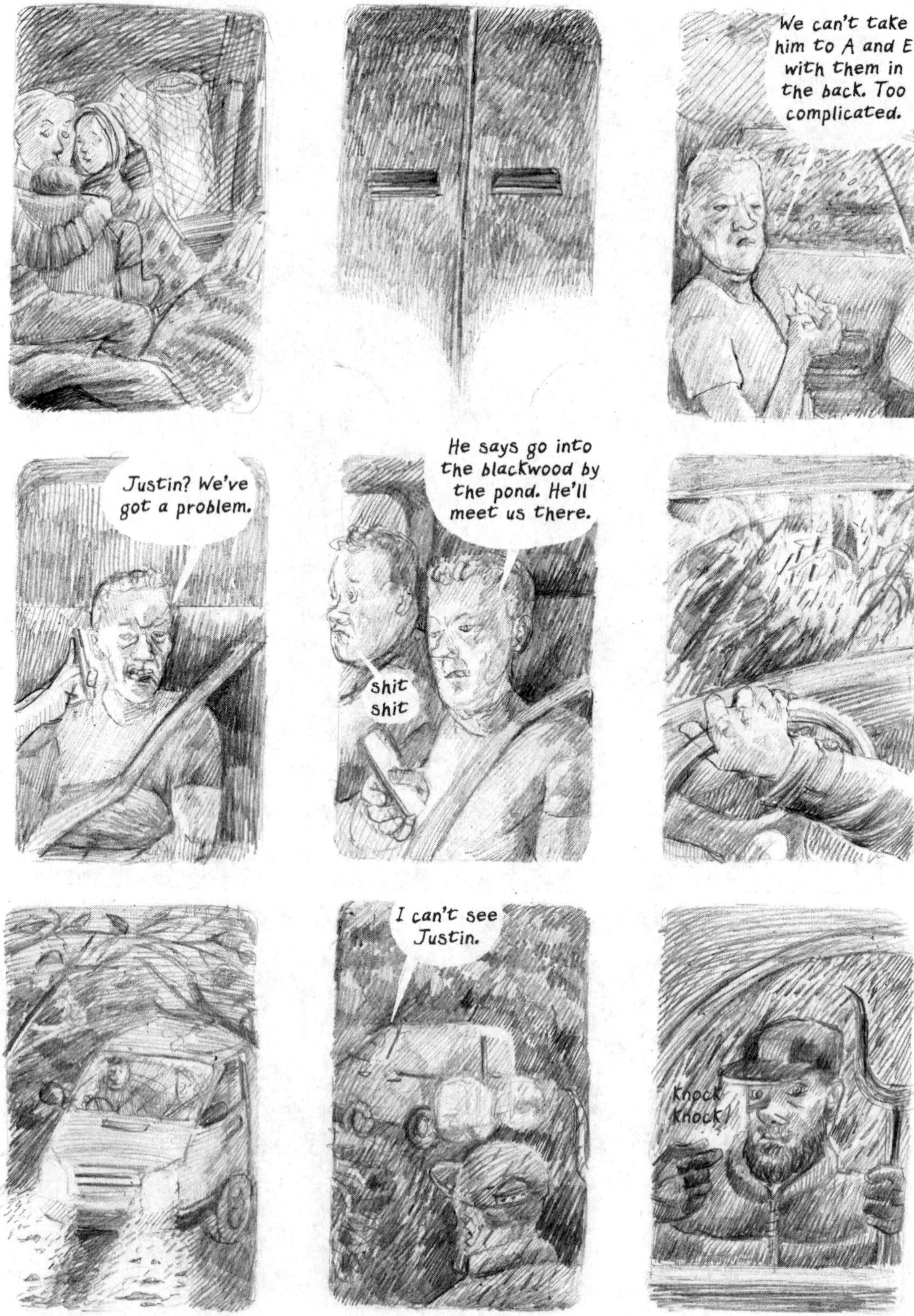
We can't take him to A and E with them in the back. Too complicated.
Justin? We've got a problem.
He says go into the blackwood by the pond. He'll meet us there.
shit shit
I can't see Justin.
Knock Knock!

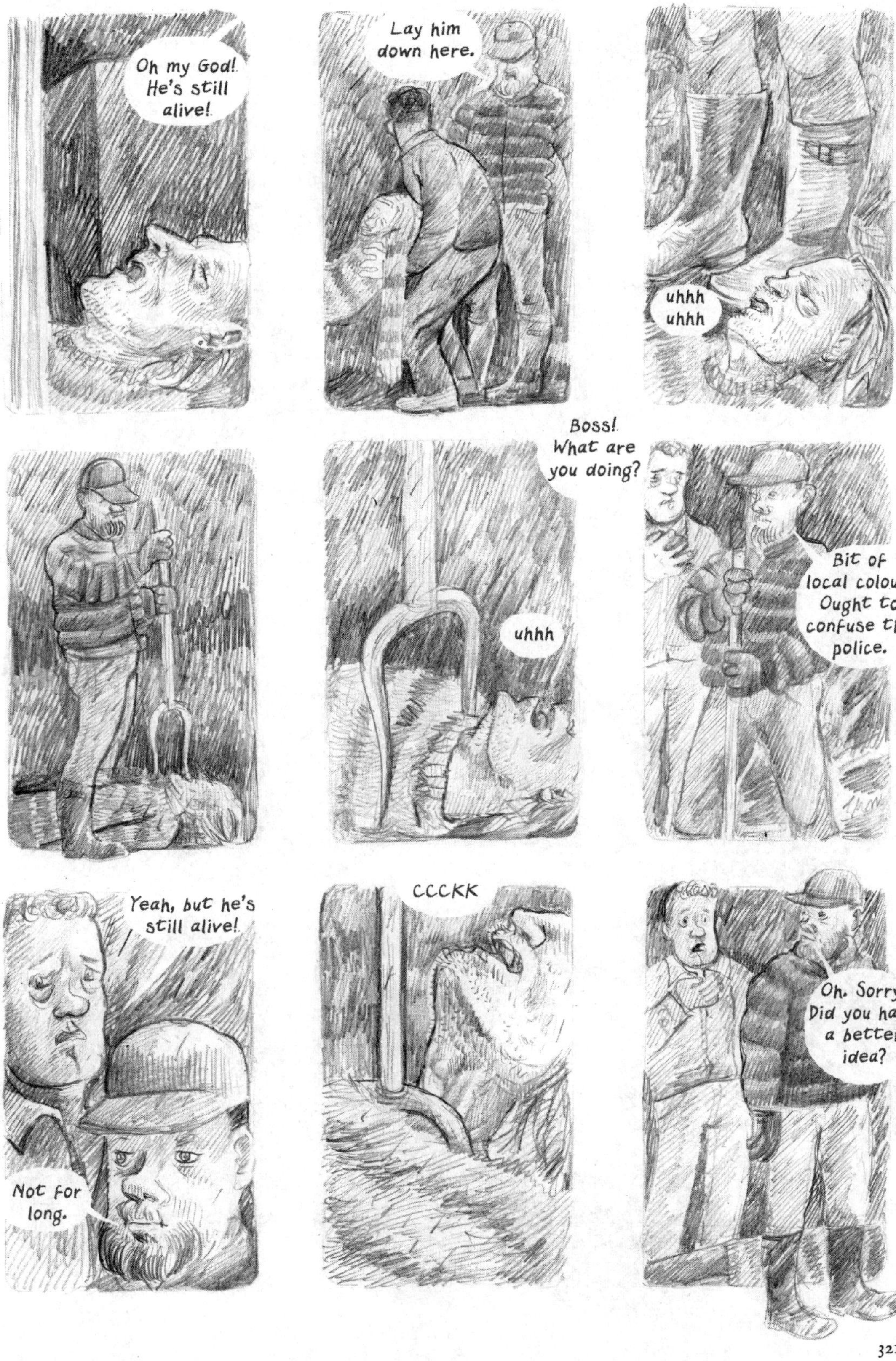
Oh my God!. He's still alive!.
Lay him down here.
uhhh uhhh
Boss!. What are you doing?
uhhh
Bit of local colour. Ought to confuse the police.
Yeah, but he's still alive!.
Not for long.
CCCKK
Oh. Sorry. Did you have a better idea?

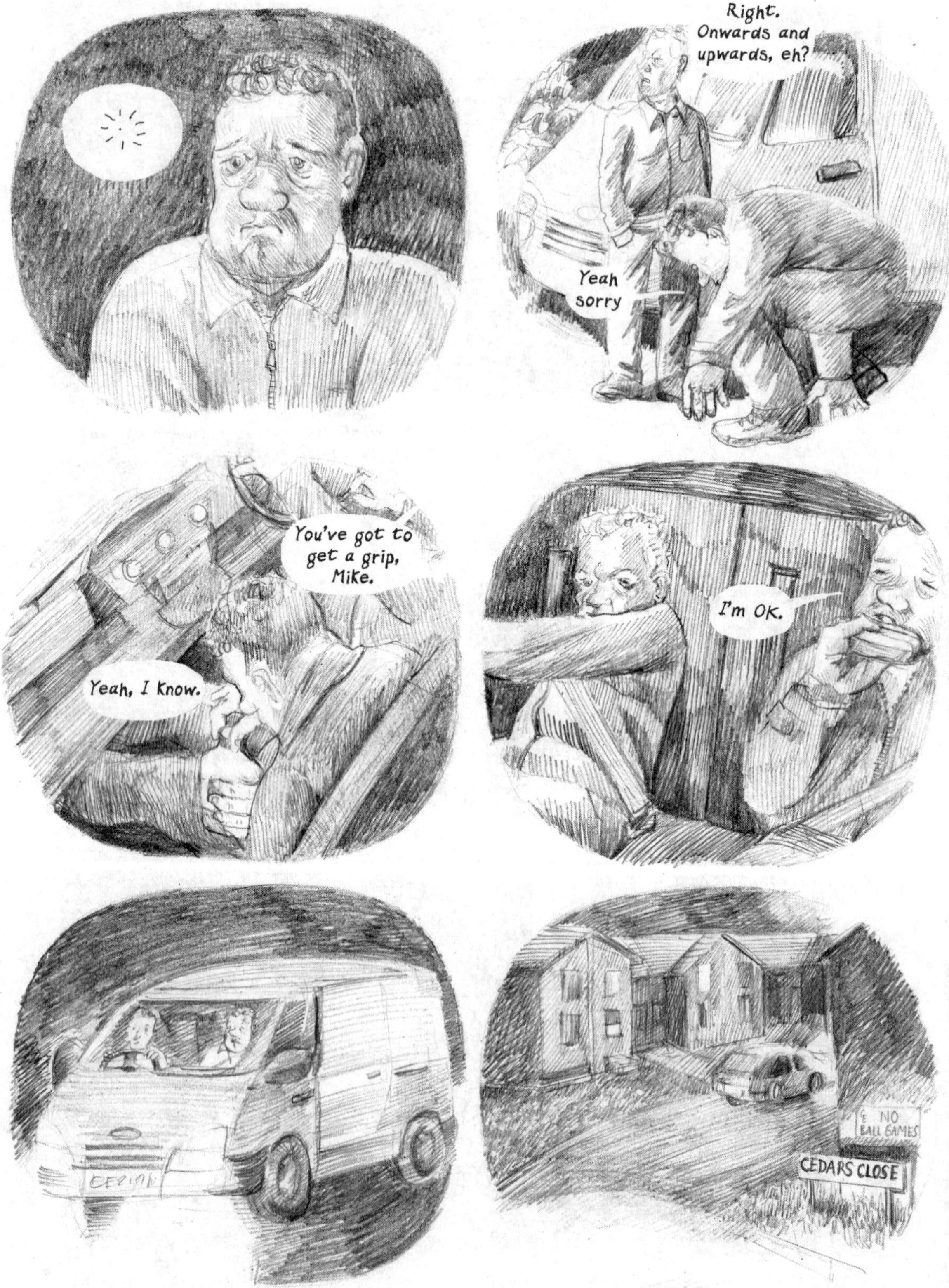
Right. Onwards and upwards, eh?
Yeah sorry
You've got to get a grip, Mike.
Yeah, I know.
I'm OK.
NO BALL GAMES
CEDARS CLOSE

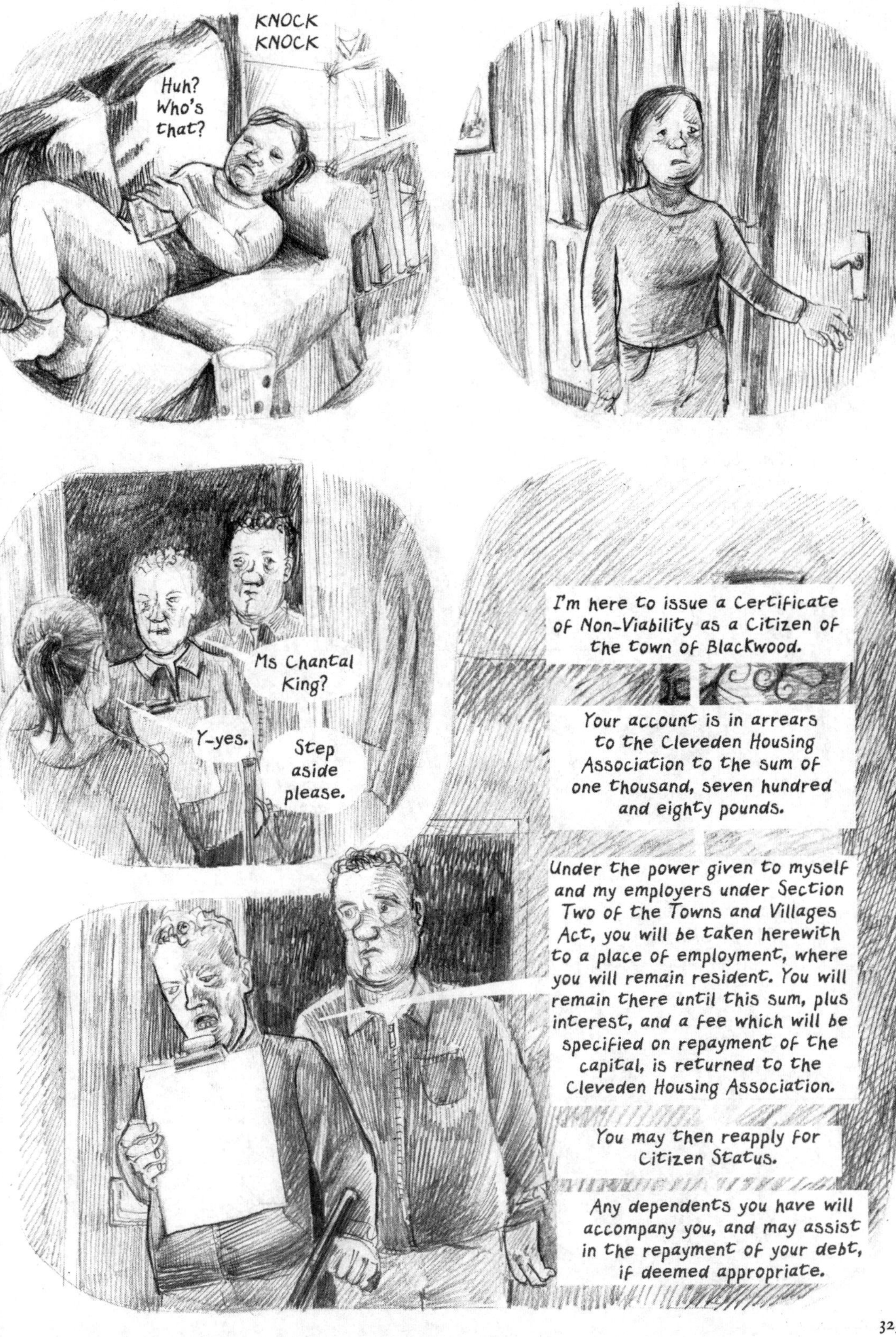
KNOCK KNOCK
Huh? Who's that?
Ms Chantal King?
Y-yes.
Step aside please.
I'm here to issue a Certificate of Non-Viability as a Citizen of the town of Blackwood.
Your account is in arrears to the Cleveden Housing Association to the sum of one thousand, seven hundred and eighty pounds.
Under the power given to myself and my employers under Section Two of the Towns and Villages Act, you will be taken herewith to a place of employment, where you will remain resident. You will remain there until this sum, plus interest, and a fee which will be specified on repayment of the capital, is returned to the Cleveden Housing Association.
You may then reapply for Citizen Status.
Any dependents you have will accompany you, and may assist in the repayment of your debt, if deemed appropriate.

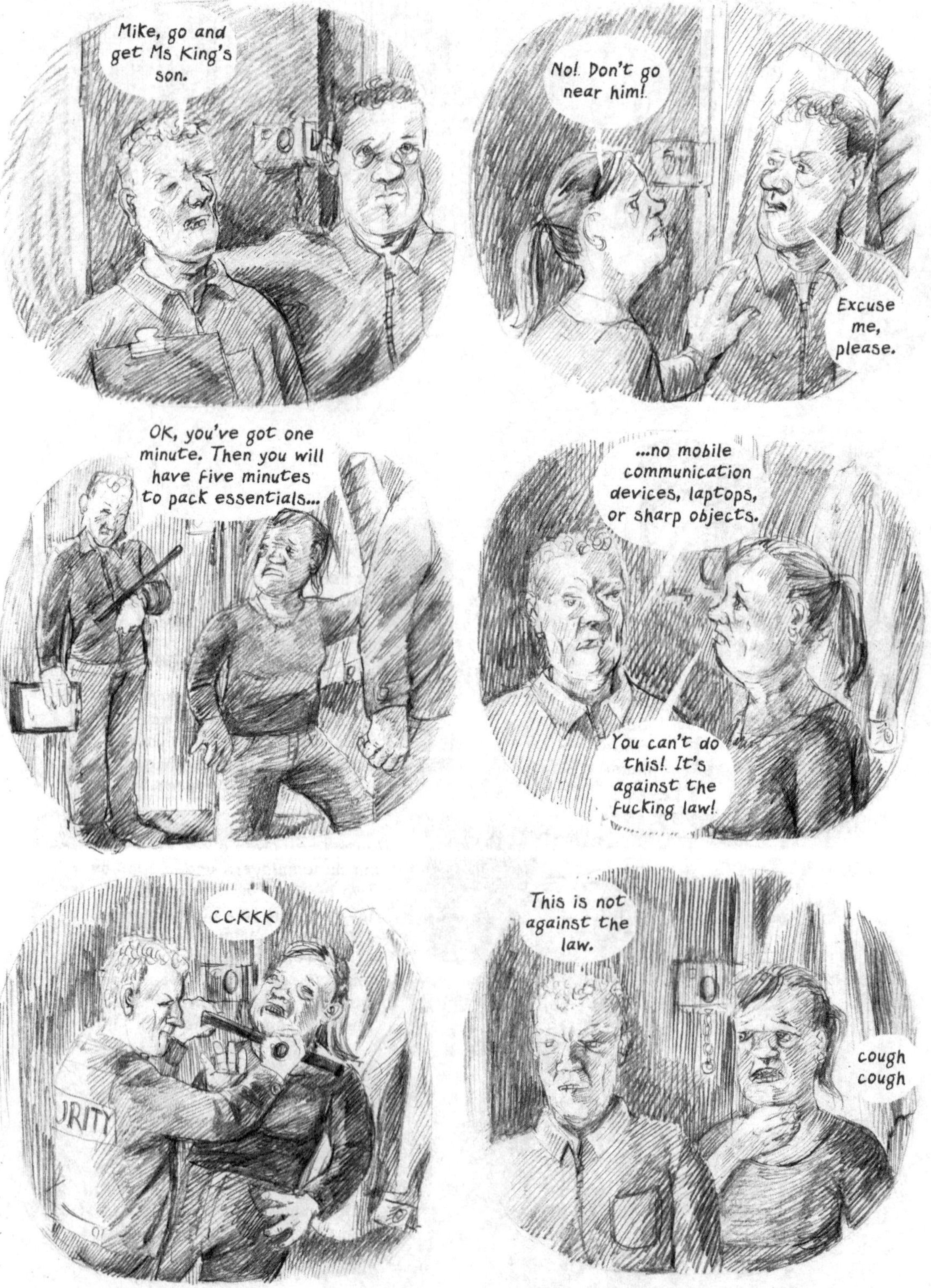
Mike, go and get Ms King's son.
No!. Don't go near him!.
Excuse me, please.
OK, you've got one minute. Then you will have five minutes to pack essentials...
...no mobile communication devices, laptops, or sharp objects.
You can't do this!. It's against the fucking law!.
CCKKK
URITY
This is not against the law.
cough cough

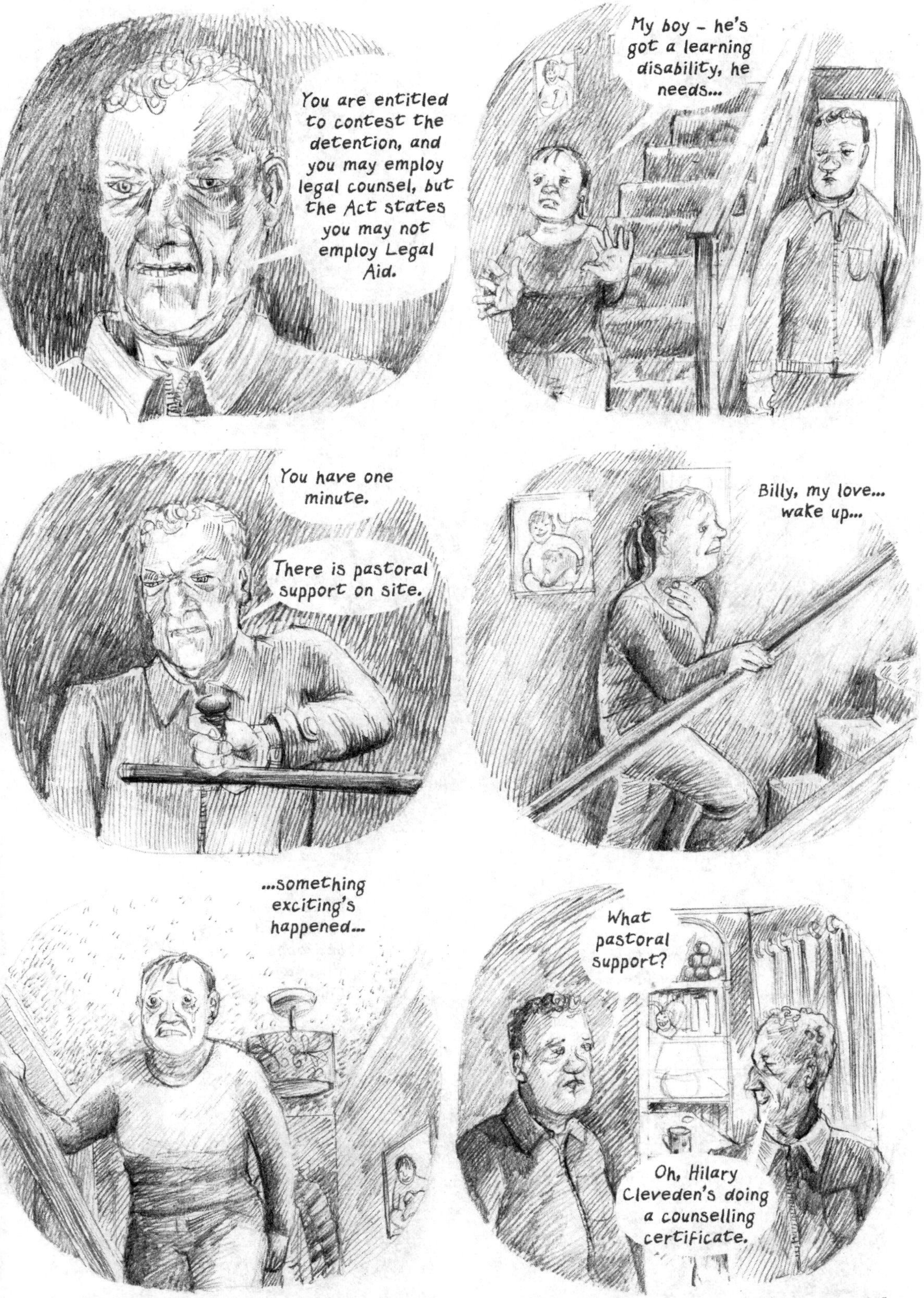
You are entitled to contest the detention, and you may employ legal counsel, but the Act states you may not employ Legal Aid.
My boy - he's got a learning disability, he needs...
You have one minute.
There is pastoral support on site.
Billy, my love... wake up...
...something exciting's happened...
What pastoral support?
Oh, Hilary Cleveden's doing a counselling certificate.

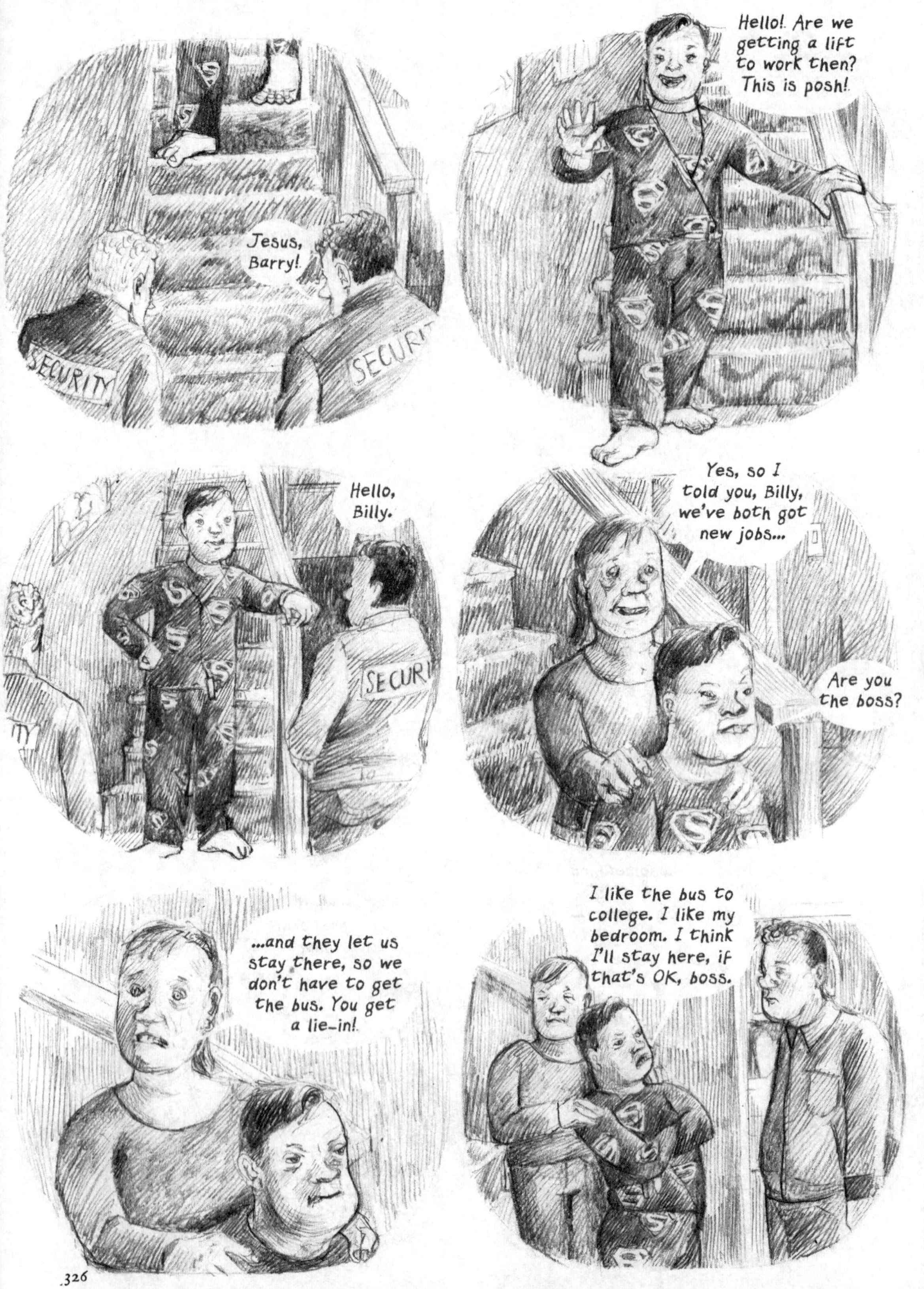

Jesus, Barry!
SECURITY
SECURI
Hello!. Are we getting a lift to work then? This is posh!.
Hello, Billy.
SECURI
Yes, so I told you, Billy, we've both got new jobs...
Are you the boss?
...and they let us stay there, so we don't have to get the bus. You get a lie-in!.
I like the bus to college. I like my bedroom. I think I'll stay here, if that's OK, boss.

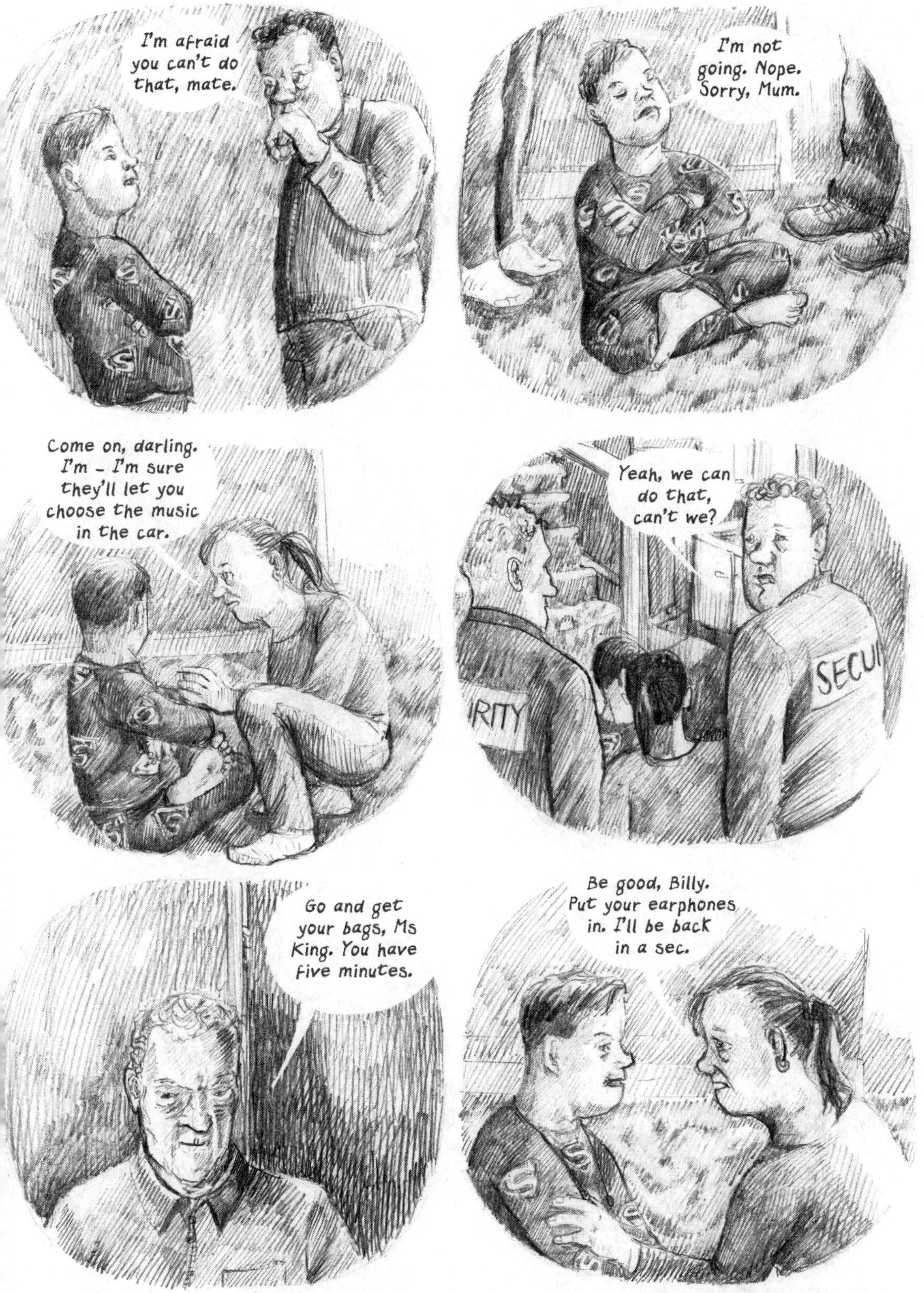
I'm afraid you can't do that, mate.
I'm not going. Nope. Sorry, Mum.
Come on, darling. I'm - I'm sure they'll let you choose the music in the car.
Yeah, we can do that, can't we?
SECU
RITY
Go and get your bags, Ms King. You have five minutes.
Be good, Billy. Put your earphones in. I'll be back in a sec.

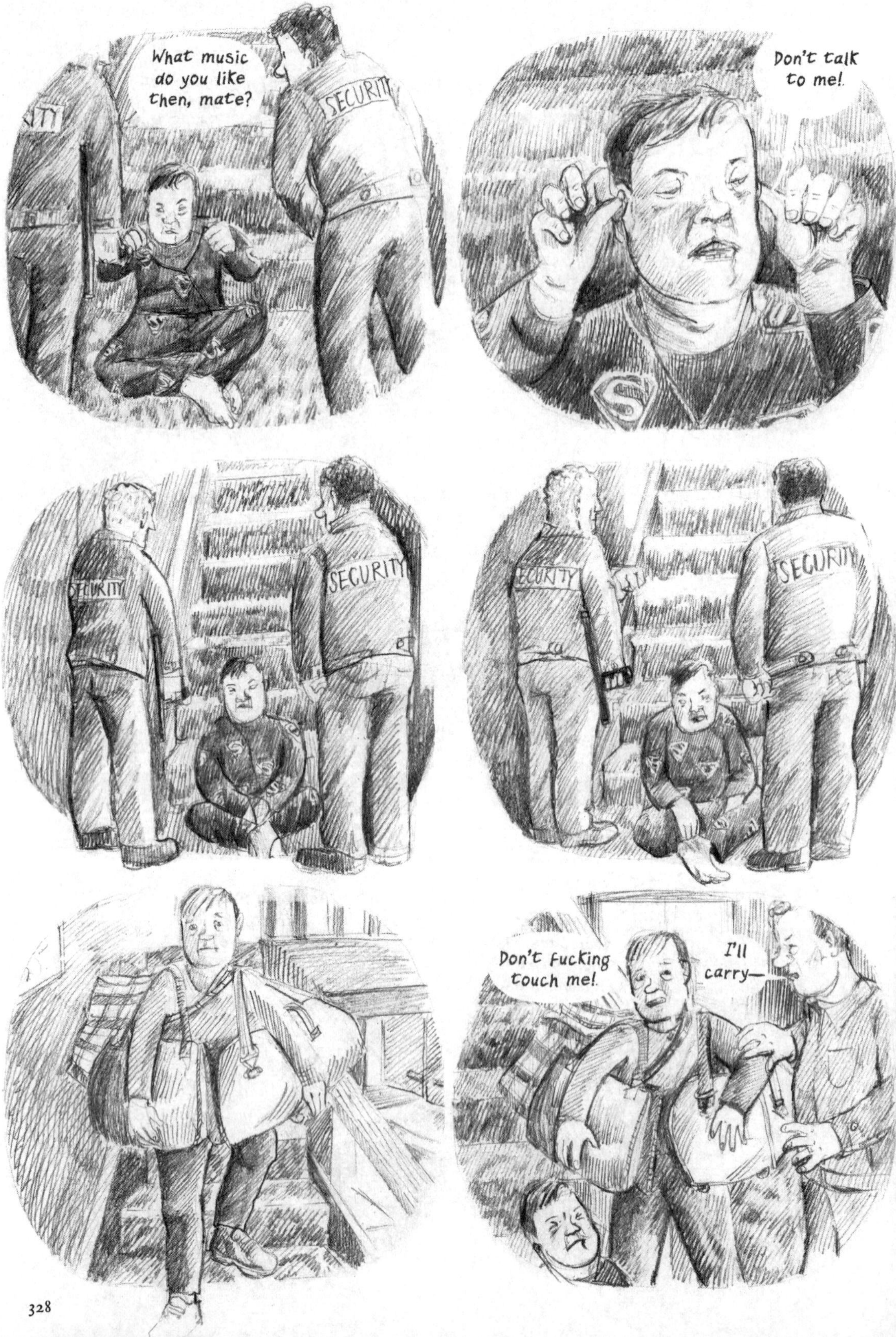
What music do you like then, mate?
SECURITY
Don't talk to me!
SECURITY
SECURITY
SECURITY
SECURITY
Don't fucking touch me!
I'll carry—

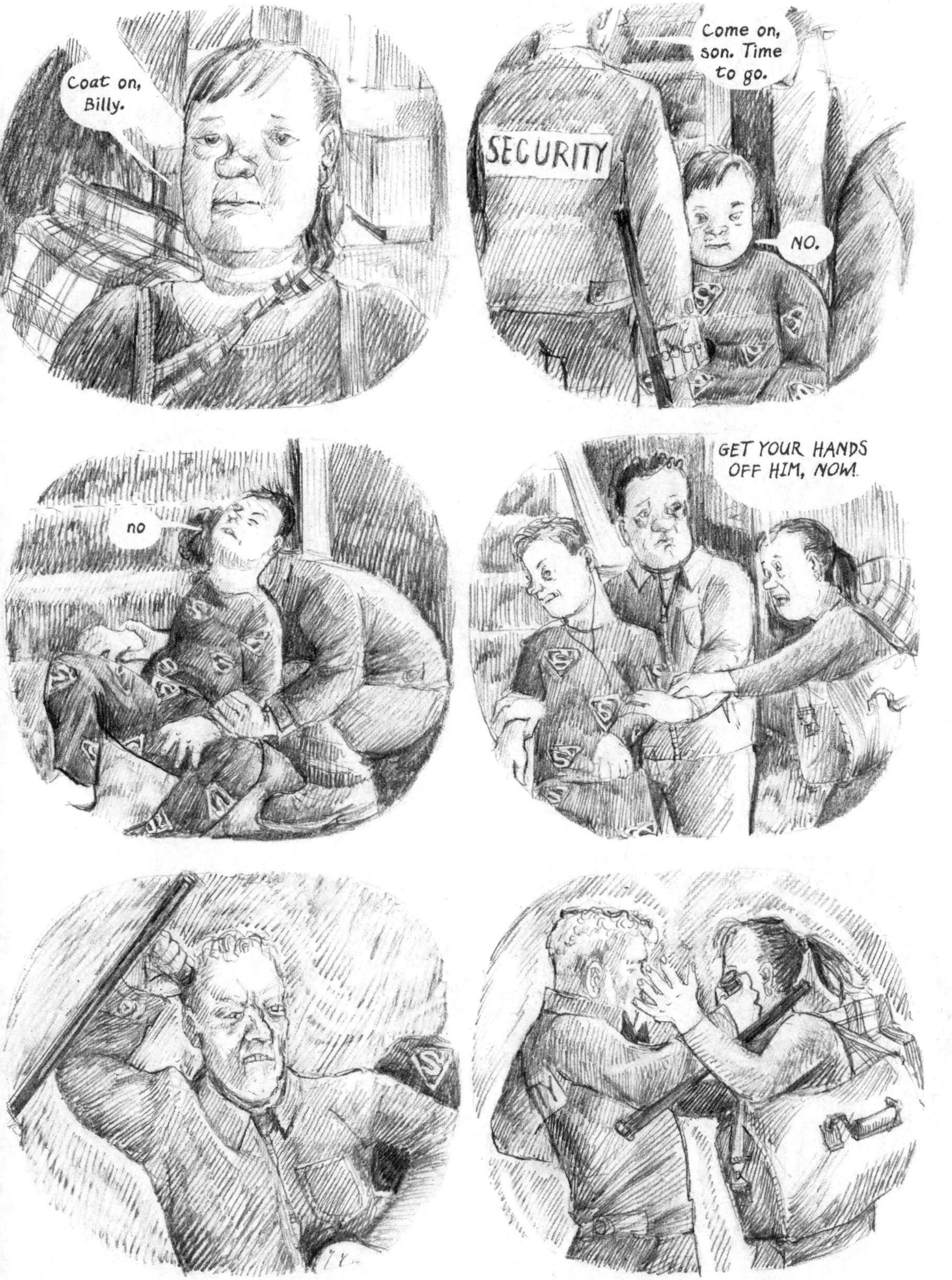
Coat on, Billy.
Come on, son. Time to go.
SECURITY
NO.
no
GET YOUR HANDS OFF HIM, NOW.

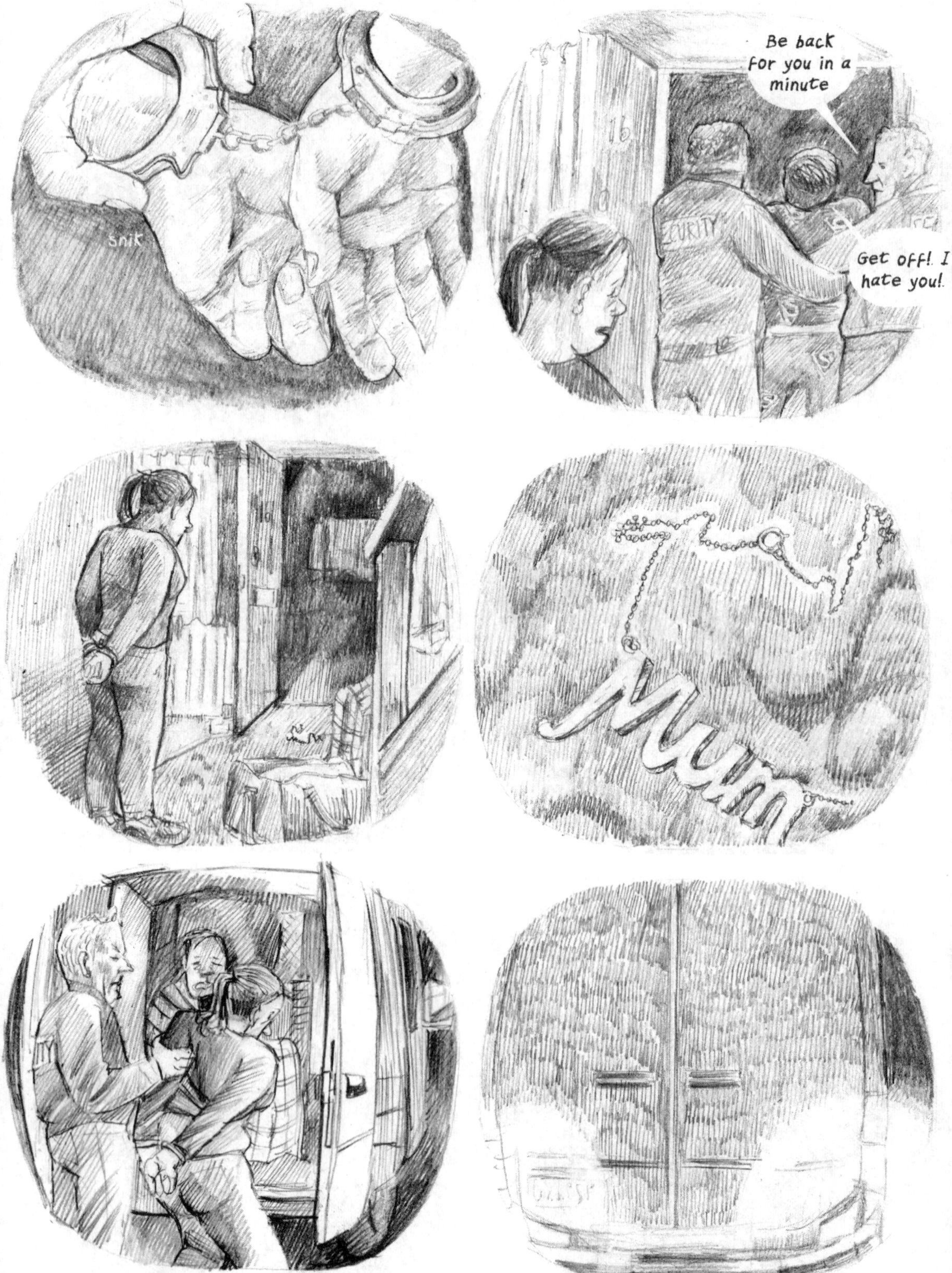
snik
Be back for you in a minute
Get off!. I hate you!.
Mum

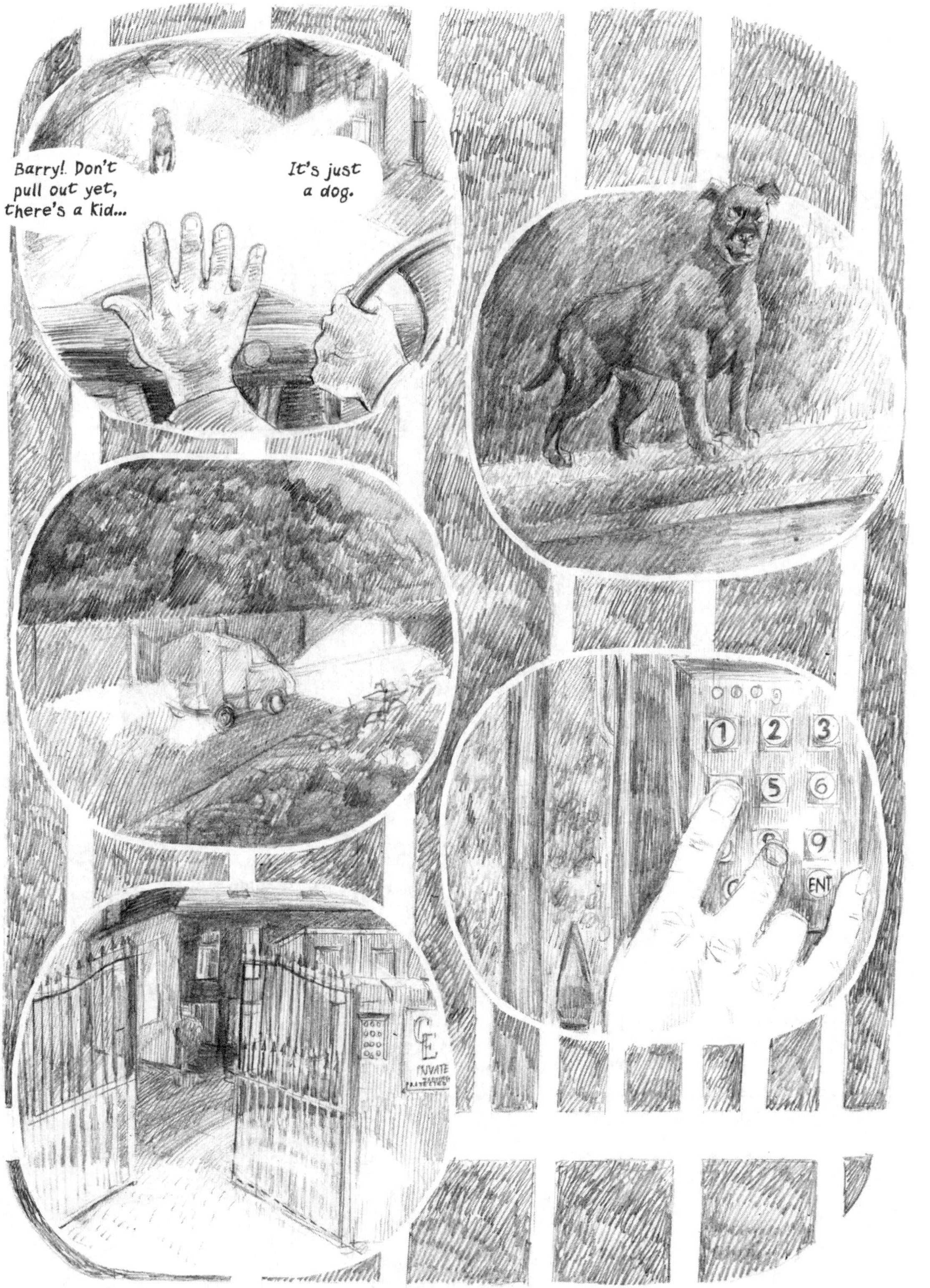
Barry!. Don't pull out yet, there's a kid...
It's just a dog.

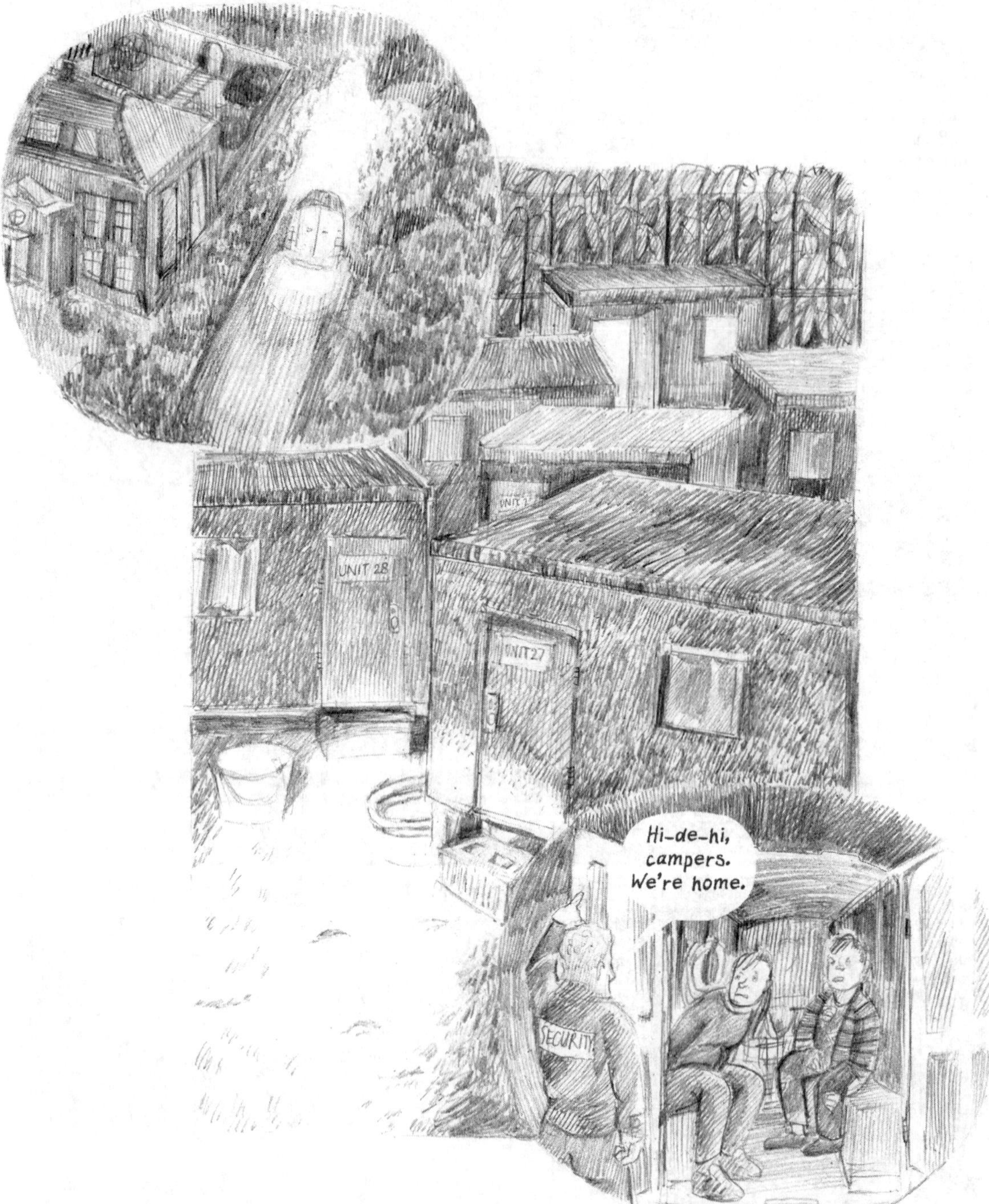
UNIT 28
UNIT 27
SECURITY
Hi-de-hi, campers. We're home.

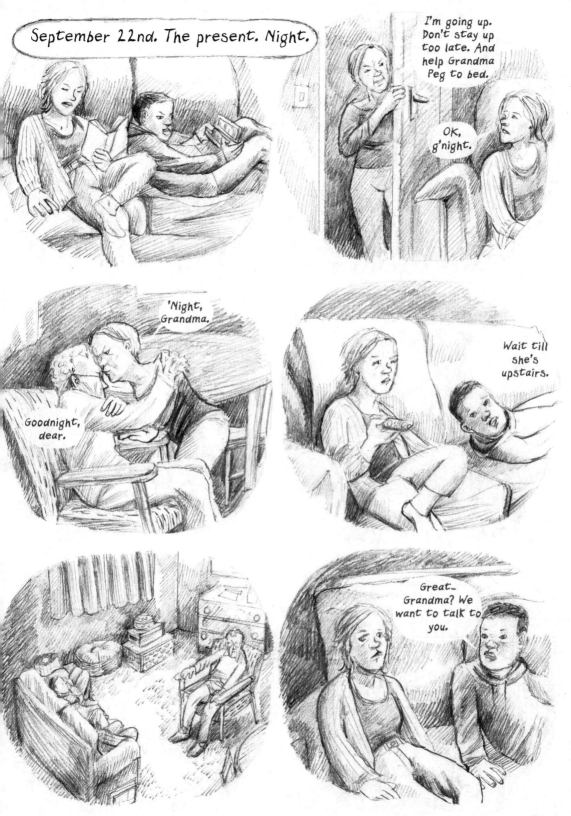

September 22nd. The present. Night.

I'm going up. Don't stay up too late. And help Grandma Peg to bed.

OK, g'night.

'Night, Grandma.

Goodnight, dear.

Wait till she's upstairs.

Great-Grandma? We want to talk to you.

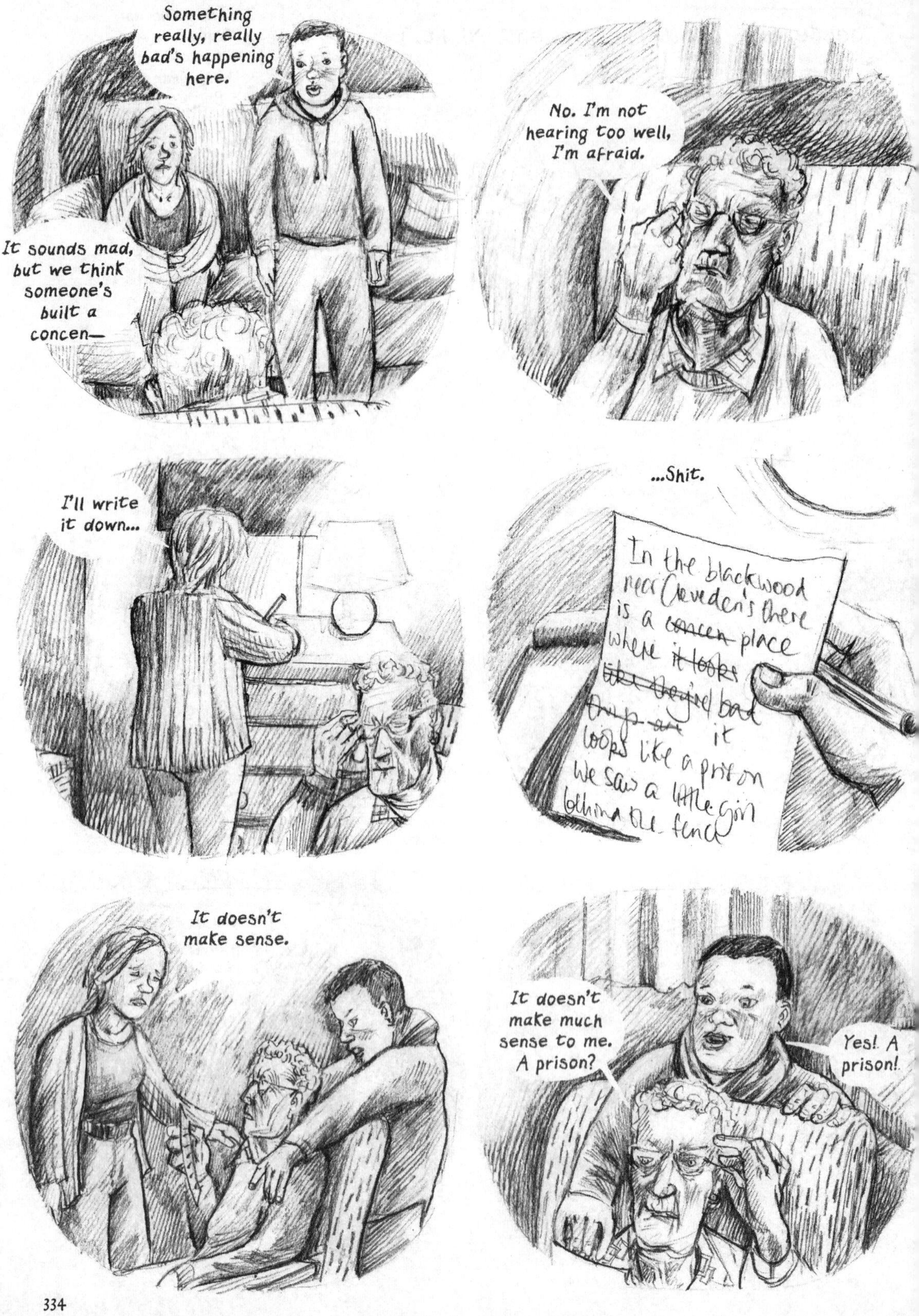
Something really, really bad's happening here.
It sounds mad, but we think someone's built a concen—
No. I'm not hearing too well, I'm afraid.
I'll write it down...
...Shit.
In the blackwood
near Clevedon's there
is a concen place
where it looks
it
looks like a prison
We saw a little girl
behind the fence
It doesn't make sense.
It doesn't make much sense to me. A prison?
Yes! A prison!

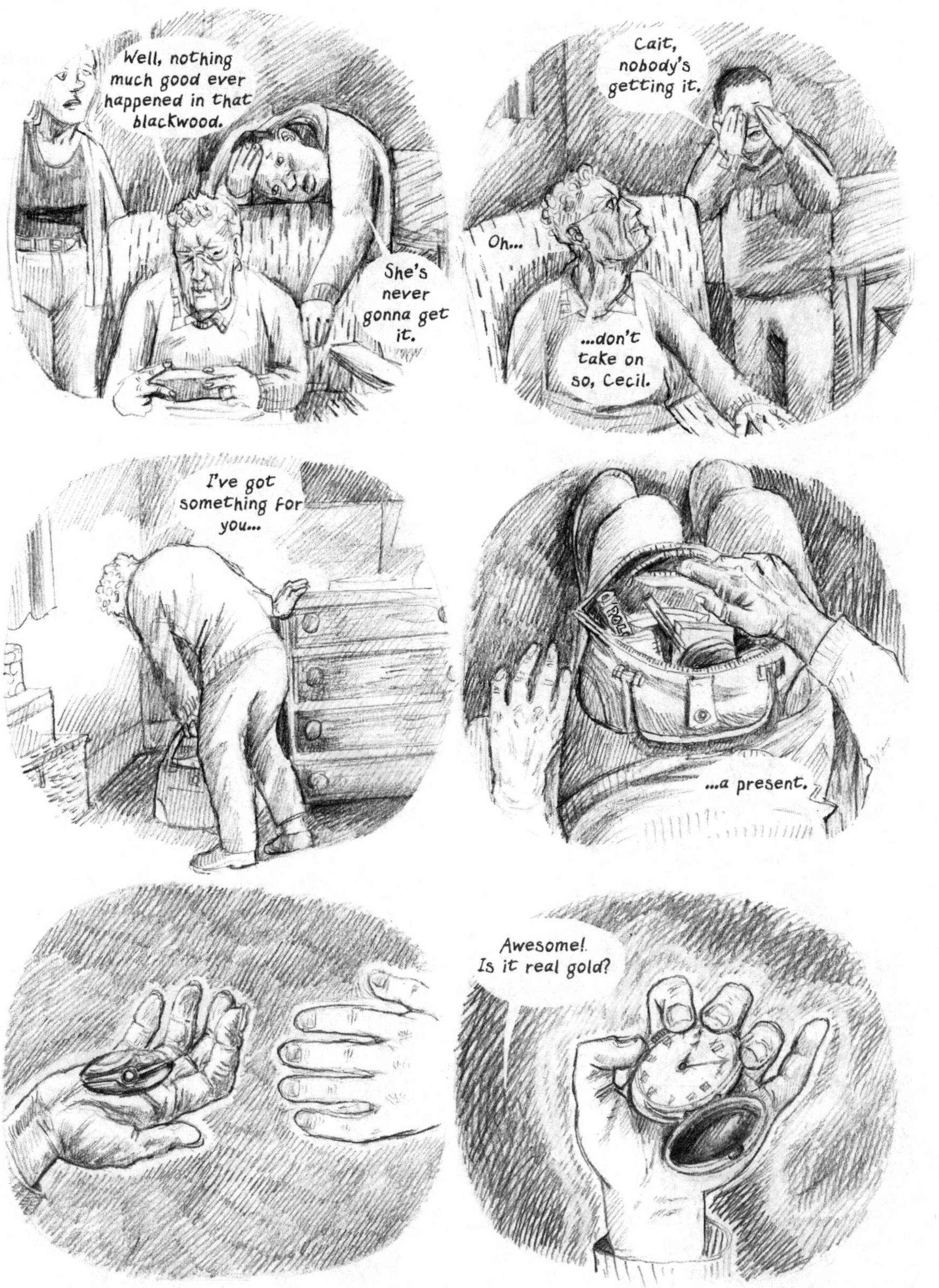
Well, nothing much good ever happened in that blackwood.
She's never gonna get it.
Cait, nobody's getting it.
Oh...
...don't take on so, Cecil.
I've got something for you...
...a present.
Awesome! Is it real gold?

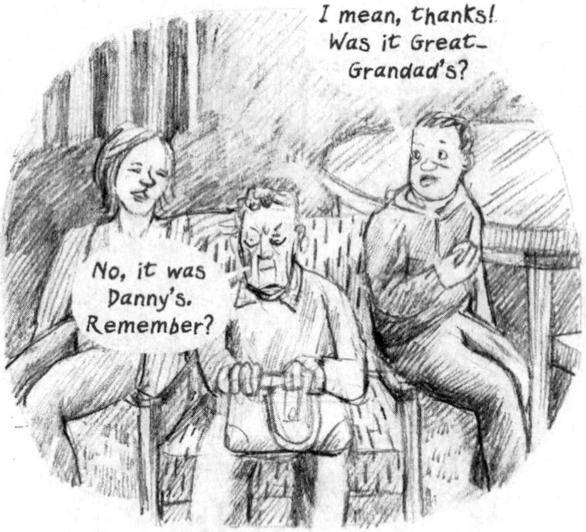
I mean, thanks! Was it Great-Grandad's?
No, it was Danny's. Remember?

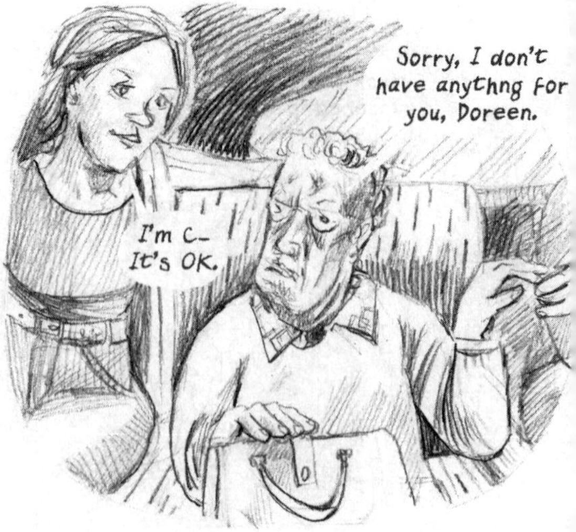
Sorry, I don't have anythng for you, Doreen.
I'm C— It's OK.

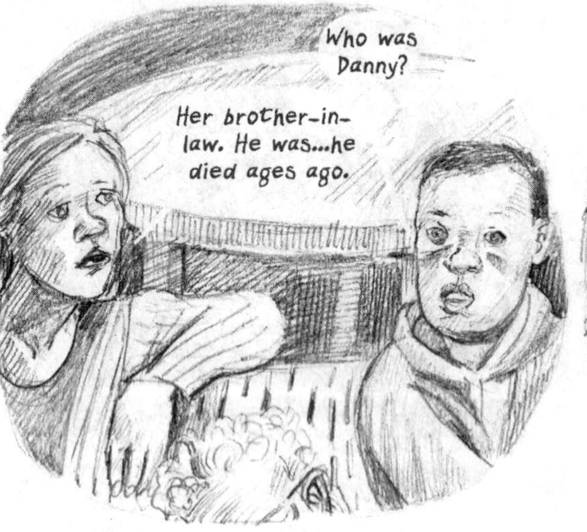
Who was Danny?
Her brother-in-law. He was...he died ages ago.

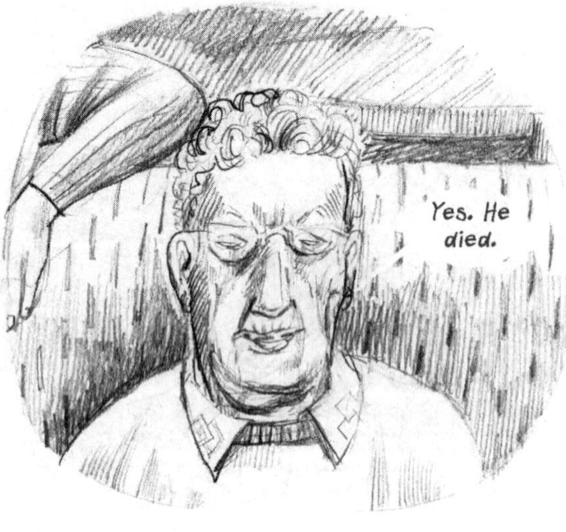
Yes. He died.

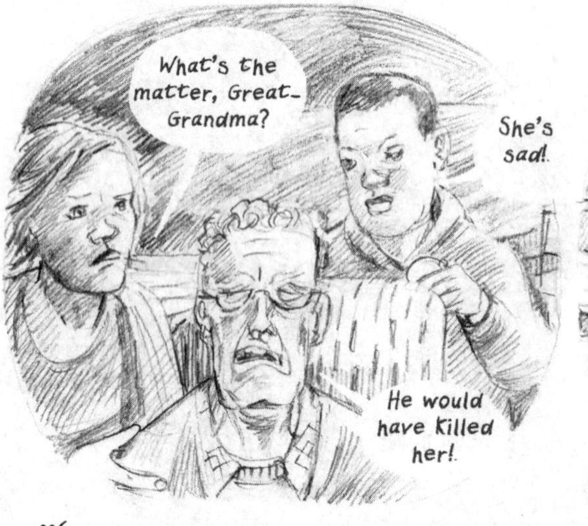
What's the matter, Great-Grandma?
She's sad!
He would have killed her!

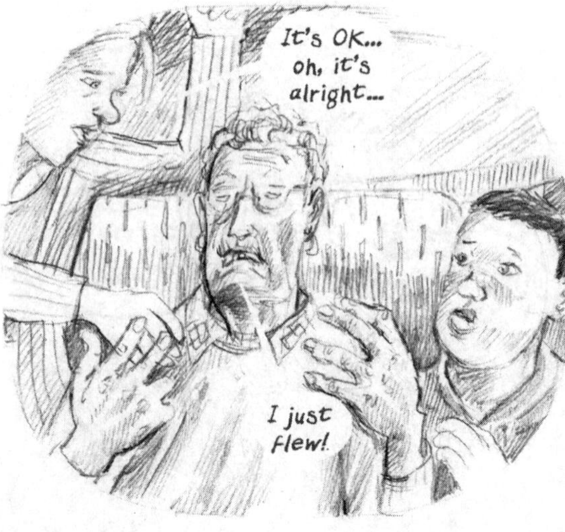
It's OK... oh, it's alright...
I just flew!

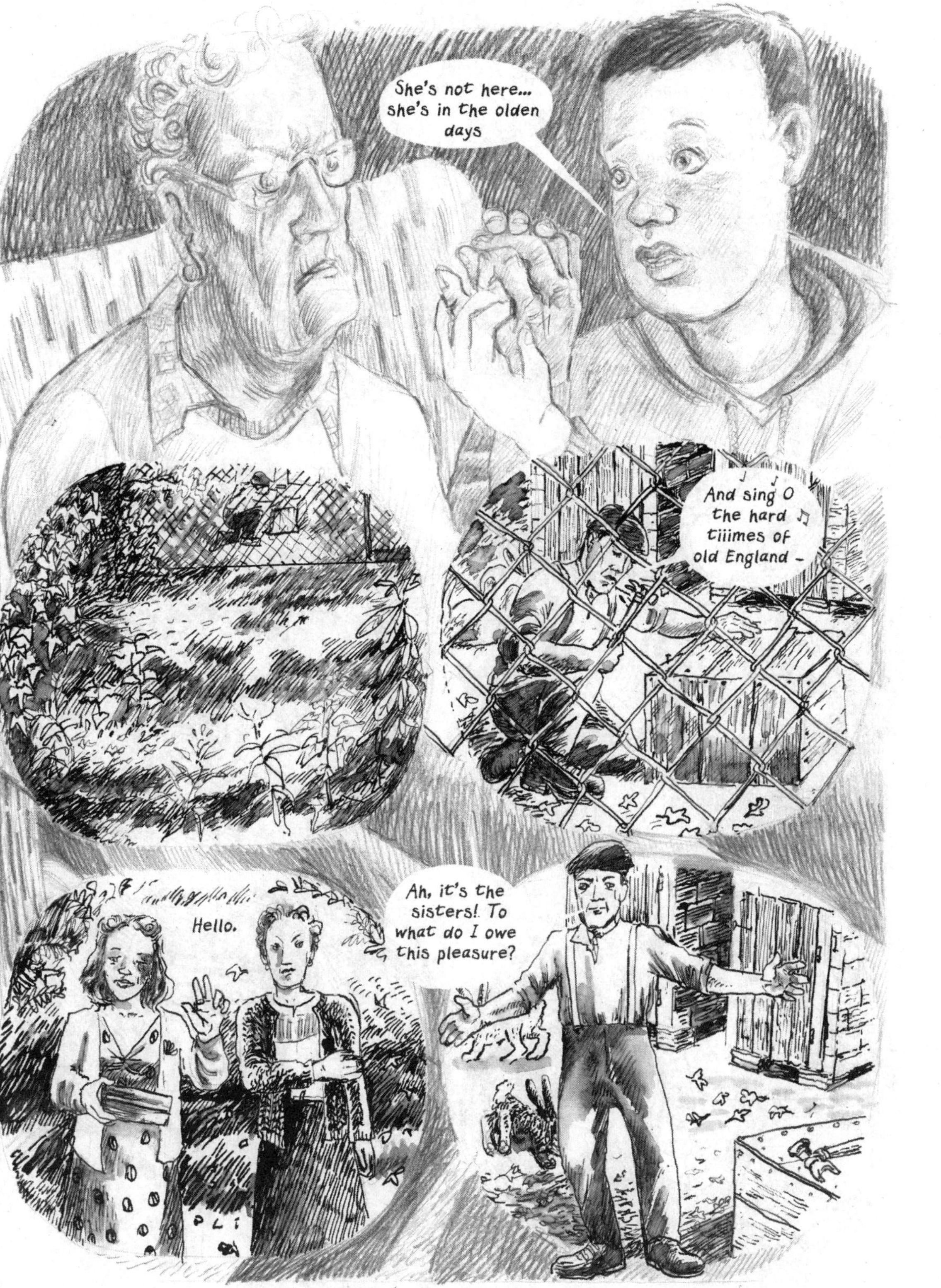
She's not here... she's in the olden days
And sing O the hard tiiimes of old England -
Hello.
Ah, it's the sisters! To what do I owe this pleasure?

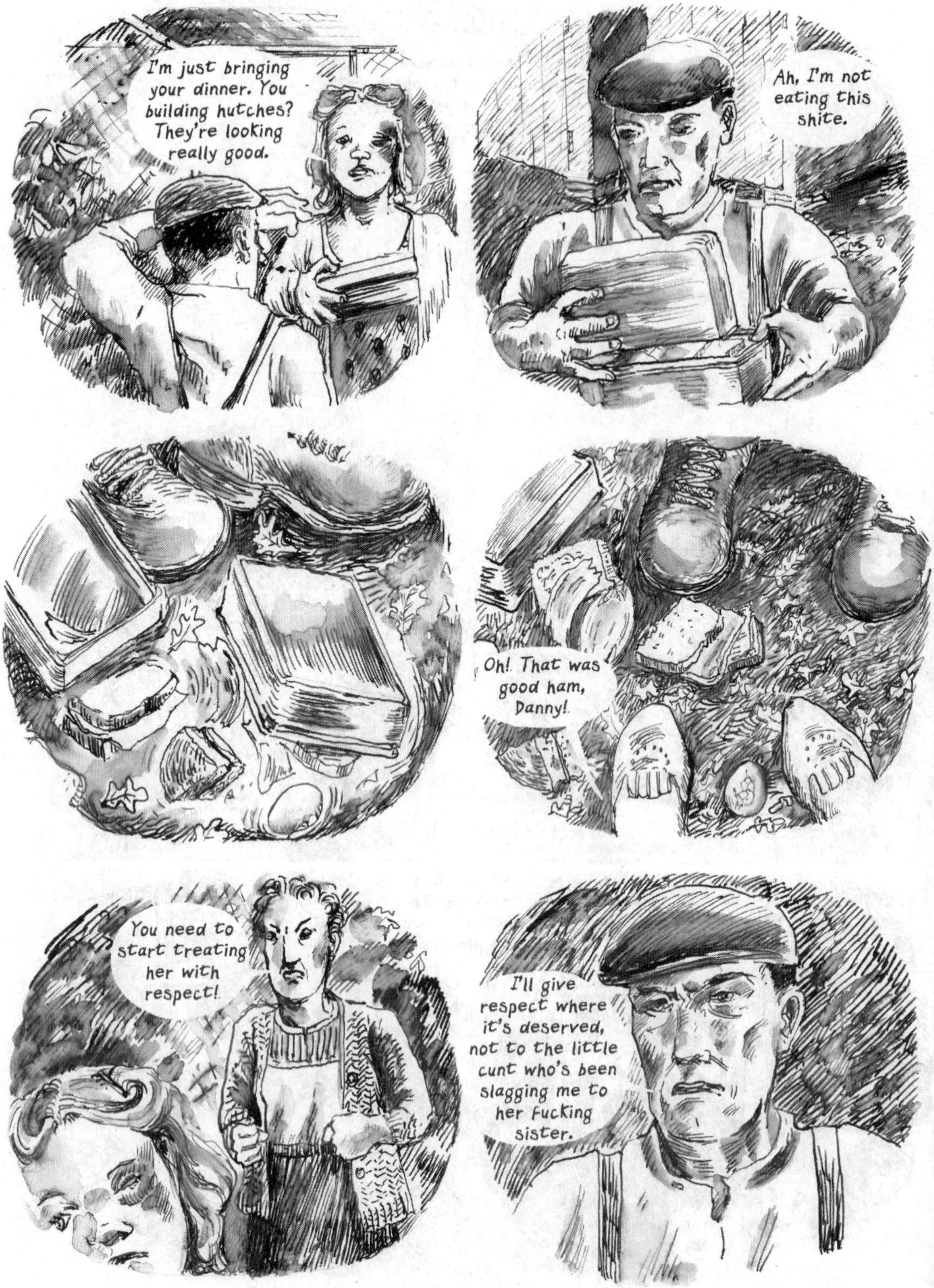
I'm just bringing your dinner. You building hutches? They're looking really good.
Ah, I'm not eating this shite.
Oh! That was good ham, Danny!
You need to start treating her with respect!
I'll give respect where it's deserved, not to the little cunt who's been slagging me to her fucking sister.

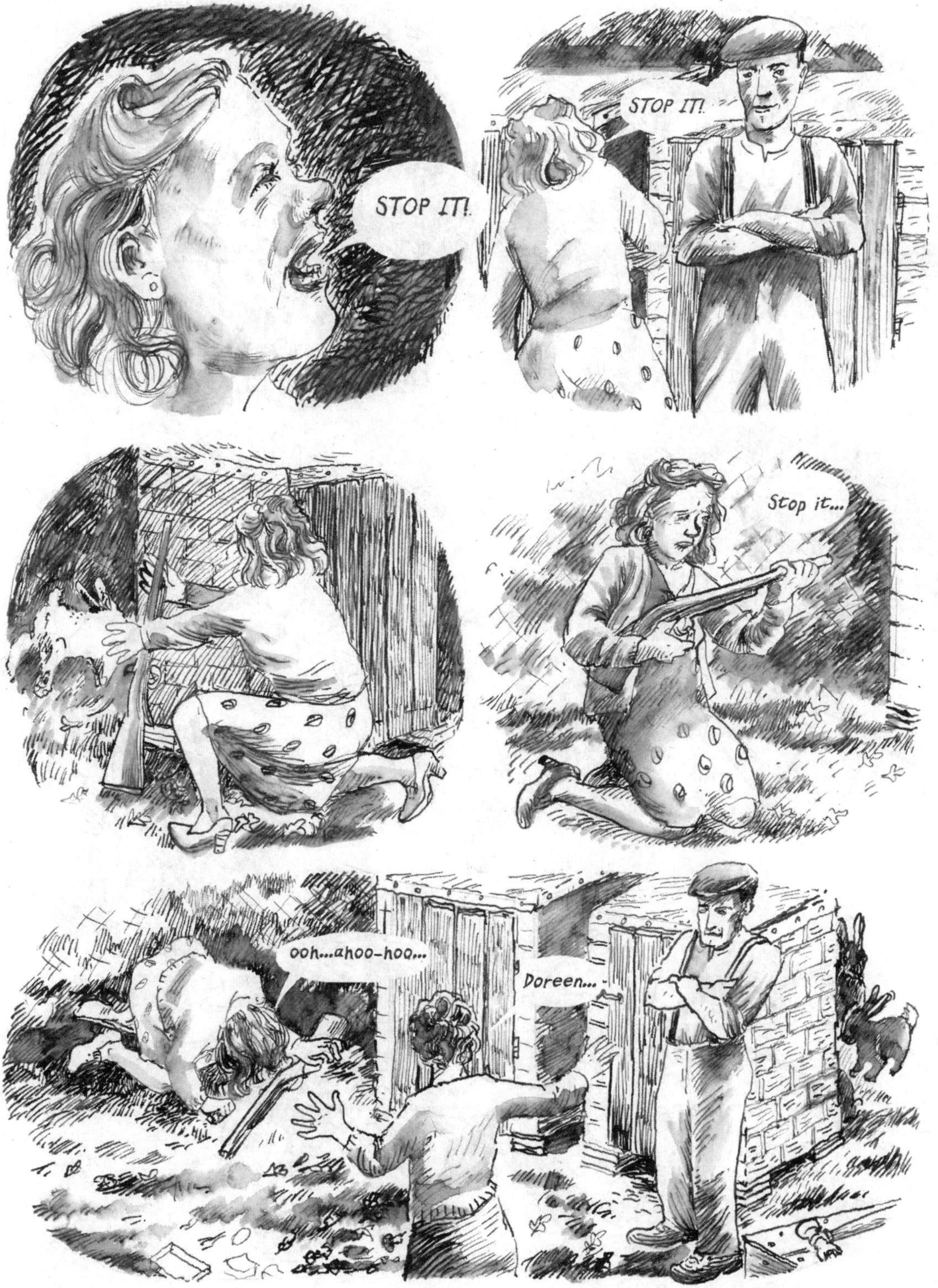
STOP IT!
STOP IT!
Stop it...
ooh...ahoo-hoo...
Doreen...

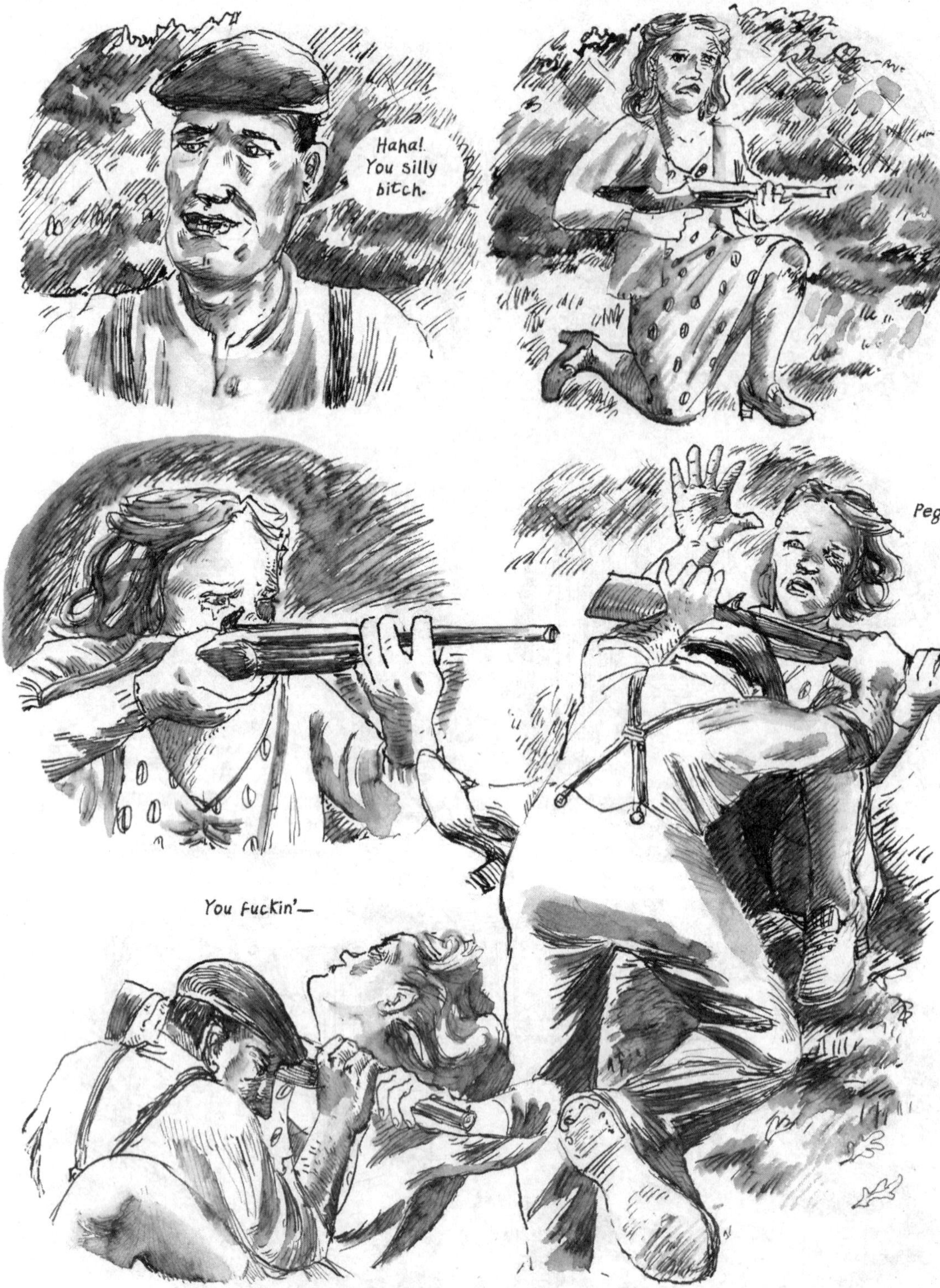
Haha! You silly bitch.
Peg!
You fuckin'—

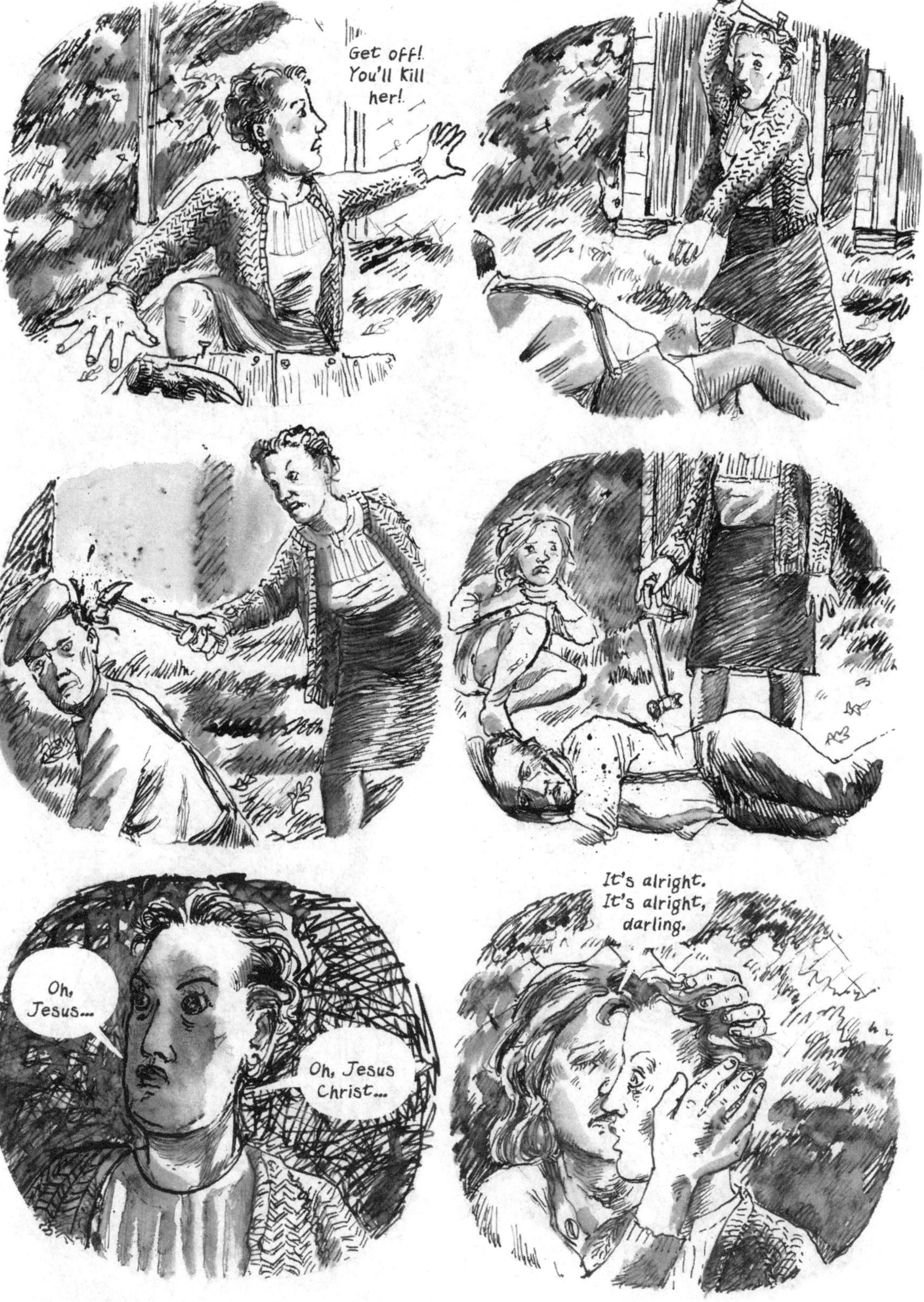

Get off! You'll kill her!
Oh, Jesus...
Oh, Jesus Christ...
It's alright. It's alright, darling.

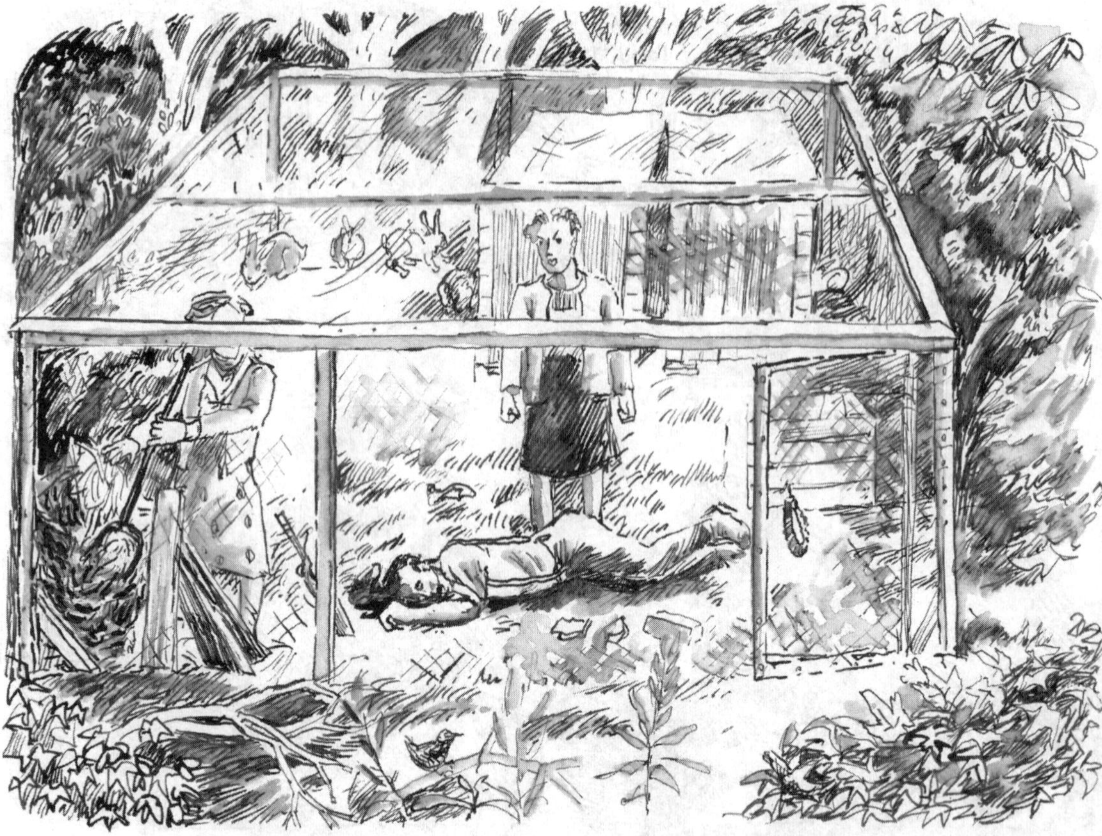

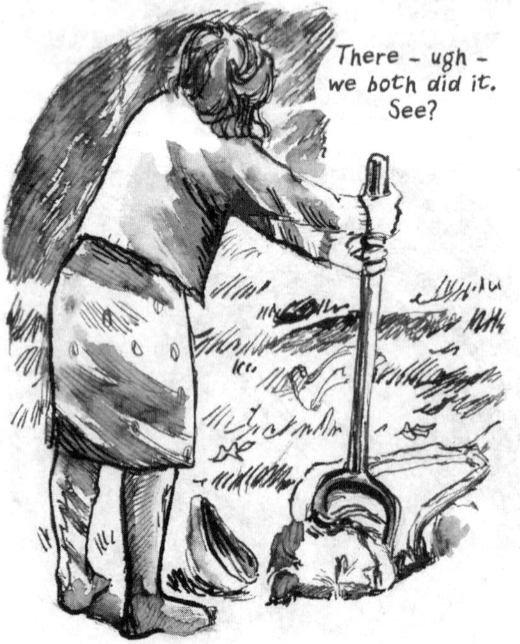
There - ugh - we both did it. See?

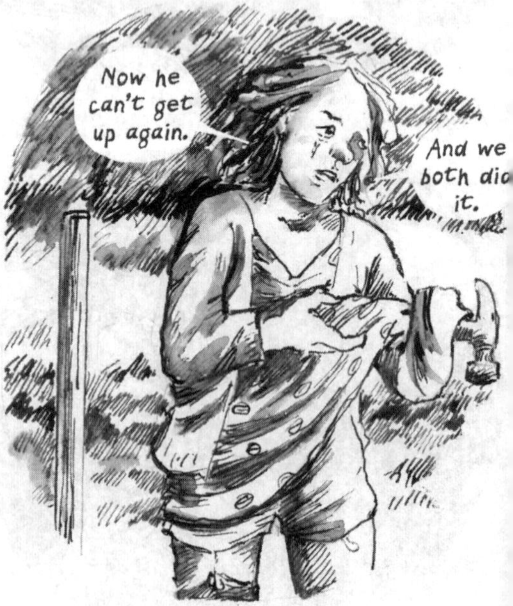
Now he can't get up again.
And we both did it.

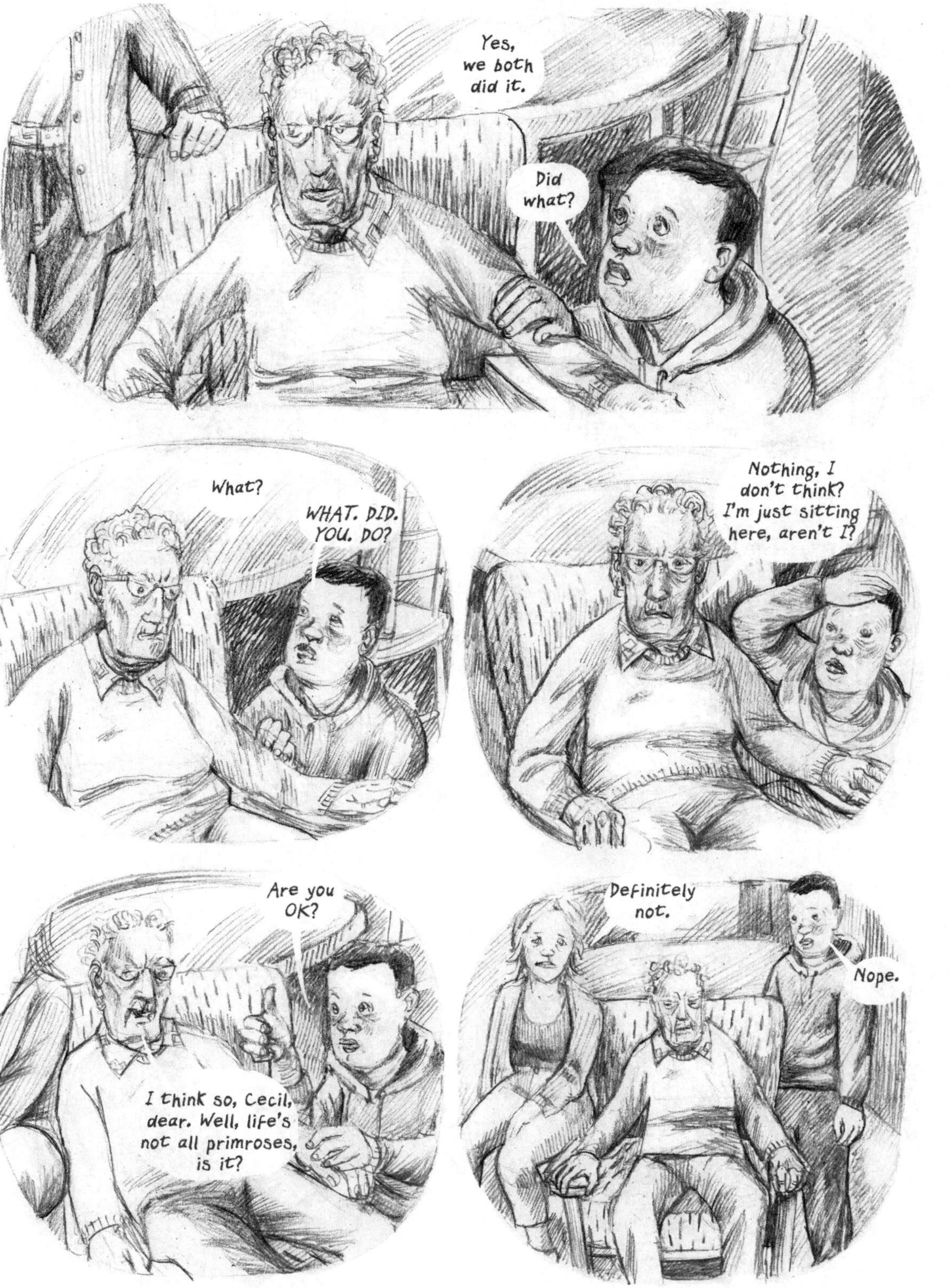
Yes, we both did it.
Did what?
What?
WHAT. DID. YOU. DO?
Nothing, I don't think? I'm just sitting here, aren't I?
Are you OK?
I think so, Cecil, dear. Well, life's not all primroses, is it?
Definitely not.
Nope.

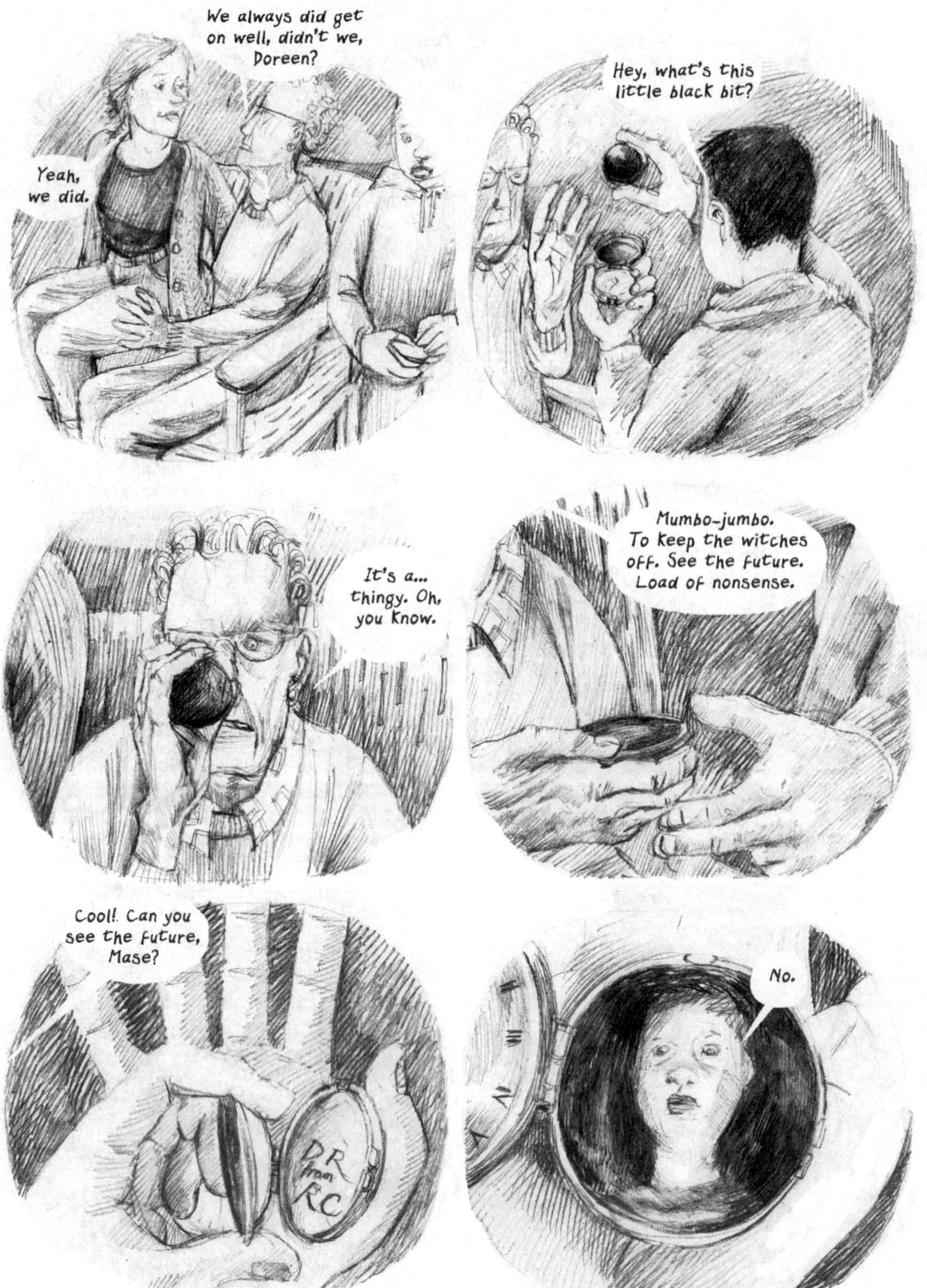
We always did get on well, didn't we, Doreen?
Yeah, we did.
Hey, what's this little black bit?
It's a... thingy. Oh, you know.
Mumbo-jumbo. To keep the witches off. See the future. Load of nonsense.
Cool! Can you see the future, Mase?
DR from RC
No.

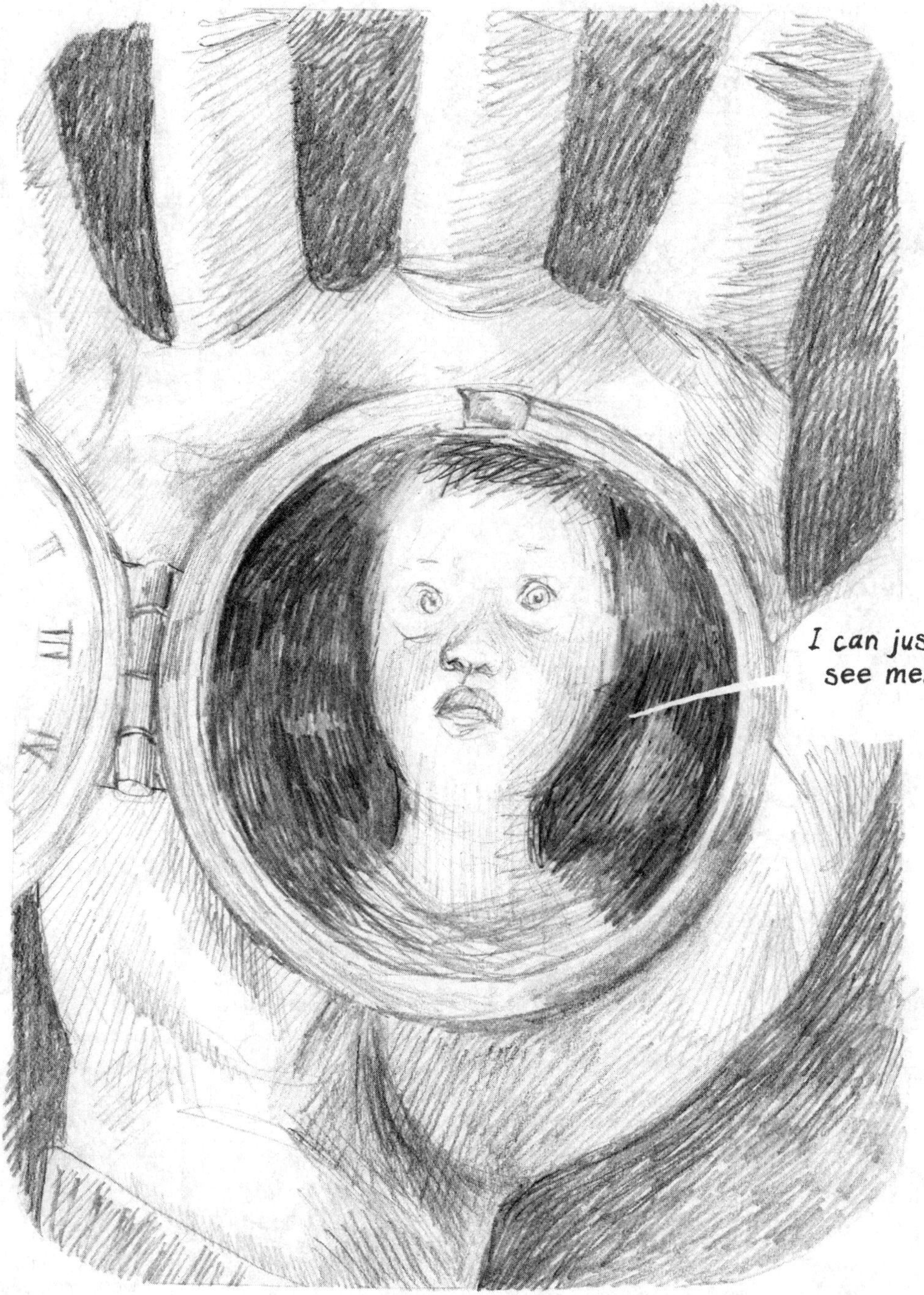
I can just see me.

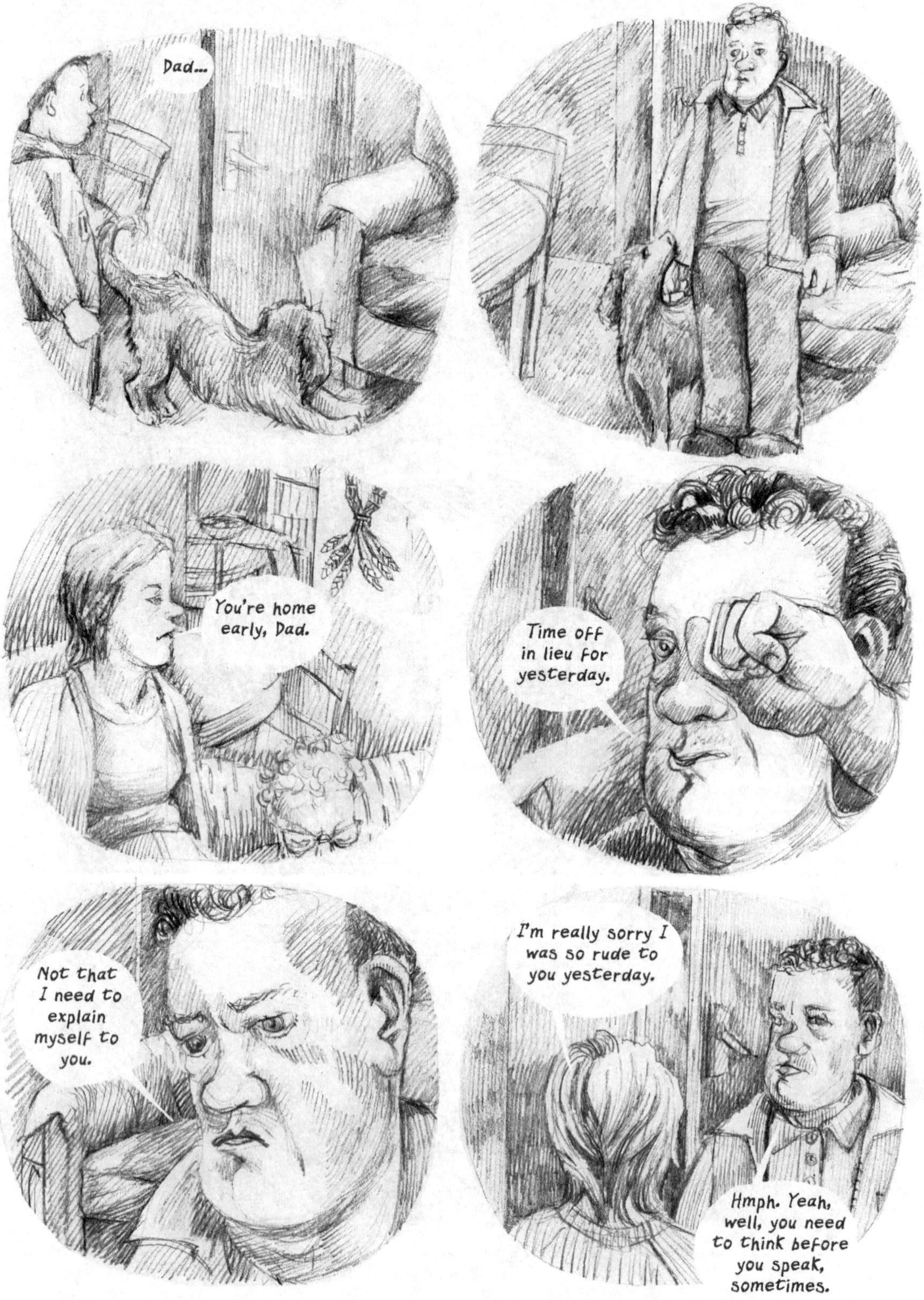
Dad...
You're home early, Dad.
Time off in lieu for yesterday.
Not that I need to explain myself to you.
I'm really sorry I was so rude to you yesterday.
Hmph. Yeah, well, you need to think before you speak, sometimes.

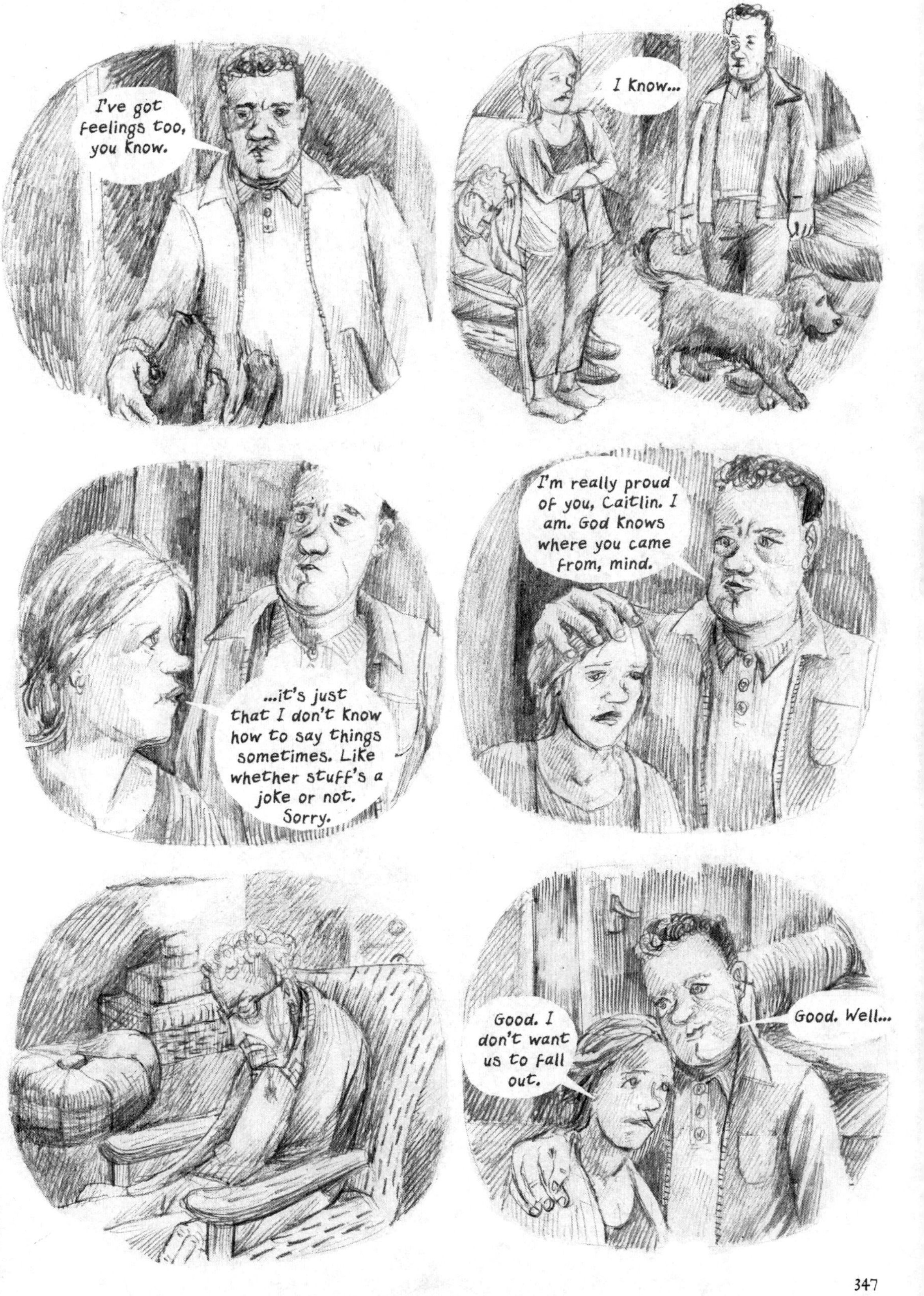
I've got feelings too, you know.
I know...
...it's just that I don't know how to say things sometimes. Like whether stuff's a joke or not. Sorry.
I'm really proud of you, Caitlin. I am. God knows where you came from, mind.
Good. I don't want us to fall out.
Good. Well...

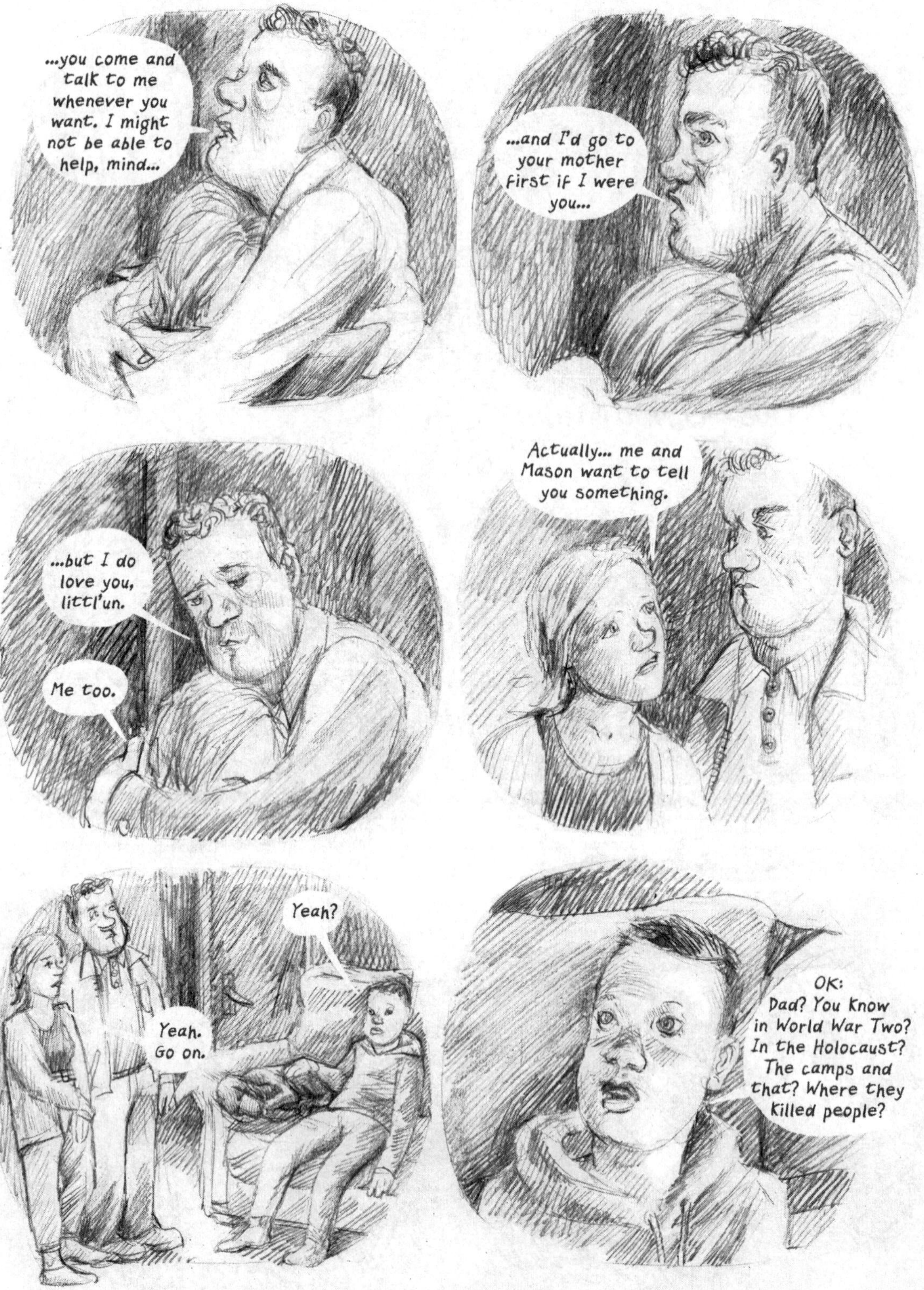
...you come and talk to me whenever you want. I might not be able to help, mind...
...and I'd go to your mother first if I were you...
...but I do love you, littl'un.
Me too.
Actually... me and Mason want to tell you something.
Yeah?
Yeah. Go on.
OK:
Dad? You know in World War Two? In the Holocaust? The camps and that? Where they killed people?

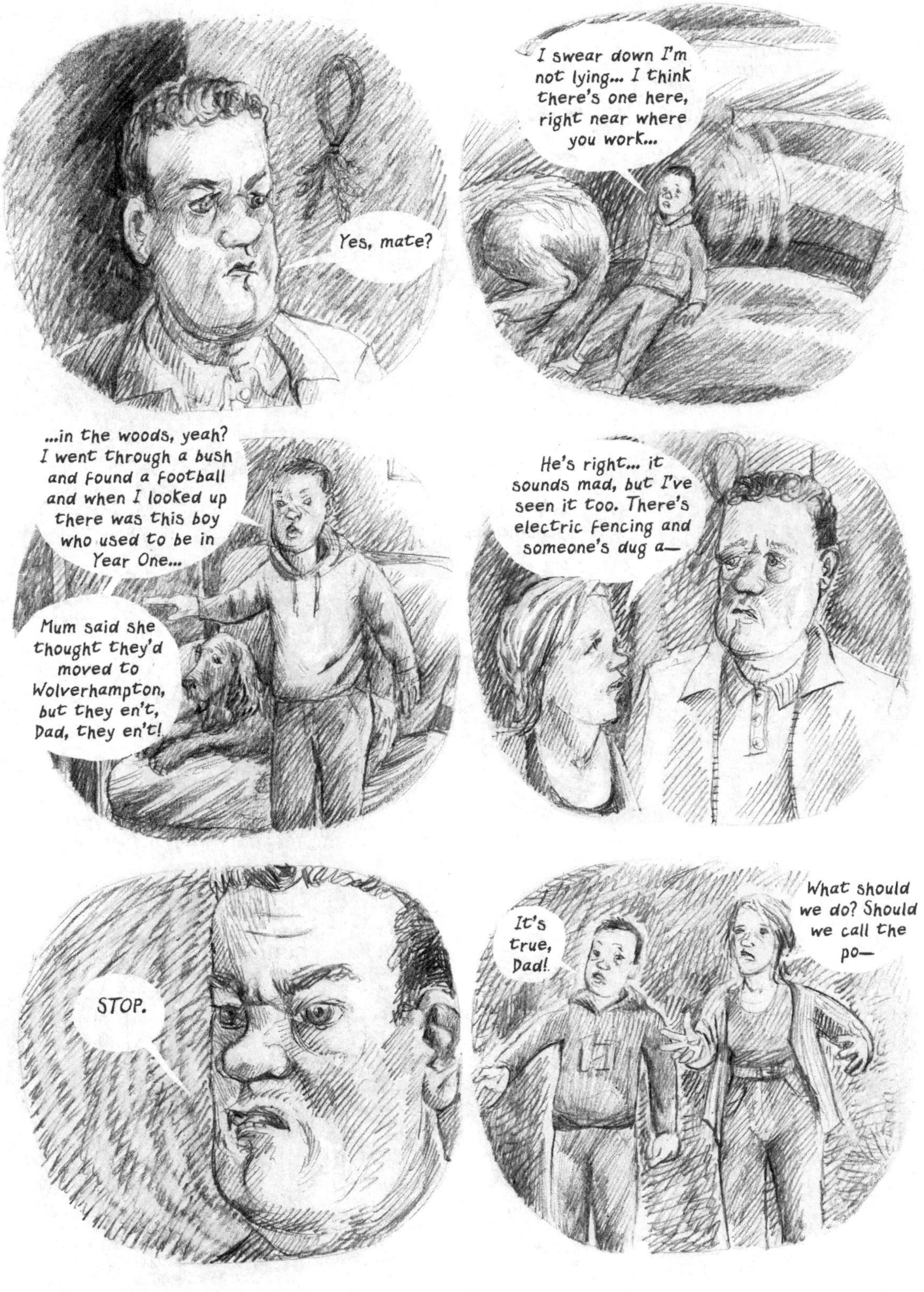
Yes, mate?
I swear down I'm not lying... I think there's one here, right near where you work...
...in the woods, yeah? I went through a bush and found a football and when I looked up there was this boy who used to be in Year One...
Mum said she thought they'd moved to Wolverhampton, but they en't, Dad, they en't!
He's right... it sounds mad, but I've seen it too. There's electric fencing and someone's dug a—
STOP.
It's true, Dad!
What should we do? Should we call the po—

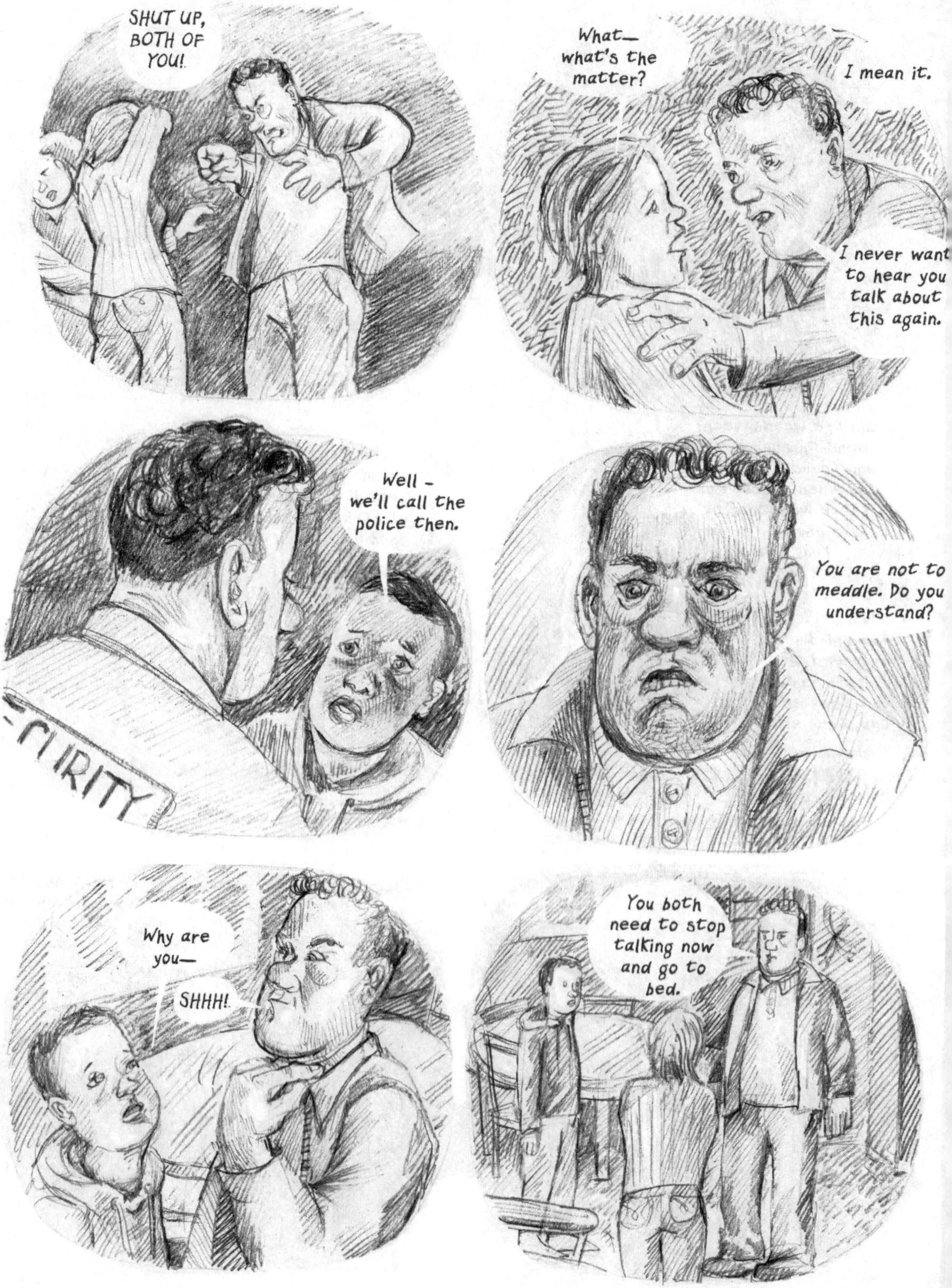
SHUT UP, BOTH OF YOU!.
What— what's the matter?
I mean it.
I never want to hear you talk about this again.
Well - we'll call the police then.
You are not to meddle. Do you understand?
Why are you—
SHHH!
You both need to stop talking now and go to bed.

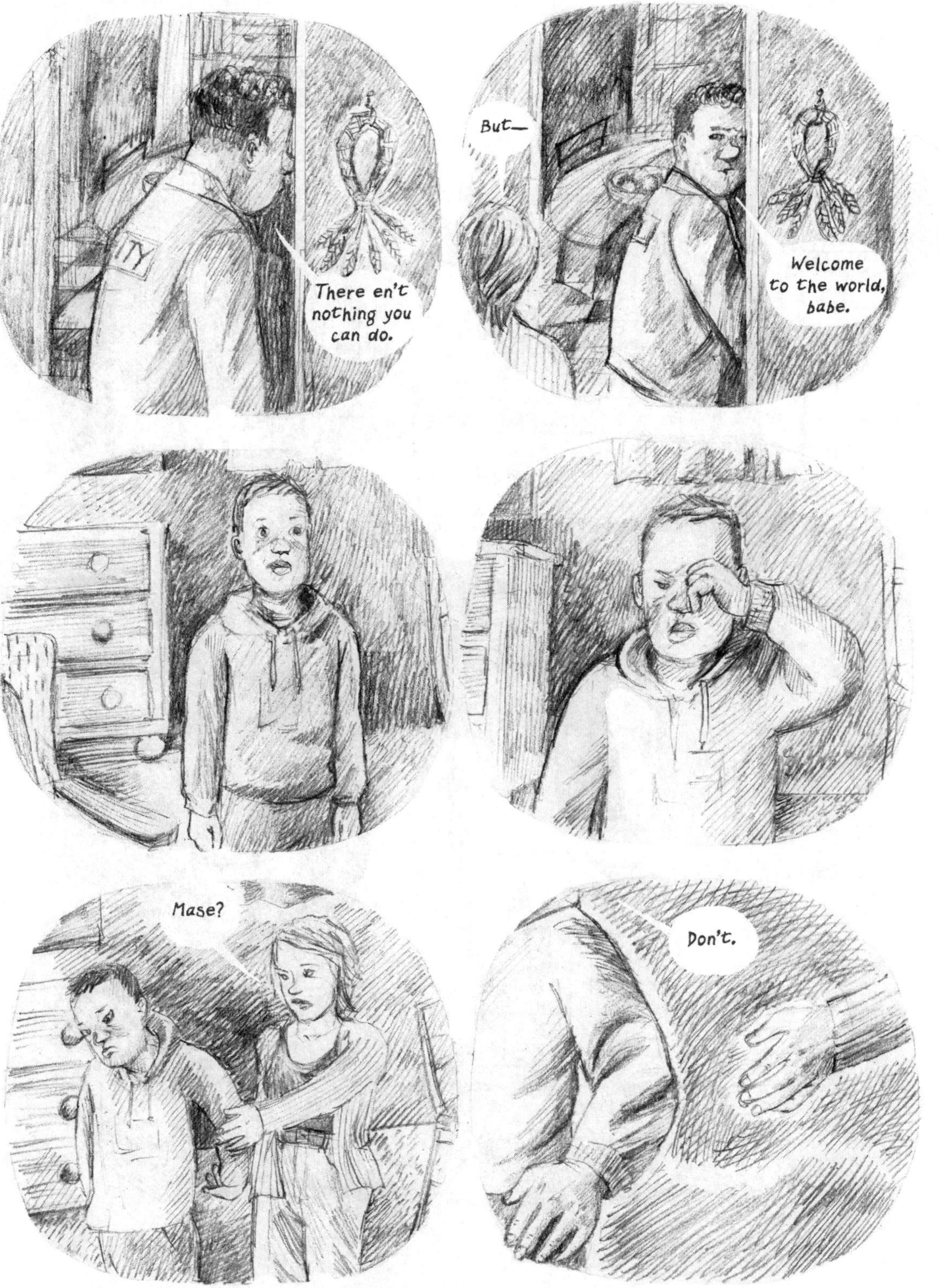
There en't nothing you can do.
But—
Welcome to the world, babe.
Mase?
Don't.

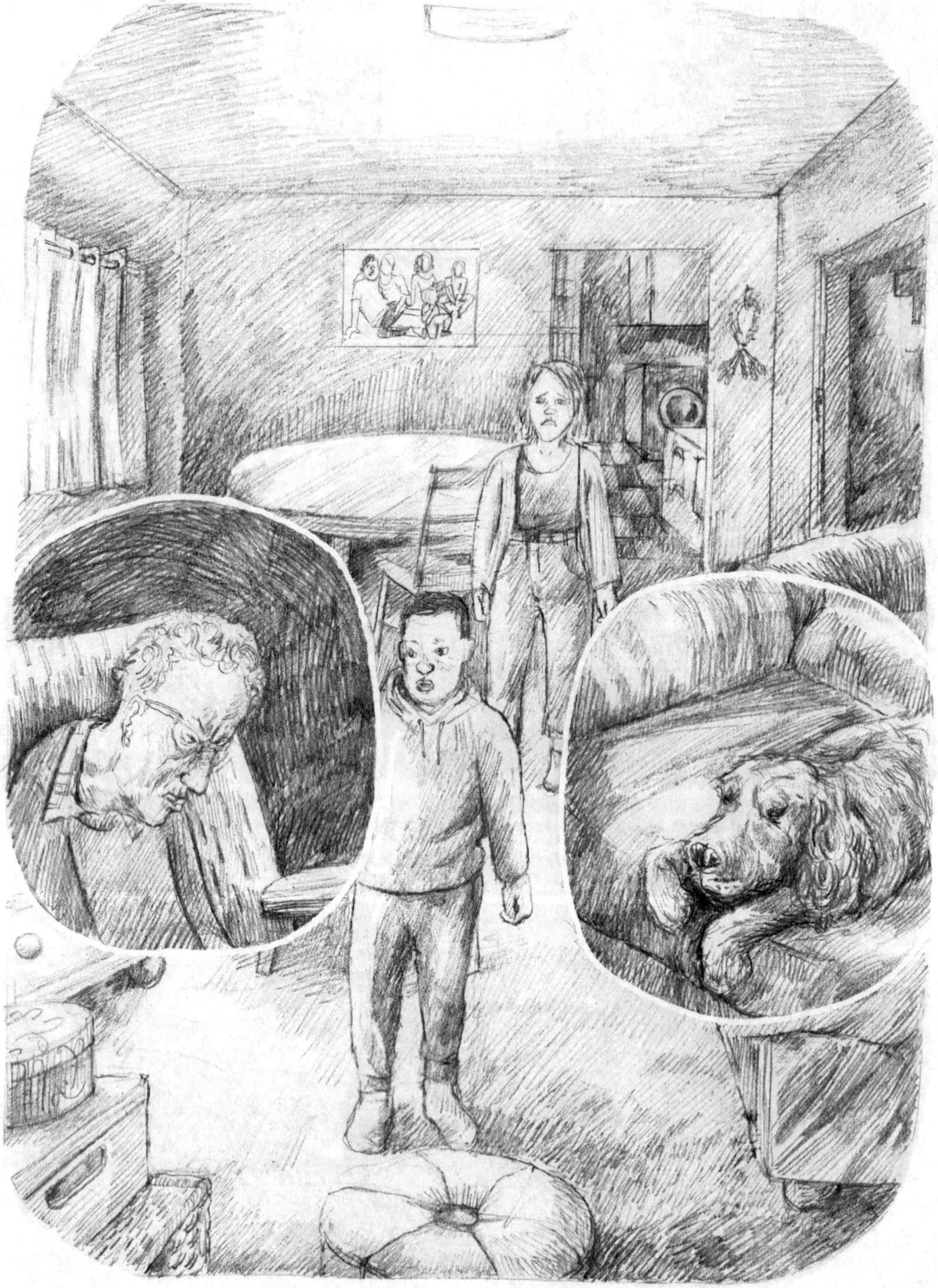

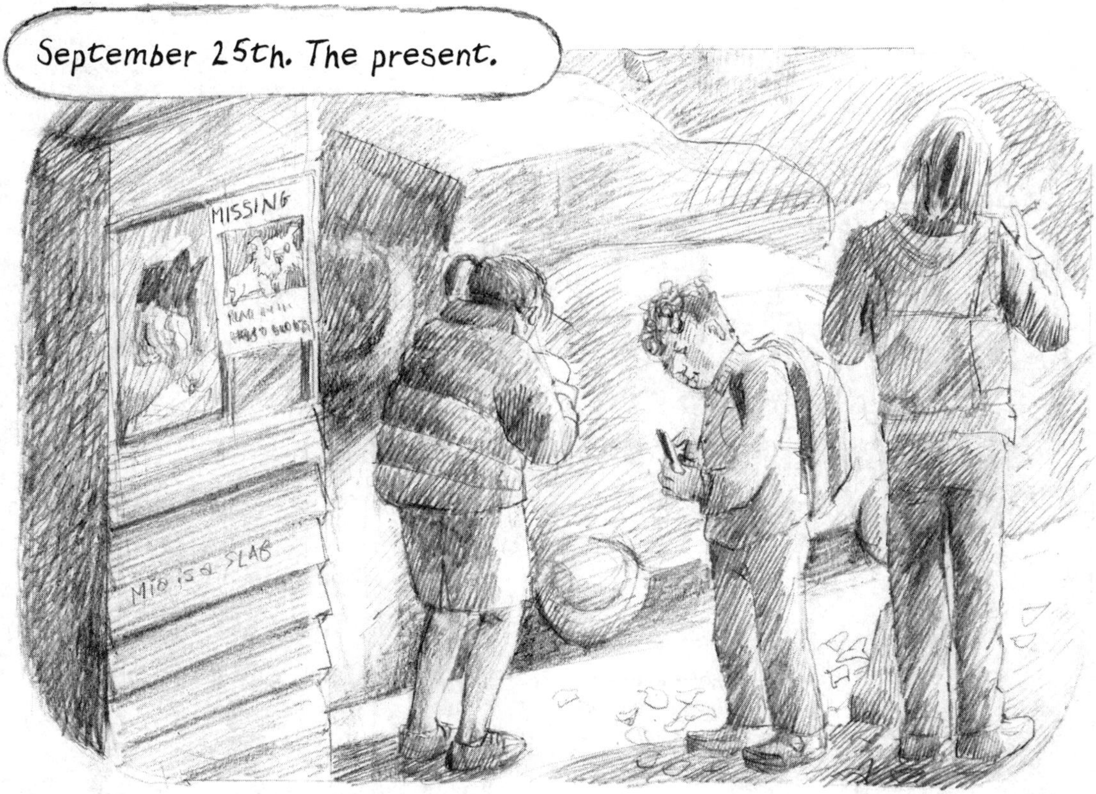
September 25th. The present.
MISSING
MIA IS A SLAG

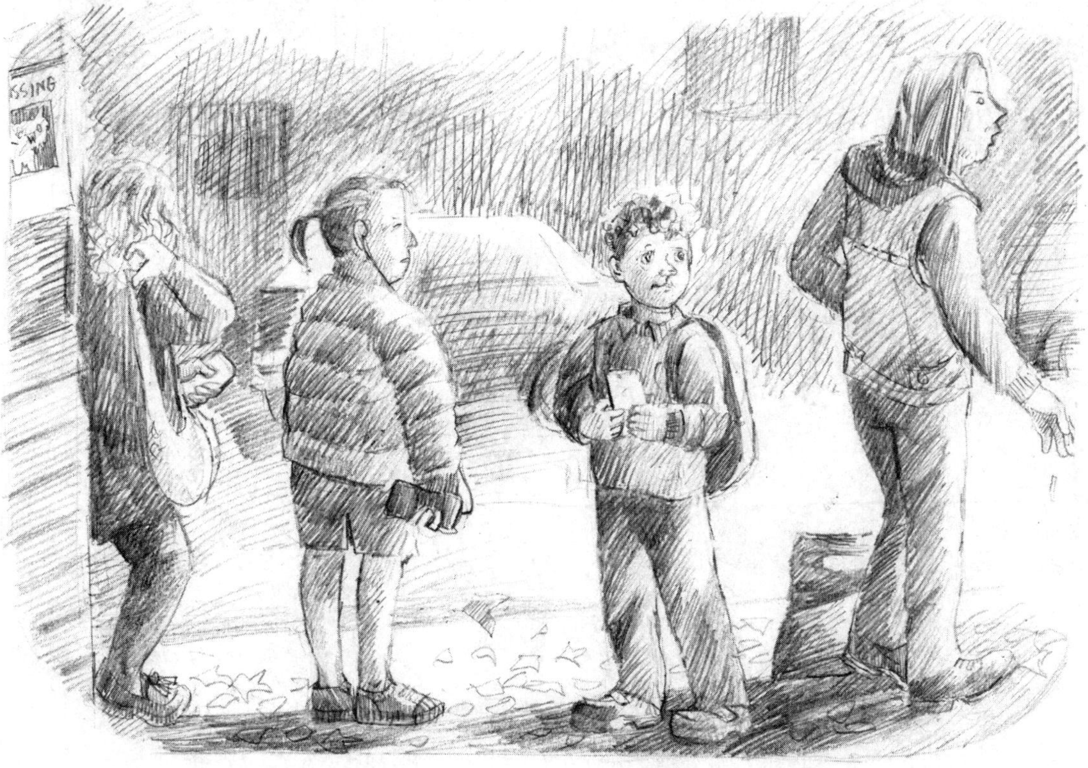
MISSING

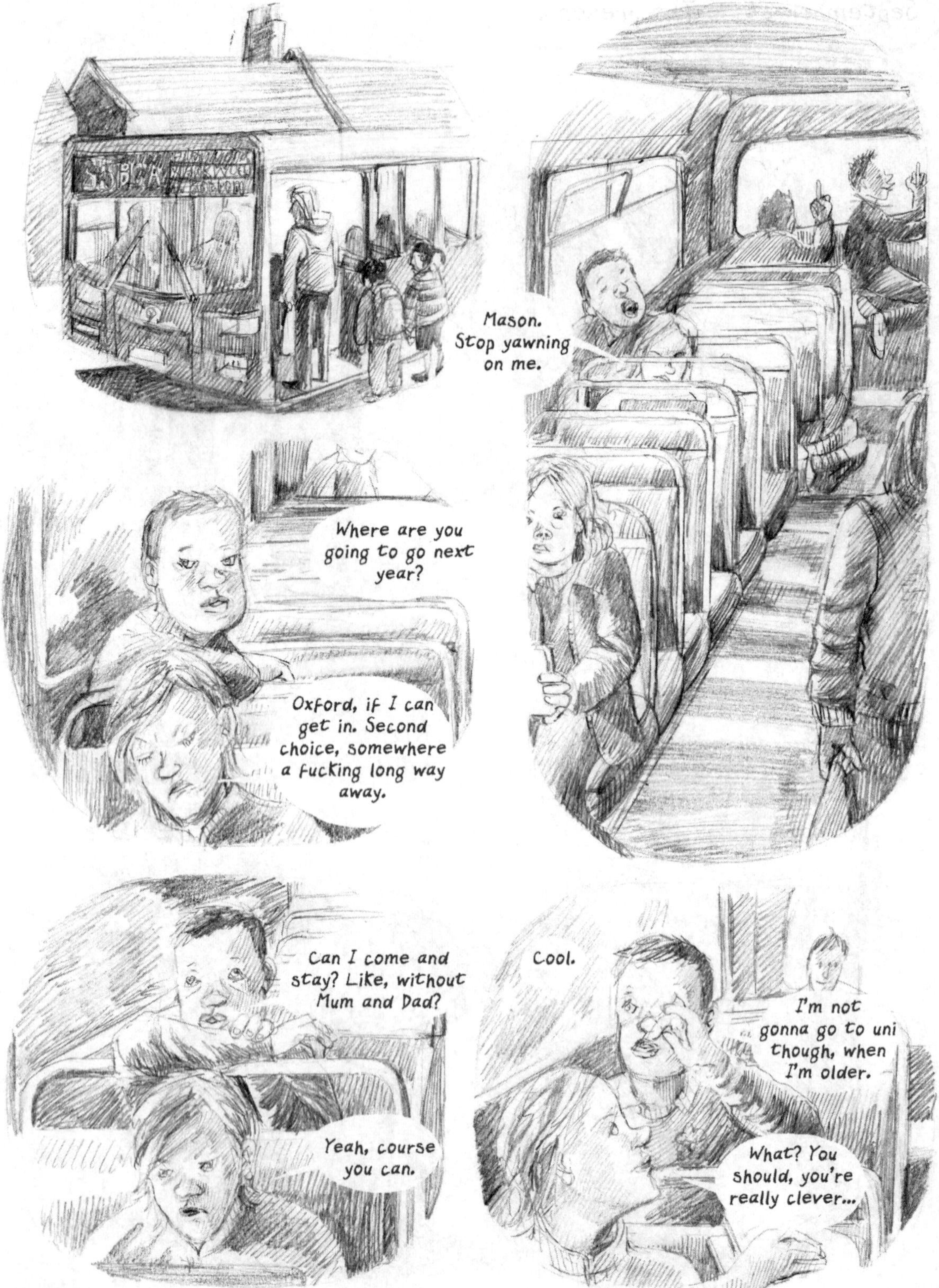
Mason. Stop yawning on me.
Where are you going to go next year?
Oxford, if I can get in. Second choice, somewhere a fucking long way away.
Can I come and stay? Like, without Mum and Dad?
Yeah, course you can.
Cool.
I'm not gonna go to uni though, when I'm older.
What? You should, you're really clever...

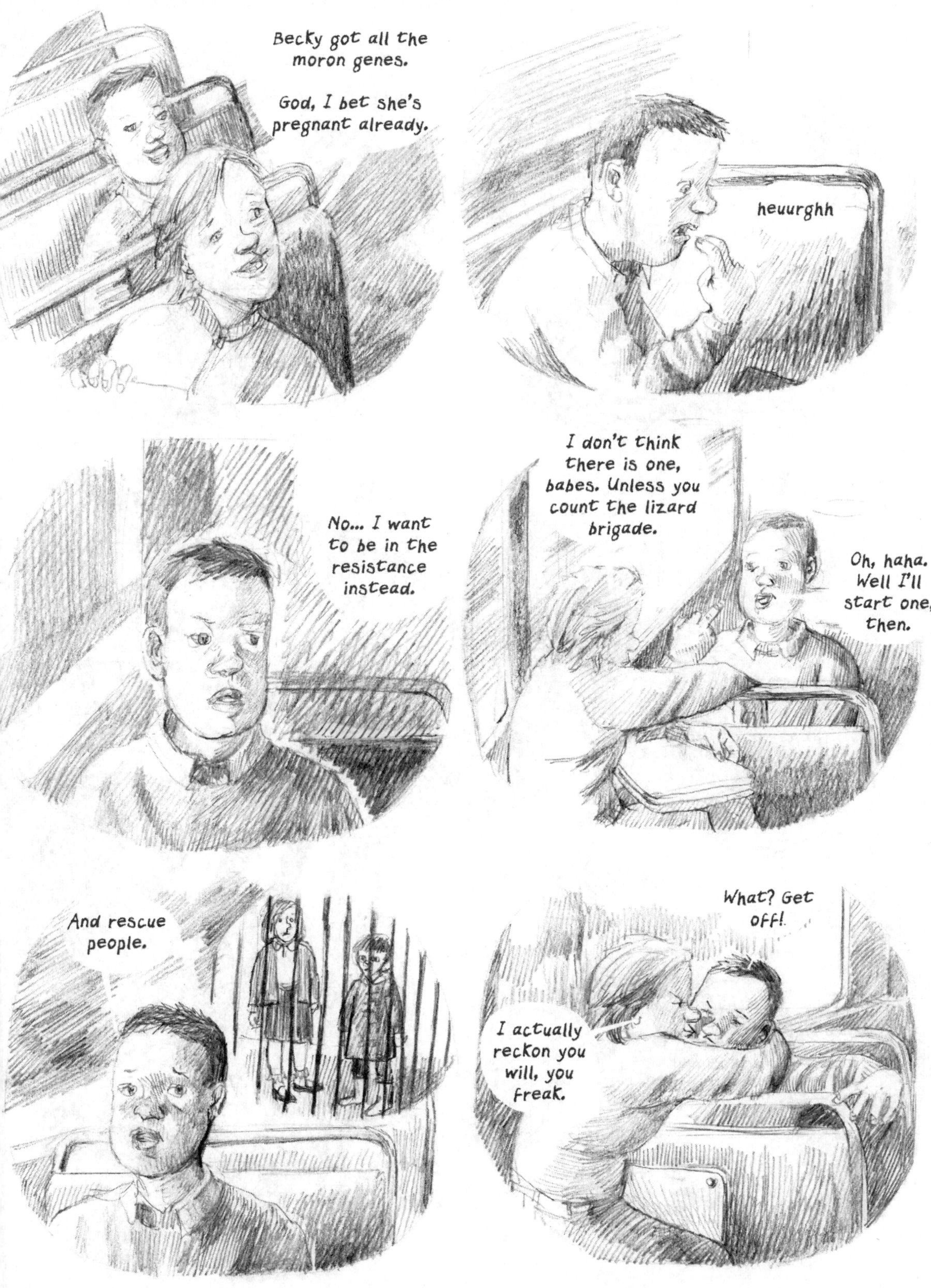
Becky got all the moron genes.
God, I bet she's pregnant already.
heuurghh
No... I want to be in the resistance instead.
I don't think there is one, babes. Unless you count the lizard brigade.
Oh, haha. Well I'll start one, then.
And rescue people.
What? Get off!
I actually reckon you will, you freak.

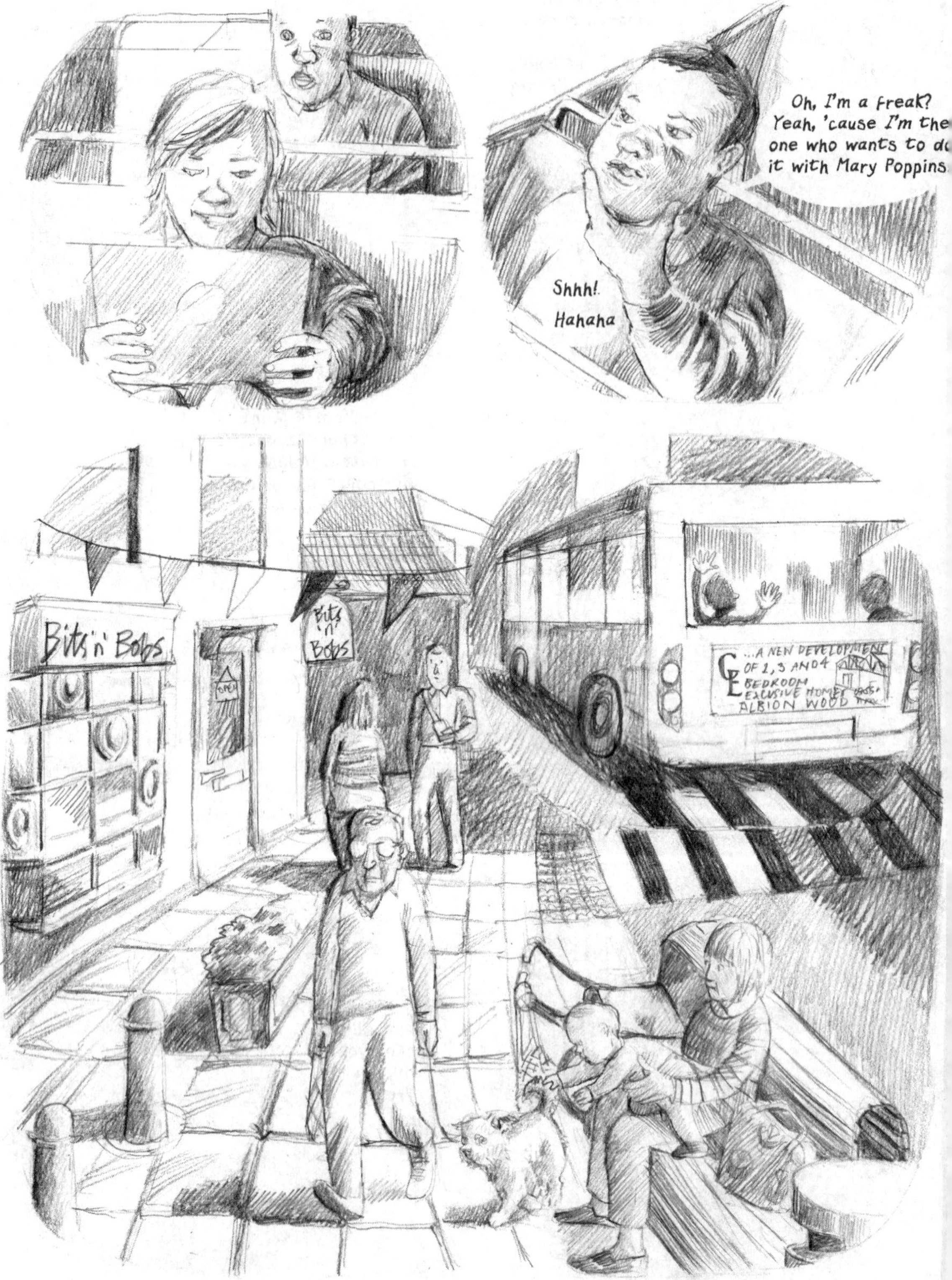
Oh, I'm a freak? Yeah, 'cause I'm the one who wants to d it with Mary Poppins.
Shhh!
Hahaha
Bits 'n' Bobs
OPEN
Bits 'n' Bobs
...A NEW DEVELOPMENT OF 1, 3 AND 4 BEDROOM EXCLUSIVE HOMES
ALBION WOOD

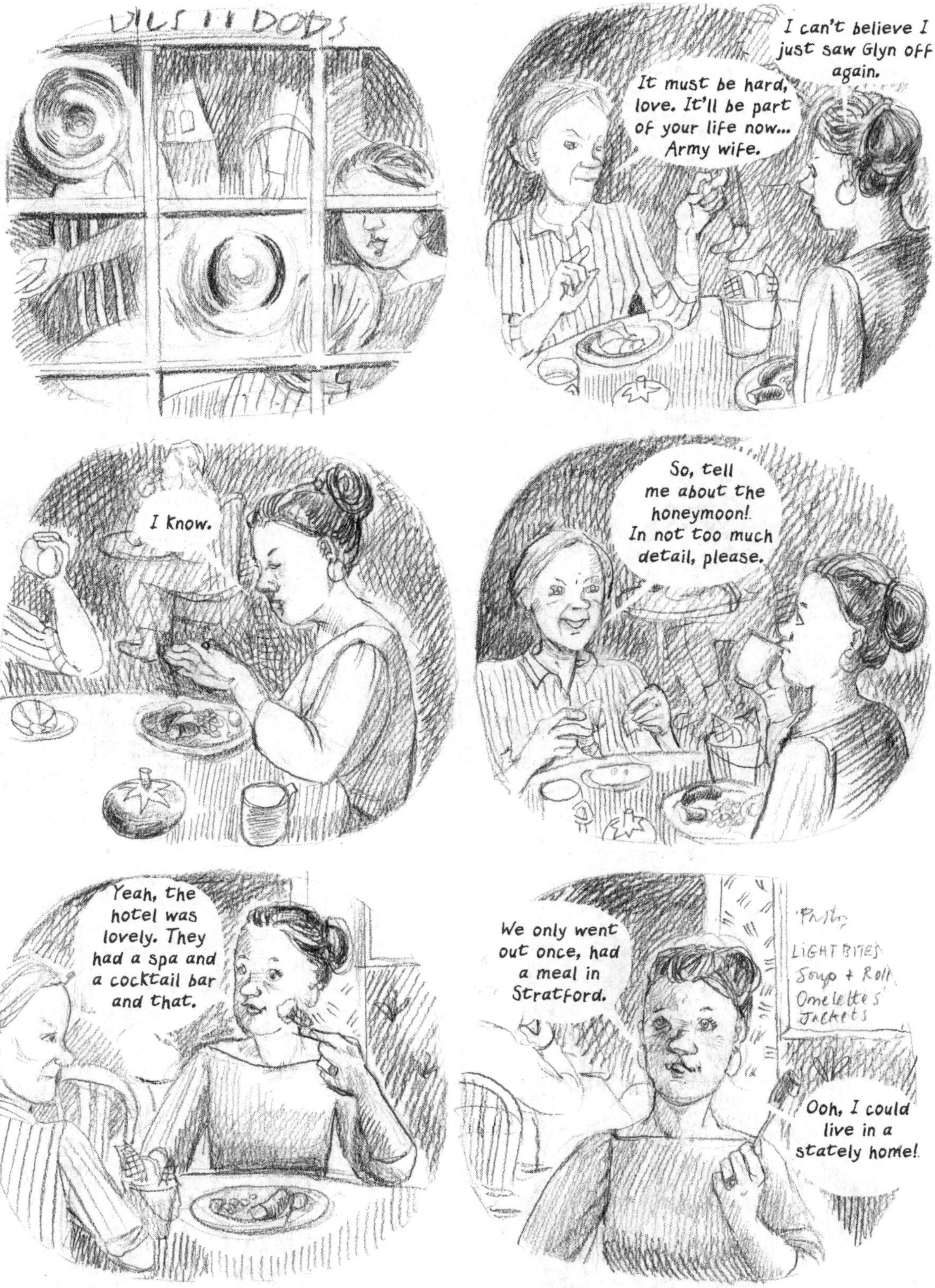
I can't believe I just saw Glyn off again.
It must be hard, love. It'll be part of your life now... Army wife.
I know.
So, tell me about the honeymoon! In not too much detail, please.
Yeah, the hotel was lovely. They had a spa and a cocktail bar and that.
We only went out once, had a meal in Stratford.
LIGHT BITES
Omelettes
Jackets
Ooh, I could live in a stately home!

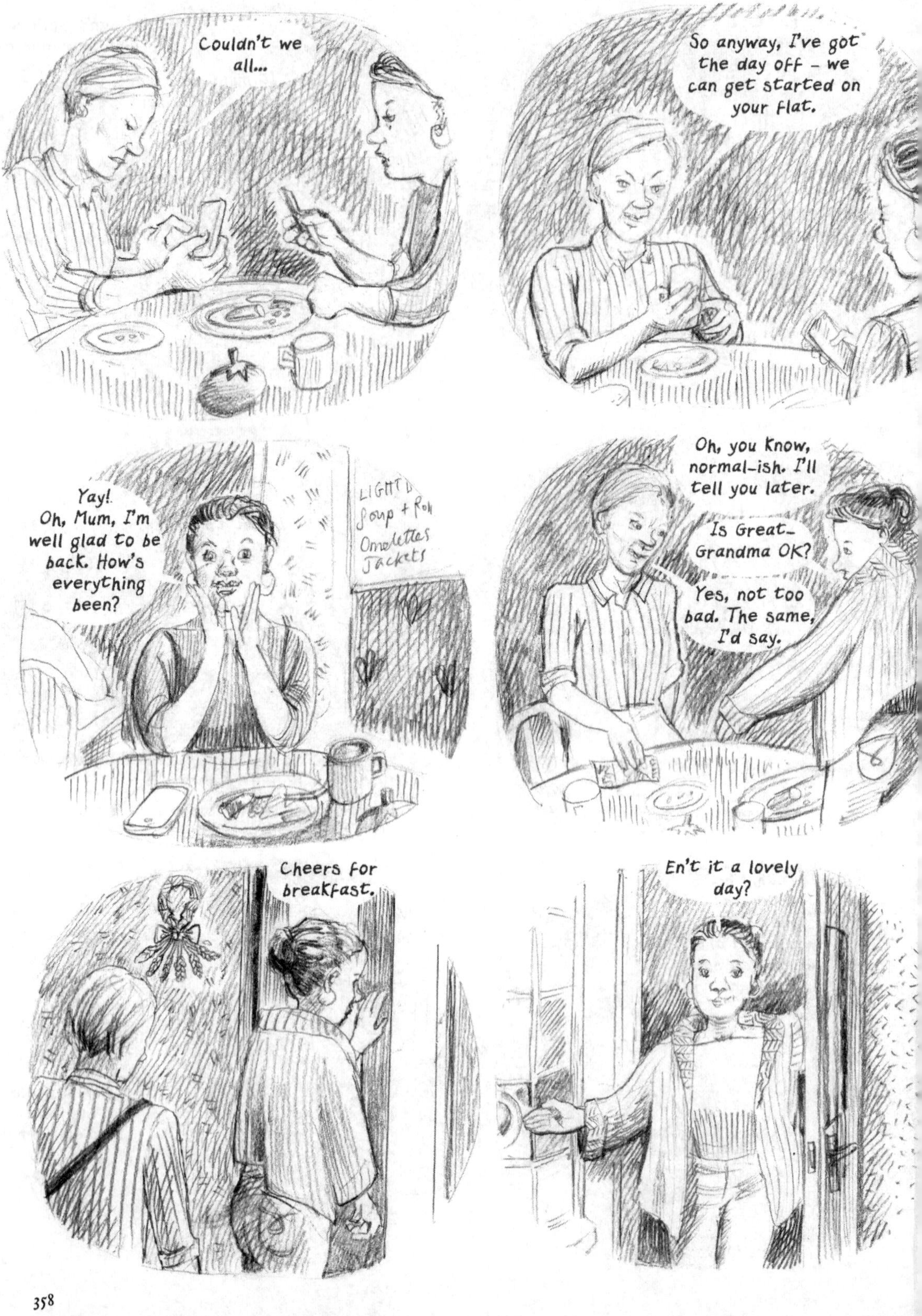
Couldn't we all...
So anyway, I've got the day off – we can get started on your flat.
Yay! Oh, Mum, I'm well glad to be back. How's everything been?
Omelettes
Jackets
Oh, you know, normal-ish. I'll tell you later.
Is Great-Grandma OK?
Yes, not too bad. The same, I'd say.
Cheers for breakfast.
En't it a lovely day?

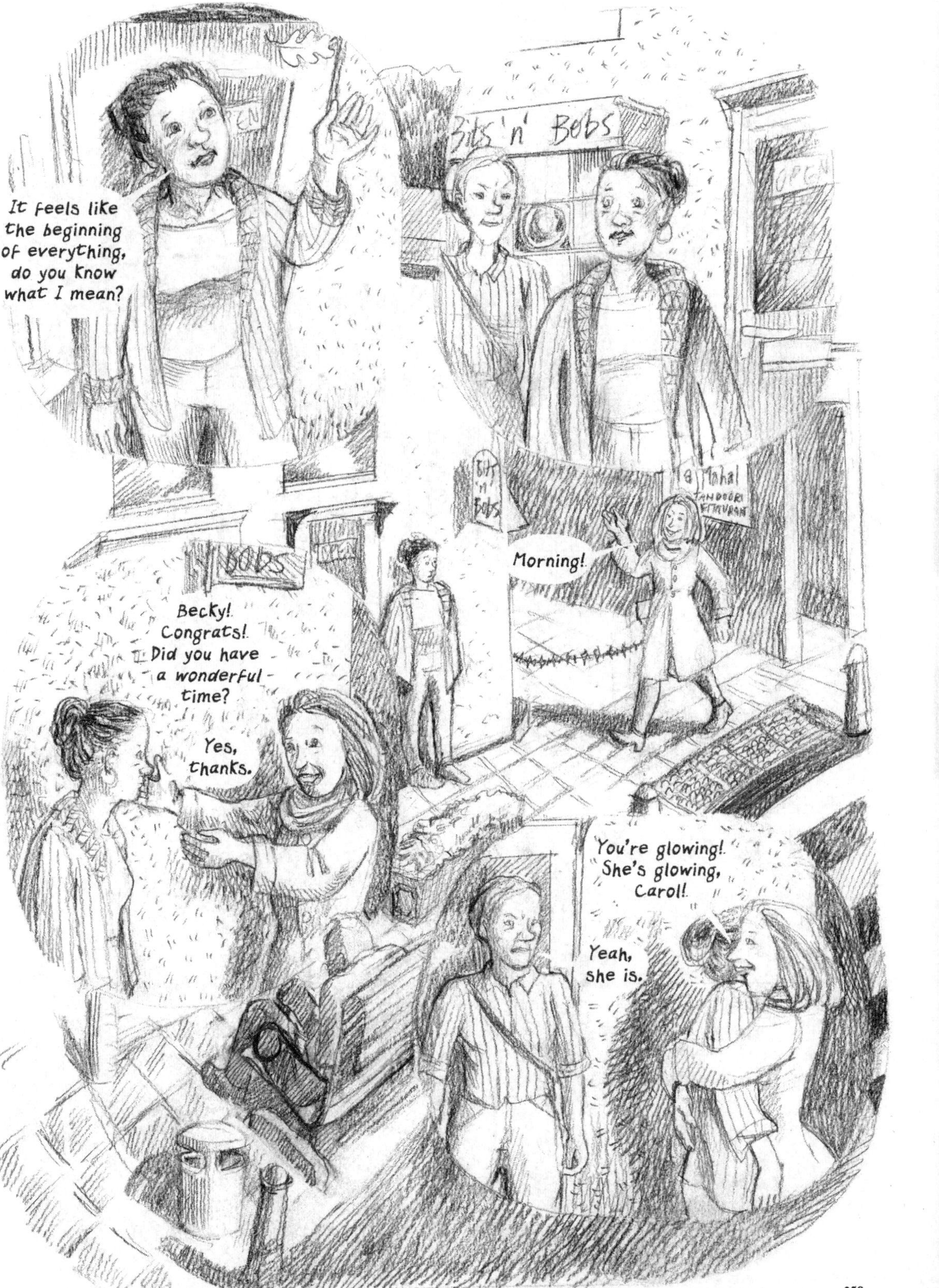
It feels like the beginning of everything, do you know what I mean?
Bits 'n' Bobs
OPEN
Bits 'n' Bobs
Morning!
Becky! Congrats! Did you have a wonderful time?
Yes, thanks.
You're glowing! She's glowing, Carol!
Yeah, she is.

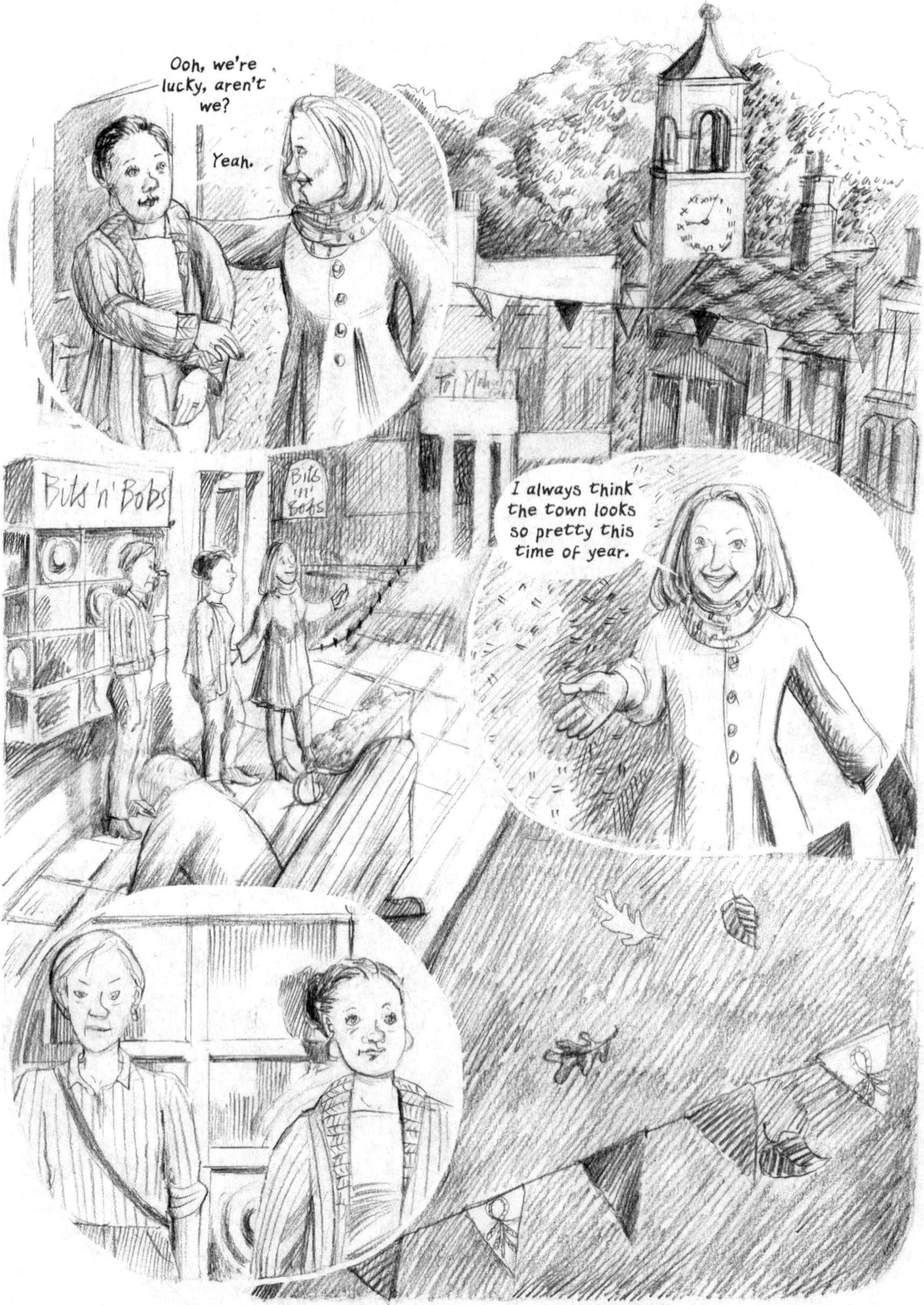
Ooh, we're lucky, aren't we?
Yeah.
Bits 'n' Bobs
Bits 'n' Bobs
I always think the town looks so pretty this time of year.

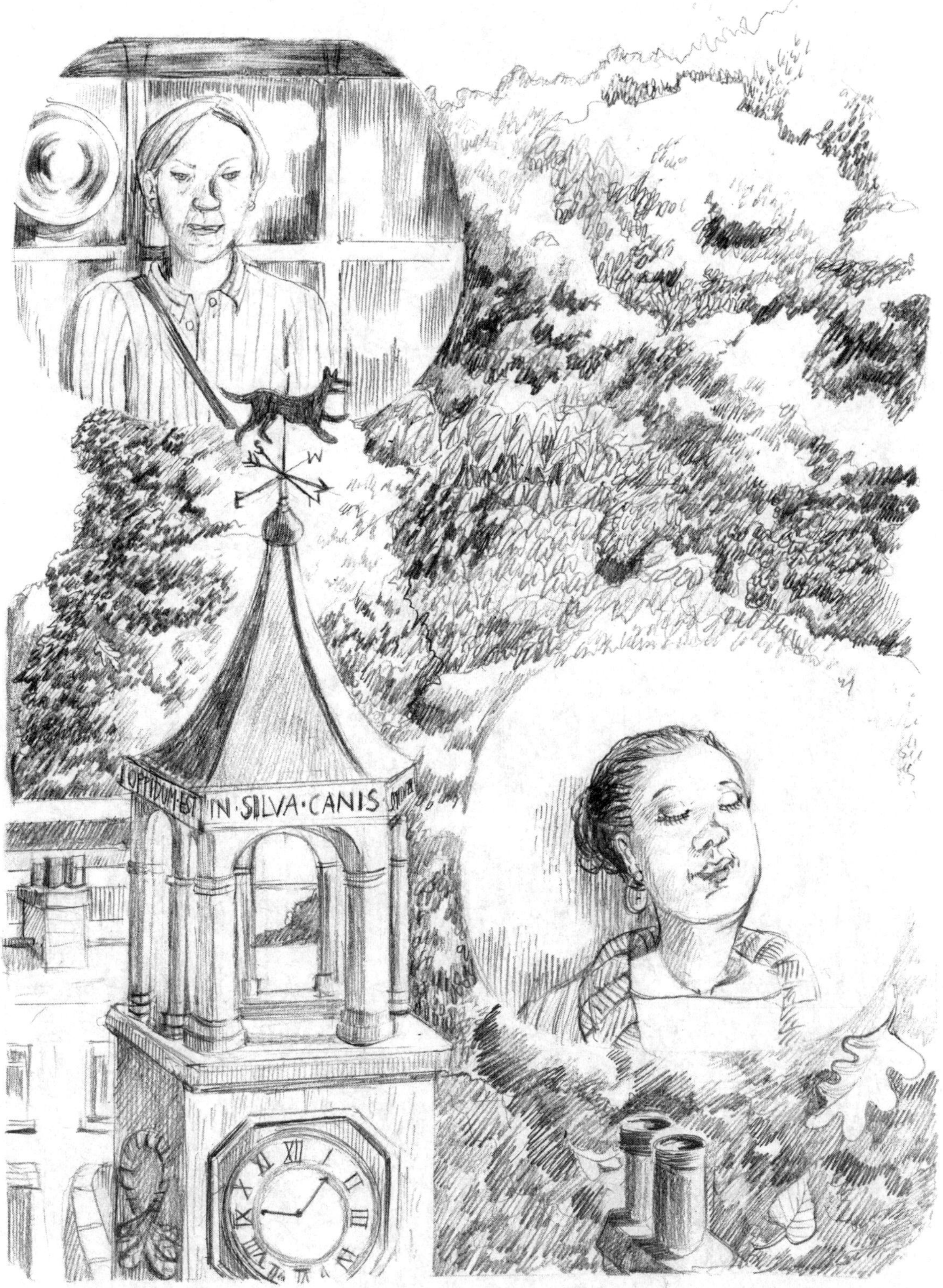
OPPIDUM·EST
IN·SILVA·CANIS

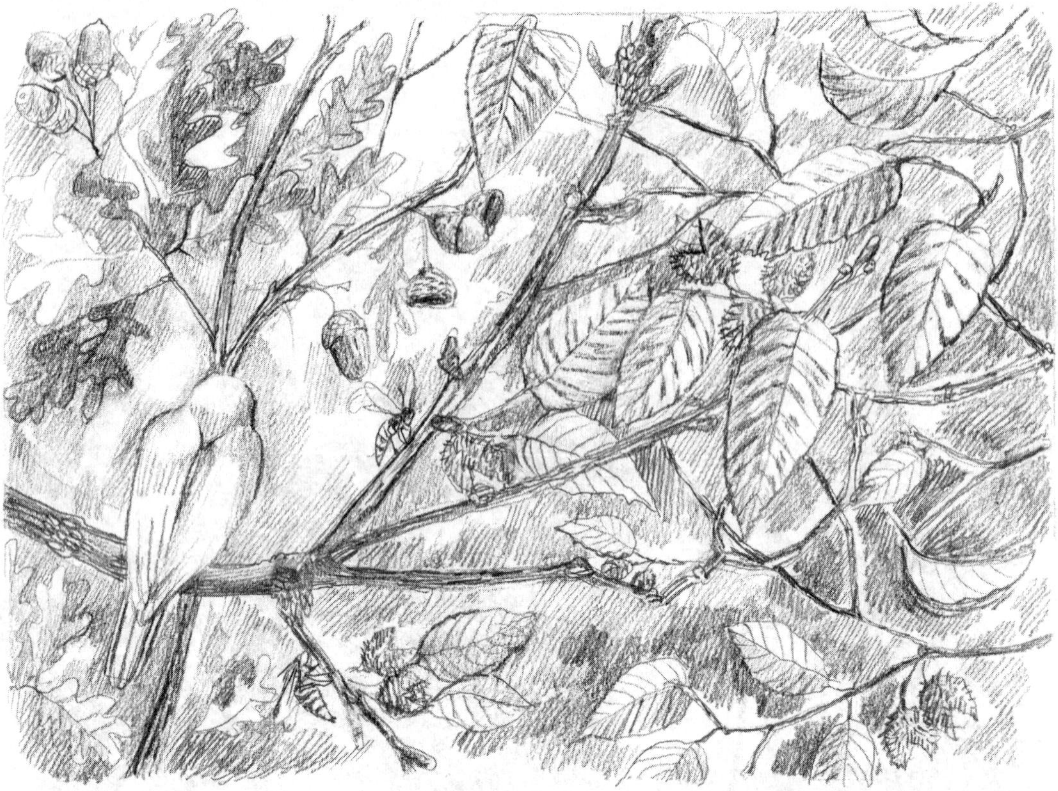

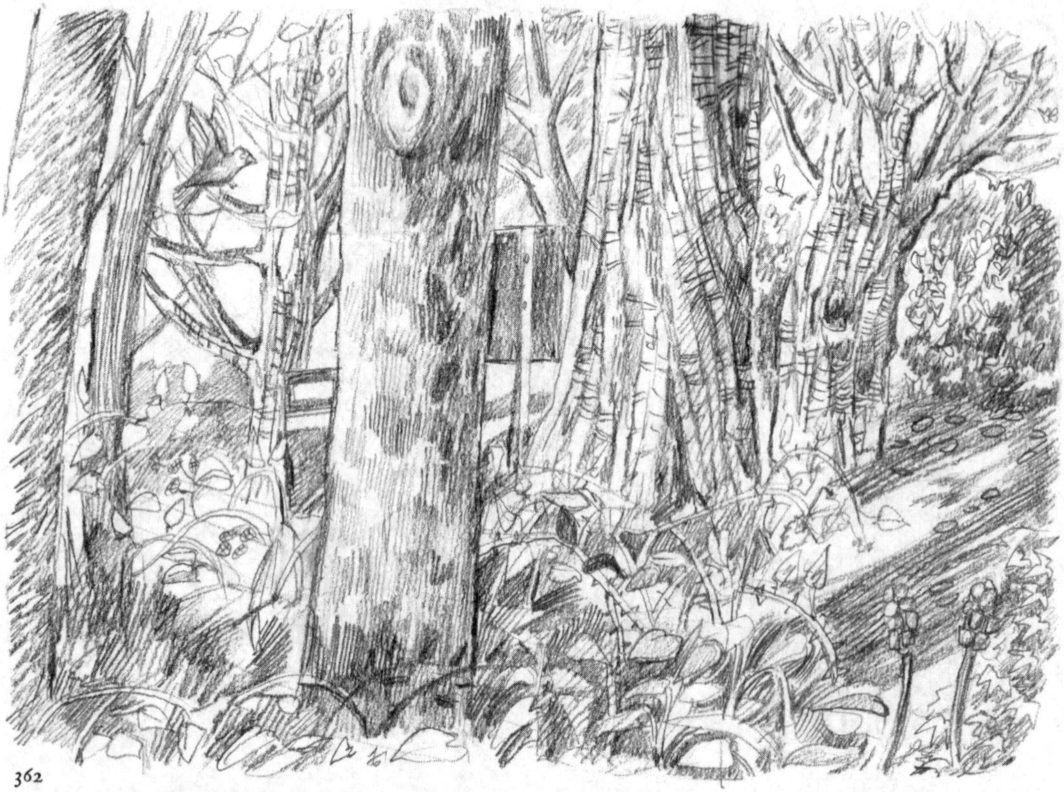

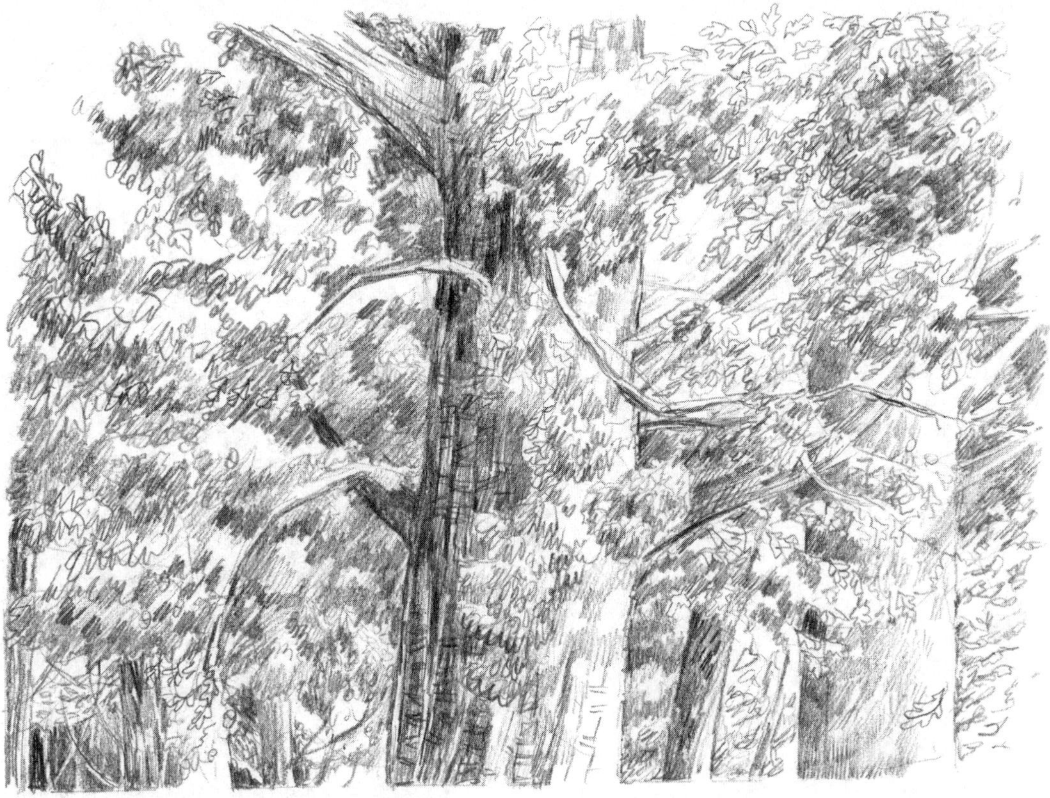

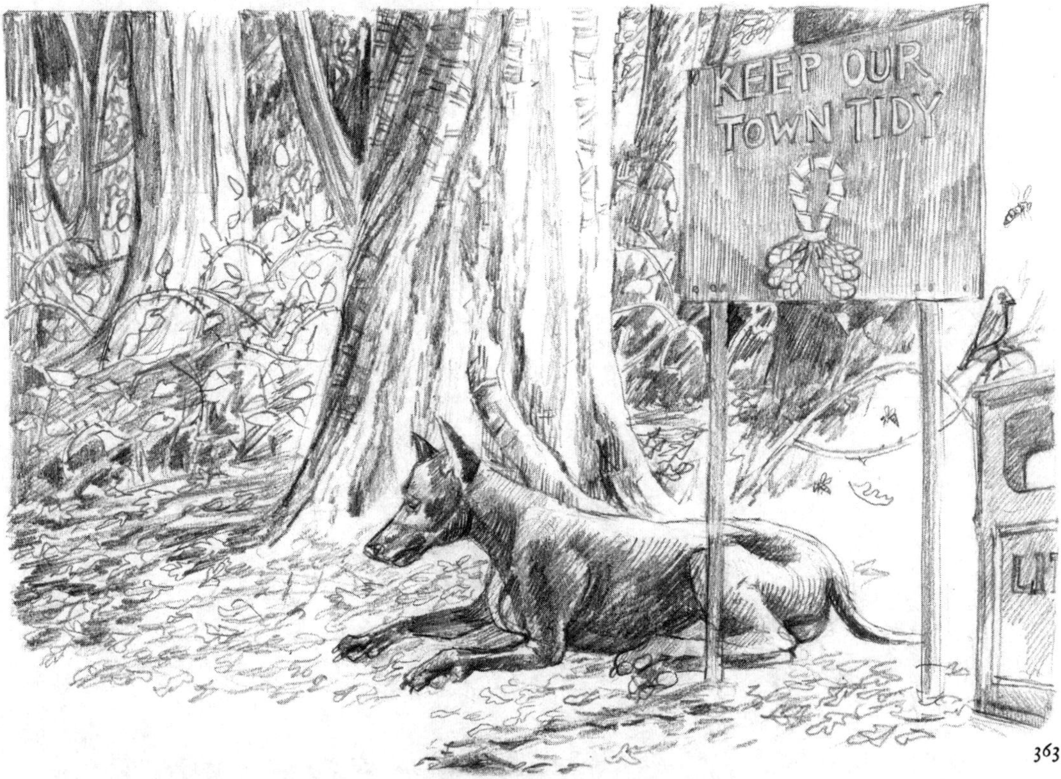
KEEP OUR
TOWN TIDY

Acknowledgements

Thanks to—

the amazing team at Myriad: Corinne Pearlman, supereditrix, Candida Lacey, Lauren Burlinson, Emma Dowson, Vic Heath-Silk, Anna Burtt, Dawn Sackett

Dan Locke, Hannah Chater, Alex Fitch, Hannah Berry, Ian Williams for your friendship, generosity and professional support

Tiff for the photo and a great deal else

the Brighton Seabirds, Helena, Fran, Vicki, Andrew and Sue for the light and sometimes the darkness

Janet for the help, four years ago, to get the whole thing started

Jay D for the loan of part of your 11-year-old self, with much love

George R and Max G from West Blatchington… I told you I'd put you in the acknowledgements!

Afterword

Blackwood was inspired by two things: a dream, of people tying baby shoes to an apple tree in a country town run by a sinister guild, and this photograph. It's a picture of a family wedding in the 1930s, near Dartford, in what was then rural Kent.

I don't know who most of the people are, but the little bridesmaid on the far right is my grandma Peggy; the one far left her big sister, Audrey; and the ghostly babe-in-arms near the back is their younger brother, Gordon, who appears to be decked out for the occasion in a shroud, like Michael Jackson's blanket baby.

Predictably, Gordon became quite a weird adult. He rarely wore a shirt above fifteen degrees, lived with his mother until she died, and was a member of a cultish group called the Swedenborgians who practised amateur dramatics, religion and polyamory. Plus, he spent a portion of the seventies in blackface, a baritone in *The Black and White Minstrel Show* on ITV.

You can also see the joyless face of their mother, Constance Dyble (holding Gordon) – owner of a sixth sense and a violent temper. Her fanatical Methodism and belief in her own psychic gifts led her to read fire-and-brimstone prophesies in the tea leaves for a queue of neighbours.

She hated my mother, for no reason. When my mum was little and whiling away boring 1950s afternoons at her grandma's house, she would try to pass the time – and a meek and sensible child, she was, with a Sunday school temperance pledge in her knicker drawer – with a quiet game of patience.

'There's fifty-two soldiers in Satan's army!' Constance would shriek, belting the playing cards to the floor with the back of her hand.

As my existence is a projection of my ancestors' conscious and unconscious wishes, I am quite obsessed with these little family stories, the ones that shine tiny beams of light on an unknowable past.

With *Blackwood*, I wanted to write a completely fictional story about mostly true stories, to create a fictional family of real people, in a fictional universe almost exactly like our own. I wanted to shine a light on the unspoken things, the traumas and secrets that ripple out from the individual, the family, the town, the ruling system – shaping people's lives and political choices. The way fathers who did not talk about one war behave towards sons who do not talk about another. What this and other kinds of denial lay the ground for.

I wanted this book, among other things, to be a story about the twentieth century – and our own – that reflects this richness and complexity, and preserves the memory of certain objects, philosophies, folklore and rhythms of speech, while maintaining an ambivalence about it, also reflecting on quiet insularity, inscrutable whiteness, NIMBYism: what lies beneath Keep Calm and Carry On.

The England the Brennans and Westons live in seems perhaps to be a whimsical dystopia. There are the unsolved murders with occult overtones, and the group of naked magicians erecting a psychic border control. There is the local peer who keeps a menagerie and a staff of attractive young men who are made (among other things) to don livery and ride around town on pigs for his pleasure and gratification. There is the detention of human beings, including children, without legal process. The murder of a Black man by white men as he waits for a bus.

Apart from the bits I borrowed overtly from *The Wicker Man* – which is my own urtext – all these origin stories are true, but some have just been bent slightly to keep the whole thing legal.

The murders of Danny Reilly and Pete Chapman, and their investigation, are inspired by the Meon Hill 'witchcraft murders' of 1948, a real life slice of Warwickshire folk horror investigated by the celebrity Scotland Yard detective Robert Fabian and still unsolved – due in part to the buttoned lips of villagers and the credulousness of the investigating team when it came to rumours of ancient rites and omens. I had heard of this case initially as a spooky yarn told to me by my aunt, who lived nearby – a family story from the collective oral story bank of an adopted hometown.

There are also fragments begged from older relatives and friends since childhood, not plump enough for story status but preserved in speech, like put-up jam from weedy summer fruit. This is my late grandad, Jack Woodcraft – to whom this book is dedicated – speaking aged eighty-nine: 'My earliest recollections were men singing in the street for money, work was scarce… my father gave a pair of his old boots to one. I also remember going out to the middle of the road and giving one a grape, which he accepted: such dreadful days.' The coda to such remarks about the deep past would invariably be some sentimental parlour ballad about the conversion of a tramp, or 'Old Man River', sung in a droll, quavery baritone and left floating in his wake as he went to busy himself. I gave this fragment to Cecil, the younger brother of Peg (who I only realised afterwards I had named after my grandma) to explain the Great Depression to his friend, and why he kept chickens as insurance against unemployment. Jack also left school at thirteen to work ('the unfairness of it turned me Socialist'), initially looking after poultry like Cecil, although his charges numbered a hundred.

Jack lived all his ninety-four years in a small market town in the south Midlands. The fabric of his life and his history in this town is of a sort that has nearly completely vanished. He knew the very soil of the place. A walk to the fields, to break up a blurry dementia-sculpted day of napping over rum, seeing ghosts, and accidentally setting small kitchen fires would give him clarity and a sense of time.

'They're about two weeks late ploughing that ground,' he would say.

'Those potatoes haven't had enough frost yet.'

'I never did like my mother very much.'

He remembered pony-carts; old maids shut away in Victorian parlours; magic lantern slideshows; childhood hay-making; hare for tea; Jarrow; Cable Street; being beaten by teachers in primary school; war and starvation.

Strangely, my grandfather's last earthly view, four years ago, through the window of a nursing home miles away from his own small town, was of the inhospitable slopes and the dark copse – where the witches held their Sabbats – at the brow of Meon Hill. It felt for a moment like *Blackwood* was escaping its pages, like an inside-out dream – but, as descendants, there will always come a time when we have to dream our ancestors back to us, and hope they won't mind too much about the way we do it.

Hannah Eaton, Brighton
July 2020